Amy Klobuchar

ANTITRUST

Amy Klobuchar is the senior senator from Minnesota and a long-time member of the Senate Judiciary Committee. She is the first woman from her state to be elected to the U.S. Senate and is a former candidate for president of the United States. She was born in Plymouth, Minnesota, and graduated from Yale University and the University of Chicago Law School. She lives in Minneapolis, Minnesota, with her husband, John Bessler, a law professor, and they are the proud parents of their daughter, Abigail.

ANTITRUST

Taking on Monopoly Power from the
Gilded Age to the Digital Age

Amy Klobuchar

VINTAGE BOOKS
A DIVISION OF PENGUIN RANDOM HOUSE LLC
NEW YORK

FIRST VINTAGE BOOKS EDITION, JANUARY 2022

The Library of Congress has cataloged
the Knopf edition as follows:
Names: Klobuchar, Amy, author.
Title: Antitrust : taking on monopoly power from the gilded
age to the digital age / Amy Klobuchar.
Description: First edition. | New York : Alfred A. Knopf, a division of Penguin
Random House LLC, 2021. | Includes bibliographical references and index.
Identifiers: LCCN 2020044843 (print) | LCCN 2020044844 (ebook)
Subjects: LCSH: Antitrust law—United States. | Antitrust law—United States—
History. | Competition, Unfair—United States—History. | Restraint of trade—
United States—History. | United States. Sherman Act. |
Roosevelt, Theodore, 1858–1919.
Classification: LCC KF1649 .K58 2021 (print) | LCC KF1649 (ebook) |
DDC 343.7307/2109—dc23
LC record available at https://lccn.loc.gov/2020044843
LC ebook record available at https://lccn.loc.gov/2020044844

Vintage Books Trade Paperback ISBN: 978-0-525-56399-0
eBook ISBN: 978-0-525-65490-2

Author photograph © Christopher Gregory Rivera
Book design by Cassandra J. Pappas

www.vintagebooks.com

Printed in the United States of America
10 9 8 7 6 5 4 3 2 1

To my husband, John, a true scholar of the law
who has a monopoly on my affections

Corporations, and especially combinations of corporations, should be managed under public regulation. Experience has shown that under our system of government the necessary supervision can not be obtained by State action. It must therefore be achieved by national action. Our aim is not to do away with corporations; on the contrary, these big aggregations are an inevitable development of modern industrialism. . . . We are not hostile to them; we are merely determined that they shall be so handled as to subserve the public good. We draw the line against misconduct, not against wealth.

—PRESIDENT THEODORE ROOSEVELT,
State of the Union address (1902)

Antitrust laws in general, and the Sherman Act in particular, are the Magna Carta of free enterprise. They are as important to the preservation of economic freedom and our free enterprise system as the Bill of Rights is to the protection of our fundamental personal freedoms. And the freedom guaranteed each and every business, no matter how small, is the freedom to compete—to assert with vigor, imagination, devotion, and ingenuity whatever economic muscle it can muster.

—JUSTICE THURGOOD MARSHALL,
United States v. Topco Associates, Inc. (1972)

Contents

Author's Note
to the Vintage Books Edition

Since the publication of the hardcover edition of this book in April 2021, a lot has happened in the world of antitrust. And then again, a lot has not.

On the positive side, the Biden administration has signaled a commitment to aggressively enforce the antitrust laws. On July 9, 2021, President Biden issued an executive order, Promoting Competition in the American Economy, promising a multiagency strategy on competition policy and antitrust enforcement in all economic sectors from tech to telecommunications to health care to agriculture. The plan takes a comprehensive, all-hands-on-deck approach to the problem of monopolization and consolidation: "excessive market concentration threatens basic economic liberties, democratic accountability, and the welfare of workers, farmers, small businesses, startups, and consumers." It also zeroes in on a subject this book discusses at length: the economic freedom of workers to switch jobs. "Robust competition is critical to preserving America's role as the world's leading economy," the executive order emphasizes.

In addition, progressive antitrust leaders have been appointed to key positions in the Biden administration, with Lina Khan taking the reins as chair of the Federal Trade Commission (FTC). She is discussed several times in this book because of her prior work putting forth groundbreaking theories on the dominant tech platforms (most notably Amazon), producing one of the few law review articles in history that actually "went viral." Tim Wu, a Columbia Law School professor and the author of *The Curse of Bigness*, is now President Biden's new special assistant for technology and competition policy and sits on the president's National Economic Council. And Jonathan Kanter, an experienced antitrust lawyer and Google critic, is slated to head up the U.S. Department of Justice Antitrust Division under Attorney General Merrick Garland. At his own confirmation hearing, Garland described antitrust law as his "first love in law school" and, citing the U.S. Supreme Court, called antitrust "a charter of American economic liberty."

In Congress, several pieces of federal legislation that had previously stalled out are on the move. The bill Senator Chuck Grassley of Iowa and I have long championed to change the merger fee statute and up the agency review fees on megamergers was passed unanimously out of the Senate Judiciary Committee. I then got the bill attached to a major commerce-focused competition bill, which passed the Senate and is expected to pass the House of Representatives. My bill—which also passed the House Judiciary Committee—will increase the FTC and DOJ Antitrust Division combined budgets by well over $100 million. My colleagues and I agree: you can't take on the world's biggest companies with duct tape and Band-Aids.

Other bills that are making headway?

Pharma-related anticompetitive conduct legislation, including one aimed at Big Pharma paying off its generic competitors to keep less costly products off the market (Klobuchar/Grassley); a bill making it harder for Big Pharma companies to file "sham" safety petitions to try to ward off generic competition (Klobuchar/Grassley); and bills led by Senators Richard Blumenthal of Connecticut, John Cornyn of Texas, and others to get at nefarious anticompetitive patent practices. And of key interest to the country, my longtime proposal (as in I ran political ads on this way back in 2006) to require pharmaceutical companies to negotiate prescription drug prices under Medicare is finally being seriously considered as one of many solutions to bring down drug prices. Why? America's prescription drug prices are far higher than those in other nations, in part because Congress banned any negotiations for prescription drug prices for seniors enrolled in Medicare. I think forty-six million seniors could get a much better deal on prescription drugs, and in the end that will help all of us.

Several bipartisan tech bills regarding discriminatory conduct and anticompetitive mergers—many of which are led and/or supported by the bipartisan duo of David Cicilline of Rhode Island and Ken Buck of Colorado in the House of Representatives—have made it through the House Judiciary Committee. This effort was not without controversy, with several Democrats from California raising issues and opposing the bills. In the Senate, Senator Grassley and I and a bipartisan group of senators across the ideological spectrum have introduced an important tech bill aimed at exclusionary conduct. Why should Amazon be allowed to use data from sellers on its platform to create knockoff products? Why should Google be allowed to self-preference its own products? This bill would stop many of these anticompetitive practices.

Of course, the most notable development on the tech front this past year was the congressional testimony of Facebook whistleblower Frances Haugen. In testimony that captivated lawmakers and the nation, she demonstrated the clear harm that a dominant company's platform and algorithms can cause when profits are prioritized over people. "I am here today because I believe that Facebook's products harm children, stoke division, weaken our democracy and much more," she testified. Her testimony may very well be the catalyst for change on the privacy, algorithm transparency, and competition policy fronts that has thus far eluded Congress.

From a broader antitrust legal perspective, some minimal progress has been made. In 2021, I reintroduced sweeping legislation making it easier to bring and prove antitrust cases (and former telecom businessman, now-senator Mark Warner of Virginia came aboard as a sponsor in addition to many others). Senator Grassley and Republican Senator Mike Lee of Utah also introduced general antitrust reform legislation, and while the bills are very different, there are some commonalities.

Also, a bill to stop companies from delaying litigation by changing the venue of state-filed antitrust lawsuits to another state has broad support. In Congress, it is led by Representatives Cicilline and Buck and Senator Lee and myself, and it is supported by state attorneys general across the country. Under existing law, antitrust actions filed by the U.S. government cannot be transferred via a judicial multidistrict litigation process, but *states* filing antitrust cases don't get the same treatment—something our State Antitrust Enforcement Venue Act of

2021 would change so state attorneys general can remain in the court they select.

Finally, the in-depth Senate antitrust hearings Senator Lee and I held in 2021 were most unusual for the Senate Judiciary Committee. One, they were strikingly bipartisan. Two, they were actually interesting. And three, they garnered much participation with many rounds of questions. Nearly every senator on the Judiciary Committee, including Democratic Chairman Dick Durbin of Illinois, attended the hearing on anticompetitive conduct in the meatpacking and food supply chains. Hearings on pharma, hospitals, big data, and home tech devices were equally notable.

One Senate antitrust hearing that made big news was on app stores. The average American now spends about four hours a day on mobile devices, and for many Americans app store use has bigfooted the web itself. The issue? Two companies completely dominate: Apple for iPhones and Google for everything else.

Maybe that's why Apple initially refused to even send a witness to our hearing. Their reason? Pending litigation. (If, by the way, that was an allowable reason, we would never have congressional hearings at all.) But we didn't even need to get to that question since after Senator Lee and I called out Apple for the bogus nature of this excuse (their own CEO had discussed this very topic on Kara Swisher's *New York Times* podcast only the week before), Apple changed course.

But the monopoly "we can do whatever we want whenever we want" behavior didn't end there. We learned at the hearing that a Match.com witness, who appeared in the Senate to testify about the high charges Apple and Google assess for access to their app stores (often *30 percent of revenue*), had actually received a call from a Google businessperson the night before the hearing attempting to intimidate him by claiming his written testimony submitted in advance differed from claims the company had made in its earnings reports to shareholders (which was a far-fetched assertion at best).

In the end the hearing served its purpose: many senators had been unaware of (1) the exorbitant rates the two dominant app stores charge companies, which are oftentimes already their own competitors (think Spotify versus Apple Music); (2) the self-preferencing behavior the app stores engage in; and (3) the inability of those trying to sell their products in app stores to alert consumers that they can get better prices or rates from the companies' own websites. As a result of the hearing, Senator Marsha Blackburn of Tennessee joined Senator Blumenthal and me to introduce legislation to bring competition and fairness to the app store market. And with a mixed court ruling in September 2021 in the *Epic Games v. Apple* lawsuit, the bill is even more important.

So to sum up the good news of the past several months:

Major promises from the Biden administration and progressive leaders appointed to key antitrust positions; bipartisan congressional interest in giving the agencies the resources to pursue the complex cases (i.e., duct tape and Band-Aids won't work anymore); excellent hearings that have informed the public and upped the interest of members of Congress in competition and privacy issues; active pushback at monopolies; and some actual progress on both new and long-pending antitrust bills.

Now the bad news.

One of the themes of this book is how conservative U.S. Supreme Court decisions have taken antitrust law further and further from its original congressional intent. In passing the Magna Carta of antitrust laws—the Sherman Act—Ohio Republican Senator John Sherman, an ally of Abraham Lincoln, would have never thought that his bill (and the subsequent Clayton Act) could be interpreted to allow one or two companies to dominate in major parts of the economy. Sadly, a series of cases, from the Supreme Court on down, led one federal judge this past summer to throw out antitrust cases brought by the FTC and state attorneys general against Facebook. The procedural posture is complicated, and the judge's decision is subject to further review. But it is a troubling sign for the ability of the current antitrust laws, at least as presently interpreted, to rein in the Big Tech companies. The judge's decision cited Supreme Court precedent significantly narrowing the ability of government enforcers (from blue and red states alike) and private plaintiffs to bring their antitrust cases.

While the court's dismissal of the Facebook case is being fought by state attorneys general and the FTC—which, under the leadership of Chair Lina Khan, has refiled the case—it is clear that court decisions have not only betrayed the original intent and clear purpose of the antitrust laws but also make it very difficult to pursue future cases without amending the federal statutes themselves (which is what I've been trying to do for some time now). The law, as I point out in this book, must be as sophisticated as the monopolists who continue to find new and innovative ways to profit off their dominant positions.

Another problematic development?

In April 2021, the U.S. Supreme Court decided *AMG Capital Management, LLC v. Federal Trade Commission*, ruling that a section of the Federal Trade Commission Act does not authorize the FTC to seek, nor a court to award, equitable monetary relief such as restitution or disgorgement. After several companies, including AMG Capital Management, had provided borrowers with short-term payday loans and misled many customers as to the essential terms of those loans and what was in the fine print, the FTC—seeking to recover approximately $1.3 billion in deceptive charges—filed suit alleging unfair or deceptive practices.

Although the FTC had used the section of the FTC Act at issue since the late 1970s to win restitution and other forms of equitable monetary relief in court, the Supreme Court ruled in *AMG Capital Management* that the statute's language does not authorize the FTC to obtain court-ordered monetary relief. After the Court's decision, then-acting FTC Chair Rebecca Kelly Slaughter—lamenting how consumers had been bilked out of roughly $1.3 billion through the deceptive payday lending scheme—issued this statement: "With this ruling, the Court has deprived the FTC of the strongest tool we had to help consumers when they need it most. We urge Congress to act swiftly to restore and strengthen the powers of the agency so we can make wronged consumers whole."

Unless Congress acts, the FTC's ability to enforce the FTC Act and antitrust laws will be thwarted and seriously impaired. Already, on July 30, 2021, the FTC was compelled to withdraw a claim against pharmaceutical company AbbVie—one alleging that AbbVie and another company, Besins Healthcare, used sham litigation to illegally maintain a monopoly—in light of the *AMG Capital Management* decision. As the FTC's Holly Vedova emphasized: "Here, the FTC would have been able to return almost a half billion dollars directly to AndroGel consumers. Instead, AbbVie and Besins can retain all of the ill-gotten gains resulting from their illegal anticompetitive conduct. This case highlights the pressing need for legislation reinstating the FTC's authority to seek equitable monetary relief for consumers in competition cases."

Given these recent decisions as well as many more handed down over the past decades, thinking the answer to our country's monopoly woes is to simply wait for the courts to catch up and take up the antitrust torch would be as naive as believing Donald Trump will suddenly take responsibility for his role in the January 6 insurrection at the U.S. Capitol. And while the answer to America's "curse of bigness" must be found in the halls of Congress (building, of course, on increasingly active state legislatures and state attorneys general), there are days when it feels like for every step forward there is another one backward, driven by the strong monopoly forces against us.

Take the bipartisan bill Republican Senator John Kennedy of Louisiana and I have introduced (led by Representative Cicilline in the House) to give news organizations the power to negotiate better rates for their products. As more and more newspapers and local news organizations die off—mainly because they are not appropriately paid for their content by the social media platforms—not even the combined power of the National Association of Broadcasters and the country's newspapers could convince California Republican Congressman and House Minority Leader Kevin McCarthy to support the bill that so many members of his own party like.

Then there is the pushback from Democrats close to tech, or the pushback from congressional members of both parties close to Big Pharma. Or the faux claims that the reason someone opposes a bill is loftier than the truth. Or the realization that my preferred approach—to make, oftentimes modest, commonsense changes to the laws so that all antitrust actions are easier to bring—would garner even more enemies. So many days it feels like we are playing a high-stakes congressional game of Whac-A-Mole (actually, more like Whac-A-Behemoth) with a never-ending parade of monopoly obstacles popping up in every corridor—and around every corner—on Capitol Hill. But when dealing with the world's largest companies with unending resources for ad campaigns and lobbyists, one should hardly be surprised. (Yes, that includes you, the tech-funded and ill-named Chamber of Progress.)

So that's the reason I ask you to read this book and pass it on to friends. Now you don't have to read every footnote (although my husband, John—who wrote them—would love it if you did). Just remember that the public is on our side. People understand that a lack of competition and choice is not good. And as you will learn after reading this book, time and time again past generations of Americans have stood up for capitalism and true competition. They have stood up for better wages and innovation and product choice. And now, my friends, this is our moment. We can do it again. As Jason Sudeikis's character Ted Lasso would say, "Believe."

Amy Klobuchar
October 2021

ANTITRUST

Introduction

My work with our nation's antitrust laws started with a phone call in 2008. More than a year after I was sworn in as Minnesota's junior U.S. senator, a pharmacist at Children's Hospital in Minneapolis called our office. He told our staff that the price of a life-saving drug used to treat premature babies with heart valve defects had suddenly gone up astronomically, and he was calling for help.

A few weeks later I met with Alan Goldbloom, then president of Minnesota's Children's Hospitals and Clinics. He confirmed everything the pharmacist had said. Ovation Pharmaceuticals—a company headquartered in Deerfield, Illinois—had bought the drug indomethacin from the mega drug company Merck and was selling it under the brand name Indocin IV. He also confirmed that Ovation had inexplicably jacked up the price. This was a drug used to treat low-birth-weight infants born with an abnormal opening between the two major blood vessels leading to the heart. The condition—called patent ductus arteriosus, or PDA—can lead to major health problems for vulnerable newborns, including heart failure. The price had skyrocketed since Ovation had bought the drug, going from $78 per treatment to $1,614—a price increase of more than *twenty times* its original cost.

Doctors and hospitals throughout the nation were experiencing the same price hike. And, when more than thirty thousand babies are born every year with PDA and the only other life-saving option is surgery (not only the most expensive treatment, but also less safe), this drug price hike was exorbitant for both families and hospitals. If a baby's family couldn't afford the drug, the hospital would eat the costs, and in the case of Minneapolis Children's, the total cost of the treatment for all newborns with PDA amounted to hundreds of thousands of dollars per year.

I sent a letter to Ovation. The company responded by saying that it had purchased the drug from Merck a few years before and that the huge price increase was due to "moving manufacturing from one plant to another."

Moving expenses?

Three years before, Ovation had in fact bought the rights to indomethacin from Merck. A year after that purchase Ovation had also acquired the rights to the other drug used to treat the same condition. It was called NeoProfen, and Ovation bought the rights to that drug from Abbott Laboratories before Abbott had even started to sell it.

With the second deal, Ovation essentially cornered the PDA market. The Illinois company hit the monopoly jackpot because the only way doctors across the United States could help thirty thousand sick infants each year was by buying one of only two drugs that the U.S. Food and Drug Administration (FDA) had approved to treat it. Ovation now owned both. Two days after purchasing the other drug, Ovation raised the Indocin IV price from $109 per treatment to $1,500, eventually moving it to above $1,600. Ovation also priced NeoProfen at more than $1,500 per treatment.

After learning these facts, I held a public event at Minneapolis Children's Hospital, a place near and dear to my heart since our daughter Abigail was treated there at birth with a significant swallowing disorder. How many times had I paced those hallways, not sure if she would live, not knowing what kind of life she would lead if she did. The one thing my husband John and I didn't have to worry about back then was paying her medical bills because my law firm's health insurance covered the drugs and care she needed. Not so with many of the babies born with heart defects.

At the hospital press conference were doctors and pharmacists as well as little Sophia Benson. Now healthy and rosy-cheeked, Sophia and her twin sister Anna had been born prematurely in the hospital two years before at twenty-eight weeks. Both baby girls spent time in the hospital's neonatal intensive care unit, the same place where, a decade earlier, our daughter had been treated. Sophia had been hospitalized for life-threatening PDA back when Minneapolis Children's was covering only about $200,000 worth of the heart drug for more than 150 babies a year due to the initial cost increase. The next year—with no changes to the makeup of the drug—the hospital paid out more than $400,000 because of the price increase. Only about one-third of the drug's jacked-up price was covered by insurance. Nationwide estimates were that the price increase was costing families, hospitals, and the taxpayers tens of millions of dollars per year.

At the hospital that day I took on Ovation's price gouging. I called on the Federal Trade Commission (FTC) to investigate. I also asked the FDA to quickly approve generics for the life-saving drug since at the time there were no generic versions of indomethacin on the market.

The price of the two branded drugs nevertheless remained high, with a spokeswoman for Ovation explaining that keeping the prices at the previous affordable levels "wouldn't be sustainable." A letter and a call to action from the junior senator from Minnesota to a drug company in Illinois clearly had no effect whatsoever on the company's conduct.

A month later I sent a letter to William Kovacic, then the chairman of the FTC under President George W. Bush, and asked for a formal investigation into Ovation's price gouging. At a routine Commerce Committee FTC oversight hearing, I held up the small packaging box used for a vial of Indocin IV and asked the FTC commissioners what they thought I should do. "As someone who is new to the Senate," I said, "what can we do to try to get at this problem?" As I noted at the hearing, "I just want to help some babies in my state and some doctors in my state want to just do their jobs."

One commissioner, Jon Leibowitz, later the chair of the FTC under President Obama, pledged he would look into it. He called the price hike "appalling" and said he could understand why my constituents and others were so concerned about it. "Investigations are very labor intensive," he testified, adding that it would help the long-understaffed FTC "when we have sufficient number of personnel and good attorneys."

"I'm on a crusade to fix this," I told him.

In July of that year, to keep up the pressure, I convened a hearing of the U.S. Senate and House Joint Economic Committee to examine the skyrocketing prices of prescription drugs. At the hearing, which we titled "At What Cost? Egregious Price Increases in the Pharmaceutical Drug Industry," I called Alan Goldbloom to testify. In his testimony, he said that Children's Hospital had treated 110 babies with PDA the previous year and that Indocin had once been a "low cost, safe, non-surgical way to treat these infants" and that "the cost for Indocin up until January of 2006 was just over $108 per unit." Goldbloom further noted that the price had jumped to $1,500—a 1,278 percent increase. He explained that because Indocin is "an old drug" that had "been on the market for more than three decades," the "dramatic price increase cannot be attributed to the high cost of research and development." "Effectively," he emphasized, "one company has a monopoly and can use it to price-gouge." At the hearing, I noted that Ovation was selling Indocin IV in the United States for forty-four times the amount it was selling for in Canada.

Five months later—in December 2008—the FTC sued Ovation for price gouging, asking the company to disgorge its "unlawfully obtained profits." The agency asserted that Ovation's acquisition of the second similar drug, NeoProfen, violated the Federal Trade Commission Act, the major federal antitrust laws—the Sherman and the Clayton Acts—and Minnesota's antitrust law. The State of Minnesota sued the company, too. "Ovation's profiteering on the backs of critically ill premature babies is not only immoral, it is illegal," decried FTC commissioner Leibowitz at the time of the lawsuit's filing. "Ovation's behavior," he observed, "is a stark reminder of why America desperately needs health care reform and why vigorous antitrust enforcement is as relevant today as it was when the agency was created almost one hundred years ago in 1914."

I had my own take on the pharmaceutical company's actions that day: "A company like Ovation knows that when it comes to saving a baby's life, price is no object." "They bank on that, literally," I said, knowing from my own fourteen years of experience as a private practice lawyer, followed by eight years as a prosecutor and chief legal officer for Minnesota's largest county, that it would take months, if not years, before the FTC's litigation against Ovation would play out in the courts. During that lengthy time, the company could continue to rake in dollars by overcharging the families of premature babies and the hospitals that treat them.

The FTC's case against Ovation—which was now against the Danish company Lundbeck, which had bought Ovation for $900 million in cash in the middle of this mess—did not end well. After a trial in December 2009, a federal district judge in Minnesota, drawing upon conservative Eighth Circuit precedents, found that Indocin IV and NeoProfen were not in the same product market and that there was no viable antitrust claim. This ruling came even though Ovation had cornered the market and Michael Burke, a vice president at Lundbeck, had the gall to send an email to others at the company stating that when it came to Indocin IV and other drugs it was acquiring, "we can price these almost anywhere we want given the product profiles." Burke's email described the drugs that were being purchased as "a group of medically niche small volume products that don't have substitutes and that are significantly under priced to the market."

While lawyers at the FTC thought that they had a strong case, the trial judge—a George W. Bush appointee—felt differently. Concluding that neonatologists, and not hospitals, are the consumers for the pharmaceuticals, she found that it was the perceived clinical advantages or disadvantages of Indocin IV versus NeoProfen that affected the doctor's choice and that those decisions were made "without regard to price." In dismissing the actions brought by the FTC and the State of Minnesota, the judge found that the plaintiffs had failed to prove that Lundbeck, through the acquisition of NeoProfen (via its purchase of Ovation), had willfully acquired or maintained monopoly power or substantially lessened competition.

But it was Ovation that had made the unilateral decision to raise the prices so high. And because there was no competition for the drugs, neither the hospitals nor the neonatologists had any choice. If they wanted either drug—and the newborns absolutely needed one or the other to avoid the riskier surgical procedure—they were compelled to prescribe and dispense either Indocin IV or NeoProfen at a price dictated by the same company.

The adverse ruling in the FTC's case attracted national attention. On appeal to the U.S. Court of Appeals for the Eighth Circuit, the attorneys general of ten states—Missouri, Illinois, Arkansas, Iowa,

Maryland, Nevada, New Mexico, North Dakota, and West Virginia—filed a friend-of-the-court brief, asking the appellate court to overturn the trial court's decision. The states' top attorneys argued that the district judge had erred. The facts of the case, they contended, led to only one reasonable conclusion: that Indocin IV and NeoProfen were in the same market, not different ones. The drugs, after all, were reasonably interchangeable for purposes of treating PDA, and both drugs had been approved by the FDA for just that purpose. Different treating physicians might prefer one drug over the other because of brand loyalty or some product differentiation, with the drugs having different side effects. But Indocin IV and NeoProfen were clearly substitutes for each other, with studies finding both to be equally effective in addressing neonatal PDA.

Ultimately, and to my dismay and the dismay of the FTC and the states, the famously conservative Eighth Circuit—in an August 2011 ruling—affirmed the district court's decision. Citing a U.S. Supreme Court precedent, *Brown Shoe Co. v. United States* (1962), the Eighth Circuit ruled: "The outer boundaries of a product market can be identified by the reasonable interchangeability, or cross-elasticity of demand, between the product and possible substitutes for it." All three judges sitting on the Eighth Circuit panel voted to affirm the district court's ruling, citing U.S. Supreme Court and Eighth Circuit precedents and basically deferring to the district court's decision.

Even now it is hard for me to fathom how the federal courts could have allowed the actions of Ovation Pharmaceuticals to go unchecked. A later published critique of the courts' decisions emphasized that the district court, in making its ruling, did not consider evidence of the "actual price rise" associated with the life-saving drug "as an alternative to the market definition approach." "In a situation such as *Lundbeck*, where the drug treatments in question were the only two available options and price/cost margins were very high," another prominent antitrust expert, Herbert Hovenkamp, wrote in a harsh critique of the decision in the case, "condemnation should have been an easy call." "The post-merger price increase," he observed, should have provided "a clear answer."

Because of its market power, Ovation had indeed taken advantage of the purchasers of its newly acquired products. The company had, through its acquisitions, put itself in total control of the only two pharmaceutical products used to treat PDA. And then, inexplicably, it was allowed—by the U.S. courts and the law (at least as interpreted by those courts)—to exploit an incredibly vulnerable group of people: the families of premature babies.

It took years after Ovation acquired indomethacin for robust generic competition to emerge, although that did eventually happen. And even with the introduction of generic drug competitors, as is often the case, the price of the life-saving PDA treatment didn't immediately go down. As with so many products, it is only with true and vigorous competition that drug prices fall.

The story of the heart valve drug for newborns is not a five-year fairy tale with a "happily ever after" ending that new market entrants finally brought the prices down. The real story is that for years the company had a complete monopoly over the drug and its sole competitor and that its owners chose to bleed hospitals, families, and the U.S. government for cash to fill their coffers at the expense of the health of newborn babies.

They did it because our current antitrust laws, at least as applied by the federal courts, were unable to check them. They did it because the laws in place simply didn't work to stop the anticompetitive behavior.

That's why I have written this book.

When a U.S. senator, the FTC, and the attorneys general of multiple states can't bring down the price of a life-saving drug for newborn babies, the deck is stacked against all of us. It means our laws aren't working. It means unchecked monopoly power, unless stopped in its tracks, makes vital medicines unaffordable to American families and—quite literally—threatens lives.

The stakes are high, and the facts are stark: American firms engaged in $10 trillion in acquisitions from 2008 to 2017, and globally the value of mergers and acquisitions (M&A) in U.S. dollars from 2014 to 2019 nearly topped $24 trillion. From 2009 to 2018, there was nearly a tripling of the number of mergers—from 716 in 2009 to 2,111 in 2018—reviewed by the FTC and the Antitrust Division of the U.S. Department of Justice (DOJ). In 2018, not one but two American companies (Apple and Amazon) reached more than $1 trillion in worth, while Google and Facebook continue to dominate their respective markets. Indeed, Apple's market capitalization crossed $2 trillion in 2020, with Amazon not far behind as it continues to grow. Meanwhile, countries around the world are questioning these companies' competitive practices as well as their privacy policies.

And while mergers and acquisitions, like all commerce, might have temporarily slowed at the onset of the coronavirus pandemic, the COVID-driven closure of so many small businesses will, many believe, lead to even more consolidation and less competition in the long run. In mid-May 2020, *The Washington Post*—reporting on a study done by economists at the University of Illinois, Harvard Business School, Harvard University, and the University of Chicago—noted that more than 100,000 small businesses had already permanently closed their doors since the pandemic escalated in March of that year. "Tearful, heartfelt announcements about small-business closures are popping up on websites and Facebook pages around the country," the article observed, with analysts projecting a wave of small-business bankruptcies and closures not seen since the days of the Great Depression. As of August 31, 2020, 163,735 businesses, including 32,109 restaurants, bars, and nightlife venues, had indicated on Yelp that they had closed. With fewer small businesses, not only can big companies engage in COVID-driven price gouging, but those big companies are also poised to swallow up more and more competitors and grow even larger.

And what is the effect of a decade of mergers, runaway corporate consolidation, and all in all concentrated growth? You wonder why cable TV rates are so high, and why—despite some competition from satellite TV and new internet streaming services—they've climbed at double the rate of inflation for two decades? Why airline fares have been so much higher in airports in midsized cities compared with competition-heavy urban areas like New York and L.A.? You wonder why pharma prices for commonly used insulin jumped in the United States from $40 a vial in 2002 to $130 a vial in 2013, and then up to $340 per vial in 2019, more than ten times its price in Canada? Why is this kind of price gouging not being stopped?

The effects of monopoly power can be felt everywhere, raising all sorts of questions for the American economy. Why do farmers pay so much for seeds and fertilizer? Why is health care so expensive? Why is it so costly to ship goods by rail in certain places? And why are so few incentives in place for Big Tech companies to protect your private information? If you haven't wondered about any of this, you need to. And if you have, you should also start thinking long and hard about the state of the nation's antitrust laws.

Americans today understand that there's too much business consolidation in this country. They understand that it's not necessarily good for them. They understand that businesses both big and small bring us enormous opportunities and innovations but that, at some point, monopolies and what have been called too-big-to-fail businesses don't promote entrepreneurship; they stifle it. Americans understand that the benefits of many big corporate mergers go largely to the investors and stockholders of the merged companies and not to the factory line worker or the customer ordering the product, the student buying an airline ticket, or the farmer trying to ship crops to market.

The majority of Americans are displeased with the way the economic and political system is working. Before the COVID-19 pandemic, a 2019 poll showed that 70 percent of Americans were angry because the system seems to work only for those with connections, money, and power, with two-thirds of Americans believing that the economy "unfairly favors powerful interests." While a 2017 Gallup poll showed that small businesses enjoy a 70 percent approval rating (the highest in three decades), the big business approval rating (and I say this coming from a state with a lot of strong, good big businesses) has remained below 10 percent for those who say they are "very satisfied" with "the size and influence of major corporations" in every year from 2001 to 2019 in which polling was done.

Part of the public's wariness of big business can be found in the increasing income disparities in the United States. As corporate consolidation continues and the wages for American workers remain flat, the top 1 percent have gotten richer. A recent study of executive compensation at America's 350 largest companies revealed that the average pay for top executives—much of it consisting of stock grants or stock options—surged to $18.9 million in 2017. As income inequality has risen, the middle class has been squeezed, and those on the lower rungs of the income scale, and in particular people of color, have fallen into even more dire circumstances. The 2020–2021 COVID pandemic has exacerbated those disparities and put our economy and public health system under one big magnifying glass: the rich, for the most part, can protect themselves, while the poor cannot. "Racial disparities in who contracts the virus have played out in big cities like Milwaukee and New York, but also in smaller metropolitan areas like Grand Rapids, Michigan," *The New York Times* reported in July 2020.

In this book I make the historical and present-day argument that one way to remedy the growing monopolization in our country is to actually do something to counteract consolidated business power. I make the case that by allowing one or two, or three or four, companies to rule over major sectors of our economy, and by allowing monopolies to get away with unbridled price gouging, we are not furthering competition. Instead, we are squelching it.

Nowhere do the modern-day competition issues come into sharper focus than with today's Big Tech companies. Their success and innovation are unparalleled in recent history. No one can doubt that. But at some point, when the sheer size and dominance of companies like Facebook and Google allows them to buy out and scare away their closest or nascent competitors, and when their political dominance allows them to put a virtual stranglehold on necessary regulation, change must come. And, as the recent major antitrust lawsuits filed by the FTC, the Department of Justice, and state attorneys general against Facebook and Google demonstrate—to quote Minnesota's own Bob Dylan—when it comes to tech, the "times they are a-changin'." As one *New York Times* reporter noted with regard to Amazon (although this principle could apply to other companies as well), when a company amasses "structural power that lets it exert increasing control over many parts of the economy," the company "should not get a pass on anticompetitive behavior just because it makes customers happy."

The consumer case for updating and better enforcing the nation's antitrust laws is straightforward: it will bring down prices by giving the citizens of this country some much-needed leverage, and it will give Americans more choice. The business case is equally compelling: squeezing out competitors through consolidated dominance is not good for capitalism. To quote Adam Smith, the godfather of our capitalist system, the "invisible hand" of competitive entrepreneurship is the key to a strong capitalist economy, but only if we have a government that effectively takes on the "overgrown standing army" Smith labeled the monopolists.

America's laws have not been updated to track the changes in America's monopoly landscape. Our Congress refuses to do it. Our enforcement tools are getting rusty. Our competition enforcers don't have enough resources to effectively take on multibillion-dollar, much less trillion-dollar, companies. And America's courts are increasingly populated by conservative judges, including on the U.S. Supreme Court, who interpret the antitrust laws so narrowly that their decisions have created a dampening effect on the ability of the government and private plaintiffs to litigate antitrust claims.

The remedy? Our antitrust laws—and our enforcers—need to be as sophisticated as today's corporate titans, and we need judges who will interpret the antitrust laws in a reasonable fashion, from the U.S. Supreme Court on down. The laws were written to put a brake on the power of big businesses, not to let them get away with whatever they want whenever they want it. And most important, everyday Americans—"We the People"—must rise up to insist on new laws and much better enforcement to take on monopoly power, just as Americans did in the days of Teddy Roosevelt and even before that, at the very establishment of this nation.

From the founding of our country, Americans have eschewed monopoly power. From the colonists' rejection of the British monarchy dictating from whom they bought their tea, to worker strikes from Chicago to Texas against monopoly robber barons, to America's farmers' and ranchers' rebellions against monopoly agricultural and transportation interests, this book shows how the antimonopoly prairie fire ultimately made its way to Washington, D.C., where John Sherman, a Republican senator from Ohio, finally passed America's first federal antitrust law in 1890.

Over the years it became clear that when it comes to antitrust, there is—and should be—a lot of power lodged in the hands of the federal government. The Department of Justice's Antitrust Division enforces our two basic antitrust laws—the Sherman and Clayton Acts—while the Federal Trade Commission Act of 1914—also known as the FTC Act—empowers the Federal Trade Commission to police any unfair methods of competition, including Sherman Act and Clayton Act violations and unscrupulous business conduct. In addition, the states have their own seats at the antitrust table, with all fifty of them as well as the District of Columbia having passed laws designed to prevent unfair competition. Over time, twenty-eight states have adopted FTC Act equivalents, commonly referred to as the Little FTC Acts. These laws give state attorneys general the broad authority to police anticompetitive conduct, but because commerce is increasingly interstate—indeed, global—in character, the federal antitrust laws are often better suited for legal action.

While hard-fought legal victories like the breakup of the Bell System companies were prevalent years ago, they have recently given way to failed Justice Department antitrust litigation like the 2018 court decision allowing the $85 billion AT&T–Time Warner merger to proceed. Meanwhile, an increasingly pro-monopoly U.S. Supreme Court has made it more and more difficult to litigate antitrust cases, and the growing dominance of mega data search and social media firms continues to make virtual mincemeat out of our existing legal standards and American antitrust enforcement. In this highly charged monopoly environment, there is a fair case to be made that the *only* thing that hasn't changed over the last decade are the laws and policies that are supposed to police market dominance.

My own personal story, like that of so many Americans, traces back to much of this changing economic landscape. My relatives came to America to work for the mining industrialists of the Gilded Age. Yet their ultimate success story—based in better mining wages and safer working conditions—was a direct result of unions taking on the organizing and antitrust battles against their employers. Our family rode those better wages all the way downriver to the Twin Cities, allowing my dad to go to college and me to go to law school. My dad's job as a newspaperman and columnist was a steady one, but the changing tides of newspaper sales and purchases, and the merger of the morning and afternoon papers, always made for some lively dinner conversation.

Then, as a brand-new lawyer in a Minneapolis law firm in 1985, I embarked on a fourteen-year legal journey in the private sector, including representing MCI Telecommunications. During that time, the company was constantly taunting the regional Bell monopolies (formerly owned by AT&T), suing across the United States and ultimately pushing its way into their territories while bringing more competition, more innovation, and certainly lower prices to the market.

Ten years later, as a new mom, I got into politics as a citizen-advocate. I took on the insurance companies and helped to pass one of the first state laws in the country guaranteeing new moms and their babies a minimum forty-eight-hour hospital stay. I was later elected as the county prosecutor in Minnesota's largest county and, for the past decade in the U.S. Senate, have served as either chair or lead Democrat on that chamber's Antitrust Subcommittee.

Nearly every American can trace their economic story in sync with the market changes of their time. But how we as a country respond to those changes can well define the economic fortunes of our citizens today. This book explains the consequences for our democracy and our economy if we fail to act. It is a basic citizen's primer on how all of this has worked and can work in the future. But it is also a plea for help.

The one institution I still have confidence in is our democracy—the one our Founding Fathers set up back in 1776, and which, nearly 250 years later, in the midst of a public health crisis and despite an actual insurrection at our nation's capitol incited by a U.S. president, has endured. In fact, Americans cast the highest number of votes ever in the 2020 U.S. presidential election. The preamble of the U.S. Constitution—the document that has long structured our representative democracy—begins, "We the People of the United States, in Order to form a more perfect Union." It's time for "We the People" to get engaged once again—to take on the systemic issues of money in politics, greed and corruption, and, yes, collusion, cartels, and the state of our nation's antitrust laws. That's one way to strive to form that more perfect Union.

With monopolies, megamergers, and corporate consolidation on the rise, we need to put the trust back into our nation's antitrust laws. From America's Founding Fathers to the trustbusters of the early twentieth century to the once-active Justice Department that broke up AT&T, American history is replete with examples of how Americans successfully took on monopoly power. And in the era of Big Tech and Big Pharma, we have no choice but to do it again.

1

Monopoly—It's Not Just a Game

The Roots of America's Antimonopolist Movement

A TRIP DOWN MONOPOLY LANE: THE GAME, THE COLONISTS, AND THE BOSTON TEA PARTY

My favorite game growing up was Monopoly. While my dad, then a journalist with *The Minneapolis Star,* would sometimes convince my sister and me to play Scrabble, and the neighborhood kids loved our home version of Jeopardy! (complete with little metal clickers to take the place of the TV buzzer), Monopoly was in a class of its own. For one, it was endless, with weekend marathons at my friends' houses, especially when it rained. For another it had weird tokens like a thimble and a wheelbarrow (now sadly replaced by the game's "updated" tokens, which include a rubber ducky and *T. rex*).

With Monopoly, you could collect hotels and houses. You could moan when you paid exorbitant rents for landing on the superchic Park Place, and rejoice when you missed the dreaded Income Tax square. The basic concept was this: the more you owned, the more you controlled, the more you made, the more you squeezed your opponents out of existence. This was assumed to be the true—and the one and only—model of American capitalism. If you managed to monopolize the board by buying up multiple properties of the same color and covering them in rent-producing real estate, you took your opponents out of the game. Whole corners of the game board became debt traps, and with each roll of the dice and trip around the board your opponents would sell off more and more of their meager holdings just to afford your escalating rents. It was all about winning with monopolies, and there were no competing "antitrust enforcement" cards to get you out of the soup (line).

When I first started running that thimble token around the Monopoly board at the kitchen table of my best friend Amy Scherber's family cabin, I never imagined I would end up as one of the two U.S. senators heading up the committee dealing with antitrust policy for our country. Yet when people ask me as a senator what monopolies and antitrust policy have to do with their lives, the answer I give now is the same one I gave back then as I raked in the Monopoly money rent on my railroads. *Everything.*

The answer is everything. Antitrust and monopolies have everything to do with our economy, the prices we pay, and the way we live.

The freedom to buy and sell goods and succeed on your own merit has long been at the core of American antitrust policy. But more important, a century before antitrust laws were even considered, the freedom to participate in a competitive market was a central guiding tenet of the American economy. It was one of the major reasons our country was founded in the first place when a ragtag group of settlers and colonists decided to start a new life in a new land. They were fiercely independent and entrepreneurial. And they wanted nothing to do with monopolies—especially government-controlled monopolies—dictating their economic choices.

The American colonists were well aware of the dangers of monopoly power. At the time of America's birth as a nation, most of its people were farmers, many of them immigrants or descendants of immigrants who'd fled Europe to get a new beginning. They'd purposefully come to a country where they could practice their religion, politics, and entrepreneurship without rules and regulations and without a king telling them what to buy and whom to buy it from. While the European nations financed American exploration and settlements to expand their land acquisitions and trading markets, the actual people who settled America had a different plan in mind. They wanted liberty.

American colonists, as best exemplified by Benjamin Franklin, prized new inventions, but they despised monopoly power. The 1641 laws of colonial Massachusetts, known as "The Body of Liberties," contain an audacious expression of the early Americans' aversion to monopolies: "No monopolies shall be granted or allowed amongst us, but of such new Inventions that are profitable to the Countrie, and that for a short time." Maryland's first constitution, adopted in November 1776, just a few months after the Second Continental Congress's issuance of the Declaration of Independence, specifically recited in its Declaration of Rights, "That monopolies are odious, contrary to the spirit of a free government, and the principles of commerce; and ought not to be suffered." North Carolina's constitution of December 1776 similarly asserted in its Declaration of Rights that "monopolies are contrary to the genius of a free state, and ought not to be allowed."

In England, monopolies were technically illegal, except there was one gaping hole in English law: Parliament itself had the right to grant monopolies. In *Darcy v. Allen* (1602), which came to be known as "The Case of Monopolies," the Court of the King's Bench ruled that while members of the royal family could not grant monopolies to individual subjects, Parliament had free rein to do so. In that case, Edward Darcy (no relation to the fictional Mr. Darcy of Jane Austen's novel *Pride and Prejudice*) had received from Queen Elizabeth an exclusive right to import, make, and sell playing cards. The queen felt that playing cards were too popular among servants and apprentices and had reduced productivity. Her solution? She put the entire playing card trade into one person's hands. The beneficiary was Darcy, who held a position in the royal household known as groom of the privy chamber. After Thomas Allen, a representative of the Worshipful Company of Haberdashers, started making and selling his own line of playing cards, Darcy sued Allen for damages. While Darcy had manufactured "400 grosses of cards" at a cost of 5,000 pounds sterling, Allen, responding to public demand, had produced an additional 180 grosses of playing cards without any royal license to do so.

In what is now regarded as a foundational case in antitrust law, the English court ruled that Darcy's patent to manufacture and sell playing cards was "utterly void" and constituted a violation of the English common law and acts of Parliament. As the decision was reported by the English jurist Sir Edward Coke, "The queen could not suppress the making of cards within the realm, no more than the making of dice, bowls, balls, hawks' hoods, bells, lures, dog-couples, and other the like, which are works of labor and art, although they serve for pleasure, recreation, and pastime, and cannot be suppressed *but by Parliament,* nor a man restrained from exercising any trade, *but by Parliament.*" The court thus squarely rejected Darcy's argument that Queen Elizabeth could—on her own—restrict the production and distribution of playing cards to moderate their use by servants or laborers or for any other reason. But Parliament kept the power to bestow monopolies for itself, later codifying and cementing its sole right to grant monopolies in what was aptly called the Statute of Monopolies (1624).

In the British Empire, the monopolies conferred by Parliament were the product of corruption, influence peddling, and outright bribes. By 1621, the year after the *Mayflower* had brought the Pilgrims to the New World, there were approximately seven hundred British monopolies in operation. As Christopher Hill writes in *The Century of Revolution* (1961), a typical seventeenth-century Englishman was "living in a house built with monopoly bricks, with windows (if any) of monopoly glass; heated by monopoly coal (in Ireland monopoly timber), burning in a grate made of monopoly iron." As Hill further observed, "He slept on monopoly feathers, did his hair with monopoly brushes and monopoly combs. He washed himself with monopoly soap, his clothes in monopoly starch. He dressed in monopoly lace, monopoly linen, monopoly leather, monopoly gold thread." A man's clothes, Hill wrote of that time, "were held up by monopoly belts, monopoly buttons, monopoly pins," with the man's food "seasoned with monopoly salt, monopoly pepper, monopoly vinegar." Even mice, Hill stressed of royal patents, "were caught in monopoly mousetraps."

It makes perfect sense then that a major motivation of those sailing to the New World was to leave their monopoly handcuffs—not to mention their monopoly mousetraps—far behind. Just as the Pilgrims came to America in search of religious freedom, many settlers came to our shores in hopes of gaining economic freedom—the ability to buy land and farm on their own, get a new job and a fresh start. They were rewarded economically when other countries' businesses bought their crops and goods, and they, in turn, wanted the freedom to do business with whomever they wanted, whenever they wanted. In *Rights of Man* (1791), a book dedicated to President George Washington,

Thomas Paine—often described as the father of the American Revolution because of his authorship of *Common Sense* (1776)—lamented that England "is cut up into monopolies." Paine's ideal: "That there shall be no monopolies of any kind—that all trades shall be free, and every man free to follow any occupation by which he can procure an honest livelihood, and in any place, town and city throughout the nation."

Thus, our country's Declaration of Independence from England was not only a political Declaration of Independence from a foreign country but also an act of economic rebellion against monopoly power. Back then, colonists who even tried to compete against the British monopoly mercenaries could be fined or imprisoned by the Crown's prosecutors. And when the economy got tough in England, the king—who, at the time of the American Revolution, was George III—would inevitably resort to more demands dictating from whom the colonists could purchase their goods. His purpose? To bring more profits back across the pond to the mother country in order to shore up England's eroding economy.

One memorable example back in the 1770s of British efforts to impose a monopoly on America's colonists? Tea.

The most common takeaway from the 1773 Boston Tea Party—in which colonists threw 342 chests of British East India Company tea into the Atlantic Ocean—was one of taxation without representation. That was most certainly part of the story. The colonists were protesting the English Parliament's Tea Act because they believed it violated their rights to "no taxation without representation." The Tea Act, which provided that tea imported into the colonies would be taxed, was the brainchild of Lord North, who'd become the prime minister of Great Britain in 1770. The East India Company, the monopoly established by England in 1600, was in dire financial straits, and Lord North—the British politician who was later said to have "lost America"—was attempting to rescue that failing enterprise with more American tax dollars after a severe drought in India drastically reduced its revenue.

But there was also an underlying monopoly issue that led the Sons of Liberty—men like the Boston silversmith Paul Revere—to toss all that tea into Boston Harbor. During the lead-up to that act of rebellion, the colonists were buying lots of their tea from Dutch traders, with that untaxed tea illegally smuggled on ships from Holland, the Caribbean,

The Boston Tea Party (1773) galvanized opposition to British rule and the British East India Company, a powerful monopoly. The War of Independence (1775–1783) soon followed.

and elsewhere. But the Tea Act sought to change things to favor the East India Company's monopoly. As the historian Mary Beth Norton explains in her book *1774: The Long Year of Revolution,* seven ships carrying East India Company tea had set sail from Great Britain to North America in October 1773 under the auspices of the newly adopted Tea Act. That law allowed the East India Company, for the first time, to sell its tea directly to colonists. Prior to that time, the law required the East India Company to sell its tea at London auctions to wholesalers, who then marketed it to retailers.

By December 1773, five of the ships carrying the East India Company tea had arrived in American ports—in Boston, Charleston, and Philadelphia—while one wrecked off Cape Cod and still another blew off course and got stranded in Antigua for the winter. The American colonists, however, had grown accustomed to getting a large portion of their tea illegally from other merchants. One historian has estimated that just a quarter of the tea consumed in the colonies actually came from the East India Company, with another scholar saying the figure might be as low as 10 percent. Even before the arrival of the ships at American ports, the colonists—in published writings in October 1773—vociferously attacked the Tea Act. One American merchant,

Alexander McDougall, in five broadsides titled *The Alarm,* called the East India Company a "corrupt" monopoly obtained through "bribery" that would "rob" colonists.

The Tea Act was extremely unpopular. And when George III and Lord North insisted on handing over control to one enterprise—the East India Company—it was the proverbial last straw. The East India Company had been founded by royal charter nearly two centuries earlier and given a permanent monopoly in exchange for a £400,000 annual payment to the Crown. But the colonists were not impressed with the company's long pedigree. They sought liberty. And they wanted it so much that they even shunned their beloved tea, shifting their consumption to coffee, in protest, even though colonists were described by one contemporary as "probably the greatest tea drinkers in the universe." "Tea must be universally renounced," John Adams would write to his wife, Abigail, in 1774 in the midst of the patriotic fervor, which came to be known as the "anti-tea hysteria."

When ships loaded with British tea arrived in Boston Harbor in the days before the Boston Tea Party, the American patriot Samuel Adams organized mass protests. More than five thousand people responded to the call, and on the evening of December 16, 1773, the protest meeting was so large that it had to be relocated from Faneuil Hall to the larger Old South Meeting House. Being forced to buy this tea—and to pay taxes on it to prop up a government-sponsored private monopoly—incensed the colonists. As if it weren't enough that they were paying taxes to a British-sponsored foreign merchant, their ability to trade with the Dutch was now stifled and a monopoly foisted upon them.

On December 17, 1773, the day after the Boston Tea Party, John Adams took note in his diary of the "3 Cargoes" of tea that "were emptied into the Sea." "This is the most magnificent Movement of all," he wrote, observing that "there is a Dignity, a Majesty, a Sublimity, in this last Effort of the Patriots, that I greatly admire." "This Destruction of the Tea is so bold, so daring, so firm, intrepid and inflexible," he emphasized, that "it must have so important Consequences, so lasting."

And the response of the king? To quote Lin-Manuel Miranda's evocative words from the musical *Hamilton* (as captured in King George's witty solo "You'll Be Back"), the Crown's basic reaction to the colonists' tea hurling was this: "Remember we made an arrangement when you went away" and "Remember, despite our estrangement, I'm your man." The refrain of the song includes what was the common belief of the royals at the time—"You'll be back, soon you'll see / You'll remember you belong to me"—capped off by the punchy warning that "when push comes to shove / I will send a fully armed battalion to remind you of my love."

In the wake of the Boston Tea Party, the British Parliament passed the Boston Port Act in 1774, resulting in the blockade of Boston Harbor. Parliament demanded that the city's residents pay for all the tea that had been dumped into the harbor. In the end, of course, that demand backfired, and the colonists, defiantly donning their tricorne hats, would stand up to the Brits' monopoly "arrangement" and their "fully armed battalion." And the flags they carried into battle—bearing blunt messages like "LIBERTY OR DEATH" and "DON'T TREAD ON ME"—captured much of the antitax and antimonopoly sentiment of their time.

EARLY OPPOSITION TO MONOPOLIES: ADAM SMITH, THOMAS JEFFERSON, AND JAMES MADISON

The colonists' revulsion against monopoly rule was, in fact, backed up by economics. Three years after the Boston Tea Party, and during the very year that the United States of America formally declared its independence from Great Britain, Adam Smith, a Scottish moral philosopher and economics professor, published his famous book, *The Wealth of Nations*. Smith would later be known as the father of capitalism, with many of America's Founding Fathers—Madison, Jefferson, and Hamilton among them—regularly citing him in letters and speeches. Like America's founders, Adam Smith believed passionately in the power of entrepreneurship, innovation, and self-interest to drive both wealth creation and societal progress. As he famously put it, "It is not from the benevolence of the butcher, the brewer, or the baker that we expect our dinner, but from their regard to their own interest."

Smith argued in *The Wealth of Nations* for the power of the "invisible hand" to increase a nation's riches by improving the lives of everyone. By that he meant that those at the top—even when acting entirely in their own self-interest to amass wealth—will naturally (and with-

Adam Smith's *Wealth of Nations* was published in 1776, the same year that the Continental Congress issued the Declaration of Independence. It became a popular book among America's founders.

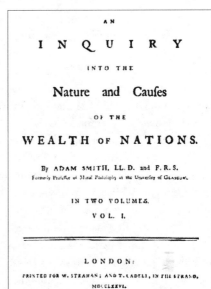

AN

INQUIRY

INTO THE

Nature and Caufes

OF THE

WEALTH OF NATIONS.

By ADAM SMITH, LL. D. and F. R. S.
Formerly Profeffor of Moral Philofophy in the Univerfity of GLASGOW.

IN TWO VOLUMES.

VOL. I.

LONDON:

PRINTED FOR W. STRAHAN; AND T. CADELL, IN THE STRAND.
MDCCLXXVI.

out even realizing it) lift up those whom Smith called the "labouring poor." At the same time, Smith made it very clear that he feared the "wretched spirit of monopolies." He saw the intrinsic evil of monopoly power and specifically warned about how monopolies could greatly constrain competition in the marketplace. He went so far as to compare a monopoly to "an overgrown standing army" that could "become formidable to the government, and upon many occasions intimidate the legislature." He spoke of the "insolent outrage of furious and disappointed monopolists" that politicians were all too often afraid to cross. He explained how monopolists, "by keeping the market constantly understocked, by never fully supplying the effectual demand, sell their commodities much above the natural price, and raise their . . . wages or profit, greatly above their natural rate." And he worried about collusion and the power of cartels, explaining, "People of the same trade seldom meet together, even for merriment and diversion, but the conversation ends in a conspiracy against the public, or in some contrivance to raise prices." In other words, a check and balance on monopolies and price-gouging cartels in a free-enterprise system was not only welcome, it was indispensable.

The founders of our country and the drafters of our Constitution, who spoke ardently of liberty but who, paradoxically, enslaved countless human beings, shared many of Smith's concerns about monopoly power. George Mason and Thomas Jefferson, both slave owners, tried valiantly, but in vain, to include a clause in the U.S. Constitution to check monopoly power. Mason, the Virginia plantation owner, feared that "Congress may grant Monopolies in Trade and Commerce" and that northern and eastern merchants would, to the ruin of the southern states, charge "exorbitant Freight" and "monopolize the Purchase of the Commodities at their own Price, for many years." Jefferson, in a letter written in 1787 while he was serving as a diplomat in Paris, complained vehemently about the lack of a Bill of Rights and unsuccessfully sought a specific "restriction against monopolies."

Jefferson and Madison—the Virginians and U.S. presidents who shared a long, cordial friendship—in fact exchanged multiple ideas on the subject of monopolies in the founding era. Jefferson was an inventor (his design for a new moldboard plow revolutionized agriculture and was awarded a gold medal by the Agricultural Society of Paris), but he still opposed the idea of granting monopolies. As U.S. Supreme Court Justice Tom Clark later wrote in *Graham v. John Deere Co.* (1966), "Jefferson, like other Americans, had an instinctive aversion to monopolies. It was a monopoly on tea that sparked the Revolution and Jefferson certainly did not favor an equivalent form of monopoly under the new government."

Madison, while also concerned about monopoly power, cautioned Jefferson against overreacting. A year after receiving Jefferson's 1787 letter bemoaning the lack of a constitutional restriction against monopolies, Madison responded. In his 1788 letter, Madison labeled monopolies "among the greatest nuisances in Government" but made the case to Jefferson that with democracy, where the power is "in the many, not in the few," monopolies would be constrained and the "danger can not be very great." Jefferson, in yet another letter to Madison, conceded in 1789 that he was pleased to see constitutional protections "to persons for their own productions in literature & their own inventions in the arts" for a term of years. Jefferson later wrote, "Certainly an inventor ought to be allowed a right to the benefit of his invention for some certain time. . . .

Nobody wishes more than I do that ingenuity should receive a liberal encouragement."

In the end, neither the U.S. Constitution nor the Declaration of Independence made explicit reference to monopolies or slavery—the ultimate monopoly over a person's labor. The Constitution did not allow Congress to ban the slave trade until 1808, thereby entrenching the "peculiar institution" of slavery, and the fugitive slave clause prevented free states from emancipating enslaved persons who tried to escape human bondage. The Declaration of Independence, though speaking of equality while remaining silent about slavery, is centered on individual citizens' "Liberty" and "pursuit of Happiness," both of which are, themselves, inimical to slavery and monopoly power. In terms of monopolies, the Declaration of Independence contains—in indictment-like fashion—explicit mention of King George III's many "injuries and usurpations," two of which pertain to the British trading monopolies of the time: "cutting off our Trade with all parts of the world," and "imposing Taxes on us without our consent." Of course, those English taxes were aiding private royal monopolies.

The Constitution does confer on Congress the power to "promote the Progress of Science and useful Arts, by securing for limited Times to Authors and Inventors the exclusive Right to their respective Writings and Discoveries." The purpose of that provision was succinctly explained by Madison in *The Federalist* No. 43: "The utility of this power will scarcely be questioned. The copyright of authors has been solemnly adjudged, in Great Britain, to be a right of common law. The right to useful inventions seems with equal reason to belong to the inventors. The public good fully coincides in both cases with the claims of individuals." Because "the States cannot separately make effectual provisions for either of the cases," Madison explained, Congress was given the power to pass laws in those two arenas.

The Founding Fathers' concerns about monopolies were real and well documented. But aside from the Constitution's intellectual property clause, there were no monopoly-related provisions in the country's founding documents. It is no surprise, then, that the Constitution's lack of clear guidance—and the failure of Congress to act in a timely way at the Republic's outset—soon led to an expansion of monopolies. As

America's 90 percent agrarian economy of the late eighteenth century gave way to the Industrial Revolution in the first half of the nineteenth century, the nation's economy grew with every new machine and each new manufacturing process. From Eli Whitney's cotton gin, patented in 1794, to Robert Fulton's creation of the first commercial steamboat in 1807, America's invention-fired economy expanded rapidly. As our country's gross national product increased, the standard of living went up for many Americans, creating what was once called the "middling class."

Yet at the same time, this major economic transition—which included much economic disruption, and then consolidation, during the Civil War (1861–1865) and its aftermath—led to the accumulation of wealth in the hands of the few over the many. And the very thing Madison had argued to Jefferson would be a check on the growth of monopolies in America—the voices of the many as reflected in our system of government—floundered in the face of the new economy. The country's leaders were seemingly inept, unprepared, or, in some cases, deliberately uninterested (due to corrupt arrangements between monopolists and politicians) in dealing with the dramatic changes brought about by the industrial age. Tammany Hall and William "Boss" Tweed, the nineteenth-century politician who took bribes and stole millions from New York City, have become synonymous with the political corruption of the time.

Through the next century, as robber barons and oil magnates bought up much of America's natural resources (from western land to Texas oil to Minnesota iron ore), little was done to check what was clearly a pro-monopoly economic transition. Much of Adam Smith's and Thomas Jefferson's early warnings about monopoly power went unheeded during the nineteenth century, with a few exceptions. There was, for example, the ongoing debate over the First Bank of the United States, which had a twenty-year renewable charter that began in 1791 and which was set up as a private institution that had the monopoly power to print money. The Second Bank of the United States, also a private corporation, was owned, in part, by the federal government. It was chartered by James Madison in 1816, with the national bank receiving a twenty-year charter and opening its main branch, in Philadelphia, in 1817. As the bank's charter was nearing the end of its term, however, President

Andrew Jackson vetoed it. In his veto message of 1832, Jackson railed against monopolies and "exclusive privileges" granted "at the expense of the public." Ultimately, the bank's charter was not renewed, and after becoming a private corporation in 1836, it was liquidated in 1841.

As antimonopoly sentiment spread, the country's political leaders became extremely wary of market consolidation, and for good reason. In 1888, President Grover Cleveland noted that corporations, which had successfully obtained a number of court rulings that allowed them to maintain their monopolies, "should be the carefully restrained creatures of the law and the servants of the people." Such corporations, he warned, "are fast becoming the people's masters."

Despite this ominous warning, the few bills that passed the U.S. Congress at the time were sufficiently watered down so as to have little impact on the well-heeled and well-connected monopolists. With mounting abuses and concerns coming from their constituents, the governors and legislatures of various states tried to step in. Yet these efforts had little effect without a strong national standard and the necessary resources and enforcement wherewithal to give the laws the force they

This 1889 political cartoon from *Puck,* a humor magazine published from 1877 to 1918, depicts the U.S. Senate debating the Sherman Antitrust Act. The monopolists, through their campaign contributions, had such power in that era that even the passage of the Sherman Act did not spell the demise of the trusts. For years, the courts themselves refused to enforce the law's plain language.

needed to make a difference. And, in the case of the one major federal law passed by Congress, the 1890 Sherman Antitrust Act, the executive branch and judges, through their rulings, effectively refused to enforce it or give it effect for years. The result? As the nineteenth century came to a close, none of the reform-minded politicians' actions had slowed down the monopoly express barreling through the American countryside.

The twentieth century ushered in a new era. As prescient as Adam Smith's and Thomas Jefferson's dire predictions of monopoly shenanigans would be, a new century finally kicked off the coming of age of Madison's stubborn, 110-year-old reply to Jefferson's pleas: that America's democracy, in which the power in the hands of the many can eventually overcome the power in the hands of a few, could act as a restraint on monopolies. For in the decades spanning the turn of the century, a strong populist progressive movement against the consolidated monopolies tore through American politics.

The nationwide union strikes and heartland farmer rebellions gave rise to antitrust powerhouses like William Jennings Bryan, a popular Nebraska congressman who became the Democratic Party's nominee in three presidential elections, and President Theodore Roosevelt. It was in fact President Roosevelt—a Republican—who took on the trusts with such gusto that by 1904, in a case originally brought in my home state (*Minnesota v. Northern Securities Company*), the U.S. Supreme Court finally said that the federal government could sue to dissolve companies that violated the antitrust laws.

ELIZABETH MAGIE AND THE GAME OF MONOPOLY

It was, of course, no coincidence that the year the U.S. Supreme Court finally heeded Adam Smith's dire warnings about monopoly power—1904—was the same year that the earliest known version of my favorite childhood game, Monopoly, was patented by a woman from Macomb, Illinois, named Elizabeth Magie. It was only recently (and, in part, through a 1970s-era lawsuit and some good old-fashioned sleuthing by the former *New York Times* and *Wall Street Journal* reporter Mary Pilon) that the myth that the game was created in the 1930s by a down-on-his-luck salesman, Charles Darrow, was officially debunked. It was Lizzie Magie, a startlingly progressive woman for her time, and an outspoken creative sort and women's rights advocate who never married until her forties, who actually invented and filed the first patent for the game. In fact, back when Magie filed the patent under its original name, the Landlord's Game, she would be one of the less than 1 percent of all early twentieth-century patent applicants who were women.

Lizzie Magie designed the Landlord's Game to promote the ideas of Henry George, an American journalist and economist who had written a wildly popular book, *Progress and Poverty* (1879), that sold millions of copies. George's book, which spawned a form of economic populism known as Georgism, explored the puzzle of increasing poverty and income inequality in the midst of the technological advances of the Second Industrial Revolution. To remedy the ills of abject poverty and to try to level the playing field, George—a man who had worked as a seaman and a gas-meter inspector and who had experienced destitution during California's gold rush as an unsuccessful prospector—believed that the rents paid to landowners were sapping the working class. He thus promoted the idea of a "single tax" on land, with other goods, including the necessities of life, to go untaxed. The idea: if working people and the poor (a description that fit most working people back then) could keep all of their wages, poverty would be eradicated more quickly. *The New York Times* reported in 1881 that George—an avowed antimonopolist—not only had "put down clearly in black and white" the causes of poverty but had "offered a cure." Martin Luther King Jr. would himself later quote from *Progress and Poverty,* which made declarations about the equality of all races. George had written of "a state of society where want is abolished," with King quoting from that passage of George's book and adding that the problems of education and housing would be solved by the elimination of poverty. The poor, King observed, would gain dignity and be "transformed into purchasers" who would "do a great deal on their own to alter housing decay" when "they have the additional weapon of cash to use in their struggle."

Henry George, who had visited Ireland in 1882 as part of his *Progress and Poverty* book tour and who had taken the side of the poor against their landlords, was persuaded to enter the political arena just a few years after publishing the book. It was a fateful decision that would, ultimately, shape the views of the future American president Teddy

Elizabeth Magie, the daughter of an Illinois newspaperman who knew
Abraham Lincoln, became fascinated by the ideas of Henry George, an
American economist who wrote a best-selling book, *Progress and Poverty,*
that advocated for a single-tax system. She invented and in 1904 patented
a board game, the Landlord's Game, that was the predecessor of the
wildly popular board game Monopoly.

Roosevelt, who once ran against George himself. In the 1886 race for
New York City mayor, George was the Labor Party candidate who
accepted his party's nomination at Cooper Union, the venue that had
vaulted Abraham Lincoln to the presidency. George and Roosevelt,
the Republican nominee and then a twenty-eight-year-old former state
assemblyman, squared off in a three-way race with Jacksonian Democrat Abram Hewitt, a congressman who represented the Lower East
Side and Gramercy Park. Although both George and Roosevelt campaigned heavily for the job, delivering stump speeches to promote their
ideas, Hewitt—the Tammany Hall candidate—prevailed in the end.
The final vote tally: Hewitt, 90,552; George, 68,110; and Roosevelt—
the third-place finisher—60,435. A disappointed Roosevelt thought his
political career was over, but instead it turns out he had learned a valuable lesson about politics: the importance of populism and paying attention to the wants and needs of the electorate.

The connection between Henry George, Lizzie Magie, and the
Monopoly game is a fascinating one. Lizzie Magie was born in 1866,

twenty years before George's and Roosevelt's spirited mayoral campaigns. She grew up in a middle-class family, though the family's fortunes ebbed into crisis after the panic of 1873, a financial crisis that triggered a depression that lasted until the end of the decade. Lizzie had to drop out of school to bring in some extra money for the family, and with the growing popularity of typewriters she dutifully found work as a stenographer. When, around 1890, the family relocated to Washington, D.C., she continued that work, finding employment as a typist in the Dead Letter Office—the office tasked with handling undeliverable U.S. mail. By the 1890s, that office processed twenty thousand to twenty-five thousand letters or packages on a daily basis. In 1893, Lizzie—the always enterprising young woman—applied to patent a device she engineered to allow different sizes of paper to pass more easily through typewriter rollers. But her real passion was for Georgism, writing, and inventing games.

When Elizabeth Magie created the Landlord's Game, she drew upon her personal experiences, including "absolute necessity" spaces for bread, clothing, shelter, and coal. American families relied on coal to heat their homes, and the bitter, hard-fought Coal Strike of 1902 in Pennsylvania's anthracite coalfields—one led by the United Mine Workers of America—was very much on her mind when she filed her patent application for the game. When the players of Magie's game

Henry George, a critic of the immense power of the railroads, wrote a global best seller, *Progress and Poverty* (1879), that inspired an economic philosophy known as Georgism. George wrote of the paradox of inequality and poverty at a time of great industrial and technological progress. He supported antimonopoly reforms and a land value tax to help remedy the social ills he saw.

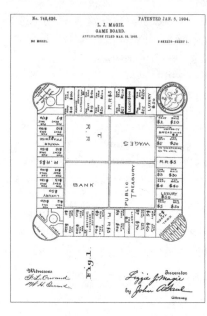

In 1903, Lizzie Magie filed a patent application for a new game, the Landlord's Game, to help bring further attention to the economic ideas of Henry George, whose book *Progress and Poverty* sparked reforms during the Progressive Era. Enthusiasts of Monopoly will recognize similarities between that board game and this one—featuring four places for railroads—that Magie designed.

landed on the "absolute necessity" spaces, they had to pay $5 each time to the "public treasury." The Landlord's Game was designed—above all else—to interest players in Henry George's economic theories, with players earning $100 each time they went around the board.

We now know that Magie developed the first version of what she patented as the Landlord's Game—which later became Monopoly—complete with four railroad squares, Chance cards, a "Go to Jail" stop, and a luxury tax, all to protest the big monopolies of her time. Magie's original Chance cards even had quotations on them, including this one from the wealthy industrialist Andrew Carnegie: "The greatest astonishment of my life was the discovery that the man who does the work is not the man who gets rich."

But here's the monopoly twist: Elizabeth Magie actually created two sets of rules for the game. The first set of rules are those of the current game I played growing up, in which a monopolist can crush opponents by virtue of monopoly holdings, while the other—the antimonopolist version—didn't stand the test of time (or the preferences of the game's promoters). The antimonopoly version of the rules actually spread wealth in a more egalitarian fashion across the board and rewarded all

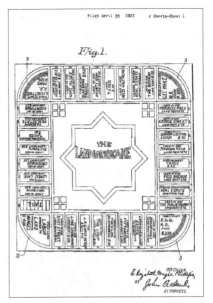

The 1923 patent application—filed by Lizzie Magie after she married Albert Phillips—for a revised version of the Landlord's Game. Her game, which featured named streets, was used at the University of Pennsylvania and other colleges to teach Georgism, a then-popular economic theory. Lizzie later sold the rights to her game to Parker Brothers.

wealth creation. That version of the rules was, in truth, the whole reason Magie invented the game. She wanted to focus Americans' attention on the unequal distribution of wealth created by the monopolists of her time.

Despite Elizabeth Magie's 1936 interview with *The Washington Post* in which she made the case that she—and not Charles Darrow—actually invented the Monopoly game, the pioneering female inventor died in relative obscurity in 1948. Darrow, who'd learned to play the game from Charles Todd, a neighbor who'd enjoyed playing a version of the game in Atlantic City, had simply modified it in 1933 by sprucing up the board and then sold it at department stores like F. A. O. Schwarz before Parker Brothers bought it in 1935 and licensed it worldwide. "While Darrow made millions and struck an agreement that ensured he would receive royalties," *The New York Times* later reported, "Magie's income for her creation was reported to be a mere $500." It was Parker Brothers—the game company that made those millions for Darrow and, of course, for itself—that paid Magie the $500 (with no residuals) in 1935 to ensure that she would not be able to make any legal claims against Parker Brothers in the future.

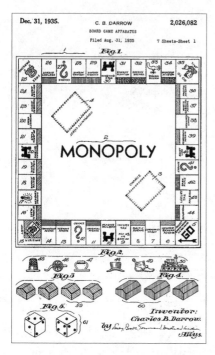

After playing a version of Lizzie
Magie's game, Charles Darrow
began to make, distribute, and sell
a modified version of the game.
Darrow unsuccessfully attempted
to sell it to Milton Bradley, but he
then persuaded Parker Brothers to
buy the game in 1935. In that year,
Darrow filed a patent application for
the game of Monopoly, with Parker
Brothers purchasing Lizzie Magie's
1924 patent, marketing the game
of Monopoly, and turning it into a
blockbuster success.

Two days after signing the agreement with George Parker, the man
who'd built the company and who had traveled all the way from Salem,
Massachusetts, to Arlington, Virginia, to acquire the rights from her,
Magie sent him a letter saying of her invented game, "Farewell, my
beloved brain-child. I regretfully part with you, but I am giving you to
another who will be able to do more for you than I have done." Sadly
for Lizzie Magie, Parker Brothers was much more interested in making
money than in promoting Georgism. And although the company, as
promised, dutifully brought out the Landlord's Game in 1939, four years
after bringing out Monopoly, Magie's version never took off.

Later dubbed by *The New York Times* as "the progressive who didn't
pass go," Lizzie Magie must have been smiling from the heavens above
when, in 1973, a San Francisco economics professor tried to recapture her
original idea and developed an antimonopoly version of the game. The
Anti-Monopoly game developer, San Francisco State University professor Ralph Anspach, was then sued by the then owners of the Monopoly
game (yes, by that point, Minnesota-based General Mills owned Parker

Brothers, the game manufacturer) for trademark infringement. It was over the course of that lawsuit, with all its claims and counterclaims, that Lizzie Magie's pivotal role in the creation of the storied Monopoly franchise was unearthed.

The Monopoly versus Anti-Monopoly case went on for ten years with both verdicts and appeals. At one point, after a trial court judge, the Nixon-appointee Spencer Williams, ruled that Anspach had committed trademark infringement, Anspach was ordered to "deliver up for destruction" any remaining copies of his game. In a demonstration of its corporate power in the David-versus-Goliath litigation, representatives of Parker Brothers invited the media and buried approximately forty thousand Anti-Monopoly games in a landfill in Mankato, Minnesota, the place where my husband, John, grew up. Anspach, by then deeply in debt, had flown to Mankato to witness the demoralizing spectacle, but he was utterly helpless to stop the destruction of the games. Ultimately, General Mills sold Parker Brothers to Tonka (later bought by Hasbro), and the San Francisco professor's game was finally allowed to move forward after years of legal wrangling.

As a quick aside, in January 1980, after Anspach won a victory on appeal in the years-long litigation, he decided to try to dig up the Anti-Monopoly games. He traveled back to Mankato in an attempt to unearth his buried games—this time, with his own press in tow. The trip to Mankato got Anspach some publicity, but the Anti-Monopoly games would remain in the landfill. What Anspach, the fifty-three-year-old Californian, quickly discovered is that the Minnesota soil was frozen solid at that time of year and that, by then, the land on which the games had been interred had been sold to a real estate developer who was constructing houses in the area. Six hours of digging in near-zero temperatures failed to turn up anything.

Today, the website for the Anti-Monopoly board game notes how it is played: "Players choose free enterprise or monopoly, then play under different rules. Competitors charge fair market value while monopolists take over whole neighborhoods and jack up rents. In real life, monopolists have an unfair advantage. But in Anti-Monopoly, competitors have a fair shot at coming out on top!"

During my late-night 1970s Monopoly marathons, I knew none of this. Back then, the Landlord's Game was no longer in production.

And Anti-Monopoly—the more modern, equally disruptive version—certainly wasn't an option either.

The result? The only Monopoly game available to me growing up taught me and millions of Americans a clear economic lesson about the virtues of making money by going big. Yes, I played Monopoly in the 1970s as I was supposed to, with the simple goal of buying Park Place and Boardwalk and the Railroads and then collecting the exorbitant rents. I learned capitalism one way—the Monopoly way. And all I ever wanted to do was to beat my mom, my sister, my friends, and even my grandma (something I did more than once). Despite Elizabeth Magie's historical purpose in creating the game—to teach the masses about the dangers of monopoly power—I didn't even know what "antitrust" was. Counter-monopoly, antitrust laws didn't even merit a square on the board. And they were definitely not contained in any of the Chance cards stacked in the pile in the middle of the game board.

But in the real world, where the U.S. Department of Justice has an Antitrust Division and we have something called the Federal Trade Commission charged with protecting consumers, the cards don't have to be stacked against us. We can change the rules of the game. Looking back through American history shows us that antimonopoly fervor and antitrust enforcement were once our ways out of the mess. Now it is our job to do it again.

2

Don't Trust the Trusts

James J. Hill, the Gilded Age, and the Labor Movement

"GIVE ME SWEDES, SNUFF AND WHISKEY,
AND I'LL BUILD A RAILROAD TO HELL."

The James J. Hill House is one of Minnesota's most famous houses. But to call it a "house" is a lesson in Minnesota understatement. It is in fact a grandiose mansion. But how do you know that if you're not a student of robber-baron history? It's that middle initial. Normal houses aren't owned by people whose names are referenced with middle initials. Especially *J*s.

In fact, that middle initial *J* can mean only one thing: it's a really big house.

And it is.

The James J. Hill House is located on tree-lined, mansion-filled Summit Avenue in St. Paul, where it stands out as a massive edifice, all in stone and brick with arches, pillars, and multiple chimneys. Once called the "showcase of St. Paul," the property includes a spectacular view of the city and the Mississippi River. The man who built it— James J. Hill—was a railroad magnate who made his fortune going big. His Great Northern Railway, running from St. Paul to Seattle, covered America's northernmost transcontinental route. James J. Hill was known for his hands-on business acumen and his willingness to build railroads in one of the largest and most untamed regions of the country.

The James J. Hill House, in St. Paul, is a thirty-six-thousand-square-foot mansion built for the railroad titan known as the Empire Builder.

"Give me Swedes, snuff and whiskey," he once reportedly boasted, "and I'll build a railroad to hell!"

In his day, James J. Hill was a figure to be reckoned with—and, in fact, a legend in his own time. In the novel, *The Great Gatsby*—written by another famous St. Paul native, F. Scott Fitzgerald—Gatsby's father notes at his funeral that his son had a great future in front of him: "If he'd of lived he'd of been a great man. A man like James J. Hill. He'd of helped build up the country." When Fitzgerald was a teenager, his family rented a home down the street from Hill's stately mansion, and it had clearly made an impression on him.

That's how famous Hill was at the time. Known as the Empire Builder, Hill not only consolidated multiple railroads across the country but also bought land, banks, and mines. He and many industrialists like him—J. Pierpont Morgan (yes, another *J*), E. H. Harriman, Henry Clay Frick, Cornelius Vanderbilt, Andrew Mellon, and John D. Rockefeller—controlled entire sectors of the ever-expanding American economy from railroads to oil to steel.

To cement their control, Hill and other wealthy business owners used the legal concept of a "trust," in which the stockholders of multiple companies transferred their shares to a single set of trustees. The stock-

James J. Hill, a Canadian American railroad titan, became known in his own lifetime as the Empire Builder. Hill controlled the Great Northern Railway and the Northern Pacific Railway, and formed the Northern Securities Company in 1901 along with other captains of industry, including E. H. Harriman and J. P. Morgan, in an effort to monopolize railroad traffic.

holders of the "holding company" would then receive a certificate entitling them to a share of the earnings of the jointly managed companies. Trusts were useful to their owners because they could be used to (1) buy out and thus eliminate competitors; (2) bring down prices in the short term to make it hard for others to compete while leaving open the possibility of raising prices in the long term; (3) force long-term contracts on customers and require them to buy products they didn't really want in order to get the ones they did want; and (4) get more control over employees because with trusts there is less competition to negotiate over wages and working conditions.

Trusts developed in the petroleum, meatpacking, railroad, sugar, lead, coal, whiskey, and tobacco industries, among others, during this era. The multimillion-dollar American Thread Company became known as the Thread Trust; the American Sewer Pipe Company, combining thirty-three firms with a 40 percent market share, was termed the Sewer Pipe Trust; and the National Biscuit Company was called the Cracker Trust. Probably the most famous trust was the Standard Oil Trust, formed in 1882 to control prices and destroy competition in the oil markets. Through the trust, John D. Rockefeller's Standard Oil Company and its affiliates controlled more than 90 percent of the country's refining capacity and much of the country's oil marketing

A Standard Oil Trust certificate from 1896. Standard Oil
Company was started in 1870 as an Ohio corporation and soon
became the world's largest oil refiner, with its affiliated companies
located all over the United States. John D. Rockefeller ran the
company until his retirement in 1897, but in 1911 the U.S. Supreme
Court found that the Standard Oil Trust was an unlawful
monopoly and the massive entity was broken up.

facilities. To highlight its enormous power, the stock certificates for the
Standard Oil Trust actually featured an etching of the U.S. Capitol (I
kid you not).

James J. Hill and his frenemies (business "competitors" who simultaneously became business "associates" in the trusts) made a lot of
money off their trusts. Their combined monopoly power allowed them
to dominate not only the financial markets but also the labor markets,
the political markets (as in state legislatures and the U.S. Congress),
and the legal markets (with many judges rendering favorable court rulings for the industrialists for years). One example? In *United States v.
E. C. Knight Co.* (1895), better known as the Sugar Trust Case, the U.S.
Supreme Court, in an 8–1 ruling, held that even though the American
Sugar Refining Company controlled 98 percent of the manufacturing
of a single commodity—refined sugar—its monopoly violated *no law.*

The Gilded Age, as it was dubbed by Mark Twain's 1873 novel of the
same name, stretched from the 1870s to about 1900. It was characterized
by rapid economic expansion, Jim Crow racial segregation, employment
and housing discrimination, and an additional influx of immigrants
to run the engines of that expansion. In addition to James J. Hill, this
was the age of Andrew Carnegie (1835–1919), the Scottish American

New York American.]

The Railway Trust.

The owners of American railroads, including Cornelius Vanderbilt, James J. Hill, Jay Gould, and Edward Harriman, became some of the most powerful men in the country. The people noticed but in the early years had little ability to push back. This cartoon, from 1904, appeared in the *New York American.*

industrialist who dominated the steel industry and became a leading philanthropist; Jay Gould (1836–1892), the ruthless American railroad developer and land speculator who got involved with Tammany Hall, the New York City political organization once led by the corrupt New York politician William "Boss" Tweed, convicted of stealing millions of dollars from local taxpayers; J. P. Morgan (1837–1913), the banker and financier who, in 1892, arranged the merger of the companies that formed General Electric; John D. Rockefeller (1839–1937), the oil magnate who co-founded Standard Oil Company with his younger brother William and became the wealthiest person in the country; and John Jacob Astor IV (1864–1912), the capitalist and great-grandson of America's first multimillionaire who lost his life on the maiden voyage of the *Titanic,* leaving behind an estimated $200 million fortune. It was a period of great wealth and excess, but also abject poverty. The massive disparities of wealth between the art-collecting and world-traveling industrialists and the typical laborer or immigrant seeking a new life in America could not have been starker.

And the James J. Hill House is—as they say—the Gilded Age Exhibit A.

A TRUSTWORTHY BEAST.

The public may regard trusts or combinations with serene confidence."—ANDREW CARNEGIE, in an interview in *N. Y. Times*, Oct. 9.

Titans of industry like Andrew Carnegie defended trusts. In this cartoon, Carnegie presents the Steel Trust, the Lumber Trust, the Salt Trust, the Oil Trust, the Sugar Trust, and the Coal Trust to Uncle Sam.

As a little girl growing up in the Twin Cities, I never got to go inside that house until it opened for public tours. It's now considered a historic landmark. Built between 1888 and 1891, it's a thirty-six-thousand-square-foot mansion designed to showcase Hill's collection of French landscape paintings. It comes complete with a grand staircase, gymnasium, forty-two rooms, twenty-two fireplaces, sixteen chandeliers, thirteen bathrooms, and a hundred-foot-long reception hall. In the mid-1970s my mom used to drive me by that imposing house in her red Ford Comet to look at the Christmas decorations and lights. While James J. Hill was long deceased when we drove past his home, other prominent Minnesota families (the Shorts, the Pillsburys) were quite alive, and I have a strong recollection of ducking down in the passenger seat of my mom's car as we also peered through their windows, hoping to catch a glimpse of their Christmas trees.

But my family's history with the James J. Hill House was more than that of passing voyeurs. No, it was a lot more than that: our family— at least on my dad's Slovenian iron ore miner side—built that house.

Metaphorically of course, but we did. Because for Hill to build that house, he needed the monopoly railroads, the iron ore, and the steel to create his wealth. And he needed the cheap labor to do the work. That's where we fit in.

1,500 FEET UNDERGROUND:
A HARDSCRABBLE LIFE ON MINNESOTA'S IRON RANGE

My great-grandparents came to America from Slovenia along with many immigrants for one reason: jobs. Their story was repeated a million times over as people immigrated to the United States from all over the world to fill job openings in many industries. The industrialists like James J. Hill needed the inexpensive labor to build their railroads, to mine their mines, and to work their oil fields. So many Americans can trace their immigrant roots to the American business need for an influx of labor, including many in recent decades. But in the case of my relatives at the turn of the nineteenth century, the additional reason they ended up in Minnesota was quite simple: it looked like Slovenia. There were mines in Slovenia, and the Slovenians were used to a landscape of forests and lakes. And with their high tolerance for snow and cold weather, my relatives were recruited by these businesses and trusts (along with Serbs, Croatians, Finns, and other hardy souls) to work as miners in northern Minnesota.

My great-grandpa Mikhail (later Americanized to Michael) Klobuchar came from the southern Slovenian town of Črnomelj, right near the Croatian border. He first arrived in steerage aboard the SS *Aller* in the port of New York on June 9, 1888, the same year James J. Hill started building his big house in St. Paul. Mikhail made his way to Minnesota, just as mining operations were opening in Ely, a town just a few miles away from the Canadian border. Ely is on the Vermilion part of northeastern Minnesota's Iron Range, a series of four stretches of iron ore deposits—the Cuyuna, the Mesabi, the Vermilion, and the Gunflint, the last of which goes straight into Canada. The iron ore my great-grandpa and the other Iron Range immigrants mined was critical to the times. It fueled U.S. manufacturing in the new century. It was made into steel and built our cars and our factories. It was used to produce our tanks and our planes and our ships. It won our wars.

John D. Rockefeller, the American oil tycoon, used hardball and predatory tactics to eliminate his competition. After founding the Standard Oil Company, he became the country's richest person. In addition to monopolizing the petroleum and oil refinery industries in the post–Civil War period, he exerted enormous influence over the railroad industry as the country expanded westward. "The growth of a large business is merely a survival of the fittest," Rockefeller said.

By no coincidence, 1888 also marked the first time that the Duluth, Missabe, and Iron Range Railway came to Ely via the neighboring town of Tower, named for the prominent East Coast industrialist Charlemagne Tower, who pioneered Minnesota's mining industry. "Amid a burst of industrial expansion," one historian noted, "scores of Finnish and Slovenian immigrants arrived by train to work in Ely's six underground mines," with Ely's population growing rapidly from 901 in 1890 to 3,717 in 1900. The high-quality iron ore deposits of Minnesota's Iron Range had to be transported by rail through rugged wilderness that included swamps, rocky terrain, and thick forests. By 1894, however, those railroad tracks had been wrested from Tower's control and came to be owned by John D. Rockefeller.

James J. Hill himself had bought the Duluth, Superior & Winnipeg Railroad in 1897 along with ten thousand acres of land on the Mesabi Range. Two years later, Hill had written a $2 million personal check to acquire another twenty-five thousand acres of iron-ore-rich land, with Hill and his sons later raising their stake in Iron Range property to sixty-seven thousand acres. In 1912, James J. Hill told a congressional committee that land he'd acquired for $4 million would produce $750 million in iron ore. Hill himself hobnobbed with the East Coast's wealthiest men: the financier and railroad magnate William H. Vander-bilt; the banker J. Pierpont Morgan; and, naturally, the patriarchs of the Rockefeller family.

Unlike James J. Hill, the Klobuchar family owned no railroads, but they did get to ride on them from their port of arrival to northern Min-nesota. On my grandma's side, her dad, Joseph Pucel, was a Slovenian farmer's son who had been recruited to come to America by a railroad agent who worked with the mining companies. He arrived at Ellis Island in 1903, with his wife, Rose, following in 1905, arriving in New York with her name pinned to her collar. As the Ely native and later *Stars and Stripes* and *Time* magazine correspondent Simon Bourgin once reported on his own mom's arrival in the town around the same time, "She got on a train and she got on a train and she got on still another train, and finally she got on the last train. It was the most godforsaken country—nothing but pine trees and boulders."

Northern Minnesota's landscape was scenic but austere, and the liv-ing cold, hard, and unforgiving. In the words of my dad, "The men went into the mines. The women hung the family clothes on the line when the temperature was 15 degrees below zero." But as he would always remind me, "There was one abiding difference between the times and places that had squashed them down before they came to America." It was the hope that their kids could "escape the shantytowns" and even-tually find a better life for their families.

But as happened time and time again, the immigrant miners' sons would quickly follow them into the mines, as many of the turn-of-the-century miners died at an early age due to either mine-related acci-dents or lung cancer or respiratory illnesses. As one historian noted, "A strapping young immigrant who appeared fit could easily get a job in the mines and would often be hired on the spot." Yet the immigrant miner's life span was not promising, and he "might last only a short time." "Fatalities were common," the historian Ann Goldman notes, "and it was dark, wet, miserable work with little or no opportunity for advancement."

On my dad's side of the family, both my great-grandpa Mikhail Klobuchar and his wife, Barbara, would die relatively young, within two years of each other, leaving behind ten children, all born within fourteen years. In fact, according to the 1920 census recorded a few

My grandfather Mike Klobuchar worked fifteen hundred feet underground in the mines of Ely, Minnesota. After the mines closed, he worked as a logger on Minnesota's Iron Range. As a young man, he supported his nine orphaned brothers and sisters.

years before they both died, the Klobuchar family included Mary, aged sixteen; Mike (my grandpa and the oldest son), aged fifteen; Kate, aged fourteen; John, aged thirteen; Annie, aged eleven; Matthew, aged nine; Agnes, aged eight; Frank, aged seven (who would die of a toothache that same year); Joseph, aged six; Frances, aged three; and Hannah, aged two. Their address? Pioneer Mine Location, part of nondescript housing for miners affiliated with Ely's Pioneer Mine.

When my great-grandparents died, my grandpa, then nineteen and the family's oldest son, was responsible, along with the next oldest brother, Johnny, for supporting their younger siblings. My grandpa had already had to quit school years before to help the family make ends meet. He had gotten excellent grades in school and dreamed of a life at sea in the navy, but instead, at age fifteen, he went to work as a teamster pulling a wagon. Later, after his parents died, he took a better-paying job as a miner at the Zenith Mine, where he worked for most of his life. Over the years, he got promoted to be one of the foremen of the mine, where he was well respected. As a man I met on the campaign trail years after my grandpa died told me, "Your grandpa wasn't like the other

Miners in 1936 at the Zenith Mine, an underground iron ore mine in Ely, Minnesota. My grandpa Mike Klobuchar worked at the mine and is in the photo.

foremen. Whenever it was time to explore a new part of the mine, all the miners knew it would be dangerous. That's why most of the mine foremen would stand at the top of the mine and radio down to the miners below, telling them where to go. Not Mike Klobuchar. He would always go with the miners. He would always go with his guys. And he would always go first."

For decades, my grandpa would go down in the mining cage, fifteen hundred feet underground, black lunch bucket in hand. His youngest sister, Hannah, had to be taken to an orphanage in Duluth for two years because after their parents died, the oldest Klobuchar boys just didn't have the means to raise her. But my grandpa promised he would come back for her. And he did. Two years later, he borrowed a car from an uncle and brought her home to Ely.

My grandma Mary Pucel, also the child of a Slovenian miner, graduated from Ely Memorial High School in 1925, met my grandpa, and married him in 1927. They had two kids—my dad and his brother, Dick. They raised their two boys on a modest miner's salary while also helping out with my grandpa's many siblings. At some point when my

I loved visiting my grandpa and grandma in Ely. They lived out their lives in this small house in the heart of Minnesota's Iron Range. My grandfather originally bought the house in another town after a mine had closed down. That's me on his lap in 1962. He moved the house on the back of a flatbed truck, dynamited a hole in the ground for the basement, and put the house on top of it.

dad and his brother were very young, my grandparents were able to purchase a small two-bedroom house for $100 after a mine closed down in the neighboring town of Babbitt. My grandpa loaded that house on the back of a flatbed truck and brought it to a lot on Ely's Madison Street, using dynamite to blow a hole for the basement. To the day he died at age seventy-four of lung cancer, that basement contained the house's one and only shower. I would note it was a far cry from the thirteen bathrooms of the James J. Hill House, but that's just too obvious.

My dad and my uncle Dick would both spend some of their summers working in the mines, but a long-term mining job was not in my grandma's ambitious plans for her sons. Two generations of the Klobuchar family had worked underground in servitude to the mining interests, with a big chunk of Minnesota's Iron Range owned by the wealthiest men in the country, including the trust that James J. Hill and his business partners set up in 1906. The Klobuchar family's history of enriching James J. Hill and John D. Rockefeller, she resolved, would end with her sons.

Yes, Mary Klobuchar's sons would never stop working to improve their lots, but they would do it according to *her* plan, not James J. Hill's.

My dad, Jim Klobuchar, in 1974. He grew up on Minnesota's Iron Range and became a newspaperman in the Twin Cities. He often wrote about ordinary people doing extraordinary things and was not afraid to take on powerful interests in his daily columns.

She was bound and determined that her two boys would (1) graduate from high school; (2) go to college; (3) graduate from college; and (4) make something of themselves with the savings she and my grandpa had painstakingly collected in coffee cans in the basement.

Through hard work and a little good fortune, my grandmother Mary's dreams came true. My uncle became an engineer for the Minnesota Department of Transportation. In his spare time, he wrote a book about Pearl Harbor. My dad attended an Iron Range community college and, later, the University of Minnesota, where he got a degree in journalism, serving in Germany during the Korean War. He would go from that hardscrabble mining town to a life as a reporter, traveling the world, climbing mountains, and covering professional sports and politics. As a Minneapolis *Star Tribune* columnist, he took on the issues and tribulations of everyday people who called or wrote to him, using his daily column as a bully pulpit of sorts, all the while covering the Minnesota Vikings and interviewing everyone from the legendary Chicago Bears coach Mike Ditka to Ginger Rogers to Hubert Humphrey and Ronald Reagan.

STRIKES AND PICKET LINES:
THE LABOR UNIONS TAKE ON THE MONOPOLISTS

As I look back at it all, I now know why the stories of Teddy Roosevelt (and later his cousin Franklin Delano Roosevelt) were passed on from one Klobuchar generation to the next—and why standing up for workers' rights and "the little fellers, not the Rockefellers" (as Paul Wellstone, one of my predecessors in the Senate, so beautifully put it), and against economic and racial injustice, were so important to our family. While my ancestors were willing to sacrifice, they were not going to be used. And taking on monopoly power meant union organizing and fair laws and genuine competition for their labor.

You see, competition doesn't just mean competition for prices. It also means competition for workers and better wages and working conditions. And that means the opportunity for collective bargaining, antidiscrimination protections, and rules of the road for worker safety. My dad still remembers the coffins of miners lined up in Ely's St. Anthony's Catholic Church and how well into the twentieth century women and children would run to the mines every time a siren went off, fearing it was their loved one lost in a cave-in. The emergence of labor unions meant safer mines with better pay during much of my grandpa's time in the mines. Antitrust and antidiscrimination laws and pro-labor legislation passed by elected officials who were looking out not only for American business but also for American workers meant improved lives for both my grandpa and grandma's generation and my mom and dad's.

Of course, the stories of industrialists' clashes with laborers were never pretty, but those battles and the formation of labor unions were absolutely necessary to gain some balance for workers. In the case of the iron ore mines, before labor unions gained a foothold on the Iron Range, meager wages and dismal working conditions led to great strife and bitter strikes—sometimes even violence and death. The big industrialists were incredibly hostile to unions and collective bargaining, with the rules and regulations set forth by the Minnesota Iron Company in 1884 reading as follows: "No person belonging to any combination or union to control wages or regulate time or manner of service will be employed; and any employee entering such combination or union, or endeavoring

The trusts and their owners were virulently anti-union as seen in this cartoon by Frederick Burr Opper. The formation of unions such as the Knights of Labor (1869), the American Federation of Labor (1886), and the United Mine Workers (1890) helped to improve wages and working conditions for workers and restored much-needed balance to the American economy.

to control wages . . . will be discharged promptly and finally, and will forfeit all money earned by him at the time of such discharge." When union organizers came to the Iron Range, the Minnesota Iron Company posted notices saying that "no union men would be employed."

In 1888—the same year my great-grandpa Klobuchar arrived to work in the mines and James J. Hill was building his house—*The Industrial Age* of Duluth described the Minnesota Iron Company as a tyrannical and cruel monopoly, but the state's then governor called out the militia to quash labor disturbances and to round up their "ringleaders." Laborers were convicted of "rioting" and sent to prison. After mine operators turned down miners' demands for higher pay, laborers went on strike. Their demands were fairly basic and similar to demands of laborers across the United States: wages that took account of the dangers of mining (in one Minnesota mine in 1893 the going rate was a measly seventy-five cents for ten hours of work); safety measures in mines related to air and water; an eight-hour workday; and state- and county-employed mining safety inspectors.

But it was in 1901, with the formation of J. P. Morgan's U.S. Steel, that things really got ugly. Back only a few decades before, more than five hundred independent iron and steel firms competed and operated in the United States. But by 1892, the largest of the steel companies— Andrew Carnegie's operation—began trying to secure control over ore supply and ore prices by integrating backward, through acquisitions, into iron ore mine ownership. The trusts wanted to control raw materials, labor costs, and production and distribution, and both Carnegie and John D. Rockefeller began buying out mines at bargain prices. By 1900, eight steel companies controlled almost three-quarters of northern Minnesota's iron ore production. The largest was U.S. Steel. Its mining subsidiary, the Oliver Iron Mining Company, controlled more than half of the iron ore produced in the area, which itself accounted for around 80 percent of U.S. production.

The effect on labor? As historian Rhoda Gilman explains, "In 1901 the formation of the United States Steel Company established monolithic control over most of the Mesabi. The steel trust did little to improve the conditions of labor or reduce the danger of the work, which claimed the lives of five in every one thousand men between 1905 and 1910." Two hard-fought strikes—one in 1907 organized by the Western Federation

THEY CAN'T KEEP IT FROM RINGING!

The Industrial Workers of the World, whose members were called Wobblies, was founded in Chicago in 1905. One of the union's founders was Eugene V. Debs, a socialist. A Finnish-language newspaper, *Industrialisti,* published in Duluth, was the union's only daily newspaper. Shipments of iron ore from Minnesota's Iron Range made their way through the port of Duluth. The IWW was involved in scores of strikes, including on the ore-rich Mesabi Iron Range.

of Miners and led mostly by Finnish workers, and one in 1916 led by the Industrial Workers of the World, or IWW—were both crushed. Union sympathizers were replaced with strikebreakers, workers were arrested or blacklisted, and one miner, striker John Alar, was shot in front of his home by an "unknown person" who was never indicted.

U.S. Steel—the nation's first billion-dollar corporation—was, like the Minnesota Iron Company, vehemently anti-union in its early years, announcing in the very year of its formation, "We are unalterably opposed to an extension of union labor and advise subsidiary companies to take firm position when those questions come up." During the 1916 strike, one union organizer, twenty-six-year-old Elizabeth Gurley Flynn, traveled throughout the Iron Range to speak to miners and their families. "I read in today's papers," she said in a speech in Hibbing, "that the Steel corporation made between $80,000,000 and $90,000,000 in profits in the past year. The range miners have given their labor and lives to help make that profit and we desire our share in the $90 million." In another speech, delivered in the midst of World War I, she noted that on the Iron Range there were "English, French, Austrians, Italians, Finns and a dozen other nationalities. In Europe these people are fighting like h——. Here . . . they are calling one another fellow workers and all co-operating to fight one big enemy—the 'Steel Trust.'"

Of course it wasn't just Iron Rangers who were striking at the turn of the century. The late nineteenth and early twentieth centuries were an era of great labor unrest and management/labor conflicts in nearly every part of the U.S. economy. Laborers from sugar workers to shoemakers were going on strike and taking on the monopolies. There was a cotton mill strike in New York; cowboy strikes in Texas and on the Great Plains; a tobacco workers' strike in Virginia; textile, collar laundresses', and longshoremen's strikes; and rail strikes throughout the nation. In 1881 workers formed the Federation of Organized Trades and Labor Unions, the predecessor of the American Federation of Labor, with the actual American Federation of Labor taking shape in 1886 and becoming a powerful force in the labor movement.

While many but not all of these strikes involved workers' struggles against powerful trusts or with monopoly interests, two notorious strikes stand out as classic examples of man versus monopoly: the Pullman Strike of 1894 and Chicago's McCormick Harvesting Machine

Strike. Tragically, the latter strike led to what has become known as the Haymarket Massacre of 1886. Both strikes captured the attention of the nation, and they were seen as a turning point for the labor movement. Each of the strikes began in Chicago, and one—the Pullman Strike— was the reason we now have Labor Day on the first Monday of September every year. The other, which led to the Haymarket Massacre, is largely the reason that May Day events in the United States have come to be so closely associated with workers' rights.

In May 1894, four thousand factory employees of the Pullman Company (then the manufacturers of Pullman railcars) began a strike in Pullman, Illinois, in reaction to wage cuts. George Pullman was an industrialist from James J. Hill's era who founded his company town of Pullman on the South Side of Chicago for the workers who built the cars. The Pullman Company was also known for hiring Black workers to work in the cars, and they came to be known as the Pullman porters. The grandfather of my friend Melvin Carter, the mayor of St. Paul, was a navy veteran and a Pullman porter, and his family knew firsthand about racial discrimination and degrading treatment. As Mayor Carter said of his grandfather, the first Melvin Carter in his family, "As a Pullman porter, it didn't really matter what your name was or how much experience you had or what your rank was. Everyone was named George." A 2002 movie, *10,000 Black Men Named George,* gets its title from the custom of all Pullman porters being generically addressed as "George." In talking about the tragic murder of George Floyd in Minneapolis, Mayor Carter offered these sobering thoughts: "I was reflecting today on the fact that the killing, the murder of George Floyd, I think it's so painful for us and so personal because for every black man in America, whether you're a lawyer or an architect or an accountant or a mayor, we know that there's no amount of credentials. There's no amount of accomplishments. There's no amount of money that can change the fact that we literally are all George."

In the Pullman Strike, the American Railway Union, founded by Eugene Debs, took on the Pullman Company, the railroads, and the U.S. government, then led by President Grover Cleveland. The company had reduced the workers' wages, laid off employees, and wouldn't reduce the rent on their company-owned homes despite the reduction in wages. At the same time, Pullman refused to allow his employees

The employees of the Pullman Company were squeezed, faced with low wages and high rent, the same concerns that drove Lizzie Magie to create the Landlord's Game, the predecessor of the popular board game Monopoly.

to buy and own their own homes. The 1894 strike and rail boycott shut down both freight traffic and passenger trains west of Detroit. Chaos ensued and thirty people died in rail-related riots and train sabotage incidents. The U.S. government got an injunction against the union, and President Cleveland ordered the army to stop the strikers from disrupting the trains when the strikers refused to honor the injunction. Debs—a trade unionist and one of the IWW's founding members— was arrested and later went to prison in spite of his lawyer Clarence Darrow's spirited defense.

Public opinion was, for the most part, aligned against the Pullman strikers. Years later, however, President Cleveland's national commission to investigate the strike and its aftermath established that there was plenty of blame to go around. Pullman's operations and his company town were found to be a major source of unrest and were said by one economist, Richard Ely, to be "un-American" because Pullman's rules

Eugene Debs, a trade unionist, was a founding member of the Industrial Workers of the World. He began his political career as a member of the Democratic Party, serving in the Indiana General Assembly. Convicted of defying a court injunction in the Pullman Strike, Debs was sent to prison for six months. In prison, he turned to socialism and ultimately became a founding member of the Socialist Party of America, running for president of the United States five times as a Socialist candidate.

were so undemocratic. In 1898, the Illinois Supreme Court specifically required the Pullman Palace Car Company to divest itself of all of its residential properties. All of the homes in the town were sold by 1907, and today Pullman is a residential neighborhood on the South Side of Chicago.

Like the Pullman Strike, the Haymarket Massacre arose out of labor unrest and was equally violent. The labor protest in Chicago's Haymarket Square started as a peaceful workers' strike on May 3, 1886, in support of an eight-hour workday. It ended in a deadly riot. Workers were striking against the McCormick Harvesting Machine Company, an agricultural equipment manufacturer owned by one of the country's wealthiest industrialist families, the McCormicks, dubbed by the press as the Reaper Kings. The strike was part of the union movement's national campaign where 350,000 workers demonstrated in favor of an eight-hour workday. At the end of the May 3 strike in Chicago one person was killed and others injured when police shot into the crowd.

A flyer calling for a rally in Haymarket Square on May 4, 1886. What began as a peaceful rally in support of a nationwide strike of workers seeking an eight-hour workday ended with an unknown person throwing a bomb at police as they tried to disperse those in attendance. Between the bomb blast and the gunfire that ensued, seven police officers and four civilians were killed.

The next day, May 4, thousands gathered to protest what had happened the day before. At around 10:30 p.m., after police arrived to disperse the crowd, someone threw a handmade bomb, constructed of dynamite in a metal casing, at the police as they advanced to break up the rally. The bomb blast and the ensuing gunfire led to the deaths of seven police officers and four civilians, with dozens more injured in the crowd of approximately three thousand people. A series of trials ensued, and four men were later hanged for their actions, while other sentences were commuted. Like the Pullman Strike, the Haymarket Massacre was seen as a seminal turning point for the labor movement and, not too far behind, as a blazing symbol of the public's distrust of the trusts—the monopolies that were making tons of money off their backs. In 1888, just two years after Chicago's Haymarket Massacre, the first major antitrust legislation in U.S. history—what became the Sherman Antitrust Act of 1890—was introduced for consideration in the U.S. Senate.

As the years went by, the McCormicks, Pullman, Rockefeller, Hill, and their industrialist frenemies kept buying more and controlling more. And the more they dominated, the greedier they got. And while much of this country's antitrust history focuses on issues related to monopoly-driven high prices or competitors being denied market access, the monopolists' penchant for cheap labor, racially discriminatory practices, limiting wages, and basically making way too much money on the backs of others is what finally led to the downfall of their trusts.

As the monopolists got richer, the public got angrier. The seeds for a growing populist movement and for laws limiting the power of the trusts were sown by the outrage Americans felt as they experienced monopoly-produced disparities in power and wealth. As competitors were being forced out of markets, the industrialists were given a virtual monopoly over their employees. When working people saw how much money their bosses were raking in and the kinds of mansions they were building, workers eventually started to rebel against the industrialists who wouldn't raise their wages or improve their working conditions.

Like the stories of so many American families, my family's journey is tied inextricably to this tumultuous chapter in American history. That's why I often end my own speeches with this: "I stand on the shoulders of those before me. I am the granddaughter of an iron ore miner who saved money in a coffee can in the basement to send my dad to college. I am the daughter of a newspaperman and a teacher, and the first woman elected to the United States Senate from the State of Minnesota. That's the American Dream."

What am I getting at here? The simple proposition that the America envisioned by so many who have sacrificed for this country—and by my parents and grandparents—was one of shared prosperity, not greed and monopoly power.

In telling my story, I know very well that I wouldn't be here today were it not for the jobs opened up for my immigrant relatives by James J. Hill and his business cohorts. My ancestors knew that too, and it's one of the reasons they rarely complained about their lots in life. They toiled away in the mines and in the cold, but they always had hope—and much reason to hope—for a better future, at least for their kids. As my dad once told me, "If the New World was not deliverance to them, then it would be for their children. They would study in American schools, understand this country, and not only work for it but make it work." For them, Ellis Island and the Statue of Liberty stood for economic opportunity and another simple proposition: that immigrants don't diminish America, they *are* America.

But it truly isn't fair to end the journey there, as only a tribute to the American Dream and the virtues of American capitalism and free enterprise. It isn't just a benevolent, Horatio Alger rags-to-riches story line with a neat happy ending of "hard work pays off in the end." *My story*—like that of so many Americans—is also a story of how our American democracy can work to even the playing field to ensure economic opportunity for the many instead of only the privileged. It is a story of how when economics get out of whack and greed shoves too many people down, in this country, in this democracy, the people push back. Hard-fought cases can be won, laws passed, and seemingly all-powerful trusts busted.

Americans have never been ones to tolerate too much consolidated power. America's founders and framers insisted on economic competition and separation of powers, assigning different powers to the legislative, executive, and judicial branches. They opposed monopolies, and they divided power between the federal government and the states while reserving rights and power to the people themselves. The U.S. Bill of Rights and the American republic's system of checks and balances were, like the antitrust laws, specifically designed to ensure that too much power would never be placed in the hands of a ruling few. As James Madison wrote in *The Federalist* No. 47, "The accumulation of all powers, legislative, executive, and judiciary, in the same hands, whether of one, a few, or many . . . may justly be pronounced the very definition of tyranny."

From the days of Benjamin Franklin and Robert Fulton to Thomas Edison, Lewis Latimer, and Alexander Graham Bell, Americans have strongly embraced entrepreneurship, innovation, and capitalism. Those economic pillars have made our economy the envy of many around the world. But that economy is also strong because a democracy gives the people a say to check monopoly power and to balance things out so that everyone has that right to pursue happiness. Not just one guy with a big house on a hill. Everyone.

3

A Heartland Rebellion

The Grangers, a Political Prairie Fire,
and a Republican Authors the Sherman Act

"THE REVOLT OF THE COMMON MAN":
THE MIDWEST'S PRAIRIE POPULISM

Justice Louis Brandeis once called America's states our laboratories of democracy. Like so many other American political movements, the story of this country's antitrust laws begins not with the mother of all democracies in Washington, D.C., but with her sons and daughters in the states. And while Delaware may be the "First State" and New Hampshire may have as its motto "Live Free or Die," it was lawmakers in Iowa—the home of corn dogs, cows, and cantankerous politics—who first answered America's pitchforked cry to pass a general law aimed at freeing its agricultural economy from monopoly rule.

The heartland's farmers, laborers, and disgruntled proprietors vociferously and relentlessly demanded legislation to counteract America's massive nineteenth-century trusts. As big business agriculture moved in and started taking over the distribution of agricultural products with price and production demands, and railroad companies upped their shipping prices, small-town farmers across America rebelled. In the end, the combination of politically active rural farmers and striking urban laborers lit a central states' activist prairie fire that was impossible to douse. Those closest to the flame—the frontline local elected representatives from the midwestern states—had more than enough impetus to act. Their very political survival depended on it.

Between 1888 and 1890, more than a dozen states, beginning with Iowa, passed general antitrust laws prohibiting combinations or monopolies that raised prices or limited output to protect a monopoly interest. In addition to Iowa, other agricultural states passing antitrust laws at the time included Kansas (first out with a grain-only antitrust provision), Maine, Michigan, Missouri, Nebraska, Tennessee, Texas, Kentucky, Mississippi, North Dakota, and South Dakota.

The states' actions were clearly fueled by Washington's inability to act. Despite a century of congressional rumblings against monopolies, federal efforts to pass trust-busting legislation did not advance. Democratic congressman Henry Bacon, a lawyer from Goshen, New York, and the chair of the Committee on Manufactures, did, however, conduct extensive, unprecedented congressional hearings into both the Standard Oil Trust and the Sugar Trust in 1888. Those investigations were initiated after the adoption of a January 25, 1888, congressional resolution that criticized monopolies, noting that they were created "for the purpose of controlling or curtailing the production or supply" of goods with the intent of "increasing their price to the people of the country."

As I have learned from my time in the U.S. Senate, well-crafted congressional resolutions and hearings are laudable and often a sign of action to come. But unless there is a law on the books that can be enforced, and an administration willing to enforce it, not much changes. It was somewhat comforting to learn that the state legislators back in the late nineteenth century felt the same: they were tired of congressional inertia, and they began to take concrete actions to combat the trusts.

In 1888, Iowa's lawmakers took matters into their own hands, passing the country's first state antitrust law of general application. Of course, the 1888 Iowa antitrust bill did not just sprout up spontaneously one day in the middle of an Iowa cornfield. In fact, the seeds for the legislation were planted two decades earlier by the Grangers—a spirited national antimonopoly farmers' movement that began when a Minnesota farmer named Oliver Hudson Kelley started a social organization, the National Grange of the Order of Patrons of Husbandry, better known as the Grange, focused on monopoly practices affecting grain prices. As one

Oliver Hudson Kelley, the son of a Boston tailor, became a Minnesota farmer, a clerk for the U.S. commissioner of agriculture in Washington, D.C., and a legendary figure in agricultural history. In 1867 he and six other men founded the National Grange of the Order of Patrons of Husbandry, better known simply as the Grange. By 1873, as farmers fought rising railroad rates and dealt with falling commodity prices, there were nine thousand Grange chapters with almost 700,000 members.

historian notes, the farmers "were chronically in debt, and after 1870 the general tendency of the prices of agricultural products was downward." In colonial America, the word "grange" was used to refer to a farmhouse and its outbuildings, with farmers referred to as grangers.

Though he had grown up in Boston as the fifth child of a New England tailor, Oliver Hudson Kelley, then in his early twenties, boarded a steamboat bound for St. Paul in 1849, determined to be a farmer. He did well for himself in Minnesota and quickly earned a reputation as an innovator. "Kelley," it has been reported, "gained local fame for boldly experimenting with new crops, installing an elaborate irrigation system, and buying one of the first mechanical reapers in the state." A natural leader, he started his social organization to both share best agricultural practices and unify farmers behind the goals of improved living conditions and a better standard of living. As Kelley wrote in a letter to a friend in 1867, "I long to see the great army of producers in our country, turn their eyes up from their work; stir up those brains, now mere machines . . . set them to think, let them feel that they are human beings, and the strength of the nation, their labor honorable, and farming the highest calling on earth." It was that impulse that led

Kelley and six other men to create their social organization in 1867, not long after the conclusion of the Civil War, with the agricultural economy—not unlike the country's democracy at the time—extremely fragile, languishing in a postwar malaise.

Within just two years, Minnesota had forty Grange chapters and an active statewide organization. But while Kelley was the brains behind the Grange, he was out in Washington, D.C., working as an agent at the Bureau of Agriculture for much of its early years, and its leadership duties fell into the hands of another Minnesotan—Ignatius Donnelly—who took the baton from Kelley and soon built the Grange into a national political phenomenon. Donnelly, the son of Irish-Catholic immigrants, was born in Philadelphia. He became a lawyer in 1852 and then made his way to the Minnesota Territory in 1857, speculating in land and running a cooperative farm. The panic of 1857—triggered by inflation and speculative railroad investments—led to a major depression in America and Europe and scuttled Donnelly's agricultural enterprise, leaving him deeply in debt. That's when he turned to politics. An antislavery Radical Republican and an early supporter of women's suffrage, he served as Minnesota's lieutenant governor and in Congress.

In those early political years, speaking at Grange meetings around

Ignatius Donnelly moved from Philadelphia to Minnesota in 1856. He became a Republican politician, serving as the second lieutenant governor of Minnesota and a member of Congress, but then became active in the antimonopoly and populist movements and edited a weekly paper, *The Anti-monopolist*. One of his dystopian, science fiction novels, *Caesar's Column: A Story of the Twentieth Century* (1890), portrayed the United States of 1988—nearly a century into the future—as a corrupt capitalist oligarchy with a poverty-ridden working class.

The Grange movement played a big role in fueling the antitrust movement. This Farmers' Alliance political cartoon from 1873 is titled "The Farmers and the Railroads: The Grange Awakening the Sleepers." The words on each railcar— "Consolidation Train," "Extortion," "Bribery," and so on—illustrate the farmers' anger toward monopoly interests.

the state, Donnelly delivered a blunt and powerful message that served to transform the social organization into a political one. As he said in one speech:

> In 1860 it cost *nineteen cents* to carry a bushel of wheat from Chicago to New York. In 1873 it costs *thirty-seven cents—nearly double!*
>
> Why? There are now more railroads to carry the produce and more produce to be carried than in 1860. The reason is *there is more robbery!*

Not satisfied with the Republican Party's positions on monopoly issues, Donnelly and his political supporters gathered in Owatonna, Minnesota, in September 1873 to form the People's Anti-Monopoly Party, later known as the Anti-Monopoly Independent Party. Their platform: taking on monopolies, regulating railroads, and fighting post–Civil War corruption. Donnelly also produced a weekly newspaper, *The Anti-monopolist,* that decried "plutocracy and wage slavery." "Liberty must overcome all her foes," Donnelly dramatically implored party members in one issue, "or perish from the earth." A lithograph, published in 1875, depicted a Granger plowing his field and making the simple declaration "I FEED YOU ALL!"

Minnesota's Anti-Monopoly Party was a forerunner of the short-lived national Anti-Monopoly Party founded in 1884 at a convention in Chicago. That convention nominated Benjamin F. Butler for president of the United States that year, but Butler—who'd been a Union army major general and the thirty-third governor of Massachusetts—ended up running as the Greenback Party's nominee, going on to be beaten badly by Grover Cleveland, the Democratic Party's nominee. "With Grover Cleveland's election in 1884," historian Ron Chernow writes in *Titan,* his biography of oil tycoon John D. Rockefeller, "many business-men braced for reform in Washington," but Cleveland "turned out to be quite moderate." "Nonetheless," Chernow explains of the time, "the public revulsion against monopolies steadily gathered force, produc-ing an Anti-Monopoly Party that condemned railroad pools and rate discrimination."

While the Anti-Monopoly Party might not have won on the national level, under Oliver Kelley's and Ignatius Donnelly's leadership, the Grange movement caught on state by state in a big way. By 1873, with farmers battling falling crop prices and rising railroad shipping rates, there were nine thousand Grange chapters in the United States with nearly 700,000 members. It was truly prairie-fire populism. "At its peak in the 1870s," one source observes, "the Grange had 860,000 members in some 21,000 lodges across the country." Interestingly, at a time when many political organizations were exclusively male—with women not even having the right to vote until 1920—the Granger clubs included women among their ranks from the start. In fact, the women were often the organization's most dedicated members. "Sentiment over black participation in the movement," it's been noted, was "divided" by geography, with "a Northern view" permitting the admission of African American farmers while "the Southern view" excluded membership. Racially integrated Grange chapters existed, with the National Grange's bylaws and constitution silent as to racial issues, but Black farmers in the South and elsewhere were regularly excluded from Grange member-ship and thus had to join separate organizations such as the Council of Laborers or the Colored Farmers' Alliance.

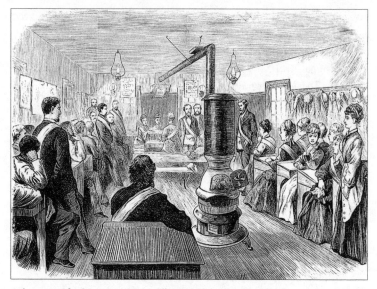

A depiction of a Grange meeting in Illinois (1900). Meetings like this one occurred all over the country as farmers, acting in solidarity, took on grain elevator operators and the railroads. The Granger movement led to the passage of laws in the Midwest—in Minnesota, Iowa, Illinois, and Wisconsin—that regulated escalating crop transport and storage fees being charged by railroads and grain elevator companies.

The importance of the Granger movement to antitrust policy cannot be overstated. In a book chapter titled "The Revolt of the Common Man," historian Holland Thompson points out that the country's farmers were in debt, their commodities garnering rock-bottom prices. In addition to monopoly transportation and storage challenges, grasshoppers were destroying frontier farms and the financial panic of 1873 resulted in runs on banks, a chain of bank failures, the New York Stock Exchange's temporary closure, and severe hardships on the backs of working-class Americans. In those days, there was no crop insurance or disaster loans or even Social Security. One woman from Alexandria, Minnesota, tellingly wrote at the time, "We have not bought any clothing since we came here, for it has took all we could raise to live, without buying clothes. My husband has not had a sock on his feet this winter, and he suffers very much with the cold."

Despair and destitution were in fact at the core of the states' antimonopoly movement. In August 1873, in Des Moines, with the Grange movement at its height, the Farmers' Anti-Monopoly Convention proclaimed, "All corporations are subject to legislative control; that such legislative control should be an express abrogation of the theory of the inalienable nature of chartered rights, and that it should be at all times so used as to prevent moneyed corporations from becoming engines of oppression." Upset by the collusive actions of the railroads and the grain dealers, one man in Dubuque, Iowa, lamented that "the railroads often play into the hands of the grain speculators, to the injury of the farmers." "There is little or no competition between rival buyers," he said, "because they either agree each morning to pay a certain fixed price that day, or else agree not to outbid each other, and divide their profits in proportion to the amount each man has bought."

The Granger movement and Supreme Court cases it produced set the stage for antitrust laws enacted later at both the state and the federal levels. The pioneering 1888 Iowa antitrust law serves as just one example of how the Granger movement affected policy. Similar to later enacted laws in other states, it provided that businesses or individuals who entered into a trust or combination "to regulate or fix the price of oil, lumber, coal, grain, flour, provision, or any other commodity or article whatever" or sought to "fix or limit the amount or quantity" of goods would be "deemed guilty of a conspiracy to defraud."

Iowa's governor at the time of the passage of the historic law was a Republican who later supported Teddy Roosevelt and the party's progressive "Bull Moose" faction. Governor William Larrabee—whose campaign slogan was "a schoolhouse on every hill and no saloons in the valley"—was a strong advocate for antitrust laws. In his first biennial message to the Iowa legislature, delivered on January 11, 1888, Governor Larrabee urged the General Assembly to pass an antimonopoly law: "I recommend that prompt measures be taken to protect the people against the abuses under the cover of combinations generally known as 'trusts' or pools. There is a common belief that these and similar combinations suppress competition, enhance the cost of the necessaries of life, and lay heavy burdens upon those least able to bear them." Months later, Iowa passed the law.

Minnesota's and Iowa's leading roles in the antimonopoly movement come as no surprise to a senator from Minnesota. Minnesota and Iowa share lots of farms, cross-border relatives, cross-border college football rivalries (with the Minnesota Gophers and the Iowa Hawkeyes vying every year for the Floyd of Rosedale pig trophy), and a penchant for state fair butter carvings (Iowa has its cow; Minnesota boasts "Princess Kay of the Milky Way" and her heavenly court, with the princesses' heads carved out of individual ninety-pound blocks of butter in a revolving refrigerator housed in the Minnesota State Fair's Dairy Building).

While the shared central states' agricultural economy best explains *why* the antitrust movement got its start in the heartland, it is the midwestern states' long-standing tradition of grassroots politics and populist activism that best explains *how* it became effective.

Like many of the midwestern states, the Grangers' initial organizing in Iowa and Minnesota occurred not long after the states' conversion from territory to statehood. With Iowa becoming a state in 1846, Wisconsin in 1848, Minnesota in 1858, Nebraska in 1867, and South and North Dakota in 1889, the heartland states' antimonopoly movements of the 1870s, 1880s, and 1890s literally formed the basis of the Midwest's populist political culture. The Grangers were in many ways a harbinger of things to come—from the unique caucuses held in fire stations, church basements, schools, and living rooms across the states, to the bully pulpit firebrand politics exemplified by generations of midwestern politicians with national standing.

WILLIAM JENNINGS BRYAN BARNSTORMS THE COUNTRY ON AN ANTIMONOPOLY PLATFORM

One of the most prominent midwestern politicians of the time was Nebraska's William Jennings Bryan, also known as the Boy Orator of the Platte. A Presbyterian who cared deeply about the rights of farmers, workers, and women, Bryan began practicing law in 1883 in Jacksonville, Illinois, but later relocated to Nebraska, moving westward as so many Americans had before him.

The rights of people to have a say in their own government was of chief concern to William Jennings Bryan. In 1890, at a bar association banquet in Lincoln, Nebraska, he observed of the Gilded Age, "This is an age of rapid accumulation of wealth, and the multiplication of corporations gives to money an extraordinary power." In defending America's jury system (a major check, along with the right to vote, on govern-

William Jennings Bryan (circa 1910) delivering a campaign speech. A Nebraska politician, Bryan captured the hearts of the Democratic Party with his crusade against the power of the "trusts." He served in the U.S. House of Representatives, ran for president multiple times, and became President Woodrow Wilson's secretary of state. He was known for his oratorical skills. His "Cross of Gold" speech, delivered at the Democratic National Convention in Chicago in 1896, is still studied today. He put his oratorical skills to use in excoriating monopoly power and the trusts.

mental power), he emphasized in that speech, "One million dollars in the hands of one man or one company will outweigh, in the political and social world, ten times that sum divided among a thousand people." Instead of accepting lucrative legal work from the railroads, Bryan opposed and occasionally sued them, once representing a seven-year-old girl who'd been hit by a Missouri Pacific train in Lincoln, Nebraska. Bryan sought—as one humanities professor puts it—"to realign the Democratic Party so that it represented the broad working and middle classes in an aggressively growth-oriented political economy."

After getting elected to Congress by his fellow Nebraskans, becoming only the second Democrat to represent the state, Bryan served in the U.S. House of Representatives from 1891 to 1895 before setting his sights on the U.S. Senate. He refused to accept money from railroads or to represent them, and in the days before the direct election of U.S. senators his principled stance cost him dearly. Despite his actively campaigning in 1894 to join the U.S. Senate, the Republican-controlled state legislature chose a former Republican congressman, John Mellen

THE VULTURES' ROOST

DRAWN BY E. W. KEMBLE

This 1905 cartoon, titled "The Vultures' Roost," depicts the trusts roosting on the roof of the U.S. Senate. With the vultures led by the Standard Oil Trust, the cartoon—drawn at a time when state legislatures, not voters, selected U.S. senators—makes the point that Senate seats were for sale and the powerful trusts were wielding corrupt influence over the selection process.

William Jennings Bryan captured the Democratic Party's presidential nomination three times, but he never made it to the presidency. This cartoon, drawn by Clifford Berryman, is titled "Mr. Bryan in 1899—'I stand just where I stood four years ago!'" The "16 to 1" slogan on his bag recalled a popular Democratic slogan and Bryan's "Cross of Gold" speech at the 1896 Democratic National Convention in Chicago, in which Bryan called for the free coinage of silver to aid debt-burdened and cash-poor farmers, with the ratio of silver to gold to be pegged at sixteen to one.

Thurston, the Union Pacific Railroad's general counsel. After hitting that roadblock, Bryan—a man who quickly became the darling of the Democratic Party—decided to run for the presidency.

Throughout his political career, Bryan continually spoke out against the trusts—the industrialists' adaptation of a legal concept that dated back many centuries. The idea for a business "trust" was first cooked up by John D. Rockefeller's lawyer, Samuel Dodd, in 1882. A trust basically eliminated the competition by combining competitive companies into one entity, with the trustees then managing it themselves. More to the point, the trusts gave monopolists like Rockefeller the ability to consolidate their power even further.

With Rockefeller's most trusted lawyer's guidance, the Standard Oil Trust was highly successful, ruthlessly cornering the market through hardball tactics. "It was probably a carping critic," one magazine quipped of John D. Rockefeller's confidence in his lawyer, "who said that the Standard Oil Company had revised our national expression to read: 'In Dodd we trust.'"

In the heartland, hardworking midwesterners got exasperated by the power of Standard Oil, the railroads, and the rest of the trusts. Their anger, led by Bryan, fomented a full-scale political rebellion. In his famous "Cross of Gold" speech, one that mesmerized the delegates at the 1896 Democratic National Convention in Chicago, William Jennings Bryan vigorously spoke out for the interests of farmers, small business owners, and miners:

> The farmer who goes forth in the morning and toils all day, begins in the spring and toils all summer, and by the application of brain and muscle to the natural resources of this country creates wealth, is as much a businessman as the man who goes upon the Board of Trade and bets upon the price of grain. The miners who go 1,000 feet into the earth or climb 2,000 feet upon the cliffs and bring forth from their hiding places the precious metals to be poured in the channels of trade are as much businessmen as the few financial magnates who in a back-room corner the money of the world.

In that 1896 presidential campaign—his first—the youthful William Jennings Bryan, who had just turned thirty-five in 1895, making him barely eligible to be president, captured the hearts of Democrats by taking on the trusts. "The Democratic party is opposed to trusts," he said in accepting his party's nomination and in supporting the party's platform.

But while Bryan was willing to take on powerful interests, those interests still prevailed in the 1896 presidential election. In spite of all his barnstorming and soaring oratory, and in spite of the fact that Bryan won more than twenty states and got 6.5 million votes to the Republican William McKinley's 7.1 million, the trust juggernaut, driven by the big industrialists' desire to dominate whole sectors of the economy, continued unabated. "From 1898 to 1900," Michael Kazin, one of Bryan's biographers, observes, "industrialists engaged in a flurry of mergers, with a total capitalization of close to $6 billion."

Though he ended up losing not one, not two, but all three presidential elections (that would be 1896, 1900, and 1908), William Jennings Bryan had given a voice to the voiceless, and he had pioneered a new kind of politics. From Nebraska's Bryan and Wisconsin's "Fighting Bob" La Follette, to South Dakota's George McGovern and Iowa's Tom Harkin, to Illinois's Jesse Jackson and Minnesota's Hubert Humphrey, to the late great Paul Wellstone, the legacy of the early progressives and antimonopoly grassroots Grangers was passed on from one political generation to another. These midwestern leaders were known to command the stage for hours without a note card in sight. As my mentor, former vice president and Minnesota senator Walter Mondale, likes to remind me, the stories of Hubert Humphrey's Minnesota Democratic-Farmer-Labor dinner speeches were legendary. Every aspiring Minnesota politician has heard it: Hubert would start his speech when people were eating dessert and wind up at about the time they were ready for bacon and eggs.

And it was those very bacon and eggs that were at the root of the midwestern obsession with monopolies. For while monopolies were a challenge for the entire U.S. economy, in the end it was the farmers and laborers of the Midwest—from the railroad strikers in Chicago to the wheat growers in Nebraska—who had both the economic imperative to take them on *and* the populist organizing tools to put their ideas into action.

OHIO REPUBLICAN SENATOR JOHN SHERMAN CARRIES THE BILL (AND THE ANTIMONOPOLY TORCH) OVER THE FINISH LINE

Despite the states' good antimonopoly work and resulting antitrust laws, the enthusiasm for state action was not always matched by actual impact. In the end, the state laws simply didn't have enough jurisdiction and breadth of enforcement to deter monopolies.

Over time it became clear that while state antitrust laws were a good start, the real enforcement actions aimed at complex monopoly trusts could only effectively occur at the federal level. To go head-to-head with the moneyed monopolists, the country needed *national* laws and the federal investigatory, prosecutorial, and civil and criminal resources to enforce them. States with small legal departments trying to enforce laws with meager penalties (with fines ranging between $100 and $5,000) did not exactly strike fear in the hearts of business moguls at J. P. Morgan & Company's Wall Street offices or at Standard Oil.

Fortunately, the demand for action didn't end at the statehouses. In fact, it was out of the midwestern cauldron of angry farmers, striking workers, and state-based grassroots action that the Sherman Antitrust Act emerged. That antitrust legislation was first introduced in 1888 in the U.S. Senate by its namesake, John Sherman, a Republican U.S. senator from Ohio whose tough, matter-of-fact manner earned him the "Ohio Icicle" moniker. As William Kolasky, a former deputy assistant attorney general in the Justice Department, described Sherman's motivation in introducing his legislation before the 1888 election, "Sherman likely wanted to assure that the Democrats would not be able to ride the swelling public antipathy towards trusts to victory in November." At age sixty-five, Sherman was a seasoned veteran of American politics, he understood the public's anger about the trusts, and he knew the extraordinary power of the country's antitrust movement.

Although Congress recessed shortly after the bill's introduction, Sherman was persistent, reintroducing his bill with only minor changes on January 25, 1889, the very first day of the next Congress. There was fierce debate over the proper wording for the antitrust legislation, and two committees—Finance and Judiciary—got into the act. There was initially a dispute over what constitutional authority Congress had to regulate the trusts, but Sherman was intent on getting something passed, even if it was not exactly what he had originally proposed. The resulting compromise language was not—Sherman said—"precisely what I want," but he announced that he would vote for it because it was "the best under all the circumstances that the Senate is prepared to give."

Interestingly enough, while the United States' populist movement may currently be associated with the Democratic Party, back in Sherman's time the antimonopoly populist work was led by politicians of both parties. Even William McKinley—the Republican who beat William Jennings Bryan in both the 1896 and the 1900 presidential elections—had himself come out in opposition to the trusts as an Ohio congressman, saying in 1888, "I have no sympathy with combinations, organized for this or any purpose, to control the supply and therefore control prices." Back then the pro- and anti-monopoly forces were much more divided by geography and political/business connections than they were by political parties.

John Sherman, who has been called America's "first—and original— trustbuster," is a case in point. He was born in Lancaster, Ohio, in 1823, the eighth of eleven children. When his dad, an Ohio Supreme Court justice, died unexpectedly, Sherman's mother was suddenly left to care for eleven children. John's older brother—William Tecumseh Sherman—who was raised by a neighbor, became a famous Union Civil War general. He was the General Sherman of "March to the Sea" fame, leading the Union army on a scorched-earth rampage from Atlanta to Savannah, burning down everything in his path and destroying much of the Confederacy's economic and transportation systems. Despite the destruction it wrought, the march is still widely viewed as the major game changer for the Union forces.

Meanwhile, General William Sherman's brother John chose a tamer but no less ultimately important route, beginning his career as a surveyor, becoming a successful lawyer in Cleveland, Ohio, and then running for office. His political career spanned nearly the entire second half of the nineteenth century, during which time he represented Cleveland in the U.S. House of Representatives as well as the State of Ohio in the Senate. As a member of the powerful Senate Finance Committee, he was a leading voice in shoring up the U.S. economy during the Civil

War. In the war's aftermath he was tasked to serve as U.S. secretary of the Treasury under President Rutherford B. Hayes, during a tumultuous time not only for the democracy but also for the economy. Sherman's duties at the time included stabilizing both the war-torn U.S. economy and the country's financial system. After serving as Treasury secretary, Sherman returned to the Senate, where he continued to lead on financial issues.

Given his brother's famed military leadership in the Union war efforts, one would guess that John Sherman was a big Abraham Lincoln fan. He was. He belonged to the antislavery wing of the Republican Party and was one of Lincoln's allies in Congress. Lincoln wanted to incentivize innovation, but he also wanted to make sure people had the means to buy the necessities of life. "The Patent System added the fuel of interest to the fire of genius," Lincoln declared in 1859, with Lincoln himself having received a patent in 1849 for a device to lift boats over shoals. In 1862, in the midst of the Civil War, Lincoln also signed into law the Homestead Act—a law supported by George Washington Julian, an Indiana antislavery Republican who fiercely opposed "land

John Sherman, a Republican from Ohio, served in both houses of Congress and became the thirty-fifth U.S. secretary of state under President William McKinley. He sponsored the legislation that became known as the Sherman Antitrust Act (1890).

monopoly" and who believed that the Homestead Act would "rescue thousands from the jaws of the land monopoly, and impart to them happiness and independence." The Homestead Act offered settlers up to 160 acres of land so long as they lived on the land and improved it. Hundreds of thousands of farms were established under the Homestead Act in the decades to come.

While there were most likely high-level discussions between John Sherman and Lincoln on the country's economic and monetary policies, one less interesting discussion was forever cemented in the history books. John's older brother William told the story of Senator Sherman taking him to meet President Lincoln: "John walked up, shook hands, and took a chair near him, holding in his hand some papers referring to minor appointments in the State of Ohio, which formed the subject of the conversation. Mr. Lincoln took the papers, said he would refer them to the proper heads of departments, would be glad to make the appointments asked for, if not already promised." Okay, you'd kick yourself if that was how you used your five minutes with Abraham Lincoln. But that was the story recounted by John Sherman's brother William.

John Sherman, though he privately questioned Lincoln's executive abilities to his brother in the midst of the Civil War, was a loyal supporter of Lincoln to the end. Looking back at the president's service after his assassination, Sherman wrote, "Mr. Lincoln possessed all the qualities required to inspire confidence and to unite all the loyal elements of our much-divided people in the great conflict of our civil war, when the possibility of Republic institutions, in a wide extended country was on trial." He further noted with great introspection how his views of Lincoln had changed over time: "At first I thought him slow, but he was fast enough to be abreast with the body of his countrymen, and his heart beat steadily and hopefully with them."

After Lincoln's death and his own stint as Treasury secretary under President Hayes, Sherman returned to the Senate and got involved in antitrust matters. As Treasury secretary, he had had a front-row seat to the increasing economic consolidation of America's post–Civil War period. It was during that time that key businesses got bigger and more powerful, trusts were formed, union laborers were striking, farmers were organizing, and states were acting. In Sherman's mind, the federal government could no longer be dormant. As he explained in a speech in

The trusts were controlled by powerful businessmen, including Andrew Carnegie, J. P. Morgan, and William and John D. Rockefeller. Three of these men are portrayed here as kings in a 1903 cartoon by Franz Albert Jüttner for the satirical journal *Lustige Blätter*.

March 1890, his intent in regulating the monopolies was not to "cripple combinations of capital and labor" but "to prevent and control combinations made with a view to prevent competition, or for the restraint of trade, or to increase the profits of the producer at the cost of the consumer." In a nod to the disgruntled workers of the time, he noted that monopolies' "bad" combinations dictate "the price of labor without fear of strikes," because they allow no competitors and they allow a monopolist to "control the market" by raising or lowering prices "as will best promote its selfish interests."

In an ode to the American Revolution and the break from the Brits, then more than a century old, Sherman was very clear: "If anything is wrong this is wrong. If we will not endure a king as a political power, we should not endure a king over the production, transportation and sale of any of the necessaries of life. If we would not submit to an emperor we should not submit to an autocrat of trade with power to prevent competition and to fix the price of any commodity."

That's why in 1888 John Sherman introduced the country's first federal antitrust legislation, one that—in the prevailing political climate—attracted lots of bipartisan support as the legislation was debated and made its way through Congress. Federal antitrust legislation drew the support of both President Grover Cleveland, a Democrat, in his 1887 and 1888 annual messages and President Benjamin Harrison, a Republican, in his first annual message to Congress in 1889.

Sherman's legislation built on state and local efforts across the country. "The purpose of this bill," he said on the Senate floor, "is to enable the courts of the United States to apply the same remedies against combinations which injuriously affect the interests of the United States that have been applied in the several States to protect local interests." In its final form, the law that became known as the Sherman Antitrust Act allowed the U.S. government to contest—and even prosecute—those who restrained trade or monopolized an industry. Section 1 prohibited contracts, combinations, or conspiracies, including in the form of trusts, that are in "restraint of trade." And section 2 prohibited monopolization, attempted monopolization, or any conspiracy to do the same, making it a felony to engage in such conduct.

During the Senate and House floor debates on the bill, a number of senators and House members spoke out in favor of the bill with a major emphasis on rising inequality and the agricultural side of the antimonopoly equation. In 1890, on the Senate floor, Sherman said that his bill would "prevent and control combinations made with a view to prevent competition, or for the restraint of trade, or to increase the profits of the producer at the cost of the consumer." "The popular mind," he declared, "is agitated with problems that may disturb social order, and among them all none is more threatening than the inequality of condition, of wealth, and opportunity that has grown within a single generation out of the concentration of capital into vast combinations to control production and trade and to break down competition." Trusts and combinations, he emphasized, quoting a Mississippi senator's remarks with approval, "increase beyond reason the cost of the necessaries of life and business, and they decrease the cost of the raw material, the farm products of the country."

Republican senator William Allison of Iowa—a politician who had been a delegate to the party's 1860 convention, which nominated Abraham Lincoln—also spoke of "a combination in the city of Chicago which not only keeps down the price of cattle upon the hoof" but also makes "the consumers of beef pay a high price for that article." "The beef trust," his congressional colleague Representative Ezra Taylor of Ohio asserted, "fixes arbitrarily the daily price of cattle, from which there is no appeal, for there is no other market." Lamenting that farmers "get from one-third to half of the former value of their cattle and yet beef is as costly as ever" and calling the beef trust a "monster," Taylor concluded that it "robs the farmer on one hand and the consumer on the other." Representative John Heard of Missouri added that the trusts had "stolen untold millions from the people." And finally, Representative George Fithian of Illinois read a letter from a constituent—a farmer "ordinarily of conservative views"—complaining about "plutocracy and giant monopolies" and declaring that the trusts were "so impoverishing the people that they are compelled to place mortgages upon their homes."

As a sign of the popularity of the populist movement at the time, no member of the House of Representatives voted against the Sherman Act. The bill passed the House of Representatives by a vote of 242–0, though 85 congressmen abstained from voting. "The overwhelming public support for the anti-trust bill," one scholar writes, "made voting against it a risky choice for politicians with aspirations for reelection." Only one U.S. senator voted against the bill, with 29 choosing not to vote. Although John Sherman had originally wanted much stronger language, the watered-down version of the bill—which essentially tracked the long-standing common-law prohibition against monopolies—managed to make its way through the House and Senate. The final vote in the Senate was 52 yeas, 1 nay, and 29 absent.

The lone dissenting vote? Senator Rufus Blodgett of New Jersey. While it appears Senator Blodgett was quiet about the reasons for his dissent, historians attribute his vote as one to protect the railroad industry and his belief that the Sherman Act would negatively affect it. Blodgett was in fact a superintendent of the New York and Long Branch Railroad for twenty-five years until his death in 1910; railroads played an important role in New Jersey politics at the time; and Blodgett was elected as a "railroad man." As for the twenty-nine nonvoting senators? Twenty appeared to be simply absent, and of the nine who were present, three had connections to monopoly industries.

John Sherman's bill was signed into law by President Benjamin Harrison on July 2, 1890, which also happened to be the 115th anniversary of the *signing* of the Declaration of Independence, a date that John Adams had wrongfully predicted would be the date that changed history (as opposed to the date two days later—the Fourth of July—when the declaration was actually issued). Whether the timing was deliberate or not, President Harrison ended up signing Sherman's antitrust bill—the country's first federal antimonopoly legislation—on the very anniversary of the signing of America's independence from England and its monopoly control over America's economy. It had in fact been 115 years since Thomas Jefferson and George Mason tried to include an antimonopoly amendment to the Constitution, with little result. Now, 115 years later, with the passing of the Sherman Act, their wish to legally rein in monopolies was granted. Under headlines like "Republican Pledges" and "The Pledge Redeemed," newspapers wrote in July 1890 that the Republican Party—then headed by President Benjamin Harrison, a former U.S. senator from Indiana, the grandson of President William Henry Harrison, and the great-grandson of a signer of the Declaration of Independence—had "honorably redeemed its pledge" to the people by passing the "Anti-trust bill."

4

Teddy Roosevelt and the
Antitrust Enforcers

The Trustbusters Take Over the White House

THE DISAPPEARING ACT: A DISAPPOINTING
FIRST DECADE FOR THE SHERMAN ACT

Despite the Sherman Act's supporters' grandiose ambitions to bring down prices and create more robust competition, for more than a decade the landmark antitrust law essentially lay dormant. The Sherman Act was rendered meaningless mainly because of a lack of enforcement and because U.S. courts, including the nation's highest court, sided over and over again with monopolists. When John Sherman—the act's namesake—died in 1900, his *New York Times* obituary didn't even bother to mention the Sherman Antitrust Act. Sadly, throughout the nineteenth and early twentieth centuries, a lot of politicians remained in the pockets of the moneyed interests that controlled the trusts (sound familiar?).

To be clear, there were skeptics from the very beginning about how effective the new Sherman Act would be. Just months after its passage, *The New York Times* had declared that the "so-called Anti-Trust law was passed to deceive the people and to clear the way" for a "Pro-Trust law" relating to tariffs. "It was a humbug and a sham," the *Times* editorialized, adding its view of the newly enacted Sherman Act: "It was projected in order that the party organs might say to the opponents of tariff extortion and protected combinations, 'Behold! We have attacked the Trusts. The Republican Party is the enemy of all such rings.'"

The early court cases were particularly disappointing for those seeking to dethrone the monopolists and put an end to their Gilded Age market dominance. In 1895, the U.S. Supreme Court notoriously turned aside the U.S. government's effort to block the American Sugar Refining Company's acquisition of four Philadelphia refineries, giving American Sugar a 98 percent market share. And in another case, federal courts held that the Sherman Act applied to labor unions. The latter decision, coming out of a case from Louisiana, flew in the face of express promises that had been made during the legislative debate. The law that was intended to take on monopolists and help workers was thus interpreted to limit workers' rights to combine their economic power by forming unions.

In fact, in the protracted Senate debate before the Sherman Act's passage, a number of senators had expressed concern that the legislation might be used—or later construed—to outlaw labor unions. For example, Senator Henry Teller of Colorado had voiced this trepidation: "While I am extremely anxious to take hold of and control these great trusts, these combinations of capital which are disturbing the commerce of the country and are disturbing legitimate trade, I do not want to go to the extent of interfering with organizations which I think are absolutely justifiable." He also declared, "We can not deny to the laborers of the country the opportunity to combine either for the purpose of putting up the price of their labor or securing to themselves a better position in the world. . . . I do not believe the mere fact of combining to secure to themselves a half-dollar a day more wages or greater influence and power in the country can be said to be an unlawful combination."

In response to such concerns, Senator Sherman assured his fellow senators that labor unions seeking higher wages and better working conditions for their members would not be impacted by his legislation. As Sherman emphasized, "Combinations of workingmen to promote their interests, promote their welfare, and increase their pay . . . are not affected in the slightest degree, nor can they be included in the words or intent of the bill." In the face of continued skepticism, Senator Sherman even proposed an amendment to the bill—an amendment that was initially adopted without a roll call vote but later dropped after the bill and its amendments were sent to the Judiciary Committee for further drafting. Had Senator Sherman's amendment remained part of the bill's language, it would have been crystal clear that unions were not intended to be covered by the law. "This act," Sherman's amendment had read, "shall not be construed to apply to any arrangements, agreements, or combinations between laborers, made with the view of lessening the number of hours of their labor or of increasing their wages."

Despite Senator Sherman's assurances, it is certainly telling that the first person to actually go to prison for a Sherman Act violation was *a union leader*—Eugene Debs—and not a robber baron. Debs and others were charged with contempt of court in mid-December 1894 for disobeying a preliminary injunction issued pursuant to the Sherman Act, and they were found guilty the same day and sent to prison. Clarence Darrow, the famed defense attorney, called Debs "the bravest man I ever knew," but not even Darrow's representation of him would keep Debs from being put behind bars for his role in the Pullman railway strike (1894). In defending Debs, Darrow had argued in vain that the Sherman Act did not address labor strikes and that "to deprive workingmen of this power would be to strip and bind them and leave them helpless as the prey of the great and strong." To deny the right to strike, Darrow had contended, "would leave each individual worker completely isolated and unaided to fight his battle alone against the combined capital."

In the years and decades after the Sherman Act's passage, businessmen were intent on squashing unions. And if that meant intimidating factory workers or putting union leaders in prison, industrial monopolists were more than willing to resort to such tactics. Debs, who had fought pay cuts for workers, was seen as nothing less than an existential threat to the establishment, and he was sent to prison for his union organizing activities. Over time, Debs—a man focused on improving the wages and the lives of working people—would not give up on politics, even from his prison cell. He had begun his political career as a member of the Democratic Party, serving in the Indiana General Assembly in the second half of the 1880s. Angered by the treatment of American workers, Debs would go on to found the Social Democratic Party of America (1898) and the Socialist Party of America (1901), run-

Eugene Debs, one of the founders of the American Railway Union and the Industrial Workers of the World, ran for president of the United States in 1920 while in prison. In the early days of antitrust enforcement, courts frequently issued injunctions to stop strikes, and labor leaders who violated such injunctions would be put behind bars.

ning for president of the United States five times. In 1920, the final time he was a presidential candidate, he ran from a prison cell.

Debs, like many labor leaders at the time, had good reason to believe that the courts were carrying the water for big business. In one case brought in the post–Sherman Act era, *Loewe v. Lawlor* (1908), the U.S. Supreme Court—siding with business over labor—outlawed secondary boycotts. A secondary boycott—an attempt to influence the actions of one company by putting pressure on another—is a group's refusal to purchase from, work for, or handle a company's products with which that group has no dispute. The Danbury Hatters' Case, as that case is better known, involved a strike against a hat manufacturer in Danbury, Connecticut, in which the union called a boycott against suppliers of that company. In the case, the U.S. Supreme Court gave a judgment in favor of the company for more than $250,000 and made secondary boycotts illegal.

Labor leaders operated in an extremely hostile environment, and the anti-union interpretation of the Sherman Act by the courts was seen by labor organizers as another example of a duplicitous betrayal. In 1910, Samuel Gompers—the son of a cigar maker and a laborer himself who rose to become the president of the American Federation of Labor from 1886 to 1924—articulated the bait and switch that so stung American labor organizers. "We know the Sherman law was intended by Congress to punish illegal trusts and not the labor unions," Gompers wrote, "for we had various conferences with members of Congress while the Sherman Act was pending, and remember clearly that such a determination was stated again and again."

It wasn't only the judges who were responsible for antitrust inaction in the last decade of the nineteenth century, however. "During the 1890s," historian James Olson explains in *The Industrial Revolution* (2015), "the Sherman Antitrust Act had little impact because conservative presidents Benjamin Harrison, Grover Cleveland, and William McKinley refused to enforce it." As Tim Wu writes of the last president in that list in *The Curse of Bigness: Antitrust in the New Gilded Age*, "Under President McKinley, *laissez-faire* was the unannounced,

William McKinley, the twenty-fifth president, kept the United States on the gold standard and did very little to enforce the Sherman Antitrust Act. "The Trusts" are portrayed here as a cigar-smoking boss crushing "The Common People" while President McKinley and his future vice president, Theodore Roosevelt, simply look on. Cartoonist: Frederick Burr Opper, 1900.

"Yes, Willie, this is Papa's exercising machine. Papa can twist it to beat the band."

but nonetheless evident, economic policy of the United States. . . . The doctrine of *laissez-faire,* a cousin to Social Darwinism, suggested that economic problems would tend to work themselves out, and hence government intervention would usually do more harm than good." One poignant example of McKinley's failure to enforce the law? Instead of using the Sherman Act to take on J. P. Morgan's creation of a steel trust, McKinley held a dinner to honor Morgan's business acumen.

AT LONG LAST, ANTITRUST ENFORCEMENT: TEDDY ROOSEVELT'S BIG STICK

In 1901, things changed dramatically on the antitrust front when William McKinley was assassinated. That's because after McKinley's death, a new Republican president, Teddy Roosevelt, entered the fray. Roosevelt became the twenty-sixth president of the United States after McKinley, its twenty-fifth, was shot by an anarchist in Buffalo on September 6, 1901. McKinley, a staunch supporter of the gold standard, died from the gunshot wounds eight days later. Suddenly thrust into the presidency, Roosevelt was determined to right the monopoly wrongs by seizing upon the issue that William Jennings Bryan had articulated so forcefully, and to carry on the legacy of John Sherman and the earlier midwestern state legislative leaders' antimonopoly efforts. Roosevelt recognized that many Americans were suffering, and he resolved to do something about it.

As a candidate and elected leader, Roosevelt had long rallied the public around the popular idea of breaking up the business trusts. And when he became president after briefly serving as governor of New York and McKinley's vice president, Roosevelt had the opportunity to turn his words into action. And he did it.

Theodore Roosevelt was at first blush an unlikely trustbuster. He grew up in a wealthy Republican family in New York and was neither from the Midwest (where much of the antimonopoly populist movement was grounded) nor extensively exposed to populist thinking in his youth.

But a few influences made him an agent of change. First, while he was born into money, he was raised to believe in the merits of hard work and pulling yourself up by your bootstraps. Second, as a New York state assemblyman, he fought corruption in Albany and had—to a large extent—built his reputation that way. Third, he had a significant base of support in the Midwest and the West, having traveled and hunted extensively in areas far away from the wealthy environs of New York. As a twenty-four-year-old, he was already hunting buffalo in the Badlands of North Dakota, where, he once said, "the romance of my life began." "I never would have been President," he observed, "if it had not been for my experiences in North Dakota."

In fact, it was that part of his Badlands background and legacy that ultimately led to the recent decision by New York City's American Museum of Natural History to remove a long-disputed statue of Roosevelt on horseback at the museum's entrance—one originally installed in 1940 in which Roosevelt was flanked by, and lorded over, an African man on his left and a Native American man on his right. "The statue," the museum said in a statement when it was announced the statue would come down, was originally "meant to celebrate" Roosevelt as a hunter, collector of scientific specimens, and "devoted naturalist and author of works on natural history," but instead "communicates a racial hierarchy that the Museum and members of the public have long found disturbing." "Over the last few weeks," Ellen Futter, the museum's president declared in making the announcement of the statue's removal, "our museum community has been profoundly moved by the ever-widening movement for racial justice that has emerged after the killing of George Floyd." "Simply put," she said, speaking of the statue as a symbol of systemic racism, "the time has come to move it."

Theodore Roosevelt's own views on race and ethnic minorities reflected the overt racial prejudices of his time. In a 1905 speech on race relations, Roosevelt observed "our effort should be to secure to each man, whatever his color, equality of opportunity, equality of treatment before the law," but then he backpedaled, saying that "the working out of this problem must necessarily be slow."

While Roosevelt failed to properly address discrimination and racial prejudice, he was ahead of his time when it came to monopoly power and its relationship to economic inequality. Of course, he also knew that the Midwest and industrial laborers so affected by monopoly power would be key to his electoral success as a national candidate. In the Midwest, the people—from farmers to small-business owners—despised the trusts, and President Roosevelt earned the respect of workingmen for the part he played in resolving a major coal strike in 1902 in which fifty thousand Pennsylvania miners had successfully fought for higher wages and an eight-hour workday. In his winning 1904 presidential election campaign, Roosevelt—riding the wave of his antitrust rhetoric and actions—would in fact sweep the Midwest and the West in addition to his home base in the Northeast. Even in his unsuccessful 1912 election when, seeking to regain the presidency after he became dissatisfied with his successor's performance, he ran on the Progressive "Bull Moose" Party ticket against the Democrat Woodrow Wilson and the incumbent president, William Howard Taft, he still managed to eke out victories in Michigan, Minnesota, South Dakota, California, Washington, and Pennsylvania.

Another core reason for Roosevelt's trust-busting? As governor of New York, he had seen the greed of the financial and oil tycoons and the power they wielded. He was familiar with their kind and knew how to deal with them. He knew firsthand that the business tycoons were doing little to address the workers' and farmers' concerns or to remedy the economic repercussions of monopoly power. He saw how the great disparities of wealth and the industrialists' arrogance toward workers were resulting in strikes, riots, and overall chaos throughout the nation. In the long term, taking on the monopolists would increase trust in business and government and reduce the riots and strikes aimed at those who had acquired too much power over their workers.

And finally, Teddy Roosevelt—not unlike my late colleague Senator John McCain—loved a good fight, and this was a just and popular one. If he didn't do it, who would? Bucking the standard pro-business positions of many senior members of his own party, he made the regulation of railroad rates and the guarantee of safer foods and drugs a central corner of the "square deal" he promised Americans. In his 1903 Labor Day speech to farmers at the New York State Agricultural Association, Roosevelt said that "the welfare of each of us is dependent fundamentally upon the welfare of all of us." Harkening all the way back to republics in ancient Greece and medieval Italy, he also made this dire warning: "The death-knell of the Republic had rung as soon as the active power became lodged in the hands of those who sought, not to do justice to all citizens, rich and poor alike, but to stand

On September 2, 1901, Vice President Teddy Roosevelt delivered his "Speak Softly and Carry a Big Stick" speech at the Minnesota State Fair. When he became president less than two weeks later after William McKinley's assassination, he famously used that stick against the trusts. This cartoon, by Minnesota cartoonist Perry Carter, was published in the March 16, 1907, edition of *The Minneapolis Tribune,* where my dad, Jim Klobuchar, was later a sportswriter and daily newspaper columnist.

THE VERY SIMPLE MESSAGE OF THE BIG STICK. HE WHO RUNS MAY READ

From the *Tribune* (Minneapolis)

for one special class and for its interests as opposed to the interests of others."

Campaign promises are one thing, but Americans at the turn of the century were looking for action, not mere words. After Roosevelt was abruptly sworn in as president after McKinley's assassination, the people were anxious, but so too were the eastern industrialists and tycoons who had experienced Governor Roosevelt's unpredictable nature. Just two weeks before McKinley's assassination, Roosevelt had given a speech at the Minnesota State Fair calling for state power to be used to rein in the trusts. "The vast individual and corporate fortunes, the vast combinations of capital which have marked the development of our industrial system," he emphasized, "create new conditions, and necessitate a change from the old attitude of the State and the nation toward property." In his September 2, 1901, speech, Roosevelt praised hard work and derided "unscrupulous competitors who have no conscience," further offering that "it is not only highly desirable, but necessary, that there should be legislation which shall carefully shield the interest of wage workers."

When it came to trust-busting, Roosevelt was in fact often at odds with the power brokers in his own political party. Although J. P. Morgan, as a member of New York's power elite, had contributed $10,000 to

At his 1901 speech at the
Minnesota State Fair, Vice
President Theodore Roosevelt—
then forty-two years old—
praised Minnesota's pioneers
and the state's next generation
of workers. The caption of
this front-page cartoon in *The
Minneapolis Tribune:* "Teddy
takes his hat off to Minneapolis
labor." Labor is portrayed as
an oversized steel milk can.

Roosevelt's campaign for New York governor, once Roosevelt won that election, the forty-year-old "boy governor" did not always play along. As *The Wall Street Journal* writer Gerard Helferich explains in his book, *An Unlikely Trust: Theodore Roosevelt, J. P. Morgan, and the Improbable Partnership That Remade American Business,* Roosevelt "showed his independence from party bosses and business interests." Helferich explains that as New York's governor from 1899 to 1900, Roosevelt "shepherded through the legislature several bills attacking what he called 'the combination of business with politics and with the judiciary which has done so much to enthrone privilege in the economic world.'"

Governor Theodore Roosevelt had made New York's Republican Party bosses so leery of what he might do next that one of them, Thomas Platt, confessed privately, "I want to get rid of the bastard. I don't want him raising hell in my state any longer. I want to bury him." The Machiavellian solution? Add him to William McKinley's Republican presidential ticket as vice president. As Helferich observes, the plan of the entrenched party bosses to place Roosevelt on the ticket as vice president was "not in hopes of advancing his career but to shunt him to a largely ceremonial position where he could do little harm." Before Walter Mondale and several who followed him transformed the modern vice presidency, the office was—as Texan John Nance Garner, FDR's vice president, once famously put it—"not worth a bucket of warm piss," though the press bowdlerized and toned down the swipe to say "warm spit."

After Theodore Roosevelt was unexpectedly elevated to the presidency, a nervous J. P. Morgan confessed to a journalist, "I am afraid of Mr. Roosevelt, because I don't know what he'll do." After getting wind of the remark, the new president parried back, "Mr. Morgan is afraid of me because he does know what I'll do."

In his very first message to Congress, Roosevelt didn't waste any time in articulating exactly what he aimed to do. Even as the nation mourned the death of President McKinley, Roosevelt expressed his vision for the future, rallying lawmakers to discard "old customs" that were no longer sufficient "to regulate the accumulation and distribution of wealth." Roosevelt praised "the captains of industry who have driven the railway systems across the continent, who have built up our commerce, who have developed our manufactures," but he worried about "the wage-worker" who "may be deprived of even bare necessities" in periods of hard times. "There is a widespread conviction in the minds of the American people that the great corporations known as trusts are in certain of their features and tendencies hurtful to the general welfare," Roosevelt said, calling for the trusts to be "supervised and within reasonable limits controlled."

During his first term as president, Roosevelt was itching for that fight. And it wasn't long before he finally found his foil: James J. Hill of St. Paul and his industrialist friends E. H. Harriman, J. P. Morgan, and John D. Rockefeller. Hill's Northern Securities Company—a New Jersey corporation whose purpose was to monopolize western railway transportation—was in fact the first trust Roosevelt and his attorney general, Philander Knox, sued in court and successfully disbanded. The case was initially brought in Minnesota, Hill's home state, in March 1902.

The formation of the Northern Securities Company was a classic monopoly scheme. James J. Hill was the president of the Great Northern Railway and the Northern Pacific Railway. He wanted to be able to use his railroads to ship goods from the Twin Cities to Chicago, and he found himself in a major bidding war for the route with his industrialist

The people of my home state of Minnesota recognized the immense power of railroad men like E. H. Harriman. This 1906 cartoon ran in the *Duluth Evening Herald*. Harriman controlled the Union Pacific Railroad and a number of other railroad and transportation companies, including the Illinois Central Railroad, the Pacific Mail Steamship Company, and the Wells Fargo Express Company.

rival E. H. Harriman. Harriman controlled the competing rail provider for the route—the Union Pacific Railroad.

The bidding war went on and on, threatening to cost much more money than either industrialist wanted to spend. But then, with the financial help of the Wall Street banker J. P. Morgan and the financier John D. Rockefeller, the two robber barons found a way to end their bidding war, reduce their costs, and own the route: they simply *eliminated* the competition between them. Instead of fighting between themselves, they combined their two competing rail companies, along with the Chicago, Burlington, and Quincy Railroad, under the ownership of one trust, dubbed the Northern Securities Company.

By the time of the establishment of the Northern Securities Company, J. P. Morgan was America's most famous banker, having arranged in 1895—as the head of an international syndicate of bankers—to sell the U.S. government 3.5 million ounces of gold valued at $65 million, thus saving the U.S. Treasury from imminent bankruptcy. The quid pro quo: the issuance of valuable thirty-year bonds that Morgan and his fellow bankers marketed. The panic of 1893 had brought on the financial crisis—a crisis precipitated by the failure of the Philadelphia and Reading Railroad—that resulted in a stock market crash and massive unemployment. By the fall of 1893, almost a million workers had been laid off, 141 banks had failed, and other railroads were going bankrupt. One historian suggests, however, that Morgan himself might have actually engineered and provoked the crisis "because he would benefit from it by building his railroad trust and electrical trust."

After a public outcry arose over the J. P. Morgan–backed formation of the Northern Securities Company, legal proceedings against it started in Minnesota. The Minnesota lawsuit drew greater attention to the issue, and everything ultimately ended up in Roosevelt's lap as the case made its way through the courts. In January 1902, Minnesota's Republican attorney general, Wallace B. Douglas, petitioned the U.S. Supreme Court for leave to file a complaint against the Northern Securities Company as an unlawful monopoly. On February 19, 1902, though, before the Supreme Court had ruled in that case, President Roosevelt's attorney general, Philander Knox, announced that the U.S. government was also preparing a suit against the Northern Securities Company. "Some time ago," Knox's prepared statement read, "the President requested an opinion as to the legality of this merger, and I have recently given him one to the effect that, in my judgment, it violates the provision of the Sherman Act of 1890, whereupon he directed that suitable action should be taken to have the question judicially determined."

The American banker and financier J. P. Morgan dominated mergers and acquisitions in the late nineteenth and early twentieth centuries. It was not hyperbole to say that he held the world—at least the industrial world—in his arms, as portrayed here by the cartoonist Albert Turner Reid. Morgan played a pivotal role in the creation of the U.S. Steel Corporation and AT&T. He also helped to capitalize the Northern Securities Company, the corporation sued by the Roosevelt administration, to the tune of $400 million.

NORTHWEST: "I reckon I'll be safer inside the coach."
From the *Ohio State Journal* (Columbus).

The combination of major railroads into a single trust attracted
the attention of both federal and state officials. The Northern
Securities Company, organized in New Jersey on November 12,
1901, soon ran into major obstacles: Minnesota's attorney general,
Wallace B. Douglas, and President Theodore Roosevelt. Cartoon
by Harry Westerman, 1902.

More than a decade after the passage of the Sherman Act, inaction
was finally giving way to action. In 1902, less than a year after Roosevelt
assumed the presidency, the U.S. Department of Justice announced
that it was filing a suit under the Sherman Antitrust Act against the
newly formed trust. The named defendants in the Minnesota case
included the Northern Securities Company, the railroads, James J. Hill,
and J. P. Morgan. Even though Roosevelt had said in the past that he
favored agency regulation of monopolies over the use of the court system, it was his own attorney general, Philander Knox, who brought the
suit.

J. P. Morgan had known Roosevelt for years, and Roosevelt's connections to eastern industrialists ran deep. In fact, Attorney General Knox
was the lawyer who, in private practice, had handled the sale of Carnegie Steel to J. P. Morgan. At a meeting at the White House on February 23, 1902, Morgan took advantage of his friendship with Roosevelt to
deliver a blunt message: he was not pleased with the lack of notice he'd
received about Roosevelt's decision to sue the Northern Securities Com-

President Roosevelt got credit for "taking the bull by the horns" in bringing suit against the Northern Securities Company. Cartoons such as this one, published in 1906 in *The Minneapolis Tribune,* must have greatly pleased him.

TAKING THE BULL BY THE HORNS

pany. "This is just what we did not want to do," Roosevelt replied with his usual directness, pointing to the desire to not provoke stock market fluctuations, or even panic, by giving the banker early notice.

Thinking that the parties could amicably settle the case, J. P. Morgan pressed the president further. "If we have done anything wrong," Morgan said, "send your man to my man and we can fix it up." "That can't be done," Roosevelt replied. "We don't want to fix it up, we want to stop it," Attorney General Knox eagerly added. Morgan then asked if Roosevelt was going to also go after his steel trust and his other business interests. "Certainly not," the president said, adding the cautionary note "unless we find out that in any case they have done something we regard as wrong." "I am the President of the United States, and am sworn to uphold the law," Roosevelt reminded an infuriated J. P. Morgan, the high-powered financier accustomed to getting what he wanted. "Mr. Morgan," Roosevelt would later remark, "could not help regarding me as a big rival operator who either intended to ruin all his interests or could be induced to come to an agreement to ruin none."

The president refused to settle the case, and the Northern Securi-

Philander Knox, the forty-fourth attorney general of the United States, became friends with William McKinley while attending college. As a prominent lawyer in Pittsburgh, Knox served as a director of the Pittsburgh National Bank of Commerce alongside Henry Clay Frick and Andrew Mellon. As the attorney for the Carnegie Steel Company, Knox played a key role in organizing the U.S. Steel Corporation in 1901 shortly before being tapped to serve as attorney general. He later served as a U.S. senator from Pennsylvania and U.S. secretary of state.

ties Company did not fare well in the courts. In 1904, in a stunning reversal for the trusts that had long gotten their way in the halls of justice, the U.S. Supreme Court, in a 5–4 vote, found that monopolies restrain trade and "deprive the public of the advantages that flow from free competition." The Supreme Court thus ordered Northern Securities to be broken up into independent railroads. Morgan's request to the president that "your man talk to my man" just didn't cut it in Washington anymore. And while Roosevelt did, in fact, distinguish between "good trusts" and "bad trusts" and showed favoritism toward Morgan's interests in other cases, a new moniker was born. "The President of the United States," the Washington *Star* reported, "is the original 'trustbuster,' the great and only one for this occasion."

But it didn't end there. Over his eight years as president, Roosevelt's Justice Department would file lawsuits to shut down more than forty monopolies, including the American Tobacco Company, Chicago's "Beef Trust" (controlled by meat packers like Swift & Company), and the DuPont Chemical Corporation. The cases would go on for years, with many of the monopolies not actually dissolved until the administration of Roosevelt's successor, William Howard Taft.

THE BREAKUP OF STANDARD OIL: JOHN D. ROCKEFELLER, PRESIDENT TAFT, AND MUCKRAKER IDA TARBELL

If the monopolists were looking for a friend in the new president at the helm, they left sorely disappointed. President Taft, who followed Roosevelt and was sworn in inside the U.S. Capitol because of a blizzard the night before, had served as a judge on the U.S. Court of Appeals for the Sixth Circuit and as Roosevelt's secretary of war. Continuing in T.R.'s trustbusting tradition, Taft was even more aggressive about pursuing court actions to address monopolies than Roosevelt. Taft insisted on "the continuous prosecution of all these combinations until they learn better," and he expressed the view that "the methods of business ought not to include combinations for the purpose of suppressing competition

The "Beef Trust" became a target of President Theodore Roosevelt in 1902 when he directed his attorney general, Philander Knox, to bring an antitrust action. Americans blamed meat packers for high food prices, and "Down with the Beef Trust" became a popular slogan in the early twentieth century. Roosevelt sympathized with the plight of poorly compensated cattlemen, and the power of the Beef Trust, which hit both producers and consumers, was described in the muckraker Upton Sinclair's best-selling novel, *The Jungle* (1906).

and driving other people out of business." To a friend and critic of his antitrust policies, Taft protested, "You seem to think that unfair competition is essential to progress in business." And he curtly added: "I deny it, and I am strongly in sympathy with the principle of the antitrust law that denies it."

In fact, the biggest trustbusting prize of all occurred during the Taft presidency—the breakup of John D. Rockefeller's Standard Oil Company. While this was a case originally brought to court in 1906 during the Roosevelt administration, it was carried on and ultimately successfully resolved in 1911 by President Taft's Justice Department. Taft called Standard Oil "the greatest monopoly and restraint of trade in the world," describing the company as "an octopus that held the trade in its tentacles."

Just as the Northern Securities Company was established to allow Hill and Harriman to control the rail industry, the Standard Oil Trust was created to allow Rockefeller to completely monopolize the refining, distribution, and marketing in the oil industry.

For years, Rockefeller monopolized the oil business through acquisitions and threatened to eliminate competitors through predatory pricing and the manipulation of railroad rates. The Standard Oil Trust was, of course, the ultimate competition crusher, giving Rockefeller control of about 90 percent of U.S. oil. By 1907, historian Keith Miller notes, the vertically integrated Standard Oil Company "owned or controlled 67 subsidiary businesses, which included 3 producing companies, 12 pipeline companies, 9 refining companies, and 6 marketing companies."

In 1892, the Ohio Supreme Court outlawed the Standard Oil Trust from operating Standard Oil of Ohio, which had been founded in 1870, but that decision simply led Standard Oil to incorporate its business in New Jersey, a state that allowed large holding companies. Although ten states, along with the Oklahoma Territory, brought a total of twenty-four cases against Standard Oil Trust members between 1890 and 1906, it would take a federal case to dissolve the Standard Oil Trust. The Justice Department's 170-page complaint ultimately led to a trial in which 444 witnesses were called to testify and 1,371 exhibits were entered into evidence. The end result? The breakup of Standard Oil.

The Standard Oil case is also notable because it is a prime example of how that era's pioneering journalists brought much-needed attention to

President Theodore Roosevelt became known as the trustbuster for his willingness to take on powerful trusts. During his administration, forty-five antitrust suits were brought against a variety of industries, including beef, oil, railroad, and tobacco. This cartoon, by L. D. Bradley, appeared in the *Chicago Daily News* and the *Oakland Tribune* in 1907 with the caption "Utilizing the squeal."

business/government backroom deals and political and corporate corruption. Those Progressive Era journalists and writers, from Nellie Bly to Upton Sinclair, became known as muckrakers.

One of the most well-known muckrakers from the early twentieth century was Ida Tarbell. After writing a two-volume biography of Abraham Lincoln, Tarbell turned her investigative prowess to Standard Oil. Published in 1904, the two-volume *History of the Standard Oil Company* was a hard-hitting work of investigative journalism serialized in *McClure's Magazine* before its release in book form. A writer and the editor of that popular magazine, Tarbell pioneered the field of investigative reporting, using reams of documents and extensive one-on-one interviews to meticulously document her findings. She uncovered a host of abuses, including an exchange between Rockefeller and an independent refiner in which Rockefeller threatened, "If you refuse to sell, it will end in your being crushed."

Ida Tarbell's interest in her subject was much more than that of a disinterested journalist. When she was a teenager, John D. Rockefeller's newly incorporated Standard Oil Company had, through aggressive tactics and collusion with the three major railroads that ran through Cleveland, crushed almost all of its competitors in Ohio and western Pennsylvania, including her own father's business. "Tarbell would never forget the wretched effects of 'the oil war' of 1872, which enabled Rock-efeller to leave Cleveland owning 85 percent of the city's oil refiner-ies," a recent *Smithsonian* article notes of this dark chapter in American history, recounting how Tarbell's father came home "grim-faced, his good humor gone," his contempt—and justifiably so—directed at the Standard Oil Company. The company's actions forced her father to mortgage the family home to meet his own company's debts, and those actions made a lasting impression on Ida. In her words, Standard Oil "never played fair."

Ida Tarbell's earthquake-like 1904 exposé on the company has been credited with ultimately bringing about the dissolution of Standard Oil and sullying the reputation of its founder, who—as his biographer Ron Chernow notes—became "the world's richest man." As Steve Weinberg writes in *Taking On the Trust: The Epic Battle of Ida Tarbell and John D. Rockefeller* (2008), "Tarbell's masterpiece, *The History of the Standard Oil Company,* influenced the U.S. Supreme Court—where the justices mandated the breakup of multinational trusts—as well as the court of public opinion, where Rockefeller's reputation disintegrated." Her book also created great public momentum for the passage of key post–Sherman Act antitrust bills, the Clayton Antitrust Act and the Federal Trade Commission Act, as well as the passage of the Hepburn Act, which authorized the Interstate Commerce Commission (ICC) to set maximum rail rates.

Now, Ida Tarbell never got the chance to interview John D. Rock-efeller, who derisively referred to her as "Miss Tarbarell." But Tarbell was relentless in her research, even tracking down a book, *A History of the Rise and Fall of the South Improvement Company* (1872), that exposed the Standard Oil Company's shady schemes and origins. The Standard Oil Company had attempted to destroy all of the copies of that book, but Tarbell found a remaining copy at the New York Public Library.

The History of the Standard Oil Company became a popular title. Tar-bell noted in its preface that she chose to examine the company because, as the first trust, it had "furnished the methods, the charter, and the traditions for its followers." As she wrote of Standard Oil, "It is the most perfectly developed trust in existence; that is, it satisfies most nearly the trust ideal of entire control of the commodity in which it deals. Its vast profits have led its officers into various allied interests, such as railroads,

Ida Tarbell, photographed here in 1905, was an investigative journalist. She exposed the abuses of the Standard Oil Company and became known as one of the nation's muckrakers. Tarbell used modern investigative journalism techniques—digging up documents and conducting scores of interviews— to expose Standard Oil's monopolistic practices. Her work, along with antitrust enforcement actions, led to the breakup of Standard Oil.

shipping, gas, copper, iron, steel, as well as into banks and trust companies, and to the acquiring and solidifying of these interests it has applied the methods used in building up the Oil Trust."

Ultimately, John D. Rockefeller's Standard Oil Company of New Jersey, which controlled 91 percent of oil production in 1904 and 85 percent of all final American sales, was broken into thirty-four separate entities, or "Baby Standards." Now, they didn't all stay "babies" for long, with Standard Oil of New Jersey transitioning to today's ExxonMobil; Standard Oil of California, now Chevron; Continental Oil Company, now ConocoPhillips; and Standard Oil of Indiana, currently known as Amoco, later purchased by British Petroleum. Nevertheless, the breakup of America's biggest trust was both good for competition and consumers. It also sent a clear message that aggressive antitrust enforcement did not end with Teddy Roosevelt's presidency.

THE PROGRESSIVE ANTITRUST ERA CONTINUES:
"GET ON THE RAFT WITH TAFT" AND
WILSON'S "BUST THE TRUSTS"

All in all, the Sherman Act and the legal victories initiated by Theodore Roosevelt and his handpicked Republican successor, William Howard Taft, signaled an end to the ascendancy—but not the political power and already accumulated wealth—of the robber barons. After the passage of the Sherman Antitrust Act—a law put in place to fight business combinations and the big, Rockefeller-style trusts of their time—the federal government, after a decade of inaction, brought a number of antitrust enforcement actions before the onset of World War I. From 1901 to 1909, Theodore Roosevelt's administration sued forty-five companies under the Sherman Act, while William Howard Taft's administration (1909–1913) brought even more, initiating a total of seventy-five enforcement actions. President Taft's attorney general, George Wickersham, aggressively pursued the trusts despite his Wall Street background and boasted that the Taft administration had turned the Sherman Act into "an actual effective weapon to the accomplishment of the purposes for which it was primarily enacted."

One of the most notable Progressive Era actions was *United States v. American Tobacco Co.* In 1907, the Roosevelt administration's Department of Justice indicted twenty-nine individuals and sixty-five corporations, including the American Tobacco Company, for antitrust violations under the Sherman Act. At the time the Department of Justice filed suit against the American Tobacco Company, that company was manufacturing roughly 86 percent of all cigarettes produced in the United States. Only in 1911, after years of litigation, did the U.S. Supreme Court (following its precedent in the *Standard Oil* case) finally find an illegal combination in the tobacco industry. As a result of the Supreme Court's decision, the American Tobacco Company was carved into four separate entities: American Tobacco Company, Liggett and Myers Tobacco Company, R. J. Reynolds, and P. Lorillard. "By the end of the 1910s," an antitrust expert at Columbia Law School notes, "just about every one of the major trusts had been broken into pieces or had some encounter with the antitrust law, making it, for a while at least, a primary level of federal economic policymaking."

When antitrust actions were litigated, however, the outcomes were not always ideal, shaped in part by the influence of political interests. For example, after a five-year Sherman Act case against the powerful "Powder Trust," the E. I. du Pont de Nemours Powder Company—the country's biggest manufacturer of explosives and gunpowder—was finally broken up in 1912. The Powder Trust had been formed in 1872, and the DuPonts monopolized the post–Civil War market for gunpowder, driving their rivals out of business. For years, the Powder Trust controlled roughly 70 percent of U.S. production, with the power of one family and one U.S. senator from that family—Henry DuPont, a Delaware senator from 1906 to 1917—helping to shield the family business from legitimate competition in the lucrative military government contracting arena. As one history observes of the powerful DuPont family, "By World War I, the DuPonts, under the leadership of P. S. (Pierre Samuel) DuPont (1870–1954), completely dominated Delaware politics, controlling newspapers, a Senate seat, and the turnpike system, and their political clout averted an antitrust suit in 1906." The June 17, 1906, edition of Wilmington's *Sunday Star* expressly noted that "the powder trust knows the new senator intimately, as a child knows its father, and he knows the powder trust."

President Roosevelt himself had close ties to the DuPont family, taking in $70,000 in campaign contributions from them, with Coleman DuPont—as one history emphasizes—being "a liberal contributor" to the Republican Party, coming "into frequent and friendly contact with powerful administration officials and members of Congress." It was only on June 13, 1912, that a federal district court in Delaware ordered that the DuPont Powder Company be broken up, though—as one commentator recounts—"the outcome was less dramatic than it looked" because the newly formed competitors that received DuPont assets "were still effectively controlled by DuPont through back channels." "Moreover," that commentator, Erik Sass, observes, "DuPont itself got to keep its monopoly on the manufacture of gunpowder for the U.S. military—supposedly the object of the anti-trust action in the first place." In fact, it had been alleged in 1906 by Robert Waddell, a former DuPont Powder Company sales agent, that the DuPont Powder Company had engaged in price-fixing and colluded to restrain competition. Waddell asserted that the Powder Trust had bilked the U.S. government out of

Henry DuPont, a member of the Republican Party, graduated from the U.S. Military Academy at West Point and was an artillery officer in the Union army during the Civil War. Before serving as a U.S. senator for Delaware from 1906 to 1917, DuPont was the president of the Wilmington and Northern Railroad Company.

more than $2.5 million a year in illegal profits from its contacts through its monopoly power.

The DuPont family fought the idea of dismantling their lucrative company, with Coleman DuPont writing a letter in early August 1907 stressing what he perceived to be the extreme difficulty of breaking up the family business. "I do not think you can unscramble an egg," he wrote. It was only under tremendous public pressure that Roosevelt's Justice Department finally decided to act, with the headline in the Hearst family–owned *San Francisco Examiner* blaring, "U.S. Sues Powder Trust,—Senator Its Chief." That paper reported that Senator Henry DuPont was "the real power in the Trust," with progressives like William Randolph Hearst—a Democrat who served as a member of the U.S. House of Representatives from New York from 1903 to 1907—leading the charge for change. After being appointed to the U.S. Senate in 1886, George Hearst—a wealthy entrepreneur and California politician—had given the *Examiner* to his twenty-three-year-old son, William Randolph Hearst, who got into the publishing business and successfully built the country's largest newspaper chain and media empire.

The progressives' long fight against powerful interests was very public and—thanks to writers like Ida Tarbell—well documented. In 1906, William Randolph Hearst's *Cosmopolitan* magazine had itself run a series of news stories titled "The Treason of the Senate." The writer, David Graham Phillips, characterized the U.S. Senate as a club for rich men who regularly sold out the common man, enriching themselves at the expense of the constituents they purported to represent. Although a U.S. district court in Delaware ultimately ordered the breakup of the DuPont Powder Company, decreeing the formation of two new companies—Hercules Powder Company and Atlas Powder Company—the DuPont Powder Company, as noted, inexplicably managed to maintain its monopoly as the manufacturer of gunpowder for the U.S. military. "The company," one brigadier general wrote in a history of World War I, "went on to make a fortune during the Great War by supplying the European Allies and later the U.S. Army with high-powered explosives for artillery shells. . . . When the United States entered the war in 1917, DuPont provided a remarkable 100 percent of its explosives."

The DuPont Powder Company story well illustrates that when U.S. senators were appointed by state legislatures, as they were when Henry DuPont was put in office, they were often the tools of the trusts themselves. As Paul Douglas, a U.S. senator from Illinois, later reflected of the era before U.S. senators were elected directly by the voters of their states, "In the cartoons of that period, the Senate Chamber was depicted as an assembly of representatives of the trusts. I have seen cartoons of that period in which Senators were labeled as representatives of the steel trust, of the express companies, and of tobacco interests. I have seen them labeled as 'sugar' Senators, 'petroleum' Senators, and 'copper' Senators." Pointing out that by 1904 the number of combinations and trusts had grown to 318 with capital assets of $7.2 trillion, Douglas observed that those senators "were regarded as being on the floor merely the embodiments of the trust interests which sent so many to this body." It was only after a hard fight that the Seventeenth Amendment, requiring the direct election of U.S. senators, was added to the U.S. Constitution in 1913.

The power of wealthy families who controlled the trusts prior to the ratification of the Seventeenth Amendment explains why early trust-busting activities were not always completely effective. While the Roosevelt and Taft administrations' antitrust enforcement cases were great in number, the legal efforts of that time produced decidedly mixed results. Only certain industries were targeted, favored industries got favored treatment, and for the most part incredibly powerful industrialists continued to wield great power. In *Truths About the Trusts* (1916), William Randolph Hearst would expressly complain about what he called "the Roosevelt method." "The Roosevelt method," he lamented, "was to divide the trusts into good trusts and into bad trusts and to go to extreme lengths in assailing those that were declared by him to be the bad trusts, and to equally extreme and sometimes illegal lengths in aiding and protecting those that were declared by him to be the good trusts." "The good trusts," Hearst wrote, "were the trusts that politically supported Roosevelt and the bad trusts were the trusts that politically opposed Roosevelt."

Teddy Roosevelt came under criticism in his 1912 bid for the presidency for being too close to the owners of certain trusts. In that 1912 campaign, the *New-York Tribune* reported under the headline "Roosevelt Halted Harvester Suit" that Roosevelt had shown favoritism to businessmen, like George W. Perkins, who worked for J. P. Morgan. The article reported that "President Roosevelt looked on" various businesses "as 'good trusts' against which the stringent provisions of the Sherman anti-trust law should not be enforced."

Thus, while Roosevelt clearly shook up the establishment trusts in a series of game-changing lawsuits resulting in high-profile monopoly takedowns, there is still room for some justified criticism. Indeed, when an indignant J. P. Morgan—in the wake of the decision to take on the Northern Securities Company—had demanded to know of President Roosevelt whether his behemoth U.S. Steel Corporation would become a target, too, Roosevelt had offered his personal assurance that that was not his intention. "Roosevelt," as one historian observes, "was in fact intimately tied to big-business interests, especially the Morgan corporate empire, through members of his administration as well as the Oyster Bay Roosevelt clan to which he belonged." "Roosevelt's 'bad trusts,'" another historian, Philip H. Burch Jr., has written, "were basically 'non-Morgan trusts,' such as the Rockefeller-controlled Standard Oil Co. [or] the Harriman-dominated Union Pacific Railroad," while "Roosevelt's 'good trusts' usually turned out to be big Morgan-controlled companies, such as U.S. Steel Corp. and International Harvester Co." In the case of the latter two enterprises, Burch writes, "no action was taken against either of these giant concerns (although some federal officials were so inclined), partly because of Roosevelt's implicit trust in Morgan-backed firms and the quiet, though highly effective pressure applied by such influential Morgan men as George W. Perkins and Elbert H. Gary, board chairman of the U.S. Steel Corp."

The issue of trusts dominated the political landscape during this period. It was, in fact, a disagreement between Teddy Roosevelt and William Howard Taft over antitrust enforcement that helped set the stage for the hotly contested 1912 presidential election. In October 1911, the Taft administration sued the U.S. Steel Corporation in federal court for violating the Sherman Act. The lawsuit charged that U.S. Steel's 1907 acquisition of the Tennessee Coal and Iron Company—one of U.S. Steel's biggest competitors—was anticompetitive and had reduced competition. In 1907, Roosevelt had entered into a gentlemen's agreement with J. P. Morgan—made in the midst of a stock market panic—that the acquisition of the Tennessee Coal and Iron Company would not be challenged. To persuade Roosevelt to let U.S. Steel acquire its rival, U.S. Steel's officers—eager to gain control of its rival's iron ore reserves and thus extend the company's dominance—told Roosevelt that the acquisition was necessary to help stabilize the markets. Taft and Roosevelt, onetime friends, had already become estranged from each other, and the Taft administration's decision to sue U.S. Steel not only violated the gentlemen's agreement but further exacerbated their personal rift. Taft's Justice Department revealed information suggesting that Roosevelt had approved the lucrative deal involving U.S. Steel and Tennessee Coal and Iron for political reasons, thus damaging Roosevelt's reputation. As one historical summary describes Roosevelt's reaction to the suit, "Breaking this gentlemen's agreement further enraged Roosevelt, and led directly to his decision to try to wrest the Republican presidential nomination away from Taft in 1911."

It was the 1912 election waged between the incumbent, William Howard Taft, the third-party candidate Theodore Roosevelt, and the Democrat Woodrow Wilson that brought about the first sweeping change to America's federal antitrust laws since the passage of the Sherman Act. In that election, Wilson beat the Republican nominee, William Howard Taft, and Theodore Roosevelt, the former president who had formed his Progressive "Bull Moose" Party in an effort to make a political comeback.

As he campaigned for the presidency once again, Roosevelt proudly

The 1912 election turned into a three-way contest. It pitted the Democratic candidate, Woodrow Wilson, against the incumbent Republican, President William Howard Taft, as well as the former Republican president Theodore Roosevelt, running that year under the Progressive "Bull Moose" Party moniker. Ultimately, Taft and Roosevelt split the Republican vote, putting Woodrow Wilson in the White House. Cartoon by Clifford Berryman, November 5, 1912.

spoke of his antitrust record. Roosevelt was in fact so devoted to trust-busting that he once gave a speech on the subject immediately after being shot. On October 14, 1912, Theodore Roosevelt grittily delivered a speech in Milwaukee—one emphasizing his antitrust record—after an attempt on his life was made. As Roosevelt left the city's Gilpatrick Hotel that evening to address an awaiting crowd, he was shot by an angry saloon keeper, John Schrank, with a revolver. The .32-caliber bullet lodged in Roosevelt's chest, but thankfully it was slowed by Roosevelt's thick coat, a glasses case, and the fifty-page folded speech he carried in his breast pocket. Before getting medical attention, Roosevelt insisted on giving an abbreviated version of his prepared speech, the one that the would-be assassin's bullet had just torn through. In his speech, Roosevelt said that he "stood by labor-unions" and touted, in these words, what he had done as president to encourage more competition: "When I took the office the antitrust law was practically a dead letter and the interstate commerce law in as poor a condition. I had to revive both laws. I did. I enforced both. It will be easy enough to do now what I did then, but the reason that it is easy now is because I did it when it was hard."

In the 1912 campaign, however, Roosevelt was dogged by the charge that George Perkins, one of his key economic advisers and a major campaign contributor, had removed from the Progressive Party platform a strong antitrust plank. Perkins, a top aide and financier J. P. Morgan's business partner who handled affairs for U.S. Steel and International Harvester, saw competition as wasteful and inefficient. Perkins donated $263,000 to Roosevelt's 1912 campaign coffers, and the Progressive Party's platform—because of Perkins's actions—ended up declaring, "The concentration of business, in some degree, is both inevitable and necessary for national business efficiency."

Woodrow Wilson, on the other hand, had Louis Brandeis as an economic adviser, and both men embraced a strong antitrust position. Wilson's biographer John Milton Cooper notes that Wilson had been "criticizing the shortcomings of the existing anti-trust law for some time" and spent many hours strategizing with Brandeis, who was on record with his well-voiced concerns about the "curse of bigness." Yet Wilson carefully distinguished between "a big business and a trust" even as he declared that the "ideals of absolutely free opportunity" were

President Woodrow Wilson is portrayed in this cartoon as an enemy of big business. Instead of using President Roosevelt's big stick, Wilson, a former professor, uses a ruler. Cartoon by Robert Carter, circa 1913.

being undermined by large businesses. Wilson differentiated between the two: "A trust is an arrangement to get rid of competition, and a big business is a business that has survived competition by conquering in the field of intelligence and economy." In railing against "artificially created" trusts run by businessmen "who wished to make their power secure against competition," Wilson—in calling for a New Freedom— pointed to men who "were put 'out of business by Wall Street,' because Wall Street found them inconvenient and didn't want their competition." "The little man is crushed by the trusts," he emphasized, noting how "the big concerns come in and undersell him" and drive him out of business. As president, Wilson—worried about the outsized power of trusts and nationwide financial panics—thus called Wall Street's financial power "the most pernicious of all trusts."

The antitrust enforcement efforts of Presidents Roosevelt, Taft, and Wilson cannot of course be viewed in isolation. They were part of the Progressive Era—a period of American history that ran from the 1890s to the 1920s and led to major changes in American life. Progressives sought to eliminate political corruption and the power of political bosses, and their social activism transformed countless aspects of political and economic life, although African Americans and other minorities continued to experience segregation and rampant discrimination in education, employment, and housing. The Equal Justice Initiative, in fact, has documented how thousands of Blacks were lynched after the Civil War through the mid-twentieth century, with lynchings especially prevalent in the South, where the Ku Klux Klan, formed in 1865, terrorized whole communities. As history shows, each of those three U.S. presidents held racist and antiquated views that were not "progressive" in any way in the sense that we use that word today. Although Theodore Roosevelt once invited Booker T. Washington to dinner at the White House, he did so only once and he privately expressed the belief that Blacks "as a race and in the mass . . . are altogether inferior to whites"; his successor, William Howard Taft, while insisting in his inaugural address that he did not have "the slightest race prejudice or feeling," refused to support the hiring of African Americans in the South and later, as the chief justice, wrote a unanimous opinion for the U.S. Supreme Court in 1927 that upheld a Mississippi law providing for segregated schools, citing the Court's now-overruled *Plessy v. Ferguson* (1896) "separate but equal" decision as a precedent; and Woodrow Wilson arranged for a private screening of *The Birth of a Nation* (1915), a widely protested film originally called *The Clansman* that glorifies the Ku Klux Klan and that used white actors in blackface, and his administration adopted and pursued overtly discriminatory and segregationist policies.

The Niagara Movement—led by W. E. B. Du Bois, William Trotter,

Louis Brandeis, a graduate of Harvard Law School, became known as "the People's Lawyer" for fighting corruption, the railroads, and monopoly power. A social reformer, Brandeis published an article in the *Harvard Law Review* on the right to privacy and engaged in a years-long fight to prevent the financier J. P. Morgan from securing monopoly power in New England's railroad industry. Brandeis believed that monopolies and trusts were not inevitable and backed Woodrow Wilson in the 1912 presidential campaign. In 1916, President Wilson nominated Brandeis to serve as an associate justice on the U.S. Supreme Court—a position he held until 1939.

The Progressive Era saw the formation of major civil rights organizations. After the founding of the Niagara Movement in 1905 by W. E. B. Du Bois and others, the NAACP was formed in 1909 to advance equality for African Americans. The NAACP itself later got involved in antitrust litigation. This photograph was taken in 1929, twenty years after the organization's formation and during the NAACP's annual conference.

Charles Bentley, and a pioneering St. Paul lawyer, Fredrick McGhee—opposed racial segregation, and its formation in 1905 ultimately led to the creation, in 1909, of the National Association for the Advancement of Colored People (NAACP). During the Wilson administration, the NAACP protested *The Birth of a Nation,* saying it stoked racial prejudice, with NAACP officer Walter F. White and his allies writing that the film was "part of the campaign of the Ku Klux Klan to recruit members." Also, the suffrage movement, spearheaded by women like Susan B. Anthony, Elizabeth Cady Stanton, Lucy Burns, and Alice Paul, led to the ratification, in 1920, of the Nineteenth Amendment guaranteeing women the right to vote. And in 1921, Margaret Sanger—an advocate for women's access to contraceptives—founded the American Birth Control League, which later became Planned Parenthood Federation of America. A major feature of the Progressive Era was union and middle-class participation in efforts to modernize and transform society, and legislation and activism sought to improve public schools and to ensure food safety and the quality of drinking water.

PASSAGE OF THE CLAYTON ACT AND
THE ESTABLISHMENT OF THE FTC

On the Progressive Era's antitrust front, Roosevelt, Taft, and Wilson led the way when it came to trust-busting. When Taft signed into law the Panama Canal Act (1912), that legislation denied access to the canal to any Sherman Act violator. Woodrow Wilson's victory in the 1912 election led directly to the creation of the Federal Reserve System in 1913 and to new legislation designed to take on the trusts. Through its Federal Reserve Act, Congress sought to prevent financial crises, to stabilize prices and the financial system, and to maximize employment in the labor force. Wilson's election also gave impetus to a new law, the Clayton Antitrust Act of 1914, that remains a cornerstone of the nation's antitrust enforcement efforts.

Wilson also signed into law the Federal Trade Commission Act of 1914, which created the Federal Trade Commission and outlawed unfair practices and methods of competition affecting interstate commerce. The law's prohibition against "unfair methods of competition" covers conduct violative of the Sherman and Clayton Acts but also sets forth a broader prohibition that applies, more generally, to unscrupulous business conduct. The successor to Roosevelt's Bureau of Corporations, which had been created in 1903 to study monopolistic practices and write reports, the FTC opened its doors on March 16, 1915. Today, the FTC remains an independent agency of the U.S. government whose mission is to prevent fraudulent or anticompetitive business practices and to protect consumers against everything from false and deceptive advertising to monopolistic behavior. It also is tasked with protecting the privacy rights of Americans.

President Wilson, like his Republican predecessors Roosevelt and Taft, felt strongly that the trusts had accumulated far too much power. "Without the watchful interference, the resolute interference, of the government," Wilson wrote in *The New Freedom,* "there can be no fair play between individuals and such powerful institutions as the trusts." With Louis Brandeis as the architect of Wilson's economic policies, Wilson decided to press for new competition policy legislation in the wake of his victory despite much opposition from big business interests. "Brandeis helped to shape the reforms of the Wilson administration, which set out to break up some of the trusts rather than to manage them from the top down," Brandeis's biographer Jeffrey Rosen aptly writes. "The Brandeisian reforms," Rosen emphasizes, included the Clayton Antitrust Act and the creation of the Federal Trade Commission. "In endorsing the Federal Trade Commission bill, introduced by Wisconsin progressive Senator Robert La Follette," Rosen stresses, "Brandeis argued that it would strengthen enforcement of the Sherman Antitrust Act and perform an invaluable role in educating the public about facts that would prevent anticompetitive behavior."

Wisconsin's Robert La Follette, a Republican politician and lawyer also known as Fighting Bob, opposed monopolies because of their harmful effects. In the 1912 presidential election, he had challenged Taft for the nomination, but his effort, in which he accumulated some delegates for the national nominating convention, was overshadowed by Theodore Roosevelt's own campaign to take back the presidency.

In his 1913 autobiography, La Follette—a politician Theodore Roosevelt considered too radical—spoke out against monopoly power and was critical of President Roosevelt himself for not using the Sherman Antitrust Act more aggressively during his presidency. After observing that he had reviewed "Roosevelt's course upon trusts and combinations," La Follette wrote, "The American people believe private monopoly intolerable. Within the last dozen years trusts and combinations have been organized in nearly every branch of industry. Competition has been ruthlessly crushed, extortionate prices have been exacted from consumers, independent business development has been arrested, invention stifled, and the door of opportunity has been closed, except to large aggregations of capital." La Follette continued, excoriating monopolists, "The public has not, as a rule, received any of the resultant economies and benefits of combination which have been so abundantly promised." Although La Follette believed that the passage of the Sherman Act had "placed in the hands of the Executive the strongest, most perfect weapon which the ingenuity of man could forge for the protection of the people of this country against the power and sordid greed of monopoly," he thought Roosevelt had missed an opportunity to crush and destroy all of the trusts then in existence.

Until his death in 1925, La Follette railed against monopolies. "The Government," he said in 1919 in a speech in the U.S. Senate, "must

Robert La Follette, of Wisconsin, served as the Dane County district attorney before getting elected as a Republican to the U.S. House of Representatives. After serving as Wisconsin's governor from 1901 to 1906 and emerging as a progressive leader, he was appointed to serve in the U.S. Senate—a seat he held until 1925. In the Senate, La Follette sought to break up the railroad trust. Cartoon by John T. McCutcheon, 1911.

destroy private monopoly wherever it exists in this country or monopoly will destroy government." "We must curb this mighty monopoly power," he said in another speech, "and give to the people of this country a free, open, competitive market, and free, open, competitive conditions under which they may buy the products of all manufacturing and producing organizations in this country at reasonable prices regulated by competition." "I have said on the floor of the Senate again and again that there is not any way of accounting for the increase in the cost of living excepting that we are in the grip of monopoly," he observed in yet another speech passionately delivered in 1919.

While La Follette's brainchild, the Federal Trade Commission, became the agency that had the power to stop fraudulent or anticompetitive conduct, the Clayton Act closed Sherman Act loopholes, prohibited sellers from entering into exclusive arrangements with purchasers or product distributors, and allowed for the recovery of treble damages against violators of the antitrust laws. One of the pre-1914 tactics of big industrialists to evade the Sherman Act had been to create interlocking directorates, in which ostensibly competing companies would share a board of directors to set the direction of those corporations. This, as one history of America's Industrial Revolution puts it, had the effect of creating monopolies "in all but name." The Clayton Act buttressed

In the election of 1912, the voters elected Woodrow Wilson, the
Democratic candidate, in a wild election that featured a sitting president,
William Howard Taft, a former president, Teddy Roosevelt, running
as a third-party candidate, and a socialist and union organizer, Eugene
V. Debs. Wilson took almost 42 percent of the popular vote, Roosevelt
garnered more than 27 percent, and President Taft—seeking reelection—
came in third with just 23 percent. Debs, who ran five times for president,
got 6 percent of the popular vote. The antitrust issue played a major role
in the campaign.

the Sherman Antitrust Act by making monopolistic price discrimination unlawful and by outlawing interlocking directorates in companies
valued in excess of $1 million. The Clayton Act also provided for civil
and criminal penalties for corporate officers who violated the law, and
legalized boycotts, strikes, peaceful demonstrations, and picketing. In
other words, union activity was protected, but the underhanded tactics
of owners of the trusts were not.

Woodrow Wilson, like William Jennings Bryan, understood the
political power of the antitrust movement. In fact, his successful 1912
presidential campaign came complete with a "Bust the Trusts" theme
song. Wilson specifically contended that despite all that *had* been done,
not enough had been done—not even by the trustbuster Teddy Roosevelt or his Republican successor, William Howard Taft—to dismantle
the trusts. The song's chorus: "So we'll have to Bust the Trusts / Or

they'll grind us in the dust / Yes, if we want to prosper / We'll have to Bust the Trusts. / Bust the Trusts! Bust the Trusts! / This we surely must / So vote for Woodrow Wilson / And he soon will Bust up the Trusts."

For our purposes today, it is important to remember that the Sherman, Clayton, and FTC Acts—as well as many of the court cases that interpreted them and thus gave them life—have withstood the test of time. The enthusiasm of the public and of political leaders for pushing the antitrust issue, however, has not, though the issue of antitrust enforcement has gotten some much-needed attention in recent times. When's the last time you heard a "Bust the Trusts" song as a backdrop for a political candidate? Yet at this point in history—with more and more mergers and consolidations, with court cases turning against enforcement and inertia winning out against efforts to change the laws to match the times we're in—we would do well to remember that political candidates actually used to *run* and *win* on the issue of antitrust. And, as far as making progress on the issue, don't forget the words of John Sherman in describing Abraham Lincoln after his assassination: "At first I thought him slow, but he was fast enough to be abreast with the body of his countrymen, and his heart beat steadily and hopefully with them."

Taking on the big interests of our time means harnessing the political energy—and the hearts—of Americans. The people in this country are ready for change on a host of issues, from racial injustice and policing reforms, to health care and climate change, to gun safety. Now, when it comes to antitrust, it is in vogue to say "no one really understands this stuff, so it isn't worth taking on the fight as a political issue." Well, that's not what Teddy Roosevelt, William Jennings Bryan, John Sherman, or the Grangers said. No, they rallied the prairie populists and charged up the hills and busted the trusts. They did it not with legal mumbo jumbo or fancy briefs (albeit a part of their strategy in court cases certainly involved them) but with simple words and steady hearts. They didn't hate business; in fact they respected it and wanted capitalism to succeed. In the end, they just wanted a "square deal" and economic liberty and fairness. That's how—and why—they busted the trusts.

5

The Last One Hundred Years

A Century of Antitrust Action (and Inaction)
in the Courts and Congress

POST–PROGRESSIVE ERA PRESIDENCIES
AND LEGISLATION

Compared with Teddy Roosevelt's antimonopoly crusades of more than one hundred years ago, America's remaining antitrust history is notably tamer, with newspaper headlines turning from workers' strikes and farmers' protests to court filings and FTC investigations. While political opposition to corporate consolidation never exited our democratic dialogue, the quiet drama of legal maneuvering is certainly no match for barnstorming speeches. Yet during much of the hundred-plus years since the Progressive Era, our nation's antitrust focus shifted to closing statutory loopholes, shoring up enforcement with resources and statutory authorities, and establishing numerous legal exemptions to our nation's antitrust laws, which have included everything from agricultural cooperatives to Major League Baseball.

So for those looking for more antitrust presidential campaign songs or Roosevelt-style theatrics, approach this chapter—and this past century—with patience. As tedious as the legal side of antitrust may be (I have tried to make it both interesting and understandable), the history of the law's development is in fact key to an enlightened understanding of how we got where we are and how we can get ourselves out of it. That's because while the past century had its share of landmark cases in which the federal government, state attorneys general, and courts aggressively engaged in antitrust enforcement, there were equally lengthy periods where antitrust laws stood largely dormant, failing to adapt to the changing monopoly dynamics of the times. The reasons for enforcement inaction were varied: economic stagnation meant more immediate needs took preference (think the Great Depression); wars (World Wars I and II are examples of time periods during which enforcement lulled); the political bent of those running the agencies (see Ronald Reagan and George W. Bush eras); and a dominant conservative ideology in the courts, particularly in the nation's highest court (see the present).

But whether a person favors or opposes strong antitrust enforcement, there can be one point of agreement: what has clearly faltered since the era of William Jennings Bryan and Presidents Roosevelt, Taft, and Wilson is a national movement led by those willing to consistently make the public case for more aggressive antitrust enforcement. Instead, the past century of antitrust history is mired in dense regulatory filings, bureaucratic decision making, industry-driven special interest lobbying, the promulgation of complex merger guidelines, a profusion of econometric analyses by economists and statisticians, and the issuance of complex, expert-witness-driven court opinions. The antitrust movement went from one grounded in the body politic to one led principally (and "led" is probably too strong a word) by academicians, lawyers, and highly paid experts and PhD-trained economists hired to explain the nuances of market definition, allocative efficiency, and cross elasticity of demand—in-the-weeds arguments that simply don't carry the same political juice as colonists throwing chests of tea into Boston Harbor, union workers leading national protests at factory gates, and farmers with pitchforks reaming out their elected representatives about exorbitant rail rates.

The slow decline in antitrust enforcement began after Woodrow Wilson's presidency, with three Republican presidents—Warren Harding, Calvin Coolidge, and Herbert Hoover—ascending to power. The onset and aftermath of World War I (1914–1918) brought on what has been called an era of antitrust "neglect," with one antitrust expert, Daniel Crane, reporting that "the impetus for antitrust's hibernation lay in two successive crises—war and depression." World War I brought a suspension of major antitrust cases until the end of the war, with Crane explaining that "the Republican administrations that succeeded Wilson during the Roaring Twenties had little interest in enforcing antitrust law and largely did not." And during the Great Depression, few political leaders worried about antitrust violations, with the national priorities focused on creating jobs and getting the American economy moving again.

In his 1920 presidential campaign, Warren Harding promised to usher in an era of "less government in business and more business in government." Although the Harding administration—as one presidential history notes—"continued a moderately aggressive antitrust policy," under Calvin Coolidge antitrust enforcement fell into such decline that Gilbert Montague, a leading antitrust attorney, called the Sherman Act a dead letter. President Herbert Hoover did little to change that trend, though his attorney general—the Minnesota native William Mitchell—announced at the beginning of his term that his department would "deal vigorously" with antitrust violators and, in fact, brought a variety of antitrust cases against companies manufacturing and selling gasoline, asphalt shingles and roofing tiles, poultry, sugar beets, Norwegian sardines, saw frames and blades, and yarn and wool products, as well as against companies selling outdoor advertising, radios and "built-in" kitchen equipment, and producing and distributing motion pictures. Hoover's own biographer Joan Hoff Wilson noted that the Hoover administration's "quantitative record" of antitrust prosecutions "is unimpressive," pointing out that Hoover—despite a clear interest in the subject, one that predated his presidency—never managed to elevate antitrust enforcement to its heyday in the Roosevelt, Taft, and Wilson presidencies. Hoover's "personal encouragement of such actions and his continued criticisms of what he had always considered illegal, oligopolistic associationalism shocked and dismayed many large and small businessmen alike," Joan Hoff Wilson explains, while cautioning that Hoover "did not satisfy those reform groups who wanted a return to Woodrow Wilson's New Freedom trustbusting approach."

Despite the lack of presidential and congressional emphasis on antitrust issues starting with Harding, Coolidge, and Hoover, Congress did continue to pass a number of antitrust-related bills in the century that followed. While the Progressive Era's Sherman and Clayton Acts are still considered the granddaddies of antitrust enforcement, there are other, much lesser-known federal antitrust laws that were enacted after that era ended. These include the Capper-Volstead Act of 1922, the Norris-LaGuardia Act of 1932, the Robinson-Patman Act of 1936, the Celler-Kefauver Act of 1950, and the Hart-Scott-Rodino Antitrust Improvements Act of 1976. Each of these laws was designed to address particular issues or respond to specific problems identified at the time of their passage. Some of them created antitrust exemptions—including for the benefit of farmers and union members—while others closed loopholes.

Under the 1922 Capper-Volstead Act, named for its legislative sponsors, Senator Arthur Capper of Kansas and Representative Andrew Volstead of Minnesota (better known as the lead sponsor of the ill-fated National Prohibition Act of 1919 prohibiting the manufacture and sale of alcohol), agricultural cooperatives are exempt from the antitrust laws. Likewise, the 1932 Norris-LaGuardia Act, along with portions of the Clayton Act, created what is known as the "labor antitrust exemption." The reason behind these exemptions? Congress found that agricultural cooperatives and unions were formed to protect farmers and employees from unfair business practices, and allowing workers to collectively bargain for wages, benefits, and better working conditions was, in fact, critical to ensuring their fair treatment, just as farm co-ops better allowed small farmers to compete. Because agricultural cooperatives and unions involve groups of farmers and employees acting collectively, Congress established their exemption from the antitrust laws, finding that their collective action should not become a basis for enforcement.

The changes in the law brought about by the Clayton Act, and then by the Capper-Volstead Act and the Norris-LaGuardia Act, were long overdue. As noted in previous chapters, in the earliest days of antitrust enforcement, the provisions of the Sherman Act were frequently perverted to favor big business at the expense of labor unions and agricultural workers—the very people the Sherman Act was put in place to protect. Ironically, although the Sherman Act was passed to curb monopolistic abuses of *large* business combinations, the law was initially used against organized labor, to stop strikes, working people, and union leaders in their tracks. The exemptions passed by Congress fixed that perversion of the Sherman Act.

A number of other laws that shaped America's antitrust landscape were passed before the onset of World War II. It was, in fact, the Wall Street crash of 1929 and the Great Depression that produced the 1936 Robinson-Patman Act—another pillar of American competition law. In an effort to save small mom-and-pop retailers, that statute bars price discrimination and predatory pricing. Requiring sellers to charge all retailers the same price unless there is a justification for a price differential, the Robinson-Patman Act became known as the Anti-chain Store Act because it was intended to combat the immense purchasing power of large-chain retailers like Sears, Roebuck and grocer A&P (these days, think Walmart). As one federal appellate court put it, "The Robinson-Patman Act stands on entirely different footing than the Sherman Act and Clayton Act. While the framers of the Sherman and Clayton Acts intended to proscribe only conduct that threatens consumer welfare, the framers of the Robinson-Patman Amendments intended to punish perceived economic evils not necessarily threatening to consumer welfare *per se*." While price discrimination involves businesses charging lower prices to larger, more powerful customers than to smaller companies, predatory pricing involves selling goods at below cost to drive out competition with the goal of later recouping the resulting losses through monopoly-driven prices after a competitor is wiped out.

After World War II, the landmark Celler-Kefauver Act of 1950 was passed. It closed a couple of gaping loopholes in the Clayton Act—provisions that companies had been exploiting to skirt the antitrust laws. While the Clayton Act prohibited stock purchase mergers that substantially reduced competition, businesses were able to evade that law's requirements by simply buying a competitor's assets instead of purchasing its stock. The Celler-Kefauver Act barred such acquisitions if competition would be reduced as a result of the asset purchase. Also known as the Anti-merger Act, the Celler-Kefauver Act strengthened the Clayton Act to prevent activities that reduced competition. In the words of one antitrust expert, it "gave the government new tools to prevent the buildup" of giant firms "in advance, by controlling—or undoing—mergers," with the legislative intent being that "instead of trying to break up the giants decades later, its idea was to prevent their formation in the first place." The law sought to erect a barrier to increasing corporate concentration.

The Celler-Kefauver Act also allowed the government to prevent vertical and conglomerate mergers that could lessen competition. While the Clayton Act, as originally written, prevented horizontal mergers— that's when two companies producing similar products combine into one (imagine, for instance, if the companies that own Coke and Pepsi merged)—the Celler-Kefauver Act barred vertical mergers in cases where buying the assets of competitors—including those in the company's own supply chain—would lead to reduced competition. "The legislative history of Section 7 of the Clayton Act, and particularly of its amendments in 1950 by the Celler-Kefauver Act," one Federal Trade Commission practice guide notes, "shows that a motivating force behind the legislation was an apprehension about the social consequences that would flow from the concentration of economic and political power in fewer and fewer corporate hands."

One particularly noteworthy vertical merger occurred nearly a half-century later, in the mid-1990s, when Time Warner, a major cable company, merged with Turner Broadcasting, the successful media company responsible for channels such as Cartoon Network, CNN, TBS, and TNT. The $7.5 billion deal, forged between two companies that accounted for approximately 40 percent of all U.S. cable programming, gave Time Warner control over additional content. The deal raised significant concerns at the Federal Trade Commission, which ultimately approved the acquisition in 1996 subject to acquisition restructuring. The acquiring company, Time Warner, agreed to the restructuring to settle FTC charges that the merger would restrict competition in cable television programming and distribution.

The FTC's concern: the acquisition would allow Time Warner to unilaterally raise consumer prices for cable television and potentially limit programming choices. In announcing the settlement, Robert Pitofsky—then the FTC's chairman—made this statement: "While the proposed merger of Time Warner and Turner Broadcasting is one of the biggest and most complicated deals that antitrust officials have reviewed, the central issue it raises can be summarized in one word: access. This settlement would preserve competition and protect consumers from higher cable service prices and reduced programming choices by ensuring that competing cable operators, new technologies and future programmers can gain access to Time Warner/Turner's customers and programming." Since the mid-1990s, however, the price of cable TV has steadily climbed. In fact, a 2016 report of the Federal Communications Commission found that price increases for cable TV had outpaced inflation for every single year of the past twenty years. And not only have rates increased, but consumer groups and content providers have repeatedly come to my office over the last few years raising concerns about cable company access issues. The words of consent decrees are one thing; effectively implementing them, enforcing compliance, and getting actual results to ensure vigorous competition can at times be another.

Finally, the Hart-Scott-Rodino Antitrust Improvements Act of 1976—enacted in the year of America's bicentennial—further amended the Clayton Act. With its name derived from its principal authors, U.S. senators Philip Hart and Hugh Scott Jr. and Representative Peter Rodino, the Hart-Scott-Rodino Act provides that parties cannot complete certain acquisitions, mergers, or transfers of assets or securities until they have made nonpublic filings with the Federal Trade Commission and the Antitrust Division of the U.S. Department of Justice. If a Hart-Scott-Rodino, or HSR, filing is required, then a deal cannot close until the waiting period has expired. The purpose of HSR filings is to give the federal government a chance to review large acquisitions before closings take place, allowing antitrust enforcement actions to be brought ahead of time, not just reactively. A failure to comply with HSR filing requirements can lead to severe monetary penalties. Before the passage of the Hart-Scott-Rodino Antitrust Improvements Act, there were so-called "midnight mergers" that took place. In those situations, the government had to persuade judges to unwind already-completed mergers that the government had gotten no notice of, putting antitrust enforcers in the unenviable position of advocating for unscrambling already scrambled eggs.

"THE GREAT SWISS CHEESE": THE ANTITRUST EXEMPTIONS

With their long history and amendments over the years, the major federal antitrust laws appear, on their face, to be comprehensive in scope. In truth, though, antitrust laws have so many exemptions that one expert, the Cleveland-Marshall law professor Christopher Sagers, has likened them to "the great Swiss cheese." As Sagers explains, "Antitrust actually turns out to be subject to quite a bristling profusion of little exemptions and limitations, and each of those limits has spawned its own case law, history, and idiosyncrasies." There are both statutory and non-statutory antitrust exemptions and a number of immunity doctrines, so American antitrust law might be thought of as a particularly complex Swiss cheese.

In fact, antitrust exemptions are the product of historical circumstances, legislation, and judicial decisions. In all, there are more than twenty statutory exemptions from antitrust law enacted by Congress. For example, until very recent legislation passed in 2020, the 1945 McCarran-Ferguson Act—adopted under pressure from the insurance industry after the U.S. Supreme Court decided in 1944 that the industry was part of "interstate commerce" and thus subject to the federal antitrust laws—exempted "the business of insurance" from the antitrust laws. Let's note that that was one whopper of an exemption. Other statutory exemptions exist for everything from railroads and the actions of local government officials to electric power, sports broadcasting, and anti-hog-cholera serum.

The federal courts have also created a web of judicial exemptions, even though the U.S. Supreme Court has suggested elsewhere that the antitrust laws should be uniformly applied across industries. One of the most famous judicially created antitrust exemptions started in the 1920s when the U.S. Supreme Court went out of its way to exempt the entire sport of baseball from the antitrust laws—a judicial exemption that (somewhat inexplicably) continues to exist to this day. In 1922, the Court specifically ruled that the federal antitrust laws were inapplicable to baseball, America's national pastime. In that case, *Federal Baseball Club v. National League,* Oliver Wendell Holmes Jr.—writing for a unanimous Court—held that "the business is giving exhibitions of baseball, which are purely state affairs." More than thirty years later, in *Toolson v. New York Yankees, Inc.* (1953), the Court reaffirmed baseball's antitrust exemption. In declining to overrule its 1922 decision, the Court found that "Congress had no intention of including the business of baseball within the scope of the federal antitrust laws" and that "if there are evils in this field which now warrant application to it of the antitrust laws, it should be by legislation." Subsequently, in *Flood v. Kuhn* (1972), the Court again reaffirmed its earlier rulings, holding that baseball is exempt from state antitrust laws, too. Although other professional sports, such as football and boxing, have no blanket antitrust exemption, professional baseball—because of this judicial quirk of history—still does, even though Major League Baseball (with its multimillion-dollar players' contracts and TV broadcasting deals) is big business and now clearly operates squarely within the realm of interstate commerce.

Interestingly enough, in *Radovich v. National Football League* (1957), the U.S. Supreme Court ruled that professional football *is* subject to the country's antitrust laws under certain circumstances. Even though three justices dissented, finding the ruling inconsistent with its baseball antitrust decision in *Toolson v. New York Yankees,* the majority found that while the antitrust laws don't apply to baseball, they do apply to football. It's a somewhat complicated story when it comes to pro football, as I explain below, but the fact that professional baseball and professional football are treated differently speaks volumes about the law's complexity and, it must be said at times, its irrationality.

The case brought by pro-football player Bill Radovich against the National Football League (NFL) involved an interesting set of facts. Radovich was an all-pro guard who had played five seasons for the NFL's Detroit Lions in the 1930s and 1940s. He got into his dispute with the NFL after asking to be traded to another NFL club, the Los Angeles Rams, so he could be closer to his dad, who lived in the L.A. area and was sick and uninsured. After the Lions' owner, Fred Mandel, rejected his request, telling Radovich he either would play in Detroit or "wouldn't play anywhere," Radovich broke his player's contract and went to play for the Los Angeles Dons, which was part of a competing, now-defunct football league, the All-America Football Conference (AAFC), that operated from 1946 to 1949.

Radovich played for the Dons through the 1947 season, but the NFL blacklisted players like Radovich who left the NFL to play for the AAFC. As one history notes of Radovich's fate, "In 1948, with his playing career winding down, he was offered a position as player-coach with a minor league team, the San Francisco Clippers. He was on the verge of accepting the offer when it was withdrawn." The San Francisco

Clippers, a farm team that was part of the NFL-affiliated Pacific Coast Football League, was prohibited from hiring players, such as Radovich, who'd been put on the NFL's blacklist. Any team signing Radovich would suffer severe consequences.

After the San Francisco Clippers refused to sign him as a coach, Bill Radovich found work as a waiter in L.A. and eventually sued the NFL. His lawyer on the case was none other than Joe Alioto, a former Justice Department antitrust litigator who went on to be a successful lawyer and, eventually, to serve as San Francisco's mayor. Radovich, unable to get a job in professional football, met Alioto—who represented high-profile clients like Walt Disney and Samuel Goldwyn—while waiting tables at L.A.'s Brown Derby restaurant. The Supreme Court ultimately sided with Radovich and Alioto, ruling that the volume of interstate business involved in professional football placed it squarely within the provisions of the nation's antitrust laws. The NFL ultimately settled with Radovich, paying him $42,500, but he never played again in the NFL.

In the wake of the *Radovich* decision, the NFL's commissioner, Bert Bell, and his successor, Pete Rozelle, lobbied Congress to pass an antitrust exemption for professional football. While the NFL was unsuccessful in getting a blanket exemption, Congress did pass the Sports Broadcasting Act of 1961, which granted an antitrust exemption to allow for the sharing of television revenues. A court had ruled that NFL teams could not negotiate broadcasting rights as a group because that would violate the antitrust laws, but Rozelle persuaded a New York congressman to introduce the bill that became the law allowing sports teams to pool their negotiation efforts. The new law, signed by President Kennedy, permitted the NFL to enter into a $4.65 million television broadcast deal with CBS. Five years later, Congress also approved the merger of the two competing football leagues of the time, the NFL and the AFL, thus exempting the merger agreement from the federal antitrust laws.

The congressional deal allowing the NFL–AFL merger was reportedly made after Louisiana congressman Hale Boggs and Louisiana senator Russell Long, then chair of the powerful Senate Finance Committee, were secretly promised that the next NFL franchise would come to their home state. Commissioner Rozelle announced that New Orleans had been granted an NFL franchise, the Saints, on November 1, 1966, with

Boggs's friend John Mecom Jr.—an oil tycoon from Houston, Texas—becoming the team's principal owner. After the NFL and its players' union got into a dispute, a non-statutory labor exemption from the anti-trust laws was also recognized in the 1970s in the context of professional football for certain of the NFL's activities.

Thus, even a cursory review of the legislative and judicial history of America's antitrust exemptions—one peppered with backroom deals in the halls of Congress—demonstrates that this area of the law is, at its best, incoherent and confusing, and, at its worst, corrupt and unfair. In either case, the statutory and judicially created antitrust exemptions add yet another layer of complexity to the nation's antitrust laws and to the public's ability to understand how they work in practice and to have faith in their application. "Antitrust law is complicated," Ben Sheffner once wrote in *Slate*, though he also clarified that "one principle is very simple: Competitors cannot get together and agree on price or the terms on which they will offer their services to their customers."

THE COURTS INTERPRET THE LAWS

While legislative exemptions and judicial decisions have defined and limited the contours of America's antitrust laws, a century of enforcement decisions—and the ability or inability to go forward with cases—has also greatly influenced the current state of the law. In deciding whether the antitrust laws should apply (or not apply), FTC and Justice Department lawyers, as well as economists and judges, must analyze the facts and the laws and make judgment calls—some harder than others. In Sherman Act and Clayton Act cases, one of the long-standing enforcement difficulties is that the laws aren't written in such a specific fashion to facilitate easy or mechanical decision making. The Sherman Act, though it contains unique statutory language, made use of common-law concepts, with Senator George Hoar—one of its chief proponents—saying in the legislative debate, "We have affirmed the old doctrine of the common law in regard to all inter-state and international commercial transactions and have clothed the United States courts with authority to enforce that doctrine by injunction."

Of course, as in any instance in which discretionary decisions are made, the government wins some cases and loses others. For example, even as federal regulators broke up the meatpacking and tobacco trusts in *Swift & Co. v. United States* (1905) and *United States v. American Tobacco Co.* (1911), the U.S. government lost its antitrust battle against the U.S. Steel Corporation. In *United States v. United States Steel Corp.* (1920), the U.S. Supreme Court ruled that it was "unable to see that the public interest will be served by yielding to the contention of the government respecting the dissolution of the company or the separation from it of some of its subsidiaries." In other cases, settlements are reached between the Department of Justice or the Federal Trade Commission and the companies in the antitrust crosshairs. Federal judges then either accept or reject such settlements.

Because the Sherman Act, the Clayton Act, and other antitrust laws are subject to interpretation, and because American presidents have dedicated widely differing amounts of time and energy to antitrust enforcement, it is not surprising that different eras of American history have involved more or less attention to that subject. Some examples? While President Herbert Hoover was described as both a "trustbuilder" and an "antitruster" for his unprincipled, often conflicting approach to big business and the antitrust laws, the Great Depression—and FDR's New Deal—ushered in major new changes. The five-member National Labor Relations Board was a product of the National Labor Relations Act, though its history is rooted in the National Labor Board, a creation of the National Industrial Recovery Act of 1933. The National Industrial Recovery Act, signed into law by President Franklin D. Roosevelt but declared unconstitutional by the U.S. Supreme Court in 1935, was a short-lived effort by Congress to authorize the president to regulate industries to produce fair wages and prices.

After World War II, antitrust enforcement continued to ebb and flow, with the policy and judicial divide over the proper application of the antitrust laws coming into stark view. As antitrust expert Douglas Broder puts it, "Antitrust enforcement returned to the fore in the late 1940s and 1950s as American corporations, revived by the war effort and the beginnings of the postwar economic boom, began to increase their power. As they grew in size, corporations once again came to be seen as threats—potential or actual—to the public welfare." Broder writes of this period of antitrust enforcement, "Government antitrust authorities began to increase antitrust prosecutions. In the late 1950s and into the

1960s, the government began to bring and win criminal prosecutions against major corporations for nationwide price-fixing conspiracies and, for the first time, to send corporate executives to jail."

The case of *United States v. Columbia Steel Co.* (1948) highlights the diverging judicial views that emerged. In that case, the United States sued under the Sherman Act to stop the acquisition by U.S. Steel of the assets of Consolidated Steel, the West Coast's biggest independent steel fabricator. U.S. Steel, with all of its subsidiaries, was the largest producer of rolled steel products, with average sales of more than $1 billion per year from 1937 to 1947, whereas Consolidated Steel had average sales of only $20 million per year. In a 5–4 vote, the U.S. Supreme Court held that the proposed acquisition would not violate the Sherman Act despite the government's argument that the sale, if carried out, would restrain competition for rolled steel and fabricated steel products. Although the majority opinion took note of "the evils and dangers of monopoly and attempts to monopolize that grow out of size and efforts to eliminate others from markets, large or small," those in the majority found that "no direction has appeared of a public policy that forbids, *per se,* an expansion of facilities of an existing company to meet the needs of new markets."

In the dissenting opinion in *Columbia Steel,* Justice William O. Douglas—writing for the four dissenters—took issue, emphasizing, "This is the most important antitrust case which has been before the

The Steel Trust was very powerful, and it had friends in high places. Over time, the value of the Steel Trust reached into the billions.

Court in years. It is important because it reveals the way of growth of monopoly power—the precise phenomenon at which the Sherman Act was aimed." As Douglas explained, "Here, we have the pattern of the evolution of the great trusts. Little independent units are gobbled up by bigger ones. At times, the independent is driven to the wall and surrenders. . . . We have here the problem of bigness." Invoking the memory of Louis Brandeis (1856–1941), the late Supreme Court justice, Douglas added, "The Curse of Bigness shows how size can become a menace— both industrial and social. It can be an industrial menace because it creates gross inequalities against existing or putative competitors. It can be a social menace because of its control of prices. Control of prices in the steel industry is powerful leverage on our economy. For the price of steel determines the price of hundreds of other articles."

THE "CHICAGO SCHOOL" VERSUS THE "HARVARD SCHOOL"

Cases like *United States v. Columbia Steel*—a legal dispute that so divided the U.S. Supreme Court justices—set off a lively and long-standing academic debate about the true purpose of America's antitrust laws. This debate, which pitted adherents of what became known as the Chicago school against members of what has been called the Harvard school, might be considered esoteric and elite by some. What side of the debate (Chicago or Harvard) regulators and judges take in actual cases, however, has had real-world consequences for consumers.

From the 1950s onward, the so-called Chicago school—a group of economists, lawyers, and judges at or associated with my alma mater, the University of Chicago—advocated for more limited enforcement of the antitrust laws. Among them, Robert Bork, Richard Posner, Frank Easterbrook, and Antonin Scalia. In *The Antitrust Paradox* (1978), for example, Robert Bork offered a critique of then-existing law, including of a series of Supreme Court precedents—*Brown Shoe Co. v. United States* (1962), *United States v. Von's Grocery Co.* (1966), and *Utah Pie Co. v. Continental Baking Co.* (1967)—that rejected mergers and acquisitions or excoriated predatory pricing. Bork believed that the Supreme Court was using antitrust law not to protect competition but to make what he saw as legitimate competition illegal. Richard Posner—another leader of the Chicago school who once worked at the FTC and in the Office of the Solicitor General and who participated in the Antitrust Division's seminar series—offered a similar critique in his *Antitrust Law: An Economic Perspective* (1976).

In his treatise *The Antitrust Paradox,* Bork argues that "antitrust policy cannot be made rational until we are able to give a firm answer to one question: What is the point of the law—what are its goals? Everything else follows from the answer we give." Bork's book became a bible for conservative antitrust lawyers, and in it Bork raised these questions: "Is the antitrust judge to be guided by one value or by several? If by several, how is he to decide cases where a conflict in values arises?" "Only when the issue of goals has been settled is it possible to frame a coherent body of substantive rules," Bork asserts, complaining that "the federal courts in over eighty years have never settled for long upon a definitive statement of the law's goals." Bork contends that "the whole task of antitrust can be summed up as the effort to improve allocative efficiency without impairing productive efficiency so greatly as to produce either no gain or a net loss in consumer welfare." For Bork, the accumulation of wealth in the hands of a few is not a relevant consideration for antitrust law, even though the Sherman Act's original author, Senator John Sherman, expressed concern about inequality in advocating for the law's passage. As Bork—in sharp contrast to Sherman, as well as the assessment of scholars who have studied the Sherman Act's origins—wrote, "It seems clear the income distribution effects of economic activity should be completely excluded from the determination of the antitrust legality of the activity. It may be sufficient to note that the shift in income distribution does not lessen total wealth."

In his writings, Bork popularized the nice-sounding phrase "consumer welfare." In particular, he expressed the view that "the only legitimate goal of American antitrust is the maximization of consumer welfare." But Bork—it must be said—articulated an incredibly bizarre definition of "consumer welfare," defining it as "minimizing restrictions of output and permitting efficiency, however gained, to have its way." He equated "consumer welfare" not with welfare for actual living, breathing consumers (in terms of prices paid for goods and services) but with pure efficiency and the "maximization of wealth." Indeed, in a twisted argument designed to suit his own ideology, Bork included the owners of monopolies as "consumers" and expressed the view that higher prices paid by American consumers were to be classified not as a loss of consumer welfare but merely as an income transfer. In short, Bork grossly perverted the whole history of the Sherman Act, which was to protect American farmers and workers and consumers from the power of monopolists.

Bork—in ignoring the intent and history of the Sherman Act even as he purported to document it—employed (to put it mildly) much sleight of hand in his analysis. As two antitrust experts, John Kirkwood and Robert Lande, explain, "Bork used 'consumer welfare' as an Orwellian term of art that has little or nothing to do with the welfare of true consumers. His desire to maximize 'consumer welfare' (which he defines as economic efficiency) carries with it no concern about the wealth extracted from consumers and transferred to firms with market power as a result of the higher prices that arise from cartel or other prohibited behavior." "Bork," they stress, "thus defined 'consumers' to include monopolists and cartels!" Instead of seeing monopolies and corporate consolidation as long-term structural problems for America's economy, Bork saw wealth creation—even if all that wealth was going into the bank accounts of rich monopolists—as the be-all and end-all. He stressed market efficiencies over "market failures," and he envisioned a limited role for judges and Congress, believing that plaintiffs and their attorneys often brought meritless antitrust cases, particularly class actions, and that antitrust rules and their enforcement should be relaxed. Courts already burdened with other types of cases and responsibilities might have found Bork's approach—advocating for less intervention and a more hands-off approach—attractive, even though the result led to more industry concentration in the long run.

In contrast to the Chicago school, the so-called Harvard school of antitrust arose out of the writings of prominent academics such as Phillip Areeda, Herbert Hovenkamp, Donald Turner, and Stephen Breyer. For example, in their book, *Antitrust Policy: An Economic and Legal Analysis* (1959), Donald Turner, a Harvard Law School professor, and the economist Carl Kaysen, President John F. Kennedy's deputy national security adviser, wrote about their own preferred approach to antitrust law. While Turner and Areeda wrote their own influential treatise, *Antitrust Law* (1980), and developed the arcane "Areeda-Turner rule" relating to predatory pricing, Breyer—the Harvard professor who later became a U.S. Supreme Court justice—wrote in *Regulation and Its Reform* (1982), "Antitrust seeks to create or maintain the *conditions* of a competitive marketplace rather than replicate the *results* of competition or correct for the defects of competitive markets."

In stark contrast to the Chicago school, members of the Harvard school focus on market failures caused by excessive concentrations of market power. They argue that too much market power in the hands of one company (a monopoly), two companies (a duopoly), or a small number of market players (an oligopoly) leads to poor market performance and excessive profit taking, all to the detriment of the consumer. Adherents to the Harvard school concentrate their efforts on maintaining effective competition by maintaining competitive market structures. Professor Herbert Hovenkamp sums up the difference between the two competing schools: "While the Chicago School emphasized the way firms would continue to compete notwithstanding imperfect structures, the Harvard School emphasized the ways that firms could avoid competing."

The pitched "Battle for the Soul of Antitrust"—to use the words of one lawyer who has described the conflict between the Chicago school and the Harvard school—has now played out for decades. While members of the Harvard school, concerned about concentrated markets, have long been skeptics of mergers and joint ventures that allow companies to accumulate too much market power, the Chicago school adherents take a far more laissez-faire approach. While the Harvard school dominated what has been called "the activist era of antitrust enforcement that extended from the middle of the twentieth century to the 1970s," the Chicago school rose to prominence in the courts—and in the country's antitrust enforcement agencies—in the 1980s after the publication of Bork's *Antitrust Paradox* and Ronald Reagan's election. Reagan tapped a prominent antitrust critic, the Stanford University law professor William F. Baxter, to head up the Justice Department's Antitrust Division, with Baxter once claiming that the U.S. Supreme Court had used "wacko economic propositions" and "outmoded, jerry-built, amateur, pseudo-economic propositions" to decide its antitrust cases. Speaking on the subject of antitrust, Baxter himself would later describe Robert Bork as "a first-rate thinker who made a real contribution."

Bill Baxter's appointment to lead the Antitrust Division was celebrated by Richard Posner and other Chicago school adherents but
bemoaned by many others, including leading Democrats. "The Baxter
policies are a single-minded application of University of Chicago style
economics," Senator Howard Metzenbaum of Ohio warned at the very
beginning of Baxter's tenure in the Reagan White House, pointing out
in an op-ed for *The New York Times* that Baxter had announced that he
would ignore "clear judicial precedent" from the U.S. Supreme Court.
Baxter described Supreme Court rulings as "misguided," "not well
informed," or "rubbish," also pledging to intervene in private antitrust
suits *but on behalf of defendants.* "Of even greater concern," Metzenbaum
wrote, "is Mr. Baxter's complete disdain for Congress' repeated emphasis on the social and political dimension of the antitrust laws." For its
part, the Supreme Court then went along and began to cite Bork's book,
with the outcomes of the Court's antitrust cases changing dramatically.

Academics and jurists, of course, do not hold monolithic views, and
there are some who take a more blended approach to antitrust. But the
rise of the Chicago school during the Reagan administration and the
decades that followed is undeniable. The shift in antitrust philosophies
that occurred in the post–World War II era can be measured in part by
the number of enforcement actions brought by the U.S. Department
of Justice. Whereas case filings were brisk from the 1940s through the
1970s, the numbers soon dropped off significantly. The Department of
Justice instituted 157 cases from 1945 to 1949 (Truman administration);
159 cases from 1950 to 1954 and 195 cases from 1955 to 1959 (Truman and
Eisenhower administrations); 215 cases from 1960 to 1964 (Eisenhower,
Kennedy, and Johnson administrations); and 195 cases from 1965 to 1969
(Johnson administration). The first half of the 1970s saw an even greater
uptick in litigated matters. From 1970 to 1974, during the Nixon administration, there were 220 antitrust cases filed by the Department of Justice, with 89 involving Fortune 500 companies, while from 1975 to 1979,
during the end of the Ford administration and into the Carter administration, there were 161 cases brought, 46 of which involved Fortune
500 cases. In the 1980s, though, the number of antitrust cases filed by
President Reagan's Department of Justice fell substantially. From 1980
to 1984, the Department of Justice filed 127 cases, 36 of which involved
Fortune 500 companies, while from 1985 to 1989, the last half of the

Reagan administration, the number of antitrust cases brought fell to 83, only 12 of which involved Fortune 500 companies.

Both the Chicago school and the Harvard school have their critics. But if we put aside that fierce academic debate for the moment, two things are clear: *first,* despite all the academic debate about the two schools of thought, America now has a monopoly problem that remains unaddressed; and *second,* who is put in charge of antitrust enforcement matters, with the heads of the Justice Department's Antitrust Division and the FTC—operating within whatever budgetary constraints they face—setting the direction and character of that enforcement.

Debates over economic theory and between leading antitrust experts are critically important, but ultimately pragmatic results are what matter the most. And there is—at this moment—plainly a need for much more rigorous antitrust enforcement than we have seen over the last few decades. In the United States, both government and private actors can bring antitrust cases, and consequently each has a role to play in solving the problem, though the U.S. government obviously can bring more resources to bear than many private parties if it chooses to do so. The statistics show that the government's share of civil antitrust cases in relation to private antitrust cases has been below 10 percent since 1964, with Democratic administrations filing slightly more civil antitrust cases than Republican administrations over the decades. But this much is clear: regardless of who is to blame for America's existing problem with monopoly power, the only way to fix it going forward is to be much more aggressive in updating and enforcing the antitrust laws.

THE BREAKUP OF AT&T

The high point for modern antitrust enforcement was the breakup of AT&T, which began in 1974 when AT&T's upstart would-be competitor, MCI, filed a thirty-six-page civil antitrust complaint against the behemoth telecommunications company. Later that year, the Ford administration's Department of Justice then brought its own antitrust lawsuit against AT&T. At the time of the lawsuits AT&T was the country's monopoly provider of both local and long-distance telephone service. AT&T had a monopoly not only over phone service but also over most of the telephone hardware produced in the United States through its equipment-producing subsidiary, Western Electric. Thus, in a truly antitrust-defying monopoly trapeze act, AT&T held both a horizontal advantage over telephone service (as in there wasn't another provider across the street or even across the country to compete with the mammoth phone company) and vertical dominance (as in the company producing the hardware for the service was literally stacked right under it, as in AT&T owned it).

The American Telephone and Telegraph Company, founded in 1885 and better known as AT&T, had established its monopoly position over time and with the early blessing of Congress and the Federal Communications Commission. The ownership of the company formed to sell Alexander Graham Bell's telephone, known in the 1880s and 1890s as the American Bell Telephone Company, was transferred to its subsidiary, AT&T, at the end of 1899. AT&T and its Bell Telephone equipment subsidiary then expanded rapidly, soon becoming known—because of its pervasive impact on everyone's lives—as Ma Bell, with its network of subsidiaries called the Bell System. AT&T sought to provide "universal service," and the company built out its monopoly network using tactics that rivaled those once employed by the Standard Oil Company.

The sheer size of AT&T nonetheless made regulators nervous. In 1949, the Justice Department's Antitrust Division decided to pursue an antitrust case against AT&T because its subsidiary, Western Electric, had a "captive monopoly" in the phone equipment business. That suit—which dragged on until 1956—ended after Harry Truman, a Democrat, was replaced by Dwight Eisenhower in the White House. Eisenhower's attorney general, Herbert Brownell Jr., was persuaded by one of Brownell's friends, whom AT&T had hired to lobby on its behalf, to end the antitrust lawsuit. To settle the case, AT&T—in exchange for being permitted to keep its manufacturing subsidiary—agreed not to enter the computer industry, then only in its infancy. The sweetheart consent decree deal outraged the public and many members of Congress, but the deal had already been made. One California congressman, James Roosevelt, the oldest son of President Franklin D. Roosevelt and Eleanor Roosevelt, openly lamented, "The only conclusion possible from the facts is that AT&T has been given favored and special treatment by the present Administration and Attorney General Brownell." However, the seventeen days of investigative hearings on the scandalous deal,

Throughout most of the twentieth century, AT&T Corporation—originally known as the American Telephone and Telegraph Company and, more popularly, as Ma Bell—had a monopoly on telephone service and was once the world's largest company. By the 1970s, AT&T had approximately one million employees and three million shareholders. Its affiliated telephone companies provided local telephone service to approximately 90 percent of the country.

agreed to at a West Virginia resort in a private meeting, only embarrassed and shamed the Justice Department's Antitrust Division and did nothing to unravel AT&T's monopoly stranglehold on both telephone service and telephone equipment. The deal did keep AT&T out of the computer industry for many years until that restriction was lifted.

The federal government's 1970s antitrust case against AT&T finally righted the monopoly wrong. That case was overseen by Judge Harold Greene, one of President Jimmy Carter's judicial appointees who, when the matter was pending, was still a relatively new judge on the U.S. District Court for the District of Columbia. As an attorney in the Justice Department's Civil Rights Division, Greene had worked closely with Attorney General Robert F. Kennedy. In that job, Greene also played a key role in drafting the Civil Rights Act of 1964 and the Voting Rights Act of 1965. After being appointed to the bench and assigned to handle *United States v. AT&T,* which pitted the federal government against what was then the world's largest corporation, Judge Greene gave final approval in 1982 to a new consent decree: one that broke up AT&T into one long-distance company and seven independently owned regional companies—Ameritech, Bell Atlantic, BellSouth, NYNEX, Pacific Telesis, Southwestern Bell, and US West.

The breakup plan for AT&T and the Regional Bell Operating Companies (RBOCs), or "Baby Bells," as they were (not-so-affectionately) called, was formalized in 1983 while I was still studying law at the University of Chicago Law School. Little did I know then that the breakup of that mammoth company would launch my private sector career as a newly minted lawyer in Minneapolis. After I graduated from law school, I went to work at the Minnesota law firm of Dorsey & Whitney, in part because former Minnesota attorney general Warren Spannaus, whom I worked for as a college intern, practiced law there. As a young associate, I was given the opportunity to represent MCI, which was originally Warren's client—and later mine. The maverick company was upending the decades-long monopoly in the telephone industry by aggressively suing and agitating to get into the local markets to compete with the post-breakup spin-offs, including our local exchange monopoly, Northwestern Bell (later known as US West).

At one administrative hearing during that time, I made the contrast between the historic beginnings of AT&T's monopoly empire and MCI's new-kid-on-the-block status by quoting the first words Alexander Graham Bell said over the telephone: "Come here, Watson, I need you." In contrast, in the Wild West world of MCI, when they were getting ready to relay the first communication between St. Louis and Chicago, the investor Irwin Hirsh memorialized that great moment by saying, "I'll be damned, it actually works." Yet without antitrust law, MCI would never have worked. It simply would have been impossible for MCI to compete against AT&T had that powerful monopoly not been broken up.

As an associate and later a partner, I managed the telecommunications law practice at Dorsey & Whitney and did the same during my last five years in private practice at the Minneapolis law firm of Gray Plant Mooty. I was MCI's and other smaller local exchange competitors' lead lawyer in our state. When Congress passed the Telecommunications Act of 1996—the first major overhaul of telecommunications law in more than sixty years—MCI and my other clients were finally able to compete with the existing monopoly companies to serve more customers at lower rates. In the fights to gain access to markets, I was often on the same side as the Minnesota attorney general and the consumer groups, and I had a front-row seat as AT&T's decades-long monopoly finally came to an end, spurring more competition in long-distance

The U.S. District Court judge Harold Greene oversaw the breakup of AT&T, supervising the consent decree that broke AT&T into several regional operating companies.

rates, not to mention the beginnings of the cellular phone market. At that time, we were modern-day trustbusters, pushing case by case and state by state for more competition and lower rates.

The breakup of AT&T—the gigantic corporation that, in its pre-divestiture form, had approximately one million employees—has been widely viewed as a historical success, spurring competition and inno-vation, leading to even more jobs and cheaper phone service. While the decision to break up AT&T was controversial at the time, the facts don't lie: since the breakup, we have gone from high-cost long-distance phone calls and rotary dial phones to smartphones, wireless technol-ogy, and the development of the internet. As one account notes of the breakup, "In the aftermath, AT&T reduced long distance rates by 40% over six years, though local carriers added access charges that prevented consumers from seeing all of the cost reduction. The local operating companies (led by Ameritech, beginning in the Chicago area that was home to Motorola, which helped develop the radio technology) also began offering mobile service in the 1980s after it had been developed by Bell Labs."

The Reagan administration followed through with AT&T's forced restructuring that had been sought by the Ford and Carter adminis-trations. The Justice Department's Antitrust Division sought to spur innovation, and officials in the Reagan administration wanted to dereg-ulate the telecommunications industry, even though the Department of Defense and other AT&T allies in the administration argued strenu-

The breakup of AT&T in 1982 transformed the telecommunications industry and led to greater innovation. Despite fear that phone bills would go up, the breakup of the Bell monopoly actually led to greater competition and dramatically lower consumer prices.

ously against AT&T's divestiture. In 1981, Caspar Weinberger—the secretary of defense—told U.S. senators that AT&T's network "is the most important communications network we have to serve our strategic system in this country" and that it was thus "essential" that it be kept together.

AT&T's actual breakup only came about after an extensive delay, which included an effort by AT&T to suspend the court case pending a search for a legislative solution, with Senate Republicans actually passing legislation that would have allowed AT&T to avoid divestiture. In the end, though, prominent Reagan advisers, including James Baker, worried about the negative political consequences of not moving forward with the breakup, the new head of the Antitrust Division ultimately promised to litigate the case "to the eyeballs," and the Justice Department and AT&T agreed that the company would be split up. Attorney General William French Smith was forced to recuse himself from the case because of his prior affiliations with Pacific Telephone, and it was Assistant Attorney General William Baxter who brokered and put together the deal to break up AT&T. As one source describes the deal that was reached, which led to the Regional Bell Operating Companies, "AT&T would get rid of its local operating companies (which later were formed into the seven RBOCs, such as US West and

NYNEX) but would keep its long-distance services, Western Electric, Bell Labs, and its Yellow Pages."

THE REAGAN ADMINISTRATION:
ANTITRUST ENFORCEMENT LANGUISHES

Although it ultimately broke up AT&T, the Reagan administration—as one Federal Trade Commission representative put it—took "a strong swing towards the 'right'" in its approach to antitrust enforcement in general. "The broad bipartisan consensus that protected antitrust for much of its history," Marc Allen Eisner has written in *Antitrust and the Triumph of Economics,* "disintegrated by the 1980s."

The Reagan administration, in fact, dismantled and defunded important antitrust infrastructure, leading to increased corporate consolidation and a neglect of the long-standing social and policy goals of antitrust law. As David Balto, former assistant director of the FTC's Office of Policy and Evaluation, emphasized of the 1980s and the Reagan administration, "A major part of that administration's economic program was to reduce government regulation. Antitrust enforcement was perceived as being overly intrusive, out of control, and highly regulatory." "The resources of the antitrust enforcement agencies were substantially reduced during the Reagan Administration," Balto has said, with antitrust enforcement efforts—in line with Bork's vision—moving away from a focus on the conduct of big businesses during that time. In what has been called its relatively "hands-off approach to antitrust enforcement," the Reagan administration's Justice Department fully embraced the Chicago school of antitrust and economics and focused its enforcement activities mostly on the brazen activities of cartels and harms caused by clearly collusive, price-fixing agreements.

One example of how antitrust enforcement efforts languished during the Reagan administration: the U.S. Department of Justice's 1982 Merger Guidelines, which replaced the much-stricter 1968 Merger Guidelines. The purpose of the 1968 Merger Guidelines was to "acquaint the business community, the legal profession, and other interested groups and individuals with the standards currently being applied by the U.S. Department of Justice in determining whether to challenge corporate acquisitions and mergers under Section 7 of the Clayton Act."

But the Reagan administration's updated 1982 Merger Guidelines differed substantially from the preceding guidelines, and they made it far less likely that proposed mergers would be challenged by federal regulators. One antitrust commentator wrote in 1983 after the new guidelines were put in place that "a significant relaxation of the 1968 rules was both warranted and necessary" and "the political climate was already prepared to tolerate a more lenient attitude toward mergers." "The isolation of efficiency as the sole goal of antitrust," another antitrust scholar wrote in the wake of the adoption of those new Merger Guidelines, required "a conscious rejection of equally dominant values that underlie the antitrust statutes"—a rejection of values that set the stage for anticompetitive mergers.

And in a triumph for Bork, that is exactly what happened. From 1982 to 1987, the Reagan Justice Department's Antitrust Division received 11,547 premerger notifications, but it challenged a minuscule fraction—33, to be exact—of those mergers. The resources devoted to antitrust enforcement were also decimated, something that continued throughout the Reagan administration and into the George H. W. Bush administration. As Brent Huber wrote in the *Indiana Law Journal* back in 1991, "The FTC currently has 442 staffers assigned to antitrust matters, down from 531 in 1980. The number of antitrust lawyers in the Justice Department has fallen from 429 in 1980 to the current level of 236." "In recent years," it was noted, "the Antitrust Division of the Justice Department and the Federal Trade Commission have undergone significant budget cuts and have challenged few corporate acquisitions." Perhaps most significantly, in 1982, after thirteen years of litigation, the Reagan Justice Department also dropped an antitrust case filed against IBM in 1969 alleging that IBM dominated the mainframe computer market.

Although the U.S. government's abandonment of the antitrust case against IBM was seen, at the time, as an "unqualified victory" for the corporate giant, James Stewart, a business journalism professor at Columbia, later wrote that "nearly everyone in the computer industry agrees that, following its antitrust victory, IBM complacently retreated into the mainframe world it dominated—a strategy that was rewarding in the short term but has now proved disastrous." As Stewart wrote in *The New Yorker* in 1993 of how IBM fell into the doldrums while AT&T thrived, "On January 28th, 1993, four days after IBM posted a quarterly loss of $4.97 billion, AT&T reported record quarterly earnings of $1 billion and a yearly profit of $3.8 billion on sales of $65 billion." "We were forced by divestiture to make changes that probably were good for us," Robert Allen, AT&T's chairman, told the magazine, adding, "We went through some tough years, but it paid off. We may have been more fortunate than IBM in that change was forced on us."

Ironically, though it was simply abandoned in 1982, that antitrust lawsuit against IBM, which forced it to spend tens of millions of dollars in legal fees, allowed just enough breathing space in the marketplace for the birth of Apple, a company created by Steve Jobs and Steve Wozniak—both college dropouts—in 1976. Before the lawsuit's abrupt abandonment in 1982, Robert Bork derisively labeled the case against IBM "the antitrust division's Vietnam." The court case included 726 trial days, 950 witnesses, and 17,000 exhibits, with the trial transcript exceeding 104,000 pages. The case, which led to $200 million in legal costs, also necessitated, however, that IBM scrupulously avoid any anticompetitive conduct throughout the 1970s lest the case against it grow stronger. While the case went on, it also gave room for more competition from Japanese and U.S. companies, including for a brand-new start-up, Microsoft, a company—now a household name—founded in 1975 by Bill Gates and Paul Allen. It was thus partly due to a U.S. antitrust suit—albeit one started long before President Reagan came into office—that the modern, personal computing age likely matured so quickly.

Another example of the early 1980s shift in focus away from rigorous antitrust enforcement came with the elimination of an FTC initiative—one that gathered data on lines of business—that was designed to monitor corporate consolidation. "The conglomerate merger experience of the late 1960s," a history of the FTC's Bureau of Economics reports, "led academics and merger enforcers to desire better data on market level activity that is often hidden in firm-level data." For example, Caspar Weinberger—chosen to chair the FTC in 1969—suggested that such line-of-business data would be helpful to have. The FTC—the nation's watchdog for unfair practices—felt that gathering data would aid policy makers in determining how to allocate scarce antitrust enforcement resources and that the dissemination of reports and studies might engender more competition. Public reports might, say, incentivize investors to enter concentrated and profitable markets or, at the very least, increase public awareness of anticompetitive conduct.

In 1974, the Federal Trade Commission—seeking to increase the relevance of its work—thus began collecting this data on large diversified manufacturers. Its first survey forms were sent to 453 large manufacturers covering 261 manufacturing industry categories. However, the FTC's inquiries were criticized as unduly burdensome and costly, with some contending that the data collection program was based on structuralist economic theory unsubstantiated by empirical evidence. Court challenges ensued, even as the FTC released reports in 1977, for instance, on everything from prescription drugs, the petroleum industry, and health maintenance organizations to mergers and acquisitions and market share relationships. In 1978, the U.S. Court of Appeals for the District of Columbia—often referred to as the second most powerful court in the country—held that the FTC had the power to collect this data. In *FTC Line of Business Report Litigation* (1978), the D.C. Circuit explicitly held that the FTC's reporting programs were within its investigatory powers because they would be useful for economic studies, policy planning, and the selection of enforcement priorities. "The Line of Business program," one source emphasizes of the agency's victory in the courts, "provided the FTC with the most extensive set of figures on American industry ever collected."

But the FTC program proved to be short-lived, and regulators soon largely closed their eyes to the creeping problem of corporate consolidation, choosing not to pay attention—or recklessly paying insufficient attention—to what was happening in America's economy. After President Reagan's FTC transition team targeted the line-of-business data collection program for reevaluation in 1981, it was abruptly canceled, eliminating the snapshot of American business activity that it had provided for at least a few years. The program was deemed too costly, with big companies fearing that the FTC would use the data to bring antitrust actions. A continuation of the line-of-business program, however, would have allowed the FTC and antitrust officials to define relevant markets with much greater precision. Accurate data, of course, has the power to expose concentrated markets and monopolistic behavior, something that apparently made the powers that be in the 1980s extremely nervous.

The clarity of hindsight shows that the late 1970s and early 1980s were a major turning point in weakening America's antitrust enforcement regime. Not only was the Republican Party less receptive to aggressive enforcement efforts pioneered by their own party's Teddy Roosevelt and William Howard Taft, but certain factions of the Democratic Party were becoming less interested as well. As noted by the antitrust expert Matt Stoller in a 2016 *Atlantic* article, during that time "young liberals did not perceive financial power as a threat, having grown up in a world where banks and big business were largely kept under control." "It was the government—through Vietnam, Nixon, and executive power—that organized the political spectrum," Stoller explains, noting that the seeds of change were planted as far back as the Carter administration, when Congress and the president deregulated the trucking, banking, and airline industries based on the argument that archaic rules were stifling competition.

This philosophical shift in the approach to antitrust issues reached its zenith, however, during the Reagan administration as big companies—in unprecedented fashion, all with the cover of Bork's ideology and the now-discredited theory of trickle-down economics—exerted their corporate power and the regulators more or less folded to the pressure. Senator Howard Metzenbaum, the Ohio Democrat who sought more vigorous antitrust enforcement, was appalled and genuinely perplexed by the Reagan administration's antitrust policies. As Metzenbaum said, "If you are for free enterprise, then you must be for antitrust. You just can't be for one and against the other—that is, unless you are the Reagan Administration."

The Reagan administration's policies, which would have consequences for decades to come, were notoriously anti-union. They also favored those at the very top of the income scale, thus tilting the field against American workers. In the 1980s, trickle-down economics truly prevailed, and the Chicago school economists had taken over the FTC and the DOJ's Antitrust Division, putting the antitrust litigators in the backseat. As one commentator notes, "President Reagan and his antitrust appointees espoused the Chicago School theories and acted on those beliefs. They quickly reduced the budgets of the antitrust enforcement authorities." At one meeting, James Miller—then the chair of the Federal Trade Commission—even joked that "at the FTC, the lawyers work for the economists and not the other way around." Miller was the first economist to head up the FTC.

THE CLINTON, GEORGE W. BUSH, AND OBAMA YEARS— AND A SHORT HISTORY OF THE MICROSOFT CASE

During the Clinton administration there was an effort to reverse the lax antitrust enforcement of the Reagan and George H. W. Bush administrations, but the damage—with the dismantling of America's antitrust infrastructure—had already been done. Indeed, fewer people were talking about monopolies in the 1980s and 1990s as the work of the Justice Department became the domain of "lawyers and economists." While the Democratic Party's 1900 platform had publicly declared that "monopolies are indefensible and intolerable," the Democratic Party's 1992 platform removed its antitrust language—the first time the party's platform had not referenced monopoly power since 1880. Written by the founder of the Democratic Leadership Council in the lead-up to that year's presidential election, the 1992 platform represented an effort to remake the Democratic Party's image after lopsided losses in prior presidential elections. "The last significant mention of antitrust in the Democratic Party's platform," the antitrust professor Daniel Crane pointed out in 2011, before the Democratic Party's 2016 platform renewed the party's explicit call to beef up antitrust enforcement, "was in Walter Mondale's 1984 platform"—a platform that emphasized that "the FTC has run roughshod over the nation's antitrust laws, allowing 9 of the 10 largest mergers in history to occur," that called for "vigorous enforcement of our antitrust laws," and that promised that "no Democratic Administration will forget the use of the old fashioned antitrust policy to keep markets competitive and prices down."

To try to reverse the lax antitrust enforcement under Republican administrations, Anne Bingaman—a graduate of Stanford Law School and the spouse of former U.S. senator Jeff Bingaman of New Mexico—was tapped to lead the Antitrust Division of the U.S. Department of Justice, and there was, again, talk of more vigorous enforcement. The election of Bill Clinton, whose appointments were—as one source puts it—"less inclined than Republican predecessors to base their trust in unfettered markets," did in fact lead to a reawakening of interest in antitrust enforcement. In a July 1993 profile of Anne Bingaman, titled "Rousing Antitrust Law from Its 12-Year Nap," Georgetown University law professor Robert Pitofsky took note of Bingaman's more activist approach to antitrust enforcement, observing that "closer calls are going to be decided in favor of action rather than inaction." Antitrust enforcement made a comeback, with Bingaman giving talks on topics like criminal antitrust enforcement, but with lower staffing levels and fewer resources it was hard to bring antitrust enforcement back to its heyday in the 1970s.

With the end of the Clinton-Gore era, George W. Bush's administration ushered in yet another period of lax antitrust enforcement at the Justice Department's Antitrust Division. In a May 2006 article titled "When It Comes to Antitrust, Washington Is Antibust," Stephen Labaton of *The New York Times* reported that the Bush administration "is handling U.S. antitrust cases with the most relaxed and least aggressive approach since the final years of the Reagan presidency." Other academics have observed that the Bush administration had "one of the weakest records of antitrust enforcement in the last half century." There were, however, a few bright spots at the Federal Trade Commission, which had a balance of both Republican and Democratic commissioners. The FTC blocked some oil mergers and brought several pay-for-delay cases in the pharmaceutical industry.

The George W. Bush administration's handling of the antitrust case against Microsoft Corporation illustrates how a change in administration can adversely affect antitrust enforcement. In 1998—during the Clinton administration—the U.S. government, the District of Columbia, and twenty states had sued Microsoft, alleging that the company had monopolized the market for operating systems by engaging in anticompetitive behavior. IBM, an early computer industry powerhouse, had faced a series of antitrust lawsuits of its own from 1969 to 1982, but Microsoft's conduct had targeted Netscape's web browser and Sun Microsystems' Java technologies. The allegation: Microsoft sought to unlawfully use monopoly power by restricting the ability of PC makers to uninstall Internet Explorer or to use Netscape or Java. The resolution of the Microsoft case was, in fact, ultimately affected as much by the change in administration as by the facts. After Judge Thomas Penfield Jackson—a Reagan appointee—had ruled for the government

More than two decades ago, the U.S. government's antitrust case against Microsoft made big headlines. Netscape Communications Corporation, originally headquartered in Mountain View, California, developed its Netscape web browser. However, its competitor, Microsoft's Internet Explorer, emerged as the dominant browser. Netscape was acquired by America Online, better known as AOL, in the late 1990s, but the development of the Netscape browser was later discontinued.

and ordered that Microsoft be broken up into two companies, a group of seven judges on the U.S. Court of Appeals for the D.C. Circuit, in a unanimous 2001 per curiam opinion, reversed Judge Jackson's liability ruling and his remedial order. The appellate ruling didn't end the case, but the seven judges had sent it back for further consideration. As with all matters, of course, it was up to the Justice Department's Antitrust Division to decide how to handle it.

The government's antitrust dispute with the Seattle-based software giant, Microsoft Corporation, actually predated 1998 and went on for years until the George W. Bush administration ended the case. Microsoft originally settled different antitrust charges with the Clinton Justice Department in 1994, ultimately entering into a 1995 consent decree later approved by Judge Jackson. That consent decree forbade the company from using its operating system dominance to quash competition. In 1997, that same Clinton Justice Department sued Microsoft for an alleged violation of that consent decree, asserting that the company violated its terms by demanding that PC manufacturers bundle the Internet Explorer web browser with its Microsoft hardware before obtaining a Windows 95 license. Judge Jackson issued a preliminary injunction, ordering that Microsoft stop requiring PC manufacturers to include Internet Explorer with its Windows product. Microsoft appealed, but when faced with a contempt citation, the company agreed to give PC makers the freedom to install Windows 95 without an icon for Internet Explorer. The following year, in May 1998, an appellate court ruled that the injunction did not apply to the launch of Windows 98, with a 2–1 majority ruling that Microsoft could integrate whatever it wanted into its operating system so long as it benefited consumers.

But the antitrust dispute involving Microsoft did not end there. In fact, the drama—both in and out of the courtroom—was just beginning. Days after the appellate court ruling, the U.S. Justice Department and twenty state attorneys general sued, alleging that Microsoft abused its market power to restrain competition. It was an epic battle, pitting public agencies against a powerful private litigant. Bill Gates—Microsoft's chairman, known today for his public health work around the globe with the Bill and Melinda Gates Foundation—was famously deposed for three days in late August and early September 1998. His videotaped testimony would later be shown in court over the course of the antitrust trial, with the first video clips played in early November 1998. Among other things, Gates testified over the course of more than twenty hours about his own email messages, often saying he had no recollection of them. "The famously hands-on Microsoft chief answered deposition questions with 'I don't know,' 'I don't remember' or 'I don't recall' more than 200 times," James Grimaldi reported for *The Seattle Times*. The deposition, conducted by David Boies, did not go well for Gates, then the world's richest man.

As it developed, the case against Microsoft was so strong that even Robert Bork—an unlikely ally who had become a paid legal consultant for Netscape Communications Corporation—sided with the Clinton Justice Department's antitrust officials. "The antitrust case brought by the Department of Justice against Microsoft is rock solid," Bork wrote in a seventeen-page white paper titled "The Case Against Microsoft" and released two months after the Justice Department had initiated its case against the tech giant. After Bork unexpectedly weighed in, going so far as to tell reporters at a lunch in January 1999 that Microsoft should be broken into three companies at the end of the trial, Microsoft—the next month—was accused of manipulating videotaped evidence in a courtroom demonstration. In his remarks, Bork—the very person who had induced a relaxation of antitrust enforcement but who was concerned about Microsoft's monopoly power and dominance—made this observation even before the conclusion of the Microsoft trial: "My own opinion is that I think structural relief is probably going to be required. . . . I think three companies would be perfectly adequate to restore competition." Microsoft itself had initially sought to retain Bork as a lawyer, but Bork ended up supporting the U.S. government's antitrust lawsuit and representing Netscape in the dispute.

As the legal dispute dragged on, Microsoft changed its public relations strategy, and politicians got into the act as well. In March 1999, Senator Slade Gorton, a Republican from Microsoft's home state of Washington, specifically called on the Justice Department to drop the case. The eight-month trial against Microsoft did not finish until June 1999 after seventy-six days of testimony, an extraordinarily long legal proceeding. It would, in fact, take many more months before the district court even announced its ruling. In early November 1999, Judge Jackson finally issued his much-anticipated findings of fact, concluding that Microsoft had impermissibly used its monopoly power to harm rivals and consumers. Microsoft, naturally, took issue with Judge Jackson's findings; U.S. Court of Appeals judge Richard Posner—the former FTC staffer and Chicago school adherent—then unsuccessfully attempted to mediate and settle the case; and the appeal ultimately went forward, with the seven judges sitting in judgment on the federal appellate court reversing Judge Jackson's breakup order in late June 2001, more than three years after the case had originally begun. The Court of Appeals for the D.C. Circuit determined that "some but not all of Microsoft's liability challenges have merit," but the D.C. Circuit specifically got rid of Judge Jackson's remedies decree, stating in part that he had "failed to provide an adequate explanation" for the relief he had ordered.

In what the D.C. Circuit acknowledged to be an "extraordinary" order, Judge Jackson was disqualified from further handling the case based on public statements he had made about it. When a different trial judge was later put in charge of the matter, the Bush administration's Department of Justice (George W. Bush was sworn into office in January of 2001)—along with some of the states—chose to settle the case on extremely lenient terms, refusing to insist on the harsher remedy that Judge Jackson had sought and that even former judge Bork had thought appropriate.

As a result of the Department of Justice's settlement with Microsoft, Microsoft entered into a new consent decree, a settlement approved by the U.S. Court of Appeals for the District of Columbia in 2004. The District of Columbia and nine states (California, Connecticut, Florida, Iowa, Kansas, Massachusetts, Minnesota, Utah, and West Virginia), having objected to the terms of that settlement, pushed for stiffer penalties, but Microsoft escaped the kind of accountability and liability that many felt it deserved. Although the objecting states extracted another $1.5 billion from Microsoft, the harsher penalties sought by the holdout states were rejected, and Microsoft, for the most part, was allowed to go about its way with only mild restrictions. In some cases, Microsoft was actually allowed to donate computers and its own software to schools in lieu of cash payments, with the expectation that it would actually be gaining customers in the long term. The end result? After protracted, hard-fought litigation, multiple Congresses, and more than one presidential administration, it was a change of presidents—with the George W. Bush administration essentially forsaking concerns about Microsoft's enormous market power—that basically ended the government's case. For several years, Microsoft operated under the consent decree. But after the company was later determined to be in compliance with its terms, it expired in 2011, leaving Microsoft to once again operate without its constraints.

It has been noted that since the Sherman Act's passage in 1890, "U.S. antitrust policies have oscillated back and forth between vigorous and lax enforcement." With the Microsoft case resolution marked as Exhibit A, the George W. Bush years are best described as a lax period of antitrust enforcement.

After the Bush years, antitrust enforcement once again emerged as a priority during Barack Obama's administration, though a number of high-profile mergers were still approved. "While the Obama administration blocked high-profile mergers of AT&T and T-Mobile, the energy giants Halliburton and Baker Hughes, Sysco and US Foods, and Comcast and Time Warner," Alan Neuhauser wrote in *U.S. News & World Report* in December 2016, "Comcast was ultimately allowed to join forces with NBC Universal, Charter Communications was permitted to acquire Time Warner, and U.S. Airways was able to buy American Airlines." In addition, the combination of Random House—

America's largest publisher—with another large publisher, Penguin, a deal announced in late October 2012, received the Justice Department's approval by mid-February 2013, with the transaction closing on July 1, 2013. And, most notably, the Obama administration's allowance of multiple tech mergers and apparent lack of interest in full-scale tech investigations allowed Big Tech to . . . well . . . get even bigger.

On the upside, the Obama administration brought an average of twenty-one antitrust challenges a year compared with sixteen per year brought during the George W. Bush presidency, showing more diligent, if moderate, pursuit of antitrust issues. But, given the lack of early focus on tech, the Justice Department's antitrust enforcement was largely seen as middle of the road. As John Briggs, an antitrust attorney, summarized the Obama years, "If we go through long-term trends, the Obama administration could be thought of as in the center of things—a 5 on the scale out of 10. Nothing unusually aggressive, nothing irregular about their policies or practices."

There are, certainly, significant highlights in the Obama administration's antitrust enforcement efforts, including, under then U.S. assistant attorney general Christine Varney, blocking the AT&T/T-Mobile merger (something the Trump administration failed to do with regard to Sprint/T-Mobile years later), holding major corporations accountable for violations, and prosecuting culpable individuals for anticompetitive conduct. During Bill Baer's subsequent leadership of the Justice Department's Antitrust Division in President Obama's second term, certain controversial mergers that would have hurt consumers were blocked. Also, the Antitrust Division filed criminal charges against seventy-seven corporations, convicted sixty-seven of them, and obtained $6.3 billion in criminal fines and penalties. The average prison sentence more than doubled from a decade earlier, and five banks were successfully prosecuted for manipulating foreign currency, paying criminal fines totaling more than $2.7 billion. Finally, over at the FTC, under the leadership of Chairman Jon Leibowitz, the FTC brought multiple cases against pharmaceutical companies, including winning three major health-care cases in the U.S. Supreme Court.

There were successes and there were failures. While the Obama administration was criticized for allowing Comcast to join forces with NBCUniversal, most notably by my former Minnesota colleague Senator Al Franken, the Obama Justice Department did block the Comcast–Time Warner merger. Bill Baer explained why: "In Comcast/Time Warner, we really were worried that having one firm responsible for delivering content, providing high-speed Internet to almost 60% of U.S. homes, had the potential to distort competition both upstream and downstream." As Baer explained, "It's not unlike, I think, some of the issues that play out in the net neutrality debate. You have this 'one pipeline' problem, where one entity controls the last mile connecting almost 60% of U.S. homes with high-speed Internet service, and it would give that one entity—Comcast—significant and disproportionate leverage in dealing with content providers that Comcast competes against in its video business."

The high cost of cable and issues pertaining to access to content are things I've also heard about repeatedly from my constituents. At the close of the Obama administration, on December 7, 2016, I co-chaired an antitrust hearing on the proposed Comcast–Time Warner merger with Senators Patrick Leahy, Chuck Grassley, and Mike Lee. As was made clear at the hearing, if the merger was approved, the combined company would have controlled 60 percent of the country's high-speed broadband customers. In addition, there were significant concerns raised about equal access to content and increasing prices. All too often, megamergers are about creating market dominance, not about lowering prices for customers. As I said at the hearing, "The solution for less competition is not even less competition."

That simple concept—that the solution for less competition is not even less competition—was in fact the foundation for my immediate opposition to another proposed merger that popped up at the time. That proposed merger was between Norfolk Southern Railway and Canadian Pacific and was later called off. Why? Even without the merger, 90 percent of today's freight traffic is handled by only four Class I railroads. Just as airline customers deserve lots of competition to keep down airline fares, businesses and farmers deserve competition in the rail industry.

One area, as I've noted, where much more could have been done? Tech. During the Obama administration, there were many acquisitions by companies like Facebook and Google that led to increasing market domination in the tech sector. Looking back, Gene Sperling—the director of President Obama's National Economic Council—acknowledged that now more must be done and offered these reflections in a conversation with the *New York Times* opinion writer and journalist Kara Swisher in 2020: "A lot of these problems became more apparent in the last few years." "If I was advising a new president what to do," Sperling said, "I would say you should have a bias for competition. . . . [I]t's not clear to me that Facebook needs to own WhatsApp and Instagram." Sperling also pointed out, "It is clear to me that when Facebook was making bad decisions about political ads or bad decisions about privacy we would have been a better country if Instagram and WhatsApp could have offered competitive alternatives." "So you're in favor of new, fresh thinking on antitrust for some of these companies?" Swisher asked. Sperling's one-word reply: "Absolutely."

"Fresh thinking" is long overdue when it comes to tech platforms. I have been concerned for years about the enormous power these companies wield and have taken them on on numerous fronts: disinformation and political ads, privacy violations, misuse of data, opposition to platform regulation, and, of course, anticompetitive tech acquisitions and conduct. As explained more in chapter 8, we must build the political will to take this on, invest in the necessary complex investigations and enforcement actions, and push Congress to pass new antitrust legislation.

There were also, unfortunately, many health-care mergers that took place during the years of the Obama administration that led to increased consolidation in that field. Chairman Mike Lee and I held an Antitrust Subcommittee hearing on September 22, 2015, on the effects of such mergers on consumers. I thought it was incredibly important to air publicly what so many of my constituents were telling me privately, especially in regard to the impact of that consolidation on the cost of their health care. As I said at the hearing in my opening statement, "I want to make sure that these deals do not harm consumers by increasing premiums or reducing benefits." The Affordable Care Act laudably extended health-care coverage to millions of Americans, but health-care industry consolidation remains a major problem. The Obama administration's Antitrust Division did successfully litigate two megamergers in the health-care insurance industry, stopping Anthem's attempt to merge with Cigna and Aetna's effort to buy Humana. Nevertheless, the reduced number of players in the health-care market is troubling because fewer providers generally mean higher prices, something we do not need more of in the health-care arena.

MALFEASANCE, MIXED MESSAGES, AND—FINALLY—
SUITS AGAINST BIG TECH: THE VOLATILE TRUMP ERA

Every new presidential administration brings a new set of players into the antitrust arena. The Trump administration did that, but it also—to a unique and unprecedented degree—brought a whole lot of chaos, with President Trump treating antitrust like a political plaything to be toyed with, instead of the serious, nonpartisan lever of competition policy that it should be. As a result, the Trump administration produced decidedly mixed results in the antitrust arena.

The most significant antitrust actions brought by the Trump Justice Department and FTC under the leadership of veteran Antitrust Division head Makan Delrahim and FTC chair Joe Simon occurred at the very end of the administration's four years in office. The first was a major Department of Justice antitrust action where the Department, joined by eleven states, alleged that Google violated section 2 of the Sherman Act by "unlawfully maintaining monopolies in the markets for general search services, search advertising, and general search text advertising in the United States through anticompetitive and exclusionary practices." "The Google of today," the complaint contends, "is a monopoly gatekeeper for the internet, and one of the wealthiest companies on the planet, with a market value of $1 trillion and annual revenue exceeding $160 billion."

Unfortunately, the government's antitrust complaint against Google was filed just two weeks before the 2020 presidential election, guaranteeing a less than bipartisan coalition and a lack of joint action at the outset by state attorneys general. That being said, the filing of the suit was in my mind a net positive and long overdue. As I said to Google CEO Sundar Pichai at a Commerce Committee hearing after the antitrust lawsuit was filed and he defended Google's monopolistic practices while saying the company was open to feedback, "I think you have gotten feedback from the lawsuit."

Secondly, the FTC, which has a long history of bipartisan decision-making at the commissioner level, filed a major antitrust action against Facebook about a month after the election. Following a long investigation and joined by the attorneys general in forty-six states as well as the District of Columbia and Guam, the suit alleges that Facebook has "engaged in a systemic strategy" to "eliminate threats to its monopoly." As outlined in the complaint, that strategy included its 2012 acquistion of "up-and-coming rival" Instagram, its 2014 purchase of the mobile messaging app WhatsApp, and "the imposition of anticompetitive conditions" on a whole host of software developers. The remedy? The FTC and states, under the leadership of New York State Attorney General Letitia James, requested that Facebook sell off certain assets, including Instagram and WhatsApp, that it be prohibited from imposing anticompetitive conditions on software developers, and that it seek prior approval for future mergers and acquisitions.

While lawyers at the Trump Justice Department's Antitrust Division and the Federal Trade Commission brought a number of additional high-profile antitrust cases, including ones involving physician services, fantasy sports, and canola and vegetable oils, they also participated in a number of failed endeavors. For instance, the Trump Justice Department's opposition to the gigantic $85 billion AT&T–Time Warner deal was famously rejected by Judge Richard Leon in June 2018, with Judge Leon not imposing any conditions on the merger's approval. Then, in December 2018, the Justice Department appealed Judge Leon's order, contending that AT&T's acquisition of Time Warner should be reconsidered. The Justice Department argued before the U.S. Court of Appeals for the District of Columbia that AT&T, which owns DirecTV, could harm competitors, such as Dish, by blacking out channels such as CNN, HBO, TBS, and TNT, which AT&T had acquired in the Time Warner merger. The appeal was firmly rejected by the appellate court. "The government's objections that the district court misunderstood and misapplied economic principles and clearly erred in rejecting the quantitative model are unpersuasive," the appellate court held in February 2019.

And the Trump administration's refusal to challenge the Sprint/ T-Mobile merger set yet another new low in enforcement as America's No. 3 and No. 4 mobile phone companies—in a baffling move that is very bad for consumers—were given the go-ahead to combine. The

Trump administration's weak record on cartel enforcement is equally problematic. "Applying traditional metrics," one analysis concludes, "cartel enforcement has markedly slowed in 2017–2018."

Then there is the issue of the administration's lack of advocacy for resources. While in the last few months of the Trump administration antitrust chief Delrahim worked valiantly with Chuck Grassley and me to try to include a megamerger fee charge that would have added significant resources to both the incoming Biden administration DOJ Antitrust Division and the FTC for competition policy enforcement, for years neither the Trump White House nor the Attorney General advocated for more antitrust resources. In February 2019, the *Financial Times* reported that "staffing in the antitrust division of the US Department of Justice has fallen since Donald Trump took office despite a boom in big corporate mergers, according to phone directories for the division." For example, an analysis by the *Financial Times* of directories showed a 13 percent decline in staffing, "with more severe attrition in units responsible for civil and criminal enforcement of competition laws." David Cicilline, my Democratic counterpart in the U.S. House of Representatives and the current chair of the House Antitrust Subcommittee, called the decline in staffing "alarming," adding, "We need to both modernize our existing antitrust laws and make sure that they're working in the current economy, and also ensure that antitrust agencies have the resources and personnel to do their work effectively." The analysis by the *Financial Times* reported these disturbing statistics: "Across the six units that review mergers, the directories showed 18 per cent fewer trial attorneys, paralegals, and other support staff. In two Washington-based units that investigate criminal price-fixing conspiracies, the decline was 27 per cent."

Former president Trump talked about antitrust-related issues from time to time when he was in office, but the numbers don't lie, and the federal government's budget—and agency budgets—showed his actual priorities. For fiscal year 2018, the Trump administration's budget request for the Justice Department's Antitrust Division was a congressional appropriation of $164.7 million. That represented 830 positions, including 380 attorneys—a request that anticipated 135 *fewer* positions, including 45 *fewer* attorneys, for the division than the year before. The Trump administration's fiscal year 2019 budget request for the Antitrust

Division was likewise for $164.7 million—a sum that was completely inadequate to do the job right. The budget allocation evidenced the administration's less-than-benign neglect of antitrust enforcement at a time when Big Tech was—in fact still is—employing scores of lawyers and lobbyists. Finally, in February 2020, and with the anticipated filings of major actions against Big Tech companies, the Trump administration announced that it would be asking for more money in congressional appropriations for the Antitrust Division—enough to reportedly hire 87 additional staffers. As noted above, DOJ antitrust head Makan Delrahim also worked personally with me to advocate for more resources to bolster the Antitrust Division's work. In the end, Congress increased the budget for the DOJ Antitrust Division by $18 million and the FTC by $20 million, which was of course helpful, although House Republicans, including Rep. Jim Jordan, blocked us from passing the Klobuchar/Grassley megamerger fee bill, which would have increased the budgets by more than double that amount. While the Trump administration demonstrated a willingness to take on Big Tech in the closing part of the president's term, the bulk of that work only came in an election year, with the Democratic-led U.S. House of Representatives also conducting its own eye-opening investigation.

No history of the Trump administration's antitrust work could be written without a discussion of President Trump's own highly improper meddling in antitrust decision making, including efforts to harm CNN, the cable news network with which he so often sparred. The president's comments and, at times, actual actions and involvement repeatedly raised serious questions about the integrity of his administration's antitrust work, no matter how hard the DOJ and FTC's antitrust staff worked. As Joe Nocera, writing for Bloomberg, emphasized in March 2019, "The evidence continues to mount that the antitrust department of the Justice Department has become just another federal agency willing to serve as a weapon the president can wield against his enemies. Is there anyone left in the administration who will stand up for the rule of law? Increasingly, the answer appears to be no." In June 2020, another expert, Eleanor Fox, a professor at New York University School of Law, had this to say on the subject: "When the Trump Justice Department sued to stop AT&T's acquisition of Time Warner, many progressives heralded the lawsuit as one that should be

President Donald Trump approached antitrust enforcement by
seeking to use it to further his petty and personal vendettas. Instead,
we need to beef up the professional staffs at the Antitrust Division
of the Department of Justice and at the Federal Trade Commission.
Cartoon by Mike Smith, *Las Vegas Sun,* 2017.

brought; yet a cloud hung over the lawsuit, for the decision to sue did
not align with the administration's business-friendly philosophy and
President Trump seemingly had a vendetta against CNN for its unfavorable coverage of him, and CNN was owned by Time Warner."

Another example? After automakers announced plans to comply
with California's pollution and emissions standards, which are tougher
than the federal standards sought by Donald Trump, the Justice
Department opened an antitrust probe into the automakers. "My suggestion is you're doing this for political reasons," my colleague Senator
Sheldon Whitehouse told the DOJ's antitrust chief, Makan Delrahim, at a hearing in September 2019 as the Trump administration—
contending that only the federal government could regulate greenhouse
gas emissions—planned to revoke California's authority to set automobile emissions standards. The probe looks like "bullying," I said, adding,
"Quite frankly the antitrust investigation into these automakers appears
to have less to do with protecting competition than with intimidating
parties that don't fall into line with the Trump administration's plan
to relax emissions standards." Aside from antitrust, the Trump administration's willingness to routinely disregard the rule of law, leading to

scores of lawsuits, including by state attorneys general, is something that we saw across the board. That undermining of the rule of law was a brazen effort to undermine institutions and democratic norms that we—as Americans—so proudly cherish.

In June 2020, before the House Judiciary Committee, a whistleblower, the Antitrust Division lawyer John Elias, testified that the Justice Department's Antitrust Division inappropriately conducted indepth antitrust reviews of ten marijuana industry mergers that posed no competition concerns. "These mergers were not even close to meeting established criteria for these kinds of investigations," Elias said, testifying that a "personal dislike for the industry" was what prompted the investigations. Elias also testified that the investigation into an agreement between the State of California and four automakers was not based on bona fide concerns, noting that "the career staff who examined it saw some very obvious defenses—things like state action and *Noerr-Pennington*." Elias added, "You really have to twist things to get around those so it did not appear to be in good faith." The whistleblower said assistant attorney general Makan Delrahim told those present at an all-staff meeting in September 2019 that the cannabis-related investigations were motivated by the industry being unpopular "on the fifth floor," a reference to the attorney general's suite of offices. Both Jeff Sessions and William Barr were extremely hostile to efforts to legalize marijuana. Although Delrahim, in a public letter, said "federal antitrust agencies had no prior experience—let alone subject matter expertise—in the cannabis industry," and although he challenged the whistleblower's complaints as "misleading," the fact remains that the Justice Department's Antitrust Division spent a whole lot of taxpayer money delving into prospective mergers that the professional antitrust staff essentially saw as a waste of government resources.

The political smoke swirling around the Trump administration's antitrust decisions wafted way beyond the lawyers' offices in the Justice Department. Although the department contended that it was evaluating the automakers' agreement in early August *before* President Trump tweeted about the issue, the whistleblower, Elias, testified that Antitrust Division staff were instructed to open an investigation into the automakers' agreement the day after President Trump tweeted about it in August. "It didn't feel like a good faith calling of balls and strikes that

I had been used to seeing," Elias observed. It was also asserted that an astonishing 29 percent of the Antitrust Division's merger probes targeted the cannabis industry, meaning that the division would not have been able to conduct costly—yet much needed—merger reviews for other industries.

In the end, there is no question that the work of the Justice Department's Antitrust Division and the FTC was continually marred by President Trump's highly politicized comments about pending mergers. Even before he became president, during the 2016 presidential campaign, Trump inappropriately announced that he would block AT&T's acquisition of Time Warner simply because he didn't like CNN, and he attacked Jeff Bezos, who runs Amazon, after receiving unfavorable coverage in *The Washington Post*, which Bezos owns. It is one thing to oppose a merger on the merits; it is quite another to create a Nixon-style enemies list or to go after a business simply because of one's politics. Yet in 2017, in speaking of the proposed AT&T–Time Warner deal, Trump—in highly inappropriate behavior motivated by his clear animus toward CNN—reportedly told his then chief of staff, John Kelly, "I want that deal blocked!"

As has been reported by many, Trump's unethical and unseemly behavior didn't just start in the White House. It can be traced throughout his business career, including, as it turns out, in the unexpected area of antitrust. Driven by his personal dislike of particular companies or people, Trump, as a businessman, played on both sides of antitrust lawsuits. In a case against the National Football League, the United States Football League (USFL)—with Trump as the owner of a USFL franchise, the New Jersey Generals—brought antitrust claims in 1984. In that case, the USFL won its antitrust case against the NFL but infamously was awarded just $1 in damages, tripled to $3 because the antitrust laws allowed the recovery of treble damages. In the end, the paltry award, plus some bad business decisions that had been pushed by Trump, ended in the USFL's bankruptcy.

The USFL, founded in 1982, had gotten off to a good start, envisioned by its founder, David Dixon, as a springtime complement to the NFL. In 1983, Trump got involved, bought the New Jersey Generals, and hired some high-profile players like Heisman Trophy winners Herschel Walker and Doug Flutie. In what turned out to be a disastrous

There are many legitimate reasons for antitrust officials to examine
the monopoly power of Amazon. Unfavorable news coverage in *The
Washington Post*, which Jeff Bezos owns, is not one of them. Cartoon
by Ingram Pinn, *Financial Times,* 2019.

business decision, Trump then persuaded the USFL to move from a
spring to a fall schedule, putting it head-to-head with the NFL. You
see, what Trump really wanted—and what he never got—was an NFL
team. Trump had unsuccessfully attempted to buy an NFL franchise in
1981, and he hoped to merge his USFL franchise into the NFL and thus
increase the value of his investment, but that never came to fruition.
At one point, Trump arranged to meet with NFL commissioner Pete
Rozelle, but according to one account the meeting ended by Rozelle
telling Trump, "Mr. Trump, as long as I or my heirs are involved in the
NFL, you will *never* be a franchise owner in the league."

At the 1986 antitrust trial, in which the jury ultimately awarded
the $1 in damages despite the USFL's lawsuit seeking $1.69 billion in
the case, the USFL called Trump as one of its star witnesses. Trump
questionably testified that the NFL commissioner, Pete Rozelle, had
offered him an NFL expansion franchise if he (Trump) would persuade
the USFL to stick with a spring schedule and pursue no legal claims.
Rozelle vehemently denied that he had ever offered Trump a franchise.

In the end, many believed Trump's involvement and selfish motives
sunk the USFL. According to one of the NFL's lawyers, Frank Rothman, Trump was a "snake" who would've sold his fellow USFL owners

down the river so he could get an NFL franchise. "Donald didn't love the USFL," Jerry Argovitz, the then owner of the Houston Gamblers, later observed, adding, "We had a great league and a great idea. But then everyone let Donald Trump take over. It was our death." One of the jurors—Miriam Sanchez, a Yonkers, New York, high school English teacher—said, "Trump had us completely befuddled. Why would he call Rozelle if he wasn't meeting him with some ulterior motive." Another juror, Patricia Sibilia, emphasized that Trump "was not believable in anything he said" and that he "came off as arrogant and unlikeable." "He did not do the USFL well," Sibilia reflected. "What's funny, in hindsight," she said in an interview, "is that his so-called business genius ruined it for them."

As a fitting end to his sketchy antitrust business involvement, just two years later, in 1988, after the bankruptcy and demise of the USFL, Trump found himself on the receiving end of an antitrust lawsuit, this time as a defendant. In that case, Trump agreed to pay a $750,000 fine to settle a claim that he failed to make the required Hart-Scott-Rodino Act filings with the FTC and DOJ in connection with his 1986 acquisition of stock in Holiday Corporation and Bally Manufacturing.

Trump's business career had one major thing in common with his ultimate antitrust impact: a whole lot of bluster with limited results. On the one hand, the highly charged rhetoric from President Trump did, at times, harken back to the trust-busting era of Teddy Roosevelt, and the willingness of lawyers in the Trump administration to at least aggressively challenge some mergers was a clear break from the laissez-faire attitudes of Republican administrations over the past several decades. Yet in the end, the integrity of the hard work of professionals and career staff devoted to enforcing the country's competition policy was decidedly undermined by President Trump in both words and actions. And while his antitrust and FTC chiefs—Makan Delrahim and Joe Simons—were willing to launch long-overdue investigations of tech companies and major groundbreaking complaints against Google and Facebook, the late-blooming nature of those actions limited their impact during Trump's time in office.

One glaring example of how President Trump's antitrust rhetoric was more TV/rally talk than reality: the appointment of two U.S. Supreme Court justices—Neil Gorsuch and Brett Kavanaugh—with extremely conservative views on antitrust. At the Senate Judiciary Committee's hearing for then nominee Gorsuch, I asked him about the Supreme Court's antitrust jurisprudence and the antitrust classes he'd taught at the University of Colorado. Despite antitrust being an area of expertise for Gorsuch, at the hearing I did not get answers to my substantive questions. At one point, I asked about three Court decisions—*Verizon Communications Inc. v. Law Offices of Curtis V. Trinko LLP* (2004), *Credit Suisse Securities (USA) LLC v. Billing* (2007), and *Leegin Creative Leather Products Inc. v. PSKS Inc.*: "As you know, although the Supreme Court has not addressed the merits of a merger case in decades, recent court decisions, *Trinko, Credit Suisse,* and *Leegin,* have made it more difficult to bring antitrust cases challenging anti-competitive conduct," I noted. "Do you think the courts have made antitrust enforcement too difficult? What do you say to your classes about this specific issue?" I asked.

Instead of getting answers to my questions about the increasing challenges associated with antitrust enforcement, I got anecdotes from Judge Gorsuch about how he'd represented both plaintiffs and defendants in lawsuits, about how he tried "not to take a view" in the classroom. When pressed again on the issue of antitrust enforcement, Judge Gorsuch did bring up, in a generic fashion, the problem of "lack of competition between competitors" that can affect consumers. But Judge Gorsuch never addressed my specific questions about the Supreme Court cases that had been making antitrust enforcement more and more difficult.

At the initial Kavanaugh hearing, I also asked Judge Kavanaugh about the series of U.S. Supreme Court decisions that made it much harder to enforce our nation's antitrust laws. As I said at the time, "This could not be happening at a more troubling time. We're experiencing a wave of industry consolidation. Annual merger filings increased by more than 50% between 2010 and 2016." Before that initial hearing, I'd examined Judge Kavanaugh's antitrust opinions, and I was not impressed by what I saw—something I communicated to President Trump's then White House counsel, Don McGahn. As I said at the hearing, "I'm concerned that the Court—the Roberts Court—is going down the wrong path and your major antitrust opinions would have rejected challenges to mergers that majorities found to be anticompetitive. I'm afraid you're going to move it even further down the path."

I asked specifically about Judge Kavanaugh's dissent in *Federal Trade Commission v. Whole Foods Market Inc.*, a case examining Whole Foods' $565 million acquisition of another grocer, Wild Oats Markets. The FTC had moved to block that merger, one involving the two largest operators of premium, natural, and organic supermarkets. In eighteen cities, the FTC had asserted, the merger would create monopolies because Whole Foods and Wild Oats were the only supermarkets in that category of grocery stores. An expert for the FTC had provided direct evidence that the opening of a Whole Foods in the vicinity of a Wild Oats store caused Wild Oats' prices to drop, with the expert likewise finding that the presence of a Wild Oats lowered Whole Foods's margins significantly. The U.S. Court of Appeals for the District of Columbia had remanded the case back to the district court to more fully consider the FTC's evidence, which included a February 15, 2007, email from Whole Foods CEO, John Mackey, to his company's board explaining that Wild Oats "is the only existing company that has the brand and number of stores to be a meaningful springboard for another player to get into this space. Eliminating them means eliminating this threat forever, or almost forever." Mackey's email also stated that by buying Wild Oats, "we will . . . avoid nasty price wars."

Despite such compelling evidence, Judge Kavanaugh had dissented in the case, citing—surprise, surprise—Robert Bork's book *The Antitrust Paradox* and writing that "the FTC's position . . . calls to mind the bad old days when mergers were viewed with suspicion regardless of their economic benefits." In his dissent, Kavanaugh, calling *The Antitrust Paradox* a "landmark antitrust book," said that "the FTC's case is weak and seems a relic of a bygone era when antitrust law was divorced from basic economic principles" and worried aloud about upending "modern merger practice." At his nomination hearing, Kavanaugh said of that Whole Foods case that it was "very fact specific" and that he "would have affirmed the decision by the district judge in that case which allowed the merger."

But that was not the only opinion—or piece of writing—that I found extremely troubling and questioned Judge Kavanaugh about at his 2018 nomination hearing. In preparing for the Kavanaugh hearing, I also learned about his dissenting opinion in *United States v. Anthem* (2017). In that case, the U.S. Court of Appeals for the District of Columbia heard an expedited appeal from the government's successful challenge to the largest proposed merger in the history of the health insurance industry. In July 2015, Anthem—a company licensed to operate under the Blue Cross Blue Shield brand in fourteen states, and a company serving approximately 38.6 million members—entered into an agreement to merge with Cigna, Anthem's competitor in those states and a company serving approximately 13 million members. After the U.S. Department of Justice, the District of Columbia, and eleven states sued to stop the merger on the ground that it was likely to substantially lessen competition, a district court, after a six-week trial, stopped the merger, rejecting Anthem's defense that the merger's anticompetitive effects would be outweighed by efficiencies.

In affirming the district court's ruling, the majority decision of the U.S. Court of Appeals pointed out that "our dissenting colleague"— Judge Kavanaugh—believed that an existing U.S. Supreme Court precedent that was never overruled could be "disregarded by this court" and that he "applies the law as he wishes it were, not as it currently is." As the majority opinion emphasized, it is not a lower court's role "to ignore on-point precedent so as to adhere to what might someday become Supreme Court precedent." Yet in his dissent, Judge Kavanaugh expressed the view that the U.S. Court of Appeals should follow "the modern approach" to antitrust—one in which, per his dissenting opinion, "the fact that a merger such as this one would produce heightened market concentration and increased shares . . . is not the end of the legal analysis." While Judge Kavanaugh noted in his dissent that "the Government could still ultimately block this merger based on the merger's effects on hospitals and doctors in the upstream provider market" (an issue he thought should be sent back to the district court), his willingness to ignore an on-point precedent in preference to reliance on Robert Bork's work (which he cited in his dissent) was something that I found particularly problematic.

The composition of the U.S. Supreme Court is incredibly important, and the extreme views of Neil Gorsuch and Brett Kavanaugh on antitrust issues were one of the many reasons why I fought so hard to keep them off the Court. Their views, including on antitrust issues, are too far out of the mainstream to warrant lifetime appointments to the highest court in the land. And in the end, the addition of Justices

Gorsuch and Kavanaugh has shifted—as I feared—the U.S. Supreme Court even further to the right in the antitrust arena. For instance, in June 2018, in a 5–4 decision in which Justice Gorsuch provided the deciding vote, the Court held that American Express did not violate the antitrust laws by putting provisions in its contracts with merchants that force them to promise that they will do nothing to encourage customers to use other credit cards with lower swipe fees. In his dissent, Justice Breyer called the majority opinion in the *American Express* case "contrary to basic principles of antitrust law."

The only recent bright spot in the Supreme Court's antitrust jurisprudence came in May 2019, when, in a 5–4 decision, the Court decided that iPhone users would be allowed to sue Apple in a lawsuit alleging that Apple had unlawfully monopolized the aftermarket for iPhone apps. In that case, *Apple Inc. v. Pepper* (2019), Apple had contended that iPhone users could not sue, because they were not direct purchasers from Apple. The Court, however, rejected Apple's argument, with Justice Kavanaugh joined by the Court's four more liberal justices finding that under the Clayton Act iPhone owners were direct purchasers who could sue for alleged monopolization. Apple's App Store, the Court emphasized, "now contains about 2 million apps that iPhone owners can download" and that "by contract and through technological limitations, the App Store is the only place where iPhone owners may lawfully buy apps."

Now, of course, one of those liberal justices—the beloved RBG—is no longer with us, and not much is known about the antitrust views of her conservative replacement, Amy Coney Barrett. But at her nomination hearing, in response to my questioning, she said that antitrust has "largely been left to judicial development, that is controlled by precedent for the most part." While I hope Justice Barrett will not follow in the antitrust footsteps of other conservative Supreme Court justices, I think most would agree that she is far more likely to side with her conservative colleagues than with the views of her pioneering predecessor, Ruth Bader Ginsburg.

In the closing year of the Trump administration—which included the highly charged 2020 presidential campaign—its competition agencies were confronted by two highly significant but somewhat interrelated challenges: the lack of appropriate antitrust, privacy, and consumer regulatory regimes to rein in the ever-expanding power of Big Tech, and the massive repercussions of the global pandemic. The COVID-19 pandemic, of course, itself created new health and economic challenges—ones that will reverberate across our country for years. In addition to facing increasing consolidation across America (a long-standing problem), the Trump Justice Department encountered many other merger requests during the pandemic.

The COVID-19 pandemic changed everything for Americans and business owners. The closure and reduced competitive abilities of so many small businesses during the pandemic, as well as the growth and strengthening of Big Tech companies, further exacerbated the "have and have-not" nature of American capitalism today. The antitrust enforcement agencies were confronted in 2020 by potential mergers that might never have been suggested absent the pandemic. One example? Back in May 2020, Reuters reported that there were ongoing merger talks between Uber Technologies Inc., the ride-hailing company, and Grubhub Inc., the online food delivery company. "A merger," Reuters reported, "would give Uber Eats' money-losing food delivery service a leg up on market leader DoorDash at a time when the coronavirus pandemic has upended Uber's business of shuttling people from place to place."

Upon getting word of the Uber-Grubhub merger talks, I immediately took it on, writing, "If Uber takes over Grubhub it isn't good for competition and it isn't good for you. When big companies corner the market it usually means more for them and less for you, especially in a pandemic." I also sent a letter to Assistant Attorney General Delrahim and FTC chairman Simons, urging them to scrutinize the potential acquisition of Grubhub. Uber's market capitalization of $59 billion far exceeded Grubhub's market capitalization of $5.3 billion, and in the letter—in which I was joined by Senators Patrick Leahy, Richard Blumenthal, and Cory Booker—we noted that "a merger of Uber Eats and Grubhub would combine two of the three largest food delivery application providers and raise serious competition issues in many markets around the country." In New York City, we noted, a combination of Uber Eats and Grubhub would result in a staggering 79 percent market share. Had the Uber Eats and Grubhub merger gone forward, just two brands—DoorDash and Uber/Grubhub—would've commanded approximately 90 percent of the national market.

Ultimately, in the wake of those objections, the merger talks fell apart, with one news report observing that a merger of Uber and Grub-hub would have resulted "in a single company with nearly half the U.S. market" at a time when many restaurants, because of the pandemic, have come to rely on online food delivery services. "News that the Uber/Grubhub deal may not materialize," I said around that time, is "good for both consumers and restaurants."

Undeterred, in June 2020, Grubhub announced that it had reached a merger deal with a European food delivery company, Just Eat Take-away. "Just Eat Takeaway Acquires Grubhub for $7.3 Billion to Create Largest Food Delivery Firm Outside China," one headline blared. Just days later, Uber announced its acquisition of Postmates in a deal worth $2.65 billion. The combination of Postmates and Uber Eats, one story reported, created "the country's second-largest delivery Goliath."

Throughout the pandemic the Big Tech companies expanded and grew. And while the Trump administration, as noted earlier, announced major antitrust investigations and brought antitrust cases against Google and Facebook at the tail end of 2020, the actual results of Trump's four years in office were underwhelming. Last-minute sub-poenas of tech companies for a Senate Commerce Committee hearing, scheduled one week before the election, only added to the narrative that this was all purely political to the then Republican-led White House and Senate. The bipartisan work that could have been done on privacy and consolidation got left on the committee room floor with not a slice of monopoly power actually taken out of the companies. All that came out of it was political talking points.

You see, although Donald Trump relished going after individual companies for highly political and personal reasons, when it came to actually enforcing the law, he hardly brought down the hammer. I was particularly outraged by the FTC's July 2019 settlement with Facebook over its handling of user information that led to the Cambridge Analytica scandal. Back then, Facebook was fined $5 billion by the Republican-led Federal Trade Commission on a 3–2 vote, with not a single executive being put under order for a violation of a consent decree. Both Democratic FTC commissioners sought heightened penalties given that the data privacy of eighty-seven million Facebook users was violated. That sum—as I said at the time—simply "doesn't fit the offense." "A onetime

$5 billion fine for a company whose profits are in the tens of billions a year is not enough to deter Facebook and force them to put consumers' privacy before profits," I observed, adding, "A good indication that the fine isn't enough is the fact that Facebook's stock increased following reports of the fine. This is another win for Facebook at the expense of consumers." My colleague Representative David Cicilline of Rhode Island perhaps said it best: "The FTC just gave Facebook a Christmas present five months early. It's very disappointing that such an enormously powerful company that engaged in such serious misconduct is getting a slap on the wrist."

In summary, despite some good work at the agency level when it came to tech investigations and the filing of tech lawsuits at the very end of his administration, Donald Trump did not deliver on the promises he made to voters in the 2016 presidential election, including many related to antitrust and consumer protection. During his time in office, President Trump did nothing to update the nation's antitrust laws or add significant resources to enforce them. And to make matters worse, he appointed many judges who are blatantly skeptical of aggressive antitrust enforcement. This has only led to more drift in this important area of law, just when concerted and significant changes are warranted.

Despite Trump's inaction, the public, I believe (as demonstrated by

"I need your Facebook password before I can hire you. If you're not on Facebook, I need you to join and post a bunch of personal stuff you don't want me to know about."

Facebook has affected the way people communicate with one another, and it should make all of us think a whole lot more about our privacy rights. Many people still don't know how their information is being used—and often sold—by the social media companies. Cartoon by Randy Glasbergen.

an increasing focus on this topic by both Democrats and Republicans in Congress and in state governments), is clearly—and quite rightfully—anxious about the effects of corporate consolidation and anticompetitive conduct. It is high time for Congress to act. After roughly a hundred years of political dormancy, it is time for Washington, D.C., to turn the page to a new chapter—a *new* progressive era of competition policy and antitrust law and enforcement.

6

We the People

*Why Antitrust Matters for Our Democracy
and Our Economy*

TOO BIG

A few years ago, I was in a diner in Albert Lea, Minnesota. An older woman at a neighboring booth with her retired farmer husband and his brother turned around and blurted out, "I know who you are. I saw you on TV."

Having just completed a round of cable show interviews on Russian interference in the 2016 presidential election, I quickly shot back, "Yep, that was me. Was the interview about Russia?"

"No," she said firmly, "it was on local news about something we could relate to right away. It was about . . ."

She paused, trying to get the right word. She finally gave up trying to capture it at length and went for the word that probably described the local interview about an agriculture merger better than any other.

"It was about big," she said. "It was about how things are getting too big and it makes it harder for us to make it."

"Too big." A phrase that harkens back to Justice Brandeis's prescient 1914 warning about the "curse of bigness"—a pointed critique that is a lot easier to understand than the entire body of law called "antitrust." Brandeis eloquently railed against "the evils of monopoly" more than one hundred years ago, but the problem has only gotten a whole lot worse since that time. The corporate consolidation that America has witnessed in recent decades has led to bigger—and much more powerful—companies. Antitrust scholars have been warning about corporate consolidation for a very long time, but those calls have largely gone unheeded.

Not surprisingly, large companies have been more than willing to exert their vast accumulated power in elections and in the halls of Congress. Big companies can hire expensive lobbyists, with Open Secrets—a website run by the Center for Responsive Politics—documenting the tens of millions of dollars in lobbying expenditures made by industry associations and companies such as AT&T, Blue Cross Blue Shield, Comcast, ExxonMobil, General Electric, Lockheed Martin, and Northrop Grumman. From 1998 to 2019, the U.S. Chamber of Commerce alone spent more than $1.5 billion on lobbying activities. The tsunami of money that has flooded American politics has perverted the country's laws and our whole electoral and political system, and, no surprise, has meant a lack of much-needed changes to our antitrust laws.

While the next chapter will focus on our nation's specific antitrust and competition policy challenges, and chapter 8 is all about the solu-

From the days of J. P. Morgan to the rise of the Koch brothers, money has long flooded American politics. Sadly, it is American workers and consumers who have most often been harmed by the tsunami of special interest campaign contributions.

tions to those challenges, the hard truth is that nothing of real consequence will change unless we take back our democracy and our politics. And that means seeing the issues of corporate power, consolidation, and monopolies through the broader lens of necessary economic, electoral, and democratic changes that must be made in America. Despite the implications of the U.S. Supreme Court's ruling in *Citizens United,* corporations are not people. People are people.

When a corporation transforms itself from a competitor to a monopoly, it wields outsized power—power over wages, power over markets, and power over the economy itself. Just as railroad companies had vast influence in the late nineteenth and early twentieth centuries, the power now wielded by today's monopolies poses a major challenge to America's representative democracy because individual voices are being drowned out. Thriving competitive companies are essential to our economy and to our American way of life, but we must never forget who built America—its workers—and who the U.S. Constitution puts in charge of the government: "We the People," not "We the Corporations" or "We the Monopolies." When America's founders set up our country, they railed against the power of the British East India Company and worried about other abuses of power. But truth be told, they could never have conceived of the sheer size of modern, multinational companies or of the enormous influence they now have.

In fact, the corporate consolidation narrative of the twenty-first century repeats itself across industries; only the names of the players—the CEOs, the specific companies—are different. "From Beer to Airlines, Corporate Consolidation Is All Around Us," one 2018 news headline blared, giving a snapshot of the problem. "The American beer industry is mostly controlled by a handful of breweries that control nearly 90 percent of the American beer market," that story reported. "The biggest four U.S. airlines reap 65 percent of the industry's revenue, compared to ten years ago, when they only took in 41 percent," it noted. It's also plagued the press, where "corporate consolidation and conglomeration increasingly define American media ownership." And monopolization has even hit—get this—cat food. Just four companies control 97 percent of the dry cat food market, with Nestlé owning major brands like Fancy Feast, Friskies, and Purina.

Both as a U.S. senator and during the 2020 presidential campaign,

"It's from CorpCo. I think they want a merger."

The absence of competition leads to less choice and higher prices for American consumers. In the twenty-first century, large, multinational companies wield monopoly power rivaling that exercised by the railroads and the Standard Oil Trust more than a century ago. Cartoon by Mark Anderson.

I've worked to draw attention to the growing problems of runaway corporate consolidation and monopoly power, including by holding Senate hearings, trying in as many creative ways as I can to draw attention to the often esoteric topic of antitrust. In 2015, for example, Republican senator Mike Lee and I held a hearing titled "Ensuring Competition Remains on Tap: The AB InBev/SABMiller Merger and the State of Competition in the Beer Industry." "This merger," I said in our hearing announcement, calling for scrutiny of the AB InBev–SABMiller proposed deal, "could have negative consequences for consumers, including increased cost, and could deprive our thriving craft and independent brewers of distribution channels critical for reaching retail consumers." I pointed out that the growing "beerhemoth" consolidation in the industry is concerning and that efforts must always be made to protect the emergence of craft brewers that have brought some much-needed competition back into the beer market. As of the end of 2018, more than 7,000 breweries and brewpubs were operating in the United States (with more than 170 in my home state of Minnesota), and those independent craft breweries must be allowed to compete effectively against the industry's biggest players. And the best part? The independents mean American jobs.

But one thing I know for sure is that while congressional oversight of beer and everything else is necessary, on its own it won't change the status quo. Day-to-day oversight must be accompanied by structural reform. That's why I've co-sponsored the constitutional amendment to overturn the U.S. Supreme Court's decisions in *Citizens United v. Federal Election Commission* (2010) and *McCutcheon v. Federal Election Commission* (2014). *Citizens United* held that corporations have a First Amendment right to make independent expenditures to influence elections, while *McCutcheon*—on a 5–4 vote—struck down a provision of federal law that imposed a limit on individual contributions that could be made over a two-year period to party and candidate committees. As I've said in calling for a constitutional amendment that would allow Congress and the states to set limits on the raising and spending of money and in calling for campaign finance reform to include passage of the DISCLOSE Act to bring transparency, "This outside money is undermining our elections and shaking the public's trust in our elections." In dissenting from part of the *Citizens United* decision, Justice John Paul Stevens pointed out that "corporations have no consciences, no beliefs, no feelings, no thoughts, no desires," and that "they are not themselves members of 'We the People' by whom and for whom our Constitution was established."

The woman I met at the diner was certainly onto something: the American people intuitively understand that there is too much bigness— too much corporate power and concentration in this country—and that it is affecting our democracy and the ability of people to afford things. Just as the Gilded Age ushered in a disturbing wave of mergers that led to a concentration of private power, the same is happening again today. From 1895 to 1904, an estimated 2,274 manufacturers merged with other companies, resulting in just 157 corporations dominating their respective industries. It was only after President Theodore Roosevelt and his successors started taking on the trusts that a little balance was restored. But the wave of corporate consolidation is now continuing apace. Since 2000, a leading index measuring U.S. market concentration has shown an increase in concentration in more than 75 percent of industries. In this global, twenty-first-century economy, businesses are bound to be bigger and more complex than they were more than a hundred years ago. But in the end, if you want to have true competition, you need to have lots of innovators and competitors.

Doing something about all this consolidation isn't easy. Antitrust is a complicated field, and because the future is impossible to predict with 100 percent accuracy, innumerable judgment calls must be made by lawmakers and antitrust officials. The sheer complexity of antitrust law, however, doesn't mean Americans should shut their eyes when the parade of mergers and acquisitions just keeps getting longer. Just as schoolchildren are taught to "stop and look both ways" before crossing the street, Americans need to carefully assess what's going on with corporate consolidation and Wall Street megamergers and the rising economic inequality that they fuel. In truth, Americans—just as they did in Teddy Roosevelt's time—need to kick-start a full-throated public debate about competition policy before they and their small businesses get run over by the big guys.

CORPORATE CONSOLIDATION:
BAD FOR CAPITALISM, BAD FOR CONSUMERS

On December 3, 1901, in his very first State of the Union message, President Theodore Roosevelt warned of the perils of industrial power and defended the legitimacy of taking on the trusts of his time even as he cautioned against demonizing businesses. "The tremendous and highly complex industrial development which went on with ever accelerating rapidity during the latter half of the nineteenth century," Roosevelt said after lamenting the assassination of William McKinley by an anarchist, "brings us face to face, at the beginning of the twentieth, with very serious social problems." "The old laws, and the old customs which had almost the binding force of law," he observed, "were once quite sufficient to regulate the accumulation and distribution of wealth." Concluding that those laws and customs were "no longer sufficient," Roosevelt spoke about "very large" individual and corporate "fortunes," about "abuses connected with the accumulation of wealth," and about the need to compete internationally.

Although Roosevelt praised capitalism and the accomplishments of commercial enterprises, he also recognized that "there are real and grave evils, one of the chief being overcapitalization because of its many baleful consequences." "A resolute and practical effort must be made to correct these evils," Roosevelt concluded. "It is no limitation upon property rights or freedom of contract," he emphasized of the responsibilities associated with receiving protection from liability for incorporators, "to require that when men receive from government the privilege of doing business under corporate form, which frees them from individual responsibility, and enables them to call into their enterprises the capital of the public," they do so "upon absolutely truthful representations." "Corporations engaged in interstate commerce," he urged, "should be regulated if they are found to exercise a license working to the public injury." "Great corporations," Roosevelt added, "exist only because they are created and safeguarded by our institutions; and it is therefore our right and our duty to see that they work in harmony with these institutions." He specifically noted that "the government should have the right to inspect and examine the workings of the great corporations" because "the first requisite" to remedy the problem of trusts "is knowledge, full and complete."

When you start viewing antitrust and Roosevelt's competition safeguards as a positive for our economy, you start seeing the world through a different set of eyes. We live in a world in which individual companies or just a handful of companies already control large segments of particular markets or have the power to dictate boilerplate terms and conditions or terms of use. For example, Google—a successful enterprise that is the subsidiary of the multinational conglomerate Alphabet Inc., headquartered in Mountain View, California—controls approximately 90 percent of the search engine market and half of all online commerce. Google is now so dominant that "google" is a verb recognized by the venerable *Oxford English Dictionary* in 2006.

Amazon—another mega-company that already possesses monopoly power—grew even more powerful during the COVID-19 pandemic, with its stock price skyrocketing as demand for its services rose. Meanwhile, Amazon's reach has only grown wider. In 2017, for example, Amazon purchased the grocer Whole Foods for $13.7 billion, raising important new questions about its ambitions and growing corporate power. Not only is the Amazon Echo now sold at Whole Foods, but Amazon Prime members get special discounts for shopping in the grocery stores. Amazon's plans to rapidly expand the number of Whole Foods locations, coupled with its ongoing efforts to get grocery buyers to shop online, is already fundamentally reshaping the grocery industry. Industry innovation is welcome, but we must also make sure that

Google has become a household word around the world. It has
also drawn the attention of antitrust officials, with both Congress
and the U.S. Department of Justice investigating the company and
its practices. The Justice Department sued Google for antitrust
violations in 2020. Cartoon by Henry Payne, 2019.

industries remain highly competitive and that anticompetitive conduct
is not allowed.

In this era of corporate consolidation and megamergers, one- or two-
or three-company control of major industries or technology platforms is
unacceptable. Americans deserve choice, and the law should safeguard
that principle. That's why I've opposed anticompetitive mergers. For
example, in June 2019, nine states and the District of Columbia filed a
lawsuit to block the merger between T-Mobile and Sprint—a number
that by September 2019 grew to sixteen states, with the state attorneys
general calling it an "anticompetitive megamerger." As I said in my own
statement at the time, "I have repeatedly raised serious antitrust concerns about the harmful effects of merging T-Mobile and Sprint, two of
the four remaining nationwide wireless carriers."

Unfortunately, in spite of the opposition, the $26.5 billion T-Mobile/
Sprint merger was approved by the Trump administration's Department of Justice after the Federal Communications Commission gave
the go-ahead to the deal in May 2019, though the state attorneys general
still sued—albeit unsuccessfully—to block it. With more than half of
the U.S. population now represented by those state attorneys general,
that lawsuit raised very serious issues, with the merger of the companies
affecting tens of millions of Americans. "With fewer companies com-

peting," Illinois attorney general Kwame Raoul said, "customers would face fewer choices, higher prices, less innovation and lower-quality service." Despite all of the objections, T-Mobile completed its acquisition of Sprint in April 2020, with the deal valued at $31.6 billion, after a federal court blessed it in February 2020.

In the telecommunications industry, as in other industries, bigger does not mean better. I saw firsthand the ill effects of monopoly power back when I was a lawyer representing what was then a relatively young company, MCI, when it was trying to break into the local telephone market. While we ultimately prevailed, that experience taught me how hard monopolies will fight to keep competitors out. So I've seen this movie before, and it doesn't usually end well. Fewer competitors mean less competition, and less competition means higher prices for consumers. That's not a good outcome for anyone but the monopolies.

With a lack of adequate competition in industries ranging from cable and telecommunications to health care and transportation, we must ask ourselves this million-dollar (*strike that*) . . . this trillion-dollar question: What are we going to do about it? "Too big to fail" was the catchphrase after the near collapse of the world's financial system (recall the sudden demise of Lehman Brothers in 2008) that led to TARP and the massive economic stimulus package. These days, we should also be thinking about "too big to succeed"—that is, about companies that have grown so big and powerful that they threaten innovation and harm consumer choice, lead to price gouging, and pose challenges to the very essence of the free-enterprise system. "I think these companies are too big, and we've allowed them to exercise monopoly power," Congressman David Cicilline, the House's antitrust chair, has lamented of the tech companies. The capitalist system works only if there is true competition in that system and if the system itself is monitored for abuses and anticompetitive conduct.

One glaring example of corporate consolidation—though one somewhat hidden from view—comes from the state of the online travel industry. Consumers go online all the time to try to get a good deal on hotels and airfares. Picking from a multitude of choices (Hotels.com, Hotwire, Orbitz, Travelocity, Trivago, Booking.com, Kayak, Priceline), they look for the best rates. The monopoly secret they don't usually know is this: following the merger of Expedia and Orbitz, there are really only two major online travel companies, Expedia Group Inc. (which runs branded websites such as Orbitz, Trivago, Hotwire, Hotels .com, Travelocity, HomeAway, Classic Vacations, Traveldoo, SilverRail, and CarRentals.com) and Booking Holdings (which runs Booking .com, Priceline, Kayak, OpenTable, and Rentalcars.com). A new report from an advocacy group known as Consumers' Checkbook points out that much of the purported competition is thus an "illusion." Many of those websites, that group observes, actually show the same airfare and hotel prices because they all go to the same database to get their results.

This is a major problem that deserves more attention. Back in 2015, I specifically called on the U.S. Department of Justice to closely scrutinize the then-proposed $1.6 billion acquisition of Orbitz by Expedia. Joined on the request by Republican U.S. senator Mike Lee, I noted that "with Expedia's acquisition of Travelocity earlier this year, Expedia and Orbitz control over 75 percent of the online travel bookings." As we wrote, "Increased consolidation among online travel agencies could transform a market that has benefited consumers into one that stifles competition. While to consumers it appears that there are dozens of options for comparing travel prices, over thirty of the identifiable website names are owned by the three largest competitors: Expedia, Orbitz and Priceline.com."

Senator Lee and I weren't the only ones with serious concerns about that merger. Hotels both small and large—from bed-and-breakfasts to the American Hotel & Lodging Association—pointed out that the merger would limit bargaining leverage for hotel commission rates. "The merger means less competition, and that is never a good thing for consumers," said Katherine Lugar, then the chief executive of the American Hotel & Lodging Association. Nevertheless, the Justice Department approved the merger, and we now have—in essence—a "duopoly" in the online travel industry.

The health-care industry is another example of massive corporate consolidation. Everyone needs health care, but a wave of mergers—as in other industries—has led to increased costs for businesses and consumers. "Mergers are creating giant health care systems that can wield their market power to drive up prices," one 2019 news story, titled "Rx for Merger Madness," observes, adding, "For businesses buying health care for their employees, such consolidation means it's tougher than ever to control health costs." Prominent health insurers, Robert Reich points out, have consolidated too, leading to higher health-care costs for Americans because of the lack of robust competition. Leemore Dafny, a former FTC official and an expert on health-care industry consolidation at Northwestern's Kellogg School of Management, wrote in *The New England Journal of Medicine* in 2014 that "the last hospital-merger wave (in the 1990s) led to substantial price increases with little or no countervailing benefit." "Since the primary driver of growth in private spending in recent years has been price increases for health care services," Dafny explains, "a compelling argument can be made for putting the brakes on consolidation."

Sadly, consolidation in the health-care industry continues at a brisk pace. The American Medical Association released a study in 2019 showing that state and local health insurance markets became more concentrated in 2018 than they were in 2014, with 75 percent of the 382 metropolitan statistical areas found to be "highly concentrated" as measured by the Herfindahl-Hirschman Index that the Justice Department and FTC use to measure market concentration. CVS's $69 billion acquisition of Aetna and Cigna's $67 billion acquisition of Express Scripts, the country's largest pharmacy-benefit management company, both completed in late 2018, are just two of the latest examples of health-care industry consolidation that have raised serious concerns among lawmakers on both sides of the aisle. For instance, Senator Chuck Grassley of Iowa called on the Justice Department to conduct a "rigorous review" of those mergers, citing a Kaiser Family Foundation report that found that the combined companies—in addition to Humana and UnitedHealth—would control 71 percent of all Medicare Part D enrollees and 86 percent of stand-alone drug plan enrollees. Before Walgreens acquired nearly two thousand Rite Aid stores in a $4 billion deal that closed in 2017, Senator Mike Lee of Utah and I raised similar concerns about that merger.

A lot of economists and advocates for labor—as well as businesspeople simply interested in having healthy markets for goods, services, and workers—have already gotten into the act to educate the public about the perils of monopolies. In one short video, titled *The Monopolization of America*, Robert Reich, President Bill Clinton's secretary of labor, effectively laid out the problems Americans face—not only with corporate consolidation, but with how it has redistributed money and power from the American people to a small cadre of corporate executives and ultra-wealthy shareholders. In the eleven-minute, easily digestible video, Reich points out, for example, that the profits of Missouri farmers are disappearing. Why? Because "Monsanto alone owns the key genetic traits to more than 90% of the soybeans planted by farmers in the United States and 80% of the corn." That market power allows Monsanto to charge farmers much higher prices. In addition, the food processors that farmers sell their crops and products to have consolidated into "mega-companies" with so much market power that they can dictate—and unilaterally cut—the prices they pay to farmers.

In walking through supermarket and retail store aisles, Reich emphasizes that what looks like a lot of choice is, in reality, just more evidence of extensive corporate consolidation. He notes that the four largest food companies control 82 percent of beef packing, 85 percent of soybean processing, 63 percent of pork packing, and 53 percent of chicken processing. Seventy percent of toothpaste sales go to just two companies, Crest and Colgate; another company, Mainetti, now makes practically every plastic hanger that is sold in the United States; and Luxottica controls 80 percent of the market for sunglasses. Luxottica sells them under popular brand names such as Ray-Ban, Prada, Oakley, and DKNY while simultaneously owning retail stores such as LensCrafters, Sunglass Hut, and Pearle Vision. What may appear, on the shelves or in shopping malls, as competing brands or competing stores are actually all owned by the exact same company. As one book, *Maximizing Corporate Value Through Mergers and Acquisitions,* describes Luxottica's 2007 hardball acquisition of Oakley, "When Oakley would not accept Luxottica's offer to be acquired, Luxottica stopped carrying the Oakley brands in its Sunglass Hut stores. This could not happen to Luxottica the manufacturer, as its distribution was controlled by Luxottica the retailer. Oakley did not have this power, and it eventually succumbed to Luxottica's pressure."

With power, as America's founders themselves fully recognized, comes the opportunity for abuse of that power. Who can forget the famous line uttered by Gordon Gekko, the character played by Michael Douglas in *Wall Street* (1987): "Greed, for lack of a better word, is good"? Competitors are allowed to compete fiercely, but anticompetitive conduct, or what is termed "exclusionary" behavior, is prohibited by the antitrust laws. If the FTC, the Justice Department, or state attorneys general identify such conduct or behavior, they have—under existing federal and state laws—multiple arrows in their quivers to take on the power of BIG. In addition, the country's laws can be strengthened further to make it easier to aim those arrows at the ever-changing, ever-moving monopoly targets dominating our country's current economic landscape. When it comes to powerful companies, the government must make clear to them that if they engage in anticompetitive conduct, there will be consequences. As Uncle Ben most famously advised his nephew Peter Parker in *Spider-Man,* "With great power comes great responsibility."

THE HAVES AND HAVE-NOTS: HOW GOVERNMENT POLICY, INCLUDING STRONG ANTITRUST LAWS, CAN REDUCE INCOME INEQUALITY AND RACIAL DISPARITIES

America's democracy—and America's economy—should work for everyone, not just the privileged few. This is an economy that works extremely well for the wealthy but leaves so many American families and working people behind, causing anger and resentment that is dividing our country. In an article titled "A Rigged Economy," Joseph Stiglitz—a winner of the Nobel Prize in economics, a Columbia University professor, and the chief economist at the Roosevelt Institute—explained in November 2018, reviewing the past forty years of American history, "The U.S. has the highest level of economic inequality among developed countries. . . . Whereas the income share of the top 0.1 percent has more than quadrupled and that of the top 1 percent has almost doubled, that of the bottom 90 percent has declined. Wages at the bottom, adjusted for inflation, are about the same as they were some 60 years ago!"

According to the Economic Policy Institute, income inequality has risen in every American state since the 1970s, with the top 1 percent, in 2015, receiving 26.3 times as much income as families in the bottom 99 percent. And the divide has only worsened in recent decades. According to the AFL-CIO's new Executive Paywatch database, a CEO of a Fortune 500 company hauled in, on average, $13.94 million in 2017—an

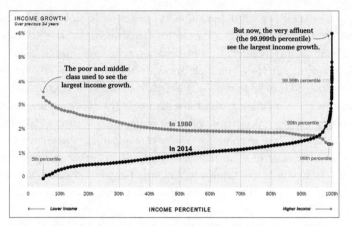

In August 2017, this chart appeared in David Leonhardt's opinion piece "Our Broken Economy, in One Simple Chart." The two lines on the graph, which depicts the economy in 1980 versus 2014, just about say it all. In 1980, the poor and the middle class saw the biggest gains in income growth. Now, however, it is just the opposite, with the ultrarich reaping massive income gains while the poor struggle mightily.

average that was *361 times* the compensation of the average American worker. "When adjusted for inflation," the AFL-CIO notes of production and nonsupervisory workers, "the average wage has remained stagnant for more than 50 years."

And it isn't just urban and suburban workers who have been affected by the nation's economic policies. For farmers in rural America, net income has dropped nearly 50 percent over the past five years. Most people are actually surprised by this one: the poverty rate for kids in rural areas is more than four percentage points higher than in urban areas. And in many parts of our country, both in inner-city and in rural communities, living in poverty is an intergenerational problem. This poverty involves more than a lower income level, it also means a lack of quality schools, health care, and jobs. Poverty is clustered in specific regions and in specific rural, suburban, and city neighborhoods.

Communities of color have been particularly impacted by low wages, persistent poverty, lack of access to capital, and lax antitrust enforcement. In a 2017 article published in *Washington Monthly,* Brian Feldman traced the decline of Black-owned businesses in the era of corporate consolidation. "The decline of black-owned independent busi-

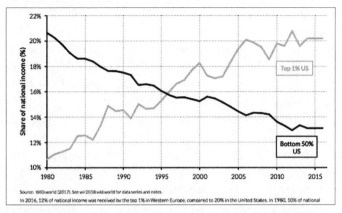

The lack of vigorous U.S. antitrust enforcement has exacerbated the problem of income inequality in the United States. The decline in antitrust enforcement since the 1980s corresponds to the phenomenon of the rich getting richer and the poor getting poorer.

nesses traces to many causes," he explains, "but a major one that has been little noted was the decline in the enforcement of anti-monopoly and fair trade laws beginning in the late 1970s." In 1985, there were sixty Black-owned banks. By 2017, that number had fallen to twenty-three. While there were, in the 1980s, fifty Black-owned insurance companies, that number has plummeted to just two companies. The country saw an uptick in Black-owned businesses after the Great Recession, but the number of minority-owned start-ups and companies should be much higher, with access to capital being a major issue. The pandemic has hit minority-owned businesses particularly hard. "The number of active Black-owned businesses in the U.S.," a columnist for the *Chicago Tribune* reported in mid-July 2020, citing research done at the University of California, Santa Cruz, "plummeted 41 percent during the early months of the pandemic from February to April, more than twice the 17 percent level of white-owned businesses."

Twelve percent of the U.S. population is Black, yet statistics show that just 3.3 percent of new businesses—that is, those less than two years old—are Black-owned. This is especially troubling for our democracy, because business ownership is tied to economic and political power. Yet the nation's history of racism has made it very hard for Black businesses to succeed. One horrific example? In what became known as the Tulsa

Race Riot of 1921, a prosperous African American community, Green-wood, known as Black Wall Street and full of churches, homes, schools, and an array of Black-owned businesses, was tragically destroyed by a white mob, with hundreds of people killed in the violence. Yet Black entrepreneurs, through the decades, have built—or had to rebuild—valuable businesses. Minority-owned businesses, in fact, played a significant role in the success of the civil rights movement, including in the Montgomery bus boycott, so ensuring that minority-owned businesses remain vibrant—and continue to be able to compete effectively in today's marketplace—is critical to social and economic justice and to keeping American communities strong.

The growing inequalities of wealth in America need to be remedied, and concrete actions must be taken to drive this change. In addition to changes to the nation's antitrust laws and enforcement, we need tax reform and other changes that would ask our wealthiest citizens to pay their fair share of taxes and that would strengthen labor unions and the American economy. For example, I've been a big supporter of Representative Jim Clyburn's legislation to fight persistent poverty. House majority whip Jim Clyburn has urged Congress to adopt a "10|20|30 formula" that would direct that at least 10 percent of federal investments be made in persistent poverty communities where 20 percent or more of the population has lived below the poverty line for the last 30 years. "In the United States," Clyburn notes, "there are 485 counties where 20 percent or more of the population has been living below the poverty line for the last 30 years." Representative Clyburn and I have also introduced comprehensive broadband infrastructure legislation to expand access to affordable high-speed internet in an effort to combat the digital divide.

While the COVID-19 pandemic shed a gigantic spotlight on income and racial disparities, these disparities have been with us for a long time. To reduce income and racial disparities, there are, in fact, all kinds of additional tax, education, health-care, and wage policies that we must champion, including to make the tax system more fair. For example, we need to roll back the excesses of the 2017 Trump tax bill and raise the corporate tax rate from 21 to 25 percent so that we can fund and rebuild American infrastructure and create good-paying jobs. The wealthiest members of our society, as well as big corporations, need to pay their fair share of taxes so that we can make necessary investments in education, infrastructure, and health care and in people and communities in need.

We need to make one- and two-year community college degrees and training certifications free for those who pursue them so that we can incentivize people to go into fields where there are or will be job openings. We need to make four-year college degrees more affordable and help with student debt. We need to fix our roads and bridges and rail and expand broadband. We need to expand access to health care and make prescription drugs and medical treatments more affordable, and we need to get to *universal* health care as a moral imperative. After all, health care is a right, not a privilege. We also need to invest in impoverished communities and in quality child care, protect people's retirements, raise the minimum wage to $15 an hour, and pass the Paycheck Fairness Act to ensure the payment of living wages and to help eliminate gender and racial pay disparities.

But to truly ensure that the gains of competition and free enterprise go to entrepreneurs and workers (as opposed to the monopolists who seek to stifle competition), we must also focus on our competition policy and thus even the playing field for small businesses and workers. Today, many Americans are saddled with credit card debt and are working long hours to keep up with paying their bills, while some Americans need to work two—or even three or more—jobs just to get by. During the Great Recession, more than 5 percent of Americans held multiple jobs, with the rate of multiple job holding declining just slightly, to 4.9 percent, as of 2017. Many people started "side hustles" such as driving for Uber or Lyft to supplement their income or added another job as a waitress or independent contractor.

To help American workers, in addition to all of the tax, education, and social services changes that rightfully dominate economic discussions, we must also zero in on a new competition policy for America. As with all things, to truly make it better for workers, this issue of antitrust enforcement and reform must be pushed to the center and included up front in political debates and discussions, in party platforms, and in candidate stump speeches. We can make change, but only if we push for it.

FIXING WAGE AND LABOR POLICIES

If the free-enterprise system is devoid or bereft of competition, it is no longer—in actuality—a free-enterprise system. And if workers are not allowed to collectively bargain for higher wages and better working conditions, big corporations will continue to dictate wages even as the productivity of American workers continues to climb. The "fight for $15"—the quest for a $15 minimum wage—is, in truth, about making sure Americans have *living* wages and about honoring what my Senate colleague Sherrod Brown aptly calls "the dignity of work." Just as labor strikes in past decades sought higher wages and better working conditions for American workers, increasing federal, state, and local minimum wages will help to rebalance American capitalism so that workers are more fairly compensated for their labor.

Union workers earn, on average, roughly 20 percent more than non-union workers in similar jobs, making unions a crucial counterweight to the enormous power of big corporations in terms of the operation of the U.S. labor market. However, union and workers' rights have been under relentless attack over multiple decades, with the enactment of so-called "right-to-work" laws whereby workers receive the benefits of union contracts without having to pay the union dues that support union activities. Congress and the states must act to protect collective bargaining rights, to safeguard unions, and to increase the minimum wage so that workers can earn a living wage.

Strengthening unions is a key component of rebalancing American capitalism. Federal and state laws must always protect, not hinder, collective bargaining rights and the right to organize and unionize. Without strong unions and a fully functioning National Labor Relations Board that enforces the country's labor laws, employers can ride roughshod over employees and job seekers. Better antitrust enforcement and better laws protecting unions, collective bargaining, and economic security, such as pension and retirement benefits, will lead to stronger competition, a more solid economy, and higher wages. That, in turn, will allow consumers to better afford the products and services they need or want and will reduce income inequality in our country.

Responding to the gig worker economy is also key. More and more workers in America are working one or more "gig" jobs. As my friend and

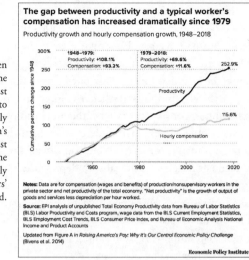

The gap between productivity and a typical worker's compensation has increased dramatically since 1979

Productivity growth and hourly compensation growth, 1948–2018

1948–1979:
Productivity: +108.1%
Compensation: +93.2%

1979–2018:
Productivity: +69.6%
Compensation: +11.6%

Productivity — 252.9%

Hourly compensation — 115.6%

Notes: Data are for compensation (wages and benefits) of production/nonsupervisory workers in the private sector and net productivity of the total economy. "Net productivity" is the growth of output of goods and services less depreciation per hour worked.

Source: EPI analysis of unpublished Total Economy Productivity data from Bureau of Labor Statistics (BLS) Labor Productivity and Costs program, wage data from the BLS Current Employment Statistics, BLS Employment Cost Trends, BLS Consumer Price Index, and Bureau of Economic Analysis National Income and Product Accounts

Updated from Figure A in *Raising America's Pay: Why It's Our Central Economic Policy Challenge* (Bivens et al. 2014)

Economic Policy Institute

The gap between productivity and the wages of workers must be attributed, in part, to the failure to aggressively enforce the nation's antitrust laws. As antitrust enforcement fell off in the 1980s, and monopoly power rose, workers' wages stagnated.

former businessman Senator Mark Warner of Virginia has reminded me many times: we need new rules of the road for an expanding number of workers in our gig economy, including the ability to save for retirement and obtain health and child care.

America's economy is driven by its businesses and its workers—some of the most productive in the world. While wages and productivity rose in tandem from the 1950s to the early 1970s, the gap between productivity and an average worker's wages has diverged substantially since 1973. From the 1980s onward, the pay-productivity gap has widened a lot, and this has much to do with the failure to vigorously enforce the antitrust laws. "From 1973 to 2017," the Economic Policy Institute points out, "net productivity rose 77.0 percent, while the hourly pay of typical workers essentially stagnated—increasing only 12.4 percent over 44 years (after adjusting for inflation)." In short, while Americans are working harder and more efficiently than ever, the fruits of their labor are mostly going to those at the very top—the corporate CEOs, the shareholders, and the wealthiest among us. Where modest wage increases have occurred for those in lower-paying occupations, it is mainly due to increases in the minimum wage at the state and local levels.

Monopolies depress wages. Increased corporate concentration has already dramatically impacted the American labor market, and it is part of the reason for the wage stagnation we've seen. Summarizing the work of Harvard economist and President Obama's top economic adviser, Jason Furman, Marina Bolotnikova writes in a 2019 article, "The New Monopoly," "Today's labor markets increasingly look like a monopsony: a market in which there is only one buyer—the inverse of a monopoly, in which there is only one seller. The more an industry is dominated by a small number of corporations, the more those companies can control the cost of labor." A small number of companies in an industry allows those companies to more easily coordinate their actions, whether by agreement or less overt means, to depress the wages of workers in that industry. As Bolotnikova explains, "Think of a town with two big-box retail stores: each store knows what the other pays its cashiers, and neither wants to raise wages. Firms can also use noncompete agreements, which ban employees from taking jobs at rival companies, to prevent workers from finding new jobs elsewhere."

Antitrust officials have made a major mistake by almost totally ignoring labor markets, which have been affected by corporate consolidation. Just as companies conspire to set prices for products and services, they sometimes get together to depress wages for their employees.

Monopoly power and corporate consolidation are bad for American consumers and workers. In this baseball-themed cartoon from 1901, "the common people" get pelted with higher prices and lower wages by the trusts. Cartoon by Frederick Burr Opper, 1901.

Back in 2006, for example, a headline in *The New York Times* blared, "Suit Claims Hospitals Fixed Nurses' Pay." The story's opening line: "Nurses filed class-action lawsuits yesterday against hospitals in Chicago, Memphis, San Antonio and Albany, asserting that the hospitals had violated federal antitrust laws by conspiring to hold down nurses' wages." Hospitals, the lawsuit contended, exchanged information about nurses' pay and agreed not to pay their registered nurses above a set amount. "Nurse pay should be set by the market, not by a secret agreement among hospitals," Daniel Small, the lead lawyer for the nurses, declared. One Albany, New York, health system ended up paying out $1.25 million to settle the claims, with a Detroit health system—to settle similar claims—agreeing to a $13.6 million settlement. The Service Employees International Union, which represented the nurses, alleged that the hospitals had exchanged the relevant information about nurses' pay through meetings, telephone conversations, and surveys.

Only rarely have the U.S. Department of Justice and private litigants successfully taken on powerful corporations in the labor market arena. In 2010, tech companies—Adobe, Apple, Google, Intel, Intuit, Pixar, and Lucasfilm—agreed to settle a Justice Department probe into an alleged conspiracy to hold down the salaries of Silicon Valley software engineers. The companies agreed not to enter into no-hire agreements with their competitors. The precipitating reasons for the case were fascinating (unless you are a software engineer). Apple's co-founder Steve Jobs, Google's CEO Eric Schmidt, and others stood accused of entering into antipoaching agreements to depress software industry wages. Steve Jobs, in response to Google's practice of cold-calling Apple's software engineers, reportedly threatened that if any of his employees were hired away, it would mean "war." Later class-action litigation, filed on behalf of approximately sixty-four thousand workers, followed in 2011, with software engineers seeking as much as $3 billion in damages—an amount that, under the antitrust laws, could have been tripled to $9 billion had the case gone to trial and the plaintiffs won. Ultimately, Intuit, Lucasfilm, and Pixar settled in May 2014 for $20 million, with Adobe, Apple, Google, and Intel settling in September 2015 for $415 million.

In sum, labor antitrust enforcement is an area ripe with possibility if our government truly wants to help workers. That, in addition to increasing the minimum wage, strengthening unions, creating a better safety net for gig workers, encouraging more women- and minority-owned businesses, and investing in economic development in impoverished areas, would even the playing field for many Americans.

MEDIA CONSOLIDATION AND MISINFORMATION: WHY OUR DEMOCRACY NEEDS A FREE AND ACCURATE PRESS TO SUCCEED

America was built on freedom of speech and freedom of the press. There are now countless websites and bloggers, with more content being produced than ever before. But these days, the consumers of news are often struggling mightily to sort out real facts from doctored videos, the real story from false tweets. The truth matters, and good legislation and good public policy outcomes are not possible if the American people do not have all of the facts or are not debating a common set of agreed-upon facts.

Politicians now use platforms such as Twitter, Facebook, and Instagram to communicate directly with their constituents and the public at large, but when politicians, PACs, and interest groups distort and manipulate the facts—or tell outright lies—it is civility and the public discourse that suffer. The social media landscape—plagued by constant disinformation attempts to manipulate platform users—continues to change, and new threats to our democracy must be addressed. With the rise of "deep fakes," election disinformation leading to the insurrection at the capitol, and former president Donald Trump's racist and mean tweets, including his retweeting of a crudely edited video of Nancy Pelosi falsely depicting her as struggling to speak, the difficulty Americans face in sorting out fact from fiction is only getting worse.

One of the cornerstones of our country is the right to speak one's mind. The First Amendment protects freedom of speech, freedom of assembly, and freedom of the press, but in the digital era public officials have a unique duty to respect the truth and not to falsify or misrepresent information, just as journalists have a vocational responsibility to endeavor to be accurate in what they report.

Compounding the social media issue, and of course related to it, is the decline of traditional media, which most often involves journalistic standards and fact checking. The First Amendment will only be protected if we have lots of trained journalists, lots of press outlets to allow people to be heard, and an independent judiciary to protect First Amendment freedoms. The more truthful voices that are heard (regardless of viewpoints) in America's marketplace of ideas, the better our democracy works, and it is not good for our representative democracy when only a small number of media companies control what people hear about and see. Whenever too much power is put in one company's—or one person's—hands, there is a greater risk of abuse, especially when a profit motive is involved. If barriers to media consolidation are eroded, the diversity of voices dwindles, and the vibrancy of our democracy suffers as a consequence.

To make the problem even more difficult, the Trump administration's repeal of federal net neutrality rules in 2017—something that allows big companies such as AT&T, Comcast, and Verizon to block or slow down access to content from competitors—has further restricted the competitive environment for the news dissemination that is so necessary to accurately inform the American electorate. Without accurate information that is freely accessible, American citizens and voters cannot make good, well-informed decisions. As James Madison warned way back in 1822, "A popular Government, without popular information, or the means of acquiring it, is but a Prologue to a Farce or Tragedy; or, perhaps both. Knowledge will forever govern ignorance: And a people who mean to be their own Governors, must arm themselves with the power which knowledge gives."

Net neutrality—the simple idea that internet service providers must treat all internet traffic and communications equally and refrain from discriminating based on the website, platform, user, or content—must be restored and zealously protected. After the Federal Communications Commission scrapped the net neutrality rules, I emphasized that the commission's vote "will harm consumers, particularly in rural areas." As I said at the time of that FCC vote, "It will limit competition. And it will hurt small business entrepreneurship and innovation. I will continue to push for a free and open internet." This is an issue that I care a lot about, as do millions of other Americans. When comedian John Oliver urged all of his *Last Week Tonight* viewers to join forces to contact the FCC to tell that agency "to preserve net neutrality," the internet traffic it generated famously caused the FCC's website to crash for two straight days. American voices must be heard loud and clear on this issue, and we must have a sense of urgency in making sure rural communities get high-speed internet and broadband as we simultaneously restore the commitment that the internet is for everyone. The internet must be equally accessible to all households and families—without discrimination, without regard to whether a person lives in a big city or on a farm, and without favoring big companies over small businesses and individual citizens.

Americans love freedom, and they deserve to have plenty of choices—with products, services, and media content—as they go about their daily lives. Indeed, protecting consumer choice is critical not only for American consumers but for the structural health of America's representative democracy. A society without a free flow of information is not free, and the more choices that Americans have the better. Antitrust officials must thus pay particularly close attention when evaluating any policy or merger that would curtail the availability of information or eliminate a news outlet. If "all politics is local," as the famous expression of the former Speaker of the House Tip O'Neill goes, a local community without a vibrant news-gathering scene and a diversity of news outlets will never produce a healthy political environment. A diversity of media outlets allows everyone to be an important part of the conversation, and it is very important for people—indeed, for *all* people—to be heard.

Although newspapers and TV stations now compete against podcasts and internet sites, they should certainly not be seen—for antitrust law purposes—as operating in the same relevant market. The "new" media outlets are not substitutes for a diverse, traditional media environment; they should be seen, instead, as an entirely separate category in the marketplace. For that reason, steps must be taken to combat and reverse the Trump administration's efforts to open the door to further media consolidation. Most disturbingly, the Federal Communications Commission (FCC) voted in December 2018 to begin a review of its media ownership rules, which currently ban a company from owning more than one of the top four stations in a market. Right now, a business can own two stations in a given market, but only one of the top four unless the FCC waives that prohibition—a waiver that should not be easily or readily obtained.

Media consolidation poses grave challenges to America's republic. In May 2017, John Light—a reporter and producer for the famed journalist Bill Moyers—wrote an article for the Moyers team about how media consolidation is threatening our democracy. "Media consolidation," he wrote, pointing out that a 2016 Gallup poll showed that only about 20 percent of Americans have confidence in newspapers and television news, "is the concentration of ownership of our news sources into the hands of fewer and fewer corporations." Donald Trump, Light observed of the 2016 election and what followed, "effectively harnessed this distrust during his campaign, and still attacks the media before his fans when he wants to prompt applause." As Light framed the serious problem we face, "Americans recognize that the media does not represent their views, and media consolidation is largely to blame. In the early 1980s, journalist Ben Bagdikian calculated that the majority of US media was held by just 50 corporations—and the number has dropped to only a handful since then."

How we got here is a long story—like so many others—about lax antitrust enforcement and relaxing regulatory structures designed to stop the power of BIG. "From the time the Federal Communications Commission was created in 1934, through the 1970s," Light pointed out, "the US government largely acted to preserve media diversity and prevent media consolidation, putting in place regulations that discouraged any one corporation from owning too many newspapers or television stations or from reaching too large an audience." For example, in *Associated Press v. United States* (1945), the U.S. Supreme Court considered a Sherman Act case brought against the Associated Press. The Court found an unreasonable restraint against trade where member newspapers had, through bylaws, been prohibited by the AP from selling or providing news to nonmembers. Writing for the Court, Justice Hugo Black had this to say: "The First Amendment, far from providing an argument against application of the Sherman Act, here provides powerful reasons to the contrary. That Amendment rests on the assumption that the widest possible dissemination of information from diverse and antagonistic sources is essential to the welfare of the public, that a free press is a condition of a free society. Surely a command that the government itself shall not impede the free flow of ideas does not afford nongovernmental combinations a refuge if they impose restraints upon that constitutionally guaranteed freedom. Freedom to publish means freedom for all, and not for some."

But the long-standing commitment to diverse sources of news came under attack during the Reagan administration. As John Light wrote, "In the 1980s, Ronald Reagan's FCC Chairman Mark Fowler brought a new, deregulatory view into vogue, and the federal government's efforts to prevent media consolidation began to unravel." That perspective gained traction and accelerated in the 1990s. Although the Telecommunications Act of 1996 helped bring about much-needed competition to the market for telephone services, it also brought about media consolidation in the radio and television industries. That law lifted the forty-station cap on how many radio stations one corporation could own, and it lifted the twelve-station limit on the number of local TV stations one company could control. Two political scientists explain what transpired in the world of television in the wake of the passage of the Telecommunications Act of 1996: "One company had been allowed to own stations that reached up to a quarter of U.S. TV households. The Act raised that national cap to 35 percent. These changes spurred huge media mergers and greatly increased media concentration."

In 1983, fifty companies owned 90 percent of American media, but by 2011 just six media giants—GE, News Corp, Disney, Viacom, Time Warner, and CBS—controlled that same 90 percent share. As of 2016, five large companies controlled 37 percent of local TV stations, with local TV news programs collectively garnering twenty-five million viewers nightly. A new study shows that local stations—driven by the trend toward conglomerate ownership—are more and more covering national politics at the expense of local politics. That study, co-authored by Gregory Martin at Stanford's School of Business and Joshua McCrain at Emory University, focused on conservative-leaning Sinclair Broadcast Group, which owns 191 stations in eighty-nine markets that reach nearly 40 percent of Americans. Sinclair was founded in 1986, went public in 1995, and delivers its content through multiple platforms.

In the 2016 presidential campaign, Sinclair stations aired fifteen "exclusive" interviews with then candidate Donald Trump, and in 2018 all of its news anchors were directed to read a script that made reference to Trump's rhetoric about "fake news." In analyzing fourteen stations that Sinclair acquired in 2017, Martin and McCrain found that the newly acquired stations upped the time they devoted to national politics by approximately 25 percent—a shift that came at the expense of local news items. The reason? Almost certainly financial. As one summary of the study emphasized, "Each local story has to be produced by a local station and requires its own reporter, camera crew, and editor. A national story, by contrast, can be produced from just one source and sent to an unlimited number of stations. For a conglomerate with hundreds of outlets, national news offers huge cost savings." Martin and McCrain also found, in analyzing the language that aired on the stations, that the newly acquired Sinclair stations showed a rightward political shift.

While millions of Americans still get their news from TV and other traditional news sources, 62 percent of Americans also get news from popular social media sites, including Facebook, Instagram, and Twitter. In addition to the fast-shifting trend away from traditional news sources such as newspapers, magazines, and local TV news programming to more nationalized programming and online platforms, another trend is emerging: within the digital platform business there is substantial consolidation, too. In terms of monthly active users, Facebook has 2.41 billion, Instagram has 1 billion, LinkedIn has 575 million, and Twitter has 320 million. The top two online platforms (Google and Facebook) account for 56.8 percent—or more than half—of the U.S. digital ad market. While Google brought in almost $40 billion in total U.S. digital ad sales in both 2018 and 2020, and while Facebook's U.S. ad revenue for those two years was estimated to be $21 billion and $31 billion respectively, their fastest-growing competitor—the ubiquitous Amazon—saw its U.S. ad revenues climb 63 percent in 2018. Amazon's ad revenues jumped to nearly $14.1 billion in 2019, with analysts projecting growth for Amazon's market share of digital ad revenues.

The rise of digital platforms clearly has benefits by improving the way, and the speed with which, we can communicate and share information. These platforms have created a 24/7 conduit for news sharing. Yet the rise of these digital platforms has put the squeeze on more traditional news outlets and has had other consequences, too. Newspapers are shuttering at an alarming rate, and the digital revolution we've witnessed has exacted a price when it comes to digital distraction, with American society now grappling with issues like distracted driving, which took

2,841 lives in 2018 alone, and smartphone addictions, with 60 percent of U.S. college students considering themselves cell-phone addicts.

In addition, the shift to digital news platforms has cost us dearly in another way: the decline of traditional content producer ad revenue has led to both a reduction in news content providers on the local level and decreasing standards when it comes to news gathering on all levels. People are consuming news at unprecedented rates, but the news we consume is, increasingly, being generated not by credentialed, well-paid journalists but by a whole host of individuals—from bloggers to self-interested political consulting firms to political hacks. And there is a major trust deficit. A poll conducted by NBC News and *The Wall Street Journal* in 2019 found that 60 percent of Americans no longer trust Facebook with their personal information.

The numbers and the number of anecdotes show the massive shift that has occurred from the "old" media to the "new" media. Between 2000 and 2016 newspaper advertising revenue fell from $65 billion to $18 billion, with advertising revenue falling further to $14.3 billion in 2018. Newspaper print circulation is nearly half of what it once was, with the estimated total U.S. newspaper circulation—for print and digital combined—down to thirty-one million for weekdays and thirty-four million for Sunday in 2017. This has meant newspaper closures and major reductions in newsroom staffs even as the newspaper industry itself has consolidated. In August 2019, it was announced that the country's two largest newspaper groups, Gannett and GateHouse Media's parent, New Media Investment Group, planned to merge in a deal valued at $1.4 billion—a deal completed in November 2019.

Consolidation and the financial struggles faced by newspapers have had major adverse effects. The *Pottstown Mercury* in Pennsylvania, for instance, cut its staff from 73 to 10, and the *St. Paul Pioneer Press* in my own state reduced its staff to below 60 employees. The most famous example of an employee reduction in force came from Colorado, where *The Denver Post* terminated the employment of scores of journalists in 2018. In fact, an ad taken out by *Denver Post* employees showed the haunting image of the newspaper's employees once gathered together for a team photo; years later, in the new version, the staffers who had been laid off by the paper, or who had simply left, were featured only as ghosted silhouettes.

In 2018, an editorial in *The Denver Post* urged its hedge fund owner, Alden Global Capital, to provide more support to the newspaper amid layoffs of journalists. The editorial was accompanied by this 2013 staff photo, with former staffers depicted in black silhouette. In 2007, the newsroom of *The Denver Post* employed more than 200 journalists. After downsizing the staff and 25 additional layoffs announced in March 2018, the number of journalists had plummeted to approximately seventy.

Another problem for this industry? Dominant digital platforms hold tremendous power over newspaper publishers. They may not provide sufficient branding, or a proprietary algorithm can entirely determine which users are exposed to content and what they see, thus allowing a digital platform to exercise near-total control over news content that reaches readers. Equally troublesome, you may have a platform that does not support a publisher's ability to attract subscribers or that has instituted certain click-through policies that force publishers to provide free content. According to a Pew Research Center report from December 2018, "Social media sites have surpassed print newspapers as a news source for Americans: One-in-five U.S. adults say they often get news via social media, slightly higher than the share who often do so from print newspapers (16%) for the first time since Pew Research Center began asking these questions."

So why not just say it doesn't matter, attributing the shift to changing times and newer technology racing past older technology? Well, the truth does matter and quality matters and at this moment a lot of the stories floating around internet sites that people take as truth are either blatantly fake or misleading. The shift in the way news is delivered, combined with the fact that media outlets have consolidated, means of course less competition, which can also lead—as shown by the studies—to more bias and fewer investigative reports. As one op-ed reported, warning of the downside of dominant digital platforms that can, through their power, exploit newspaper publishers, "Facebook does not employ reporters. Google does not send people to state capitals to uncover corruption. Neither dispatches correspondents to conflict zones. Yet those websites make towering piles of money while using the work of another industry that is in a death spiral." In criticizing the $1.4 billion GateHouse-Gannett merger, Michael Copps—a former FCC commissioner—emphasized, "Less journalism and less deep-dive investigative reporting will only lead to less informed citizens."

Media consolidation, because it involves the flow of information, is particularly atrocious for America's democracy. Unlike monopolists that operate solely in the business realm (always maintaining a financial incentive to sell or offer a particular good or service, albeit at unlawful, supra-competitive prices, whether just one, two or three companies exist in an industry), news outlets and broadcasters who possess monopoly power may, because of their owners' views and biases, never actually report the news that Americans deserve to hear. For example, if there were just two or three companies making yogurt, at least there would be major financial incentives for those companies not to make and sell lousy-tasting yogurt. But if media companies were permitted to merge down to just two or three massive companies, the idea of "freedom of the press" would truly resemble an Orwellian dystopia. A vibrant democracy requires freedom of speech and freedom of the press, and there should be innumerable, independently run media outlets for the American people.

The solutions? Enforce and update the antitrust laws, and allow for net neutrality with legal rules of the road for truth and privacy. Why? Because Americans deserve better. And the American people should demand better—from the antitrust laws, from the way those laws are implemented and enforced, and from our leaders.

I have already introduced a bill with bipartisan support to help even the playing field for news organizations desperately trying to survive the gale-force triopoly headwinds created by Facebook, Google, and Ama-

Facebook and its CEO, Mark Zuckerberg, have come under fire for the use—and misuse—of consumers' private data. We need more congressional oversight when it comes to Big Tech, and we need to be asking more sophisticated questions. Cartoon by Rob Rogers, *Pittsburgh Post-Gazette,* 2018.

zon, with those three companies taking in more than 70 percent of all online advertising dollars. The Journalism Competition and Preservation Act was introduced in the House by Representatives David Cicilline (D-R.I.) and Doug Collins (R-Ga.). Senator John Neely Kennedy (R-La.) and I introduced the Senate version, with the bill establishing a forty-eight-month safe harbor for news publishers to band together to negotiate with the online platforms to improve access to, and the quality of, news online. Such coordination would only be permitted if it directly relates to the accuracy, attribution or branding, interoperability, or quality of news; benefits the entire industry rather than just a few publishers and is not discriminatory; and is directly related and reasonably necessary for the negotiations, instead of being used for other purposes. The bill has attracted a lot of support from those who care about the health of the journalism industry and the freedom of the press.

PROTECTING OUR DEMOCRACY: GETTING
DISINFORMATION AND DARK MONEY
OUT OF OUR POLITICS

It is paramount that we protect our democracy. If American elections and ballot boxes are not secure and free from foreign interference, our voters aren't able to make decisions based on truthful information, and then America's democracy—and the right of every American to have a say in their own government—is not secure either.

To ensure fair and honest elections free from both foreign interference and misleading and false information, we must do all we can to secure our election system with backup paper ballots and audits and the like. But we must also establish and enforce clear rules of the road for political advertising and truthtelling on major internet platforms. In the 2016 presidential year election, approximately $1.4 billion was spent on online political advertising, yet there were no rules in place to catch the fraudulent ads (some actually paid for with Russian rubles) that sought to sow discord and division among Americans over gay rights, guns, race, immigration, and their religious beliefs. In 2020, on the other hand, thanks to the good work of people like Chris Krebs, the first director of the Department of Homeland Security's Cybersecurity and Infrastructure Security Agency (CISA), we had an election that CISA called "the most secure in American history"—a declaration that ultimately led Krebs, who refused to peddle in conspiracy theories and disinformation, to be fired by Donald Trump via Tweet.

My Honest Ads Act—a bipartisan bill I authored that was co-sponsored by Senators John McCain and Mark Warner, and is now co-sponsored by Senator McCain's longtime friend Republican senator Lindsey Graham—would put in place sane advertising rules for political ads on social media sites similar to the ones already in place for newspapers, TV, and radio. The tech companies originally opposed this bill, but in the wake of the Cambridge Analytica scandal, some of these companies and their CEOs (including Facebook and its leader, Mark Zuckerberg) committed to support the legislation. Several of the major tech platforms, including Facebook, are now voluntarily disclosing both campaign and issue ads and requiring disclaimers.

Voluntary disclosures are a good start. But federal legislation must be passed because each company is using different disclosure and disclaimer rules, with some using none at all. I look at it this way: if a radio station in Thief River Falls, Minnesota, is able to track political ads and is required to keep them available to the public, large social media companies should be able to do so. Social media companies such as Facebook have enormous power, and with that power should come responsibility. Spending on political ads in the 2020 election cycle totaled a whopping $8.5 billion. At a 2020 post-election hearing, I continued to ask the hard questions and specifically asked Zuckerberg about misleading ads that had fallen through the cracks. In our increasingly algorithm-driven digital landscape, I also pushed for actual human review of political ads and, of course, passage of my Honest Ads Act.

An additional threat to our democracy is the enormous power of well-financed special interests. Washington, D.C., has long been deluged with highly paid lobbyists (many of them former cabinet secretaries and members of Congress) for special interests. Those lobbyists regularly dole out big-dollar campaign contributions on behalf of their corporate and industry association clients, literally flooding the seat of our democracy with checks that distort—and in some cases downright corrupt—lawmakers' decision-making. Some politicians have even been convicted of crimes, including bribery. Political campaigns cost a lot of money to run, and because there is not yet public financing for federal elections, members of Congress are forced to spend an outsized portion of their time raising money. Instead of spending all of their time representing their constituents and doing the people's business, they are—quite literally—often sitting in windowless offices dialing for dollars. If we want to fix America's democracy, we must make law and politics about good government and helping people, not doing endless "call time" to raise money.

I still remember the effective campaign ad of one of my friends, the late U.S. senator Paul Wellstone of Minnesota. The ad depicted little kids in their high chairs writing oversized checks to Paul's Republican opponent using colored markers. One boy wrote out a check for "10000000" and signed it "Sam." A girl wrote out another check for "zillion" and signed it "Jessica." Paul wanted to make the point—and it was a good one to make—that kids, some of our society's most vulnerable members, don't have the resources to compete against well-funded special

"It's Still There"

Dark money ominously hangs over American law and politics. To save our representative democracy, we must pass campaign finance reform, get the states to ratify a constitutional amendment to reverse *Citizens United,* and get money out of politics.

interests and slick, well-oiled lobbying operations—whether lobbyists are representing Big Pharma, Big Oil, or some other interest. "Politics," Paul said, "is not just about power and money games"; it's "about the improvement of people's lives." Or, as one of our predecessors, Hubert Humphrey, put it just as evocatively, "The moral test of government is how that government treats those who are in the dawn of life, the children; those who are in the twilight of life, the elderly; and those who are in the shadows of life—the sick, the needy and the handicapped."

To clean up Washington, D.C., we need to take bold and decisive actions. First, we need to pass a constitutional amendment to overturn *Citizens United*—the disastrous U.S. Supreme Court decision that opened the floodgates to dark money in our politics. Second, to ensure private citizens maintain control of our democracy, we need to make sure that every eligible voter has the right to cast his or her vote without any barriers or interference. We need to reauthorize the Voting Rights Act, pass my bill to automatically register every eligible voter at age eighteen, and fight back against gerrymandering, voter ID laws, and the purging of voter rolls so that what happened to Georgia's gubernatorial candidate Stacey Abrams never happens again. We also need to make voting easier, including by passing the bill I introduced with Senator

Ron Wyden, so all voters can exercise their right to vote and do so conveniently and safely, with early in-person and mail-in voting allowed across the board. Voters shouldn't have to decide between their right to vote and their right to be healthy, especially in a pandemic.

When it comes to campaign finance, in one decision after another the U.S. Supreme Court has enabled—not fought back against—big money in politics. In *McCutcheon v. Federal Election Commission* (2014), for instance, the Supreme Court—in a 5–4 decision—ruled that aggregate limits restricting how much a donor can give to candidates or political committees violated the First Amendment. The Court specifically held that "Congress may regulate campaign contributions to protect against corruption or the appearance of corruption," yet it determined in that case that "Congress may not regulate contributions simply to reduce the amount of money in politics." Of course, it's all the money flooding American politics that has actually led to all the corruption and that has so distorted the outcomes produced by our political system. We need a

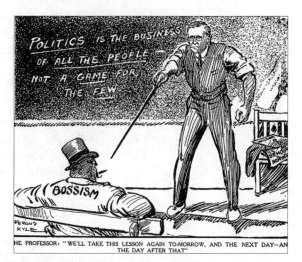

THE PROFESSOR: "WE'LL TAKE THIS LESSON AGAIN TO-MORROW, AND THE NEXT DAY—AND THE DAY AFTER THAT"

President Woodrow Wilson, a former professor, became a strong advocate for the enforcement of the nation's antitrust laws. My late friend Senator Paul Wellstone was another former professor—and a much more progressive one—who long recognized that politics is about the improvement of people's lives. "The people of this country, not special interest big money, should be the source of all political power," he once said.

U.S. Supreme Court that gets it—that money itself has corrupted our democracy and that the best way to save our republic is to get big money and dark money out of our campaigns and elections. Yet, no one believes that the Court's current majority views will change anytime soon. That's why *Citizens United* must be reversed with a constitutional amendment and why we must pass the For the People Act, which includes campaign finance and voting reforms. The Constitution puts "We the People" in charge of our democracy, and it should be the people—not private corporations with lots of cash—setting public policy.

Former president Trump and the leaders of his party have sadly chosen to try to win elections by resorting to disenfranchising voters instead of actually trying to appeal to them with policies and new ideas. In short, instead of voters choosing their elected officials, elected officials, through gerrymandering and discriminatory practices, are now trying to pick their voters. Unfortunately, Donald Trump's false claims of systemic voter fraud in the 2020 election and dangerous attempts to invalidate legally cast ballots may be the most obvious examples but in fact are just the latest in a string of attempts by Republican leaders to undermine our democracy. In North Carolina, for instance, a Republican state legislature passed a voter ID law in 2013 that was ruled to be unconstitutional, with the U.S. Court of Appeals for the Fourth Circuit finding that the law was an effort to "target African Americans with almost surgical precision."

That Republican Party leaders, for years, hired an operative who became known as the "Michelangelo of gerrymandering" for engineering gerrymandered maps speaks volumes about what is going on. It was only after that operative died and his estranged daughter turned over his hard drives to Common Cause—a nonpartisan, grassroots organization—that the true extent of his hyper-partisan intent and malignant activities was revealed. Gerrymandering has created ideologically extreme districts, which is exceedingly bad for our democracy because it only fuels the tribalization of our politics. We should have as many competitive congressional districts as possible, not be creating safe seats for Democratic and Republican politicians where the only thing those politicians ever worry about is drawing primary challengers.

The time has come to tackle once and for all the problems of gerrymandering, immoral voter disenfranchisement, and the corrupting influence of dark money on American politics. This isn't a Democratic or a Republican issue—this is an American issue. Indeed, it is long past time that we, as Americans, solve these vexing problems, lest the cancer on our capitalist system, our electoral system, and our body politic grow even bigger over time. When the political system protects Big Pharma's profits at the expense of citizens who can't afford their insulin and other life-saving drugs, it is clear that the system is broken. When that same political system continues to hand out subsidies to Big Oil and the fossil fuel industry when the climate crisis threatens our planet, it is the American people—and future generations—who lose and suffer the dire consequences. Not only are we seeing rising sea levels (and, as a direct result, a rise in insurance costs for homeowners), but extreme weather events—tornadoes, hurricanes, floods, and hailstorms—have become more common. Our federal and state governments should work for the people of this country, not irresponsibly dole out corporate welfare to titans. Decisions—as the Ojibwe people say—should be made not just for the present but for how they will impact the future seven generations from now.

LETTING THE PEOPLE BE HEARD: MAKING A GOVERNMENT FOR "WE THE PEOPLE" A REALITY

Politics has long been dominated by those seeking to profit from it, but it has gotten worse over the decades. In Frank Capra's *Mr. Smith Goes to Washington* (1939), Jimmy Stewart's character—a naive, newly appointed U.S. senator—has to fight against a corrupt political system, one controlled by graft and political bosses intent on building a dam instead of passing Smith's bill to create a wholesome campsite for boys. The level of nefarious political corruption that Stewart's character encounters in the movie—the conduct that leads to his now famed twenty-five-hour fictional filibuster fight—is exponentially dwarfed by the sheer scale of shady backroom deals that now regularly get made in the nation's capital and in lobbyists' offices in the shadow of the U.S. Capitol dome. In the movie, Smith faces long odds as he confronts a corrupt and unresponsive political system. Indeed, the Washington, D.C., powers that be try to portray him as a lightweight and a country bumpkin whose bill is jeopardizing their own dam project in a larger appropriations bill.

The stakes of the movie's fictional conflict, which include an effort to smear Smith through a manufactured scandal, are of course small beans compared with the very real-world consequences of what regularly takes place today. Good bills are killed by bad actors. Oftentimes, good legislation never even gets a floor vote or a committee hearing. For example, in 2018, after my bipartisan Secure Elections Act, cosponsored with Republican senator James Lankford, was scheduled for a committee markup, the Trump White House made calls to stop it. Likewise, the National Rifle Association (NRA) has co-opted the Republican Party, with the former Senate majority leader, Mitch McConnell, refusing to hold votes on sensible gun safety legislation.

Whereas in prior decades legislative horse-trading was never pretty, it was at least usually about making compromises in a good faith effort to further the public good—whether for the benefit of our education system, our soldiers and veterans, our seniors, our interstate highway system, or another good cause. Today, however, legislation is routinely driven by rampant self-interest, runaway greed, and the massive infusion of money into American politics. Special interests like the NRA buy influence and scare politicians, and it is the American people who lose out. Only if the American people band together and collectively insist on bold action to fight corruption and influence peddling will they eventually succeed in getting the much-needed reform they so rightfully deserve. It is extremely hard to amend the U.S. Constitution. But I believe the American people are finally so fed up with Congress and Washington, D.C., that it is now possible to gather enough public support to actually amend the Constitution to overturn *Citizens United* and fix our democracy, as well as legislatively pass the For the People Act—a series of reforms to put the people back in charge of our democracy.

Those with great power, history shows, are likely to abuse it. Because of their vast resources, billionaires, giant multinational corporations, and special interest groups now have an outsized amount of power and control in our nation's capital. And they have, in fact, grossly abused their power. Powerful corporations have purchased influence, and that has resulted in bad public policy outcomes—something the American people know is happening but, all too often, feel powerless to stop. In fact, almost two-thirds of Americans, including many Republicans, have come to believe that the economy "unfairly favors powerful interests." This is not good for our country, and it is not good for the vast majority of Americans who are daily harmed by all the monopoly power. For Louis Brandeis, the whole idea of democracy was about advancing the public good, rather than the aggregation of capital or putting market power in the hands of a few. As Brandeis put it, "We must make our choice. We may have democracy, or we may have wealth concentrated in the hands of a few, but we can't have both."

I have heard the words "too big" across America and from many of my own constituents, words repeated in diners and cow barns, on college campuses and manufacturing floors. For more than a decade I've made annual visits to all of Minnesota's eighty-seven counties, and those trips and my travels around the country as I ran for president have given me a unique perspective on the day-to-day problems Americans face. I've spent a lot of time in rural America, and many rural counties voted for Donald Trump in both 2016 and 2020. In fact, in a state that Donald Trump nearly won in 2016—where he came a little over 1 percent short of beating Hillary Clinton—many of my constituents voted for him because they felt that no one had their backs and that the "system" had left them behind. Big interests were against them; the government wasn't working for them; and they felt as if they had to disrupt the whole system. For a number of my rural and exurban supporters who cast their votes for Barack Obama in 2008 and 2012, the only way they felt they could get a fair shake was to shake things up with Donald Trump.

I didn't agree with Donald Trump's policies and divisive style of leadership then or now, and I honestly never predicted the full extent of the chaos, incompetence, racism, and brazen corruption he would bring to the White House and, ultimately, to our country. But the economic argument these American voters made in 2016 was grounded in the reality of their daily struggles to get by. By 2020, though, in the midst of a global pandemic and economic crisis, a still highly divided country—with the greatest number of citizens casting their ballots in our nation's history—made a much different choice: by a margin of more than seven million votes, they voted for Joe Biden. It is now on his shoulders—and ours—to bring about the necessary economic and democracy reforms. As I said when I announced my own campaign for president along the

Mississippi River in the middle of a Minnesota blizzard, we need to rise to the occasion and meet the challenges of our day—we need to cross the river of our divides to reach higher ground.

The world has changed a lot since *Mr. Smith Goes to Washington* first hit movie theaters. The advent of the digital age has greatly accelerated the pace of change, and corporations have gotten a whole lot bigger than they were in the late 1930s. Large media companies, in fact, have accumulated more power than ever before—power that allows those companies to shape the American agenda and to pick and choose who or what gets news coverage and who or what does not.

The American people are reawakening to the idea that too big is really bad—bad for them, and bad for the economy in general. Monopoly power is corrosive to America's free-enterprise system, and American consumers are, inevitably, the ones who end up paying the price. The good news? Antitrust is finally back on the American agenda, with members of Congress finally paying more attention to the growing problems of corporate concentration and its resulting abuses.

If Americans are to rebalance our democracy, we must recapture the spirit of the antitrust movement. Nineteenth- and early twentieth-century farmers and workers were not shy about expressing themselves, and twenty-first-century Americans should not be either. We have seen more concentrated markets in numerous industries, including agriculture, medical and pharmaceuticals, social media and telecommunications, transportation, and online ticket sales. To take on the power of BIG, individual citizens must act collectively, just as labor unions do in negotiations with large corporations. It is only through determination and citizen advocacy that representative democracies change, and it will only be through such commitment and action that America's democracy—when confronted with corruption and influence peddling—will change for the better. Antitrust became a very hot topic during the Progressive Era, and it should once again take center stage in American political life.

The woman in the diner in Albert Lea, Minnesota, was definitely onto something when she talked about the problem of big. Now we need to think big to solve it.

7

Modern-Day Antitrust Challenges

Corporate Consolidation, Congressional Inertia,
and the Conservative Courts

ormer vice president and Minnesota senator Hubert Humphrey, whose desk I'm now honored to have in the Senate chamber, believed in the strict enforcement of America's antitrust laws to stop "the growing concentration of economic power." In 1952, on the Senate floor, Humphrey asked, "Do we want an America where the economic marketplace is filled with a few Frankensteins and giants? Or do we want an America where there are thousands upon thousands of small entrepreneurs, independent businessmen, and landholders who can stand on their own feet and talk back to their Government or to anyone else?"

As discussed at length in the previous chapters, throughout our history, the American people have collectively stood up to Humphrey's "Frankensteins." They did so to return economic and political power to workers and small-business owners, and they did so to ensure that their states, regions, and local communities would remain vibrant and not be left behind. Unfortunately, in recent decades, proactive, pro-competition efforts have languished. While antitrust enforcement reached its apex in the 1960s and major cases were still being pursued in the 1970s, things decidedly took a turn for the worse in the 1980s. Perhaps the declining counterweight of antitrust enforcement was best encapsulated by a telling statement made in 1995 by Microsoft's co-founder Bill Gates to a group of Intel executives when he was in the midst of his own battle with antitrust officials. "We haven't changed our business practices at all," he said, before adding, "This antitrust thing will blow over."

The following two charts, both based on the Antitrust Division's workload reports, pretty much tell the story of the decline in antitrust enforcement. The first chart—prepared in 2019—shows that the Antitrust Division, for all intents and purposes, basically stopped bringing stand-alone section 2 cases under the Sherman Act—the section of the law that prohibits businesses from monopolizing, attempting to monopolize, or conspiring to monopolize commerce or trade. It shows that the Antitrust Division pursued only one stand-alone monopolization case in the current century. Compare what was happening in the 1970s, and you can see the difference.

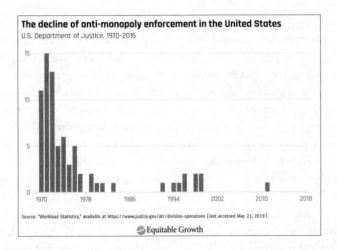

The decline of anti-monopoly enforcement in the United States
U.S. Department of Justice, 1970-2016

Source: "Workload Statistics," available at https://www.justice.gov/atr/division-operations [last accessed May 23, 2019].

Equitable Growth

Now, while this chart depicts only situations in which the Antitrust Division has brought *stand-alone* section 2 cases, a broader look at the data is equally telling. The workload statistics for section 1 cases, as shown in this second chart from 2019, also show a dramatic decline in antitrust enforcement. Either way you look at it, antitrust enforcement has fallen on hard times.

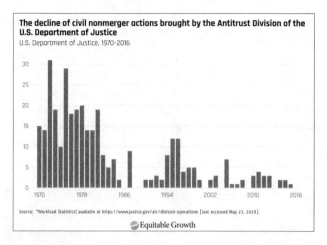

The decline of civil nonmerger actions brought by the Antitrust Division of the U.S. Department of Justice

U.S. Department of Justice, 1970–2016

Source: "Workload Statistics," available at https://www.justice.gov/atr/division-operations [last accessed May 23, 2019].

Equitable Growth

Now, we all know we can't just turn back time. But what we can do is identify the current challenges and meet them with new and innovative solutions. This chapter outlines the current challenges; the next outlines the solutions. Identifying the problems and adverse consequences associated with the current state of our antitrust laws is, actually, relatively easy. Stagnant laws, conservative court rulings, and, depending on the administration, lax antitrust enforcement have led to a series of anticompetitive mergers and acquisitions, exclusionary conduct, and industry concentration that have stifled competition. To get back to some semblance of fair competition, we must both modernize our laws to create a check on anticompetitive conduct going forward and look backward to investigate, and yes, even change, some of the past decisions.

The antitrust challenges faced by Americans today can roughly be divided into twelve categories:

1. **Runaway Corporate Consolidation,** which has led to a reduction in both start-ups and the percentage of people employed in new businesses;
2. **Greater Income/Wealth Inequality, Stagnant Wages, Higher Prices for Consumers,** and **Exacerbated Racial Disparities** (also discussed in Chapter 6);

3. **Lax Antitrust Enforcement** due to both political inaction and a lack of resources;

4. **Conservative Judges Making Conservative Antitrust Court Rulings,** which have made antitrust enforcement much more difficult and discouraged antitrust actions;

5. **Laws and Legal Standards That Don't Track the Times,** with particular industries—such as Big Tech and Big Pharma— effectively blocking changes to protect their monopoly power;

6. **The Power of Big Tech,** with the combined market capitalization of Alphabet (Google), Amazon, Apple, Facebook, and Microsoft soaring to more than $6.5 trillion in 2020;

7. **Horizontal Shareholding,** where wealthy businesspeople or large, institutional investors in the stock market own shares in multiple companies in the same industries that—at least ostensibly— "compete" against one another;

8. **Anticompetitive Practices That Hurt American Workers and Consumers,** such as the overuse of non-compete agreements, or practices that stifle innovation or consumer choice, such as patent system abuse;

9. **Big-Dollar Politics** that distort our democracy and give outsized power to corporate lobbyists and wealthy players (a subject of the last chapter);

10. **Media Consolidation** (also discussed in chapter 6), which affects the way Americans get and consume their news, as well as the content and reliability of that news;

11. **The Increasingly International Character of Commerce,** with international mergers and acquisitions making antitrust enforcement more complex than ever while leaving Americans at the whim of the global market's hurricane-force winds; and

12. **The Current Complex and Inaccessible Nature of Antitrust Issues,** which makes political and legal changes seem out of reach despite the glaring need for action.

Challenge 1—Corporate Consolidation. The first challenge involves mustering the political will to address a problem—runaway corporate consolidation—that too few, to date, even acknowledge exists. Bigness has become a major problem, and bigness means more barriers to entry for new market entrants, especially small businesses, the historic driver of so many American jobs and so much American innovation and competition.

As comedian John Oliver pointed out in 2017 on his show, *Last Week Tonight*, in a segment dedicated to corporate consolidation, every elected official regularly recites that small businesses are the backbone of the U.S. economy. However, in a well-deserved rant punctuated with both funny clips and a number of expletives about people's anger and frustration over everything from airline baggage fees (up to $4.2 billion in 2016 from $543 million in 2007) and cable companies to the monopoly power of banks and health-care companies, Oliver observed that "we seem to have forgotten how important antitrust is" because "this issue affects almost everything you do." "And if this whole story is infuriating you so much that you are yearning for the sweet escape of death," Oliver quipped toward the end of his segment, with a box popping up in the upper-left-hand corner of the screen highlighting the three players in the coffin industry (Hillenbrand, Matthews International, and Aurora), "well bad luck because the casket industry is controlled by these three companies."

In fact, Oliver is right, though after Matthews International and Aurora Casket merged in 2014 just *two* companies—Matthews and Indiana's Batesville Casket Company, owned by behemoth Hillenbrand—control 82 percent of the coffin industry. As industries have become more concentrated, the number of new businesses has fallen sharply in recent years, with CNN noting in 2016 that 452,835 firms were started in 2014, a number far below the number of new firms—614,024—started in 2006, just eight years earlier. Approximately 433,000 new firms were launched in 2016, with start-up activity—according to a recent report—falling "well below historical norms." The United States, the report noted, "continues to start and scale new firms at far lower rates and in far smaller numbers than it did in the past." That trend, the report's authors observed, "has serious implications for the future potential of the economy to generate wage growth, productivity advances, and a balanced geography of economic development." The pandemic, of course, only exacerbated the difficulties faced by small entrepreneurs to start new businesses and access venture capital and reduced the financial stability and number of small businesses at an even greater rate, with

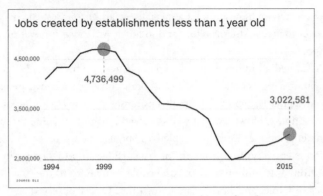

New businesses have traditionally been major drivers of employment. In the past two decades, the American economy experienced a decline in the number of people employed by new businesses.

Bloomberg News reporting in July 2020 that "Covid-19 Is Bankrupting American Companies at a Relentless Pace."

In mid-July 2019 testimony before the Antitrust Subcommittee of the Judiciary Committee of the U.S. House of Representatives, Tim Wu—a Columbia University professor—outlined what is at stake. "For more than a century now," he testified, "the key economic advantage of the United States has been its startup economy and capacity for launching new industries." As he explained in his testimony, "This is innovation, yes, but of a particularly important kind. It is not just the improvement of mousetraps, but rather the pioneering of entire industries that, in time, come to employ millions and generate trillions. Being the place companies get their start has given the United States an extraordinary advantage over the last century, and helped make it the world's preeminent economic power." "But this advantage, which we sometimes take for granted," Wu cautioned, "is now threatened by excessive consolidation in the U.S. economy. The most obvious symptom is the decline of the American startup."

Wu's message is clear: we need to do more to combat corporate consolidation, and the enforcement of the nation's antitrust laws should be part of that. Citing a June 2018 study conducted by the Brookings Institution, Wu—after examining the data—reminded Congress, "Startup rates have declined drastically across the economy. In an extraordinary development, the number of companies shutting down has grown to match the number that are starting up." As Wu also told the House Antitrust Subcommittee members that day, "The Department of Labor shows a declining number of people working for startups, while the Center for American Entrepreneurship documents a relative decline in American [venture capital] funding relative to the rest of the world." Even before the pandemic, Wu predicted, "We may, in short, be entering a 'startup winter.'"

While the new start-up data Wu cited in his testimony is extremely troubling, the COVID-19 pandemic has, perhaps counterintuitively, recently led to more new start-ups, with new business applications increasing. Wharton management professor Ethan Mollick explains, "In a normal recession, we see that business starts to drop." But he points to the reality that "people are being forced to start new businesses" as their places of work shut down, adding this optimistic note: "We find that during college breaks, the number of startups launched goes way up because college students have idle time to launch companies." "Typically," Mollick cautions of the new uptick in start-ups, observing that there are, of course, always exceptions to the general rule, "if you launch a company during a recession, your company does worse in the long term."

Along with a general concern about entrepreneurial activity and the health, quality, and staying power of American start-ups, there's also no denying a related problem—as discussed in chapter 6—that big businesses are getting bigger. Amazon's $50 billion valuation in 2010 jumped to more than $1.5 trillion by 2020, with one analyst predicting its market capitalization will soon exceed $2 trillion; Walmart went from a $179 billion valuation in 2010 to a $339 billion valuation in 2020; and Home Depot's valuation skyrocketed from $47 billion in 2010 to $267 billion in 2020. As of mid-2020, Apple and Microsoft both had market capitalizations of more than $1.6 trillion, with Apple's market capitalization quickly climbing to more than $2 trillion that same year in the midst of the pandemic.

The news reports—and the reports of nonprofits—help tell the story. In October 2015, a *Wall Street Journal* article, titled "Wave of Megadeals Tests Antitrust Limits in U.S.," noted that "a growing number of industries in the U.S. are dominated by a shrinking number of companies." "Big companies are much more dominant than they were even 15 years ago,"

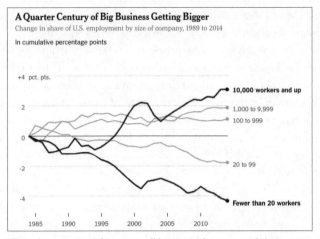

A Quarter Century of Big Business Getting Bigger
Change in share of U.S. employment by size of company, 1989 to 2014

In cumulative percentage points

+4 pct. pts.

2 — 10,000 workers and up

1,000 to 9,999

100 to 999

0

20 to 99

-2

-4 — Fewer than 20 workers

1985　1990　1995　2000　2005　2010

Throughout America's history, small businesses have powered the country's economy. Since the 1980s, however, a smaller percentage of Americans actually work for small businesses. The main culprit: corporate consolidation. Source: David Leonhardt, "The Charts That Show How Big Business Is Winning," *New York Times,* June 18, 2018.

David Leonhardt reported in *The New York Times* in 2018, with the Open Markets Institute—a nonprofit that advocates for antitrust reform—also releasing employment data to prove it. In 1989, 21 percent of the American workforce was employed by companies with fewer than twenty workers; by 2014, only 18 percent of the workforce worked for such employers. By contrast, the percentage of Americans working for companies employing more than ten thousand workers increased from 24 percent in 1998 to 28 percent in 2014. The Open Markets Institute, in analyzing twenty-six different industries, found that in more than half of those industries just two firms now control more than half of the market.

One glaring consolidation example is what we're seeing with pharmacies. The three largest pharmacy chains—CVS Health, Walgreens Boots Alliance, and Walmart—collectively operate more than 20,000 stores in the United States, generating hundreds of billions of dollars in annual revenue, while approximately 1,230 independent rural pharmacies have closed, with fewer than 6,400 remaining as of July 2018. A total of 630 rural communities that had at least one independent, chain, or franchise retail pharmacy in 2003 had none just fifteen years later. As

Lisa Esposito, a writer for *U.S. News & World Report,* wrote in 2018 of small towns in America now without pharmacies, "Residents may need to travel far to fill prescriptions, or turn to mail-order arrangements without the benefit of in-person counseling or easy ability to ask questions about taking medications safely." And often, life-saving drugs are controlled—and thus priced—by a dwindling number of companies. Finally, as if it wasn't hard enough for small pharmacies, in November 2020 Amazon launched its own online pharmacy, putting in further jeopardy independent retail pharmacies in small towns and rural communities.

Small independent pharmacies are being forced out of business not only by the Walmarts and the Amazons but by pharmacy benefit managers. "If your local small town pharmacy is shut down, this is probably a big reason why," observes Representative John Forbes, an Iowa legislator who runs an independent pharmacy and closely tracks developments in the industry. Even before the COVID-19 pandemic, a University of Illinois study published in a respected medical journal found that one in eight U.S. pharmacies closed between 2009 and 2015 and that the majority of them were independent pharmacies located in low-income neighborhoods.

And it doesn't end with pharmacies. There is no question that over

Independent pharmacies are struggling to survive as the industry has become highly concentrated. Cartoon by George Russell, *Marin Independent Journal,* 2019.

the past few decades, almost all industries—from consumer products, to professional services, to online platforms—have witnessed corporate concentration to one degree or another, often on an unprecedented scale. Take accounting. Back in the 1970s and 1980s, when I was in high school and college, there were eight large, multinational accounting firms. The "Big Eight" consisted of Arthur Andersen; Coopers & Lybrand; Deloitte, Haskins & Sells; Ernst & Whinney/Ernst & Ernst; Peat Marwick; Price Waterhouse; Touche Ross; and Arthur Young. In 1988, the Big Eight did the audits for approximately 98 percent of U.S. public companies by sales. But the Big Eight became the Big Six, then decreased to just five firms. In 2002, following the Enron scandal, Arthur Andersen's collapse turned the Big Five into the Big Four. We are now down to just Ernst & Young, Deloitte Touche, KPMG, and PricewaterhouseCoopers, the firms now cynically referred to, in a nod to college basketball, as the Final Four.

Or take the publishing industry, where—due to a series of mergers and acquisitions that shuttered or combined major publishing houses—we were taken down to the Big Five: Penguin Random House (which is in fact controlled by a German media company, Bertelsmann), HarperCollins, Simon & Schuster, Hachette Book Group, and Macmillan. One recent megamerger occurred in October 2012, when the parent companies Pearson and Bertelsmann agreed to combine Penguin and Random House—then the country's two largest trade publishers—in a joint venture that, according to those pushing for it, would allow them to better compete in the e-book market against Amazon and Apple. During this same time period, an antitrust dispute involving Amazon's $9.99 e-book pricing policy and Apple's agreement with major publishing companies to up the price of e-books led to a protracted court battle in which Apple ultimately paid out $450 million for its anticompetitive conduct. After ViacomCBS announced that its subsidiary publishing arm, Simon & Schuster, was up for sale and that final bids were due before Thanksgiving Day in 2020, the Society of Children's Book Writers and Illustrators aptly posed this question: "Will the 'Big Five' Become the 'Big Four'?" As of this writing, it appears that there will be an attempt to do just that since it was announced in late November 2020 that Bertelsmann—which now owns *all* of Penguin Random House—would buy Simon & Schuster for $2.18 billion in what was described as an "all-cash deal" that was "expected to close" in 2021.

Americans may still love an underdog or a David-versus-Goliath story, but these days the publishing industry has become—truth be told—a Goliath-versus-Goliath story. It pits one Goliath, Amazon, against other big companies. Indeed, Penguin Random House's main competitor, Amazon, has itself—in the words of one commentator, Alex Shephard—"spent the past several years accruing significant power in the industry." When people shop for books these days, they often shop online through Amazon.com, spelling the demise of many local bookstores while putting others at risk of closure, especially with the onset of the pandemic. "When it comes to publishing," Shephard observes, "Amazon has arguably never been more powerful." According to *Wired,* Amazon remains "the most dominant force in American bookselling today," accounting for more than "90 percent of ebooks and audiobooks, and around 42 to 45 percent of print sales."

The consolidation and reduction in publishing competition have, quite obviously, been bad news for most authors, those who use their creativity to inform, entertain, and inspire us. A June 2018 report, released by the Authors' Licensing and Collecting Society, found that author

Consumers are buying more online than ever before, and the 2020 COVID-19 pandemic in the United States accelerated that trend, resulting in a lot more economic power for the Big Tech companies and a lot more challenges for small businesses. Cartoon by Kim Warp, *The New Yorker,* 2019.

"It warms my heart to see their look of hope that we might not just buy it online."

earnings have fallen by 42 percent over the past ten years. That means fewer people can make their living by writing books. Back in 2015, the Authors Guild, the American Booksellers Association, and the Association of Authors' Representatives all asked the Justice Department to look into how Amazon's dominance has affected the book business and the interests of writers. In 2019, in a twenty-two-page letter, Oren Teicher, the CEO of the American Booksellers Association, wrote this to the Justice Department: "When examining the company's history and present business model, it is clear that Amazon is able to use its dominance to manipulate market structures, suppress competition, and harm consumers and other stakeholders. In turn, Amazon is able to further expand its market share."

The issue is not, of course, just about authors and books. Amazon has changed America's entire retail landscape, and the pandemic has increased its market power even more. In 2020, Amazon's stock price skyrocketed to more than $3,000 per share, with one analyst—after taking note of an Amazon earnings report that far exceeded expectations—observing that "COVID-19 has been like injecting Amazon with a growth hormone." Also, Amazon has opened brick-and-mortar bookstores across the country and is competing ever more with independent bookstores.

As evidenced by the sheer number of Amazon deliveries, Amazon has clearly forever changed the way Americans shop—as well as the way individuals and businesses store digital information. During the pre-pandemic 2018 holiday shopping season, more than 80 percent of surveyed consumers said they would be searching on Amazon, with online shopping accounting for more than 46 percent of gift purchases. On its platform, Amazon sells books and electronics, but also everything from tools and home and kitchen products to digital music and automotive parts and accessories. After Amazon in 2018 bought PillPack, an online pharmacy, for $753 million, making a move into yet another industry, it followed up—as noted previously—with Amazon Pharmacy's launch in November 2020, adding to its online empire. One of Amazon's subsidiaries, Amazon Web Services (AWS), now has one million active users, customers in 190 countries, and five times more developed cloud infrastructure as its next fourteen competitors combined. According to recently published statistics, "one-third of people who visit websites on the Internet daily access websites which are powered by AWS," and AWS now has a 41.5 percent share of the public cloud market, more than Microsoft, Google, IBM, and Rackspace combined. AWS, it has been reported, "has decreased its prices at least as many as 60 times since its launch" in 2002 yet has "generated a whopping $26 billion in revenue for parent Amazon in 2018."

Of course, once a company achieves dominance in a market, it can decide to raise prices, too. That is the recurring problem with market dominance throughout history. Using one dominant firm's services can be easy, convenient, and sometimes even cheap, but over time, with no competition to push it, the dominant firm inevitably raises its prices because it has no incentive to do otherwise (see the cable industry example, where rising cable prices have far outpaced inflation).

Ironically, when big companies attempt to merge with other big companies, they now often cite the need to compete against Amazon—in what might be called "the Amazon defense." The line of reasoning they employ: Amazon is so big and powerful that we must become so much bigger and so much more powerful to possibly compete. For example, when Office Depot and Staples sought to merge, in what would have been a $6.3 billion deal, the two companies contended that Amazon was ramping up its corporate supply business, thus supposedly necessitating the merger. The FTC, which thankfully blocked the proposed Staples–Office Depot merger, didn't buy—and successfully beat back—that argument in federal court. The FTC challenged Staples' proposed acquisition of Office Depot because it would have effectively eliminated direct competition for large business-to-business customers, with the FTC contending that the combined firm would account for 70 percent of that market and would thus be anticompetitive. The entry of Amazon as an online office supply competitor thus did not deter the FTC from suing to stop the merger, which was ultimately called off in May 2016.

A surge of corporate power has swept across the American landscape over the past few decades. And while the consolidation and merger trends and growth have been most dramatic in the tech area, where Google, for instance, now controls more than 90 percent of the global online search market, it is by no means solely in the purview of tech. Consolidation has threatened—or even ended—some people's way of life as companies, concerned about quarterly earnings or short-term

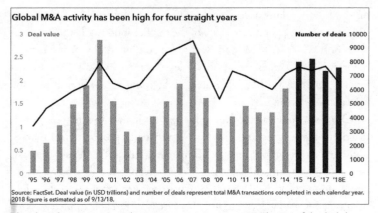

Global M&A activity has been high for four straight years

Source: FactSet. Deal value (in USD trillions) and number of deals represent total M&A transactions completed in each calendar year. 2018 figure is estimated as of 9/13/18.

This chart depicts merger and acquisition activity since 1995. The size of the deals has gotten bigger in recent years. Consolidation is a global phenomenon, and it is affecting scores of industries. If capitalism is to work for everyone, it is critical that antitrust laws be more rigorously enforced.

profits, suddenly decide to close individual factories or entire divisions. As companies have combined, Americans in states like Michigan, Ohio, Pennsylvania, and Wisconsin have gotten caught in the crosshairs when manufacturing plants have closed, small farms have shuttered, and mom-and-pop diners and stores have been put out of business. Certain regions and localities have been hit particularly hard, leading to economic inequality and considerable hardship. Over the years, the rich have gotten richer, and the poor have gotten poorer, with hardworking farmers running smaller farms hit particularly hard. In 2018, my hometown paper, the *Star Tribune,* reported these startling statistics about our country's farm economy: "While the vast majority of dairies in the U.S. are still small with an average of about 240 cows, farmers have been quitting for decades. The number of U.S. dairies fell from 678,000 in 1970 to fewer than 40,000 this year." This massive upheaval in the economy has—and rightfully so—led to anger and resentment as people just do their best to stay afloat.

At the Heartland Forum in Storm Lake, Iowa, where I spoke in March 2019, Aaron Lehman, the president of the Iowa Farmers Union, gave his own dire warning about the treacherous waters ahead. As he put it, "Farm income has been dropping for 5 years. According to USDA statistics, the median farmer is losing money again this year. The average age of the Iowa farmer is over 59 years old. Agribusiness consolidation is at an all-time high." He closed with a statement that describes the anxieties and concerns of so many small-business owners, whether they be farmers on the prairie, workers on the manufacturing lines, or American entrepreneurs struggling to bring a new and innovative product to market. "Our challenges," as Lehman said in referring to the across-the-board consolidation we are seeing, "are huge."

Challenge 2—Increased Income/Wealth Inequality, Stagnant Wages, Higher Prices for Consumers, and Exacerbated Racial Disparities. Corporate consolidation and the market power of monopolies lead to higher prices for consumers and lower or stagnated wages for American workers and have fueled runaway executive compensation and income and wealth inequality. A *Wall Street Journal* analysis showed that the median compensation for 132 CEOs of S&P 500 companies was $12.4 million in 2018, but the wages of American workers have not kept pace with the growth in productivity—not by a long shot. "From 1979 to 2017," a February 2019 report of the Economic Policy Institute notes, "productivity grew 70.3 percent, while hourly compensation of production and nonsupervisory workers grew just 11.1 percent." From 1978 to 2018, another report of the Economic Policy Institute finds, CEO compensation grew by 940 percent, while the wages for the typical worker rose by just 11.9 percent.

America's antitrust laws, as originally designed, were intended to decrease such inequality. As Republican senator John Sherman, in defending the law that bears his name, emphasized in 1890, no social problem "is more threatening than the inequality of condition, of wealth, and opportunity that has grown within a single generation out of the concentration of capital into vast combinations to control production and trade and to break down competition." Indeed, if the antitrust laws are vigorously enforced, Americans will once again be in a better position to confront the challenges of wealth and income inequality. "Antitrust is an important policy tool for addressing labor and inequality problems," Diana Moss, the president of the American Antitrust Institute has observed. Although Moss notes that "lax antitrust enforcement is hardly the sole cause of America's labor and inequality problems," she emphasized that antitrust enforcers can—and should—use the tools they have at their disposal to block mergers that would, for example, create monopoly power capable of depressing wages.

As also discussed in the last chapter, taking on monopoly power by reinvigorating antitrust enforcement will also help to confront the challenges of a shrinking middle class and the racial disparities in America. Monopoly pricing robs American communities and consumers of their hard-earned money, with monopoly power subject to multiple forms of abuse, thereby exacerbating inequality and racial disparities. Big businesses have engaged in racial profiling, discriminatory hiring and promotion practices, and redlining, whereby minority communities were systemically denied credit, insurance, or other financial services. Wealth and income inequality especially hurts low-income workers—so many of them people of color—struggling to get by paycheck to paycheck, making it difficult to access capital to start a new business. For those already in poverty, increased consolidation, fewer start-ups, and less small-business employment mean less opportunity for them.

As a report of the Open Markets Institute observes of the relationship between monopoly power and income inequality, "The rapid rise in monopolization over the last generation has increased inequality in several ways. Monopolization means the powerful can charge citizens more for such basic goods as health care, housing, and travel." "In concrete terms, monopoly pricing on goods and services turns the disposable income of the many into capital gains, dividends, and executive compensation for the few," Lina Khan and Sandeep Vaheesan write in the *Harvard Law and Policy Review.* "Monopolization," the report of the Open Markets Institute emphasizes, "also means that the people who control corporations can pay workers less, knowing workers have fewer places to sell their labor." As the report further notes, "Monopoly, like most forms of concentrated power, is often brought to bear against the least advantaged in an unequal society." Even the use of artificial intelligence and algorithms—as the Federal Trade Commission has observed of the technologies so often employed in business today—carries "the potential for unfair or discriminatory outcomes or the perpetuation of existing socioeconomic disparities." In the hands of a monopolist, of course, the risk of misuse is even greater.

Traditionally, the antitrust laws helped *fight* discrimination, whether it was price discrimination or racial discrimination. People may not commonly associate antitrust laws with antidiscrimination efforts, but they should. The antitrust laws were, in fact, used effectively in the 1960s to stop discrimination in housing and employment. For example, the Sherman Act was used to integrate African Americans into the medical profession by stopping the abhorrent practice by Chicago-area hospitals and medical organizations of barring Black physicians from joining their staffs and their ranks. "In 1964," one commentator, Brian Feldman, observes, "Reginald Johnson, secretary of the National Urban League, encouraged the use of antitrust laws to break up housing segregation in the nation's cities. . . . Antitrust actions taken by the American Civil Liberties Union, the NAACP Legal Defense and Educational Fund, and other organizations helped force desegregation of neighborhoods and realty boards in cities including Trenton, St. Louis, Pittsburgh, Akron, and New York City."

Such antitrust actions opened up greater economic opportunities in cities and towns throughout the country, including in the Deep South, where the legacy of slavery had such deep roots. "While there were 70,000 black-owned businesses in the United States in 1920," one working paper notes, "their total more than doubled across the civil rights era so that by 1969 they totaled 163,000. . . . Just under 1,000 of these businesses, totaling 988, were in Birmingham, Alabama, . . . which was a focal point of the Civil Rights Movement when Martin Luther King led nonviolent marchers against Chief Eugene Connor's high-pressure water hoses, cattle prods, and attack dogs."

Just as historically Black colleges and universities give educational opportunities to African American communities, minority-owned businesses give communities of color economic power that translates into real political power, and that has made a major difference in lifting up members of those communities. Proper enforcement of the nation's antidiscrimination and antitrust laws is one tool that we, as a country, have at our disposal to stamp out discrimination and exclusionary conduct and discriminatory barriers to competition. We should use that tool to make our society better.

Tilting the economic playing field against entrepreneurs, small-market participants, individual consumers, and those who have faced historical discrimination in favor of monopolists, cartels, and billionaire corporate titans is not only unfair; it is unconscionable. Everyone—

from minimum-wage workers to the owners of small businesses and start-ups—should have an equal chance and an honest opportunity to compete in the American economy.

Challenge 3—Lax Antitrust Enforcement and a Lack of Resources. While Congress must act decisively to correct the imbalance of power that exists between large corporations and American consumers and workers, the antitrust laws must be enforced with much greater vigor by the executive branch to ensure that inequalities of wealth and power are not further exacerbated by unfair or anticompetitive conduct. As President Theodore Roosevelt once put it, "The great corporations which we have grown to speak of rather loosely as trusts are the creatures of the State, and the State not only has the right to control them, but it is in duty bound to control them wherever the need of such control is shown."

In fact, small businesses, workers, and consumers should be able to depend upon steady and vigorous enforcement of the laws, including the antitrust laws, to safeguard their ability to compete, to earn living wages, and to make goods and services affordable. If market participants, working people, and consumers are to have a fighting chance, antitrust enforcement is indispensable to foster free competition, fair wages, more fluid labor markets, and innovation. As Justice Thurgood Marshall put it in *United States v. Topco Associates, Inc.* (1972), "Antitrust

In 1967, Justice Thurgood Marshall became the first African American justice to serve on the U.S. Supreme Court. A graduate of Howard University School of Law, he founded the NAACP Legal Defense and Educational Fund, arguing cases such as *Brown v. Board of Education* before the U.S. Supreme Court before becoming an associate justice of the Court, serving in that role until 1991.

laws in general, and the Sherman Act in particular, are the Magna Carta of free enterprise. They are as important to the preservation of economic freedom and our free enterprise system as the Bill of Rights is to the protection of our fundamental personal freedoms. And the freedom guaranteed each and every business, no matter how small, is the freedom to compete—to assert with vigor, imagination, devotion, and ingenuity whatever economic muscle it can muster."

Recent research shows that the failure to beef up antitrust enforcement will have serious consequences for America's economy and innovation. Writing in the *Harvard Business Review* in 2016, Justus Haucap, an economist, and Joel Stiebale, a professor of empirical industrial economics, describe how their analysis of sixty-five pharma mergers found that antitrust authorities have been "too lenient" when it comes to drug company mergers. Such mergers, they found, not only reduce innovation and research and development at the merging firms but also are "having a sizable negative impact on innovation and R&D *at the combined firm's rivals.*" As they explain, "It's not unexpected that merging companies reduce their R&D spending following a merger. That may be due to the cost savings of pooling efforts and combining their labors. Research has shown that pharma mergers reduce innovation. But what's surprising and troubling is that our new evidence shows that merging companies' *competitors* also spend less on R&D after the merger. . . . On average, patenting and R&D expenditures of non-merging competitors also fell—by more than 20%—within four years after a merger."

Or take the cable industry. Back in 2011, Comcast entered into a consent decree with the Department of Justice and the Federal Communications Commission to limit the harmful competitive effects of its acquisition of NBCUniversal—an acquisition that many opposed altogether. There were competition issues while that decree was in effect, but they got even worse after those conditions expired in September 2018, leading consumer advocates to worry about Comcast's prioritizing the delivery of its own content online or withholding NBC content from competitors. In fact, in 2018, the American Cable Association—a group that represents smaller broadband and cable providers—urged the Justice Department's Antitrust Division to investigate Comcast's practices, specifically asking it to look into "harms stemming from the dominant communications firm's control of cable systems, TV stations,

The pharmaceutical industry, like so many industries, has consolidated over the last few decades. The result? Higher prices for consumers and for life-saving medications. Cartoon by John Darkow, *Columbia Daily Tribune*, 2016.

and regional sports networks concentrated in some of the largest local markets in the country." The association pointed out that with the expiration of restrictions imposed on Comcast, Comcast's "ability to raise programming prices in local markets is unmatched."

A healthy capitalist economy thus depends on antitrust enforcement. Antitrust actions, it must be remembered, are not designed to destroy competitors; they are designed to protect competition. And new competition can work wonders by inspiring new products and services. As antitrust expert Tim Wu points out, the breakup of corporations can spawn innovation and "transform a stagnant industry into a dynamic one." "In reality," he observes, making the analogy to corporate spin-offs that occur all the time in business, "a large corporation is made up of sub-units, whether functional or regional, or independent operations that have been previously acquired." Just as weeding a garden or thinning a forest can allow new plants or trees to grow, sometimes the solution to reinvigorating competition is to unwind transactions (see resulting consumer benefits from the breakup of AT&T) that have crowded out vigorous competition.

The country's antitrust laws, which were intended to keep the American economy in balance for the benefit of all, have not been updated—or interpreted or enforced—in a manner to keep up with the times. That needs to change, and I'll offer some concrete prescriptions for change in the next chapter, including the appointment of government antitrust enforcers who will assiduously and aggressively enforce competition policy. But right now, the U.S. government's antitrust enforcers don't even have the resources they need to monitor compliance with the existing laws. Staffing levels at the Federal Trade Commission and the Justice Department's Antitrust Division have been woefully inadequate, and lax enforcement has led to megamergers on an unprecedented scale—megamergers that enforcers, in large part because of the lack of resources, are not even well positioned to adequately evaluate, much less go back in time and reinvestigate previously approved or unexamined mergers and acquisitions if competition in the industry lags. Now, not every merger or acquisition is bad for competition and consumers. But every proposed major merger, as well as efforts by dominant firms to gobble up nascent competitors (see Facebook's acquisition of Instagram and WhatsApp), should certainly be scrutinized properly. The antitrust enforcers must have the proper allocation of resources to do their work

For two decades, cable TV rates have outpaced inflation, rising at more than double the rate of inflation. Cartoon by David Sipress, *The New Yorker*, 2016.

"*We're a cable giant, you're a cable giant. Together we can be a giant cable giant.*"

before a proposed deal gets approved, rejected, or allowed to go forward with appropriate conditions.

Agency budgets matter, and how budgets are funded—or not funded—has real-world consequences. The Justice Department's Antitrust Division is now heavily dependent on filing fees to pay its attorneys, staff, and experts. From the very first $500,000 appropriation for antitrust enforcement in 1904 until the $44,937,000 congressional appropriation in fiscal year 1989, the Antitrust Division was funded solely by direct appropriations from Congress. Starting in 1990, pursuant to a change in the Clayton Act, however, the Antitrust Division began to get a portion of its funding from filing, or user, fees. In 1990, while Congress gave the Antitrust Division a direct appropriation of $34,317,000, it got $13,519,000 of its revenue from filing fees. Since then, the Antitrust Division's dependence on filing fees—money shelled out by companies eager to acquire other companies—has only grown.

Fast-forward to changes to premerger filing notification requirements of the Hart-Scott-Rodino Antitrust Improvements Act (1976), which became effective February 1, 2001, and the Antitrust Division became even more dependent on the payment of "user fees" that don't even cover the cost of what's required to be analyzed. The Hart-Scott-Rodino Act provided for the creation of a tiered fee structure and the payment by companies of graduated premerger fees (split equally between the Justice Department's Antitrust Division and the FTC) depending on the size of the deal in question. In fiscal year 2017, while Congress directly appropriated $39,977,000 to the Antitrust Division, the Antitrust Division's total budget of $164,977,000 was heavily dependent on the collection of $125,000,000 in filing fees.

When it comes to staffing levels, the U.S. government statistics are sobering. At the end of 1980, there were 453 full-time attorneys employed in the Justice Department's Antitrust Division. At the end of fiscal year 2017, the Antitrust Division had only 330 attorneys on staff along with 136 paralegals, 50 economists, and 150 other professional staff. The staffing levels at the Federal Trade Commission's Bureau of Competition, which is also tasked with enforcing the nation's antitrust laws, have also remained flat. In fact, the overall number of employees at the FTC has fallen off since the Reagan presidency. In fiscal year 1980, the FTC had 1,719 employees. But over the course of the 1980s, the FTC essentially became a shadow of its former self. By fiscal year 1989, the FTC's full-time staff had fallen to 894 employees, with the number of full-time employees not cracking 1,000 again until fiscal year 2001. It was not until 2009 that the FTC's staffing level climbed above 1,100 full-time employees, with that number fluctuating only slightly since that time. In 2019, the total number of the FTC's full-time equivalents stood at only 1,101 employees, a staffing level far below what it had been four decades earlier. And in its fiscal year 2021 budget request, submitted in February 2020, the Trump Administration's FTC asked for enough money to cover only 1,140 full-time equivalent positions. While both the FTC and the Antitrust Division of the Justice Department were finally given more resources at the end of 2020 ($18 million for DOJ's Antitrust Division and $20 million for the FTC), the agencies, who we now expect to take on mammoth companies like Facebook and Google and their droves of lawyers, are still significantly underfunded for the task at hand. Without sufficient personnel levels, it's simply impossible to do all the work that needs to be done.

In September 2019, the Washington Center for Equitable Growth—a nonprofit research organization dedicated to advancing evidence-backed ideas and policies to promote strong, stable, and broad-based economic growth—issued a sobering report titled "The State of U.S. Federal Antitrust Enforcement." It found that criminal antitrust filings have fallen to historic lows, that U.S. merger enforcement actions have not kept pace with increased merger filings, that U.S. GDP growth had outpaced growth in antitrust appropriations, and that civil non-merger actions and U.S. antitrust enforcement resources had recently fallen, too.

And we all know this: while the antitrust staffing levels have decreased, the quantity and complexity of the work the agencies *should* be doing has increased exponentially. First, the American economy has expanded, which greatly adds to the work to be done by the U.S. government's antitrust officials. The United States has seen recessions and a major financial crisis since the early 1980s, but (with the exception of the pandemic, which plunged U.S. gross domestic product, or GDP, in the second quarter of 2020, with the U.S. economy contracting by 3.5 percent in 2020), the country's GDP has grown over the decades, giving those who investigate anticompetitive conduct much more to do. And even with the economic contraction brought on by the pandemic, companies are still either merging or contemplating mergers with startling regularity.

Second, with the sophisticated and uniquely situated technology industry growing rapidly, the nature of commerce has grown ever more complex. The thought of a small number of government antitrust lawyers going head to head with legions of lawyers at Facebook and Google is very concerning. Because of the Hart-Scott-Rodino Act, premerger notifications must be filed for certain transactions, providing valuable data to gauge just how much antitrust enforcement work there actually is to do. In 2009, the Justice Department's Antitrust Division received 716 Hart-Scott-Rodino (HSR) premerger notifications. In 2017, by contrast, the number of HSR premerger notifications had climbed to 2,059, although the number of HSR investigations initiated stayed flat (no doubt, in part, because of the lack of sufficient resources). While forty-nine HSR investigations were initiated in 2009, a slightly smaller number of such investigations—forty-eight—were initiated in 2017. When the number of HSR filings has almost tripled, one would expect to see far more investigations to follow. That simply has not happened.

To add to everything else, the FTC and the Justice Department's Antitrust Division now routinely need to review multi*billion*-dollar deals, not just multi*million*-dollar deals. In May 2016, before the November 2016 presidential election, *The Economist* reported that "a $10 trillion wave of mergers since 2008 has raised levels of concentration" in America's economy. Between 2015 and 2018, there were, in fact, sixty-one mergers or acquisitions where the acquiring firm was valued at more than $10 billion, only four of which were successfully blocked by the antitrust laws. Noting the fury of voters, *The Economist* pointed out "a corrosive lack of competition" in America's economy—something that surely drove a fair number of voters to the polls. "Microsoft," the article's author emphasized, "is making double the profits it did when antitrust regulators targeted the software firm in 2000. Our analysis of census data suggests that two-thirds of the economy's 900-odd industries have become more concentrated since 1997." The magazine lamented, "America is meant to be a temple of free enterprise. It isn't."

Keeping a better eye on corporate consolidation—and then checking and rolling back such consolidation—are critical to the long-term health of America's economy. If no one is paying attention—and if no one is stepping up to ask the tough questions of market participants and demand a halt to anticompetitive actions—then massive corporations will continue to steamroll the public. As Barry Lynn warns in *Cornered: The New Monopoly Capitalism and the Economics of Destruction* (2010), "The making of monopoly—the imposition of complete or near-complete control over an activity that had been organized in an open or semi-open market—is once again the business of business in America." Instead of monopoly power, the American people need and deserve a vibrant labor market and vibrant markets for goods and services to keep innovation levels high, prices low, and the middle class strong. Without adequate monetary resources for antitrust enforcers, the FTC and the Justice Department's Antitrust Division will never be able to monitor, investigate, and prosecute the anticompetitive conduct as they should.

The laudable goal of antitrust law is—at its core—simply to ensure free and fair competition, the most important pillar of American capitalism. If America's economy is to work for everyone (and it must), then entrepreneurship should be rewarded, competition must be robust, and monopolists and cartels (for example, sellers operating under a price-fixing agreement for purposes of inflating prices and restricting competition) must be held accountable. Those who violate the law should not be getting a real-world version of the Monopoly game's get-out-of-jail-free cards.

Challenge 4—Conservative Courts and Conservative Antitrust Rulings. This is a big one. The federal courts, including the U.S. Supreme Court, have become increasingly hostile to antitrust claims. Erwin Chemerinsky—a highly respected voice in the legal academy and now the dean at Berkeley's law school—has called the current U.S. Supreme Court "the most pro-business Supreme Court there has been since the mid-1930s" (and that was before Ruth Bader Ginsburg died and was replaced by Amy Coney Barrett). And through the years, other prominent experts have concurred. For example, Adam Feldman, who specializes in sophisticated empirical analysis of Supreme Court decisions for the well-known *SCOTUS* blog, called the Supreme Court of the United States "the big business court."

The golden age of antitrust enforcement, which relied heavily on the willingness of the courts to enforce the law, is thus now far back in the rearview mirror, replaced by what has been called a New Gilded

Age. My colleague Senator Sheldon Whitehouse of Rhode Island has in fact meticulously documented how, in more than seventy recent cases, "justices appointed by Republican presidents have, with remarkable consistency, delivered rulings that advantage big corporate and special interests." At the Kavanaugh hearing, Senator Whitehouse showed and spoke about how, as a D.C. Circuit Court judge, Brett Kavanaugh had "voted to advance far-right and corporate interests a striking 91 percent of the time."

The Trump administration, by coordinating with the former Senate majority leader, Mitch McConnell, appointed three new Supreme Court justices, along with a slew of lower federal court judges. Notoriously, Mitch McConnell brazenly prevented the appointment of President Obama's highly qualified nominee, Judge Merrick Garland, to the Supreme Court, an act that will have decades-long ramifications for American jurisprudence. The confirmation of Justice Neil Gorsuch instead of Judge Garland (now attorney general), coupled with McConnell's bare-knuckle tactics in ramming Judge Kavanaugh's nomination through the Senate and then reversing himself on no-election-year appointments after Justice Ruth Bader Ginsburg's death to push through conservative icon Amy Coney Barrett in one of the fastest Supreme Court confirmations in recent history, has moved the Supreme Court further to the right on business issues.

These days, the conservative U.S. Supreme Court occasionally surprises the public—and the presidents who appointed its members—with rulings protecting the Affordable Care Act, DREAMers, the LGBTQ community, and the integrity of election results. But the Supreme Court of late regularly decides disputes against workers and unions and in favor of big corporations—the trend my colleague Sheldon Whitehouse pointed out so effectively during several Senate Judiciary Committee nomination hearings. Indeed, the Supreme Court—often in close, highly divided opinions, many decided on 5–4 votes—has issued a whole host of rulings adversely affecting minority voting rights, union rights, and individual workers' rights, such as its 2007 decision against Lilly Ledbetter. In one of those 5–4 decisions, *Epic Systems Corp. v. Lewis* (2018), the Supreme Court ruled that employers could continue to require workers to sign arbitration clauses that block workers' access to the courts. Ironically, there is actually nothing "pro-business" at all—or, for that matter, particularly conservative, at least in the traditional sense—about the Supreme Court's thwarting antitrust enforcement (except, perhaps, for the individual businesses that the Court has allowed to escape antitrust liability for their monopolistic, anticompetitive conduct). Instead of defending the free-enterprise system, the Court has enabled—and thus encouraged—behavior that harms competition.

The Supreme Court's rightward shift is not new. Ronald Reagan, whose administration so thoroughly embraced Robert Bork's antitrust philosophy, was able to name four justices, including Chief Justice William Rehnquist and Justice Antonin Scalia, to the nation's highest court. Reagan's successor, George H. W. Bush, also got to make two lifetime appointments (including the ultraconservative Clarence Thomas), as did his son George W. Bush. The impact of these appointments has been felt in many areas of the law, including in the antitrust arena. In 2008, the year of Barack Obama's election to the presidency, William Kolasky—a former deputy assistant attorney general in the Department of Justice's Antitrust Division—observed, "It has been more than fifteen years since the Supreme Court last decided an antitrust case in favor of a plaintiff.

The appointment of conservative U.S. Supreme Court justices has tipped the balance of the scales of justice against antitrust plaintiffs. The nation's antitrust laws are written in general language, so who interprets those laws really matters. Cartoon by Mischa Richter, *The New Yorker,* 1963.

Over this fifteen-year period, plaintiffs have gone o-for-16, with not a single plaintiff winning an antitrust case in the Supreme Court since the first George Bush was president." This record led *Antitrust* magazine to ask whether the Supreme Court's antitrust decisions represent 'The End of Antitrust as We Know It?' "

Unfortunately, in the last couple of decades, the U.S. Supreme Court has issued a number of rulings that make it harder for litigants to successfully bring antitrust lawsuits, including antitrust class actions. Due to such decisions, it has become tougher for plaintiffs and American consumers to even get their day in court. For example, in 2007, in *Bell Atlantic Corp. v. Twombly,* the Court—contorting the law to shield big companies from antitrust scrutiny—changed what had been a very uncontroversial, decades-old pleading standard, instead forcing antitrust plaintiffs to plead more than ever before in order to survive motions to dismiss in federal courts. Suddenly changing a long-standing interpretation of the Federal Rules of Civil Procedure may sound pretty bland and inconsequential, but it's not—especially if it limits access to the courts, which is exactly what the *Twombly* decision did. Likewise, a few years later, in *Comcast Corp. v. Behrend* (2013), the Supreme Court reversed the class-action certification of a proposed class of more than two million current and former Comcast subscribers who were seeking damages for alleged federal antitrust violations. Again, the Court sided with big business instead of consumers.

In the Supreme Court's haste to shield corporate defendants from antitrust scrutiny, the majority opinion in *Twombly* dismissed the plaintiffs' class-action lawsuit out of hand, meaning that no manager or executive for any of the corporate defendants ever had to produce a single email or sit for a deposition. The plaintiffs, who alleged they'd overpaid for telephone, internet, and other services from major phone companies, were precluded from obtaining any information at all from the defendants in the case. Remarkably, the defendants didn't even have to deny the complaint's allegations; the Supreme Court simply threw out the plaintiffs' lawsuit.

Oddly enough, in the *Twombly* ruling, the Supreme Court's majority opinion emphasized that, historically, "monopoly was the norm in telecommunications, not the exception." Noting that the major telephone companies were "born in that world" and "doubtless liked the world the way it was, and surely know the adage about him who lives by the sword," the Court stressed, "Hence, a natural explanation for the noncompetition alleged is that the former Government-sanctioned monopolists were sitting tight, expecting their neighbors to do the same thing." That the Supreme Court refused to let the lawsuit proceed because former monopolists were, in effect, refusing to compete because they were accustomed to behaving like monopolists and declining to compete for that reason is very troubling. Of course, it is inconceivable that the major telephone and internet providers would publicly admit any participation in an unlawful combination or conspiracy to violate the antitrust laws. The only way to truly discover if such a combination or conspiracy existed would have been to allow at least limited discovery of documents and other evidence, which the Supreme Court summarily denied. If that discovery showed the presence of an unlawful conspiracy, the plaintiffs in *Twombly* should have been given their day in court.

Other examples of U.S. Supreme Court decisions limiting the application of the antitrust laws or the ability of plaintiffs to successfully bring antitrust cases include *Verizon Communications Inc. v. Law Offices of Curtis V. Trinko, LLP* (2004), *Leegin Creative Leather Products, Inc. v. PSKS, Inc.* (2007), and *Ohio v. American Express Co.* (2018). *Trinko* held that the refusal of a monopolist to deal with a competitor usually does not constitute unlawful exclusionary conduct and that the Sherman Act "does not give judges *carte blanche* to insist that a monopolist alter its way of doing business whenever some other approach might yield greater competition." *Leegin* overruled a landmark Supreme Court decision, *Dr. Miles Medical Co. v. John D. Park & Sons Co.* (1911), which had ruled almost a full century earlier that vertical price restraints were illegal per se under the Sherman Act. In that case, Leegin, a manufacturer of leather apparel, refused to sell to retailers if they intended to discount its products below their recommended retail price. And in the *American Express* case, the Court—in a 5–4 decision—held that company policies barring merchants from steering customers to use credit cards with lower transaction fees, thus forcing those merchants to pay the higher fees, did not violate the antitrust laws.

These decisions have far-reaching consequences, not only for litigants themselves, but also for future antitrust claims. Already, the *American*

Express decision played a detrimental role in one unsuccessful Antitrust Division challenge to a merger. In November 2018, the travel technology companies Sabre Corporation and Farelogix Inc. announced their plan to merge in a $360 million deal, but after the Antitrust Division challenged the deal, the companies beat back the Justice Department lawsuit that asserted the merger would limit competition in the airline booking industry and drive up fees. Although the deal was ultimately called off when the U.K.'s Competition and Markets Authority blocked the transaction, the adverse U.S. district court ruling—one that specifically relied on the *American Express* decision—is still out there. "Companies are likely to exploit this decision," noted Michael Kades, the director of markets and competition policy at the Washington Center for Equitable Growth, observing that while the Sabre-Farelogix deal was scuttled by the U.K. decision, the unfavorable U.S. ruling "doesn't just disappear."

In addition to decisions from the nation's highest court, other powerful courts, including the U.S. Court of Appeals for the District of Columbia, have, at times, also thwarted antitrust cases or meaningful review of mergers and acquisitions. One illustrative example is how the D.C. Circuit undermined the Antitrust Procedures and Penalties Act, better known as the Tunney Act. Its namesake, John Tunney, was a U.S. senator from California from 1971 to 1977. The 1972 film *The Candidate,* starring Robert Redford, was based on Tunney's 1970 Senate race, in which a telegenic thirty-six-year-old Tunney—a Democrat—beat a Republican incumbent. In the wake of Nixon administration scandals, including one involving an acquisition of an insurance company by International Telephone and Telegraph (ITT), Senator Tunney sought to protect the public from "sweetheart" antitrust deals by ensuring that Justice Department antitrust settlements would be subjected to appropriate judicial review and be in the public interest. The Tunney Act, the modest legislative proposal he shepherded through Congress, has been described as "a Watergate-era statute that mandates federal court approval of certain antitrust consent decrees" and was designed to stop a real-world abuse he'd encountered.

Although the Tunney Act was designed to eliminate the judicial rubber-stamping of antitrust consent decrees, the D.C. Circuit appellate court ultimately undermined the law's purpose. The law, in truth, was fairly limited in scope, and it did not address whether, for example, the Justice Department should open any particular antitrust investigation or pursue any specific antitrust case. The Tunney Act was instead intended to allow courts to stop egregious settlements that run afoul of the public interest. But even that limited purpose was thwarted by the D.C. Circuit.

Whether it is a court ruling in a case such as *Leegin* or *American Express,* the interpretation of the Tunney Act, the *Twombly* pleading decision, or a multitude of other decisions over the past few decades that have severely limited the reach of federal antitrust laws, there does not seem to be much light on the horizon if one's antitrust reform plan is to simply wait and see if these courts, including the conservative U.S. Supreme Court, will abruptly change their approaches. While presidents should be certain to consider judges' antitrust views when making federal judicial appointments at all levels, a wait-and-see-if-the-Court-changes-the-precedent approach will clearly not fix the country's antitrust problems. That's why dealing with challenge 5 below—one of changing the actual legal standards through statutes—is a much more likely path to success.

Challenge 5—Existing Legal Standards. Given that the U.S. Supreme Court's ideological rulings have been a boon to big business, the challenge of changing our laws in Congress must be met if real progress is to be made. Altering existing legal standards is one big way to put teeth back into the antitrust laws.

One everyday challenge for antitrust enforcers is actually *proving* an antitrust violation. For example, to successfully prove a violation of section 1 of the Sherman Act, one must show the existence of a "contract, combination . . . or conspiracy" in restraint of trade. As Professor Christopher Sagers of the Cleveland-Marshall College of Law points out in his guide to the antitrust laws, "Evidence of conspiracy in violation of antitrust can be hard to come by. Conspiracies in restraint of trade are illegal and can constitute crimes subject to severe penalties. True conspirators, knowing that their conduct is illegal, will normally try to keep it as secret as possible." "Nowadays," he points out, "smoking gun evidence of conspiracy is rare except where government investigators have gotten it through undercover agents or cloak-and-dagger techniques."

Courts have determined that section 1 of the Sherman Act, which targets concerted action, prohibits only "unreasonable" restraints of trade, so antitrust enforcers must also show that the defendant possesses market power and that the challenged conduct's harm is greater than any benefits to competition. Likewise, although section 2 of the Sherman Act makes it illegal to "monopolize, or attempt to monopolize," trade or commerce, the U.S. Supreme Court has made clear that simply *being* a monopoly is not an antitrust violation but that a company cannot acquire or maintain a monopoly through illegal means. It is the "willful acquisition or maintenance" of monopoly power—as distinguished from "growth or development as a consequence of a superior product, business acumen, or historic accident"—that must be proven to show a violation.

In addition to the high burden of proving Sherman Act violations, to show that a prospective merger or acquisition violates section 7 of the Clayton Act, it must currently be shown that the merger or acquisition "may substantially lessen competition or tend to create a monopoly." Horizontal Merger Guidelines and Vertical Merger Guidelines have long existed, but—as Stephen Weissman, a deputy director of the FTC's Bureau of Competition, pointed out in 2015 of section 7—"it can be hard to prove what is likely to happen in the future." In reviewing a prospective transaction, the antitrust agency will need to define the relevant market or markets, analyze how the merger is likely to affect competition in the market or markets, examine any merger-specific "efficiencies," and analyze the potential for competition from existing companies or potential new entrants into the market. As Weissman put it in November 2015 before the Washington State Bar Association, "Because Section 7 of the Clayton Act is forward-looking, the agencies must also assess whether firms not currently selling products or services should be included as 'market participants' for purposes of the competitive analysis. We also consider whether there are other firms not currently in the market that are likely to enter the market or expand their operations in a way that will counteract the potential for anticompetitive harm from the merger."

It can thus be challenging to prove a Clayton Act violation, with those seeking to acquire another company regularly arguing that the acquisition will strengthen, not weaken, competition, with lots of discretionary judgment to be exercised by antitrust enforcers and, ultimately, if necessary, by the courts. As antitrust scholars Herbert Hovenkamp and Carl Shapiro explain in *The Yale Law Journal* of the discretionary exercise of antitrust/merger review and the obvious importance of the legal procedures and standards brought to bear by antitrust officials and reviewing judges, "Merger analysis is almost always a predictive exercise involving considerable uncertainty. As a result, burdens of proof matter a great deal. The structural presumption—that a merger is anticompetitive if it leads to a significant increase in market concentration—has therefore proven essential to effective merger enforcement." To make it easier to challenge mergers, I've suggested shifting the burden of proof for megamergers and lowering the Clayton Act's standard barring mergers that "substantially" lessen competition to ones that "materially" lessen competition—a change, as Hovenkamp and Shapiro note, that "is clearly intended to strengthen the government's hand in court."

To complicate matters further, in the case of private litigants, one must have standing to sue for an antitrust violation in the first place. In its decision in *Illinois Brick Co. v. Illinois* (1977), the U.S. Supreme Court held that, with very limited exceptions, *indirect purchasers* of goods or services cannot sue to remedy antitrust violations. Indirect purchasers of goods are those who do not purchase products directly from manufacturers. Instead, the Supreme Court held in *Illinois Brick* that only *direct purchasers*—those who buy directly from manufacturers—have standing to sue. While direct purchasers pay higher prices, they often "pass on" the overcharges that arise out of the anticompetitive behavior, with indirect purchasers down the supply chain ultimately suffering the consequences. A number of state antitrust laws already reject the *Illinois Brick* doctrine, with the Antitrust Modernization Commission report (2007)—more than ten years ago—calling for Congress to overturn, through legislation, the *Illinois Brick* doctrine.

For decades now, many antitrust experts have criticized the *Illinois Brick* decision. Indeed, on January 23, 2018, Andrew Finch, a deputy assistant attorney general within the U.S. Department of Justice, announced that the then Trump Justice Department's Antitrust Division was "looking at whether or not it might be worthwhile" to recommend that the U.S. Supreme Court reverse its *Illinois Brick* decision to bring "stability and continuity" to antitrust enforcement. To date, nothing has happened in that regard or along those lines. Indeed, Trump's Justice Department went in the opposite direction, arguing before the U.S. Court of Appeals for the Ninth Circuit that state laws recognizing indirect purchaser standing pose an irreconcilable policy conflict with federal law. Although I believe *Illinois Brick* was wrongfully decided and that indirect purchasers should be allowed to sue, as the American Antitrust Institute has pointed out, a legislative repeal of *Illinois Brick* must be done in the right way so as not to unintentionally undermine private antitrust enforcement, including in class-action cases.

For predatory pricing claims, the U.S. Supreme Court has also set a high threshold that antitrust litigants must meet before they can successfully bring such claims. "Predatory pricing," one textbook notes, "occurs when a company lowers its prices below cost to drive competitors out of business. Once the predator has the market to itself, it raises prices to make up lost profits—and more besides." A plaintiff, the Supreme Court held in 1993, "must demonstrate that there is a likelihood that the predatory scheme alleged would cause a rise in prices above a competitive level that would be sufficient to compensate for the amounts expended on the predation, including the time value of the money invested in it." The adoption of this doctrinal test—known as the recoupment test—has made it much harder for antitrust plaintiffs, with the number of cases filed and won by plaintiffs falling. As antitrust expert Lina Khan writes in a chapter of *Digital Dominance: The Power of Google, Amazon, Facebook, and Apple* (2018), "Today, succeeding on a predatory pricing claim requires a plaintiff to meet the recoupment test by showing that the defendant would be able to recoup its losses through supracompetitive prices. Since the Court introduced this recoupment requirement, the number of cases brought and won by plaintiffs has dropped dramatically."

How courts actually define the relevant market and what actions Congress will require them to take to protect competition present other, very real antitrust challenges of the legal standard variety. Recall that in 1963, in *United States v. Philadelphia National Bank,* the U.S. Supreme Court established a presumption that mergers resulting in more than a 30 percent market share are presumptively unlawful. The 30 percent threshold was aimed at preventing mergers that would lead to firms having too large a share of relevant markets. As Herbert Hovenkamp and Carl Shapiro recently summarized the basic approach laid out in that case, "Since the Supreme Court's landmark 1963 decision in *United States v. Philadelphia National Bank,* antitrust challengers have mounted prima facie cases against horizontal mergers that rest on the level and increase in market concentration caused by the merger. Proponents of the merger are then permitted to rebut by providing evidence that the merger will not have the feared anticompetitive effects."

To better safeguard the approach laid out in *Philadelphia National Bank,* and to prevent the chipping away of its standard by the federal courts, legislation I've introduced in Congress—as Hovenkamp and Shapiro note—would "codify the *Philadelphia National Bank* structural presumption found in the case law." They further add that the proposed legislation "seems quite useful, as it would prevent the courts at all levels from undermining or otherwise weakening the structural presumption, as some have favored." Under the legislation, a merger would be illegal if it "would lead to a significant increase in market concentration" in any domestic market, "unless the acquiring and acquired" participant establishes, "by a preponderance of the evidence, that the effect of the acquisition will not be to tend to materially lessen competition or tend to create a monopoly or a monopsony."

How antitrust enforcement agencies and the courts define what the relevant market is can—quite literally—determine the outcome of the analysis as to whether there is an antitrust violation. For example, in 2008, the Justice Department approved a merger between satellite radio's two principal carriers, XM Satellite Radio Holdings, Inc. and Sirius Satellite Radio, Inc. "Although critics argued that the relevant market was satellite radio," one book notes, illustrating how consequential it can be to define the relevant market in a particular way, and taking specific note of how the country's seventeen million satellite radio customers would be affected by the merger, "the Justice Department concluded that satellite radio was a small slice of a larger market that included radio and other music delivery services, such as Apple iPods and online entertainment." If the relevant market is defined too broadly, mergers and acquisitions can too easily escape the scrutiny of regulators, and not only are consumers left with fewer and fewer choices, but dominant companies are permitted to escape liability for their anticompetitive conduct.

The *Philadelphia National Bank* standard has truly been undermined and eroded in the past few decades, suggesting that the passage of new legislation is needed to codify its core requirements and to combat corporate consolidation in lines of business. For example, in *United States v. General Dynamics Corp.* (1974), a case that lessened the U.S. Supreme Court's focus on market concentration as a decisive factor, the Supreme Court affirmed a trial court ruling allowing the merger of two coal producers—a merger that increased the market share of the two biggest firms from 45 to 49 percent in one geographic market and from 44 to 53 percent in another. Whereas the *Philadelphia National Bank* case focused on the compelling need to prevent market concentration, the *General Dynamics* case took a far different—and laxer—approach. As conservative justice Clarence Thomas—who has been heavily criticized for his antitrust opinions—described the shift in approach wrought by the latter case, "*General Dynamics* began a line of decisions differing markedly in emphasis from the Court's antitrust cases of the 1960s. Instead of accepting a firm's market share as virtually conclusive proof of its market power, the Court carefully analyzed defendants' rebuttal evidence. These cases discarded *Philadelphia Bank*'s insistence that a defendant 'clearly' disprove anticompetitive effect, and instead described the rebuttal burden simply in terms of a 'showing.'"

One particular issue that can be reevaluated in the Biden administration is the Vertical Merger Guidelines issued at the end of June 2020 by the U.S. Department of Justice and the Federal Trade Commission. In January 2020, the Trump Justice Department and the FTC had issued for comment long-anticipated draft Vertical Merger Guidelines to replace outdated 1984 guidelines, and on June 30, 2020, the final Vertical Merger Guidelines were issued. But two Democratic FTC commissioners—Rebecca Kelly Slaughter and Rohit Chopra—issued dissenting statements. While agreeing that the old guidelines needed to be replaced, Slaughter observed that the final version of the new Vertical Merger Guidelines "misses the mark on both process and substance." The way in which the FTC adopted the final version, she noted, "short-circuited the more thorough discussion that the public" deserved, especially in light of the COVID-19 pandemic, to "improve the final product." She also expressed her fear the new Vertical Merger

Guidelines will send a "signal" that antitrust enforcers "will view vertical mergers as likely to be procompetitive and will use the Guidelines to justify lack of enforcement against vertical mergers."

Commissioner Chopra shared many of Slaughter's concerns, asserting that "it was imprudent not to seek additional comment on this new iteration" of the Vertical Merger Guidelines. "Public forums to discuss the project were canceled and never rescheduled or replaced with an online format," Chopra stressed of the adoption of the new Vertical Merger Guidelines in the midst of the pandemic. Chopra also stated that the new Vertical Merger Guidelines "do not directly address the many ways that vertical transactions may suppress new entry or otherwise present barriers to entry" and that "the guidelines make assumptions based on contested economic theories and ideology rather than historical, real-world facts and empirical data in line with modern market realities." As Chopra argued, noting how "economic calcification" has occurred "in virtually every sector" and how, in the digital economy in particular, internet start-ups are now launched with the express goal of being bought out by one of the Big Tech players, emphasizing: "Killer apps quickly become killer acquisitions. Immeasurable innovation has been lost because the government stopped preventing dominance from blocking disruption."

As I noted in early July 2020, after the final version of the Vertical Merger Guidelines was released, I was "deeply disappointed" that the new guidelines had been finalized over the dissent of both Democratic FTC commissioners, who, like me, sought to improve the guidelines before their promulgation. The new administration can in fact redraft and reissue the guidelines, and it should do just that.

My argument when it comes to competition policy? For the sake of the American economy, the benefit of the doubt should no longer be given to big corporations and in favor of approving megamergers. Instead, the benefit of the doubt should be resolved in favor of American consumers and workers. And the only way to ensure that happens is to address the outdated legal standards by changing America's laws. Problems addressed by my bills and other solutions put forward in chapter 8 include acting to deter exclusionary anticompetitive conduct. That can be accomplished, among other ways, by changing the standard for assessing potentially anticompetitive "tying" arrangements (that is, an agreement by a party to sell one product but only on the condition that the buyer also purchase a different—or "tied"—product), creating meaningful opportunities in the law to "look back" at mergers or acquisitions to assess their anticompetitive effects and remedy any resulting harm, and increasing penalties and consequences for cartels and their conspiring participants. In general, whether it is upping the civil and criminal penalties for anticompetitive conduct to better deter it, changing the legal standard to assess predatory pricing or other exclusionary behavior (taken care of by my legislation), or creating a look-back mechanism, all of these challenges can be met by changes to existing law as well as better enforcement of the law.

Challenge 6—The Power of Big Tech. The new digital entrants in an ever-evolving twenty-first-century economy present tremendous oppor-

THE GALLOPING SNAIL

Congressional inaction is, sadly, a common theme of American history. In the antitrust arena, although U.S. lawmakers in prior decades passed laws to combat anticompetitive conduct, Congress has not recently tackled the problem of monopoly power and corporate consolidation. In the face of Big Tech monopolization, we cannot afford for Congress to operate at a snail's pace. Cartoon by Burt Thomas, *The Detroit News, 1933.*

tunities for America, but we must confront this hard reality: the nation's antitrust laws have simply not kept up with the pace of change.

As discussed earlier in this chapter in regard to Amazon and throughout chapter 6 to tech in general, there is no question that the Big Tech companies possess tremendous power. In fact, the five tech giants— Apple, Amazon, Alphabet (Google), Facebook, and Microsoft—now jointly make up a full 20 percent of the total value of the stock market. As *The New York Times* recently reported, the coronavirus pandemic has sent those five companies "to new heights, putting the industry in a position to dominate American business in a way unseen since the days of railroads." As that news report noted of what occurred in the first seven months of 2020, "The stocks of Apple, Amazon, Alphabet, Microsoft and Facebook, the five largest publicly traded companies in America, rose 37 percent in the first seven months this year, while all the other stocks in the S&P 500 fell a combined 6 percent, according to Credit Suisse."

One legal challenge when it comes to tech? Monopsonies. Most people are familiar with monopolies. A *monopoly* is where one seller controls the market for a good or a service, leading to higher prices for consumers. But a *monopsony*—a market situation in which there is only one buyer—is just as bad. Whereas a seller can monopolize a market, in a monopsony a large buyer controls the market. As Julie Young, in describing the concept of a monopsony, explains, "A monopsony is a market condition in which there is only one buyer, the monopsonist." Young writes, "Because of their unique position, monopsonies have a wealth of power. For example, being the primary or only supplier of jobs in an area, the monopsony has the power to set wages. In addition, they have bargaining power as they are able to negotiate prices and terms with their suppliers."

Professor Thales Teixeira, in a Medium blog titled "Big Tech's Power Is in Monopsony," gives this example of tech companies operating as monopsonies: "As the dominant buyers of specialized know-how, services, and supplies . . . they have wielded a power to set the prices paid to their employees, suppliers, and partners. While distinct from monopolies, these new behemoths similarly serve to undermine fair competition." While section 7 of the Clayton Act currently encompasses mergers among buyers, adding "monopsony" language would—as two antitrust scholars write—"help clarify and emphasize for the courts that harm to suppliers, such as farmers or workers, that results from a merger between their customers can violate Section 7." In 2016, the Obama administration's Council of Economic Advisers did a study of monopsony power in the labor market, and its report—which explained how monopsony power can reduce wages and overall welfare—found that "a general reduction in competition among firms" had shifted "the balance of bargaining power towards employers." The report noted that "evidence of rising market concentration and monopoly-style profits is especially strong in the health-care and technology sectors."

For good reason, long-neglected tech issues—from privacy to political ads to disinformation—are finally penetrating the public's attention. The issue of antitrust has specifically gotten more and more attention of late, with much of the interest focused on Amazon, Apple, Facebook, and Google. The four CEOs of those companies—Jeff Bezos, Tim Cook, Mark Zuckerberg, and Alphabet's Sundar Pichai, who runs Google—testified via video before a House committee in July 2020, with Zuckerberg, Pichai, and Twitter's Jack Dorsey later testifying before Senate committees. At the hearing before the Antitrust Subcommittee of the House of Representatives, the CEOs were grilled on a variety of antitrust issues, including their companies' market dominance, as well as issues pertaining to content and misinformation online, their ties to foreign governments such as China, access to their platforms (or, in Apple's case, its App Store), the use and abuse of consumer data, and section 230 of the Communications Decency Act (a provision that shields online platforms from liability for users' posts).

For example, Mark Zuckerberg faced questioning about Facebook's acquisition of Instagram and WhatsApp. Representative Jerrold Nadler of New York accused Zuckerberg of acquiring Instagram because he saw it "as a powerful threat that could siphon business away from Facebook." I later asked Zuckerberg about the same transactions in a Senate Judiciary Committee hearing, noting that he wrote in internal Facebook emails that Instagram could be very disruptive to his company and that one of Facebook's reasons for acquiring Instagram was to neutralize a nascent competitor. At a similar U.S. Senate Commerce Committee hearing, I also asked Google's Pichai about the company's control of approximately 90 percent of the search-engine market and 70 percent of the search-advertising market. And, as I noted, Google's response to public inquiries, investigations, and now lawsuits has been more than just "defensive." "It's been defiant," I said.

During the congressional hearings, each CEO got dozens of questions, with David Cicilline, the House Antitrust Subcommittee chair who has overseen an investigation of the companies, observing that all four tech companies "have monopoly power." "Some need to be broken up, all need to be properly regulated and held accountable," he said, pointing out that each company controls a "key channel of distribution," whether it be an App Store or an ad market, and uses data gathering—including from competitors—to protect and extend its power. "Their ability to dictate terms, call the shots, upend entire sectors, and inspire fear represent the powers of a private government," he warned.

In the Senate hearings, while most of the questioning focused on section 230 issues, I honed in on antitrust matters in my questioning of CEO Zuckerberg, noting that Facebook was excluding smaller competitors by either buying them or limiting interoperability with the Facebook platform. I cited a number of examples, and Jack Dorsey—Twitter's CEO—testified that Twitter itself "found it extremely challenging to compete" with Facebook using Vine, the short-form video hosting service Twitter had launched in 2013 but which it eventually shut down in late 2016. Twitter had previously acquired Vine, which grew to tens of millions of active users and competed with other social media services such as Instagram. But after Twitter launched Vine, Zuckerberg authorized a Facebook executive to block Vine's friend-finding feature. "Yup, go for it," Zuckerberg wrote.

There were many pointed questions in the House, too. "Why does Google steal content from honest businesses?" Representative Cicilline asked of Alphabet/Google's CEO, Sundar Pichai, during the House hearing, with concerns expressed about the conflict of interest inherent in a search engine directing people to websites where Google either is promoting its own services or has other financial incentives. "We need to ensure the antitrust laws first written more than a century ago work in the digital age," Cicilline concluded. Sadly, a portion of news coverage coming out of the House hearing related to Jeff Bezos's audio feed not working at the beginning of the hearing and Bezos and Mark Zuckerberg eating snacks.

What followed, however, was a 449-page report from the House Judiciary Committee's Antitrust Subcommittee. "Our investigation revealed an alarming pattern of business practices that degrade competition and stifle innovation," committee member Val Demings of Florida observed when the report was issued in October 2020. After examining nearly 1.3 million documents and hearing from 38 witnesses, 60 antitrust experts, and 240 market participants, the House Antitrust Subcommittee concluded in its report that the tech platforms "wield tremendous power" and "abuse it by charging exorbitant fees, imposing oppressive contract terms, and extracting valuable data from the people and businesses that rely on them."

The House report described in great detail the abuses of monopoly power. "Each platform," the report emphasized, "uses its gatekeeper position to maintain its market power." Pointing out that the tech companies under investigation had "acquired hundreds of companies just in the last ten years," the report specifically noted how dominant tech platforms had acquired nascent or potential competitors to neutralize competitive threats or to extend their dominance, in some cases acquiring smaller companies, only to shut them down—transactions described as "killer acquisitions." One important fact to know: of Facebook's nearly one hundred acquisitions, the Federal Trade Commission had extensively investigated only one, Facebook's 2012 purchase of Instagram. "To put it simply," the report observed, "companies that once were scrappy, underdog startups that challenged the status quo have become the kinds of monopolies we last saw in the era of oil barons and railroad tycoons."

Lina Khan, who helped lead the House Judiciary Committee tech investigation, in a much-talked-about law review article, "Amazon's Antitrust Paradox," explicitly argues that America's existing antitrust laws—at least as interpreted by the courts—are, themselves, not up to the task to tackle the antitrust challenges of the twenty-first century. Her article—and it's an interesting read—makes some fascinating points. "Due to a change in legal thinking and practice in the 1970s and 1980s," she explains, "antitrust law now assesses competition largely with an eye to the short-term interests of consumers, not producers or the health of the market as a whole; antitrust doctrine views low consumer prices,

The Big Tech companies, again and again, have asked us to trust them with our most sensitive information even as they've grown bigger and bigger. It's time for lawmakers and antitrust officials to rein in their monopoly power. Cartoon by Phil Hands, *Wisconsin State Journal,* 2019.

alone, to be evidence of sound competition." For example, although Amazon revolutionized order fulfillment, including with its popular Amazon Prime program, the failure to pay attention to antitrust issues has resulted in the accrual of unprecedented private power. "With its missionary zeal for consumers," Khan writes of Amazon's business tactics, which have regularly involved pricing goods below cost, "Amazon has marched toward monopoly by singing the tune of contemporary antitrust." Of course, once a company has cornered a market by offering low prices, that same company—now a monopoly enterprise—can then jack up prices. Avoiding that outcome is the very thing that antitrust law was and is—and should be—designed to prevent.

The challenge, of course, is how to make America's antitrust laws, already corrupted by Robert Bork's ideological worldview (and, of late, very much adrift due to judicial dismissiveness of anticompetitive conduct), relevant once more in an ever-changing business environment. Antitrust law's current framework—equating "consumer welfare" with short-term effects on price and output—simply fails to comprehend what Khan aptly calls "the architecture of market power in the twenty-first century marketplace." As Khan observes, while a

"market structure-based understanding of competition was a foundation of antitrust thought and policy through the 1960s," the Chicago
school's approach to antitrust largely decimated that structuralist view.
"The Chicago School," she writes, "claims that 'predatory pricing, vertical integration, and tying arrangements never or almost never reduce
consumer welfare.'" The experience of the past few decades, though,
shows that the same predatory pricing tactics once used by Rockefeller's
Standard Oil Company can be used just as easily by modern corporate enterprises, including Amazon, to wipe out competitors and gain
market dominance. Indeed, every predatory pricing scheme that a big
corporation uses sends a chilling message to any potential competitor
or new market entrant. The message: you will be crushed if you pose a
challenge to our market dominance.

   Challenge 7—Horizontal Shareholding. A less publicized issue, but
one that has serious implications for America's economy, is the extent
to which dominant companies have common shareholders. "By 2015,"
a Harvard Law School professor, Einer Elhauge, writes, "on average 70
percent of the stock of publicly traded corporations was held by institutional investors, with 17.6 percent on average held by the big three index
fund families alone." While individual shareholders own 30 percent of
the shares in publicly traded companies, they vote only 28 percent of
their shares—a participation rate that is dwarfed by the voting rate
of the big institutional players. The institutional investors—the stock
market's largest participants—vote 91 percent of their shares, giving
them a disproportionate share of the power in controlling firm behavior.
As of 2016, just three players—BlackRock, Vanguard, and State Street—
controlled 95 percent of all index fund assets. Whereas BlackRock held
39 percent of the assets, Vanguard held 33 percent, and State Street held
23 percent. The asset-management industry has grown more concentrated in recent years, with a November 2020 news report observing
that those three firms control $15 trillion and that, over the last decade,
they have attracted 82 percent of all investor money. That gives each of
those financial institutions incredible power. And when just a handful
of index funds and Wall Street portfolio managers have large financial
stakes in the very same companies, there are perverse incentives for the
players, and anticompetitive conduct is made more likely, even if it may
be extremely difficult to detect.

Horizontal shareholding presents a structural problem to America's free-enterprise system. The potential solutions (to be explored in the next chapter) will have to be carefully crafted so as not to jeopardize the rights of small investors, including their right to invest in mutual and index funds as part of their 401(k) or other retirement plans. But the challenge is nonetheless real and growing, as even John Bogle—the founder of the Vanguard Group who invented the index fund back in 1975—has opined. In a 2018 *Wall Street Journal* op-ed, Bogle observed that the "share of corporate ownership by index funds will continue to grow over the next decade" and cautioned that if market trends continue, "the Big Three"—Vanguard, State Street, and BlackRock—"might own 30 percent or more of the U.S. stock market." "I do not believe that such concentration would serve the national interest," he wrote.

Where the leading shareholders of industry competitors overlap, competing companies may behave differently than if the competitors were owned by completely separate owners. For example, one study found that where banks have common investors, bank fees and rates were adversely affected. The CEOs of companies care about their shareholders and thus try to maximize shareholder value. But where corporate boards and executives in an industry are working on behalf of *common* shareholders, the directors, officers, and managers of those companies have a higher incentive to price their products or services at monopoly prices, even though the public naively believes the companies are fiercely competing in the marketplace.

"Such 'horizontal shareholding,' as it's called," Jenny Luna reports in a recent *Stanford Business* article of the views of Yale economist Fiona Scott Morton, "may erode competition, boost consumer prices, and possibly violate long-standing antitrust laws." In her article "The Biggest Antitrust Story You've Never Heard," Luna traces the rise of the problem of horizontal shareholding since 1970. And it's a problem that's only grown worse. From 1999 to 2014, the probability of two competing companies in the S&P 1500 having a large horizontal shareholder increased from 16 percent to 90 percent. That's a huge shift, and one that should start setting off alarm bells.

The increasingly common phenomenon of horizontal shareholding is so concerning because it has been shown to have measurable anticompetitive effects. "The causal mechanisms by which common share-

Before the passage of the Clayton Act, it was not illegal to be an "interlocking director"—someone who sat on the corporate boards of two competing companies. Section 8 of the Clayton Act prohibited interlocking directorates for U.S. companies competing in the same industry if those companies were larger than a certain size and if, combined into a single entity, there would be a violation of the antitrust laws. Cartoon by Daniel R. Fitzpatrick, *St. Louis Post-Dispatch,* 1914.

holders might influence corporate policy," Elhauge explains, "include all of the ordinary mechanisms by which managers are incentivized to act in the interests of their shareholders: shareholder voting, executive compensation, the market for corporate control, the stock market, and the labor market." For example, a major component of executive compensation is the granting of restricted stock or stock options dependent on the value of corporate shares, and significant horizontal shareholding—by its very nature—lessens the incentives of corporate managers to compete. The better shareholders do, the better the managers do, and managers want to please their shareholders. "Horizontal shareholding," Elhauge notes, "can decrease competition through the even simpler mechanism of reducing the incentives of shareholders to pressure managers to compete."

Companies seek to maximize their profits, but if two companies—ostensibly "competitors"—are actually owned by common shareholders, those companies begin to resemble old-style "trusts" and are incentivized to compete less aggressively so that they can each reap higher profits, thus benefiting their common owners. As a result, prices rise and competition suffers. For example, higher levels of horizontal shareholding have been shown to increase pharmaceutical prices and—of special interest to farmers—the cost of seeds. A look at the U.S. seed market—in a study conducted by Mohammad Torshizi and Jennifer Clapp—reached this conclusion: "Our empirical analysis shows that, even when taking measures to fully separate the effects of market concentration and common ownership, approximately 15% of the increase in soy, corn and cotton seed prices over the 1997–2017 period are due to the rise of common ownership. These findings contribute to the current literature regarding the anticompetitive effects of common ownership and confirm the results of studies performed in other sectors, such as airlines."

Examples of decreased competition due to horizontal shareholding can be found across multiple industries. Elhauge summarizes the findings of two recent studies of the pharmaceutical industry: "One study finds that increased horizontal shareholding between an incumbent brand and an entering generic results in a 12% increase in the odds that they will enter into reverse-payment settlements that delay generic entry and produces a larger delay of entry. Another study finds that increased common ownership between drug manufacturers and potential generic entrants reduces the odds of generic entry by 9–13%." The airline industry, where higher levels of horizontal shareholding have led to higher prices in concentrated route markets, also illustrates the point. Berkshire Hathaway was once the largest shareholder in two of the country's largest airlines, United and Delta, and it was also the second-largest shareholder in American Airlines and Southwest Airlines. Large mutual fund companies (BlackRock, Vanguard, State Street, Fidelity, and T. Rowe Price) are, themselves, among the largest shareholders in airline stocks. As a group, it was once reported, the top-ten shareholders own between 39 percent and 55 percent of the stock in each airline carrier.

The ascendency of horizontal shareholding—as Einer Elhauge notes, examining contemporary American history—has coincided with a "large divergence between corporate profits and investment" that began in 2000 and "with the period during which we have had the highest growth in corporate profits and greatest decline in labor's share of national income since World War II." Pretax corporate profits have reached new highs, but the net investment by corporations has lagged far behind. The economic consequences, as explained by Elhauge:

"High corporate profits go to shareholders who are disproportionately wealthy and reflect high prices that are disproportionately borne by the non-wealthy, and the lack of corporate investment depresses employment and wages in a way that further disproportionately harms the non-wealthy."

While some don't acknowledge the anticompetitive or potentially anticompetitive impact of horizontal shareholding, and while there is no consensus as to the solutions, for anyone who is watching Wall Street investors and stock ownership patterns, the challenge associated with horizontal shareholding is clear. Horizontal shareholding presents conflicts of interest, so in addition to a potential legislative response, federal agencies must thoroughly investigate the anticompetitive effects of concentrated markets, particularly those with high levels of horizontal shareholding. "Horizontal shareholding," Elhauge writes, "poses the greatest anticompetitive threat of our times, mainly because it is the one anticompetitive problem we are doing nothing about." "Until recently," he notes, pointing out the lack of antitrust attention to date by federal agencies, "the anticompetitive potential of horizontal shareholding by institutional investors was not appreciated, and thus there would have been no motive to bring such a case." New empirical studies, however, show the clear and present danger of horizontal shareholding in concentrated markets, with high levels of horizontal shareholding associated with anticompetitive effects. This is an antitrust "sleeper" issue that deserves a federal wake-up call!

Challenge 8—Anticompetitive Practices. Over the past few decades, the United States has seen a rise in anticompetitive practices. They are varied, but they inhibit competition and economic freedom. Employers, for instance, have increasingly resorted to using non-compete agreements to stifle competition in labor markets. Non-compete clauses cover 30 million of America's 170 million workers, with such clauses serving to limit where employees can work—or what they can do—after leaving a job. One study published in 2018—an analysis of 2016 franchise disclosure documents—found that no-poaching-of-workers agreements (which prevent employees of one retail franchise from working for other franchisees) are found in 58 percent of major franchisors' contracts, including McDonald's, Burger King, Jiffy Lube, and H&R Block.

More and more Americans are being compelled to sign onerous non-compete agreements that restrict their rights and stifle competition in the labor market. Cartoon by Chris Wildt.

"The only thing wrong with Capitalism is competition. Sign this non-compete agreement."

Non-compete agreements are used to suppress the wages of both high-skilled/high-wage workers and those in low-wage jobs, with the terms of non-compete agreements almost always dictated exclusively by the employer. Employers have even attempted to use non-compete agreements to suppress the wages of minimum-wage workers who are already struggling to make ends meet. In one particularly egregious example, Jimmy John's—an Illinois-based sandwich chain—was found to be using non-compete agreements to bar departing employees from taking jobs with competitors of Jimmy John's for two years after leaving the company. That was, simply put, an outrageous effort to suppress wages by trying to deter employees from leaving for better-paying employment opportunities. In June 2016, after an investigation by the New York Attorney General's Office, the company finally agreed to stop using that anticompetitive practice—one that targeted low-wage workers, putting them in fear of being sued if they left to work for a competitor.

Forced arbitration clauses have become another obstacle hindering the rights of American workers. A 2018 study estimated that more than sixty million American employees are bound to mandatory arbitration contracts. Mandatory arbitration clauses are frequently included in the paperwork for new hires at companies, and these clauses prohibit workers from suing in court. "This trend," the Economic Policy Institute study observed, estimating that more than 55 percent of workers are now subject to them, "has weakened the position of workers whose rights are violated, barring access to the courts for all types of legal claims, including those based on Title VII of the Civil Rights Act, the Americans with Disabilities Act, the Family and Medical Leave Act, and the Fair Labor Standards Act."

The adverse consequences of forced arbitration? The most vulnerable, including low-wage workers and those who have been discriminated against or sexually harassed, can be taken advantage of. "Because arbitration is confidential, women don't know that others are experiencing the same behaviors," notes Rachel Arnow-Richman, an employment law expert. Just as the #MeToo movement has exposed abusers, observes freelance reporter Brianna Holt, "so too has it exposed the ways companies protected them"—with mandatory arbitration clauses (along with confidentiality agreements) being one of them.

Anticompetitive practices, in whatever form they take, hurt workers or hurt consumers. The practice of pay-for-delay in the pharmaceutical industry, which has been the subject of much litigation along with long-time legislative efforts I've led in Congress to stop it, is one example that directly affects countless Americans. These anticompetitive arrangements involve pharma companies actually paying generic competitors to *keep* their products off the market! The result? One pharma company avoids competition by paying off another, and the consumers and taxpayers lose. Since 2001, the FTC has filed a number of lawsuits to stop these so-called "reverse-payment" settlements of patent disputes, anticompetitive deals the FTC previously estimated may cost consumers and taxpayers $3.5 billion a year.

The litigation has been hard fought. After the U.S. Court of Appeals for the Eleventh Circuit held in 2005 that pay-for-delay settlements were generally immune from antitrust scrutiny, other federal appellate courts followed suit and the number of such settlements skyrocketed. As one source notes of what took place: "According to the FTC, there were only three pay-for-delay settlements in fiscal year 2005. In 2006, the number jumped to fourteen, and in fiscal year 2012, 40 out of 140 final resolutions of patent disputes between a brand-name and generic manufacturer involved possible pay-for delay payments." With the number of such settlements going from zero in fiscal year 2004 to more than three dozen in fiscal year 2012, it is estimated that prescription drug costs increased by $63 billion during that time period alone.

In 2013 in *FTC v. Actavis, Inc.*, the U.S. Supreme Court declined to label such arrangements either presumptively valid or presumptively violative of antitrust law. However, Justice Stephen Breyer—writing for the Court in its 5–3 decision—made it easier for the FTC to challenge these "pay-for-delay" settlements. In holding that the Eleventh Circuit should have allowed an FTC lawsuit challenging one such settlement to proceed, Justice Breyer's majority opinion stated that "five sets of considerations lead us to conclude that the FTC should have been given the opportunity to prove its antitrust claim." Among the considerations for scrutinizing such settlements in legal proceedings in spite of a mutually agreed upon resolution of a patent dispute: "If the basic reason is a desire to maintain and to share patent-generated monopoly profits, then, in the absence of some other justification, the antitrust laws are likely to forbid the arrangement." "In sum, a reverse payment, where large and unjustified, can bring with it the risk of significant anticompetitive effects," Justice Breyer's majority opinion ruled.

This issue of pay-for-delay still remains ripe for a legislative solution. For years, Republican senator Chuck Grassley and I have carried the bipartisan bill to stop this anticompetitive conduct in its tracks. The Congressional Budget Office conservatively estimates our bill would save patients and taxpayers $613 million over ten years. Delaying action to stop pay-for-delay only benefits the pharmaceutical industry while hurting consumers. It is long past time to get it done.

Another example of anticompetitive conduct? Time-limited, government-conferred patents are intended to incentivize innovation for the benefit of society, but instead drug companies have frequently abused their patent rights by blocking generics from entering the market in an attempt to illegitimately extend their monopoly or duopoly power. A bill I introduced with Senators Patrick Leahy, Chuck Grassley, and Mike Lee, the Creating and Restoring Equal Access to Equivalent Samples (CREATES) Act—to address abuses and delay tactics that prevent generic companies from getting FDA approvals—would, according to the Congressional Budget Office, result in almost $4 billion in savings. At least some provisions of this bill were incorporated into another law enacted in late 2019.

Challenge 9—Dark Money and Big-Dollar Politics. If the answer to our antitrust woes is to change the laws, there is one more major obstacle to overcome if true and lasting reform is to be achieved: the challenge of Big Dollar, Dark Money politics. As discussed at length in chapter 6, American politics is corrupted by the outsized influence of money. Dark money groups spent $308 million in the 2012 election, another $181 million in the 2016 election, $150 million in the 2018 midterm elections, and another $100 million in the 2020 election (though the Brennan Center for Justice notes that the latter figure, the amount reported to the Federal Election Commission, "likely underreports the problem" by more than 600 percent). In a late November 2020 story titled "$100 Million May Just Be the Tip of an Iceberg," it was reported, "Dark money groups have poured more than $750 million into 2020 elections through ad spending and record-breaking contributions to political committees such as super PACs." As Ciara Torres-Spelliscy, who did the reporting based on OpenSecrets research, emphasized in her story: "This could mean that $650 million is what I call 'black hole money'—money spent on politics and never reported in the campaign finance system."

And those amounts are dwarfed by the total amount of money spent on political campaigns, which run into the billions every election cycle. "Americans who are running for federal elective offices," CBS News reported in the wake of the 2016 election between Hillary Clinton and Donald Trump, "spent more than ever—about $6.8 billion—in that pursuit." While the Center for Responsive Politics estimated that $2.76 billion was spent in 2012 during the hard-fought contest between Barack Obama and Mitt Romney, nearly an equal amount—$2.65 billion— was spent on the Clinton-Trump race. The candidates themselves raised approximately $1.5 billion, with super PACs raising more than $600 million. The staggering cost of the 2020 U.S. presidential and congressional elections: an unprecedented $14 billion, double the amount of the previous record, the total spent in 2016.

In addition, the amount of money spent on lobbyists—dollars mostly spent by already highly profitable companies looking to retain

A massive amount of money is spent on lobbyists every year. The pharmaceutical/health products lobby spent $295 million in 2019 alone, and there are 2.7 pharmaceutical/health products lobbyists for each member of Congress.

their market power—is truly extraordinary. A total of $3.4 billion was spent on lobbying activity in Washington, D.C., in 2018, and the U.S. Chamber of Commerce—which represents companies—spent the most of any organization, shelling out almost $95 million, according to the nonpartisan Center for Responsive Politics. The pharmaceutical industry, as a whole, spent even more than that, with one recent news report noting that "its trade group, Pharmaceutical Research and Manufacturers of America, and individual drug companies together spent a staggering $280 million on federal lobbying in 2018, far surpassing other sectors." (There are 535 members of Congress, so that's more than $500,000 per member.) As that report added, showing how money is being spent hand over fist to influence public policy, "The record for Washington lobbying activity—$3.51 billion—was set in 2010, the year Congress passed the Affordable Care Act, overhauling the nation's health insurance system."

All of the dark money and the billions of dollars spent in American political campaigns and on issues of national legislative importance has taken its toll. For example, while the Affordable Care Act expanded health-care coverage, it didn't, much to my chagrin, take on out-of-

The corrupting influence of money in politics is nothing new, but the problem is getting worse. This 1906 *Puck* cartoon, captioned "Killed in committee," depicts Republican senator Nelson Aldrich of Rhode Island stopping an antitrust bill and other legislation in his "Senate Committee Room" spiderweb. Cartoon by John S. Pughe, *Puck,* 1906.

control pharmaceutical prices. Nor did it provide for a nonprofit, public option, something favored by President Barack Obama that would have greatly helped in bringing down U.S. health-care costs more generally. No, the public option was dropped almost entirely from the debate in 2009. Meanwhile, things have only gotten worse, with people struggling with high deductibles and a frequent inability to afford their co-pays— something a public option would help to address. The pharmaceutical industry itself has been consolidating into massive companies, which also impacts the ability of people to afford their medical care. That industry, "which had been fairly fragmented," Tim Wu writes in *The Curse of Bigness,* "underwent a major consolidation from 2005 through 2017," with mergers and acquisitions reducing the international market "from some sixty-odd firms to about ten."

The price spikes for everything from our daughter Abigail's EpiPens, to insulin (a drug my mom used to treat her diabetes) and Humira, a rheumatoid arthritis drug, as well as thousands of other drugs, includ- ing common ones, are galling and warrant continual monitoring and vigilance by regulators. Take Nicole Smith-Holt of Minnesota, who lost her son Alec at age twenty-six. After Alec, a restaurant manager in Min- nesota, aged off his mom's insurance, he tried to ration his insulin. He made $35,000 a year in his job, too much to qualify for Medicaid. But he couldn't afford the life-saving medicine he needed. He died alone in his apartment less than one month after his mom's insurance stopped covering him. Nicole was my guest for President Trump's 2019 State of the Union address, because I wanted to give her a national platform to make her case. President Trump broke his promises to bring down prescription drug prices, and legal and legislative action to reduce out-of-control drug prices is long overdue.

Real-life stories such as Nicole's mean that because of all the corporate consolidation that has already occurred, America's economy now faces big structural challenges—ones only exacerbated by all the money spent on lobbying and in elections to ensure the preservation of the status quo. Big companies don't want scrutiny of their business practices, and those companies are the very companies that are exerting so much influence in the nation's capital. These days, vigorous consumer protection and U.S. antitrust enforcement thus face hurdles that they should not just because big corporations and well-financed industry associations—from Big Oil to insurance companies to Big Pharma—have outsized power in Washington, D.C.

Challenge 10—Media Consolidation. In 1983, fifty companies owned approximately 90 percent of U.S. media assets. By 2011, however, 90 percent of American media was controlled by just six companies—GE, News Corp, Disney, Viacom, Time Warner, and CBS. And consolidation has continued, upping the stakes even more for American democracy and the entire U.S. population. As discussed in chapter 6, with fewer media companies, the media companies that do exist have much greater power—power over content and content providers, power over price (think cable bills), and power over distribution. Meanwhile, unsuspecting Americans are left holding the bag and with what might be called "the illusion of choice." What can appear to unsuspecting members of the public as separate companies are actually entities owned by the same holding company.

In addition to the reduction in competition discussed in the last chapter and a troubling incentive for less emphasis on accuracy, media consolidation can lead to censorship, a by-product of the fact that only a handful of companies control America's newspaper chains, radio and TV stations, and internet platforms. After the passage of the Telecommunications Act of 1996, which loosened media ownership restrictions,

Clear Channel grew rapidly from 40 radio stations to 1,240 by 2002. "What's happening is that Clear Channel is a great hulking Frankenstein monster gobbling things up," musician Billy Bragg said at a concert more than a decade ago, with some Clear Channel stations blacklisting artists (for example, the Chicks, formerly the Dixie Chicks) or refusing to play some songs of well-known musical groups. "There's a very narrow number of gatekeepers, and that can be very destabilizing for a democracy," another musician, Tom Morello of Rage Against the Machine fame, told *The Boston Globe*. Clear Channel rebranded itself in 2014 as iHeartMedia, reaching 275 million people in the United States every month. That broadcast and entertainment company, iHeartMedia, planned to file for a $1.5 billion initial public offering in 2019 but instead of an IPO recently opted for a Nasdaq listing.

Another radio giant, Cumulus Media Inc., which owned more than 250 stations, also temporarily banned the then-named Dixie Chicks from getting airtime in 2003 after their lead singer, Natalie Maines, took on President George W. Bush at a concert in London as the White House prepared to invade Iraq. Cumulus Media directed all of its forty-two country music stations to stop playing the group's songs. That led a number of lawmakers in Washington, D.C., to express concern about the power of large media companies. "It's a strong argument about what media concentration has the possibility of doing," my friend Senator John McCain of Arizona scolded Cumulus's chairman, Lewis W. Dickey Jr. "If someone else offends you, and you decide to censor those people, my friend," he said, "the erosion of our 1st Amendment is in progress." "This sends a chill down my spine," added Senator Byron Dorgan of North Dakota. In an interview with *Billboard* magazine, Senator McCain emphasized, "This is an aspect of media concentration that should give everyone pause. It's very disturbing."

Challenge 11—Globalization. We live in an increasingly global, interconnected world. Commerce is international in character, and goods regularly flow across borders, though various tariffs and trade regulations govern that flow as countries and their leaders fight over trade deficits and environmental and labor standards. For years, I've served as co-chair of the Canada–United States Inter-Parliamentary Group, so I've seen firsthand what international negotiations look like as I've dealt with a wide array of issues pertaining to everything from border crossings to intellectual property rights to ballast water, to wood products and beef and dairy. Canada is one of America's largest trading partners, with total trade equaling about $2 billion per day, so there is a lot at stake in such negotiations. Whenever trade deals are negotiated, it is imperative that American negotiators focus on labor standards, environmental standards, and workers' rights. As is evidenced by the pharmaceutical provisions contained in several of these deals, large, multinational corporations are very good at looking out for themselves, but American workers need champions who will ensure we have fair trade, not unfettered trade.

Extremely complex antitrust issues exist in the international arena, just as they do at the domestic level. On March 30, 2018, Reuters reported that global mergers and acquisitions reached record levels, totaling $1.2 trillion in value for the first quarter of 2018 alone. "Strong equity and debt markets and swelling corporate cash coffers," its story noted, "helped boost the confidence of chief executives, convincing them that now is as good a time as ever to pursue transformative mergers, dealmakers said." While the number of deals had dropped by 10 percent, to 10,338, Reuters reported, "the value of M&A deals globally increased 67 percent year-on-year in the first quarter of 2018," with the data showing "how deals on average are getting bigger." Reuters described the activity in the three-month period in question: "M&A volumes doubled in Europe in the first quarter, while the United States was up 67 percent and Asia was up 11 percent." "The antitrust environment for M&A transactions seems favorable today though certain deals, which catch the attention of regulators or politicians for one reason or another, can be problematic," Jack Levy, a partner at Centerview Partners Holdings LP, emphasized in the story.

International deals pose unique regulatory and national security concerns. The Reuters story took note, for example, of how Singapore-based Broadcom's hostile $117 billion bid for the U.S. chip maker Qualcomm had been blocked on national security grounds, with the proposed deal called off in light of those concerns. "If there's not a trusted domestic supplier of chips, everyone will have to go to a Huawei, or [another] foreign supplier," observed Brian Fleming, an attorney who worked in the Justice Department's National Security Division in both the Obama and the Trump administrations. In 2018, the FBI warned U.S. citizens that they shouldn't buy smartphones made by Huawei because of the tech firm's close links to the Chinese government. In December 2018, the Justice Department brought criminal charges against Huawei and its CFO, Meng Wanzhou, for trying to sell equipment to Iran in spite of the U.S. sanctions regime. The charges against Huawei—the Chinese telecom giant—also described efforts by the company to steal trade secrets.

In addition to national security considerations, the evaluation of proposed international deals means that antitrust agencies in more than one country are involved. "Effective enforcement of U.S. antitrust laws in a global economy requires cooperation with competition agencies outside the U.S.," the Justice Department's Antitrust Division notes. The Antitrust Division works with agencies in other countries on matters relating to international cartels, mergers, and civil enforcement issues. The Federal Trade Commission's Office of International Affairs, established in 2007, coordinates the activities of those personnel formerly in the International Antitrust Division of the Bureau of Competition, which was created in 1982 to investigate and prosecute cases with an international dimension.

Of course, companies that run afoul of antitrust laws, whether foreign or domestic, risk being fined for anticompetitive conduct. In March 2019, for example, Europe's antitrust regulators fined Google $1.7 billion, bringing the total fines imposed on Google by the European Union to nearly $10 billion. As the Associated Press reported, the $1.7 billion fine—"for freezing out rivals" in the online advertising business—was the third time in less than two years that Google had been hit with a sizable fine. The other two fines ($5 billion and $2.7 billion) were for Google's requiring cell-phone makers using the company's Android operating system to install Google browser and search apps, for manipulating online search results, and for directing internet users to Google Shopping, its comparison-shopping service, to the detriment of its rivals. Google is also under investigation in Europe for its job search service, with Amazon, Apple, and Facebook also facing antitrust investigations there.

Google has also been under investigation in the United States by the Department of Justice, resulting in the sixty-four-page antitrust lawsuit filed against it in October 2020. In September 2020, before that lawsuit was filed, Senator Mike Lee and I chaired our own lengthy hearing examining Google's dominance in the online ad market, raising issues pertaining to Google's market power and its purchase of DoubleClick. Among other things, the Justice Department's lawsuit alleges that "Google has willfully maintained and abused its monopoly power" in general search services, search advertising, and general search text advertising "through anticompetitive and exclusionary distribution agreements." The complaint seeks "structural relief as needed to cure" the anticompetitive harm; an injunction barring Google from engaging in anticompetitive practices; and "preliminary or permanent relief necessary and appropriate to restore competitive conditions in the markets affected by Google's unlawful conduct."

One particular and pressing global challenge America faces on competition, as well as on many other fronts, is China—a communist country that subsidizes its domestic companies, thereby creating an unfair playing field for American workers and businesses. China has manipulated its currency, stolen American intellectual property, and only relatively recently gotten into the competition law arena—and in a way that continues to favor Chinese companies over foreign competitors. "The underlying aim of China's antimonopoly law, which was put into effect on Aug. 1, 2008," one source notes, "is to obstruct foreign rivals, said a U.S. lawyer working at a Chinese law firm." Whereas the aim of U.S. antitrust law is to prevent the formation of monopolies and oligopolies, "in China's case"—one legal adviser explains of Chinese officials and their aims—"regulators are more concerned with improving the competitiveness of Chinese companies than monitoring for the establishment or abuse of dominant market position."

Discrimination against foreign companies is forbidden under World Trade Organization rules, but it is difficult to prove. China has an antimonopoly law, the stated goal of which is to promote "the healthy development" of the country's "socialist market economy." However, China's criteria for review of mergers and acquisitions are not transparent, there have been significant delays in the review process, and the most severe fines have generally been reserved for foreign companies. Clearly, much more must be done to persuade China to adopt—and then implement in a nondiscriminatory manner—its own pro-competition laws. According to a 2018 news story, "China's three main antitrust enforcement agencies were merged into a single body, the State Administration for Market Regulation, and will receive more staff." In a country of more than a billion people, very few resources are devoted to antitrust regulation, as the available evidence shows. "Only about 40 people worked on screening and probes at the old agency, according to local media reports," that 2018 news story noted, pointing out that antitrust officials "were also often considered lower ranking than the heads of state-run enterprises they were charged with regulating." Only if America works closely with its allies—and demands fair trade along with appropriate pro-competition and labor and environmental rules—will China be more effectively pressured to implement policies that are fair to American workers and businesses.

Challenge 12—Kick-Starting Public Engagement. The biggest challenge of all may be figuring out how best to get Americans engaged (historically speaking, simply reengaged) with antitrust issues. How can elected officials educate and engage the American public in a subject that even most law students and legal practitioners consider a rather dull, byzantine area of the law? What is the best way to reach the American people on the need to reinvigorate antitrust enforcement? I'm not suggesting that we need to dust off Woodrow Wilson's "Bust the Trusts" song, but we definitely need to use the technology we have at our disposal to make the American public more aware of what's going on with corporate consolidation and monopoly power. It is clear that America's long-dormant antitrust movement needs to awaken from its decades-long slumber. And I know that, by working together, we must and can right the antitrust ship. Why? I see more and more citizen advocates, and yes, even members of Congress, raising this issue in the political arena. I see this moment in history—the one described in this book—as one we must seize on now as a call to action.

It's not ever going to be easy to get the public to perk up when they hear the word "antitrust." As explained in chapter 3, that word came from America's historic 1880s social movement that rose up *against* trusts—the behemoth trusts made famous by James J. Hill, J. P. Morgan, and John D. Rockefeller, those ultra-wealthy men with their famous middle initials. It's a word that is, admittedly, somewhat outdated, even though the idea it represents—that competition must be zealously safeguarded—is as important and relevant as ever. "Antitrust," Daniel Crane, a University of Michigan Law School professor, explains, is, in reality, actually "a horrible word—so negative, so poorly descriptive of the actual field, so antiquated." Although American lawyers and judges still speak of antitrust law and antitrust violations because of the way American law developed over many decades, the antitrust terminology is not as prevalent elsewhere. "In most other countries that have an analogue to the United States' Sherman Act," Crane observes, "antitrust law is called competition law, a more positive and evocative way of describing the field."

In addition to the obvious problem with the actual word "antitrust," and in my mind, the need to replace it with the more aptly titled "competition policy," there are many other obstacles. For starters, because of the sheer complexity of antitrust law, only a few lawyers actually concentrate their practices in this field of law. The Antitrust Law Section of the American Bar Association has fewer than ten thousand members, and its annual spring meeting in Washington, D.C., offering breakout sessions and continuing legal education credits for practicing lawyers, does not, clearly, a social movement make. The Supreme Court's lengthy decisions are read by very few people; a lot of antitrust topics are so in the weeds that only the most passionate antitrust lawyers and specialists (the kind who wear red baseball caps reading "Make Antitrust Great Again"—yes, this is a thing) can understand or get excited about them; and the study of antitrust law is something that—let's be honest—few people take up as a hobby. As with the Progressive Era, I believe it's going to be the observable *effects* of a lack of competition on America's economy—and on Americans' pocketbooks—that is going to drive (and that should drive) a renewed interest in antitrust law and competition policy. Those effects are already being felt, and it's time that America's elected officials get their act together to protect the public from monopolistic behavior.

Some of the best political and legal minds, it is true, have spent considerable time thinking about antitrust issues—and, in particular, the implications of failing to enforce the antitrust laws. In fact, in a bit of trivia, two American presidents—William Howard Taft and Bill Clinton—actually once taught antitrust law. It is, however, the U.S.

Supreme Court justice Stephen Breyer, another former antitrust law professor, who once identified what may be the singular, uphill challenge ahead for those of us who have spent some time in the antitrust trenches, trying to raise public awareness of this topic's singular importance. In 2009, at the Supreme Court's oral argument in *Bilski v. Doll,* a case about the patentability of business methods, the always-witty Justice Breyer pondered aloud whether he could patent "a great, wonderful, really original method to teach antitrust law that kept 80 percent of the students awake." The quip of Justice Breyer—who, before joining the nation's highest court, worked as a special assistant in the Antitrust Division of the U.S. Department of Justice—drew laughter because of antitrust law's long-standing reputation as a dense, highly technical subject. Every lawyer in the Supreme Court chamber that day, no doubt, had a flash of recognition that antitrust law can be very dull, even though the law's application has real-world consequences of considerable public interest.

Every so often, antitrust breaks into pop culture, be it through an NPR podcast, a John Grisham novel, documentaries such as *Fair Fight in the Marketplace* (2007) or *Louis Brandeis: The People's Attorney* (2007), or the plotline of a blockbuster James Bond movie featuring a drug cartel or an evil villain seeking to monopolize a precious metal or an entire industry. Yes, that's true: In *Goldfinger* (1964), the British MI6 agent James Bond (played by Sean Connery) foils the plot of a sinister gold bullion smuggler, Auric Goldfinger, to increase the value of his own holdings by irradiating all of the gold in Fort Knox with a nuclear bomb supplied by the People's Republic of China. Likewise, in *A View to a Kill* (1985), 007 squares off against the psychopathic character of Max Zorin (played by Christopher Walken), the owner of Zorin Industries—a shady microchip manufacturer with ties to the KGB. In an effort to monopolize the microchip industry, Zorin hatches a diabolical plan to destroy his competition in Silicon Valley by planting a bomb in an abandoned mine shaft near the San Andreas Fault, scheming to trigger a massive earthquake at high tide and to flood out all of his competitors.

And it isn't just James Bond. One finds scattered allusions to antitrust throughout a number of TV shows and films. In *The Practice,* the writer and producer David E. Kelley cast the actor James Spader as Alan Shore, a character described by one TV critic as "a lecherous, twisted antitrust lawyer with a breezy disregard for ethics." In season 5, episode 7 of the Showtime series *Billions,* created by Brian Koppelman, David Levien, and Andrew Ross Sorkin, the hedge fund owner Bobby Axelrod—the head of Axe Capital who often resorts to bribery and insider trading—hatches a scheme to corner the market on rare minerals through meteor harvesting. And in perhaps my favorite film antitrust mention, in the dystopian science fiction action film *Demolition Man* (1993), set in the year 2032, one of the characters, Lenina Huxley (played by Sandra Bullock), notes that "Taco Bell was the only restaurant to survive the Franchise Wars." "So?" Sylvester Stallone's character, policeman John Spartan, replies, prompting Huxley to shoot back: "So, now all restaurants are Taco Bell."

Antitrust disputes have also made headlines in the music industry. Concerts given in connection with the World Cup soccer finals in 1990, 1994, and 1998 by the Three Tenors—the global opera stars José Carreras, Plácido Domingo, and Luciano Pavarotti—thrilled audiences and led to one of the best-selling classical music albums of all time, but the antitrust dispute over an agreement between PolyGram Holding, Inc. and Warner Communications, Inc. over one of the concert recordings ended in a lengthy judicial opinion by the U.S. Court of

Antitrust humor is in short supply. Here's one exception, which might be especially funny (or not so funny) if you live in New York City. Cartoon by Tom Cheney, *The New Yorker,* 1998.

Appeals for the D.C. Circuit. And the ongoing issue of monopoly power in the sale of concert tickets once prompted Pearl Jam to cancel its 1994 summer tour after the band became disgusted that Ticketmaster had added extra service charges to tickets. This issue, of the dominance of Ticketmaster, continues, with the coronavirus pandemic causing considerable hardship to already cash-strapped smaller venues, something I directly took on with Senator John Cornyn of Texas. Our bill, Save Our Stages, which passed as part of the 2020 Pandemic Relief package, specifically targeted help to the smaller venues and excluded the behemoth Ticketmaster.

In antitrust discussions in general, locating even a slender reed of antitrust humor, whether in the proverbial swamp of Washington, D.C., or anywhere else, is, I confess, not easy—and not going to be the path to success for the reform of our nation's monopoly problem. In fact, in 2005, the then U.S. attorney general, Alberto Gonzales, reported that after a team of researchers had worked "furiously for days" in preparation for his speech on antitrust, he could "confidently report" that "there are no jokes about antitrust law."

The closest efforts at antitrust humor that I could identify were jokes about the game of Monopoly, about a prospective merger, and a few one-line quips on Twitter. The comedian Steven Wright, known for his wry humor and deadpan delivery, once uttered this monopoly-themed one-liner: "I think it's wrong that only one company makes the game Monopoly." The prospective merger (and very dated) joke, also made years ago: "AT&T is reportedly interested in buying America Online. If this occurs, federal regulators are concerned that the merged corporation will have a total monopoly on busy signals." And a representative sample of Twitter posts, many in the same vein: "I have an antitrust joke but it would destroy the competition." "I've got an antitrust joke, but it just can't compete." "I have an antitrust joke, but I don't want to monopolize the conversation." "I have an antitrust joke, but it breaks me up when I tell it." "I have a reasonably amusing antitrust joke but it's not funny per se."

Even Comedy Central's ever-popular *Daily Show* came up dry. In 2004, *The Daily Show* did a segment on University of Wisconsin–Madison students using antitrust law to sue to protect their right to drink alcohol (at affordable, non-collusive prices, mind you). The law-student-led lawsuit was filed in Madison, Wisconsin, after two dozen local taverns teamed up with the city and the University of Wisconsin to curb drink specials and tackle the very real problem of binge drinking. Ed Helms, a *Daily Show* correspondent, went to Madison to do a segment on the very unique legal dispute. In the March 2004 class-action complaint, three UW students had sued (as the Wisconsin Supreme Court later summarized it) on behalf of themselves and any similarly situated persons who "patronize the 24 Madison taverns after 8 p.m. on Friday and/or Saturday nights." The plaintiffs accused the taverns near campus of price-fixing in violation of Wisconsin's antitrust law—a state law modeled on the Sherman Antitrust Act of 1890. Under pressure from city officials worried about excessive drinking by college students, the taverns had collectively agreed to eliminate drink specials after 8:00 p.m. It was that lawsuit that drew Comedy Central's attention, with the four-minute, twenty-eight-second segment of Jon Stewart and Ed Helms—titled "Unhappy Hour"—airing on April 26, 2004.

The segment on *The Daily Show,* introduced by Jon Stewart as an "inspiring example" of "campus activists taking on the system," focused on attempts to eliminate "weekend drink specials." It highlighted "75¢ cans of beer" offered with "free bacon all night long," "nickel shots," and "2 for 1 pints." After making light of young men—some playing drinking games—overeager to consume excessive amounts of alcohol, the segment pivoted to the proverbial "smart kid with glasses" who contended that the tavern owners hadn't gone about doing what they did "in a legal way." That young man confidently asserted that the tavern owners had violated antitrust laws, whereupon the segment cut to an interview with Mike Verveer, a Madison alderman. Verveer called the lawsuit "frivolous and outrageous" despite the lawsuit's claim that the voluntary ban on drink specials constituted a naked, per se price-fixing conspiracy. Ed Helms, a *Daily Show* correspondent, ended the segment by saying, in a tongue-and-cheek fashion, that the students planned to "fight this thing . . . until the end of the semester."

Ultimately, the Wisconsin Supreme Court determined in 2008— long after the end of the 2004 spring semester—that the tavern owners were immune from antitrust liability under what is known as the "implied repeal doctrine." The state's high court wrote that the implied repeal doctrine—another obscure antitrust exemption, part of "the great

Swiss cheese" of antitrust law—"addresses situations in which there is no explicit statutory exception to antitrust law but it is reasonably clear that the legislature intended to allow municipalities to undertake an action that is anticompetitive."

While *The Daily Show* poked fun at the Madison lawsuit, the serious subject of antitrust is a hard one to take on with jokes and banter. But the more people talk about it—on comedy shows, on the evening news, in campaigns, in class, to their neighbors and co-workers, and, of course, on the internet—the better off we will be. We must be both creative and relentless to galvanize the public behind the cause. And yes, while it may be hard to find easy and freewheeling antitrust humor, let's just embrace it: antitrust enforcement is no joke.

8

The Path Forward

The Solutions to America's Monopoly Problem

LOOKING AHEAD

I am an optimist, but I am also a clear-eyed realist. In this book I have made the argument that factors that have led to increased economic consolidation, more income inequality, and higher costs for consumers include our government's failure to prioritize and vigorously enforce the country's antitrust laws as well as the conservative interpretation of those laws by the courts over the last few decades. But in a broader systemic analysis, the lack of antitrust action is also attributable to congressional paralysis: our lawmakers have failed to adapt to the new economic landscape—including the rising monopoly power of Big Tech—and to proactively amend competition laws due in part to the political clout and sway of the very interests that should be reined in by reinvigorated competition policies. Lawmakers have also failed to take action on related measures like privacy and drug pricing. In addition to legislative inaction, American workers and new market entrants face many barriers to competing against the big guys in the twenty-first-century economy. But in the end the lack of a political movement to take on the status quo has thwarted any real change to our antitrust laws and rules.

It is critical that we take action now before corporate consolidation further corrodes America's economy. Two-thirds of U.S. industries became more concentrated between 1997 and 2012, and increasingly, powerful institutional investors own significant stock holdings in multiple companies in the same industries. The American economy is dynamic and complex, and no one should ever bet against the ingenuity—and the competitive spirit—of American workers. But given what has occurred during the past four decades—and what has only been exacerbated by the recent pandemic—it is no longer acceptable for the government to do nothing in the face of increasing levels of corporate consolidation and monopoly behavior.

Much needs to be done to rebalance America's economy for the benefit of the American people. Here's my road map for change, which starts with the steps and ideas outlined in chapter 6. Those include taking on democracy reforms like passing a constitutional amendment to overturn *Citizens United;* signing into law the For the People Act, which passed the U.S. House of Representatives (and includes several provisions I proposed to stop voter suppression and to make voting easier and more secure); and enacting my bills to set minimum federal standards for mail-in ballots and early voting access as well as the Accessible Voting Act to make voting as easy as possible for seniors and people with disabilities. It also means making long-term economic reforms, from tax law changes and increasing the minimum wage to making it easier for unions to organize. It means creating and maintaining a social safety net for gig economy workers and making major changes to health care, child care, and work-family leave so people have more security in the workforce to pursue the American Dream. It means taking on racial disparities in our economy and across our justice system to ensure economic opportunities and fairness. It means passing a meaningful data privacy law. It means embracing the First Amendment and fighting media consolidation to protect our democracy, passing legislation to make it easier for newspapers and other media content providers to negotiate fair rates with social media platforms, and ensuring that all Americans, including in rural areas, have access to high-speed broadband. And, of course, it means a new commitment to take on antitrust fights.

We must prioritize antitrust enforcement—which I argue is better called competition policy—and create new tools to get it done, as well as legislatively change the antitrust standards and related consumer laws to adapt to the new digital marketplace realities. We must better incentivize innovation and make it easier for small businesses to compete, in addition to giving workers the flexibility to change jobs. We must create the political energy—a new antitrust/pro-competition movement—to make all of this happen.

What follows is a list of my Top 25 recommendations to improve competition in our nation so that markets work better for Americans. These recommendations include many that pertain specifically to antitrust policy and enforcement, anticompetitive conduct, and better scrutiny of mergers and acquisitions. I might best call it "if I could wave a magic wand and enact some bills and make some trouble" (what the late, great congressman John Lewis, the civil rights icon, would've called "good trouble, necessary trouble"). We must recognize that corporate consolidation, concentration in industries, and the failure to adequately enforce the antitrust laws have adversely affected American consumers and the health of America's economy. Mergers and anticompetitive behavior have increased the price of everything from cable TV and beer to health care, and we must stop admiring the problem and actually start doing something about it.

When it comes to fixing our nation's problems with monopoly power, the Top 25 list of things that we need to get done can basically be divided into three to-do lists: (1) things Congress can do, including changing laws and upping the legal standards, tools, and penalties, investing in enforcement, and conducting oversight; (2) things President Biden and his administration can do, including coming forward with a brand-new "competition policy" by advocating for major law changes, continuing investigations into and taking pro-consumer actions regarding the tech and pharma industries, aggressively enforcing the antitrust laws, and appointing officials who want to "make antitrust great again"; and (3) things outside the antitrust box that can be done by lawmakers and agencies which would enhance competitive markets and help workers and consumers—for example, patent and labor law reform, comprehensive immigration reform, new privacy policies, reducing non-compete agreements, and investing in both capital and STEM education for women and minorities and their businesses. After laying out that Top 25 agenda, I've also put together a Top 10 list of things that *you* can do to make a difference.

The Top 25

What Congress Can Do . . .

No. 1—Update the Nation's Antitrust Laws, Prevent Anticompetitive Exclusionary Conduct and Activities Harmful to Competition, and Vigorously Conduct Congressional Oversight. Our nation's antitrust laws should be functional and promote robust competition. Statutory improvements to those laws should highlight a return to curbing monopolistic and oligopolistic behavior that leads to market concentration and consolidation. A top-to-bottom review of the nation's antitrust laws is in order; the laws have not been updated to keep up with the times. There are numerous ways in which companies with monopoly and market power can engage in anticompetitive and exclusionary conduct, and in the digital age we must pass new laws—such as my Anticompetitive Exclusionary Conduct Prevention Act—to combat and deter such conduct. As Michael Kades, the director of markets and competition policy for the Washington Center for Equitable Growth, says of that bill's importance, "The proposed legislation would update the previous time Congress passed legislation on the topic of dominant firm conduct, in 1914, when airplanes were new, Archduke Ferdinand's assassination (that sparked World War I) was 3 weeks away, and Ford Motor Company had just instituted an 8-hour workday."

I introduced the Competition and Antitrust Law Enforcement Reform Act in February 2021 to deter anticompetitive abuses that harm consumers and innovation. That legislation, which seeks to amend the Clayton Act, also specifically prohibits such anticompetitive exclusionary conduct that risks harm to competition. It would enhance the ability of the Department of Justice and the FTC to enforce the nation's antitrust laws. The bill, co-sponsored by Senators Richard Blumenthal, Cory Booker, Ed Markey, and others, also strives to address the reality of America's modern-day marketplace. The legislation notes that "when dominant sellers exercise market power, they harm buyers by overcharging them, reducing product or service quality, limiting their choices, and impairing innovation," and "when dominant buyers exercise market power, they harm suppliers by underpaying them, limiting their business opportunities, and impairing innovation."

After defining "exclusionary conduct" as conduct that either "materially disadvantages" one or more "actual or potential competitors" or "tends to foreclose or limit the opportunity" of one or more "actual or potential competitors to compete," the Competition and Antitrust Law Enforcement Reform Act makes it "unlawful for a person, acting alone or in concert with other persons, *to engage in exclusionary conduct that presents an appreciable risk of harming competition.*" The bill allows the attorney general to recover civil penalties of not more than the greater of 15 percent of the total U.S. revenues of the company for the previous calendar year or 30 percent of the U.S. revenues of the company in any line of commerce affected or targeted by the unlawful conduct. The bill also limits the ability of courts to imply antitrust immunity for regulated conduct and shifts the burden of proof so that companies with a market share of greater than 50 percent, or that otherwise have substantial market power, would have to prove that their exclusionary conduct in the markets they dominate does not present an "appreciable risk of harming competition."

George Slover, the senior policy counsel at Consumer Reports, observed after my initial bill's introduction in March 2020 that it "addresses a key shortcoming in our law." "Current antitrust law," he said, "doesn't apply to a company until it already has a monopoly, or is on the verge of one—even when it has enough market power to sabotage the competitive process." As Slover observed, "This targeted, measured bill would move the line where it needs to be to address the kinds of anticompetitive abuse we are seeing too much of in today's marketplace. This is particularly important as commerce and communications increasingly take place online, with dominant platforms presenting new challenges to making sure we have a competitive marketplace that works for consumers and for all who seek to reach them."

Although some very specific suggestions are laid out below as part of this Top 25 list, the nation's lawmakers and civil servants need to consistently pay attention to anticompetitive conduct and figure out how best to stop it.

In addition to lawmaking, congressional oversight is an important way to raise public awareness and drive change. In 2017, my friend Keith Ellison—then a member of the U.S. House of Representatives and now Minnesota's attorney general—formed the Antitrust Caucus with other

WEATHER PREDICTIONS FOR FEBRUARY: "Look out for a big thaw."

It is hard to pass legislation through Congress, as this 1903 cartoon from the Theodore Roosevelt era makes clear.

House members to bring more scrutiny to antitrust issues. The series of hearings my colleagues Jerry Nadler and David Cicilline conducted in 2020, as well as their subsequent report on the tech industry, are great examples of what Congress can do to build the case for change. If members of Congress aren't aware of what is happening in the realm of monopoly and monopsony power and corporate concentration, they aren't exposed to the information they need to draft good legislation—and to set good policies—in the antitrust arena. And if public hearings aren't regularly held by Congress on antitrust topics to educate lawmakers and the public, the inevitable consequence is that those lawmakers and the American public are kept in the dark.

My Senate colleague Mike Lee and I have held a number of antitrust hearings over the years, although I would have greatly increased their scope and frequency if I had been in charge. We come from different parties, and we have different perspectives and views on the law. We frequently disagree on issues, but we share a commitment to the subject of antitrust law and enforcement, and we have developed a strong, bipartisan approach to the subcommittee. We are both committed to the professionalism and independence of antitrust enforcement. (That, of course, is the minimum that we should expect when it comes to antitrust professionals.)

We can't afford an "out of sight, out of mind" attitude when it comes to the problem of corporate consolidation, and the more lawmakers and the public can hear from antitrust professionals, including at the Department of Justice and the FTC, the better. And given the importance of antitrust issues to the American economy, it certainly makes good sense to ask judicial nominees more questions about their views on the subject.

As I see it, it is not enough at this point in time to simply prevent a further deterioration of the centuries-old tradition of antitrust enforcement. The stakes are too high to play defense; we must play offense if we are to tackle the challenges of our time. And that means Congress must get into the act, with both the U.S. Senate and the U.S. House of Representatives taking steps and passing legislation to remedy the problems of monopoly power and runaway corporate consolidation.

No. 2—Increase Antitrust Enforcement Staff. The federal government has been appropriating money for antitrust enforcement since 1903, when Congress appropriated $500,000 for that purpose, enough money to hire three attorneys and two stenographers for fiscal years 1904 through 1907. The number of full-time equivalents, or FTEs, at the Federal Trade Commission, however, was slashed in the 1980s, and staffing levels have never gotten back to pre-1980 levels. Congress has appropriated money for the Justice Department's Antitrust Division in every year since 1908, with direct appropriations climbing from $100,000 in 1910 and $300,000 in 1920 to $1.3 million in 1940, $3.7 million in 1950, and $4.5 million in 1960. Although congressional appropriations to the Antitrust Division rose steadily in the two decades that followed (from $9.7 million in 1970 to $43.5 million in 1980), direct appropriations stagnated in the 1980s, with the Antitrust Division becoming more dependent on filing fee revenues starting in 1990 after a change in the law. Now the Federal Trade Commission and the Antitrust Division of the Department of Justice are woefully understaffed and underfunded. Federal antitrust authorities have simply not gotten the resources they need to do their jobs properly, and antitrust staffers thus face what Bill Baer—the former assistant attorney general for the Justice Department's Antitrust Division—calls a "daunting" workload.

We must be smart about antitrust enforcement and reform, but we need to be bold. Instead of *cutting* the Antitrust Division's staff, as the Trump administration did (with the exception of the very end of their volatile four-year tenure, when both the FTC and the DOJ Antitrust

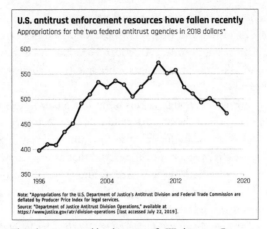

This chart, prepared by the nonprofit Washington Center for Equitable Growth, shows how antitrust-related appropriations have fallen in recent years, although there will finally be an increase in 2021.

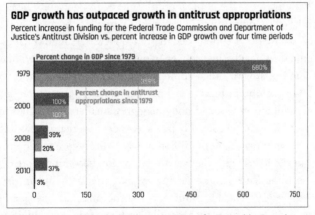

This chart, put together by Washington Center for Equitable Growth prior to the pandemic, shows how antitrust appropriations have not kept pace with GDP growth.

Division budgets were increased), we should be *strengthening* antitrust enforcement. Only by doing the latter can we ensure free, open, and highly competitive markets. In this era of BIG, now more than ever we need vigorous enforcement efforts to counterbalance runaway corporate consolidation and the outsized power of billionaires and millionaires and monopolies and monopsonies. Adding more staff and resources for FTC and Department of Justice enforcement is particularly helpful for reviewing highly complex major tech mergers and continuing and expanding upon tech investigations and legal actions.

To give federal officials the resources they need to both examine and take action against anticompetitive exclusionary conduct as well as evaluate the potential anticompetitive effects of a merger or acquisition, Congress must act and make appropriations, not just give lip service to the issue. Agency budgets matter, and the president and Congress should be willing to better fund agencies that work on antitrust issues given the importance of stopping anticompetitive conduct, protecting consumers, and safeguarding the health of America's economy. Upping the budgets of the FTC and the Justice Department's Antitrust Division—something I've long advocated for—can be done by direct appropriation or by adjusting filing fees. In either case, though, additional funding for antitrust staffing and expertise should be seen as *a good investment* with the potential *for a return* (in the form of fines and actual savings and return on investment for taxpayers), not as wasteful government spending. Major funding increases are needed, with one way to increase funding quickly being the passage of a supplemental appropriation.

As the law now works, filing fees are paid when companies file proposed mergers for review. Unfortunately, those fees have simply not kept up with the times or the growing complexity of corporate deals. In fact, the filing fees haven't been adjusted since 2001. This is a serious issue, and one that must be urgently addressed. Congress should appropriate more money to strengthen antitrust enforcement efforts—an investment that will pay off in terms of greater economic growth, better wages for workers, and more innovation.

Investing in the FTC and the Justice Department's Antitrust Division makes perfect sense. Oftentimes—it must be remembered—antitrust authorities, when functioning at their best, actually become profit makers. They don't make *actual* profits, as a traditional business does. But they do bring in money by exposing—and then fining—anticompetitive conduct, antitrust enforcement actions that, in the long run, will benefit consumers. One example? In 2015, the Obama Department of Justice obtained a record $3.6 billion in criminal antitrust fines.

Given that the entire Antitrust Division's budget is but a small fraction of that figure ($162.2 million in 2015), that eye-popping number provides a glimpse into the enormous "rate of return" that is possible when antitrust officials are simply allowed to do their jobs. Antitrust enforcement decisions should be made by antitrust professionals, not by a president or politicians with axes to grind, which is why it is so important to have high-quality, well-informed antitrust officials in place.

Increasing the budgets of the antitrust enforcement agencies by a significant amount is thus likely to be a cost saver for both the government and consumers. Look no further than the consumer benefits from long-distance telephone rates that resulted from the breakup of AT&T to see what I mean. More funds simply allow enforcers to better detect, deter, and eradicate cartels and anticompetitive conduct. And if you want action on Big Tech, these agencies need to be as sophisticated as those they are investigating. Boosting the budgets of antitrust authorities will also send a strong message to cartels and monopolists that they will not be able to get away with unlawful behavior.

A quick statistic helps illustrate the clear and present danger that under-resourced antitrust review and enforcement represents. Right now, the acquiring party to a merger is required to pay just $280,000 for a deal valued at $899.8 million or more. And even deals a hundred times that size—which require so many more resources to review and parse through in terms of the required economic and legal analysis—incur the same fees. Given the huge risks that megamergers pose to the pocketbooks of American consumers and to the long-term health of America's economy, the required filing fees are far too meager to give antitrust officials the resources they need to evaluate the propriety of mergers. The filing fees, in fact, don't come close to covering the actual costs of evaluating the proposed mergers. Thus, in addition to upping the congressional appropriation for the Federal Trade Commission and the Justice Department's Antitrust Division (something a president can propose in a new budget with new budget priorities), the filing fees paid by companies need to be updated.

To help solve the problem and to give antitrust enforcement agencies added resources and access to the information they need to do their jobs, in September 2017 I introduced the Merger Enforcement Improvement Act, a version of which is included in my 2021 bill. The legislation seeks to quickly provide the Justice Department's Antitrust Division and the FTC with more resources and better information to ensure that those who evaluate mergers and acquisitions have the tools, assets, and technical expertise they need to do their work. While the Antitrust Division has one mission (to enforce the nation's antitrust laws), the FTC basically has three mandates: consumer protection, antitrust enforcement, and protecting Americans' privacy.

In particular, the bill seeks to improve enforcement agencies' ability to assess the impact of merger settlements, require studies of new issues, and adjust merger filing fees. The current fee structure, put in place years ago, simply doesn't reflect the pre-pandemic uptick in complex, multibillion-dollar megamergers. The bill seeks to decrease fees for smaller mergers but increase them for mergers involving more than $500 million. In addition, the bill provides that the filing fees will be pegged to the Producer Price Index so that they automatically increase over time, resulting in a permanent fix to this problem. In any capitalist system, there will always be mergers. But we need to make sure that these mergers aren't anticompetitive. That's why my bill also directs the comptroller general of the United States to conduct a study "to assess the success of merger remedies required by the Department of Justice or the Federal Trade Commission in consent decrees," including "the impact on maintaining competition, a comparison of structural and conduct remedies, and the viability of divested assets."

To enable the agencies to fulfill their missions and protect competition by bringing enforcement actions against the richest, most sophisticated companies in the world, my 2021 bill would authorize a $300 million increase to each agency's budget. We've already seen some momentum for upping the agency budgets, with the appropriations for the FTC going from $310 million in 2019 to $321 million in 2020, with an additional $20 million designated in the end-of-the-year budget in 2020. The DOJ Antitrust Division also received an $18 million increase at the same time. When I introduced my original bill to increase the budgets, Senators Patrick Leahy of Vermont, Richard Blumenthal of Connecticut, Cory Booker of New Jersey, Dick Durbin of Illinois, Mazie Hirono of Hawaii, Ed Markey of Massachusetts, Kirsten Gillibrand of New York, and Tammy Baldwin of Wisconsin were the bill's co-sponsors. In addition, Senator Grassley has joined me on a bipartisan

The Federal Trade Commission should be more than "an idle threat," as portrayed by this 1934 cartoon in which the power of monopolies poses a massive barrier to small businesses and "the little fellow."

bill that would ensure antitrust officials have more resources. We were in fact close to including the Klobuchar/Grassley bill in the end-of-the-year 2020 budget agreement but it was blocked by House Republican leadership.

Whenever the American economy grows, the budgets of America's antitrust agencies should grow with it. This will allow antitrust agencies to do their jobs more effectively, whether that means collecting more information about the effects of potential or completed mergers or having the means to hire lawyers, economists, and other experts to bring cases in court. If additional appropriations and resources are not provided, antitrust officials will be unable to properly monitor and police the operations of America's free-enterprise system, resulting in more monopoly power, not less.

As the number of corporate mergers and acquisitions has grown, so have the complexities of antitrust enforcement settlements, premerger conditions, and the enforcement of those conditions. Since America's financial crisis, we often talk—and rightfully so—about the issue of firms being "too big to fail." An equally important question for modern antitrust enforcement officials, though, is whether some mergers are simply too big to fix and should not be allowed to move forward in the first place. Effective enforcement depends on accurate information and feedback, both before and after mergers take place, and agencies can make much better enforcement decisions if they understand what has worked in the past and what has not.

This much is clear: we need to give agencies the resources and sophisticated tools they need to do their jobs.

No. 3—Pass Legislation to Reduce Consolidation, Shift the Burden of Proof to Companies in Megamergers to Make It Easier to Prove Antitrust Cases, and Deal with Monopsonies. The law as currently written, and the courts as currently composed, have not stopped runaway corporate consolidation. Thus, changing the now-prevailing legal standards used to evaluate mergers and acquisitions would be very helpful to fight corporate consolidation, market concentration, and monopoly and monopsony power. Congress has the authority and power to act, and it must do so.

In September 2017, I introduced legislation—and did so again in 2021—to protect competition and prevent consolidation of industries that would be harmful to consumers. It proposes to amend the Clayton Act and seeks to (1) restore the original purpose of the antitrust laws to prevent anticompetitive mergers; (2) shift the burden of proof for megamergers and dominant firm mergers to the consolidating parties to prove that the merger does not harm competition; (3) create the Office of the Competition Advocate to encourage antitrust investigations, and to analyze and publish reports on merger activity; and (4) add the term "monopsony" to the Clayton Act so it is clear that single buyers controlling a market can be found to violate the law. A monopsony, often referred to as a buyer's monopoly, is a market condition in which there is only one buyer or in which a large buyer controls a large proportion of the market and drives down prices.

In antitrust cases, which party has the burden of proof can be decisive. The current burden of proof in merger cases is very high, making it extremely onerous to stop anticompetitive mergers. If the burden of proof in giant mergers and those involving dominant firms is shifted to the merging parties, the American public will be better protected from the consequences of monopoly power and corporate consolidation. The bill requires that the parties asking for approval of a megamerger prove it won't reduce competition, as opposed to the government having to prove that it will. If megamergers are claimed to be good for competition, then the parties to such transactions should have to prove it because the adverse impact of large anticompetitive deals can be substantial. When a megamerger has the potential to cause harm to competition, consumers, workers, and small businesses should not have to take the risk of the deal being anticompetitive.

Current law—in particular, section 7 of the Clayton Act—prohibits mergers and acquisitions if the effect "may be *substantially* to lessen competition, or to tend to create a monopoly." Courts interpreting that language have found it sets a very high threshold for challenging corporate deals, thus paving the way for mergers and acquisitions that harm consumers and have debilitating, anticompetitive effects.

In fact, in his May 2020 congressional testimony, Bill Baer—the former head of the DOJ Antitrust Division—made the specific point that while section 7 only requires the government to show that the proposed merger "may" substantially lessen competition or "tend" to create a monopoly, that is not how courts are reading the statute, with one federal court in Delaware concluding in 2020 that the Justice Department had not proven that a merger "will" harm competition—thus setting a higher bar than the statute itself currently sets forth. "A look at other court merger decisions in recent years," Baer pointed out in his testimony, "finds a similar tendency to ignore the Clayton Act mandate to prevent against risks to future competition and to hold the government to a near impossible standard."

To help address the problem, my proposed legislation would lower the applicable standard in the Clayton Act from "substantially" to "materially." The latter term is defined in the bill as that which is "more than a *de minimis* amount." The bill, which would give more federal scrutiny to mergers and acquisitions, notes that "competition fosters small business growth, reduces economic inequality, and spurs innovation," reciting at the outset that "concentration that leads to market power and anticompetitive conduct makes it more difficult for people in the United States to start their own businesses, depresses wages, and increases economic inequality."

Antitrust officials will still have to make reasoned judgments about which mergers and acquisitions should not be allowed to go forward, but if the bill is passed, they would be using a better, more workable standard than the one that prevails today. Changing the standard to "materially lessen competition" would send a signal to courts that they should more carefully scrutinize—and block—deals that would reduce competition. To date, courts have struggled or declined to interfere with vertical mergers and with mergers where the harm is to *potential* competition. For example, in *Federal Trade Commission v. Steris Corp.* (2015), a federal district court in Ohio rejected an FTC lawsuit seeking an injunction to block Steris Corporation's planned $1.9 billion acquisition of Synergy Health PLC. That lawsuit alleged that the acquisition would violate the antitrust laws by eliminating the likely future competition in the market for sterilization of medical equipment between Steris and Synergy Health. A new and lower legal standard for antitrust enforcers and the courts to consider in evaluating the consequences of prospective mergers would help to reinvigorate antitrust enforcement, not only in cases where the price of a good or service is at issue, but also in cases where quality or innovation concerns are at stake.

The bill also seeks to fight the growing power of monopsonies—a new reality in America's economy. In particular, the bill describes *monopsony power* as that which "allows a firm to force suppliers of goods or services to cut their prices to unreasonably low levels, resulting in reduced business opportunities for suppliers and reduced availability and quality of products and services for consumers." The bill also makes

The cornerstone of the free-enterprise system is competition. If there is no or only "a little" competition, the free-enterprise system simply cannot function properly. In 1912, J. P. Morgan was asked by Samuel Untermyer—counsel and investigator for a congressional subcommittee investigating Wall Street bankers and financiers— if he disliked competition. Morgan famously replied, "I like a little competition." This 1913 cartoon by Art Young depicts Morgan mixing a little competition/soda water with his big bottle of "Monopoly Whiskey."

"I Like a Little Competition"—J. P. Morgan

clear that monopsony power "can result in workers being forced to accept unreasonably low wages." The labor market and workers' wages are directly related to how much power corporate players have, and we, as Americans, need to level the playing field for our workers by taking on high-powered monopsonies. Monopsony power is just as bad as monopoly power.

The purpose of the bill is to reinvigorate competition and to ensure the health of America's economy for generations to come. Among other things, the bill would empower a competition advocate to publish periodic reports on market concentration, collect data, issue subpoenas, and recommend industry practices meriting antitrust investigations by the FTC and the Justice Department's Antitrust Division. It would also allow antitrust enforcement officials to evaluate the assurances and forward-looking promises made by those seeking merger approvals, because we would get actual data to assess whether they were made in good faith or were an attempt to defraud or hoodwink investigators and the public.

No. 4—Change the Legal Standard for Predatory Pricing Claims. Predatory pricing is but one tactic dominant market participants use to stymie new entrants or squash new market participants. And right now it is a problem that is hard to tackle because of the existing legal regime. In *Brooke Group,* the U.S. Supreme Court held in 1993 that even if a company prices below cost, an antitrust violation will only be found if the plaintiff also can demonstrate that the defendant has a reasonable prospect or "dangerous probability" of recouping its losses and that the defendant can do this in the same market in which it suffered its losses. Due in part to the evidentiary difficulties these requirements impose upon antitrust plaintiffs, it has become extremely difficult for plaintiffs to win predatory pricing cases.

The experience of the past few decades has shown that the same bare-knuckle predatory pricing tactics once used by Rockefeller's Standard Oil Company can be—and in fact are—used by large companies, including in the tech sector, to wipe out competitors and gain market dominance. Because the U.S. Supreme Court has set an incredibly high threshold that antitrust litigants must meet before they can successfully bring predatory pricing claims, that hurdle needs to be lowered by Congress so that antitrust officials can clear it more easily and stop the kind of predatory pricing that, ultimately, leads to price gouging. Dominant firms, including Amazon, should not be permitted to price below cost in a predatory manner in order to push out existing competitors or chill potential competitors from entering the market.

A little history is helpful. In *Brooke Group,* the Supreme Court held that a plaintiff "must demonstrate that there is a likelihood that the predatory scheme alleged would cause a rise in prices above a competitive level that would be sufficient to compensate for the amounts expended on the predation, including the time value of the money invested in it." This doctrinal test—known as the recoupment test—has made it substantially harder for antitrust plaintiffs to prevail, with the number of cases filed and won by plaintiffs falling dramatically. Because the Supreme Court has set the standard so high, anticompetitive conduct regularly goes unchecked, even though we know—or can easily surmise—it is occurring.

There is—to put it mildly—a major disconnect between marketplace realities and the U.S. Supreme Court's jurisprudence, which gives wide deference to conduct by dominant—or monopoly—companies. Although the Supreme Court has asserted that "predatory pricing schemes are rarely tried and even more rarely successful," empirical research dating back to the 1970s shows that predatory pricing is frequently used by dominant companies to crush or reduce competition. Predatory pricing—which already violates the nation's antitrust laws—involves a relatively simple two-step process: first, a company prices its goods or services below cost to drive competitors out of the market by forcing them to sell at a loss; second, the company—during the recoupment stage—charges a monopoly price to recoup the losses it incurred in establishing its market dominance. If the company, through monopoly pricing, is able to make more money during the recoupment phase than it was forced to expend in the initial predation phase, the company—unless deterred by law—will have employed what one scholar calls "an attractive anticompetitive strategy." For dominant companies, it is entirely rational to want to shut out or bankrupt competitors. That's because a company without meaningful competition can charge higher prices and reap monopoly rewards.

Thankfully, Congress doesn't have to accept the law as it now stands. It can pass legislation to overturn Supreme Court precedents that aren't predicated on interpretations of constitutional law. It can, therefore, change the current legal standard because the Supreme Court's *Brooke Group* holding merely represents a judicial interpretation of federal law. The Anticompetitive Exclusionary Conduct Prevention Act (discussed in item No. 1 on this list) already addresses predatory pricing in part by broadly addressing "exclusionary conduct," but Congress could go even further by eliminating or modifying the recoupment test.

A new standard for predatory pricing cases could be that pricing below cost in a well-defined market is presumed to be anticompetitive unless the entity with the market power rebuts that presumption. Presumptions can be decisive in antitrust cases, especially because interpreting the laws as written can be so subjective.

No. 5—Resuscitate the Philadelphia National Bank *Presumption.* To protect our free-enterprise system, lawmakers and regulators must constantly be on the lookout for anticompetitive conduct, and when such misconduct is found, it must be stamped out and properly punished. One thing Congress could do right away is resurrect the U.S. Supreme Court's now largely lifeless *Philadelphia National Bank* antimerger presumption. In that 1963 case, the Court established a presumption that a merger that would give one entity a 30 percent market share in the relevant market was presumptively unlawful.

The idea? Mergers that produce highly concentrated markets are inherently suspect, and it is better to stop anticompetitive harm in its incipiency when the effect of an acquisition may substantially lessen competition or lead to the creation of a monopoly. The importance of the *Philadelphia National Bank* presumption has faded over time. Once a presumption, *Philadelphia National Bank*'s holding has essentially become just an element for antitrust officials and the courts to consider. It is necessary that the government establish it to win, but establishing it is not sufficient for the government to win. Yet the central idea behind the *Philadelphia National Bank* case—that it is a very bad idea to allow corporate consolidation in a relevant market for goods or services—is actually a very worthy one.

Legislation could codify or, better yet, slightly modify that case's holding to strengthen it. The Consolidation Prevention and Competition Promotion Act (discussed above in item No. 3 on this list), in fact, already effectively codifies the impulse behind the *Philadelphia National Bank* case by requiring courts in antitrust cases brought by the United States, the Federal Trade Commission, or a state attorney general to determine that "the effect of an acquisition . . . may be materially to lessen competition or create a monopoly or a monopsony if . . . the acquisition would lead to a significant increase in market concentration in any line of commerce or in any activity affecting commerce in any section of the country." Using this approach has advantages over codifying the 30 percent threshold because the 30 percent threshold makes the finding turn on market definition. Also, in concentrated markets, mergers that result in less than a 30 percent market share can raise significant concerns, too.

Other legislative fixes are also appropriate. For example, by focusing on acquisitions that may *materially* reduce competition instead of just looking at actions that may *substantially* lessen competition (as I do in the Consolidation Prevention and Competition Promotion Act), the law could give the *Philadelphia National Bank* ruling new life and create a presumption that mergers leading to more concentrated markets are presumptively illegal. The entity seeking to counteract the presumption would have to show that the merger is not anticompetitive by, for example, showing that it would generate significant efficiencies that would be passed on to consumers for their benefit. And, of course, if a merger or acquisition did go forward, antitrust officials would be able to check to see if consumers actually benefited or ended up getting harmed by the transaction. If the latter, prompt enforcement remedial actions could be brought and taken.

Even the now-retired judge Richard Posner, a longtime Chicago school adherent who, as a law clerk for Justice William Brennan, conceived of the *Philadelphia National Bank* presumption in the first place, still finds it to be a relevant, easily understood standard. The presumption, he explains of the 1960s-era case, created a "simple" standard that could be rebutted (but only in appropriate circumstances), with Posner expressing the obvious concern that "a high degree of concentration . . . facilitates collusion." "The fewer large firms there are in a market," he notes, "the easier it is for them to collude, either explicitly or tacitly." Posner himself, on the fiftieth anniversary of the *Philadelphia National*

Bank decision, recently pondered aloud about how much "efficiency" the mergers of big companies actually bring. As he said in 2015, conveying his own skepticism in light of what he's seen over the decades, "I wish someone would give me some examples of mergers that have improved efficiency. There must be some." When it comes to protecting American capitalism, I believe we should err on the side of ensuring *robust competition* rather than running the risk of allowing the elimination of so many competitors that we *destroy competition* itself.

We have learned a lot about the problems of monopoly power and corporate consolidation in the last few decades. The approach of the Chicago school that Robert Bork advocated has, itself, in many ways been discredited. Instead of promised "efficiencies," we got monopoly power, higher prices, lower wages for workers, and runaway income inequality.

Adherents of the Chicago school, the economist Jonathan Baker writes in *The Antitrust Paradigm: Restoring a Competitive Economy*, "expected that relaxing antitrust rules would enable firms to achieve greater efficiencies." Their now decades-old wager, as Baker puts it, was this: "Firms would lower costs, possibly passing some of the savings through to lower prices. They would also improve their products and services, and innovate more quickly and extensively, boosting economic growth. . . . We now know that the Chicagoans lost their bet." Baker, the former chief economist at the Federal Communications Commission, sums it up: "Since the implementation of antitrust deregulation, market power has widened, without accompanying long-term gains in consumer welfare. Instead, economic dynamism and the rate of productivity growth have been declining. The harms from the exercise of market power have extended beyond the buyers and suppliers directly affected to include slowed economic growth and a skewed distribution of wealth."

While still embracing a conservative approach to law and economics, respected antitrust experts and jurists like Richard Posner themselves see the need for antitrust reform and more rigorous review of proposed mergers and acquisitions. The challenge now is to implement an expansion of U.S. competition policy.

Congress passed the Sherman Act to check monopoly power, and when Americans realized more had to be done, their duly elected representatives enacted the Clayton Act to plug loopholes in the law. Robert Bork's incredibly misleading "consumer welfare" misnomer—a paradigm put forward long after the nation's foundational antitrust laws were put in place, one not rooted in the actual historical record, but one inexplicably embraced by the federal judiciary—simply ignores significant harms to consumers associated with monopoly conduct, as well as Congress's clear intent in the late nineteenth and early twentieth centuries to take on monopoly power and anticompetitive mergers.

Today, the problems of monopoly power and corporate consolidation are even worse than they once were because the size of corporations is exponentially larger. For that reason, it is totally appropriate for Congress to eliminate the requirement that a merger "substantially" lessen competition and to replace that onerous standard with the "materially" lessen competition language. Congress—and then the courts—must make clear that they will not tolerate anticompetitive mergers that run afoul of that principle. As noted, section 7 of the Clayton Act already explicitly prohibits acquisitions whose effect "may be substantially to lessen competition, or to tend to create a monopoly." Given how American courts have narrowly interpreted the country's antitrust laws in an ahistorical, Borkian manner, competitive harms are occurring more and more frequently in America's economy. New steps, therefore, must be taken to stop that from happening. In particular, the antitrust laws must be reviewed and amended to make them more workable and—in some cases—to make more specific what those laws prohibit. To bring fair competition back to American industries, changes to the law—at a minimum—should make clear that any mergers or acquisitions that may materially lessen competition will not be permitted under the law. Anticompetitive deals that risk materially lessening competition are bad for America's economy. Period.

No. 6—Create a Presumption for Anticompetitive "Tying" Conduct. A related reform to combat the Chicago school's decades-old antitrust miscalculation would be to create another presumption that "tying" by dominant firms is presumptively illegal anticompetitive conduct. Tying is an arrangement whereby in order to buy one product or service, the consumer is compelled to purchase another product or service in a separate market.

The current standard for illegal tying is set forth in the U.S. Supreme

Court's 1984 decision in *Jefferson Parish Hospital District No. 2 v. Hyde*. That standard is complicated and restrictive, and unfortunately very few plaintiffs are actually able to meet it. One of its requirements is that the plaintiff must demonstrate market power or dominance. In *Jefferson Parish*, a defendant with a 30 percent market share was found *not* to have sufficient market power or dominance.

The Anticompetitive Exclusionary Conduct Prevention Act states that exclusionary conduct "shall be presumed to present an appreciable risk of harming competition" if undertaken by either a market participant with "a market share of greater than 50 percent as a seller or a buyer in the relevant market" *or* one who "otherwise has significant market power in the relevant market." A market participant with "significant" market power—a standard that could be far less than 50 percent or even 30 percent—would thus be subjected to the presumption of anticompetitive conduct. That new standard would greatly help in challenging anticompetitive "tying" conduct.

No. 7—Create a "Look Back" for Mergers and Acquisitions. To be effective, the antitrust laws should be both forward looking *and* backward looking, and the agencies that do antitrust enforcement must be much more engaged than they have been. It is not enough that antitrust regulators carefully review proposed mergers and acquisitions to decide whether they are anticompetitive; they must also periodically examine whether previous mergers or acquisitions were actually in the public interest or have materially harmed competition. Of course, the challenge with retrospective reviews is that they are expensive and time-consuming, which is why it is so critically important to block anticompetitive mergers and acquisitions before they take place. When acquiring companies enter into consent decrees, we must also ensure that those decrees are monitored and enforced, whether they are in the cable industry or the tech or pharmaceutical industries.

In the U.K., there is a market investigations law—a version of which could be adopted in the United States and enforced by the Federal Trade Commission. As Tim Wu explains in *The Curse of Bigness* as to how the enforcement of such a law could bend the trajectory of corporate concentration back to greater competition, "The prerequisite would be persistent dominance of at least ten years or longer, suggesting that a market remedy is not forthcoming, and proof that the existing indus-

More than a century ago, railroads were the monopolies everyone was talking about. Today, the Big Tech companies—Amazon, Apple, Google, and Facebook—constitute a large and ever-growing part of the world's commercial infrastructure.

try structure lacked convincing competitive or public justifications, and that market forces would be unlikely to remedy the situation by themselves. . . . The market investigation would serve as a particularly effective tool for stagnant and longstanding but not particularly abusive or aggressive monopolies or duopolies."

Though it is always better to reject anticompetitive mergers or acquisitions *before* they are consummated, a look-back approach is plainly viable, too, and is, in fact, indispensable to correct bad judgments made on prior mergers or acquisitions. As Wu suggests, "Consider a breakup of Facebook that undid the mergers with Instagram and WhatsApp. While Facebook might not like being dissolved, and might find the new competition unwelcome, it is hard to see what the great social cost, if any, would be. It is not clear that there are important social efficiencies gained by the combination of these firms." He concludes, "Reintroducing competition into the social media space, perhaps even quality competition, measured by matters like greater protection of privacy, could mean a lot to the public." If antitrust officials determine that corporate assets need to be divested to restore more effective competition (which is one of the requested remedies in the FTC/state attorneys general suit against Facebook), that divestiture should be ordered and done in a rational, commonsense fashion.

One of my antitrust bills, the Merger Enforcement Improvement Act, has an entire section on post-settlement data. That bill would amend the Clayton Act by adding language requiring the submission of data after any agreement is reached with the Federal Trade Commission or the United States to resolve an antitrust case regarding an acquisition. On an annual basis during the five-year period after the agreement is entered into, data must be submitted to the FTC or the assistant attorney general that will allow for an assessment of the competitive impact of the acquisition. The information to be submitted includes "the pricing, availability, and quality of any product or service, or inputs thereto, in any market, that was covered by the agreement"; "the source, and the resulting magnitude and extent, of any cost-saving efficiencies or any consumer benefits that were claimed as a benefit of the acquisition and the extent to which any cost savings were passed on to consumers"; and "the effectiveness of any divestitures or any conditions placed on the acquisition in preventing or mitigating harm to competition." Of course, retrospective reviews should not be excuses to limit or delay antitrust enforcement when an anticompetitive issue arises.

The Consolidation Prevention and Competition Promotion Act, which acknowledges the 50 percent increase in the number of acquisitions and mergers reviewed by the FTC and the Justice Department's Antitrust Division between 2010 and 2015, also requires companies entering into settlement agreements with the FTC or the Justice Department regarding an acquisition to report information *after the fact* that would allow a better assessment of the competitive impact of that acquisition. That way, if antitrust officials make a bad call on the basis of wrong or incomplete information, something can still be done about it. As with the Merger Enforcement Improvement Act, for the five-year period after the date of any settlement, those entering into one would have to annually submit information about the pricing, availability, and quality of the products or services in question. That information would relate to any cost-saving efficiencies or consumer benefits claimed to result from the acquisition, the extent to which any cost savings were passed on to consumers, and the effectiveness of any conditions placed on the acquisition in preventing or mitigating harm to competition.

Requiring parties to provide information on a yearly basis after a settlement makes particularly good sense because the best evidence of whether a merger has turned out to be anticompetitive is to actually check on what happened in its wake. Although more resources will be needed, agencies should be checking on mergers on a routine basis, not just when specific complaints arise. When mergers are approved, better post-merger monitoring will also ensure that industries remain highly competitive. Bottom line: more aggressive antitrust enforcement would go a long way toward preventing concentrated markets and monopoly power.

No. 8—Strengthen Penalties Against Cartels and Anticompetitive Conduct. Other provisions of antitrust law must also be updated to ensure that monopolies are not allowed to engage in anticompetitive conduct and that cartels are held accountable for illegal behavior. A cartel is a group of firms that collude so they can act as a monopoly to charge higher prices and increase their profits. As one economist, William McEachern, describes the problem of cartels, "Colluding firms, compared with competing firms, usually produce less, charge more, block new firms, and earn more profit. Consumers pay higher prices, and potential entrants are denied the opportunity to compete."

To better combat monopoly power, I introduced the Monopolization Deterrence Act of 2019 for just that purpose. That bill would authorize the Justice Department and the FTC to seek civil penalties under section 2 of the Sherman Act against corporations and individuals whose anticompetitive behavior unlawfully disadvantages a competitor. To more effectively deter monopolistic activity, a penalty could be up to 15 percent of the offending company's total U.S. revenue for the previous calendar year or, for the time that the misconduct took place, up to 30 percent of the company's total U.S. revenue related to the particular unlawful conduct at issue. The bill would also ensure that the Justice Department and the FTC coordinate their efforts to create guidelines, considering a number of relevant factors, for how they would impose monetary penalties.

This legislation is already supported by leading consumer welfare advocacy groups, including Consumer Reports, the American Antitrust Institute, and Public Knowledge. "We need to make sure we have effective enforcement tools to deter dominant corporations from engaging in anti-competitive, monopolistic practices that harm the marketplace and consumers," George Slover, senior policy counsel at Consumer Reports, announced when I introduced the legislation. "Senator Klobuchar's legislation," he added, "will put new teeth into our antitrust laws by empowering enforcers and courts to impose significant financial penalties when a corporation abuses its dominance in the marketplace."

Charlotte Slaiman, competition policy director at Public Knowledge, a group that promotes freedom of expression, an open internet, and consumer rights, likewise had this to say about the bill's importance: "Many of the important competitive concerns affecting people today are analyzed under the framework of monopolization outlined in Section 2 of the Sherman Act. This includes anticompetitive self-preferencing by vertically integrated firms, anticompetitive refusals to deal fairly with competitors or potential competitors, and anticompetitive tying or bundling." "Section 2 monopolization cases," she pointed out, "are more difficult to bring than other cases, and if the government wins at court, it usually can do no more than stop the offending company from engaging in the same anticompetitive behavior in the future." "Adding monetary penalties as a percentage of a company's U.S. revenue," she observed of the legislation, "could help deter anticompetitive conduct and give the antitrust enforcement agencies more leverage to promote competition in these types of cases."

We also need to do a much better job of taking on cartels. Right now, cartel sanctions are only a fraction as large as they should be to deter such conduct, and much more could be done to incentivize those with knowledge of cartels or anticompetitive behavior to share what they know with antitrust authorities. It is now known from academic research conducted by John Connor and Robert Lande—two leading antitrust experts—that the total expected costs of cartel activity (for example, in civil or criminal penalties) are significantly less than the sum of expected gains to cartels and individual decision makers involved in such unlawful activity. The title of their 2012 article in the *Cardozo Law Review* says it all in regard to the perverse, present-day incentives: "Cartels as Rational Business Strategy: Crime Pays." In light of their findings, increasing fines and penalties for cartel participants makes good and logical sense. Given that many cartels are never detected at all and that cartel participants are known to take extreme risks in furtherance of their illicit, greed-driven plots and objectives, it is, admittedly, hard to know the full extent of the problem and thus the optimal level for cartel sanctions. But we must try to tackle this problem, and upping the fines and penalties for cartel participants would help to better deter white-collar crime.

When violations are detected and penalties for antitrust violations are imposed, the violators should be held accountable for their actions and be banned from working in the same industry. Right now, cartel activity is not being adequately—let alone optimally—punished, and violators all too frequently just receive the equivalent of a police officer's verbal warning at a traffic stop before going right back to doing what they were doing before. Clearly, much more needs to be done to detect—and then permanently shutter—cartels.

Consider this: cartel fines have long been calculated on the basis of a U.S. Sentencing Commission formula. That formula is predicated on an estimate "that the average gain from price-fixing is 10 percent of the selling price." However, empirical data shows that the median average cartel overcharge over the last twenty years has been more than double that figure, 22 percent, with the mean, or average, cartel overcharge calculated to be 49 percent. Some cartels have raised prices very substantially for products or services, leading to the higher figure. In short, today's fines are not properly calibrated to remediating the harm. At a minimum, the U.S. Sentencing Commission should double its current presumption that cartels raise prices by an average of 10 percent. This would increase criminal fines substantially while simultaneously serving as a deterrent to future cartel activity. White-collar offenders may not be committing murders, but all too often they are getting away with murder when it comes to jacking up prices on unsuspecting American consumers.

A factual determination that someone has engaged in cartel activity should result in an order that any such person be barred from working in the same industry for a certain number of years after serving time in prison or paying the fine. As Judge Douglas Ginsburg and others, in thinking about the appropriate policy for the U.S. Department of Justice to adopt, have recommended, "As part of its plea agreements with corporations, the DOJ should insist that the corporate defendant agree not to hire or rehire anyone who has been convicted of price fixing. These bans should remain in effect for a substantial period—say, five years after the employee gets out of prison." No new legislation is needed to implement this policy, and clauses in plea agreements with offending individuals could also bar those individuals from serving on the board of directors of publicly traded companies, just as the Securities and Exchange Commission (SEC) already prohibits those convicted of violating securities laws from working for public companies.

Orders should also insist that corporations not be allowed to pay the fines of their convicted employees. Allowing ultra-wealthy companies to pay fines for corporate officers, managers, or employees—and then allowing those officers, managers, or employees to return to their jobs—would defeat the whole purpose of deterring cartel activity. Just as the SEC has disciplinary authority over industry participants and can bar corporate officers and directors from serving for reporting companies, those who run or participate in cartel activity must pay the price for what they have done. Convicted price fixers should not be able to quickly return to the same industry after they get out of prison or simply pay penalties only to pick up where they left off after they cut a check or their employer picks up the tab.

Some cartels have a global reach, and they too must be stopped in their tracks. One cartel—the Organization of the Petroleum Exporting Countries (OPEC)—has long operated openly and in plain sight. Formed in 1960 by Iran, Iraq, Kuwait, Saudi Arabia, and Venezuela, OPEC has—since its formation—curtailed oil production at various times, thus artificially manipulating the price of oil. It is time for that to end and for OPEC to be relegated to the history books. We should be investing more in clean energy and green jobs. It is far better for us, as a country, to invest in farmers in the Midwest than in oil sheikhs and oil cartels in the Mideast. Indeed, no cartel—whether domestic or international—should be allowed to operate. It is that simple.

That's why Senator Chuck Grassley and I introduced bipartisan legislation to allow the U.S. government to fight back against OPEC's brazen price-fixing. Our No Oil Producing and Exporting Cartels (NOPEC) Act—*okay, we do our best to come up with catchy titles for legislation*—would authorize the U.S. Department of Justice to sue oil cartel members for antitrust violations. It would also make clear that neither sovereign immunity nor the so-called act of state doctrine prevents judges from ruling on antitrust charges brought against foreign governments for manipulating the pricing or production or distribution of petroleum. As I said in 2018 when we rolled out our legislative proposal, "Open competition in international oil markets is critical to ensuring that American families pay fair prices at the pump."

No. 9—Allow Indirect Purchasers to Sue for Antitrust Violations. On another front, Congress could authorize so-called indirect purchasers to sue for damages under federal antitrust laws. Right now, under the U.S. Supreme Court's *Illinois Brick* decision, the federal antitrust laws permit only direct purchasers to sue for damages. Because of this judicial branch reality, indirect purchasers, who are often the ones ultimately paying a cartel's or monopolist's overcharges, currently have no standing to sue for damages.

The *Illinois Brick* decision should be reversed legislatively, especially because it has been shown that as it is now, those harmed by anticompetitive conduct so rarely recover the damages that they have suffered. Already, some state antitrust laws allow indirect purchasers to sue. Although it needs to be done very carefully, so as not to lower damage awards or unintentionally deter private antitrust enforcement, federal law could be changed by giving standing to purchasers who are end users of the cartelized or monopolized products and by holding accountable those who violate the law. The end users, after all, are often the ones absorbing much if not all of the overcharges created by cartel or monopoly activity. The new legislation would, by statute, abrogate the *Illinois Brick* doctrine while preserving the ability of private litigants to pursue class actions and explicitly allow indirect purchasers to sue for damages just as direct purchasers do now. They would still have to prove that they've been harmed, but if they can do so, they should be allowed to recover.

Even if Congress fails to act, more state legislatures could, themselves, pass indirect purchaser legislation to change state laws around the country. A model statute, which could provide the starting point for legislative debate and consideration, has already been drafted. So long as the final work product protects the rights of private litigants, including to seek class-action relief, it would be a good thing to help deter antitrust violations.

No. 10—Allow for Recovery of Prejudgment Interest for Successful Antitrust Plaintiffs. Even smaller steps, such as automatically imposing prejudgment interest on violators, could help to more appropriately punish those who violate the nation's—or a state's—antitrust laws. Violations of the antitrust laws give rise to corporate and individual penalties, and courts are authorized to award victorious private plaintiffs treble damages and attorneys' fees. If we look at the current state of federal law, though, the awardable money damages and sanctions hardly ever include an assessment of what lawyers call prejudgment interest—the sum of money that the judgment would have earned over the period of time from when the claimant was entitled to receipt of those dollars. Whereas post-judgment interest (that is, interest from the date a judgment is entered by a court of law) is currently awardable in antitrust cases, the damage caused by anticompetitive conduct starts long before a court makes a finding that there has been an antitrust violation. Although federal law states that prejudgment interest "may" be awarded, the statute puts strict conditions on its recovery so that—as a practical matter—prejudgment interest is only very rarely awarded in antitrust cases. Because of the way the statute is written, antitrust defendants hardly ever end up paying prejudgment interest.

Antitrust cases can go on for years, sometimes more than a decade, so allowing the recovery of prejudgment interest in addition to post-judgment interest would greatly increase the size of antitrust judgments and encourage malefactors to settle more quickly. It is not unusual for a big antitrust case to take five years or longer to resolve, and during that time price fixers are retaining their illegal overcharges and reinvesting—or earning interest on—that money. Legislation mandating prejudgment interest for both criminal and civil violations (that is, making antitrust violators pay interest on damage awards dating back to the date the actual harm began) would increase the effective size of money judgments for antitrust violations, thus imposing on wrongdoers the full cost of their bad behavior. That result would be fair because those who violate the law, not innocent parties or consumers, should bear the true cost of the antitrust violations. This relatively simple change in the law to add prejudgment interest to the final judgment would be especially helpful to combat the tactics of defendants who use litigation to delay—and drag out through judicial proceedings—the payment of antitrust damages or restitution before a judgment or plea bargain is entered. The amount of prejudgment interest to be awarded could be determined through the use of the Consumer Price Index or the Producer Price Index.

No. 11—Protect and Incentivize Antitrust Whistleblowers. Another good idea is for the United States to implement a whistleblower reward or bounty system for individuals who expose anticompetitive conduct or turn in cartels. This idea—which has been put forth by William Kovacic, a Republican who once chaired the FTC—reminds me of the plotline of *The Informant!*, a 2009 film starring Matt Damon that was based on a true story about a 1990s price-fixing scheme involving Archer Daniels Midland (ADM) and the company's Japanese counterpart, Ajinomoto. Mark Whitacre—the real-life ADM executive played by Damon—became an FBI informant/whistleblower who exposed serious wrongs, including market sharing and price-fixing agreements for products such as lysine (produced from corn and used for animal feed for chickens and pigs), even as he engaged in wrongdoing of his own. He recorded incriminating conversations about price-fixing in a smoke-filled hotel room using a hidden camera and microphone, and he revealed the motto of the ADM conspirators: "They always say, 'The competitors are our friends, and the customers are our enemies.'" ADM ended up paying a $100 million fine in 1996, and Whitacre spent eight years in prison for tax evasion, money laundering, and fraud that arose out of his role in the multinational lysine price-fixing conspiracy. A new whistleblower regime—a version of which was just passed into law at the end of 2020 and is described below—may help bring more antitrust violations to light and could provide that those involved in wrongdoing would forfeit the ability to receive any financial compensation.

Private parties who are injured by antitrust violations already have the right to sue—and to receive treble damages—for those violations. Further incentivizing private parties to step forward and supplement the efforts of federal and state antitrust officials, however, would help to take on—and quash—cartels and monopoly power. A whistleblower system serves to root out anticompetitive conduct and could apply to both civil and criminal matters (such as the one recently enacted in 2020). Bounties in civil actions could be introduced gradually to see how well they work, and initially they could be limited to individuals or small businesses exposing the misbehavior of companies with monopoly power who participate, for example, in price-gouging cartels or other exclusionary conduct. The optimal civil incentive structure would have to be worked out in Congress, but perhaps qualifying bounty recipients could be given a small percentage of the fines that would not have been obtained but for the whistleblowers' actions. The United States already has a long tradition of using *qui tam*—or whistleblower—lawsuits to expose fraud committed against the federal government, with individuals allowed to bring suit on behalf of the government.

In 2020 Senators Grassley and Leahy passed the Criminal Antitrust Anti-retaliation Act (of which I was a co-sponsor), which extends whistleblower protection for employees who provide information to the U.S. government relating to *criminal* antitrust violations or any act or omission that an employee reasonably believes to be a violation of the antitrust laws. "Just as whistleblower protections for government employees help root out waste, fraud and abuse, they can also help prevent misconduct in the private sector," Senator Grassley observed at a recent hearing. It should be noted that Senators Grassley and Leahy were incredibly persistent about this bill. It passed the Senate a whopping four times before finally passing the House and becoming law.

What a President and an Administration Can Lead . . .

No. 12—Presidential Appointments and Judicial Nominees. For true change in our competition policy to occur, a president must lead a major effort to put pressure on Congress to pass antitrust reform legislation, including but not limited to the ideas I recommend above. In addition, he must push for resources for antitrust enforcers, independent and well-resourced investigations of consolidated industries, and most of all action, including against Big Tech. He must put the power of the presidential bully pulpit behind these efforts.

To ensure that antitrust enforcement is as vigorous as it needs to be, the president must also appoint the most qualified antitrust officials. Appointees to the Justice Department and the FTC must actually *believe* antitrust laws and enforcement are critical to the health of America's economy. We don't need officials who are risk averse, who become nothing more than apologists for anticompetitive mergers and acquisitions, or who are simply looking to cash in after their stints at the Justice Department or the FTC. We need people with antitrust experience, but we need people who are not afraid to enforce the law without fear or favor.

The Justice Department's Antitrust Division, as well as federal agencies such as the Federal Trade Commission and the Federal Communications Commission, and state attorneys general's offices across the country should continually be on the lookout for any anticompetitive actions or practices. The major high-profile lawsuits recently filed against tech giants Google and Facebook are great examples of complex coordinated work. When bad conduct is discovered, enforcers should put a stop to it with the tools they already have and, when necessary, propose new legislation and rules or regulations to deal with novel or unanticipated forms of anticompetitive or exclusionary conduct. Although the antitrust laws were originally written to deal with railroad and oil barons, the laws were written using general language. As a 2020 editorial in *The Washington Post* points out, the antitrust laws "employ an economy of language and establish broad principles that can be adapted to specific cases," even those in a twenty-first-century marketplace that John Sherman could never have imagined. Laws must, of course, also be updated from time to time to deal more effectively with new problems and specific challenges, as described elsewhere in this chapter.

Americans must stay informed about issues that affect them, and that includes issues pertaining to competition policy. State and federal agencies themselves have the power to hold hearings, and they should continue to hold public hearings to help expose exclusionary and anticompetitive practices and keep the American people better informed about antitrust issues. The light shed by public comments and public testimony, for example, can result in changes to Federal Trade Commission or Federal Communications Commission policies. Public hearings on Big Data, common stock ownership, digital marketplaces, horizontal and vertical mergers, monopsonies, predatory conduct, the status of journalism, and privacy can inform both policy makers and the public. Of course, public hearings are not enough, especially if they don't result in follow-up. We also need antitrust enforcers to investigate anticompetitive and exclusionary conduct and to actually bring cases like the ones recently brought against the tech companies. Although the law provides for private antitrust enforcement, with some companies having the resources to pursue their own antitrust claims (including to stand up to Big Tech), that is clearly not a substitute for high-quality, government-led antitrust enforcement.

And judicial appointments, of course, are crucial to making our nation's antitrust laws work. In antitrust cases, judgment calls must be made all the time by judges, with courts—using the rule of reason doctrine—deciding what is a "reasonable" versus "unreasonable" restraint against trade. That is why it is so absolutely critical to appoint the best judges possible, and why judicial nominees should be questioned about antitrust issues. There is vast discretion and much uncertainty involved in antitrust matters, and too often judges accept outdated and discredited economic theories. Judges with common sense who are well informed on the consequences of anticompetitive and exclusionary conduct, however, can make good decisions if they take the time and effort to examine the facts and understand why the antitrust laws were put in place to begin with.

The issue today is that the decidedly conservative antitrust bent of the U.S. Supreme Court, including its newest members (Justices Gorsuch, Kavanaugh, and Barrett), is a continuing factor in calculations about whether antitrust actions should be brought. The simple question antitrust officials and private litigants must now wrestle with is this: Why go to the trouble of challenging a merger or acquisition or suing to stop anticompetitive conduct if the U.S. Supreme Court (or a lower court following the Court's precedents) is likely going to throw the lawsuit out? If, for instance, President Biden appoints more judges who recognize the importance of antitrust, the calculus of antitrust officials and private litigants will change for the better, and more cases will be brought, and brought successfully.

But no progress will be made unless the president makes antitrust enforcement and competition policy a major priority with the public, explaining why more enforcement resources and better laws are necessary to reduce prices, increase innovation, and even the playing field for American workers and consumers. The antitrust laws should not be used by a president as threats to make good on personal vendettas, something that President Trump did time and time again. Instead, the power of the presidency must be used to push for systemic change to America's competition policy. During the Trump administration, misuse of the antitrust laws for political ends became a clear and present danger to sound and fact-based enforcement of those laws. Under Joe Biden's administration this must change, with better enforcement and asset divestiture on the table as one anti-monopoly remedy.

No. 13—Take On the Big Tech Companies. Nowhere is it more clear that we need presidential leadership to take actions to change laws and lead investigations than in Big Tech. The sheer number of mergers and acquisitions, outsized monopoly power and grotesque exclusionary conduct in the Big Tech sector exemplifies what is going on with the power of BIG. The alarm bells are, at long last, finally going off, not only about Amazon, but about other tech companies such as Google, Facebook, and Apple. The two major national antitrust lawsuits against Facebook and Google, as well as the House tech investigation and report and various tech hearings in the Senate, have been more than a simple shot across the bow. This is finally real. People are actually starting to talk in earnest about what can be done—from regulation to forced asset divestiture to changes in the laws themselves—to rectify the problem. In the Big Tech sector, a Biden Department of Justice and the FTC should, among other things, reexamine the hundreds of M&A transactions to continue to provide even more evidence that the pattern of purchases and exclusionary conduct constitutes the monopolization or attempted monopolization of relevant markets in violation of our laws.

While each Big Tech platform controls different aspects of our economy, they share one undeniable quality, which the recent U.S. House investigative report summed up simply: each is a "gatekeeper" over "a key channel of distribution." Apple monopolizes the mobile app store market, where it—as noted in the House report—controls access to more than 100 million iPhones and iPads. Google completely monopolizes general online search and search advertising. Amazon controls a significant portion of the online retail market and also has major monopoly power over so many small businesses that must advertise on Amazon. And Facebook? The dominant gateway to social media.

Each "gateway"—as the House report observes—allows each company to "pick winners and losers," charge "exorbitant fees," impose "oppressive contract terms," and extract "valuable data from the people and businesses that rely on them." Not only is the dominance of the big tech companies protected by high entry barriers, but each dominant platform also is able to protect its market power by identifying potential rivals and buying them out, cutting them out, or replicating or copying their work. As the report notes of Facebook and its monopoly power in the social networking space, "Internal communications among the company's Chief Executive Officer, Mark Zuckerberg, and other senior executives indicate that Facebook acquired its competitive threats to maintain and expand its dominance. For example, a senior executive at the company described its acquisition strategy as a 'land grab' to 'shore up' Facebook's position, while Facebook's CEO said that Facebook 'can likely always just buy any competitive startups,' and agreed with one of the company's senior engineers that Instagram was a threat to Facebook."

That last point—about market dominance and stifling or chilling competition—is key to understand if we are to protect capitalism and free enterprise. We must safeguard innovation and put a stop to anticompetitive conduct that stifles it. At our Senate hearing in September 2019, the Judiciary Committee's Antitrust Subcommittee took up how Big Tech firms have become—in the words of one news report—"serial innovation killers" by "buying up tech start-up competitors before those competitors are large enough to raise red flags with regulators." At the hearing, Diana Moss of the American Antitrust Institute referred to weak antitrust enforcement over the years and said that much more attention needs to be paid to mergers not reportable under Hart-Scott-Rodino reporting requirements "that are likely to fly below the antitrust radar."

Moss came to the hearing with hard data, testifying that the American Antitrust Institute had looked at "over 700 acquisitions of nascent or potential rivals" since 1987 by Big Five tech companies—Amazon, Apple, Facebook, Google, and Microsoft. It found that just under 240 of those transactions were reportable to antitrust agencies, that more than 80 percent of those transactions closed after early stage review, and that those agencies more extensively investigated (through a second request or beyond) only 9 of the deals. Only one of those deals (Google-ITA Software Inc.), Moss pointed out, was actually challenged in federal district court. In order to acquire ITA Software, a producer of airfare pricing and shopping systems, Google was required to license ITA's software on commercially reasonable terms and to establish internal firewall procedures to protect competition for airfare comparison and booking websites. It was, in fact, a series of acquisitions, including of ITA Software, that made Google the dominant search provider and digital advertising vendor that it is today.

American antitrust enforcers must be much more vigilant in monitoring high-tech companies, just as European officials have been in investigating and monitoring any potential antitrust transgressions. In Europe, Amazon is currently under investigation for its use of data from independent retailers, and it could face a fine of as much as $28 billion if it is found to have violated the law. In addition, companies such as Qualcomm and Google have been hit with major fines for anticompetitive conduct in the European Union, with Europeans considering new laws and tactics to limit the power of Big Tech.

Bad conduct should carry consequences, and that should certainly be the case for antitrust violations. When companies engage in anticompetitive conduct, they should be made to pay, whether it be with fines to compensate for harm and wrongdoing or—if necessary to rectify ill-gotten marketplace dominance—by forcing the sale of assets or even breaking them up. The antitrust laws were designed to deter illegality so that the marketplace would be free from anticompetitive conduct. Indeed, many antitrust experts have suggested undoing, through legal actions, what has been done through anticompetitive mergers and acquisitions.

In a May 2019 op-ed in *The New York Times,* titled "It's Time to Break Up Facebook," Chris Hughes—a co-founder of Facebook—actually took direct aim at his friend Mark Zuckerberg's "staggering" influence. Zuckerberg, Hughes wrote, "controls three core communications platforms—Facebook, Instagram and WhatsApp—that billions of people use every day." Noting that Zuckerberg controls approximately 60 percent of the company's voting shares, Hughes emphasized, "Mark alone can decide how to configure Facebook's algorithms to determine what people see in their News Feeds, what privacy settings they can use and even which messages get delivered. He sets the rules for how to distinguish violent and incendiary speech from the merely offensive, and he can choose to shut down a competitor by acquiring, blocking or copying it." Contending that the U.S. government must hold Zuckerberg and Facebook "accountable" for the company's misbehavior and malfeasance—from its "sloppy privacy practices," to what happened with Cambridge Analytica, to its "slow response to Russian agents, violent rhetoric and fake news"—Hughes issued his direct and very dramatic call to action: "It is time to break up Facebook."

While Mark Zuckerberg has made clear he will vigorously oppose any effort to break up Facebook, the op-ed by Chris Hughes—which calls for the regulation of Facebook along with breaking it up—has sparked a renewed conversation about what to do about Big Tech's immense power. Elected officials from President Joe Biden to my Democratic colleague Elizabeth Warren, to all of the Democratic members of the U.S. Senate's Antitrust Subcommittee, to Speaker Pelosi and key Representatives Nadler and Cicillini, to Senator Chuck Grassley and other conservative Republicans, to business leaders, have been calling for change. Facebook acquired Instagram in 2012 and WhatsApp in 2014, and the statistics Hughes pointed to in his op-ed are especially telling with regard to Facebook's sheer size and monopoly power: "It is worth half a trillion dollars and commands, by my estimate, more than 80 percent of the world's social networking revenue." As he puts it, "About 70 percent of American adults use social media, and a vast majority are on Facebook products. Over two-thirds use the core site, a third use Instagram, and a fifth use WhatsApp. By contrast, fewer than a third report using Pinterest, LinkedIn or Snapchat." Facebook's monopoly power, Hughes contends, has had unacceptable marketplace consequences.

There are multiple things that can be done to stem the power of big corporations such as Facebook, but a necessary start, as has been done in the FTC suit, is to closely scrutinize their past acquisitions and any prior or ongoing exclusionary or anticompetitive activities as the panoply of options are evaluated. The facts show that Facebook acquired Instagram (a photo-sharing platform) for $1 billion and WhatsApp (a mobile messaging service) for $19 billion, effectively eliminating those nascent and up-and-coming competitors that were especially popular with young people—a demographic that can foretell long-term growth. Indeed, the sheer number of acquisitions by tech giants raises extremely troubling questions about why so many of these acquisitions were allowed to proceed in the first place during both Democratic and Republican administrations. "In total," Tim Wu writes in *The Curse of Bigness,* "Facebook managed to string together 67 unchallenged acquisitions, which seems impressive, unless you consider that Amazon undertook 91 and Google got away with 214 (a few of which were conditioned)." Many entities, including many small businesses, are now highly dependent on Google for internet traffic to their websites and there is not an equivalent search-engine substitute. Google even controls how many people get from point A to point B, with Google Maps capturing 80 percent of the market for navigation mapping.

Predating the DOJ lawsuit, on September 15, 2020, our Antitrust Subcommittee of the U.S. Senate Judiciary Committee held a hearing entitled, "Stacking the Tech: Has Google Harmed Competition in Online Advertising?," to shed more light on Google's practices. Before that hearing, I pointed out that for years there have been complaints that Google has used multiple acquisitions and an unmatched advantage in consumer targeting to dominate internet searches and to deliver ads, thus undermining rivals and limiting competition. I believe that additional cases should be brought against Google at both the federal and state levels when it comes to ad searches.

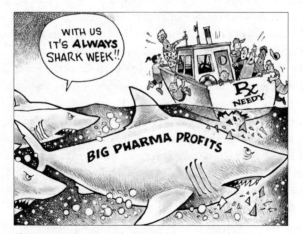

Pharmaceutical prices in the United States are out of control, making life-saving medications such as insulin unaffordable. We must do something about it because people's lives are at stake. Cartoon by Dave Granlund.

Another dominant company—Amazon—has also used acquisitions and access to competitors' data to accumulate market power. As the investigation of the House of Representatives into digital markets observes of Amazon's platform, "The platform has monopoly power over many small- and medium-sized businesses that do not have a viable alternative for reaching online customers. Amazon has 2.3 million active third-party sellers on its marketplace worldwide, and a recent survey estimates that about 37% of them—about 850,000 sellers—rely on Amazon as their sole source of income." As the House report found of Amazon's inherent conflict of interest in operating an online marketplace and hosting third-party sellers when Amazon itself is a seller, "Amazon has engaged in extensive anticompetitive conduct in its treatment of third-party sellers. Publicly, Amazon describes third-party sellers as 'partners.' But internal documents show that behind closed doors, the company refers to them as 'internal competitors.'"

Antitrust officials must address tech issues by taking concrete and pragmatic steps. Anticompetitive conduct will not stop if actions—including antitrust cases—are not taken to stop that conduct, and that also means meaningful remedies and passing new legislation to better regulate the companies going forward. We must be as vigilant as ever in sending the message that we will not tolerate any exclusionary or anticompetitive conduct by the Big Tech companies.

No. 14—Take On Big Pharma and Get Lower Prices for Consumers. This is actually a No. 1 priority for me in the Senate, and it should be for any president. The drug companies have been serial abusers of the patent system, reaping huge profits at the expense of American consumers. They have also marketed and sold addictive opioids without disclosing their highly addictive nature, and they have jacked up the prices of life-saving drugs so high that Americans have died because they could not afford life-saving medications. It is time that we, as a country, take on the pharmaceutical industry.

In a study published in 2018 in the *Journal of Law and the Biosciences,* Robin Feldman examined the practice of "evergreening," whereby drug companies artificially extend the life of their patents over products in which patent protection is about to expire. The study examined all drugs on the market between 2005 and 2015 and found that 78 percent of the drugs associated with new patents were actually not new drugs but existing ones. Noting that "drug prices have skyrocketed" and that "the cost of prescription medication is growing faster than any other form of health care spending," Feldman emphasized, "These price increases can be seen in specialty drugs—such as the antimalarial drug Daraprim, which Martin Shkreli's company famously increased from $13.50 per tablet to $750 per tablet—and in more common drugs—such as the rheumatoid arthritis drug Humira, whose price has increased by 126%. . . . Prices can drop as much as 20% when the first generic enters the market; with multiple generics, the prices may eventually drop by 80–85%." Feldman's conclusion: "Our challenge as a society is to restore the balance provided by the patent system itself, in which the inventor of a truly innovative product receives a limited period of time to attempt to garner a return, following which, open competition reigns supreme. The system has strayed far from that ideal."

For years, I have fought the pharmaceutical companies to lower prescription drug prices. I have long led a bill to lift the ban that prevents the U.S. government from negotiating cheaper prices under Medicare on behalf of forty-three million seniors. It is simply un-American—and an absolute outrage—that the government is barred from negotiating lower drug prices for tens of millions of Americans. Negotiation is an all-American activity, one that goes to the very core of the free-enterprise system. We should *demand* negotiation, not *forbid* it. When the pharmaceutical industry, in 2003, spent $116 million to persuade Congress to bar Medicare from negotiating over prescription drug prices, that industry knew exactly what it was doing. According to one assessment, that $116 million "has benefited the industry (and cost consumers) an estimated $90 billion per year"—a return on "investment" for Big Pharma of an astonishing *77,500 percent*. It's well past time that we come to terms with the pharmaceutical companies' grip on Washington and unleash the power of the people by passing meaningful legislation.

Canada—America's next-door neighbor—has much lower prescription drug prices, and there is absolutely no reason why Americans should be paying exorbitant prices for their drugs. Over the years, I have paired up with colleagues—from Senator John McCain to Senator Bernie Sanders—to try to bring in less expensive drugs from Canada. (Efforts to allow individual states to import such drugs have been defeated due to legal challenges.) After Senator McCain's death, I found another Republican lead sponsor—Iowa's Chuck Grassley—to take up this cause, one that makes perfect sense to me. Americans shouldn't be paying more for pharmaceuticals than Canadians, and as I like to say as the senior senator from Minnesota, "I can see Canada from my porch."

While the best way to deal with prescription drug prices is to pass reimportation legislation and my Medicare negotiation bill, there are several key things a president—and an administration—can do even without congressional action. As I detailed in my presidential campaign with my plan for 100 things a president can do without Congress in the first hundred days of a new administration, a president can immediately, for example, create downward pressure on prices by allowing for safe importation of prescription drugs from countries like Canada. Existing Food and Drug Administration authority allows for such waivers.

Because of a piece of legislation Senator Susan Collins and I got passed, we already allow the importation of drugs from other safe countries if there is a shortage of those drugs in the United States. But if people can't *afford* their prescription drugs, we should be equally outraged. We should allow the safe importation of drugs from other countries so people can buy, *at affordable prices,* the medications that they need to live.

The administration can also end "pay for delay" agreements that increase the cost of prescription drugs. It can also push for the passage of necessary legislation and instruct the U.S. Department of Health and Human Services to issue regulations to stop anticompetitive practices that increase prescription drug prices.

The practice of pay-for-delay is especially troubling. For many years now I've worked on bipartisan efforts with Senator Grassley and Senator Leahy and others to stop this unconscionable practice, whereby Big Pharma companies pay off generics to keep their products off the market. The legislation I have co-sponsored includes (1) the Creating and Restoring Equal Access to Equivalent Samples (CREATES) Act, which would prevent abusive tactics that inhibit affordable drugs from coming to market, and (2) the Preserve Access to Affordable Generics and Biosimilars Act, which—as noted earlier—would help stop anticompetitive payoffs in which branded companies outrageously pay their generic competitors *not* to compete as part of patent settlements. The latter bill, introduced in 2018 and 2019, would give the FTC the authority to start enforcement proceedings against pharma companies that use pay-for-delay settlements to prolong the market entry of drugs or biological products.

American pharmaceutical companies should not be afraid of competition; they should embrace it. And American lawmakers and consumers should not tolerate a practice that makes prescription drugs unaffordable; they should insist on a better way forward.

Big Pharma companies must no longer be allowed to run Washington, D.C. Their strong-arm tactics, which have included fighting tooth and nail to stop efforts to lower costs and to allow the safe importation of drugs from Canada, have driven Americans to take drastic, sometimes desperate measures to find lower-cost medications. In May 2019, one headline in my hometown paper, the *Star Tribune,* caught my attention: "Insulin Outlaws: High Cost of Medication Drives Minnesotans Across the Border to Canada." Six Minnesotans, led by Lija Greenseid, a mother of a teenage daughter with type 1 diabetes, had crossed the border into Canada to buy insulin from a Canadian pharmacy. The group spent $1,265 for insulin supplies that in the United States would have cost an estimated $12,400. One member of the group, Travis Paulson, recalled a time when insulin cost $8 a vial. He bought fifteen vials of insulin in Canada for $410—a supply of medication for three to four months that would have cost him approximately $5,250 in the United States. Nicole Smith-Holt, whose son Alec had so tragically died after trying to ration his insulin, and who had been my guest at the state-of-the-union address in 2019, made the trip too, offering moral support and encouragement and making a symbolic purchase of a single vial of insulin that might have saved her son's life. A recent Harvard study showed that insulin is very cheap to produce, costing between $3 and $7 a vial. The last major improvement to insulin came in the mid-1990s, so there is no reason whatsoever—other than corporate power and abuse—for why a single vial of insulin now costs between $300 and $400.

We all know the importance of having a strong pharmaceutical industry, especially during this pandemic. But nevertheless, the need for an industry and the success of that industry can still exist without a national rip-off. Americans shouldn't have to go to Canada to purchase affordable life-saving medications. We must pass general antitrust reform as well as pharmaceutical-focused consumer protection laws. We need presidential leadership to get this done.

No. 15—Carefully Scrutinize Both Horizontal and Vertical Mergers, and Update the Horizontal and Vertical Merger Guidelines to Improve Merger Enforcement. The first Merger Guidelines, which were intended to provide clarity to the business community and the legal profession about the standards being applied by the U.S. Department of Justice in assessing whether to challenge a corporate acquisition or merger, were issued in 1968. Those 1968 Merger Guidelines, developed by Assistant Attorney General Donald Turner, an economist and lawyer, were fairly strict but have been revised multiple times since their initial issuance, with revisions made in 1982, 1984, 1992, 1997, and 2010.

For example, the 1982 Merger Guidelines—written by President Reagan's Justice Department and heavily influenced by Robert Bork's ideas—focused on whether mergers would bring higher prices in the short term but, especially as lax antitrust enforcement became the norm, woefully neglected to consider long-term effects. The 1982 Merger Guidelines—as well as other subsequent amendments—loosened the standards set forth in 1968, delivering a one-two punch as, first, the standards in those guidelines became less strict and, second, antitrust enforcers then failed to carefully scrutinize the anticompetitive nature of specific acquisitions and mergers. On many occasions, antitrust officials

STOP THIEF!
HE WANTS THE EARTH.

Multinational corporations have become more and more ubiquitous. Global domination might make a good theme for a James Bond movie, but in the real world anticompetitive conduct—whether it occurs on a local level or on a global scale—must be combated. Fair competition is key if consumers are to get fair prices, not monopoly prices.

simply neglected to consider a merger's anticompetitive impact in the long run and, instead, just accepted the representations of an acquiring company about the proposed merger's supposed benefits to consumers or the company's argument that the merger would bring "efficiencies."

A presidential administration has the power to revise both the Horizontal and the Vertical Merger Guidelines. The Vertical Guidelines, after first being issued in 1984, were only recently revised, in mid-2020, by the Trump administration (and not in a good way). To better ensure that anticompetitive mergers and acquisitions are not approved, the Justice Department's guidelines for both horizontal and vertical mergers need to be updated. For example, the dissenting statements of Rohit Chopra and Rebecca Kelly Slaughter, the FTC commissioners who were critical of the Trump administration's new Vertical Merger Guidelines and the way they were finalized, contain major issues (including about the health of digital markets) that need to be considered in redrafting those guidelines. The Justice Department's Antitrust Division, in conjunction with the Federal Trade Commission, can prepare and then issue new merger guidelines—ones that are truly designed for the modern era—to send the message that anticompetitive mergers, of whatever type, will not be tolerated.

Horizontal and vertical mergers differ in character, though mergers of both types can be anticompetitive in nature. Whereas horizontal mergers are between companies that sell the same or similar products or services, vertical integration is a system in which a company owns or controls its supplier, distributor, and retail locations. A system of vertical integration, such as Amazon already has in the book business (creating conflicts of interest and an incentive for Amazon to preference the sales of its own authors over those of other publishers), gives companies considerable market power and clout. That's why I have vigorously questioned the wisdom of allowing vertical integration of industries and opposed vertical mergers, such as the AT&T–Time Warner merger.

At their core, the merger guidelines put out by the Justice Department's Antitrust Division and the FTC are important because their contents strongly signal what mergers will or will not be approved. Merger guidelines are also heavily relied upon by the courts. If the merger guidelines are not strong enough, mergers or acquisitions that should not be approved will be approved. In recent testimony, for example, Diana

Moss—the president of the American Antitrust Institute—emphasized that current merger presumptions may, in fact, be inadequate for digital technology acquisitions. The existing Horizontal Merger Guidelines, Moss noted, focus on narrowly defined markets and look at each acquisition separately. "The rapid series of digital technology acquisitions over the past few decades," she pointed out, "supports the idea that enforcers should attempt to expand the lens through which they evaluate serial transactions, with emphasis on the longer-term effects of such consolidation." Her suggested sensible policy prescriptions: (1) establishing rebuttable presumptions for acquisitions of nascent and potential rivals tied to highly concentrated markets, including in upstream or downstream markets; (2) retrospective analysis of consummated mergers to see if the mergers resulted in lower quality, less choice, higher prices, or slower innovation; (3) improved agency transparency so that the public and the business community know why the agencies took various actions; and (4) a blue-ribbon committee to evaluate the need for a new digital markets act.

No. 16—Conduct a Top-to-Bottom Review of Horizontal Shareholding and Use Existing Laws as Well as Advocate for New Ones to

Monopoly power can stifle economic liberty and opportunity. In this cartoon, arising out of the panic of 1907, J. P. Morgan and what was known as the Money Trust crush the Statue of Liberty.

Constrain It. As America's economy has evolved since the 1950s, new antitrust issues have emerged that warrant our urgent attention. One of those issues: the now endemic problem of horizontal shareholding, whereby Wall Street investment funds or ultra-wealthy investors own shares in multiple companies in the same industry. Just as insider trading is illegal in the securities context because it negatively affects the integrity of stock markets, allowing the same wealthy investment firms and investors to invest in multiple companies within the same industries can create problematic conflicts of interests.

As discussed in chapter 7, this is a complex problem, but one that should no longer be dismissed with a shrug of the shoulders. Seventy percent of the stock market is now controlled by institutional investors (for example, banks and hedge funds)—the very same investors who are frequently the largest shareholders in multiple companies that compete against one another. Cross-ownership coupled with industry consolidation and highly concentrated industries presents a real issue that needs to be addressed. I believe a federal commission should be convened to begin that work and make detailed recommendations to Congress. Already, I have a bill that would require the FTC to conduct studies on the broader impacts of concentration of commercial enterprises and on institutional investors' cross-ownership of competing companies.

The nation's antitrust laws, as designed, sought to preserve and protect competition, not competitors, and those laws have long restricted the right to engage in anticompetitive conduct. If we don't want the "trusts" of yesteryear to be reconstituted by allowing billionaires and large institutional investors to own big stakes in multiple companies in the very same industry, we must better understand the problem and then act. Where high-net-worth individuals or institutional investors buy a significant number of shares in multiple companies in the same industry, the prospect of anticompetitive conduct and cartel formation becomes much more likely, especially where the investments are substantial or result in controlling—or near-controlling—interests.

Einer Elhauge—the Harvard professor who has carefully studied this issue—has already meticulously documented the problem and proposed some potential antitrust enforcement solutions to counter it. In a 2019 paper, he highlights empirical studies showing that increased horizontal shareholding "explains 15% of the price increase for soy, corn, and cotton seeds from 1997–2017" and that, in the pharmaceutical industry, such horizontal shareholding "between an incumbent brand and an entering generic not only increases by 12% the odds that they will enter into reverse-payment settlements that delay generic entry, but also produces a larger delay of entry." He further explains that even when horizontal shareholders have minority stakes in corporations, horizontal shareholding often has anticompetitive effects in concentrated markets. "The new economic proofs," the abstract of his paper observes, "show that, without any need for coordination or communication, horizontal shareholding will cause corporate managers to lessen competition to the extent they care about their vote share or re-election odds and will cause executive compensation to be less sensitive to firm performance."

In light of the mounting empirical evidence, Elhauge—using antitrust jargon unfamiliar to everyday Americans—has recommended "that antitrust agencies should investigate any horizontal stock acquisitions" that have resulted or would result in a level that exceeds a certain threshold on the Modified Herfindahl-Hirschman Index, which involves a calculation measuring the degree of industry concentration taking into account the cross-ownership of investors' stakes in com-

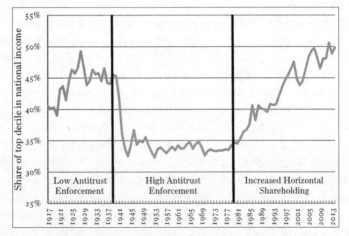

Antitrust enforcement is necessary to help fight income equality, as this chart from Einer Elhauge's article "How Horizontal Shareholding Harms Our Economy—and Why Antitrust Law Can Fix It" shows.

peting companies. His own, more easily accessible translation, using less antitrust lingo: antitrust agencies must "investigate concentrated markets with high horizontal shareholding to ascertain whether anti-competitive effects exist in those markets, so any empirical uncertainty would be resolved in enforcement actions about specific markets." His proposal, targeted at the lawyers, economists, and other antitrust professionals who review such matters: "that antitrust agencies consider horizontal shareholding when assessing mergers and cross-shareholdings and investigate any markets with a sufficiently high level of horizontal shareholding." In simple language, don't let big money players re-create Rockefeller-style "trusts" through other means.

Anticompetitive conduct, in whatever form, threatens America's free-enterprise system. And just as Elhauge sees a major problem, as have European antitrust officials, he sees potential solutions. Section 7 of the Clayton Act, Elhauge explains, already prohibits stock acquisitions that may substantially lessen competition, and that provision should be used more aggressively—even as currently written—to combat horizontal shareholding's adverse effects. "Thus," Elhauge contends, calling attention to the existing power of antitrust regulators, "the stock acquisitions that create horizontal shareholdings are illegal whenever those horizontal shareholdings are shown to have created actual or likely anticompetitive effects."

In addition, Elhauge asserts that section 1 of the Sherman Act—the 1890 law that applies to any "contract, combination in the form of trust or otherwise"—should be utilized, too, to constrain horizontal shareholding because it involves contracts between corporations and common investors. "Those contracts," he notes, "are what give horizontal shareholders rights to vote for corporate management and a share of corporate profits." Of course, only when horizontal shareholdings cause anticompetitive effects, or are likely to produce such effects, would they be found to violate the Sherman Act. We are not talking here about stopping a small individual investor from buying and owning whatever stocks he or she wants for a diversified stock portfolio—one, say, put together as part of a college savings or retirement plan. And we are not talking here about eliminating mutual funds or index funds—the kinds of funds people rely on to build a nest egg for their retirements.

A number of ideas have been floated to address the problem of hori-

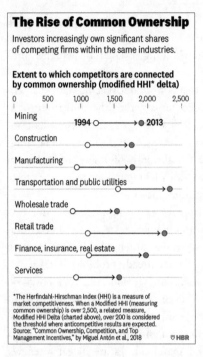

The Rise of Common Ownership

Investors increasingly own significant shares
of competing firms within the same industries.

**Extent to which competitors are connected
by common ownership (modified HHI* delta)**

0   500   1,000   1,500   2,000   2,500

Mining
            1994 ○⸺⟶● 2013

Construction
                ○⸺⟶●

Manufacturing
               ○⸺⟶●

Transportation and public utilities
                    ○⸺⟶●

Wholesale trade
            ○⸺⟶●

Retail trade
            ○⸺⟶●

Finance, insurance, real estate
             ○⸺⟶●

Services
            ○⸺⟶●

*The Herfindahl-Hirschman Index (HHI) is a measure of
market competitiveness. When a Modified HHI (measuring
common ownership) is over 2,500, a related measure,
Modified HHI Delta (charted above), over 200 is considered
the threshold where anticompetitive results are expected.
Source: "Common Ownership, Competition, and Top
Management Incentives," by Miguel Antón et al., 2018   ♡ HBR

The rise of common ownership,
as presented in this graph that
appeared in the *Harvard Business
Review* in 2019, shows the risk of
allowing common stock ownership
of competing companies in the same
industries.

zontal shareholding, including one to rein in the anticompetitive power
of institutional investors. Forbidding common stock ownership of competing firms above specified limits (or putting other rules of the road
in place to curtail the harm caused by the practice) makes good sense
if lawmakers and experts can put together a sensible and pragmatic
proposal. Just a handful of extremely large institutional investors own
large chunks of the stock of many competing corporations, including
those in key sectors such as the airline industry. This common stock
ownership distorts companies' competitive incentives and could easily
result—indeed, almost certainly has resulted—in higher prices for consumers, if not the outright formation of as-yet-undetected cartels.

New legislation—the precise details of which would need to be
worked out after additional study and transparent congressional
hearings—could prevent the same stockholders from owning large
amounts of the stock of competing companies. To reflect the realities
of how portfolios are built and real-world investing works, a carefully
crafted law would take into consideration the best available information

and contain an exception to allow individual investors, and even portfolio managers with institutional investors, to own certain amounts of stock in competing corporations up to a certain level—one to be determined through further study and research about the anticompetitive nature of horizontal shareholding. Experts must be allowed to weigh in on the problem, but perhaps an exemption might be considered—or patterned—along the lines of the current law that forbids the same individual to be an officer or director of competing firms but that allows de minimis exceptions for overlaps of less than $34 million (a figure the FTC revises annually), or 2–4 percent of sales and so on.

Again, the real concern is not about small, individual investors or those who invest in 401(k) plans or similar vehicles. The concern is about large, powerful investors and extremely wealthy individuals who own—or who in combination with a few others own—controlling or near-controlling stakes in corporate enterprises that should be competing against one another but that may not, in practice, be aggressively doing so. Some scholars have contended that the horizontal shareholding studies done to date do not yet make a sufficient case for broad and sweeping reform and have urged that more information gathering take place to better understand the issues at stake. For example, C. Scott Hemphill and Marcel Kahan of the New York University School of Law argue that while "it may be tempting to follow the principle of 'better safe than sorry'" to avoid any potentially anticompetitive effects of horizontal shareholding, "this temptation should be resisted." While this is, admittedly, a complex problem that needs to be addressed through thoughtful and pragmatic solutions, America's antitrust enforcers should not be like ostriches sticking their heads in the sand. On the contrary, they should work with diligence and speed, drawing upon the expertise of experts, to better understand the problem and then make specific recommendations to solve it.

No. 17—Better Scrutinize the Effects of Conglomerate Mergers. We should also better scrutinize the ill effects of conglomerate mergers, especially because Big Tech, Big Ag, and Big Pharma companies and other multinational companies have the power to squash smaller enterprises in local communities. From 2015 to 2019 alone, there were dozens of mergers and acquisitions where *both* of the involved firms' assets exceeded $10 billion (and even $25 billion, $50 billion, or $100 billion). Indeed, from

2015 to 2019, only three of the seventy-eight largest mergers and acquisitions (that is, those situations where both the acquiring and the acquired firm were valued in excess of $10 billion) were successfully blocked.

The sheer size of a company gives it power—economic power, political power, and the power to potentially co-opt regulatory agencies. Under existing law, the bigness of a corporation is not, in and of itself, an antitrust violation, though some scholars are beginning to advocate for outlawing conglomerate mergers above a certain size to combat corporate consolidation. "Bigness" alone, it must be acknowledged, is simply not illegal under the nation's existing antitrust laws, and it never has been throughout American history, in part because certain industries require scale to produce their products (think automobile manufacturers that compete against one another in a global environment). Indeed, patent laws actually contemplate exclusivity for patent holders for a limited period of time, allowing inventors and innovators to reap the financial rewards for their hard work and entrepreneurship.

The antitrust laws were enacted in response to the vast power of the trusts, and a showing of exclusionary or anticompetitive conduct has long been required to successfully bring an antitrust claim. As one source describes the country's antitrust laws, "The prohibition against monopolization is not violated by the mere possession of monopoly power or some predetermined share of the market. U.S. antitrust law does not include a 'no-fault' monopoly statute, and there is no 'bright line' that, once crossed, exposes an otherwise lawful monopolist to antitrust sanctions." A "no-fault approach" to antitrust was proposed by Donald Turner—President Lyndon Johnson's assistant attorney general for the Antitrust Division and the person who drafted the division's first set of Merger Guidelines—in the *Harvard Law Review* in 1969, with another article in that journal, written by Oliver Williamson in 1972, lamenting that "antitrust policy has long been plagued by the problem of continued dominance of an industry by a single firm which has obtained its position by lawful means." And in 1976, the Democratic senator Philip Hart of Michigan introduced a no-fault bill in Congress. However, the "no fault" monopolization idea and that bill went nowhere.

At the very least, however, we need accurate industry concentration data on which to ground policy decisions. The FTC used to collect industry data on lines of business in an effort to make sure particular sectors did not become too concentrated, and antitrust officials today also have a need to get accurate information so that they can closely monitor industries for monopoly power and consolidation. Although the data collection program was stopped in the mid-1980s, if antitrust agencies are adequately funded, they will be better able to use modern-day technology to effectively track anticompetitive or exclusionary conduct. Antitrust officials should closely scrutinize all industries where we know that companies are exercising monopoly power. Only if those companies know that antitrust scrutiny will occur will they be deterred from engaging in anticompetitive conduct. One model in the U.K. allows antitrust officials to conduct market studies and investigations as to why particular markets are not working well. "The most important feature of market studies and investigations," Sandra Marco Colino, a law professor specializing in competition law, writes in her book *Competition Law of the EU and UK,* "is that they focus, as the names suggest, on the operation of the market as a whole, rather than on the way in which a single firm, or agreement, operates." The goal: to remedy, mitigate, or prevent any "adverse effect on competition" or "any detrimental effect on customers so far as it has resulted from, or may be expected to result from, the adverse effect on competition."

By thinking big while paying attention to small details, we can better combat the power of massive conglomerates. We must do both, because, as history shows, big companies are frequently willing and more than able to exercise their power to corrupt our politics or to stifle free and fair competition.

No. 18—Better Coordinate International Enforcement. Since the mid-1990s, it has been recognized that we need better coordination of antitrust enforcement internationally. When Janet Reno was the attorney general of the United States, she announced a legislative proposal— the International Antitrust Enforcement Act of 1994, drafted by the Justice Department's Antitrust Division—that President Bill Clinton ultimately signed into law. Attorney General Reno said at the time of the legislation's introduction, "As more countries utilize laws to preserve competition and to stamp out cartels, the playing field is leveled and U.S. consumers and industries are the beneficiaries. Unfortunately, our antitrust enforcement tools have not kept pace with the internationalization of the marketplace." The International Antitrust Enforcement

Act allows the Justice Department and the FTC to obtain evidence from foreign antitrust agencies, including in the context of criminal and civil antitrust investigations and cases, by authorizing U.S. antitrust officials to provide reciprocal assistance where it was deemed to be in the public interest to do so.

Since the mid-1990s, of course, the globalization of commerce has only accelerated, meaning that more coordination and cooperation between the United States, the European Union, and foreign countries is needed than ever before. In 2001, the International Competition Network (ICN), an informal network of recognized antitrust authorities from both developed and developing countries, had its first meeting in New York. The United States had suggested establishing the ICN, which has been called "a network similar to" the G7 for antitrust issues. According to the ICN, which the United States continues to be a member of, the organization—"the only global body devoted exclusively to competition law enforcement"—plays a vital role: "The ICN provides competition authorities with a specialized yet informal venue for maintaining regular contacts and addressing practical competition concerns. This allows for a dynamic dialogue that serves to build consensus and convergence towards sound competition policy principles across the global antitrust community." The ICN publishes papers on everything from Big Data and conglomerate mergers and consumer protection to digital markets and privacy.

While the Department of Justice and the FTC already have in place Antitrust Guidelines for International Enforcement and Cooperation, the United States needs stronger relationships with its allies to facilitate better international antitrust enforcement. Given their experience and backgrounds, President Joe Biden and Vice President Kamala Harris will be in a uniquely good position to foster and build those ties. International networks of stakeholders in the antitrust arena can, at times, produce only esoteric discussions of the problems that lead nowhere. The activities of multinational corporations routinely cross borders, however, and in the digital age U.S. antitrust officials—at both the DOJ and the FTC—must be concerned about the activities of companies and individuals around the world, not just within the boundaries of the United States.

In addition to international enforcement, our trade policies must reflect the realities of unfair competition from China and other countries. Some countries have sovereign wealth funds and lack rigorous antitrust enforcement agencies. We need stronger trade measures—and better enforcement of trade laws—to protect American workers from unfair economic practices. For example, China's dumping of subsidized steel in the U.S. market is highly problematic—and must be stopped—because of the importance of domestic steel production. In fact, the strengthening of the enforcement of our laws starting during the Obama administration showed an emphasis on enforcement can work. Similarly, in a rare victory against the pharmaceutical industry, the Trump administration—at the urging of congressional Democrats led by Speaker Pelosi—also agreed to remove from the U.S.-Mexico-Canada trade agreement a provision that would have given the makers of expensive biologic drugs ten years of protection from less expensive generics. "This is one of the first times we've actually seen pharma lose," Representative Earl Blumenauer, an Oregon Democrat, observed.

Ideas Outside Antitrust That Would Foster More Competition and Protect Consumers . . .

No. 19—Reform the U.S. Patent System and Stop Serial Innovation Killers. Reforming the U.S. patent system is yet another way to incentivize more competition and entrepreneurship. The ability to seek and receive patent protection is a valuable incentive for inventors and innovators, but when patents last too long, they stifle competition, furthering the development of monopoly power. While patent protection is critical to our economy, the U.S. patent system can also be used by patent holders to block new market entrants from competing effectively. "Thickets of patents," Tim Wu writes in *The Curse of Bigness,* citing the work of economist Carl Shapiro, are "sometimes deployed to slow down those seeking to bring new products to market."

Instead of allowing dominant firms to create what are frequently huge barriers to entry for new market participants, the patent and antitrust laws should better take into consideration the need for more innovation, not less. In fact, the pejorative term "patent troll" has been coined to capture the situation in which a company or person acquires patent rights (often through a bankruptcy) not for purposes of manufacturing products but to aggressively sue alleged infringers.

Back in 2011, I was an original co-sponsor of the America Invents Act, which made significant changes to the U.S. patent system and was designed to deal with the backlog of more than 700,000 patent applications. That was a first step, but additional reform of the patent system is still in order. We need to make sure we are promoting innovation, not quashing or disincentivizing start-ups. And we need to make sure the patent system is not preventing life-saving drugs from getting into the hands of American consumers at affordable prices.

The America Invents Act modernized the country's patent laws and cut red tape so patents could be processed more expeditiously. And back in 2015, I co-sponsored the Protecting American Talent and Entrepreneurship (PATENT) Act. That bipartisan legislation was aimed at protecting legitimate patent holders and their rights while limiting the ability of bad actors to exploit the system. Truly frivolous lawsuits can stifle innovation, and the PATENT Act sought to deter abusive litigation practices. The PATENT Act provided for heightened penalties for those found to have violated the FTC Act by sending abusive or misleading demand letters—letters typically written by lawyers in connection with the assertion of patent rights.

Like me, New York's senior U.S. senator, Chuck Schumer, one of the bill's other co-sponsors, saw the need for something concrete to be done. As Senator Schumer said when we introduced the bill, "Patent trolls are taking a system meant to drive innovation and instead using it to stifle job-creating businesses around the country. Main Street stores, tech startups and more are being smothered by the abuse that is all too common in our patent system, and it's time for that to end." Both big companies and "patent trolls" can misuse patents to stifle legitimate competition, and when that happens, it is a real problem—and something that America's founders would not have liked one bit.

The patent laws should—as they were originally designed to do—encourage innovation, not stop it in its tracks. Intellectual property is a major driver of America's twenty-first-century economy, with China's theft of U.S. intellectual property a long-standing sticking point in U.S.-China relations and trade talks. But just as we must protect American IP from theft by foreign governments and companies, we must also ensure that patents are not misused or abused domestically to stifle legitimate competition, especially in critical areas, such as life-saving medical devices and prescription drugs. Lives should not be sacrificed on the altar of patent protection and exclusivity. The grant of a government-issued patent is not a license to engage in reckless price gouging, and when corporations exploit their patents in ways that put human lives at risk, the government has a responsibility to step in to protect people instead of abusive patent holders. The government, for example, cannot stand idly by as insulin makers charge prices that Americans cannot afford, putting their lives in jeopardy.

Congress has the authority to regulate patent rights, and it should exercise that authority to ensure that the lengths of patents are appropriate, that competition remains vigorous, and that the prices of goods and services remain affordable. The U.S. Constitution gives Congress the power "to promote the Progress of Science and useful Arts, by securing for limited Times to Authors and Inventors the exclusive Right to their respective Writings and Discoveries." Note the emphasis on "limited Times" and—as it relates to scientific advances—on promoting "the Progress of Science." This aligns with Thomas Jefferson's view that while society can "give an exclusive right to the profits" arising from an invention "as an encouragement" for inventors "to pursue ideas which may produce utility . . . generally speaking . . . these monopolies produce more embarrassment than advantage to society." The patent system, Jef-

When individuals go to work for large companies, they often have little or no negotiating power. This has resulted in an exponential increase in the number of non-compete and forced arbitration clauses that are detrimental to the rights and interests of workers. Cartoon by Jerry King.

"Before we hire you, we'd like you to sign this non-compete agreement. It basically states that you won't work anywhere else for the rest of your life."

ferson reminded a correspondent in 1813, was "for the benefit of society," with Jefferson's letter taking note of his own work for the patent board while acknowledging the difficult line-drawing problem associated with deciding when it was proper to recognize an exclusive patent and when it was not.

No. 20—Protect Workers by Restricting the Use of Non-Compete Agreements and Forced Arbitration Clauses, Strengthen Unions, and Pass Comprehensive Immigration Reform. Administratively and legislatively, there are also plenty of other things that can be done to help combat outsized corporate power vis-à-vis workers and consumers. For example, agencies such as the FTC can put reasonable restrictions on the use of non-compete agreements, and lawmakers can pass legislation to restrict their use, too. California's near ban on non-compete agreements hasn't stymied that state's diverse and robust economy, and it would make good sense to unleash the power of the American worker by restricting their use nationwide, especially for low-wage workers.

What's been going on in America with non-compete provisions deserves much more attention than it has gotten. Many American workers are at-will employees whom employers can fire at any time and for any reason. That leaves employees with little job security. To make matters worse, many of these at-will employees are forced to sign oppressive non-competes. The advantage of collective bargaining and unions, of course, is that workers get more economic security and better wages and benefits, along with the right to take any employment-related disputes to arbitration should they desire. At the state level, a few states— California being one of them (and a very prominent one given the state's size)—have afforded at least some protections to at-will employees. In California, there are specified exceptions (for example, relating to the sale of a business), but non-compete agreements are generally unenforceable. "Every contract by which anyone is restrained from engaging in a lawful profession, trade, or business of any kind," California's statute reads in part, "is to that extent void." Barring or restricting the post-termination options of workers certainly hampers their ability to earn a living, so non-compete agreements need to be used much more judiciously.

To open up more opportunities for American workers, we need to raise public awareness of the anticompetitive nature of non-compete agreements. As one example, in March 2019, I joined a letter led by my Senate colleague Richard Blumenthal along with Senators Sherrod Brown, Elizabeth Warren, Ben Cardin, and Ed Markey calling for the FTC to limit non-compete clauses for workers. These clauses, affecting approximately thirty million workers, limit the ability of employees to find new jobs in a similar industry for a significant period of time after leaving a job. As the letter, signed by six Democrats, reads, "We write to urge the Federal Trade Commission to use its rulemaking authority, along with other tools, in order to combat the scourge of non-compete clauses rigging our economy against workers. . . . Non-compete clauses harm employees by limiting their ability to find alternate work, which leaves them with little leverage to bargain for better wages or working conditions with their immediate employer." The FTC already has authority to act, and it should use that authority.

In addition to banning the use of non-competes for minimum-wage or near-minimum-wage workers and restricting their use in other contexts where they are inappropriate, Congress might consider establishing, through legislation, a rebuttable presumption that any non-compete agreement is invalid if the worker is not highly compensated or does not

Protecting the rights of workers is key to economic security and liberty. Workers must be allowed to collectively bargain, and they deserve to reap the benefits of their labor.

ROOSEVELT'S FAREWELL MESSAGE POINTS THE WAY

(President Roosevelt, in his last annual message to Congress, makes many recommendations pointing toward the betterment of social and industrial conditions in the United States.)

From the *Evening Herald* (Duluth)

have access to bona fide trade secrets or other confidential information. The bill's exact language and wage threshold could be thrashed out in congressional debate, but the idea would be to make sure powerful companies are not wielding their enormous power to restrict the mobility—and thus the earning potential—of American workers.

We also need to pass the Restoring Justice for Workers Act, legislation designed to end forced arbitration clauses and to protect workers' rights to pursue their claims in court. That legislation was introduced in May 2019 by Senator Patty Murray of Washington and two congressmen, Jerry Nadler (D-N.Y.) and Bobby Scott (D-Va.). Their bill, which I joined along with a number of my colleagues, would overturn the U.S. Supreme Court's 2018 decision in *Epic Systems Corp. v. Lewis.*

The need for this legislation is clear. As Senator Murray emphasized in proposing it, "So many workers are being forced to sign away their rights—many without even knowing they're doing so—often leaving them with little recourse if they're cheated out of their pay or harassed in the workplace." "For far too long," Representative Nadler added, "corporations have tied the hands of American workers through the use of forced arbitration clauses, which are often buried in the fine print of employment contracts and used as a precondition for employment. Forced arbitration strips working Americans of their day in court to hold employers accountable for wage theft, discrimination, harassment and many other forms of misconduct." My former Senate colleague Al Franken took on mandatory arbitration clauses that are harmful to American workers and consumers and also introduced his own legislation to crack down on such clauses.

As with issues of entrepreneurship, we should not view issues of antitrust narrowly. Human capital—the hard work of people—is a key component of a healthy economy. In addition to better enforcing the antitrust laws, we should unleash the economic power of those living within our country in order to take on the power of BIG. We need to stand up for workers and unions. That means training American workers better, ensuring that unions are strong and that people have the right to collectively bargain, increasing the federal minimum wage to $15, guaranteeing paid family leave, and ensuring that workers can earn paid sick leave.

Strong unions counterbalance corporate power, so it is important to keep unions strong. That's why I support Senator Patty Murray's Protecting the Right to Organize Act to strengthen the National Labor Relations Act and Senator Mazie Hirono's Public Service Freedom to Negotiate Act. And that's why I support rolling back so-called "right-to-work" laws by repealing the provision of the Taft-Hartley Act that gives states authority to pass such laws, and fighting to protect worker safety and employee pension benefits.

Yet another way to spur economic growth while reducing the federal deficit is to enact comprehensive immigration reform—something I have fought for over many years. People have been coming to America for centuries, and immigrants, including DREAMers, now protected by the Deferred Action for Childhood Arrivals program because of a 5–4 ruling written by Chief Justice John Roberts, have made America the vibrant place that it is today. Not only is comprehensive immigration reform a moral issue, but it is an important economic issue, because there are many workers employed in the shadow economy who receive below-minimum wages. That's one of the chief reasons the AFL-CIO and its president, Richard Trumka, support comprehensive immigration reform. Labor markets don't function properly where there is a shadow economy, and companies need and justifiably rely on workers to fuel growth. As an added bonus, comprehensive immigration reform would also lower the federal deficit. In 2013, it was estimated that the passage of a comprehensive immigration reform bill would bring down the federal deficit by $158 billion over a ten-year period.

Indeed, since its founding, America has counted on new immigrants to innovate, to start businesses, and to fuel its economy. Recently, the Center for American Entrepreneurship analyzed Fortune 500 data and found that, in 2017, 43 percent of Fortune 500 companies were founded or co-founded by an immigrant or the child of an immigrant. That data revealed, "The occurrence of first- or second-generation immigrant founders is significantly higher among the largest Fortune 500 companies—accounting for 52 percent of the top 25 firms and 57 percent of the top 35 firms. Immigrant-founded Fortune 500 firms are headquartered in 33 of the 50 states, employ 12.8 million people worldwide, and accounted for $5.3 trillion in global revenue in 2016." These statistics are a powerful economic argument for finally passing and signing into law a comprehensive immigration reform bill—legislation that would create a path to citizenship and, among other things, give economic security and legal certainty to the 800,000 undocumented DREAMers who were brought to the United States as children.

Immigrants to the United States also account for a sizable portion of Nobel Prize winners. More than 30 percent of all U.S.-based Nobel Prize winners were born outside the United States. "As in so many other aspects of national life," Bruce Stillman wrote in *Scientific American* in October 2018, "immigrants have contributed mightily to the leading position of American science." As Stillman explains, citing the impressive statistics, "One indicator is the percentage of American Nobel Prizes in the sciences won by individuals who lived and worked in the U.S. at the time of their award but were born in other lands. From the inception of the prizes in 1901 until 2017, 95 of America's 289 science laureates (chemistry, physics, physiology or medicine) have been immigrants— one in three." "Immigrants have been awarded 39 percent, or 33 of 85, of the Nobel Prizes won by Americans in Chemistry, Medicine and Physics since 2000," a recent report of the National Foundation for American Policy found.

No. 21—Encourage a Strong Small-Business Sector and Access to Capital for Minority- and Women-Owned Businesses. The U.S. Census Bureau estimates that 1.1 million employer firms—that is, those with paid employees—were owned by women and 1 million by minorities. As I mentioned in chapter 7, however, there are major disparities in access to capital for minority- and women-owned start-ups. This problem has been with us for a long time, and it needs to be remedied. As the summary of one 2015 report notes, "New and small business owners often face particular challenges, including lack of access to capital, insufficient business networks for peer support, investment, and business opportunities, and the absence of the full range of essential skills necessary to lead a business to survive and grow. Women and minority entrepreneurs often face even greater obstacles."

For decades (indeed, since the country's founding), small businesses have been the engine of America's economy and of job growth. We need to make sure that small businesses continue to power economic growth. "Small businesses," the U.S. Small Business Administration has observed, "are the lifeblood of the U.S. economy: they create two-thirds of net new jobs and drive U.S. innovation and competitiveness." In what

I see as a warning sign, however, a December 2018 report measuring the contribution of small businesses to the American economy determined that the small-business share of GDP declined from 48 percent in 1998 to 43.5 percent in 2014. "The findings," the report concluded, "indicate that small businesses did not fare as well as large businesses between 1998 and 2014." As that report found, "While small businesses continue to drive innovation and create nearly two-thirds of all new jobs, recent trends bring their future role into question." Still, small-business GDP contributed $5.9 trillion to the $13.6 trillion private economy in 2014, with productivity in terms of real GDP at $103,000 per employee for small businesses.

We need more successful small businesses if we want to have a thriving U.S. economy in the long term. In 2018, 99.9 percent of U.S. businesses were small businesses—that is, firms with fewer than 500 employees. According to the U.S. Small Business Administration, there are 30.2 million small businesses in the United States that, in 2015, employed 58.9 million people—or 47.5 percent of the private workforce. Small businesses created 1.9 million net jobs in 2015, and companies with fewer than 100 employees had the largest share of small-business employment. The smallest firms, in fact, contributed the most to job growth in the United States. The U.S. Small Business Administration cited this statistic in its "2018 Small Business Profile": "Firms employing fewer than 20 employees experienced the largest gains, adding 1.1 million net jobs. The smallest gains were in firms employing 100 to 499 employees, which added 387,874 net jobs." In other words, the smallest firms help drive employment and economic growth.

In a free-enterprise system, entrepreneurs start companies and investors have the right to buy shares in those companies. That is, in fact, the American way. Without start-ups and people investing their capital in new companies and ventures, America's economy would stagnate and never realize its full potential. Start-ups lead to innovation, and their very existence forces bigger companies to always be on guard—and to keep innovating themselves—lest they get overtaken by an upstart competitor and lose market share. Regrettably, what is happening now and what the pandemic has exacerbated is that massive companies are simply gobbling up start-ups in their incipiency or at least before they are big enough or strong enough to really take on the Big Tech companies and the other multinational corporate giants. We must do a better job of making it easier for small businesses to start and grow.

Entrepreneurship is more important than ever in this era of BIG. After Senator Tim Scott of South Carolina and I co-founded the bipartisan Senate Entrepreneurship Caucus, which serves as a clearinghouse for ideas to support entrepreneurs, we introduced the Enhancing Entrepreneurship for the 21st Century Act. That legislation, which is supported by the Center for American Entrepreneurship and the Small Business and Entrepreneurship Council, would require the U.S. secretary of commerce to conduct a comprehensive study into the "startup slump" our country has experienced in recent years. John Dearie—the president of the Center for American Entrepreneurship—emphasized that "the Enhancing Entrepreneurship for the 21st Century Act will contribute enormously to our understanding by directing the Secretary of Commerce to investigate the issue, bringing to bear all the data and analytic capacities of the Federal government." In announcing support for our legislation, Dearie observed, "After growing at an average annual rate of 3.6 percent between 1947 and 2000, the U.S. economy has not grown at 3 percent or better on a year-over-year basis since 2005. It is not a coincidence that this subpar growth is occurring at a time when startup rates have fallen near four-decade lows."

To better assist start-ups and women- and minority-owned businesses, we need to provide more support and loans through the Small Business Administration. We also need to pursue more public-private partnerships, with a 2015 Brookings report calling for an expansion of the State Small Business Credit Initiative and use of the New Markets Tax Credit to attract more private sector funding for businesses in economically distressed communities and for minority entrepreneurs. Back in 2012, President Barack Obama signed into law the Jumpstart Our Business Startups Act, or JOBS Act, which encouraged funding of small businesses in the United States by easing certain securities regulations. Title III, known as the CROWDFUND Act, created ways to use crowdfunding to issue securities.

No. 22—Incentivize and Fund STEM Education and Entrepreneurship. To promote healthy markets and vigorous competition, we need to ensure a pipeline of talent to further entrepreneurship, innovation, and start-ups. To that end, I have long been a supporter of education and apprenticeship training in the disciplines of science, technology, engineering, and math—collectively known as STEM. The Sherman Act, the Clayton Act, and other antitrust laws cannot, all by themselves, guarantee a vibrant economy. We also need to invest in people. The antitrust laws (which seek to penalize unlawful, anticompetitive conduct) must thus be paired with education and training efforts to spur more competition within relevant markets and industries.

How do we support STEM? First, the obvious: more affordable post-secondary education, better student loan rates and payback programs, and free one- and two-year degrees. Second, targeted recruitment efforts in minority areas, as well as company and nonprofit high school mentorships, career fairs, and internships. For example, in Rochester, Minnesota, home of the Mayo Clinic, Mayo medical personnel teach kids about zebra fish (the small aquatic fish used in cardiac disease, cancer, and other scientific research because of its advanced molecular genetics) in the classroom and at its Zebrafish Facility, a curriculum that starts in elementary school and continues through high school.

Innovation is stifled when there are too few STEM graduates and too little competition, leading, almost inexorably, to excessive profit taking at the expense of American consumers. When there are eight or ten competitors in a given industry, all of the firms are constantly trying to do anything new and innovative and hire all the new STEM talent that they can to get a leg up on the competition. But when there's only one firm, the status quo is just fine for that company. There's simply no incentive for a monopolist to hire the people to develop new products or services—or to innovate on price—unless that monopolist is fearful of an emerging, up-and-coming competitor. Similarly, if there are only two or three dominant firms in an industry, the competition among those firms will not be nearly as robust, and the firms may even form a cartel or conspire to violate the antitrust laws because it is (due to the small number of players) so easy to do that. Encouraging more STEM talent, particularly underutilized talent pools of women and minorities, creates new ideas and new companies that can at least attempt—in the words of a famous book by Minnesota business guru Harvey Mackay—to "swim with the [big] sharks" and compete.

No. 23—Protect Privacy and Create New Consumer-Friendly Policies for Data Use. America was founded on the idea of civil liberties and individual rights. To protect those rights we must confront the fact that privacy has been upended by Big Tech. Several legislative arenas—even beyond antitrust, though certainly related to the issue of bigness—are ripe for an overhaul. Foremost is privacy law, which has floundered in a sea of high-end lobbying by the tech companies and other special interests against privacy protections. Bigger is not better when it comes to protecting individuals' privacy rights, because without meaningful competition in the technology sector and online platforms consumers don't have the prospect of seeing much competition among companies' privacy policies either.

Americans should have control over their own data and digital lives. That means they should have greater protections than they do now. The Senate Commerce Committee's Democratic chair, Maria Cantwell, recently introduced a sweeping bill of which I'm a co-sponsor to protect Americans' data. I've also authored a bill with Republican senator John Kennedy of Louisiana that would enhance privacy rules by requiring companies to (1) give a notice of a privacy breach within seventy-two hours of its occurrence (to which Facebook's CEO, Mark Zuckerberg, himself has said, "That makes sense to me"); (2) allow online users to "opt out" of having their data shared against their wishes; and (3) make privacy and opt-out disclosures easy to understand and very, very obvi-

For years, Big Tech companies like Facebook have been using and selling our data despite consumers' belief that their privacy policies protect us. The details of the Cambridge Analytica scandal that emerged in the wake of Donald Trump's election in 2016, including the foreign interference in that election using Americans' private information, should be of concern to all of us.

ous for consumers. Americans should not have to read through dense boilerplate provisions laid out in tiny font sizes to know their rights. And with the addition of health tracking products such as Fitbit and Amazon Halo, we also need specific protections for health-related online tracking products. Alaska Republican senator Lisa Murkowski and I have a bill that would do just that.

Multiple hacks and consumer data breaches—from Equifax to Facebook and Twitter and from Yahoo to Capital One—have caught the eye of all American lawmakers over the past few years. While tech companies and social networks sell ads and want to maximize the time users spend on their platforms, there must be rules of the road for privacy. Also, there needs to be enhanced coordination between the U.S. government and businesses for cyber protection on both the domestic and the international levels so people's most sensitive data is not stolen or misused. As America learned the hard way after finding out about the Russian-led hack of 2020, which involved a significant number of government agencies and businesses, we need international best practices and workable legal standards, better-trained cyber investigators to aid in enforcement, and more cyber education. My truth-in-political-advertising and election security bills—the Honest Ads Act and the Secure Elections Act—exemplify other sensible things that we can do to protect our democracy and reduce disinformation.

Finally, holding companies liable for data acquisition—and then the selling of that data—could be accomplished through the tax code. Large platforms such as Facebook, I've noted, "use us, and we're their commodity, and we're not getting anything out of it." One possibility I've floated, in addition to making sure we better protect the privacy of consumers, is to tax Big Tech companies on the profits they make when they collect and use our data. "When they sell our data to someone else," I noted in 2019, "maybe they're going to have to tell us so we can put some kind of a tax on it."

No. 24—Stop Using the Word "Antitrust" and Start Calling It "Competition Policy." We should curtail our use of the word "antitrust," except when talking about the history of the trusts and the specific antitrust laws that were enacted in response to the power of those trusts. I know the very title of this book is *Antitrust,* but the laws that were first passed in the late nineteenth century were only called "antitrust" laws because they were passed in response to all of the "trusts" that had been formed. In truth, these laws—and the court cases they have spawned—are (or at least should be) about protecting competition. It's easier for people to think and talk about competition policy and furthering competition in the marketplace than it is to think in the nineteenth-century language of "trusts" and "antitrust."

No. 25—Build a New Pro-Competition Movement. To make progress, elected officials must find a way to elevate antitrust issues in the political discourse. Monopolies and increased corporate consolidation have led to higher prices and stagnant or lower wages for Americans, so everyone should care a lot—and should be encouraged to care even more—about the country's current competition policy landscape. We now live in a complex, global economy, so it is particularly important for Americans to understand the antitrust laws and how competition policy does—and should—work. And the American people must, themselves, get more involved to solve the problem of BIG.

Now, here's where you come in. Here are ten things *you* can do to help:

- Support local small businesses and ask your family and friends to do the same.
- Pay more attention to who actually owns the companies that make products or provide services that you use. So often you are fooled into thinking that you are choosing between competitive brands (like online travel websites), yet one internet search will show you they are owned by the same company (watch the short Robert Reich video, posted on YouTube, titled *The Monopolization of America*). Try to do what you can to support businesses that do not possess monopoly power, including on tech platforms.
- Keep up to date on what is happening in the news with proposed mergers and acquisitions and with corporate consolidation and concentration in industries, and then make your voice heard by writing op-eds or engaging in citizen activism, including by bringing up the subject of competition policy at political meetings, social and business clubs, and other civic events. Look at the websites and join the email update lists for organizations such as the American Antitrust Institute, the Open Markets Institute, the

Washington Center for Equitable Growth, the American Economic Liberties Project, and the Roosevelt Institute. These organizations, which can keep you informed, disseminate information on monopoly power and work to educate the public about the importance of antitrust law and enforcement. If you are a lawyer, join the American Bar Association's Antitrust Law Section and get a subscription to *Antitrust* magazine.

- Call and write your U.S. senators and your member of Congress, as well as your state attorney general, to tell them that you care about competition policy and express your frustration that more has not been done to stop monopoly power.

- Demand that public officials at the federal and state level do what they can to fight monopoly power (for example, by passing new laws or holding public hearings), and during political campaigns ask the candidates for office what their views are on that subject.

- Run for office yourself to remake our political system and help create the new, pro-competition landscape we need to help the American economy work the way it should. We need all the allies we can get.

- If you see or experience anticompetitive behavior, report it to antitrust officials at the U.S. Department of Justice, the Federal Trade Commission, and your state attorney general's office (and then follow up to make sure your complaint is handled appropriately).

- Submit public comments to agencies when you have the chance to do so and remember the power of collective action. Keep in mind the 21.7 million comments submitted online in 2017 during the Federal Communications Commission's public comment period about net neutrality and comedian John Oliver's on-air plea resulting in so many public comments that the FCC's server crashed, and demand greater transparency from public officials and agencies about their decision making.

- Fight for choices in tech platforms and privacy rules, and for net neutrality and high-speed broadband. Fight for lower pharma prices and to ensure that there is rigorous competition in relevant markets.

- Start a new business to take on the power of BIG yourself, and find a committed lawyer willing to represent you if you encounter any exclusionary or anticompetitive conduct. Remember: the antitrust laws give those injured by violations of law the right to sue, which is how—years ago—my former client MCI was able to take on AT&T's anticompetitive behavior, collect millions of dollars in damages, and become a major competitor in the telecom industry.

Everyone has different skills, but we all need to do our part and do what we can. In order to persuade Congress to change the laws, and thus to better deter anticompetitive conduct, we need to build a new, grassroots antitrust movement—call it a *pro-competition* agenda. Whatever we call it, that movement must involve tens of millions of people, not just a few economists, lawyers, and antitrust experts. It takes political will and the expenditure of political capital to get things done, and legislative fixes to update outdated laws or to reverse out-of-touch court rulings don't just happen all by themselves. It is only when citizens get involved—and demand action (whether it's sensible gun safety measures, antitrust reform, or to address the climate crisis)—that change comes. Just as the Granger movement, antimonopoly parties, and American presidents succeeded in past decades in pushing for more action to take on the power of BIG, we can do it again. We are living in the age of Big Pharma and Amazon and Google, but we can combat the lax antitrust enforcement that has contributed to the extreme inequality of wealth that has taken such a toll on American families and working people. We cannot go back, but we can move forward with clear-eyed policies that will rein in monopolies and once again put the American people in charge of our own destiny.

Conclusion

It is time for Americans—for "We the People"—to reclaim our power. What the United States needs now is a renewed antitrust movement—one that is grounded in competitive economic policies and sets forth a pro-competition agenda. From progressives to conservatives, from small businesses to cash-strapped workers, we must come together to right the ship of state. A rigorous competition policy evens the playing field, spurs innovation, and reduces consumer prices.

Remember it was Adam Smith who likened monopolists to "an overgrown standing army" who "have become formidable to the government" and "upon many occasions intimidate the legislature." In *The Wealth of Nations,* Smith worried mightily about lawmakers who support "every proposal for strengthening" monopolies in order to curry favor with them and to avoid "the insolent outrage of furious and disappointed monopolists." It was our own Founding Fathers who, on the night of December 16, 1773, dumped all that tea into Boston's harbor to send a message that no, they would not prop up a bloated monopoly, the East India Company, and thereby drive colonial tea merchants, like John Hancock, out of business. And it was John Sherman—an antislavery, pro-Lincoln Republican from Ohio—who wrote our country's first federal antitrust law, asserting, "If we will not endure a king as a political power we should not endure a king over the production, transportation, and sale of any of the necessaries of life. If we would not submit to an emperor we should not submit to an autocrat of trade, with power to prevent competition and to fix the price of any commodity."

While the trusts of yesteryear are no more, they have—over time—regenerated themselves, only in different guise. In place of trusts, we now have massive, multinational corporations—including larger-than-ever tech monopolies—and widespread corporate consolidation. Instead of Rockefeller's sprawling Standard Oil Company, we now have huge horizontally and vertically integrated enterprises, from Amazon to Google. And whereas we once had figures like James J. Hill and E. H. Harriman who tried to corner the railway market by issuing trust certificates, we now have horizontal shareholding, whereby wealthy investors own stocks in multiple companies in the same industry, which is, in effect, a trust, only by a different name.

The failure to prioritize—and to vigorously enforce—the country's antitrust laws has already contributed in part to what many rightfully understand to be America's "rigged" economy—one that works for the wealthy but leaves so many families and working people behind, in debt, and unable to afford health care or pay their bills. It is the anger and resentment caused by income inequality and stagnant wages and small businesses driven out of the marketplace that is, increasingly, bitterly dividing America's body politic—a division that former president Trump, on a daily basis, tried to widen and exploit. And often it is the most vulnerable—the poor, children, single mothers, people of color, new immigrants, and others who do not have an equal seat at the table—who suffer the most.

We all want a strong and vibrant competitive business community, with more innovation and choices for consumers. We want to encourage start-ups and more minority- and women-owned businesses. To get good results, we must clear away anticompetitive conduct and the often-insurmountable barriers to entry that new business entrants face. New business formation has been declining as a share of America's economy since the late 1970s, with companies in industries with the highest market concentrations reaping—not surprisingly—the highest profit margins. Any capitalist should want to fix that. Better competition policies and enforcement will also help address income inequality, which, for decades, has continued to worsen, reaching new heights in the twenty-first century. We need to reverse those trends.

To restrict and contain monopolistic behavior, there are really only two options: regulate behavior (as we do already with public utilities and other activities) or enforce the antitrust laws (which promote free enterprise, innovation and entrepreneurship, and, ultimately, promote competitive markets). Indeed, to maintain a healthy economy, it turns out that we need *both* sensible regulation and antitrust enforcement. Reasonable regulations work in tandem with antitrust laws to protect against abuses of power. To make sure we continue to grow and produce American-made agricultural products, we need both the antitrust laws and the U.S. Department of Agriculture. For safe and competitive air travel options we need the antitrust laws and the Federal Aviation Administration. Digital privacy and election security will not magically occur without appropriate regulatory structures and rules. And when it comes to tech? Bill Gates—in a speech to the Economic Club of Washington, D.C., in June 2019—himself emphasized that he fully expects "there will be more regulation of the tech sector" in the future.

It's important to note that regulation and antitrust should be about protecting consumers and the health of America's economy and our way of life, not about erecting unnecessary barriers to competition. Businesses shouldn't be forced to deal with unnecessary or overly burdensome "red tape" that stifles innovation; instead, there must be—at all times—an appropriate balance between antitrust intervention and regulation, on one side, and robust entrepreneurship, on the other. What must be conceded is that a purely laissez-faire market economy— one in which transactions are totally free from governmental review or oversight—will never produce a highly innovative and competitive marketplace, let alone a marketplace that works for everyone.

The solutions for Americans—whether they live in Brooklyn, New York, or rural Georgia or Milwaukee, Wisconsin, or Elko, Nevada—are right in front of us. We just need the political will to get them done. We need stronger laws; more antitrust enforcement and the resources to do it; divestment of tech assets and a federal privacy law; appropriate rules on cross-ownership of companies; limits on non-compete agreements for employees; the power to open up and fix consent agreements; more congressional oversight; and yes, judges who get it.

To the extent that it is conservative federal judges who are hindering legitimate antitrust enforcement, the best remedy is to have a president who will, in addition to putting forward new legislation to change the laws, nominate judges and regulators who will take antitrust laws very seriously. The antitrust laws are only as good as the quality of the agency heads and those appointed to enforce them, and those laws can serve the purposes that they were designed to serve only if fair-minded judges give those laws a fair reading and apply them without fear or favor. Without the right people in place, antitrust enforcement is doomed to fail or to be far too impotent to address the issues of monopoly power and corporate consolidation we face today.

Americans should expect the best of the best when it comes to their public servants, and that should be as true for the president of the United States as it is for members of Congress to city council members. In the antitrust arena, we need more people like the trust-busting lawyer Thurman Arnold, the Wyoming-born maverick attorney and law professor who was put in charge of the Justice Department's Antitrust Division during President Franklin D. Roosevelt's administration. Arnold—like other antitrust officials we've had at various times in the past—was not afraid to take on powerful interests, whether it be the American Medical Association, the oil industry, or powerful corporations like General Electric. During his tenure, the Antitrust Division brought 1,375 complaints involving forty industries. Arnold recognized that "size in itself is not an evil," though he aptly recognized that size "does give power to those who control it." It was that power, he knew, that had to be checked lest it be abused. As one compilation, *Great American Lawyers,* notes of his legacy in increasing fivefold the personnel devoted to antitrust enforcement, "Arnold is credited with single-handedly reviving antitrust law as a means of regulating industry." Without committed leadership to antitrust enforcement at the top, of course, the rise in corporate consolidation will only continue unabated.

Finally, competition policy is a subject that can no longer be relegated to the realm of law schools and antitrust agencies; more citizens must start voicing their concerns about BIG to their elected officials so that those officials take it much more seriously. If Americans don't act now, the "curse of bigness" that Louis Brandeis warned about will only continue to cast a longer and longer spell on the American economy and its consumers. As Hubert Humphrey, the beloved former U.S. senator from Minnesota and an outspoken advocate for antitrust enforcement, once said, "If we are unwilling to make history, others will write it for us." Unfortunately, it is the monopolists and would-be monopolists who, at the moment, are writing the modern-day history of antitrust and economic power. It is also the paralyzed Congress that, for the time being, is aiding and abetting those monopolists and the purveyors of runaway corporate consolidation. It is a story, for the most part, of law-makers and judges *not doing something* instead of *doing something* about the problem of BIG.

America's antitrust laws were first put in place more than a hundred years ago to rectify the imbalance of power between the rich and those of more modest means. It was a different time in American history, but there are important lessons from that era that must never be for-gotten. Namely, that the inevitable result of monopoly power—price gouging and stagnant wages—will continue until immense economic power is confronted head-on. The very nature of the global economy means that the operation of the American economy—with its intricate supply chains, for example—is so much more complex, making it more prone to manipulation than ever before. Potential antitrust violations must now be closely monitored by multiple countries and institutions, and in the United States at both the federal and the state levels, with regulators never losing sight of the fact that decisions made in corporate boardrooms in one place can suddenly create a monopoly in another or a price hike around the globe.

Today's gig economy workers—the people struggling to afford their health-care or education expenses, or working two or three jobs just to get by—are yesterday's grangers with pitchforks. It is now crystal clear that the antitrust laws must be seriously updated and made relevant again as part of a reinvigorated American competition policy. We need to incentivize more competition and more innovation, not less, and we need to make sure that American capitalism allows all to compete. Everyone in America deserves a fair shot—and an honest opportunity—when it comes to realizing the American Dream.

But enough words have been written. And enough experts have weighed in.

Now it's time to get to work.

Acknowledgments

This book would not exist except for two things: (1) monopolies; and (2) my husband, John Bessler. But, thinking it over again, I should really put my husband first.

John is a law professor at the University of Baltimore and the Georgetown University Law Center, and he teaches classes on everything from contracts to civil procedure to international human rights law and the death penalty. He has written ten books himself, including *The Birth of American Law: An Italian Philosopher and the American Revolution,* which won the prestigious Scribes Book Award for the best work of legal scholarship for 2014.

How he got dragged into this book project is pretty obvious, but his contributions were nonetheless remarkable. He wrote nearly every endnote (yes, there are a lot of them) and helped write and edit many of the detailed legal portions of the text. He did all this while teaching full-time, campaigning across the country with me during my presidential run, and still being a wonderful husband to me and dad to our daughter, Abigail.

While writing endless notes on an antitrust book wasn't part of our wedding vows, it was more than John's marital commitment that brought him to spend so much time on this book. Like me, my husband has a deep respect for history and the law. He actually proposed to me on Abraham Lincoln's birthday in a bookstore (in the nonfiction aisle, of course). Like me, he wants the law to work for everyone and antitrust (or, as I argue it should be called, "competition policy") is an area that cries out for more understanding and change.

He is not alone in his beliefs. So many people helped me get this book done. First and foremost, my editor, Victoria Wilson, at Alfred A. Knopf, who, despite also editing a biography of Ruth Bader Ginsburg (among many other titles), urged me to write this book and, most importantly, to not go small. She wanted a big book for a big subject that would cover not just the political wrangling but also the fascinating history, the law, and a roadmap for the future. She was patient with a crazy schedule (as in my being a full-time senator, running a Senate race, and then, yes, the presidential campaign). She kept her (and my) spirits up during the worst of the pandemic and was always willing to learn a new fact and drill down on a story. And thanks, Vicky, for also suggesting the cartoons! Thanks to others who worked on the book, including Ingrid Sterner, Rita Madrigal, Katherine Hourigan, Lisa Montebello, Cassandra Pappas, Michiko Clark, Marc Jaffee, and Ryan Ouimet, as well as my intrepid agent, Paul Fedorko.

Thanks to all of the people who reviewed the book or parts of it and made such good suggestions. They include former FTC chair Jonathan Leibowitz, former Justice Department antitrust head Bill Baer, my former staffer and now head of the Washington Center for Equitable Growth Michael Kades, University of Baltimore antitrust expert and law professor (and my husband's colleague) Bob Lande, former president of the University of Vermont (not to mention former dean of the University of Minnesota Law School) Tom Sullivan, and superstar lawyer Rosa Po, who headed up policy for my presidential campaign as well as previously serving as my deputy chief of staff.

Others who inspired me simply because they care so much about this subject (although I did not burden them with reading this more-than-500-page book) include my colleagues who have taken a special interest in antitrust: Richard Blumenthal, Dick Durbin, Patrick Leahy, Sheldon Whitehouse, Cory Booker, and Mazie Hirono on the Senate Judiciary Committee, as well as Elizabeth Warren (who should be an honorary member of the committee). Thanks to Senator Chuck Grassley (who has worked with me on antitrust legislation) and Senator Mike Lee (the two of us lead the antitrust subcommittee), my Minnesota Senate colleague Tina Smith, as well as a number of other senators who I hope will take on this fight with me on a bipartisan basis over the next few years. Representatives David Cicilline and Jerry Nadler did a great job leading the major tech investigation in the U.S. House of Representatives and I look forward to working with them to right our monopoly wrongs. While Makhan Delrahim (head of the Justice Department antitrust division under the prior administration) and former FTC Chair Joe Simons and I didn't always see eye to eye on everything, I appreciated their work in several areas, including their willingness to file major tech actions and caring enough about the future of antitrust enforcement to fight for resources for their staffs going forward into the next administration. I was always grateful for their willingness to work with me when there was common ground. Thanks also to the career DOJ Antitrust Division and FTC staff—both current and former and future—as well as so many stellar FTC commissioners.

Through the years, I have been blessed with amazing legal staff who have taught me a lot. They include antitrust lawyers Marc Lanoue, Michael Kades, and Caroline Holland, as well as counsels Jake Sullivan (who went on to serve as national security advisor to President Biden), Jonathan Becker (also my former chief of staff), Paige Herwig, Tim Molino, Craig Kalkut, Sammy Clark (who went on to become the city attorney for St. Paul), Kirstin Dunham, Elizabeth Farrar (who also served as my legislative director and deputy chief of staff), Ben Driscoll, Keagan Buchanan, and Ajay Kundaria.

Thanks also to fellow antitrust authors/reporters/experts whose work educated me on my own book-writing journey. They include Supreme Court Justice Stephen Breyer, former Labor Secretary Robert Reich, Tim Wu, Barry Lynn, Matt Stoller, Lina Khan, Sally Hubbard, Gerard Helferich, David Leonhardt, Kara Swisher, Charlotte Slaiman, Martin Gaynor, Nancy Rose, Mary Pilon, William Kolasky, Ron Chernow, Jeffrey Rosen, Richard Posner, Joseph Stiglitz, Robert Pitofsky, Cecilia Kang, John Oliver, Philip Longman, Thomas Lambert, Stephen Weissman, Paul Krugman, Robert Connolly, Steve Coll, Cass Sunstein, Herbert Hovenkamp, Einer Elhauge, Albert Foer, Christopher Sagers, Diana Moss, former FTC Chairman William Kovacic, George Slover, Eleanor Fox, John Kwoka, Gene Kimmelman, Jonathan Baker, Fiona Scott Morton, David Balto, Daniel Crane, Steven Salop, Carl Shapiro, and Jon Sallet. I could mention so many others, but you will find them in the notes.

During the time period in which I wrote this book a lot happened. That would be called an understatement. There was the pandemic (with my husband getting very sick from and thankfully recovering from COVID) and the economic downturn, three contentious Supreme Court nomination hearings, two impeachment hearings, my 2018 U.S. Senate reelection, my 2020 presidential campaign (beginning in the snow and ending with a heartfelt endorsement of Joe Biden), a prolonged and completely unsubstantiated attack on our democracy by former President Trump ultimately resulting in a failed insurrection and invasion of the U.S. Capitol, a presidential inauguration (which I co-chaired as head of the Senate Rules Committee along with my Senate colleague Roy Blunt), my work in U.S. Senate leadership as head of the Democratic Steering Committee, and visits to Minnesota's eighty-seven counties.

Through it all I was so proud to represent my wonderful state and to work on behalf of the people of Minnesota.

None of this would have been possible without my steadfast family, including our incredible daughter, Abigail, whose keen editorial eye improved this book; an extraordinary staff, some of whom I have already mentioned, although I would also add Lizzy Peluso, Lindsey Kerr, and Laura Schiller, who have led my D.C. work while still raising six children between them (including Lindsey's adorable twins); legislative director Doug Calidas and communications director Nate Evans; those who have led my state office, including Ben Hill, Clara Haycraft, and Elizabeth Ebot; the people who have made my life work every day, including Blair Mallin, Devan Cayea, Madeline Coles, Greg Swanholm, Lydia Hubert-Peterson, and Jorge Zurita-Coronado, and also former manager Hannah Hankins (thanks, Hannah, for running the office during those critical months of the pandemic); my rock and political advisor Mandy Grunwald; Justin Buoen, my presidential campaign manager and political advisor for sixteen years; my longtime communications advisor and former chief of staff, Brigit Helgen; as well as all of our "Team Amy" scrappy, happy crew.

So that's enough for now. What I would really like to have happen is that just a few short years from now I get to write an epilogue to this book that says that our nation's competition policy is strong, that we built a successful pro-competition movement, passed a bunch of new laws together, and took on the monopolies. That's what would make me truly thankful.

Stay tuned.

Notes

3 **Alan Goldbloom:** Frank Vascellaro, "Outgoing Children's Hospitals CEO Reflects on a Decade of Change," WCCO, Dec. 3, 2014, minnesota.cbslocal .com.

3 **patent ductus arteriosus:** Patent ductus arteriosus (PDA), www.mayoclinic .org/diseases-conditions/patent-ductus-arteriosus/symptoms-causes/syc -20376145; Patent ductus arteriosus (PDA), Drugs.com, Jan. 25, 2018 (content from Mayo Clinic), www.drugs.com/mcd/patent-ductus-arteriosus-pda.

3 **The price had skyrocketed:** Philip Lowe and Mel Marquis, eds., *European Competition Law Annual 2010: Merger Control in European and Global Perspective* (Oxford: Hart, 2013), p. xx n23; Findings of Fact, Conclusions of Law, and Order, Aug. 31, 2010, *Federal Trade Commission v. Lundbeck, Inc.,* Civil No. 08-6379 (JNE/JJG), ¶¶ 37–63, ia800200.us.archive.org.

3 **more than thirty thousand babies:** Jessica Chapman, "Price-Fixing Alleged in Drug for Babies," Courthouse News Service, June 25, 2009, www .courthousenews.com.

3 **option is surgery:** Patent ductus arteriosus (PDA), Drugs.com, Jan. 25, 2018 (content from Mayo Clinic), www.drugs.com/mcd/patent-ductus-arteriosus -pda; Patent ductus arteriosus (PDA), Mayo Clinic, www.mayoclinic.org /diseases-conditions/patent-ductus-arteriosus/diagnosis-treatment/drc -20376150.

4 **I sent a letter to Ovation:** "Klobuchar Questions Cost of Drug for Premature Babies," *Pioneer Press,* March 7, 2008, www.twincities.com.

4 **The company responded by saying:** Chen May Yee, "Same Drug, a New Price, but Same Old Headache in Care," *Minneapolis Star Tribune,* March 7, 2008, www.startribune.com.

4 **NeoProfen:** NeoProfen, www.rxlist.com/neoprofen-drug.htm#description. ("NeoProfen is indicated to close a clinically significant patent ductus arte-

riosus [PDA] in premature infants weighing between 500 and 1500 g, who are no more than 32 weeks gestational age when usual medical management [e.g., fluid restriction, diuretics, respiratory support, etc.] is ineffective. The clinical trial was conducted among infants with an asymptomatic PDA.")

4 **our daughter Abigail:** Amy Klobuchar, *The Senator Next Door: A Memoir from the Heartland* (New York: Henry Holt, 2015), 118.

4 **hospital press conference:** Chen May Yee, "Same Drug, a New Price, but Same Old Headache in Care."

4 **Sophia and her twin sister Anna:** Emily Kaiser, "Klobuchar Presses for Drug Pricing Scrutiny," *Minneapolis Star Tribune,* July 25, 2008, www.klobuchar .senate.gov.

5 **paid out more than $400,000:** Chen May Yee, "Same Drug, a New Price, but Same Old Headache in Care."

5 **At the hospital that day:** Amy Klobuchar, "Klobuchar Challenges Drug Company for Price-Gouging on Drug for Premature Babies," press release, March 8, 2008, votesmart.org.

5 **at the time:** "Klobuchar Questions Cost of Drugs for Premature Babies."

5 **a spokeswoman for Ovation:** Ibid.

5 **I sent a letter:** Klobuchar to Kovacic, April 25, 2008, votesmart.org.

5 **Commerce Committee FTC oversight hearing:** *Federal Trade Commission Reauthorization: Hearing Before the Committee on Commerce, Science, and Transportation, United States Senate, One Hundred Tenth Congress, Second Session, April 8, 2008* (Washington, D.C.: U.S. Government Printing Office, 2012), www.govinfo.gov.

5 **I convened a hearing:** Media Advisory, "Small Market Drugs, Big Price Tags: Are Drug Companies Exploiting People with Rare Diseases?," U.S. Congress, Joint Economic Committee, July 22, 2008, www.jec.senate.gov; Andy Birkey, "Are Drug Companies Exploiting People with Rare Diseases? Klobuchar Hearing Examines Price-Gouging," *Twin Cities Daily Planet,* Aug. 1, 2008, www.tcdailyplanet.net. At the hearing, I also called Madeline Carpinelli of the Institute for Pharmaceutical Research in Management and Economics at the University of Minnesota. She said that over the prior twenty years one in twenty brand-name drugs saw price increases of more than 100 percent and that six brand-name drugs underwent price increases of 1,000 to 3,400 percent. "Lawmakers Criticize Pharmaceutical Companies for Large Price Increases for Brand-Name Medications for Rare Diseases," khn.org; "Lawmakers to Investigate Pharma Price-Gouging," HealthImaging, July 31, 2008, www.healthimaging.com.

6 **In his testimony:** Testimony of Alan L. Goldbloom, MD, President and CEO, Children's Hospitals and Clinics of Minnesota, Joint Economic Committee, July 24, 2008, www.jec.senate.gov and www.govinfo.gov. In that testimony, Dr. Goldbloom observed that "Indocin is not the only drug Ovation has marked up in such a dramatic fashion." He said that three other drugs purchased from Merck—Cosmegen, Diuril Sodium, and Mustargen—"have seen price increases of 3,437 percent, 864 percent, and 979 percent respectively." As he explained the importance of those drugs to patients, "Cosmegen is an agent used to treat a variety of pediatric cancers, Diuril Sodium is a diuretic used to reduce fluid overload in infants and neonates, and mustar-

gen is used to treat brain tumors and certain lymphomas (another form of cancer)."

6 **At the hearing, I noted:** Opening Statement of Hon. Amy Klobuchar, "Small Market Drugs, Big Price Tags: Are Drug Companies Exploiting People with Rare Disease?," U.S. Congress, Joint Economic Committee, July 24, 2008, www.govinfo.gov.

6 **the FTC sued Ovation:** Federal Trade Commission, "FTC Sues Ovation Pharmaceuticals for Illegally Acquiring Drug Used to Treat Premature Babies with Life-Threatening Heart Condition," press release, Dec. 16, 2008, www.ftc .gov; "FTC Accuses Ovation in Lawsuit of Price Gouging," Reuters, Dec. 16, 2008, www.reuters.com; Josephine Marcotty, "Alleging Price-Gouging, FTC Sues Maker of Drug for Preemies," *Minneapolis Star Tribune,* Dec. 17, 2008, www.startribune.com.

6 **I had my own take:** Marcotty, "Alleging Price-Gouging, FTC Sues Maker of Drug for Preemies."

7 **The FTC's case against Ovation:** Overview of FTC Actions in Pharmaceutical Products and Distribution, Health Care Division, Bureau of Competition, Federal Trade Commission, June 2019, 9–10 (discussing the FTC's case), www .ftc.gov.

7 **the Danish company Lundbeck:** Jonathan D. Rockoff, "Denmark's Lundbeck to Buy Ovation Pharmaceuticals," *Wall Street Journal,* Feb. 9, 2009, blogs.wsj.com; "Lundbeck's Acquisition of Ovation Pharmaceuticals Cleared by US Federal Trade Commission," press release, March 19, 2009, investor .lundbeck.com.

7 **a federal district judge in Minnesota:** "Case Study: *FTC v. Ovation,*" Law 360, Dec. 16, 2010, www.law360.com. The district judge had earlier refused to dismiss the lawsuits brought by the FTC and the State of Minnesota on summary judgment. Leigh Kamping-Carder, "Lundbeck Fails to Escape Neo-Profen Antitrust Suits," Law 360, July 21, 2009, www.law360.com.

7 **not in the same product market:** Findings of Fact, Conclusions of Law, and Order, Aug. 31, 2010, *Federal Trade Commission v. Lundbeck, Inc.,* Civil No. 08-6379 (JNE/JJG). 1–40.

7 **send an email:** Ibid., ¶¶ 39, 43; Maxwell S. Kennerly, "'We Can Price These Almost Anywhere We Want Given the Product Profiles,'" *Litigation & Trial: The Law Blog of Plaintiff's Attorney Max Kennerly,* Oct. 1, 2010, www .litigationandtrial.com.

7 **In dismissing the actions:** "FTC Loses Merger Trial Because of Market Definition," *Antitrust Lawyer Blog,* Doyle, Barlow & Mazard PLLC, Oct. 12, 2010, www.antitrustlawyerblog.com.

7 **the judge found:** Findings of Fact, Conclusions of Law, and Order, Aug. 31, 2010, *Federal Trade Commission v. Lundbeck, Inc.,* Civil No. 08-6379 (JNE/ JJG), Conclusions of Law, 1–6, 9.

7 **On appeal:** Brief for Plaintiffs-Appellants Federal Trade Commission and State of Minnesota, *Federal Trade Commission and State of Minnesota v. Lundbeck, Inc.,* 8th Cir., Nos. 10-3458 and 10-3459 (Consolidated) (filed Dec. 27, 2010), www.ftc.gov.

8 **friend-of-the-court brief:** Brief of Amici Curiae States of Missouri, Illinois, Arkansas, Iowa, Maryland, Nevada, New Mexico, North Dakota, South

Dakota, and West Virginia in Support of Plaintiffs-Appellants, *Federal Trade Commission and State of Minnesota v. Lundbeck, Inc.,* 8th Cir. Nos. 10-3458 and 10-3459 (Consolidated) (filed Jan. 24, 2011), www.appliedantitrust.com.

8 **conservative Eighth Circuit:** "Lundbeck: The Expert Witnesses Testify," FTC Watch, www.mlexwatch.com (noting that "more than 80 percent of the judges" on the Eighth Circuit "are Republican appointees").

8 **in an August 2011 ruling:** *FTC v. Lundbeck, Inc.,* 650 F.3d 1236 (8th Cir. 2011).

8 **A later published critique:** Lowe and Marquis, *European Competition Law Annual 2010,* 46.

8 **Herbert Hovenkamp:** Herbert Hovenkamp, "Mergers with Dominant Firms: The *Lundbeck* Case," *Antitrust Chronicle,* no. 1 (Dec. 2011), 6, www.competitionpolicyinternational.com.

9 **robust generic competition:** Findings of Fact, Conclusions of Law, and Order (Aug. 31, 2010), *Federal Trade Commission v. Lundbeck, Inc.,* Civil No. 08-6379 (JNE/JJG), Findings of Fact, 19–20. After the FDA, in July 2008, approved an application by Bedford Laboratories for generic indomethacin (a generic bioequivalent of Lundbeck's Indocin IV), the company's indomethacin for injection product was first offered for sale in 2010—the same year the FDA approved another generic version of indomethacin for APP Pharmaceuticals. In 2014, Prasco Labs also entered into a distribution and supply agreement with Recordati Rare Diseases Inc., the patent holder of NeoProfen, for the right to distribute a generic version. Michael Johnsen, "Prasco Labs Gains Rights to Authorized Generic Version of NeoProfen," *Drug Store News,* May 22, 2014, www.drugstorenews.com; "Prasco to Market Authorized Generic of NeoProfen® (ibuprofen lysine) Injection," prasco.com; NeoProfen, www.drugs.com/pro/neoprofen.html; Rare Diseases, Recordati, www.recordati.com/en/rare_diseases/. And in 2016, the FDA approved a generic version of NeoProfen manufactured by Exela Pharma Sciences. "X-GEN Pharmaceuticals and Exela Pharma Sciences Receive FDA Approval for Ibuprofen Lysine Injection," press release, May 2, 2016, www.x-gen.us ("X-GEN's Ibuprofen Lysine Injection, under licensing agreement with Exela, is therapeutically equivalent to Recordati Rare Diseases' NeoProfen® Injection and is the first available generic alternative in the marketplace"). Exela, which had been sued by Recordati in 2014 for patent infringement, had long sought to make a generic version. Exela had sent Recordati a notice in June 2014 that it was seeking FDA approval to engage in the sale of a generic version of NeoProfen. Complaint, *Recordati Rare Diseases Inc. v. Exela Pharma Sciences, LLC, et al.,* U.S. District Court for the District of Delaware, 1:14-cv-00956-UNA (filed July 18, 2014), insight.rpxcorp.com.

9 **didn't immediately go down:** It has been found that—in general—"first generics" do relatively little to bring down pharmaceutical costs, and that held true for NeoProfen, one of thousands of branded drugs in the United States. As one analysis from September 2018 pointed out, in the case of NeoProfen, "the generic manufacturer prices the drug only slightly lower than the price of the brand-name drug." Jonathan D. Alpern and William M. Stauffer, "Does a Generic EpiPen Mean Lower Prices? Don't Hold Your Breath," Stat, Sept. 7, 2018, www.statnews.com. "First generics," the U.S. Food and Drug Administration notes, "are just what they sound like—the first approval by FDA

which permits a manufacturer to market a generic drug product in the United States." First Generic Drug Approvals, Food and Drug Administration, www .fda.gov. In the case of Ovation, for all the intervening time when no competition existed, the lives of premature babies were put at risk and consumers got ripped off. Prior to 2006, as Alan Goldbloom, the CEO of Minnesota's Children's Hospitals and Clinics, testified before Congress, the annual cost for Indocin for the children's hospitals was $136,426 nationally. In just the first year of the drug's dramatic price increase, as Goldbloom testified, however, those same hospitals spent "close to $2 million." Testimony of Alan L. Goldbloom, MD, president and CEO, Children's Hospitals and Clinics of Minnesota, Joint Economic Committee, July 24, 2008, 33–34. For a very significant time, Ovation—and later its acquiring company, Lundbeck—had monopoly market dominance that caused significant monetary harm. As David Wales, the acting director of the FTC Bureau of Competition, said on the topic of damages when the FTC initially filed its complaint against Ovation in federal district court, "While Ovation is profiting from its illegal acquisition, hospitals and ultimately consumers and American taxpayers are forced to pay millions of dollars a year more for these life-saving medications. The action today is intended to restore the lost competition and require Ovation to give up its unlawful profits." As the FTC's press release announcing that case further emphasized the massive harm caused by Ovation's corporate power and unconscionable price gouging, "Because there are no other drugs available to treat patent ductus arteriosus, hospitals treating babies with this critical condition have no choice but to pay Ovation's monopoly price. And ultimately, the artificially high prices paid by hospitals are passed on to families, government programs such as Medicaid, and other public and private purchasers." Federal Trade Commission, "FTC Sues Ovation Pharmaceuticals for Illegally Acquiring Drug Used to Treat Premature Babies with Life-Threatening Heart Condition," press release, Dec. 16, 2008, www.ftc.gov.

9 **true and vigorous competition:** A study conducted by the FDA found that it typically takes five generics on the market to drive a drug price down to 33 percent of the original brand-name price. Sydney Lupkin and Jay Hancock, "Trump Administration Salutes Parade of Generic Drug Approvals, but Hundreds Aren't for Sale," Kaiser Health News, Feb. 7, 2019, khn.org. "On average," the FDA study concluded, "the first generic competitor prices its product only slightly lower than the brand-name manufacturer." Generic Competition and Drug Prices, U.S. Food and Drug Administration, www.fda.gov. It takes a second generic, the FDA determined, to reduce the average generic price to nearly half of the brand-name price, with additional generics and FDA approvals also causing prices to fall, though more slowly.

9 **$10 trillion in acquisitions:** Matt Stoller, "With Amazon on the Rise and a Business Tycoon in the White House, Can a New Generation of Democrats Return the Party to Its Trust-Busting Roots?," Open Markets Institute, July 13, 2017, openmarketsinstitute.org.

9 **nearly topped $24 trillion:** "Value of Mergers and Acquisitions (M&A) Worldwide from 1985 to 2019," Statista, Feb. 24, 2020, www.statista.com.

9 **nearly a tripling of the number of mergers:** "Hart-Scott-Rodino Annual Report—Fiscal Year 2018," www.ftc.gov.

9 **two American companies:** David Streitfeld, "Amazon Hits $1,000,000,000,000 in Value, Following Apple," *New York Times,* Sept. 4, 2018.

9 **crossed $2 trillion in 2020:** Carmen Reinicke, "Apple Hits $2 Trillion Market Cap, Becomes First US-Listed Company to Reach Milestone (AAPL)," *Business Insider,* Aug. 19, 2020, markets.businessinsider.com.

10 **continues to grow:** Tezcan Gecgil, "With Its Eyes Set on $2 Trillion Market Cap, Buy Dips in Amazon Stock," InvestorPlace, Aug. 26, 2020, investorplace .com; Shannon Liao, "Amazon Has Its Most Profitable Quarter Ever, but Growth Is Slowing," *Verge,* April 25, 2019, www.theverge.com.

10 **might have temporarily slowed:** Luisa Beltran, "Mergers and Acquisitions Dropped 83% in the U.S. Because of Covid," *Barron's,* July 6, 2020, www .barrons.com.

10 **reporting on a study:** Heather Long, "Small Business Used to Define America's Economy. The Pandemic Could Change That Forever," *Washington Post,* May 12, 2020, www.washingtonpost.com.

10 **As of August 31, 2020:** Anjali Sundaram, "Yelp Data Shows 60% of Business Closures Due to the Coronavirus Pandemic Are Now Permanent," CNBC, Sept. 16, 2020, www.cnbc.com.

10 **cable TV rates:** Mike Farrell, "Cable Rates on the Rise," *Multichannel News,* Jan. 8, 2019, www.multichannel.com; see also Mark Cooper, *Cable Mergers and Monopolies: Market Power in Digital Media and Communications Networks* (Washington, D.C.: Economic Policy Institute, 2002), 1, cyberlaw.stanford .edu ("In the late 1990s, the assistant attorney general for antitrust called the cable industry 'the most persistent monopoly in the American economy.' Things have only gotten worse.").

10 **despite some competition:** Luke Bouma, "Comcast Warns That Cord Cutting Will Speed Up in 2020 and That Cable TV Prices Are Going Up," Cord Cutters News, Jan. 24, 2020, www.cordcuttersnews.com.

10 **double the rate of inflation:** Nathan McAlone, "Cable TV Price Increases Have Beaten Inflation Every Single Year for 20 Years," *Business Insider,* Oct. 31, 2016, www.businessinsider.com.

10 **airline fares:** Avi Grunfeld, "An Analysis of the Effect of Airline Mergers on Airfares: A Case Study of Delta-Northwest and Continental-United," *SPICE: Philosophy, Politics, and Economics Undergraduate Journal* (Spring 2015): 39, repository.upenn.edu; Nigel Dennis and David Pitfield, "A Tale of Two Cities: The Impact of Airline Mergers and Consolidation at London and New York," *Transportation Research Record: Journal of the Transportation Research Board,* Aug. 15, 2018, journals.sagepub.com; Bloomberg, "American Airlines to Pay $45 Million to End Consumer Antitrust Lawsuit," *Fortune,* June 16, 2018, fortune.com.

10 **insulin jumped:** Randi Hutter Epstein and Rachel Strodel, "Diabetes Patients at Risk from Rising Insulin Prices," *New York Times,* June 22, 2018. "The amount of insulin a person needs varies," that story noted, "but one vial typically lasts about a week or two."

10 **up to $340 per vial:** Alexandra Hutzler, "HHS Secretary Alex Azar Once Doubled the Price of Insulin," *Newsweek,* July 31, 2019, www.newsweek .com.

10 **Why do farmers pay so much:** Zoe Willingham and Andy Green, "A Fair

Deal for Farmers," Center for American Progress, May 7, 2019, www.american progress.org.

11 **2019 poll:** Rebecca Klar, "Poll: 70 Percent Angry at Political Establishment," *Hill,* Aug. 25, 2019, thehill.com.

11 **two-thirds of Americans:** Amina Dunn, "Partisans Are Divided over the Fairness of the U.S. Economy—and Why People Are Rich or Poor," Pew Research Center, Oct. 4, 2018, www.pewresearch.org.

11 **2017 Gallup poll:** Raymond J. Keating, "Americans Have High Confidence in Small Business," SBE Council, Sept. 21, 2017, sbecouncil.org.

11 **big business approval rating:** "Big Business," Gallup, news.gallup.com/poll /5248/big-business.aspx.

11 **executive compensation:** "The Stock Market Boom Has Given CEOs a Raise. What About Average Workers?," *PBS NewsHour,* Sept. 13, 2018, www.pbs.org (noting that the Economic Policy Institute found that "from 2016 to 2017, the average pay of CEOs from the top 350 publicly traded firms increased 17.6 percent—to $18.9 million").

12 *The New York Times* **reported:** Richard A. Oppel Jr. et al., "The Fullest Look Yet at the Racial Inequity of Coronavirus," *New York Times,* July 5, 2020.

12 **one** *New York Times* **reporter:** David Streitfeld, "Amazon's Antitrust Antagonist Has a Breakthrough Idea," *New York Times,* Sept. 7, 2018, www.nytimes .com.

12 **Adam Smith:** William O. Thweatt, ed., *Classical Political Economy: A Survey of Recent Literature* (New York: Springer Science+Business Media, 1988), 34.

13 **Over the years:** Many federal antitrust cases have been filed since the passage of the Sherman Antitrust Act. George Bittlingmayer, "Antitrust and Business Activity: The First Quarter Century," 70 *Business History Review* 363, 376 (1996) (listing by year the number of federal antitrust cases filed from 1890 to 1914, noting that 154 cases were filed over that time period, with 15 of those involving major railroads). And over the decades, the antitrust movement has had some successes. Why were we able to bring down long-distance rates and usher in decades of innovation in telecommunications? Because the Justice Department's Antitrust Division under both Democratic and Republican administrations took the AT&T monopoly to court. Kimberly A. Zarkin and Michael J. Zarkin, *The Federal Communications Commission: Front Line in the Culture and Regulation Wars* (Westport, Conn.: Greenwood Press, 2006), 65–66. Why were we able to have more competitive prices on compact discs a couple of decades ago? Because the Justice Department brought a landmark price-fixing case against music distributors. John E. Stapleford, *Bulls, Bears, and Golden Calves: Applying Christian Ethics in Economics* (Downers Grove, Ill.: InterVarsity Press, 2002), 149; David A. Balto, "Antitrust Enforcement in the Clinton Administration," 9 *Cornell Journal of Law and Public Policy* 61, 100 (1999). How did we get fairer prices for aspiring lawyers in Georgia trying to take the bar exam? *Palmer v. BRG of Georgia Inc.,* 498 U.S. 46 (1990). A group of enterprising law students took an antitrust case all the way up to the U.S. Supreme Court. James F. Ponsoldt, "Toward the Reaffirmation of the Antitrust Rule of Per Se Illegality as a Law of Rules for Horizontal Price Fixing and Territorial Allocation Agreements: A Reflection on the *Palmer* Case in a Renewed Era of Economic Regulation," 62 *SMU Law*

Review 635 (2009) (discussing the facts of the antitrust case brought by the law students).

13 **Sherman Act:** At the federal level, the FTC and the Justice Department's Antitrust Division still regularly rely on the Sherman Act to police anticompetitive conduct. In particular, there are two key sections of it that guide regulators— as well as judges and lawyers. First, section 1 of the act prohibits unreasonable contracts, combinations, or conspiracies between two or more businesses or entities that restrain trade. *Copperweld Corp. v. Independence Tube Corp.*, 467 U.S. 752, 768 (1984); Albert A. Foer and Randy M. Stutz, eds., *Private Enforcement of Antitrust Law in the United States: A Handbook* (Cheltenham, U.K.: Edward Elgar, 2012), xx. The actual text of section 1 reads, in somewhat cumbersome language, "Every contract, combination in the form of trust or otherwise, or conspiracy, in restraint of trade or commerce among the several States, or with foreign nations, is declared to be illegal." 15 U.S.C. § 1. Likewise, section 2—another staple of modern antitrust litigation—prohibits monopolization, attempted monopolization, or any conspiracy or combination to monopolize, whether by a single entity or multiple entities. *Copperweld Corp.*, 467 U.S. at 767–68. To quote its exact language, it is unlawful to "monopolize, or attempt to monopolize, or combine or conspire with any other person or persons, to monopolize any part of the trade or commerce among the several States, or with foreign nations." 15 U.S.C. § 2. It is a felony to violate the Sherman Act, and fines—and even lengthy prison terms—can be imposed on violators. *In re Mushroom Direct Purchaser Antitrust Litigation*, 655 F.3d 158, 165 (3d Cir. 2011). The law currently makes corporate violators punishable by fines up to $100 million and individual violators by fines up to $1 million or terms of imprisonment of up to ten years, or both. 15 U.S.C.A. § 1.

13 **Clayton Act:** The Clayton Antitrust Act complements the legal protections against anticompetitive conduct that Senator John Sherman originally put in place in 1890. The key provision of the Clayton Act is section 7, which prohibits mergers or acquisitions that would substantially lessen competition. 15 U.S.C. § 18; see also *U.S. v. American Bldg. Maintenance Industries*, 422 U.S. 271, 279 (1975) ("§ 7 of the Clayton Act is explicitly limited to corporate acquisitions"); compare *United States v. Philadelphia National Bank*, 374 U.S. 321, 356 (1963); *United States v. Blue Bell Inc.*, 395 F. Supp. 538, 542 (M.D. Tenn. 1975); *United States of America v. Allied Waste Industries, Inc.*, No. Civ. 1:00CV01067, 2000 WL 621130, *3 (May 12, 2000); *Fraser v. Major League Soccer, L.L.C.*, 97 F. Supp.2d 130, 139–40 (D. Minn. 2000) ("There can be no § 7 liability because the formation of MLS [Major League Soccer] did not involve the acquisition or merger of existing business enterprises, but rather the formation of an entirely new entity which itself represented the creation of an entirely new market"). For example, in the seminal case of *Brown Shoe Co. v. United States*, 370 U.S. 294 (1962), the U.S. Supreme Court stopped a merger under the Clayton Act that the Court found would have lessened competition substantially in the sale of men's, women's, and children's shoes. Likewise, in 1963, the Court held that the merger of the second- and third-largest banks in the Philadelphia area would have led to a 30 percent market share and thus ran afoul of the Clayton Act's section 7. *Philadelphia National Bank*, 374 U.S. 321.

14 **state attorneys general:** For decades, there has also been a working group, made up of DOJ and FTC representatives and state attorneys general, to coordinate federal-state antitrust enforcement cooperation. American Bar Association, Antitrust Law Section, *State Antitrust Enforcement Handbook,* 2nd ed. (2008), 51.

14 **prevalent years ago:** Steve Coll, *The Deal of the Century: The Breakup of AT&T* (New York: Open Road Media, 2017). In the first century after the Sherman Act was passed, there are many examples of antitrust policy being strengthened, both by Justice Department enforcement and by court decisions, as well as subsequent federal legislation that bolstered the original law. But over time the laws were weakened due to judicially created or legislatively inserted exemptions for industries from rail to insurance to Major League Baseball. William D. Middleton, George M. Smerk, and Roberta L. Diehl, eds., *Encyclopedia of North American Railroads* (Bloomington: Indiana University Press, 2007), 961 (entry of James W. Ely Jr., noting, "In the Transportation Act of 1920 Congress made a number of significant changes in railroad regulatory policy. Congress strengthened the power of the ICC and abandoned the notion of fostering competition. Instead, the Transportation Act sought to encourage consolidation of carriers into a limited number of systems. Not only was ICC approval now required for rail mergers, but such action by the commission conferred immunity from antitrust laws."); *Federal Baseball Club of Baltimore, Inc. v. National League of Prof. Baseball Clubs,* 259 U.S. 200 (1922) (ruling that the Sherman Antitrust Act did not apply to professional baseball). Compare *Paul v. Virginia,* 75 U.S. (8 Wall.) 168 (1868) (finding that "issuing a policy of insurance is not a transaction of commerce"), overruled by *United States v. South-Eastern Underwriters Association,* 322 U.S. 533 (1944) (holding that the Sherman Antitrust Act applied to insurance and that Congress could regulate insurance under the U.S. Constitution's commerce clause), with McCarran-Ferguson Act, 15 U.S.C. §§ 1011–15 (1945) (exempting the business of insurance from federal antitrust laws to a certain extent, but providing that the Sherman Act, the Clayton Act, and the Federal Trade Commission Act "shall be applicable to the business of insurance to the extent that such business is not regulated by State law"), and Melanie L. Fein, *Banking and Financial Services: Banking, Securities, and Insurance Regulatory Guide,* vol. 1, § 16.09 (New York: Aspen, 2006) (quoting and describing the McCarran-Ferguson Act). In 2020, Congress voted to amend the McCarran-Ferguson Act, which had exempted the business of insurance from the antitrust laws. Alan Goforth, "U.S. Senate Votes to Repeal Federal Antitrust Enforcement for Insurers," Benefits Pro, Dec. 28, 2020, www.benefitspro.com.

14 **AT&T–Time Warner merger:** Diane Bartz and David Shepardson, "U.S. Justice Department Will Not Appeal AT&T, Time Warner Merger After Court Loss," Reuters, Feb. 26, 2019, www.reuters.com; Sara Salinas, "AT&T's Merger with Time Warner Will Stand, After DOJ Loses Its Appeal and Drops the Case," CNBC, Feb. 26, 2019, www.cnbc.com.

14 **difficult to litigate antitrust cases:** See Submission of Bill Baer, Visiting Fellow, Governance Studies, Brookings Institution, before the U.S. House Committee on the Judiciary, Subcommittee on Antitrust, Commercial, and Administrative Law, May 19, 2020, 3, www.brookings.edu ("In my view the

fear of getting it wrong warped antitrust enforcement. That is my fundamental concern with the state of antitrust enforcement today. It is too cautious, too worried about adverse effects of 'over enforcement.' . . . The attitude that any uncertainty should result in inaction has caused many courts to demand a level of proof that is often unattainable.").

14 **the morning and afternoon papers:** The *Star Tribune,* where my dad worked until his retirement, is the product of a 1982 combination between *The Minneapolis Star,* an evening paper, and the *Minneapolis Tribune,* a morning paper. The new newspaper became known as the *Minneapolis Star and Tribune,* which then became simply the *Star Tribune* in 1987.

14 **suing across the United States:** Emmanuel K. Ngwainmbi, *Exporting Communication Technology to Developing Countries: Sociocultural, Economic, and Educational Factors* (Lanham, Md.: University Press of America, 1999), 51 ("In the early 1970s, MCI sought to connect its network with the Bell Telephone System. Threatened about a new competition, AT&T rejected MCI's bid to make the connection. In turn, MCI sued AT&T for three billion dollars in damage and for the right to make the connections. . . . The emergence of MCI, Western Union, ITT, and Sprint in the early 1970s forced AT&T to lower priced services."); Lynne W. Jeter, *Disconnected: Deceit and Betrayal at WorldCom* (Hoboken, N.J.: John Wiley & Sons, 2003), xxiii ("MCI's challenge to AT&T's monopoly in a March 1974 lawsuit citing violation of the Sherman Antitrust Act ultimately led to the breakup of AT&T, when Ma Bell, as everyone knew her, was laid to rest."); see also Peter Temin, *The Fall of the Bell System: A Study in Prices and Politics,* with Louis Galambos (Cambridge, U.K.: Cambridge University Press, 1989).

15 **one of the first state laws:** Kevin Breuninger, "Minnesota Democrat Amy Klobuchar Declares Bid for 2020 Presidential Nomination," CNBC, Feb. 10, 2019, www.cnbc.com.

15 **cast the highest number of votes ever:** Domenico Montanaro, "President-Elect Joe Biden Hits 80 Million Votes in Year of Record Turnout," NPR, Nov. 25, 2020, www.npr.org.

1. MONOPOLY—IT'S NOT JUST A GAME

17 **Monopoly:** I was, clearly, not alone. Rod Kennedy Jr. and Jim Waltzer, *Monopoly: The Story Behind the World's Best-Selling Game* (Layton, Utah: Gibbs Smith, 2004), 8 ("In 1935, it became the best-selling board game in America. In the seven decades since, more than 750 million sets have been sold and MONOPOLY has gained a worldwide audience.").

17 **a journalist:** Jim Klobuchar, *Minstrel: My Adventure in Newspapering* (Minneapolis: University of Minnesota Press, 1997).

17 **Income Tax square:** The enormous disparities in wealth generated by trusts during the Gilded Age spawned the passage and ratification of the U.S. Constitution's Sixteenth Amendment. That amendment, ratified in 1913, allowed Congress to levy a federal income tax without apportioning it among the states or basing it on U.S. census data. The U.S. Supreme Court, in *Pollock v. Farmers' Loan & Trust* (1895), had held that certain taxes on income (in

particular, those on property, the rents from land, and stock dividends) were unconstitutional, so a constitutional amendment, which effectively overruled *Pollock,* was needed for the creation of a graduated income tax. The income tax Congress put in place after the Sixteenth Amendment's ratification asked the country's wealthiest citizens to do their part—to pay their fair share. John D. Rockefeller had retired in 1897 after amassing a fortune of $900 million, and a 1912 congressional study of J. P. Morgan's financial empire revealed 112 companies with a valuation of $22 billion. Jeffrey A. Johnson, ed., *Reforming America: A Thematic Encyclopedia and Document Collection of the Progressive Era* (Santa Barbara, Calif.: ABC-CLIO, 2017), 1:201. The first post–Sixteenth Amendment income tax law, the Revenue Act of 1913, set up a progressive income tax system, imposing a tax ranging from 1 percent on incomes exceeding $3,000 to 7 percent on incomes exceeding $500,000. The U.S. Supreme Court upheld the constitutionality of the progressive income tax in 1916. John O. Everett, Cherie Hennig, and Nancy Nichols, eds., *Contemporary Tax Practice: Research, Planning, and Strategies* (Chicago: CCH, 2008), 1–4.

18 **people were farmers:** R. Douglas Hurt, *American Agriculture: A Brief History,* rev. ed. (West Lafayette, Ind.: Purdue University Press, 2002), 35 ("Nearly all the first colonists engaged in farming, and approximately 75 to 90 percent still practiced agriculture by the time of the American Revolution.").

19 **"The Body of Liberties":** William Whitmore, comp., *The Colonial Laws of Massachusetts* (Boston: Rockwell and Churchill, 1890), 29, 34–35.

19 **Maryland's first constitution:** Constitution of Maryland (Nov. 11, 1776), art. 39.

19 **North Carolina's constitution:** Constitution of North Carolina (Dec. 19, 1776), art. 23, in *The Constitutions of the Several Independent States of America* (New York: E. Oswald, 1786), 183, 185.

19 **technically illegal:** Steven G. Calabresi and Larissa Price, "Monopolies and the Constitution: A History of Crony Capitalism" (2012), Faculty Working Papers, Paper 214, scholarlycommons.law.northwestern.edu.

19 ***Darcy v. Allen:*** "The Case of Monopolies," Trin. 44 Eliz., in John Henry Thomas and John Farquhar Fraser, *The Reports of Sir Edward Coke, Knt.,* new ed. (London: Joseph Butterworth and Son, 1826), 6:159–66 (reported there as *Darcy v. Allein*); *Darcy v. Allen* (The Case of Monopolies), King's Bench (1603), in James Bradley Thayer, *Cases on Constitutional Law* (Cambridge [Mass.]: Charles W. Sever, 1894), 15–16; David Chan Smith, *Sir Edward Coke and the Reformation of the Laws: Religion, Politics, and Jurisprudence, 1578–1616* (Cambridge, U.K.: Cambridge University Press, 2014), 256; William Carpmael, *Law Reports of Patent Cases* (London: A. Macintosh, 1843), 1:26–27.

19 **an exclusive right:** Moïs H. Avram, *Patenting and Promoting Inventions* (New York: B. C. Forbes, 1922), 32 ("In the thirteenth year of her reign, Queen Elizabeth granted to one Ralph Bowes the exclusive privilege of making, importing or selling playing cards, for the period of twelve years, which was subsequently extended to the plaintiff, Darcy, an assignee of Bowes.").

20 **monopolies in operation:** Christopher Hill, *The Century of Revolution, 1603–1714,* 2nd ed. (London: Routledge, 1980), 31–32.

20 ***Rights of Man:*** Thomas Paine, *Rights of Man: Being an Answer to Mr. Burke's*

Attack on the French Revolution, 2nd Philadelphia ed. (Carlisle, Pa.: George Kline, 1791), 35.

21 **fined or imprisoned:** Roger A. Arnold, *Microeconomics,* 12th ed. (Boston: Cengage Learning, 2016), 279.

21 **Boston Tea Party:** Benjamin L. Carp, *Defiance of the Patriots: The Boston Tea Party and the Making of America* (New Haven, Conn.: Yale University Press, 2010).

21 **Tea Act:** Paul S. Boyer et al., *The Enduring Vision: A History of the American People,* 6th ed. (Boston: Wadsworth, 2010), 1:110.

21 **"lost America":** Peter Whiteley, *Lord North: The Prime Minister Who Lost America* (London: Hambeldon Press, 1996).

22 **East India Company's monopoly:** Phil Valentine, *Tax Revolt: The Rebellion Against an Overbearing, Bloated, Arrogant, and Abusive Government* (Nashville: Nelson Current, 2005), 95 (noting that the Tea Act of 1773 lowered taxes but that the Tea Act "really upset the colonists" because it propped up "the British-owned East India Company by giving them a monopoly on the tea market in America" and because "they had come to the conclusion that England had no authority to tax them at all").

22 **Mary Beth Norton:** Mary Beth Norton, *1774: The Long Year of Revolution* (New York: Alfred A. Knopf, 2020), xvii, 4, 7, 10, 13.

23 **Alexander McDougall:** McDougall, a native of Scotland, was a Sons of Liberty leader from New York City who later became a delegate to the Continental Congress. E. Wayne Carp, *To Starve the Army at Pleasure: Continental Army Administration and American Political Culture, 1775–1783* (Chapel Hill: University of North Carolina Press, 1984), 270n41.

23 **five broadsides:** Joseph S. Tiedemann, *Reluctant Revolutionaries: New York City and the Road to Independence, 1763–1776* (Ithaca, N.Y.: Cornell University Press, 1997), 176.

23 **£400,000 annual payment:** John Bruce, *Report on the Negociation, Between the Honorable East-India Company and the Public, Respecting the Renewal of the Company's Exclusive Privileges of Trade, for Twenty Years from March, 1794* (London: Black, Parry and Kingsbury, 1811), 20.

23 **shifting their consumption:** Mark Pendergrast, *Uncommon Grounds: The History of Coffee and How It Transformed Our World,* rev. ed. (New York: Basic Books, 2010), 15.

23 **More than five thousand people:** Katurah Mackay, "Churches and Chowda," *National Parks* 73, no. 7–8 (July/Aug. 1999): 35.

23 **in his diary:** John Adams, diary entry Dec. 17, 1773, in *Diary and Autobiography of John Adams,* vol. 2, *1771–1781,* ed. L. H. Butterfield (Cambridge, Mass.: Harvard University Press, 1961), 85–87.

23 *Hamilton:* Renee C. Romano and Claire Bond Potter, eds., *Historians on "Hamilton": How a Blockbuster Musical Is Restaging America's Past* (New Brunswick, N.J.: Rutgers University Press, 2018).

24 **the flags:** Marc Leepson, *Flag: An American Biography* (New York: Thomas Dunne Books, 2005), chap. 1.

24 **antimonopoly sentiment:** Daniel A. Crane, "Antitrust Antifederalism," 96 *California Law Review* 1, 6 (2008) ("At the Constitution's framing, the former colonies inherited from British common law a suspicion of corporate charters

based on the view that such special privileges generally led to monopoly. Further, since many of the foreign trading companies that colonized the reaches of the British Empire were explicitly granted monopoly rights—exclusive trading privileges in specific regions—in their charters, the American colonists tended to associate the corporate with explicit monopoly. Abhorrence of monopoly became an American tradition early on.").

24 *The Wealth of Nations:* Adam Smith, *An Inquiry into the Nature and Causes of the Wealth of Nations* (London: W. Strahan, 1776). Thomas Jefferson called *The Wealth of Nations* the "best book" on the subject of political economy. Jefferson to Thomas Mann Randolph, May 30, 1790, in *The Works of Thomas Jefferson,* ed. Paul Leicester Ford (New York: G. P. Putnam's Sons, 1904), 6:63.

24 **letters and speeches:** James Madison, "Report on Books for Congress," 1783; Robert L. Hetzel, "The Relevance of Adam Smith," in *Invisible Hand: The Wealth of Adam Smith,* ed. Andrés Marroquín (Honolulu: University Press of the Pacific, 2002), 25; see also Joseph A. Murray, *Alexander Hamilton: America's Forgotten Founder* (New York: Algora, 2007), 170 (noting that Alexander Hamilton, in his *Report on Manufactures,* "drew heavily" from Adam Smith's *Wealth of Nations* "to justify his pro-manufacturing stance").

25 **"labouring poor":** Smith, *Wealth of Nations,* 2:575.

25 **he worried about collusion:** Irvin B. Tucker, *Macroeconomics for Today,* 6th ed. (Mason, Ohio: South-Western Cengage Learning, 2010), 102.

26 **enslaved countless human beings:** Henry Wiencek, *Master of the Mountain: Thomas Jefferson and His Slaves* (New York: Farrar, Straus and Giroux, 2012), 13 ("In his lifetime Jefferson owned more than 600 slaves."); Robert A. Nowlan, *The American Presidents, Washington to Tyler: What They Did, What They Said, What Was Said About Them, and Full Source Notes* (Jefferson, N.C.: McFarland, 2012), 182 ("Over the course of his lifetime, Madison owned more than 100 slaves who worked on his plantation."). Many of America's Founding Fathers owned enslaved persons who toiled on their plantations. William G. Hyland Jr., *George Mason: The Founding Father Who Gave Us the Bill of Rights* (Washington, D.C.: Regnery, 2019), 240 ("Twenty-five of the fifty-five men gathered in Philadelphia owned slaves, and three-fourths of those were dependent on slave labor for their economic well-being."); Diana Turk et al., eds., *Teaching U.S. History: Dialogues Among Social Studies Teachers and Historians* (New York: Routledge, 2010), 25 ("Thomas Jefferson owned slaves but was quoted as saying that slavery was a 'hideous blot' on America, and George Mason owned more than three hundred slaves but condemned slavery as evil. In fact, 31 percent of the delegates to the Philadelphia Convention owned approximately 1,400 slaves."); Andrea Wulf, *Founding Gardeners: The Revolutionary Generation, Nature, and the Shaping of the American Nation* (New York: Vintage Books, 2012), 201 (noting that James Madison owned more than a hundred enslaved persons when he retired, with those individuals living in "rickety" cabins with dirt floors "by the fields of the 3,000-acre plantation"); Denise A. Spellberg, *Thomas Jefferson's Qur'an: Islam and the Founders* (New York: Alfred A. Knopf, 2013) (noting that Thomas Jefferson owned 187 enslaved persons by 1774 and that, at his Mount Vernon plantation, George Washington owned more than 300 enslaved individuals).

26 **Mason, the Virginia plantation owner:** Jonathan Elliot, comp. and ed., *The*

Debates in the Several State Conventions, on the Adoption of the Federal Constitution, as Recommended by the General Convention at Philadelphia in 1787 (Washington, D.C.: Jonathan Elliot, 1836), 1:535.

26 **"restriction against monopolies":** Jefferson to Madison, Dec. 20, 1787; see also Crane, "Antitrust Antifederalism," 9 ("A slew of Antifederalist writers attacked the proposed Constitution as setting up a Congressional power to grant mercantile monopolies. The ratifying conventions of Massachusetts, New Hampshire, and North Carolina requested, in their proposed bill of rights, an amendment 'that congress erect no company of merchants, with exclusive advantages of commerce' and New York proposed a similar provision. After the ratification, Thomas Jefferson, in private correspondence to Madison, expressed the need for an anti-monopoly provision in the Bill of Rights.").

26 **a long, cordial friendship:** Lee Wilkins, "Madison and Jefferson: The Making of a Friendship," 12 *Political Psychology* 593 (1991).

26 **Jefferson was an inventor:** Gregory A. Stobbs, *Software Patents,* 3rd ed. (New York: Wolters Kluwer, 2012), 1–17.

26 ***Graham v. John Deere Co.:*** *Graham v. John Deere Co.,* 383 U.S. 1 (1966).

26 **"among the greatest nuisances":** Madison to Jefferson, Oct. 17, 1788.

26 **in yet another letter:** Stobbs, *Software Patents,* 1–18.

26 **"Certainly an inventor":** Jefferson to Oliver Evans, May 2, 1807, in *The Writings of Thomas Jefferson,* ed. H. A. Washington (Washington, D.C.: Taylor & Maury, 1853), 5:74–75.

27 **the ultimate monopoly:** Ashish K. Vaidya, ed., *Globalization: Encyclopedia of Trade, Labor, and Politics* (Santa Barbara, Calif.: ABC-CLIO, 2006), 1:195 (taking note of a "slave master's monopoly over the slave's labor").

27 **The Constitution:** Junius P. Rodriguez, *The Historical Encyclopedia of World Slavery* (Santa Barbara, Calif.: ABC-CLIO, 1997), 1:664–65.

27 **royal monopolies:** John Middleton, ed., *World Monarchies and Dynasties* (London: Routledge, 2005), 634 ("More often, monarchs created economic monopolies, and it is these institutions that are most often associated with the word 'monopoly.' Industrial monopolies were frequently used to establish a new industry where none had existed before or to establish trade in a new market. . . . Royal monopolies were also used to open new markets for trade and to colonize new territories. . . . The East India Company, which operated from the early 1600s to late 1800s, had a royal monopoly on British trade with the East Indies, including the right to import tea to the American colonies. This monopoly, and the import tax associated with it, contributed to the disaffection of the American colonists, leading to the 'Boston Tea Party' and, ultimately, to the American Revolution.").

27 **confer on Congress:** U.S. Constitution, art. 1. sec. 8, cl. 8.

28 **cotton gin:** David S. Kidder and Noah D. Oppenheim, *The Intellectual Devotional: American History—Revive Your Mind, Complete Your Education, and Converse Confidently About Our Nation's Past* (New York: Modern Times, 2007), 25.

28 **first commercial steamboat:** Andrea Sutcliffe, *Steam: The Untold Story of America's First Great Invention* (Hampshire, U.K.: Palgrave Macmillan), 208, 229.

28 **America's invention-fired economy:** Harold Evans, *They Made America: From*

the Steam Engine to the Search Engine—Two Centuries of Innovators (New York: Back Bay Books, 2004).

28 **"middling class"**: James T. Kloppenberg, *Toward Democracy: The Struggle for Self-Rule in European and American Thought* (Oxford: Oxford University Press, 2016), 783n32; John D. Bessler, *The Birth of American Law: An Italian Philosopher and the American Revolution* (Durham, N.C.: Carolina Academic Press, 2014), 8.

28 **Tammany Hall**: Then New York's Democratic Party headquarters, Tammany Hall came to be associated with "sleazy, unprincipled crooks" who shook down the decent and indecent alike in pursuit of an illicit buck." Terry Golway, introduction to *Machine Made: Tammany Hall and the Creation of Modern American Politics* (New York: W. W. Norton, 2014); Corona Brezina, *America's Political Scandals in the Late 1880s: Boss Tweed and Tammany Hall* (New York: Rosen, 2004).

28 **First Bank of the United States**: Martin L. Primack and James F. Willis, *An Economic History of the United States* (New York: Benjamin/Cummings, 1980), 100.

29 **veto message**: Philo A. Goodwin, *Biography of Andrew Jackson, President of the United States* (New York: R. Hart Towner, 1835), 388–89.

29 **President Grover Cleveland**: President Grover Cleveland, Fourth Annual Message, Dec. 3, 1888, in *A Compilation of the Messages and Papers of the Presidents* (New York: Bureau of National Literature, 1897), 12:5358–59.

30 **progressive movement**: Michael McGerr, *A Fierce Discontent: The Rise and Fall of the Progressive Movement in America, 1870–1920* (New York: Free Press, 2003).

30 **William Jennings Bryan**: *Speeches of William Jennings Bryan* (New York: Funk & Wagnalls, 1913), 1:xxiii–xxvi, xxix, xxxii–xxxiii, xxxvi–xxxviii.

30 ***Minnesota v. Northern Securities Company***: *Minnesota v. Northern Securities Co.*, 194 U.S. 48 (1904); see also *Northern Securities Co. v. United States*, 193 U.S. 197 (1904).

30 **patented by a woman**: Mary Pilon, "Monopoly's Inventor: The Progressive Who Didn't Pass 'Go,'" *New York Times*, Feb. 13, 2015, www.nytimes.com.

30 **a 1970s-era lawsuit**: Ralph Anspach, *The Billion Dollar Monopoly Swindle: During a David and Goliath Battle, the Inventor of the Anti-Monopoly Game Uncovers the Secret History of Monopoly* (Redwood City, Calif.: Xlibris, 2010).

31 ***Progress and Poverty***: Henry George, *Progress and Poverty: An Inquiry into the Cause of Industrial Depressions and of Increase of Want with Increase of Wealth* (New York: Sterling, 1879).

31 **millions of copies**: John Laurent, ed., *Henry George's Legacy in Economic Thought* (Cheltenham, U.K.: Edward Elgar, 2005), 3.

31 **Martin Luther King Jr.**: Thomas F. Jackson, *From Civil Rights to Human Rights: Martin Luther King Jr. and the Struggle for Economic Justice* (Philadelphia: University of Pennsylvania Press, 2007), 273; Cornel West, ed., *The Radical King: Martin Luther King Jr.* (Boston: Beacon Press, 2015), 173.

31 **made declarations**: Edward T. O'Donnell, *Henry George and the Crisis of Inequality: Progress and Poverty in the Gilded Age* (New York: Columbia University Press, 2015), 25; Kenneth C. Wenzer, ed., *Henry George: Collected Journalistic Writings* (London: Routledge, 2015), 1:164.

32 **1886 race:** Richard Brookhiser, "1886: The Men Who Would Be Mayor," *City Journal* (Autumn 1993), www.city-journal.org.

32 **Cooper Union:** Harold Holzer, *Lincoln at Cooper Union: The Speech That Made Abraham Lincoln President* (New York: Simon & Schuster, 2006).

32 **Lizzie Magie was born:** Mary Pilon, *The Monopolists: Obsession, Fury, and the Scandal Behind the World's Favorite Board Game* (New York: Bloomsbury, 2015), 18–21, 24–25, 31, 34, 39, 41, 60–62.

33 **Dead Letter Office:** *Hearings Before Subcommittee of House, Committee on Appropriations Consisting of Messrs. Forney, Dockery, Holman, Henderson of Iowa, and Dingley, in Charge of Legislative, Executive, and Judicial Appropriation Bill for 1893* (Washington, D.C.: Government Printing Office, 1892), 139.

33 **Coal Strike of 1902:** Perry K. Blatz, *Democratic Miners: Work and Labor Relations in the Anthracite Coal Industry, 1875–1925* (Albany: State University of New York Press, 1994), 121.

33 **when she filed her patent application:** When Lizzie Magie submitted her patent for her game with the U.S. Patent Office, it was, coincidentally, filed on the very same day that Orville and Wilbur Wright filed their own patent application for their invention for a "flying machine." David McCullough, *The Wright Brothers* (New York: Simon & Schuster, 2015). Lizzie Magie's original patent application for the Landlord's Game was filed on March 23, 1903. It declared that "the object of the game is to obtain as much wealth or money as possible, the player having the greatest amount of wealth at the end of the game after a certain predetermined number of circuits of the board have been made being the winner" (landlordsgame.info/rules/lg-p04.html). The Wright brothers' application for their "flying machine" was also filed on March 23, 1903. Stephen Corda, *Introduction to Aerospace Engineering with a Flight Test Perspective* (West Sussex, U.K.: Wiley, 2017), 15. A revised patent application for the Landlord's Game, filed on April 28, 1923, stated that the game was designed to be "educational in its nature" and that "the object of the game is not only to afford amusement to the players, but to illustrate to them how under the present or prevailing system of land tenure, the landlord has an advantage over other enterprises and also how the single tax would discourage land speculation." As Lizzie Magie described the game's object, "The player who first accumulates ($3000) three thousand dollars, in cash, wins the game." Philip E. Orbanes, *Monopoly: The World's Most Famous Game—and How It Got That Way* (Philadelphia: Da Capo Press, 2006), 231–32. A good networker, Lizzie Magie later got acknowledged in the preface to the muckraker Upton Sinclair's 1915 compilation, *The Cry for Justice: An Anthology of the Literature of Social Protest.* Her own invention, the Landlord's Game, of which early, handmade copies still exist, would later become known simply as the "monopoly game."

34 **two sets of rules:** Kathy Martin, *Famous Brand Names and Their Origins* (South Yorkshire, U.K.: Pen & Sword History, 2016), 142; Marlene Wagman-Geller, *Women Who Launch: Women Who Shattered Glass Ceilings* (Coral Gables, Fla.: Mango, 2018), chap. 6.

35 **not Charles Darrow:** Martin, *Famous Brand Names and Their Origins,* 142–43.

35 **modified it:** Tristan Donovan, *It's All a Game: The History of Board Games from Monopoly to Settlers of Catan* (New York: Thomas Dunne Books, 2017), 81–82.

35 **paid Magie:** Pilon, *Monopolists,* 122–23.

35 **in the future:** The Monopoly game would be licensed by Parker Brothers for production in many other countries, and after World War II sales went from 800,000 a year to more than 1 million. By 1974, Parker Brothers had reportedly sold 80 million sets of the game, and by 1982 the game had been translated into more than fifteen languages. "Your Move, Parker Brothers," *New York Times,* Nov. 10, 1974. A number of anniversary editions and spin-offs have been produced, with Monopoly Junior first published in 1990. Monopoly is available in forty-three languages and in 111 countries, with Hasbro estimating that more than 1 billion people have played the game. Meg Wagner, "Monopoly Puts Real Money in French Game Boxes to Celebrate 80th Year," *New York Daily News,* Feb. 4, 2015, www.nydailynews.com.

36 **an antimonopoly version:** The developer of this version, a professor, had long lectured his students about the evils of monopolies. John Carman, "No Trust Should Remain After the Game," *Minneapolis Star,* May 27, 1974, 7.

37 **buried approximately forty thousand:** Pilon, *Monopolists,* 223–29. The Anti-Monopoly games had been manufactured by Mankato Industries. "Anti-Monopoly Games Destroyed After Suit," *New York Times,* July 6, 1977, 72.

37 **in January 1980:** "Anti-Monopoly Game Wins in Court," *Santa Cruz Sentinel,* Jan. 23, 1980, 11; "Judicial Dice Unbury Anti-Monopoly," *Daily Utah Chronicle,* Feb. 8, 1980, 8.

37 **his own press in tow:** "We'll be in New York with *Anti-Monopoly* in time for the Toy Fair in February," Anspach said, vowing to have his game back in production soon. He called the dig a "symbolic" move to let the maker of Monopoly know he was back. To celebrate his appellate victory, Anspach even took out a *Star Tribune* newspaper ad in 1980, titled "Anti-Monopoly.™ The game that made headlines." The ad touted that the idea of his board game was "to bust trusts instead of build them" and that Anti-Monopoly "is back (not from the dump, but in the store), and you can have this controversial game for the welcome-back price of 6.99." In January 1980, the media noted that while the immensely popular Monopoly board game had sold 80 million sets worldwide since 1935, Anspach had sold 419,000 Anti-Monopoly sets before he'd been temporarily ordered to halt production of his game, whose players are "trustbusters" who win points by breaking up monopolies. Anspach told reporters that he still had no more plans to sell out to Parker Brothers than he did four years earlier, when, he observed, he'd been offered $500,000 for his brainchild. "Ethics and principle" are involved, he emphasized.

37 **Six hours of digging:** "Six hours of digging in near-zero cold failed to turn up any sign of the games," *The Winona Daily News* reported, with Minnesota's *Star Tribune* adding that the "fruitless search" simply produced "a hole about 12 by 20 feet and 16 feet deep." "Exhumation of Games Is Failure," *Winona Daily News,* Jan. 24, 1980, 9b; "Anti-Monopoly's Inventor Fails to Find His Games in Dump," *Minneapolis Star Tribune,* Jan. 24, 1980, 32. "It's been a nightmare," Anspach said as he looked over reams of court documents, telling reporters he'd taken out a second mortgage on his house and gone deeply into debt to pay legal bills totaling between $100,000 and $200,000. Ralph Vartabedian, "Inventor Passes Go, Collects Garbage," *Minneapolis Star,* Jan. 23, 1980, 1, 11.

37 **the website:** Anti-Monopoly, www.antimonopoly.com.

37 **no longer in production:** Orbanes, *Monopoly*, 14, 24; Steven Johnson, *Wonderland: How Play Made the Modern World* (New York: Riverhead Books, 2016), 198. Magie's original game rules had been deemed unworthy of sale many decades before. A professor of economics at the University of Pennsylvania's Wharton School of Finance used the Landlord's Game from 1906 to 1915, and college students there—and at Harvard and Columbia—played it, as did Quakers in Atlantic City and Philadelphia. Kate Raworth, "Monopoly Was Invented to Demonstrate the Evils of Capitalism," BBC, July 28, 2017, www.bbc.com; Christopher Ketcham, "Monopoly Is Theft," *Harper's Magazine*, Oct. 19, 2012, harpers.org. But while Monopoly had sold more than 250,000 copies by the end of 1935, with Parker Brothers later producing 20,000 Monopoly games a week as orders poured in, allowing Darrow to live a life of leisure, sales of the Landlord's Game floundered. As one history reports of Parker Brothers and retailers' refusals to stock the Landlord's Game, "Most of the ten thousand copies of the Landlord's Game the company produced were destroyed. Magie could only look on helpless as her board game dream fell apart. The Landlord's Game was dead. Her bid to spread the gospel of Henry George had failed. All that was left was Monopoly, the Frankenstein's monster she had inadvertently created." Donovan, *It's All a Game,* 85.

2. DON'T TRUST THE TRUSTS

39 **James J. Hill House:** www.mnhs.org/hillhouse.

39 **"showcase of St. Paul":** David Goran, "A Historic Piece of Minnesotan Architecture: The James J. Hill House," *Vintage News,* Aug. 4, 2016, www.thevintagenews.com.

39 **Great Northern Railway:** Ralph W. Hidy et al., *The Great Northern Railway: A History* (Minneapolis: University of Minnesota Press, 1988).

40 **"Give me Swedes":** William M. Adler, *The Man Who Never Died: The Life, Times, and Legacy of Joe Hill, American Labor Icon* (New York: Bloomsbury, 2011), 112.

40 *The Great Gatsby:* F. Scott Fitzgerald, *The Great Gatsby,* ed. Michael Nowlin (Toronto: Broadview, 2007), 167.

40 **rented a home:** Dave Page and John Koblas, *F. Scott Fitzgerald in Minnesota: Toward the Summit* (St. Cloud, Minn.: North Star Press of St. Cloud, 1996); Dave Page, *F. Scott Fitzgerald in Minnesota: The Writer and His Friends at Home* (St. Paul: Fitzgerald in Saint Paul, 2017).

40 **Known as the Empire Builder:** Michael P. Malone, *James J. Hill: Empire Builder of the Northwest* (Norman: University of Oklahoma Press, 1996), 280.

40 **many industrialists:** Matthew Josephson, *The Robber Barons: The Classic Account of the Influential Capitalists Who Transformed America's Future* (San Diego: Harvest, 1962); T. J. Stiles, *The First Tycoon: The Epic Life of Cornelius Vanderbilt* (New York: Alfred A. Knopf, 2009); Les Standiford, *Meet You in Hell: Andrew Carnegie, Henry Clay Frick, and the Bitter Partnership That Transformed America* (New York: Crown, 2005).

41 **Trusts developed:** Bhu Srinivasan, *Americana: A 400-Year History of American Capitalism* (New York: Penguin Press, 2017), 245.

41 **Standard Oil Trust:** John Hrastar, *Liquid Natural Gas in the United States: A History* (Jefferson, N.C.: McFarland, 2014), 41.

41 **Through the trust:** Robert W. Kolb, ed., *The SAGE Encyclopedia of Business Ethics and Society,* 2nd ed. (Thousand Oaks, Calif.: SAGE, 2018), 3446 ("In adapting the legal concept of the trust to an industrial setting, Standard Oil persuaded the stockholders of 30 companies in the economically critical oil industry to turn control of their corporate stock over to 9 trustees, who then could exercise all voting rights for this stock in a coordinated fashion.").

42 **stock certificates:** Standard Oil Trust stock certificate, www.standardoiltrust .com.

42 ***United States v. E. C. Knight Co.:*** *United States v. E. C. Knight Co.,* 156 U.S. 1 (1895).

42 **1873 novel:** Mark Twain and Charles Dudley Warner, *The Gilded Age: A Tale of Today* (Hartford: American, 1874). The book first appeared in 1873.

42 **Jim Crow racial segregation:** Joel Shrock, *The Gilded Age* (Westport, Conn.: Greenwood Press, 2004), 18, 222, 247.

42 **influx of immigrants:** Sean Dennis Cashman, *America in the Gilded Age: From the Death of Lincoln to the Rise of Theodore Roosevelt,* 3rd ed. (New York: New York University Press, 1993), 74, 85.

42 **Andrew Carnegie:** Samuel Bostaph, *Andrew Carnegie: An Economic Biography* (Lanham, Md.: Rowman & Littlefield, 2017).

43 **Jay Gould:** Edward J. Renehan Jr., *Dark Genius of Wall Street: The Misunderstood Life of Jay Gould, King of the Robber Barons* (New York: Basic Books, 2005).

43 **J. P. Morgan:** Ron Chernow, *The House of Morgan: An American Banking Dynasty and the Rise of Modern Finance* (New York: Grove Press, 2001).

43 **John D. Rockefeller:** Grant Segall, *John D. Rockefeller: Anointed with Oil* (Oxford: Oxford University Press, 2001).

43 **John Jacob Astor IV:** Axel Madsen, *John Jacob Astor: America's First Multimillionaire* (New York: John Wiley & Sons, 2002), 6; Russell J. Fishkind, *Probate Wars of the Rich and Famous: An Insider's Guide to Estate Planning and Probate Litigation* (New York: John Wiley & Sons, 2011), chap. 3.

44 **French landscape paintings:** About the Art Gallery, James J. Hill House, www.mnhs.org.

45 **from Slovenia:** Gary Kaunonen, *Flames of Discontent: The 1916 Minnesota Iron Ore Strike* (Minneapolis: University of Minnesota Press, 2017) (taking note of "South Slavic" and Slovenian immigrants on Minnesota's Iron Range and observing that my dad's grandparents came from Slovenia); Amy Klobuchar, *The Senator Next Door: A Memoir from the Heartland* (New York: Henry Holt, 2015), 18–20.

45 **mines in Slovenia:** Leopoldina Plut-Pregelj et al., *Historical Dictionary of Slovenia,* 3rd ed. (Lanham, Md.: Rowman & Littlefield, 2018), 352.

45 **northern Minnesota:** Marvin G. Lamppa, *Minnesota's Iron Country: Rich Ore, Rich Lives* (Duluth: Lake Superior Port Cities, 2004).

45 **Minnesota's Iron Range:** Richard W. Ojakangas and Charles L. Matsch, *Minnesota's Geology* (Minneapolis: University of Minnesota Press, 1982), 126.

45   **iron ore:** Dave Kenney, *Minnesota Goes to War: The Home Front During World War II* (St. Paul: Minnesota Historical Society Press, 2005), 122.

46   **came to Ely:** Frank A. King, *The Missabe Road: The Duluth, Missabe, and Iron Range Railway* (Minneapolis: University of Minnesota Press, 1972), 33–34.

46   **one historian noted:** Joseph P. Schwieterman, *When the Railroad Leaves Town: American Communities in the Age of Rail Line Abandonment* (Kirksville, Mo.: Truman State University Press, 2004), 162.

46   **Hill himself had bought:** Tom Webb, "The Iron Empire: James J. Hill's Great Northern Ore Trust Terminated," *St. Paul Pioneer Press,* April 17, 2015, www .kitco.com.

47   **the Klobuchar family:** Klobuchar, *Senator Next Door.*

47   **Simon Bourgin:** Simon Bourgin, *An Odyssey That Began in Ely* (Ely, Minn.: Ely-Winton Historical Society, 2010).

47   **In the words of my dad:** Jim Klobuchar, *Minstrel: My Adventure in Newspapering* (Minneapolis: University of Minnesota Press, 1997), 27.

47   **As one historian:** Andrew Goldman and Ann Goldman, *Facing North: Portraits of Ely, Minnesota* (Minneapolis: University of Minnesota Press, 2008), xxiii–xxiv.

48   **had to quit school:** Klobuchar, *Senator Next Door,* 20–22.

49   **His youngest sister, Hannah:** Ibid., 338.

49   **My grandma:** "Mary Klobuchar" (obituary), *Ely Echo,* April 26, 1999, 4.

51   **book about Pearl Harbor:** Dick Klobuchar, *Awakening a Sleeping Giant* (Bloomington, Ind.: AuthorHouse, 2003).

51   **life as a reporter:** Klobuchar, *Minstrel.*

51   **Minnesota Vikings:** Jim Klobuchar, *Purple Hearts and Golden Memories: 35 Years with the Minnesota Vikings* (Coal Valley, Ill.: Quality Sports Publications, 1999).

52   **"the little fellers":** Bill Lofy, *Paul Wellstone: The Life of a Passionate Progressive* (Ann Arbor: University of Michigan Press, 2005), 59.

52   **the rules and regulations:** Arnold R. Alanen, "Early Labor Strife on Minnesota's Mining Frontier, 1882–1906," *Minnesota History* 52 (Fall 1991): 247–63.

54   **Oliver Iron Mining Company:** Aaron Brenner, Benjamin Day, and Immanuel Ness, eds., *The Encyclopedia of Strikes in American History* (London: Routledge, 2009), 462.

54   **As historian Rhoda Gilman:** Rhoda R. Gilman, "The History and Peopling of Minnesota: Its Culture," *Daedalus* 129, no. 3 (Summer 2000): 1–29.

55   **John Alar:** Gary Kaunonen and Aaron Goings, *Community in Conflict: A Working-Class History of the 1913–14 Michigan Copper Strike and the Italian Hall Tragedy* (Lansing: Michigan State University Press, 2013), chap. 1.

55   **first billion-dollar corporation:** Quentin R. Skrabec Jr., *The 100 Most Significant Events in American Business: An Encyclopedia* (Santa Barbara, Calif.: Greenwood, 2012), 122.

55   **vehemently anti-union:** William C. Blizzard, *When Miners March,* ed. Wess Harris (Oakland: PM Press, 2010), 258.

55   **Elizabeth Gurley Flynn:** Robert M. Eleff, "The 1916 Minnesota Miners' Strike Against U.S. Steel," *Minnesota History* 51, no. 2 (Summer 1988): 63–74; Janet Raye, "Hellraisers Journal: Elizabeth Gurley Flynn Urges Miners to Leave the

Mesabi and Head Out to Harvest Fields," July 29, 2016, We Never Forget: The Labor Martyrs Project, www.weneverforget.org.

55 **Pullman Strike of 1894:** Linda Jacobs Altman, *The Pullman Strike of 1894: Turning Point for American Labor* (Brookfield, Conn.: Millbrook Press, 1994).

55 **McCormick Harvesting Machine Strike:** Albert A. Hoffman Jr., *Some Historical Stories of Chicago* (Xlibris, 2010), 99.

56 **Labor Day:** Michael Burgan, *The Pullman Strike of 1894* (Minneapolis: Compass Point Books, 2008), 43 ("After the Pullman strike, Congress passed a law creating Labor Day, which is celebrated on the first Monday in September.").

56 **May Day:** Peter Linebaugh, *The Incomplete, True, Authentic, and Wonderful History of May Day* (Oakland: PM Press, 2016) ("The history of the modern May Day originates in the center of the North American plains, at Haymarket, in Chicago—'the city on the make'—in May 1886."). Illinois became a center of much trust activity, and the trusts could be ruthless in trying to eliminate any competition. Ernest E. East, "The Distillers' and Cattle Feeders' Trust, 1887–1895," 45 *Journal of the Illinois State Historical Society* 101 (1952) ("Illinois was the center of operations of the 'whisky trust,' one of the largest and most notorious combines in the industrial history of the United States. The combine was organized on May 10, 1887, as the Distillers' and Cattle Feeders' Trust. . . . Stockholders of sixty-five distilleries, former members of an ineffective whisky pool, formed the trust."); ibid., 105 ("Only a few independent distilleries were strong enough financially to buck the trust. Independents were attacked through underselling after they resisted tempting offers to come into the combine. Trust agents invaded their territory and secretly offered goods at less than the trust's regular prices. This practice usually persuaded the independent to surrender."); ibid., 105–6 ("Among the stubborn independents was H. H. Shufeldt & Co. of Chicago, which held out for four years against the combine. A charge of dynamite was exploded at Shufeldt's distillery in the early morning of December 10, 1888. Two packages containing the explosive were thrown on the roof of a vat-room at the distillery. They evidently were aimed at a skylight over a vat of high wines. The bombs fell short. One tore a hole in the vat-room roof, causing a fire which did considerable damage. The second package, containing seven sticks of dynamite, failed to explode and was recovered by police. No arrests were made. 'It was charged that the whisky trust was at the bottom of the conspiracy, the object of which was to rid itself of a dangerous and successful rival,' said the *Chicago Tribune*."); ibid., 110 ("The arrest of George J. Gibson of Peoria, the well-to-do and socially prominent secretary of the Distilling and Cattle Feeding Company, by United States officers at Chicago on a charge of plotting the destruction of the Shufeldt distillery furnished a front page sensation in 1891. Gibson was seized February 11, at the entrance to the Grand Pacific Hotel on information furnished by Thomas S. Dewar, an internal revenue gauger, who said the whisky trust secretary had placed an 'infernal machine' in his hands and promised him $10,000 cash and $15,000 in whisky stock if he succeeded in causing a fire and explosion that would destroy the Shufeldt plant."); ibid., 115 ("Gibson was indicted by a grand jury in the Criminal Court of Cook County on February 16, 1891. He was charged with procuring gunpowder with felonious intent—two additional indictments charged attempts to commit arson;

a fourth with procuring gunpowder for the destruction of life and property, and a fifth with conspiracy to commit murder. But Gibson never faced a trial jury—a nolle prosequi order being entered eventually in each case.").

56 **Pullman Company:** Jack Kelly, *The Edge of Anarchy: The Railroad Barons, the Gilded Age, and the Greatest Labor Uprising in America* (New York: St. Martin's Press, 2018), 98–99.

56 **Melvin Carter:** Dana Bash and Bridget Nolan, " 'We Literally All Are George': St. Paul Mayor Reflects on Generations of Pain Among African Americans," CNN, June 7, 2020, www.cnn.com.

56 *10,000 Black Men Named George:* Kathleen Fearn-Banks and Anne Burford-Johnson, *Historical Dictionary of African American Television,* 2nd ed. (Lanham, Md.: Rowman & Littlefield, 2014), 13 ("This 90-minute docudrama told the story of A. Philip Randolph (Andre Braugher), editor of *The Messenger* magazine, who led the Brotherhood of Sleeping Car porters in its fight against the powerful railroads and to be organized as a union. After Emancipation, newly freed slaves had been hired as porters by railroad magnate George Pullman. They were not always paid for their labor, but when they were, the wages were meager. Their work hours and treatment were brutal. All of them answered to the name 'George.' Randolph, who had already helped organize elevator operators and shipyard workers, had to get 10,000 signatures of porters on a petition. He not only fought the railroad officials, but he also had to battle the brethren internally to be trusted; they were afraid of losing their jobs.").

56 **In the Pullman Strike:** James S. Olson, ed., *Encyclopedia of the Industrial Revolution in America* (Westport, Conn.: Greenwood Press, 2002), 205–6; Philip Dray, *There Is Power in a Union: The Epic Story of Labor in America* (New York: Anchor Books, 2010), 187–201.

57 **national commission:** Elizabeth A. Osborne and Christine Woodworth, eds., *Working in the Wings: New Perspectives on Theatre History and Labor* (Carbondale: Southern Illinois University Press, 2015), 173.

57 **one economist:** Janice L. Reiff, "A Modern Lear and His Daughters: Gender in the Model Town of Pullman," in *The Pullman Strike and the Crisis of the 1890s: Essays on Labor and Politics,* ed. Richard Schneirov, Shelton Stromquist, and Nick Salvatore (Urbana: University of Illinois Press, 1999), 66.

58 **Haymarket Massacre:** James Green, *Death in the Haymarket: A Story of Chicago, the First Labor Movement, and the Bombing That Divided Gilded Age America* (New York: Anchor Books, 2007); Joseph Anthony Rulli, *The Chicago Haymarket Affair: A Guide to a Labor Rights Milestone* (Charleston, S.C.: Arcadia, 2016).

59 **was introduced:** Rudolph J. R. Peritz, *Competition Policy in America: History, Rhetoric, Law,* rev. ed. (Oxford: Oxford University Press, 1996), 13.

60 **Statue of Liberty:** Lines from "The New Colossus," Emma Lazarus's famous poem, "Give me your tired, your poor, / Your huddled masses yearning to breathe free," exemplify the idea that America is a welcoming country—one that offers extraordinary opportunity to all, regardless of their circumstances at their arrival on our shores. Emma Lazarus was, herself, enthralled by Henry George's best-selling book, *Progress and Poverty.* Esther Schor, *Emma Lazarus* (New York: Schocken, 2017), 116–17.

61 **opposed monopolies:** In his *Report on the Subject of Manufactures* (1791), Alex-

ander Hamilton worried about the ability of monopolies to charge "enhanced" prices. In his report, which encouraged domestic production, Hamilton emphasized, "When a domestic manufacture has attained to perfection . . . it invariably becomes cheaper. Being free from the heavy charges, which attend the importation of foreign commodities, it can be afforded, and accordingly seldom or never fails to be sold Cheaper, in process of time, than was the foreign Article for which it is a substitute. The internal competition, which takes place, soon does away every thing like Monopoly, and by degrees reduces the price of the Article to the *minimum* of a reasonable profit on the Capital employed. This accords with the reason of the thing and with experience." Alexander Hamilton's Final Version of the Report on the Subject of Manufactures, Dec. 5, 1791, Founders Online, National Archives, founders.archives .gov. Original source: *The Papers of Alexander Hamilton,* vol. 10, *December 1791—January 1792,* ed. Harold C. Syrett (New York: Columbia University Press, 1966), 230–340.

61 *The Federalist* **No. 47:** James Madison, *The Federalist* No. 47 (originally published in the *New York Packet,* Feb. 1, 1788).

61 **Benjamin Franklin:** Walter Isaacson, *Benjamin Franklin: An American Life* (New York: Simon & Schuster, 2003).

61 **Robert Fulton:** Kirkpatrick Sale, *The Fire of His Genius: Robert Fulton and the American Dream* (New York: Touchstone, 2001).

61 **Thomas Edison:** Linda Tagliaferro, *Thomas Edison: Inventor of the Age of Electricity* (Minneapolis: Lerner, 2003).

61 **Lewis Latimer:** Rayvon Fouché, *Black Inventors in the Age of Segregation: Granville T. Woods, Lewis H. Latimer, and Shelby J. Davidson* (Baltimore: Johns Hopkins University Press, 2003), chap. 3; Lewis H. Latimer, *Incandescent Electric Lighting: A Practical Description of the Edison System* (New York: D. Van Nostrand, 1890).

61 **Alexander Graham Bell:** Charlotte Gray, *Reluctant Genius: Alexander Graham Bell and the Passion for Invention* (New York: Arcade, 2011).

3. A HEARTLAND REBELLION

62 **"The Revolt of the Common Man":** The title of chapter 3 of a book containing a history of America's Granger movement. Holland Thompson, *The New South: A Chronicle of Social and Industrial Evolution* (New Haven, Conn.: Yale University Press, 1919), 31.

62 **laboratories of democracy:** In his dissent in *New State Ice Co. v. Liebmann,* 285 U.S. 262 (1932), the exact words of Justice Brandeis were as follows: "It is one of the happy incidents of the federal system that a single courageous State may, if its citizens choose, serve as a laboratory; and try novel social and economic experiments without risk to the rest of the country." Ibid., 311 (Brandeis, J., dissenting).

63 **more than a dozen states:** American Bar Association, Antitrust Law Section, *Antitrust Federalism: The Role of State Law* (1988), 3; Joseph Wilson, *Globalization and the Limits of National Merger Control Laws* (The Hague: Kluwer Law International, 2003), 65.

63	**Henry Bacon:** *Illustrated American* 9 (1891): 398; *Portrait and Biographical Record of Orange County, New York* (New York: Chapman, 1895), 746, 751.

63	**congressional resolution:** *Congressional Record: Containing the Proceedings and Debates of the Fiftieth Congress, First Session* (Washington, D.C.: Government Printing Office, 1888), 19:719.

63	**the country's first state antitrust law:** Wayne D. Collins, "Trusts and the Origins of Antitrust Legislation," 81 *Fordham Law Review* 2279, 2335–36 (2013) (listing the thirteen states that passed antitrust laws before the passage of the Sherman Antitrust Act).

63	**the Grangers:** Solon Justus Buck, *The Granger Movement: A Study of Agricultural Organization and Its Political, Economic, and Social Manifestations, 1870–1880* (Lincoln: University of Nebraska Press, 1913).

63	**As one historian notes:** Thompson, *New South*, 31.

64	**the word "grange":** Robert Longley, "The Granger Laws and the Granger Movement," ThoughtCo., Oct. 2, 2019, www.thoughtco.com.

64	**it has been reported:** "Oliver Kelley Organizes the Grange," History, www.history.com.

64	**in a letter:** O. H. Kelley, *Origin and Progress of the Order of the Patrons of Husbandry in the United States: A History from 1866 to 1873* (Philadelphia: J. A. Wagenseller, 1875), 22, 25.

65	**Ignatius Donnelly:** Thomas A. Woods, *Knights of the Plow: Oliver H. Kelley and the Origins of the Grange in Republican Ideology* (Ames: Iowa State University Press, 1991), 147–48.

66	**in Owatonna, Minnesota:** Arthur Naftalin, "The Tradition of Protest and the Roots of the Farmer-Labor Party," *Minnesota History* (June 1956): 56; William E. Lass, *Minnesota: A History*, 2nd ed. (New York: W. W. Norton & Co., 1998), 201; Franklyn Curtiss-Wedge, comp., *History of Fillmore County Minnesota* (Chicago: H. C. Cooper, Jr. & Co., 1912), 1:500.

66	**A lithograph:** "The Grange Movement, 1875," Gilder Lehrman Institute of American History, www.gilderlehrman.org.

67	**"With Grover Cleveland's election":** Ron Chernow, *Titan: The Life of John D. Rockefeller Sr.* (New York: Vintage Books, 1998), 292.

67	**one source observes:** Fergus M. Bordewich, "Replanting Democracy: Reconstruction Was Only One Part of a Broad Effort to Rebuild American Society on Egalitarian Terms," review of *The Second Founding*, by Eric Foner, *Wall Street Journal*, Sept. 21–22, 2019, C7.

67	**right to vote:** Jennifer MacBain-Stephens, *Women's Suffrage: Giving the Right to Vote to All Americans* (New York: Rosen, 2006), 25.

67	**the Granger clubs:** African American farmers were often excluded from Grange chapters, especially in the South, and they thus resorted to forming their own cooperative groups. Jenny Bourne, *In Essentials, Unity: An Economic History of the Grange Movement* (Athens: Ohio University Press, 2017) ("Regrettably, the morals of the early Grange did not extend to welcoming African Americans into the fold, particularly in the South. Given that half of the people engaged in southern agriculture were black, this excluded a large swath of farmers. The first subordinate Grange in Louisiana—a state firmly under control of the Radical Republicans since before the end of the Civil

War—reportedly let all join without regard to color, but this was not true elsewhere."); Paul S. Boyer et al., *The Enduring Vision: A History of the American People*, 6th ed. (Boston: Wadsworth, 2010), 2:460 (noting that, in time, "a parallel organization of black farmers emerged" called "the National Colored Farmers' Alliance").

67 **"Sentiment over black participation"**: Anthony J. Adam and Gerald H. Gaither, *Black Populism in the United States: An Annotated Bibliography* (Westport, Conn.: Praeger, 2004), 153. Compare Charles Postel, *Equality: An American Dilemma, 1866–1896* (New York: Farrar, Straus and Giroux, 2019), chap. 3 ("Nor did the Grange organize black farmers, although nothing in the rules mentioned race or prohibited Granges from accepting black members. . . . [D]espite reports of African Americans joining the movement, including a Grange in Louisiana that accepted black members, in reality the Grange, in the South as well as the North, was a white organization."), with Omar H. Ali, *In the Lion's Mouth: Black Populism in the New South, 1886–1900* (Jackson: University Press of Mississippi, 2010), 29 ("In terms of the Colored Granges, as early as 1867 white farmers began to organize themselves into the Order of Patrons of Husbandry (a.k.a. the Grange), a fraternal order which sought to improve the economic conditions of farmers through education and the pooling of resources. Granges thrived across the North and South. Several Colored Granges were formed, but details on them are scant. . . . The white Northern Granges had pushed their southern orders to admit African Americans, but it seems with little success."), and Susan J. Ellis and Katherine H. Noyes, *By the People: A History of Americans as Volunteers* (San Francisco: Jossey-Bass, 1990), 134 ("While women were accepted as Grange members, the question of admitting blacks was far more controversial.").

67 **Racially integrated Grange chapters**: Anna-Lisa Cox, *A Stronger Kinship: One Town's Extraordinary Story of Hope and Faith* (New York: Little, Brown, 2006) (referring to "the formation of a racially integrated Grange" chapter in Covert, Michigan, in 1873).

67 **National Grange's bylaws and constitution**: Linda Marie Thorstad, "The Historical and Cultural Geography of the Grange in Minnesota and Louisiana, 1870–1880" (PhD diss., Louisiana State University, 1999), 110, digitalcommons .lsu.edu.

67 **separate organizations**: Gina Misiroglu, ed., *American Countercultures: An Encyclopedia of Nonconformists, Alternative Lifestyles, and Radical Ideas in U.S. History* (London: Routledge, 2009), 247 ("The Colored Farmers' Alliance was established in 1886 for African American farmers, primarily in the South."); Charles W. Calhoun, ed., *The Gilded Age: Perspectives on the Origins of Modern America*, 2nd ed. (Lanham, Md.: Rowman & Littlefield, 2007), 149 ("black farmers had formed their own Colored Farmers Alliance, which spread over the South, claiming over a million members").

68 **"The Revolt of the Common Man"**: Thompson, *New South*, chap. 3.

69 **one man in Dubuque, Iowa**: Clement Le Verne Waldron, "Anti-Trust Legislation in Iowa and Nebraska with an Introductory Chapter on the Origin of the Trust" (M.A. thesis, University of Wisconsin, 1907), 20.

69 **Supreme Court cases**: *Munn v. Illinois*, 94 U.S. 113 (1877); *Wabash, St. Louis*

& *Pacific Railway Co. v. Illinois,* 118 U.S. 557 (1886); see also *The Oxford Guide to United States Supreme Court Decisions,* ed. Kermit L. Hall (Oxford: Oxford University Press, 1999), 203 (*"Munn v. Illinois* forms with the related Granger Cases a historic ruling that tests the constitutionality of state police power, through legislation, to regulate private business. Coming in the industrial upheaval of the late nineteenth century, the case gave vitality to the recently enacted Fourteenth Amendment."); *The Oxford Encyclopedia of American Business, Labor and Economic History,* ed. Melvyn Dubofsky (Oxford: Oxford University Press, 2013), 1:309 ("In 1886 the issue of state regulation of railroads again came before the courts. The Wabash railroad, an interstate carrier in the Middle West, appealed a decision of the Illinois courts to the Supreme Court. In *Wabash, St. Louis & Pacific Railway v. Illinois* (1886), the Court found for the railroad, ruling that a state court not regulate interstate commerce, since the Constitution granted that power solely to the federal government. This decision led Congress to enact the Interstate Commerce Act in 1887. That measure assigned the task of regulating railroads to the newly created Interstate Commerce Commission, the nation's first independent regulatory agency.").

69 **first biennial message:** Governor William Larrabee, First Biennial Message, Jan. 11, 1888, in *The Messages and Proclamations of the Governors of Iowa,* comp. and ed. Benjamin F. Shambaugh (Iowa City: State Historical Society of Iowa, 1904), 6:32, 82.

70 **Floyd of Rosedale:** John Grasso, *Historical Dictionary of Football* (Lanham, Md.: Scarecrow Press, 2013), 191.

70 **a harbinger of things to come:** "Granger laws" enacted in the 1870s in states like Minnesota, Wisconsin, Illinois, and Iowa represented an early effort at economic regulation. The Granger movement also played a key role in the creation of the federal Interstate Commerce Act of 1887, which regulated a major monopoly interest that was greatly affecting farmers' transportation costs—the railroads.

70 **Boy Orator of the Platte:** Mark A. Noll, *A History of Christianity in the United States and Canada* (Grand Rapids: William B. Eerdmans, 2003), 300–301.

71 **his principled stance:** William G. Thomas III, "William Jennings Bryan, the Railroads, and the Politics of 'Workingmen,'" 86 *Nebraska Law Review* 161, 161–63 (2007).

73 **in 1882:** William E. Martello and Jeffrey Gale, "Trusts," in *Encyclopedia of Business Ethics and Society,* ed. Robert W. Kolb (Thousand Oaks, Calif.: SAGE, 2008), 1:2123:

> Standard Oil Company, founded by John D. Rockefeller, pioneered the industrial trust in 1882. In adapting the legal concept of the trust to an industrial setting, Standard Oil persuaded the stockholders of 30 companies in the economically critical oil industry to turn control of their corporate stock over to nine trustees, who then could exercise all voting rights for this stock in a coordinated fashion. In return, these previous stockholders received shares in the newly created entity—the trust—which entitled them to receive financial returns based on the overall performance of the new combined entity.

73 **Standard Oil Trust:** Barr Ferree, ed., *Year Book of the Pennsylvania Society* (New York: Pennsylvania Society, 1908), 56.

73 **"It was probably a carping critic":** Albert Chandler, ed., *The Brief: A Magazine of the Law* 7 (1907): 27.

73 **"Cross of Gold" speech:** "Bryan's 'Cross of Gold' Speech: Mesmerizing the Masses," historymatters.gmu.edu.

74 **taking on the trusts:** William J. Bryan, *The First Battle: A Story of the Campaign of 1896* (Chicago: W. B. Conkey, 1896), 124–26, 261, 291, 294, 304, 365, 408, 409–12, 422, 446, 461, 509–10, 553, 586, 589.

74 **"From 1898 to 1900":** Michael Kazin, *A Godly Hero: The Life of William Jennings Bryan* (New York: Anchor Books, 2007), 96.

75 **state antitrust laws:** James May, "Antitrust Practice and Procedure in the Formative Era: The Constitutional and Conceptual Reach of State Antitrust Law, 1880–1918," 135 *University of Pennsylvania Law Review* 495, 499 (1987) ("At least fourteen states inserted antimonopoly provisions into their state constitutions prior to July 2, 1890, the date of passage of the federal Sherman Act, and at least thirteen states enacted their own antitrust legislation prior to that date. By 1900, the number of states and territories adopting such statutes rose to twenty-seven, reaching a total of at least thirty-five states by 1915.").

75 **Wall Street offices:** Gerard Helferich, *An Unlikely Trust: Theodore Roosevelt, J. P. Morgan, and the Improbable Partnership That Remade American Business* (Guilford, Conn.: Lyons Press, 2018), xiii.

75 **first introduced in 1888:** In the 1888 election, both the Democratic and the Republican platforms contained antitrust planks. William Kolasky, "Senator John Sherman and the Origin of Antitrust," *Antitrust* (Fall 2009): 86. It was shortly after the Republican convention that Sherman began his push for antitrust legislation. Ibid. ("Immediately after the 1888 Republican Convention, Sherman began his push for antitrust legislation by introducing a resolution in July, proposing to direct the Committee on Finance, of which he was a ranking member, to develop antitrust legislation designed to promote 'free and full competition,' which he saw as naturally 'increasing production [and] lowering . . . prices.'"); see also ibid. ("Before the Finance Committee could complete its work, Senator John Reagan, a Democrat from Texas, introduced his own anti-trust bill in August, which he asked to have referred to the Judiciary Committee. Senator Sherman, faced with this challenge to his leadership on the issue, immediately objected, asserting that the Committee on Finance was 'already in charge of that subject.' Senator Reagan quickly receded, saying he had no objection to the bill being referred to the Committee on Finance."). Sherman's bill was titled "A Bill to Declare Unlawful Trusts and Combinations in Restraint of Trade and Production." Ibid., 86–87.

75 **the "Ohio Icicle" moniker:** Ibid., 85.

75 **"Sherman likely wanted to assure":** Ibid., 86.

75 **reintroducing his bill:** Ibid., 87.

75 **fierce debate:** Ibid., 86–87. "The debate initially focused on what constitutional authority Congress had to regulate these trusts." Ibid., 87.

76 **resulting compromise language:** Ibid., 88. "Beginning on March 25, 1890, the Senate held three consecutive days of floor debate on the bill." Ibid., 87. On March 27, Senator George Edmunds of Vermont and Senator George Hoar of

Massachusetts—both Republicans—questioned the bill's language, and the
U.S. Senate, by a vote of 31–28, ultimately referred Senator Sherman's bill to
the Judiciary Committee. Less than one week later, that committee reported
back a new bill, a bill that "deleted all of Sherman's language except for the
title and replaced it with the language now familiar to antitrust lawyers." Ibid.;
see also ibid., 88 ("The Senate, after a brief debate, quickly passed the Judiciary
Committee's substitute bill with only minimal changes. The House subsequently approved a nearly identical bill and, following conference, both houses
passed the Sherman Act nearly unanimously."). Senator Hoar later claimed
that he, not Senator Sherman, "was the author of the bill," although Senator
Edmunds disputed that claim, reporting that the bill's language was the result
of extended debate in the Senate Judiciary Committee. Ibid., 89. "It would be
correct to say," Edmunds recalled, "that nearly every member of the committee was the author of the bill, for my work in drawing it up was merely putting
into logical shape what every member of the committee had participated in."

76   **come out in opposition:** Kevin Phillips, *William McKinley* (New York: Times
Books, 2003), 38.

76   **who has been called:** Kolasky, "Senator John Sherman and the Origin of Antitrust," 88.

77   **Lincoln declared:** Harriet A. Washington, *Deadly Monopolies: The Shocking
Corporate Takeover of Life Itself—and the Consequences for Your Health and Our
Medical Future* (New York: Anchor Books, 2012), 22.

77   **received a patent:** Lincoln's Patent, abrahamlincolnonline.org.

77   **"land monopoly":** James L. Huston, *Securing the Fruits of Labor: The Ameri-
can Concept of Wealth Distribution, 1765–1900* (Baton Rouge: Louisiana State
University Press, 2015), 208; Frederick J. Blue, *No Taint of Compromise: Crusaders in Antislavery Politics* (Baton Rouge: Louisiana State University Press,
2005), 169; Forrest A. Nabors, *From Oligarchy to Republicanism: The Great
Task of Reconstruction* (Columbia: University of Missouri Press, 2017), 62–68.
In urging "an equitable homestead policy," Congressman George Julian asked
Congress to parcel out "small farms for . . . the freedmen" instead of selling
"large tracts to speculators, and thus laying the foundation for a system of land
monopoly in the South scarcely less to be deplored than slavery itself." James
McPherson, *The Struggle for Equality: Abolitionists and the Negro in the Civil
War and Reconstruction* (Princeton, N.J.: Princeton University Press, 1964),
249. Decades later, in 1909, Winston Churchill gave his own assessment of
the dangers of land monopoly using these words: "It is quite true that land
monopoly is not the only monopoly which exists, but it is by far the greatest
of monopolies—it is a perpetual monopoly, and it is the mother of all other
forms of monopoly." Josh Ryan-Collins, Toby Lloyd, and Laurie Macfarlane,
Rethinking the Economics of Land and Housing (London: Zed Books, 2017),
chap. 7. In the United States, Henry George—the economist—also worried
about "monopolization of our land," saying that "the giant of monopolies is
the monopoly of the land." Henry George, Jr., comp., *The Writings of Henry
George: Our Land and Land Policy—Speeches, Lectures and Miscellaneous Writings* (New York: Doubleday and McClure Co., 1901), 9:345; Francis K. Peddle
and William S. Peirce, eds., *The Annotated Works of Henry George: "Our Land
and Land Policy," and Other Works* (Madison, N.J.: Fairleigh Dickinson Uni-

versity Press, 2016), 1:45, 83, 152; Henry George, *Our Land and Land Policy: Speeches, Lectures, and Miscellaneous Writings*, ed. Kenneth Wenzer (East Lansing: Michigan State University Press, 1999).

78 **who believed:** Michael Paul Rogin, *Ronald Reagan, the Movie: And Other Episodes in Political Demonology* (Berkeley: University of California Press, 1987), 182.

78 **Homestead Act:** Jason Porterfield, *The Homestead Act of 1862: A Primary Source History of the Settlement of the American Heartland in the Late 19th Century* (New York: Rosen, 2005).

78 **one less interesting discussion:** William Tecumseh Sherman, *Memoirs of Gen. W. T. Sherman* (New York: C. L. Webster, 1891), 195. A biography of Abraham Lincoln gives this account: "When Ohio Senator John Sherman pressed him about some appointments, Lincoln slumped in his seat with a look of despair. This prompted Sherman to confess his shame at bothering him with such minor concerns and to promise that he would stop pestering him about them. The president's expression abruptly brightened, he sat upright, and his entire demeanor changed." Michael Burlingame, *Abraham Lincoln: A Life* (Baltimore: The Johns Hopkins University Press, 2013), 2:477.

78 **John's older brother William:** *The Tribunal Responses to John Brown and the Harpers Ferry Raid*, eds. John Stauffer & Zoe Trodd (Cambridge, Mass.: The Belknap Press of Harvard University Press, 2012), 438.

78 **privately questioned Lincoln's executive abilities:** Burlingame, *Abraham Lincoln*, 2:477.

78 **Sherman wrote:** "Visitors from Congress: John Sherman (1823–1900)," Mr. Lincoln's White House, www.mrlincolnswhitehouse.org; Lewis E. Lehrman, *Lincoln & Churchill: Statesmen at War* (Guilford, Conn.: Stackpole Books, 2018), 108.

78 **in a speech:** Albert H. Walker, *History of the Sherman Law of the United States of America* (Washington, D.C.: Beard Books, 1910), 12–13.

80 **John Sherman introduced:** As it was introduced, Sherman's bill contained the following language: "That all arrangements, contracts, agreements, trusts, or combinations . . . made with a view, or which tend to prevent full and free competition . . . or which tend to advance the cost to the consumer . . . are hereby declared to be against public policy, unlawful, and void." Rudolph J. R. Peritz, *Competition Policy in America: History, Rhetoric, Law*, rev. ed. (Oxford: Oxford University Press), 13. The antitrust legislation had other proponents in the lead-up to its passage, but Senator John Sherman played a major role in getting the legislation enacted into law. James S. Olson and Shannon L. Kenny, *The Industrial Revolution: Key Themes and Documents* (Santa Barbara, Calif.: ABC-CLIO, 2015), 186 ("In 1890, Senator George Hoar of Massachusetts drafted legislation outlawing monopolies in manufacturing industries. Senator John Sherman of Ohio shepherded the legislation through Congress, and it became known as the Sherman Antitrust Act of 1890."); Martin J. Sklar, *The Corporate Reconstruction of American Capitalism, 1890–1916: The Market, the Law, and Politics* (Cambridge, U.K.: Cambridge University Press, 1988), 107 ("The Sherman Act was considered by its principal authors and floor managers in the United States Senate—Republican senators John Sherman of Ohio, George F. Hoar of Massachusetts, and George F. Edmunds of Vermont—as a

federal enactment of the common law with respect to restraints of trade and monopoly."); Rudolph J. R. Peritz, *Competition Policy in America, 1888–1992: History, Rhetoric, Law* (New York: Oxford University Press, 1996), 13–26 (discussing the passage of the Sherman Act and its codification of the common-law rule against monopolization and restraints of trade).

80   **annual messages:** President Grover Cleveland, Third Annual Message, Dec. 6, 1887, in *A Compilation of the Messages and Papers of the Presidents* (New York: Bureau of National Literature, 1897), 12:5165, 5173; President Grover Cleveland, Fourth Annual Message, Dec. 3, 1888, in ibid., 5358–59.

80   **first annual message:** President Benjamin Harrison, First Annual Message, Dec. 3, 1889, in ibid., 5567, 5478.

80   **"The purpose of this bill":** "Trusts," *Speech of Hon. John Sherman, of Ohio, Delivered in the Senate of the United States, Friday, March 21, 1890* (Washington, D.C.: 1890).

80   **Section 1:** 15 U.S.C. § 1.

80   **And section 2:** 15 U.S.C. § 2.

80   **on the Senate floor:** Congressional Record—Senate, March 21, 1890, 2456, 2460–61, www.appliedantitrust.com/02_early_foundations/3_sherman_act /cong_rec/21_cong_rec_2455_2474.pdf. Senator Sherman recognized that it would not always be easy to distinguish between lawful and unlawful activity. As Sherman said on the Senate floor, "I admit that it is difficult to define in legal language the precise line between lawful and unlawful combinations. This must be left for the courts to determine in each particular case. All that we, as lawmakers, can do is to declare general principles, and we can be assured that the courts will apply them so as to carry out the meaning of the law, as the courts of England and the United States have done for centuries." Ibid., 2460.

80   **William Allison:** *Congressional Record: Containing the Proceedings and Debates of the Fifty-First Congress, First Session* (Washington, D.C.: Government Printing Office, 1889), 21:2470 (March 21, 1890, statement of Senator William Allison).

81   **Representative Ezra Taylor:** Parke Wilde, *Food Policy in the United States: An Introduction,* 2nd ed. (New York: Routledge, 2018) (citing statement of Ezra B. Taylor, 21 Cong. Rec. 4098 (1890)); *Bills and Debates in Congress Relating to Trusts* (Washington, D.C.: Government Printing Office, 1903), 348.

81   **Representative John Heard:** E. Thomas Sullivan, *The Political Economy of the Sherman Act: The First One Hundred Years* (New York: Oxford University Press, 1991), 79.

81   **Representative George Fithian:** *Congressional Record: Containing the Proceedings and Debates of the Fifty-First Congress, First Session,* 21:4102–3.

81   **one scholar writes:** Barak Orbach, "How Antitrust Lost Its Goal," 81 *Fordham Law Review* 2253, 2259 (2013).

81   **common-law prohibition:** Wayne L. McNaughton and Joseph Lazar, *Industrial Relations and the Government* (New York: McGraw-Hill, 1954), 57 ("Louis B. Boudin has pointed out that Senator Hoar made the following statement concerning the intent and purpose of the Judiciary Committee in recommending to the Senate adoption of the proposed law: 'We have affirmed the old doctrine of the common law in regard to all interstate and international

commercial transactions, and have clothed the United States courts with authority to enforce that doctrine by injunction.'"").

81 **29 absent:** "Not voting on the bill," one modern commentator, Steven Lavender, points out of those who didn't vote, "may have been a middle ground for these Senators that allowed them to preserve their industry connections, yet not offend citizens of their states." Steven Lavender, "Senator Rufus Blodgett: The Sherman Anti-trust Act's Lone Dissenter," Nov. 11, 2013, works.bepress .com (unpublished paper).

81 **Senator Rufus Blodgett:** Russell Decker, "The Senator Who Voted Against the Sherman Antitrust Act," 77 *Proceedings of the New Jersey Historical Society* 256 (1959); Lavender, "Senator Rufus Blodgett."

82 **signed into law:** The Ohio congressman William McKinley—the future president—fulsomely praised its enactment as a blow to "trusts or unlawful combinations of capital" seeking "to raise prices according to their own sweet will, and extort undue profits from the mass of the people." Phillips, *William McKinley*, 38. In his inaugural address, President McKinley promised that an antitrust stance would be "steadily pursued, both by the enforcement of the laws now in existence and the recommendation and support of such new statutes as may be necessary to carry it into effect." Yet the Sherman Antitrust Act quickly fell into disuse, with his attorneys general doing little to fulfill his promise to the American public. William Letwin, *Law and Economic Policy in America: The Evolution of the Sherman Antitrust Act* (Chicago: University of Chicago Press, 1965), 137–41.

82 **Under headlines like:** "The Pledge Redeemed," *St. Albans (Vt.) Weekly Messenger,* July 31, 1890, 2; "Republican Pledges," *Chicago Inter Ocean,* July 16, 1890, 4; "Republican Pledges," *Hartford (Kans.) Call,* July 25, 1890, 2.

4. TEDDY ROOSEVELT AND THE ANTITRUST ENFORCERS

83 **the landmark antitrust law essentially lay dormant:** George F. Edmunds, "The Interstate Trust and Commerce Act of 1890," *North American Review* (Dec. 1911), 194:801, 815–16 (Vermont senator George F. Edmunds, one of the legislators involved in drafting the Sherman Act, observed in 1911, "For several years following the passage of the Act it seemed as if the Department of Justice doubted its constitutionality or was unable to find evidence of constant and increasing violations of it. Those engaged in, and profiting by, schemes to dominate and monopolize trade went boldly on."). One case alleging coal-mine owners and coal dealers in Kentucky and Tennessee had conspired to raise the price of coal was successfully prosecuted in the year after the Sherman Act's passage, however. *United States v. Jellico Mountain Coal & Coke Co.,* 46 F. 432 (M.D. Tenn. 1891); Naomi R. Lamoreaux, *The Great Merger Movement in American Business, 1895–1904* (Cambridge, U.K.: Cambridge University Press, 1985), 164 ("In the first case prosecuted under the Sherman Act, *Jellico Mountain Coal,* the United States filed suit against a combination of coal-mine owners and coal dealers in Tennessee and Kentucky which, the government claimed, had conspired to raise the price of coal. A federal court found the Nashville Coal Exchange, as the combination was called, in viola-

tion of the Sherman Act."). But as one history of antitrust enforcement notes, that case "turned out to be one of the very few government victories in Sherman Act litigation in the early 1890's." John J. Siegfried and Michelle Mahony, "The First Sherman Act Case: *Jellico Mountain Coal*, 1891," in *The Antitrust Impulse: An Economic, Historical, and Legal Analysis,* ed. Theodore P. Kovaleff (New York: Routledge, 2016), vol. 1, chap. 4.

83 *New York Times* **obituary:** "John Sherman Is Dead," *New York Times,* Oct. 23, 1900.

83 *The New York Times* **had declared:** Richard N. Langlois, "Antitrust: Where Did It Come from and What Did It Mean?" (University of Connecticut, Department of Economics Working Paper Series, working paper 2016-07, Sept. 2016), 35–36, web2.uconn.edu.

84 **a 98 percent market share:** *United States v. E. C. Knight Co.,* 156 U.S. 1 (1895).

84 **applied to labor unions:** *United States Workingmen's Amalgamated Council,* 54 Fed. 994 (E. D. La. 1893), *aff'd, Workingmen's Amalgamated Council v. United States,* 57 Fed. 85 (C. C. A. 5th 1893).

84 **protracted Senate debate:** Joseph L. Greenslade, "Labor Unions and the Sherman Act: Rethinking Labor's Nonstatutory Exemption," 22 *Loyola of Los Angeles Law Review* 151, 155–57 (1988).

85 **for further drafting:** There has long been a debate about the intended purpose of the Sherman Antitrust Act—a debate that has involved everyone from Robert Bork (the U.S. Supreme Court nominee rejected by the U.S. Senate in 1987) to leading antitrust law professors. Compare Robert H. Bork, "Legislative Intent and the Policy of the Sherman Act," in *The Political Economy of the Sherman Act: The First One Hundred Years,* ed. E. Thomas Sullivan (New York: Oxford University Press, 1991), 47 ("The views of Senator Sherman (R., Ohio), are crucial to an understanding of the intent underlying the law that bears his name. Sherman was the prime mover in getting antitrust legislation considered and pressed through the Senate. . . . [T]hough Sherman's bill was completely rephrased by the Judiciary Committee, of which he was not a member, the final bill, in its substantive policy aspects, embodied Sherman's views."), with Robert H. Lande, "Wealth Transfers as the Original and Primary Concern of Antitrust: The Efficiency Interpretation Challenged," in ibid., 71–72 ("Congress was concerned principally with preventing 'unfair' transfers of wealth from consumers to firms with market power. . . . [T]he antitrust laws embody a strong preference for consumers over firms with market power.").

85 **the first person to actually go to prison:** Richard M. Valelly, ed., *Encyclopedia of U.S. Political History* (Washington, D.C.: CQ Press, 2010), 1:351 ("In its first decade, the [Sherman] Antitrust Act actually had the effect of strengthening corporations' hand against labor. It was used to arrest labor leader Eugene V. Debs, who had organized a boycott of all railroads that bought Pullman cars in support of a Pullman railroad workers' strike."); compare Joseph C. Gallo et al., "Department of Justice Antitrust Enforcement, 1955–1997: An Empirical Study," 17 *Review of Industrial Organization* 75, 92 (2000) ("While a number of labor organizers were imprisoned for violating the antitrust laws during 1915–1937 (Posner, 1970, p. 391), it was not until 1921 that a business person, convicted of price fixing, actually served time in jail.").

85 **Debs and others were charged:** Judy L. Whalley, "Crime and Punishment—

Criminal Antitrust Enforcement in the 1990s," 59 *Antitrust Law Journal* 151, 152 (1990). A 1903 indictment against the Federal Salt Company, brought in California, became the first successful criminal price-fixing case. That company, which ended up paying a $1,000 fine, monopolized the sale of salt in western states. Four years later, in 1907, the U.S. government filed eight criminal cases, with criminal cases rising to twenty-one by 1911 before later dropping off. As one commentator has described early efforts at criminal antitrust enforcement, "This was a rocky beginning. Few cases were brought, fewer were successful, and penalties, especially jail sentences, were meager." Ibid.

85 **Clarence Darrow:** Jack Kelly, *The Edge of Anarchy: The Railroad Barons, the Gilded Age, and the Greatest Labor Uprising in America* (New York: St. Martin's Press, 2018), 256, 261.

85 **Pullman railway strike (1894):** Robert W. Kaps, *Air Transport Labor Relations* (Carbondale: Southern Illinois University Press, 1997), 17. In the Pullman Strike, employees of the Pullman Palace Car Company went on strike in 1894 to protest layoffs and 40 percent wage cuts even as the company announced a regular dividend to its shareholders. The American Railway Union, headed by Debs, acted in solidarity with the Pullman workers and declared a sympathy strike, announcing a boycott of the company's railcars. Railway workers across the country had refused to switch the Pullman cars, and railways in and out of Chicago had to be shut down.

86 *Loewe v. Lawlor:* *Loewe v. Lawlor,* 208 U.S. 274 (1908).

86 **made secondary boycotts illegal:** In 1932, Congress changed the law by passing the Norris-LaGuardia Act. The Norris-LaGuardia Act freed organized labor from the fear of federal court injunctions and banned yellow-dog contracts whereby employees were compelled to agree, as a condition of their employment, not to join a labor union. Such contracts had long been used to prevent the formation of unions.

87 **Samuel Gompers:** John H. M. Laslett, "Samuel Gompers and the Rise of American Business Unionism," in *Labor Leaders in America,* ed. Melvyn Dubofsky and Warren Van Tine (Urbana: University of Illinois Press, 1987), 62.

87 **James Olson explains:** James S. Olson, *The Industrial Revolution: Key Themes and Documents,* with Shannon L. Kenny (Santa Barbara, Calif.: ABC-CLIO, 2015), 186.

87 **As Tim Wu writes:** Tim Wu, *The Curse of Bigness: Antitrust in the New Gilded Age* (New York: Columbia Global Reports, 2018), 25, 45–46.

88 **a steel trust:** J. P. Morgan merged hundreds of steel companies into U.S. Steel and then bought out—and thus eliminated—Andrew Carnegie as a rival competitor. Ronald E. Seavoy, *An Economic History of the United States From 1607 to the Present* (New York: Routledge, 2006), 250 (noting that J. P. Morgan purchased Carnegie Steel for $480 million in January 1901); Kenneth Warren, *Big Steel: The First Century of the United States Steel Corporation, 1901–2001* (Pittsburgh: University of Pittsburgh Press, 2001), 7 ("On 1 April 1901 the United States Steel Corporation was incorporated under the laws of New Jersey. It was far and away the nation's biggest steel company and the largest industrial organization of any kind worldwide.").

88 **gold standard:** President McKinley signed the Gold Standard Act on March

14, 1900. That law established gold as the exclusive basis for redeeming paper currency and halted bimetallism, which had allowed silver to also serve as a monetary standard. As one source explains the intense battle over monetary policy in the late nineteenth century, "In the latter half of the 19th century, the populist movement sought to inflate farm prices through the wider use of paper currency. It called for using silver, which was more plentiful than gold as backing for the currency. A high point of the movement was the 'Cross of Gold' speech by William Jennings Bryan at the 1896 Democratic National Convention." Andrew Glass, "President McKinley Signs Gold Standard Act, March 14, 1900," *Politico,* March 14, 2013, www.politico.com.

89 **"I never would have been"**: John Hamilton, *Theodore Roosevelt National Park* (Edina, Minn.: ABDO, 2009), 5.

89 **the recent decision:** Nora McGreevy, "The Racist Statue of Theodore Roosevelt Will No Longer Loom over the American Museum of Natural History," Smithsonian.com, June 23, 2020, www.smithsonianmag.com.

89 **the overt racial prejudices of his time:** Neil H. Cogan, *Theodore Roosevelt: A Manly President's Gendered Personal and Political Transformations* (New York: Routledge, 2020), 18 (observing of Theodore Roosevelt, "To his great discredit, he was not receptive to the plight of African Americans, ethnic minorities, and Native Americans. Until the last years of his life, Roosevelt was unable to transform himself from his ingrained racism and took as his justification, without studied consideration, the biased 'science' in popular circulation. Roosevelt held fast to the Social Darwinist belief that African Americans were at the early stages of social development and readiness for civic engagement. He invited the prominent black educator Dr. Booker T. Washington for a political meeting and dinner at the White House. But after hateful criticism by racist Southern politicians and journalists, Roosevelt never again invited Dr. Washington or any other African American for a similar event."); Clay Risen, *The Crowded Hour: Theodore Roosevelt, the Rough Riders, and the Dawn of the American Century* (New York: Scribner, 2019), 24 ("Reading them today, Roosevelt's essays from the 1890s are noteworthy for their racism and misogyny; though he used 'race' loosely, as a synonym for nationality, he clearly thought much less of peoples not born of Anglo-American stock, and feared what would happen if too many of them immigrated to the United States.").

89 **a 1905 speech on race relations:** Theodore Roosevelt, "At the Lincoln Dinner of the Republican Club, New York, February 13, 1905," reprinted in *A Compilation of the Messages and Speeches of Theodore Roosevelt, 1901–1905,* ed. Alfred Henry Lewis (Bureau of National Literature and Art, 1906), 560–65.

90 **a major coal strike:** Walter LaFeber, Richard Polenberg, and Nancy Woloch, *The American Century: A History of the United States Since the 1890s,* 7th ed. (London: Routledge, 2013), 39. Samuel Gompers, the leader of the American Federation of Labor, called the Coal Strike of 1902 "the most important single incident in the labor movement in the United States." That strike, he pointed out, secured for workers a "shorter work-day with higher pay." "From then on," Gompers said, "the miners became not merely human machines to produce coal but men and citizens, taking their place among the fairly well-paid, intelligent men, husbands, fathers, abreast of all the people not only of their communities but of the republic." "The strike," Gompers added, "was evidence of

the effectiveness of trade unions even when contending against trusts." Gerard Helferich, *An Unlikely Trust: Theodore Roosevelt, J. P. Morgan, and the Improbable Partnership That Remade American Business* (Guilford, Conn.: Lyons Press, 2018), 98.

90   **In his 1903 Labor Day speech:** Theodore Roosevelt, "A Square Deal" (speech at the New York State Agricultural Association, Syracuse, Sept. 7, 1903), www .memorablequotations.com.

91   **at the Minnesota State Fair:** Wu, *Curse of Bigness*, 47; Ben Welter, "Sept. 3, 1901: Roosevelt 'Big Stick' Speech at State Fair," *Minneapolis Star Tribune*, Sept. 2, 2014.

92   **"showed his independence":** Helferich, *Unlikely Trust*, 34–35.

92   **John Nance Garner:** Robert A. Caro, *The Years of Lyndon Johnson: The Passage of Power* (New York: Alfred A. Knopf, 2012), 110; Gary Westfahl, *A Day in a Working Life: 300 Trades and Professions Through History* (Santa Barbara, Calif.: ABC-CLIO, 2015), 1195.

93   **a nervous J. P. Morgan:** Helferich, *Unlikely Trust*, 38–39.

93   **first message to Congress:** Theodore Roosevelt, State of the Union address, Dec. 3, 1901, www.theodore-roosevelt.com.

93   **Northern Securities Company:** Wu, *Curse of Bigness*, 48–49.

93   **the first trust:** Before Theodore Roosevelt became president, there had been very limited antitrust enforcement. The *Republican Text Book for the Campaign of 1902* pointed to just a handful of cases, including *United States v. Joint Traffic Association*, 171 U.S. 505 (1898), and *Addyston Pipe & Steel Co. v. United States*, 175 U.S. 211 (1899). In the *Joint Traffic Association* case, thirty-one railroad companies engaged in transporting freight and passengers between Chicago and the East Coast had formed an association known as the Joint Traffic Association. In that case, the Supreme Court ruled that Congress had the power "to legislate and to prohibit" combinations that restrain interstate commerce. *Joint Traffic Association*, 171 U.S. at 571. In the *Addyston Pipe* case, the U.S. Supreme Court affirmed a Sixth Circuit decision written by the then chief judge, William Howard Taft, and held "that where the direct and immediate effect of a contract or combination among particular dealers in a commodity is to destroy competition between them and others, so that the parties to the contract or combination may obtain increased prices for themselves, such contract or combination amounts to a restraint of trade in the commodity even though contracts to buy such commodity at the enhanced price are continually being made." *Addyston Pipe*, 175 U.S. at 244. The *Republican Text Book for the Campaign of 1902* argued, "The Republican administrations of President McKinley and President Roosevelt have made a good record in their efforts to execute the anti-trust law. . . . These two Republican Presidents have recognized no man or corporation as above the law." Republican Congressional Committee, *Republican Text Book for the Campaign of 1902* (Philadelphia: Dunlap, 1902), 104–7.

93   **in March 1902:** Republican Congressional Committee, *Republican Text Book for the Campaign of 1902*, 107–8.

94   **gold valued at $65 million:** Milton Friedman and Anna Jacobson Schwartz, *A Monetary History of the United States, 1867–1960* (Princeton, N.J.: Princeton University Press, 1963), 111; Helferich, *Unlikely Trust*, xix.

94 **panic of 1893:** Quentin R. Skrabec Jr., *The 100 Most Significant Events in American Business: An Encyclopedia* (Santa Barbara, Calif.: ABC-CLIO, 2012), 104–7.

95 **"because he would benefit":** By 1888, J. P. Morgan had become the largest stockholder in Edison General Electric. Quentin R. Skrabec Jr., *George Westinghouse: Gentle Genius* (New York: Algora, 2007), 97.

95 **started in Minnesota:** Hiram F. Stevens, *History of the Bench and Bar of Minnesota* (Minneapolis: Legal Publishing and Engraving, 1904), 2:207; Helferich, *Unlikely Trust,* 34–35.

96 **known Roosevelt for years:** Helferich, *Unlikely Trust,* 54–55.

97 **Roosevelt replied:** Susan Berfield, *The Hour of Fate: Theodore Roosevelt, J.P. Morgan, and the Battle to Transform American Capitalism* (New York: Bloomsbury, 2020).

97 **"If we have done anything wrong":** Ibid.

97 **Roosevelt would later remark:** Robert S. Farnsworth, *The Grand Western Railroad Game: The History of Chicago, Rock Island, and Pacific Railroads* (Pittsburgh: Dorrance, 2017), 1:312.

97 **refused to settle the case:** A 1902 newspaper item, headlined "President Is Fearless," noted that "Mr. J. P. Morgan and others of his coterie in Wall street—and among these might be mentioned Mr. Robert Bacon, who was Theodore Roosevelt's classmate in college and is now one of J. P. Morgan & Co.'s most valued partners—rushed down to Washington in a body to see what might be done" after Theodore Roosevelt's Department of Justice "began to take action so strenuously against the Northern Securities company." The newspaper story emphasized that Morgan made a personal appeal to President Roosevelt but that Roosevelt rejected the entreaty. "Theodore Roosevelt seems to be absolutely fearless in all these matters," the story reported, adding of Roosevelt, "He believes that if anybody, no matter how big, is violating the law, he must be gone after exactly as you would a horse-thief in the cattle country." "President Is Fearless," May 11, 1902, Theodore Roosevelt Papers, Library of Congress Manuscript Division, www.theodorerooseveltcenter.org.

98 **in other cases:** Jolyon P. Girard, ed., *Presidents and Presidencies in American History: A Social, Political, and Cultural Encyclopedia and Document Collection* (Santa Barbara, Calif.: ABC-CLIO, 2019), 805 ("Although known as a trust buster, Roosevelt did not seek to break up all trusts. Instead, he differentiated between 'good' and 'bad' trusts. 'Good' trusts were those that allowed some competition and treated their workers fairly, and 'bad' trusts were those that undermined competition and treated their workers poorly."); Murray N. Rothbard, *The Progressive Era,* ed. Patrick Newman (Auburn, Ala.: Mises Institute, 2017), chap. 7 ("President Roosevelt's chief business ally in driving the Bureau of Corporations bill through Congress was George W. Perkins, a Morgan partner and in the process of being Morgan's right-hand man in forming the two giant 'trusts,' United States Steel and International Harvester. Perkins agreed totally with Roosevelt's conception of federal regulation of trusts. Like Roosevelt, Perkins believed that there were 'good trusts' and 'bad trusts,' and, like T.R., he believed that his own U.S. Steel and International Harvester were conspicuous examples of the good. So influential was Perkins in establishing the Bureau that when the president signed the bill into law, he gave one of the

two pens he used to George Perkins."). There were, in Theodore Roosevelt's time, many trusts. H. W. Brands, *American Colossus: The Triumph of Capitalism, 1865–1900* (New York: Anchor Books, 2010), 592 (noting that there were "some two hundred trusts" that "arose in industries as diverse as leather and lead, copper and coal, insurance and machine tools" and further observing, "Some trusts (sugar, oil, leather, coal, insurance) touched individual consumers directly; others (lead, machine tools, farm equipment, transport) pinched producers, who then passed the monopoly prices along.").

98 **the Washington *Star* reported:** Wu, *Curse of Bigness,* 51. Along with "trust-buster," the term "octopus hunter" came into vogue. Ibid., 50.

99 **Taft insisted:** Jonathan Lurie, *William Howard Taft: The Travails of a Progressive Conservative* (Cambridge, U.K.: Cambridge University Press, 2012), 145, 197.

100 **To a friend and critic of his antitrust policies:** Ibid., 145.

100 **Taft called Standard Oil:** Barak Orbach and D. Daniel Sokol, "Symposium: 100 Years of *Standard Oil* Antitrust Energy," 85 *Southern California Law Review* 429, 431 (2012).

100 **monopolized the oil business:** Christopher R. Leslie, "Revisiting the Revisionist History of *Standard Oil,*" 85 *Southern California Law Review* 573 (2012); compare Orbach and Sokol, "Symposium," 431 ("Standard Oil invented the 'corporate trust' and played a central role in the trust movement that motivated Congress to enact the Sherman Act in 1890. More than 130 years after Standard Oil took over almost the entire market for refining of crude oil in the United States, scholars still debate how the company acquired its monopolistic position.").

100 **Keith Miller:** Keith L. Miller, "Standard Oil," in *The American Economy: A Historical Encyclopedia,* ed. Cynthia Clark Northrup (Santa Barbara, Calif.: ABC-CLIO, 2003), 1:267.

100 **in New Jersey:** M. S. Vassiliou, *Historical Dictionary of the Petroleum Industry* (Lanham, Md.: Scarecrow Press, 2009), 429 ("The Ohio Supreme Court outlawed the arrangement in 1892 and ordered the Standard Oil Trust dissolved. The trust nevertheless continued to operate from its New York City headquarters. Eventually Standard took advantage of favorable New Jersey laws allowing holding companies. In 1899, it renamed its New Jersey firm the Standard Oil Company (New Jersey) and placed it at the hub of the organization. Assets that were formerly in the Standard Oil Trust were put into the holding company.").

100 **twenty-four cases:** James May, "Antitrust Practice and Procedure in the Formative Era: The Constitutional and Conceptual Reach of State Antitrust Law, 1880–1918," 135 *University of Pennsylvania Law Review* 495, 501 (1987).

100 **170-page complaint:** Wu, *Curse of Bigness,* 65.

100 **led to a trial:** Ibid., 67.

101 ***History of the Standard Oil Company:*** Ida M. Tarbell, *The History of the Standard Oil Company* (New York: McClure, Phillips, 1904).

101 **Rockefeller threatened:** Wu, *Curse of Bigness,* 60, 64–66.

102 **a recent *Smithsonian* article:** Gilbert King, "The Woman Who Took on the Tycoon," Smithsonianmag.com, July 5, 2012, https://www.smithsonianmag.com.

102 **his biographer Ron Chernow:** Ron Chernow, *Titan: The Life of John D. Rockefeller Sr.* (New York: Vintage Books, 1998), xix, 10, 299, 308.

102 **Steve Weinberg:** Steve Weinberg, *Taking On the Trust: The Epic Battle of Ida Tarbell and John D. Rockefeller* (New York: W. W. Norton, 2008), xiv–xv.

102 **Clayton Antitrust Act:** Pub. L. 63-212, 38 Stat. 730 (1914).

102 **Federal Trade Commission Act:** Pub. L. 63-203, 38 Stat. 717 (1914).

102 **Hepburn Act:** Pub. L. 59-337, 34 Stat. 584 (1906).

102 **popular title:** William R. Nester, *Theodore Roosevelt and the Art of American Power: An American for All Time* (Lanham, Md.: Lexington Books, 2019), 142 (noting that Ida Tarbell's book *The History of the Standard Oil Company* was a "bestseller" that had "as powerful an effect on Roosevelt as Upton Sinclair's novel *The Jungle* would two years later," with Roosevelt ordering the Bureau of Corporations to investigate Standard Oil).

102 **in its preface:** Tarbell, *History of the Standard Oil Company,* 1:vii.

104 **"Get on the Raft with Taft":** Scott John Hammond et al., *Campaigning for President in America, 1788–2016* (Santa Barbara, Cal.: ABC-CLIO, 2016), 604 (noting that "Get on the Raft with Taft" became "the most popular Taft campaign song and slogan" and that "it included within the lyrics an interesting line: 'Get on a raft with Taft. . . . He'll save the country sure, boys, from Bryan, Hearst, and graft. So all join in, we're sure to win. Get on a raft with Taft.'"); ibid. ("The phrase 'from Bryan, Hearst, and graft' sought to remind voters of Bryan's failure to effectively deal with the Standard Oil influence peddling scandal, which implicated high-level officials in both parties. During the middle of September 1908, powerful newspaper publisher William Randolph Hearst released a number of letters indicating that a number of Republican as well as Democratic leaders had accepted payments from the Standard Oil Company in return for blocking legislation that the powerful company opposed.").

104 **"Bust the Trusts":** "Bust the Trusts: Democratic Campaign Song," words by F. J. Miller, music by Licco I. Liggy (published in New York by Weiss, MacEachen & Miller, and dedicated to Woodrow Wilson), levysheetmusic .mse.jhu.edu.

104 **George Wickersham:** Paul Moreno, "T.R. and T.B.T.F.," *National Review,* March 22, 2013, www.nationalreview.com; see also "George Wickersham: 'The Scourge of Wall Street,'" Historical Society of the New York Courts, May 20, 2020, history.nycourts.gov (noting that George Wickersham "began his career creating and defending large corporations, then switched sides, as US attorney general under William Howard Taft from 1909 to 1913, to become known as 'the scourge of Wall Street' for his aggressive prosecution of antitrust cases").

104 **carved into four separate entities:** Doug Brugge, *Particles in the Air: The Deadliest Pollutant Is One You Breathe Every Day* (Cham, Switzerland: Springer, 2018), 17; Jeffrey L. Cruikshank and Arthur W. Schultz, *The Man Who Sold America: The Amazing (but True!) Story of Albert D. Lasker and the Creation of the Advertising Century* (Boston: Harvard Business Review Press, 2010), 248; Peter Boyle et al., eds., *Tobacco: Science, Policy, and Public Health,* 2nd ed. (Oxford: Oxford University Press, 2010), 57.

104 **an antitrust expert:** Wu, *Curse of Bigness,* 74.

105 **five-year Sherman Act case:** Rodney Carlisle, *Powder and Propellants: Energetic Materials at Indian Head, Maryland, 1890–2001,* 2nd ed. (Denton: University of North Texas Press, 2002), 54.

105 **As one history observes:** Bill Marshall, ed., *France and the Americas: Culture, Politics, and History* (Santa Barbara, Calif.: ABC-CLIO, 2005), 1:401.

105 **Wilmington's** *Sunday Star:* Gerard Colby, *Du Pont Dynasty: Behind the Nylon Curtain* (Open Road Media, 2014), chap. 7.

105 **as one commentator recounts:** Erik Sass, "World War I Centennial: Breaking Up DuPont," *Mental Floss,* June 13, 2012, www.mentalfloss.com.

107 **formation of two new companies:** Alfred D. Chandler Jr. and Stephen Salsbury, *Pierre S. du Pont and the Making of the Modern Corporation* (Washington, D.C.: Beard Books, 2000), 292.

107 **DuPont Powder Company:** Kennard R. Wiggins Jr., *Delaware in World War I* (Charleston, S.C.: History Press, 2015), 38–39. Robert Waddell's Buckeye Powder Company later lost a court case against the DuPont Powder Company. See *Buckeye Powder Co. v. DuPont Powder Co.,* 248 U.S. 55 (1918).

107 **Paul Douglas:** Congressional Record—Proceedings and Debates of the 84th Congress, First Session (1955), vol. 101, pt. 4, p. 5430.

107 **the Seventeenth Amendment:** Wendy J. Schiller and Charles Stewart III, *Electing the Senate: Indirect Democracy Before the Seventeenth Amendment* (Princeton, N.J.: Princeton University Press, 2015), 158; see also Advisory Commission on Intergovernmental Relations, *The Transformation in American Politics: Implications for Federalism* (Washington, D.C.: Advisory Commission on Intergovernmental Relations, 1986), 36 ("The direct election of Senators, mandated by the 17th Amendment, was supposed to free that institution from the control of the political machines and the 'trusts.'").

107 **early trust-busting activities:** In the early days of antitrust enforcement, there was often reticence about breaking up companies. One Maryland federal district judge, way back in 1916, had this to say even after finding that a corporation—in that case, the American Can Company—had violated the Sherman Act: "I am frankly reluctant to destroy so finely adjusted an industrial machine as the record shows the defendant to be." *United States v. American Can Co.,* 230 F. 859, 908 (D. Md. 1916).

108 *Truths About the Trusts:* William Randolph Hearst, *Truths About the Trusts* (1916), 4.

109 **offered his personal assurance:** Wu, *Curse of Bigness,* 50.

109 **as one historian observes:** Chip Berlet and Matthew N. Lyons, *Right-Wing Populism in America: Too Close for Comfort* (New York: Guilford Press, 2000), 80.

109 **Philip H. Burch Jr.:** Philip H. Burch Jr., *Elites in American History: The Civil War to the New Deal* (New York: Holmes & Mayer, 1981), 2:164–65.

109 **a disagreement:** James C. German Jr., "Taft, Roosevelt, and United States Steel," *Historian* 34 (Aug. 1972): 598; "Split Between Taft and Roosevelt," *1912: Competing Visions for America* (exhibition), Ohio State University, ehistory.osu .edu; "Gentlemen's Agreements," *1912: Competing Visions for America* (exhibition), Ohio State University, ehistory.osu.edu.

110 **Roosevelt had approved the lucrative deal:** Paul D. Moreno, *The American State from the Civil War to the New Deal: The Twilight of Constitutionalism and*

the *Triumph of Progressivism* (Cambridge, U.K.: Cambridge University Press, 2013), 117.

110 **the 1912 election:** James Chace, *1912: Wilson, Roosevelt, Taft, and Debs—the Election That Changed the Country* (New York: Simon & Schuster, 2009); Daniel A. Crane, "All I Really Need to Know About Antitrust I Learned in 1912," 100 *Iowa Law Review* 2025 (2015).

110 **spoke of his antitrust record:** "1912: Theodore Roosevelt Shot in Milwaukee," History Channel, Feb. 27, 2019, www.history.com; Theodore Roosevelt, "I Have Just Been Shot," Oct. 14, 1912, in *Speeches of Note: An Eclectic Collection of Orations Deserving of a Wider Audience,* comp. Shaun Usher (New York: Ten Speed Press, 2018), 18–25; Oliver E. Remey, Henry F. Cochems, and Wheeler P. Bloodgood, *The Attempted Assassination of Ex-President Theodore Roosevelt* (Milwaukee, Wis.: Progressive Publishing Co., 1912), chap. 2; "Roosevelt Is Shot and Wounded by an Insane Man," *Leavenworth Weekly Times,* Oct. 17, 1912, 6. After being shot, Roosevelt was strongly advised against giving his speech, but he insisted on speaking to the assembled crowd. "I will make this speech or die," he said. "It will be one or the other." "Ball Is Turned by Manuscript—Prepared Speech Reposing in Overcoat Pocket Diverts Missile," *San Francisco Call,* Oct. 15, 1912, 2.

111 **George Perkins:** David Pietrusza, *TR's Last War: Theodore Roosevelt, the Great War, and a Journey of Triumph and Tragedy* (Guilford, Conn.: Lyons Press, 2018), 97; James MacGregor Burns, *The Workshop of Democracy, 1863–1932* (Open Road Media, 2012).

111 **the Progressive Party's platform:** "Making Faces at the Trusts," *Saturday Evening Post,* Oct. 5, 1912, 26.

111 **Woodrow Wilson:** Woodrow Wilson, *The New Freedom: A Call for the Emancipation of the Generous Energies of a People* (New York: Doubleday, Page, 1917), 165, 177, 180, 186.

111 **economic adviser:** Wu, *Curse of Bigness,* 76. Brandeis favored what he called "regulated competition." Ibid.

111 **Wilson's biographer:** John Milton Cooper Jr., *Woodrow Wilson: A Biography* (New York: Vintage Books, 2011), 163.

111 **"curse of bigness":** Louis D. Brandeis, *Other People's Money: And How the Bankers Use It* (New York: Frederick A. Stokes, 1914), 162.

111 **as he declared:** *Antitrust Impulse,* vol. 1.

112 **"the most pernicious of all trusts":** Melvin I. Urofsky, *Louis D. Brandeis: A Life* (New York: Pantheon Books, 2009), 381; Lewis J. Paper, *Brandeis: An Intimate Biography of Supreme Court Justice Louis D. Brandeis* (Open Road Media, 2014), chap. 14.

112 **Equal Justice Initiative:** Equal Justice Initiative, *Lynching in America: Confronting the Legacy of Racial Terror* (Montgomery, Ala.: Equal Justice Initiative, 2017), 4, 12–13, eji.org.

113 **Roosevelt once invited:** Deborah Davis, *Guest of Honor: Booker T. Washington, Theodore Roosevelt, and the White House Dinner That Shocked a Nation* (New York: Atria Books, 2012); Nester, *Theodore Roosevelt and the Art of American Power,* 156.

113 **Taft, while insisting:** Jeffrey Rosen, *William Howard Taft* (New York: Times Books, 2018), 126; see also Abraham L. Davis and Barbara Luck Graham, *The*

Supreme Court, Race, and Civil Rights (Thousand Oaks, Calif.: SAGE, 1995), 79 ("Thirty-one years after *Plessy*, the Taft Court reaffirmed the separate-but-equal doctrine in public education in a case involving Chinese ancestry. In *Gong Lum v. Rice*, 275 U.S. 78 (1927), the Court ruled, in a unanimous opinion, that a child of Chinese descent could be required to attend a black school in Mississippi under the separate-but-equal doctrine. 'Colored' was interpreted by the Court to mean everyone except whites, and excluding Chinese students from white schools was not a violation of equal protection.").

113 **Woodrow Wilson:** Bruce Bartlett, "Woodrow Wilson Was Even More Racist Than You Thought," *New Republic,* July 6, 2020, newrepublic.com; Dylan Matthews, "Woodrow Wilson Was Extremely Racist—Even by the Standards of His Time," *Vox,* Nov. 20, 2015, www.vox.com; Nicholas Patler, *Jim Crow and the Wilson Administration: Protesting Federal Segregation in the Early Twentieth Century* (Boulder: University Press of Colorado, 2004).

114 **the NAACP protested:** Melvyn Stokes, *D. W. Griffith's "The Birth of a Nation": A History of "the Most Controversial Motion Picture of All Time"* (Oxford: Oxford University Press, 2007), 129, 138, 227, 239. The NAACP was a litigant in some cases touching on antitrust law. For example, in *NAACP v. Button* (1963), the U.S. Supreme Court found that "the First and Fourteenth Amendments protect certain forms" of "group activity" and that "the Sherman Act does not apply to certain concerted activities" to the extent such activities involve "mere solicitation of governmental action with respect to the passage and enforcement of laws." Also, in *NAACP v. Claiborne Hardware Co.* (1982), the U.S. Supreme Court confirmed that a civil rights boycott by the NAACP against a white store owner in Claiborne County, Mississippi, was not an attempt to destroy competition in violation of a state antitrust law, but was entitled to First Amendment protection because the rights to assembly, to petition, and to free speech furthered the boycott's objectives of racial equality and integration and the NAACP was attempting to influence government action and to further racial justice.

114 **suffrage movement:** Jean H. Baker, *Sisters: The Lives of America's Suffragists* (New York: Hill and Wang, 2005); Katherine H. Adams and Michael L. Keene, *Alice Paul and the American Suffrage Campaign* (Urbana: University of Illinois Press, 2008).

115 **Panama Canal Act:** John J. Flynn, Harry First, and Darren Bush, *Antitrust: Statutes, Treaties, Regulations, Guidelines, Policies* (New York: Foundation Press, 2007), 46; compare "Antitrust Technical Corrections Act of 2001," in Report to Accompany H.R. 809, House Reports Nos. 1-36, 107th Cong., 1st Sess. (Jan. 3–Dec. 20, 2001), United States Congressional Serial Set, Serial Number 14720, 2 ("Section 11 of the Panama Canal Act provides that no vessel owned by someone who is violating the antitrust laws may pass through the Panama Canal. The Committee has not been able to determine why this provision was added to the act or whether it has ever been used. However, with the return of the Canal to Panamanian sovereignty at the end of 1999, it is appropriate to repeal this outdated provision.").

115 **created the Federal Trade Commission:** Marc Winerman, "The Origins of the FTC: Concentration, Cooperation, Control, and Competition," 71 *Antitrust Law Journal* 1 (2013).

115 **a broader prohibition:** Gilbert Holland Montague, "Unfair Methods of Competition," 25 *Yale Law Journal* 20 (1915); see also Charles Grove Haines, "Efforts to Define Unfair Competition," 29 *Yale Law Journal* 1 (1919). For a modern assessment of the FTC's power to stop unfair methods of competition and for a recitation of the history of the FTC's broadly defined powers, see Concurring Opinion of Commissioner Jon Leibowitz in the Matter of Rambus Inc., Docket No. 9302, www.ftc.gov ("Section 5 [of the FTC Act] was intended from its inception to reach conduct that violates not only the antitrust laws themselves, but also the policies that those laws were intended to promote. . . . I also address the scope of Section 5 because some commentators have misperceived the Commission's authority to challenge 'unfair methods of competition,' incorrectly viewing it as limited, with perhaps a few exceptions, to violations of the Sherman and Clayton Acts. Others are unclear just how far Section 5 can reach beyond the antitrust laws. Regardless of the reasons for these cramped or confused views, a review of Section 5's legislative history, statutory language, and Supreme Court interpretations reveals a Congressional purpose that is unambiguous and an Agency mandate that is broader than many realize.").

115 **Bureau of Corporations:** James W. Garner, *Government in the United States: National, State, and Local* (New York: American Book Company, 1913), 349 ("The Bureau of Corporations, created in 1903, was intended mainly to furnish an agency for the investigation of corporations suspected of violating the anti-'trust' laws of the United States. It is authorized to investigate the organization and methods of any corporation or joint-stock company engaged in foreign or interstate commerce (except common carriers subject to the interstate commerce act) and to report to the President such information as may be of value in enabling him to enforce the anti-'trust' laws and in making recommendations for additional legislation.").

115 **opened its doors:** Paul A. Pautler, "A History of the FTC's Bureau of Economics," in *Healthcare Antitrust, Settlements, and the Federal Trade Commission,* ed. James Langenfeld and Edwin Galeano (Bingley, U.K.: Emerald, 2018), 236n4; *Our History,* Federal Trade Commission, https://www.ftc.gov/about-ftc/our-history.

115 **Wilson wrote:** Woodrow Wilson, *The New Freedom: A Call for the Emancipation of the Generous Energies of a People* (New York: Doubleday, Page, 1917), 284.

116 **Jeffrey Rosen:** Jeffrey Rosen, *Louis D. Brandeis: American Prophet* (New Haven, Conn.: Yale University Press, 2016), 65.

116 **the 1912 presidential election:** Carol Berkin et al., *Making America: A History of the United States,* 5th ed. (Boston: Wadsworth, 2011), 496.

116 **In his 1913 autobiography:** Robert M. La Follette, *La Follette's Autobiography: A Personal Narrative of Political Experiences* (Madison, Wis.: The Robert M. La Follette Co. 1913); see also Robert M. La Follette, "La Follette's Why I Continued as a Candidate: Roosevelt Never a Progressive," *La Follette's Magazine* 4 (1912): 9, 15.

116 **railed against monopolies:** Ellen Torelle, comp., *The Political Philosophy of Robert M. La Follette as Revealed in His Speeches and Writings* (Madison, Wis.: Robert M. La Follette Co., 1920), 121, 126.

117 **Clayton Act:** James S. Olson, *Encyclopedia of the Industrial Revolution in America* (Westport, Conn.: Greenwood Press, 2002), 50.

117 **treble damages:** Albert A. Foer and Randy M. Stutz, eds., *Private Enforcement of Antitrust Law in the United States: A Handbook* (Cheltenham, U.K.: Edward Elgar, 2012), 236 ("Section 4 of the Clayton Antitrust Act of 1914 establishes both a private right of action and an award of treble damages. It states: 'Any person who shall be injured in his business or property by reason of anything forbidden in the antitrust laws may sue therefor . . . and shall recover threefold the damages by him sustained, and the cost of suit, including a reasonable attorney's fee.' ").

117 **one history:** Olson, *Encyclopedia of the Industrial Revolution in America,* 50.

118 **"Bust the Trusts":** "Bust the Trusts: Democratic Campaign Song," words by F. J. Miller, music by Licco I. Liggy (published in New York by Weiss, MacEachen & Miller, and dedicated to Woodrow Wilson), levysheetmusic .mse.jhu.edu.

119 **Abraham Lincoln:** Lincoln—the "Rail-Splitter" from humble beginnings— understood well the value of hard work and fair play because he himself had risen out of poverty to become a successful lawyer. At a speech in New Haven, Connecticut, in 1860, Lincoln spoke about capital and the rights of working people. He got cheers from the crowd when he said, "I am glad to see that a system of labor prevails in New England under which laborers can strike when they want to, where they are not obliged to work under all circumstances, and are not tied down and obliged to labor whether you pay them or not!" Lincoln was never antibusiness, but he believed in hard work and the value of labor. As Lincoln put it in his speech, again to more applause, "I don't believe in a law to prevent a man from getting rich; it would do more harm than good. So while we do not propose any war upon capital, we do wish to allow the humblest man an equal chance to get rich with everybody else. . . . I am not ashamed to confess that twenty-five years ago I was a hired laborer, mauling rails, at work on a flat-boat—just what might happen to any poor man's son!" Terence Ball, ed., *Abraham Lincoln: Political Writings and Speeches* (Cambridge, U.K.: Cambridge University Press, 2013), 239. In his first annual message to Congress, delivered on December 3, 1861, Lincoln made this observation: "Labor is prior to, and independent of, capital. Capital is only the fruit of labor, and could never have existed if labor had not first existed. Labor is the superior of capital, and deserves much the higher consideration." Abraham Lincoln Quotes About Labor and Work, Abraham Lincoln Research Site, rogerjnorton.com.

5. THE LAST ONE HUNDRED YEARS

121 **landmark cases:** One landmark case, against the Aluminum Company of America (ALCOA), a lawsuit that had been brought in 1937 before the onset of World War II, was decided in 1945 by Judge Learned Hand, of the U.S. Court of Appeals for the Second Circuit, as the war was ending. Judge Hand found that ALCOA—the sole domestic producer of virgin aluminum—was guilty of violating the Sherman Act, concluding that Congress "did not condone 'good trusts' and condemn 'bad' ones; it forbade all." The *ALCOA* case led to

the entry into the market of Reynolds Metals and Kaiser Aluminum, turning the aluminum industry into what one Wall Street analyst termed a "tri-opoly." James R. Williamson, *Federal Antitrust Policy During the Kennedy-Johnson Years* (Westport, Conn.: Greenwood Press, 1995), 19; W. Randall Jones, *The Greatest Stock Picks of All Time: Lessons on Buying the Right Stock at the Right Time* (New York: Three Rivers Press, 2002), 123–24. The *ALCOA* case broke new ground and is still studied today. See M. Sornarajah, *The International Law on Foreign Investment,* 2nd ed. (Cambridge, U.K.: Cambridge University Press, 2004), 182 ("In 1945, in the *Alcoa Case,* Judge Learned Hand changed the pre-existing view that the Sherman Act, the principal antitrust legislation in the United States, applied only within the territorial limits of the United States.").

121 **antitrust enforcement:** At times, officers or employees of major corporations have been fined or sent to jail or prison for violating the antitrust laws. For example, in September 1959, the U.S. Senate held hearings about whether U.S. electrical equipment makers were conspiring to fix prices. Soon thereafter, in January 1960, a federal grand jury sitting in Philadelphia indicted a number of businessmen for conspiring to fix prices, to "rig" bids, and to restrain competition in the electrical machinery and equipment industry. Of the individual defendants, sixteen worked as General Electric officers or managers, and ten were Westinghouse executives or managers. While GE had a 40 to 45 percent market share in heavy electrical equipment markets, Westinghouse had a market share of 30 to 35 percent. Although twenty-four of the thirty-day jail sentences that were imposed in February 1960 were suspended, seven of the businessmen—in a conspiracy that cost taxpayers $175 million annually—actually spent some time behind bars. It was the first modern case that sent major corporate executives to prison for price-fixing in violation of the Sherman Act. Myron W. Watkins, "Electrical Equipment Antitrust Cases—Their Implications for Government and for Business," 29 *University of Chicago Law Review* 97, 98, 100 (1961); Lawrence M. Salinger, ed., *Encyclopedia of White-Collar and Corporate Crime* (Thousand Oaks, Calif.: SAGE, 2005), 1:377.

121 **World Wars I and II:** At times of crisis, America's antitrust laws fell almost entirely by the wayside. For example, during World War I, the free-enterprise system became, in effect, a "command and control" economy. "Antitrust enforcement died out during World War I and was slow to resume during the probusiness euphoria of the 1920s," University of Michigan law professor Thomas Kauper observes. "Antitrust enforcement was again abandoned during World War II," Kauper explains, noting that "private actions seeking treble damages or injunctive relief . . . were not common until well after World War II." Thomas E. Kauper, "The Antitrust 'Revolution' and Small Business: On 'The Turnpike to Efficiencyville,'" in *Law and Class in America: Trends Since the Cold War,* ed. Paul D. Carrington and Trina Jones (New York: New York University Press, 2006), 122.

121 **Ronald Reagan and George W. Bush eras:** Steven Mufson, "Return of the Trust-Busters," *Washington Post,* June 17, 1990, www.washingtonpost.com ("Antitrust enforcement during the Reagan administration was the most lax since the Sherman Act's first decade. William F. Baxter, an academic from Stanford University was appointed—instead of a practicing antitrust

lawyer—to head the antitrust division of the Justice Department. At the FTC, Reagan appointed James C. Miller III, who opposed most of the agency's activities."); John D. Harkrider, "Antitrust Enforcement During the Bush Administration—an Economic Estimation," *Antitrust* (Summer 2008): 43 ("The analysis of these 200 mergers reveals that, all else being equal, transactions reviewed by the Antitrust Division during the Bush administration were approximately 24 percentage points *less* likely to be challenged than transactions reviewed by the Antitrust Division or FTC during the Clinton administration, a result that was statistically significant at the 95 percent confidence interval."); ibid., 47 ("The statistical evidence reviewed in this article is consistent with the conclusion that transactions reviewed by the Antitrust Division during the Bush administration were less likely to be [c]hallenged than transactions reviewed by the Antitrust Division during the Clinton administrations or by the FTC during either the Clinton or Bush administrations.").

121 **more aggressive antitrust enforcement:** Diana Klebanow and Franklin L. Jonas, *People's Lawyers: Crusaders for Justice in American History* (New York: Routledge, 2015) (noting that during the presidencies of Theodore Roosevelt and William Howard Taft, the federal government filed "more than 100 antitrust suits" and that "in some cases at least, the trusts that were sued were forced to divest some of their holdings—to combine less and to compete more"); compare ibid. ("By 1910, however, various leaders in thought and politics . . . were questioning the value of antitrust policy.").

121 **highly paid experts and PhD-trained economists:** Jesse Eisinger and Justin Elliott, "These Professors Make More Than a Thousand Bucks an Hour Peddling Mega-Mergers," ProPublica, Nov. 16, 2016, www.propublica.org.

121 **one antitrust expert:** Daniel A. Crane, "Antitrust Enforcement During National Crises: An Unhappy History," *GCP: The Online Magazine for Global Competition Policy,* Dec. 11, 2008, 6–7, www.competitionpolicyinternational.com.

122 **few political leaders worried:** Some of President Franklin Delano Roosevelt's initiatives, including the National Recovery Administration, which was established in 1933, allowed industries to write codes of fair competition or used government intervention in an effort to jump-start employment and economic activity. The U.S. Supreme Court declared the law setting up the National Recovery Administration to be unconstitutional in 1935. Jeff Shesol, *Supreme Power: Franklin Roosevelt vs. The Supreme Court* (New York: W. W. Norton, 2010), 80–81; James S. Olson, *Historical Dictionary of the Great Depression, 1929–1940* (Westport, Conn.: Greenwood Press, 2001), 250.

122 **Warren Harding promised:** G. Cullom Davis, "The Transformation of the Federal Trade Commission, 1914–1929," in *Business and Government in America Since 1870,* ed. Robert F. Himmelberg (New York: Garland, 1994), 4:85.

122 **one presidential history notes:** George Bittlingmayer, "The Use and Abuse of Antitrust from Cleveland to Clinton: Causes and Consequences," in *Reassessing the Presidency: The Rise of the Executive State and the Decline of Freedom,* ed. John V. Denson (Auburn, Ala.: Mises Institute, 2001), chap. 12.

122 **William Mitchell:** Ellis W. Hawley, "Herbert Hoover and the Sherman Act, 1921–1933: An Early Phase of a Continuing Issue," 74 *Iowa Law Review* 1067, 1086–88 (1989) (noting that "in a major policy address delivered at a meeting

of the American Bar Association in October 1929," Attorney General William Mitchell made it clear that his department would "deal vigorously" with every violation of antitrust law coming to its attention and that eventually "cases would be filed against groups such as the Bolt, Nut, and Rivet Manufacturers Association, the Wool Institute, the Sugar Institute, and the Asphalt Shingle and Roofing Institute").

122 **brought a variety of antitrust cases:** *The Federal Antitrust Laws with Amendments: List of Cases Instituted by the United States and Citations of Cases Decided Thereunder or Relating Thereto—December 31, 1930* (Washington, D.C.: Government Printing Office, 1931), 215–20.

122 **Hoover's own biographer:** Joan Hoff Wilson, *Herbert Hoover: Forgotten Progressive* (Long Grove, Ill.: Waveland Press, 1992), 153.

122 **clear interest in the subject:** Hawley, "Herbert Hoover and the Sherman Act," 1067 ("In the history of American antitrust law, Herbert Hoover has never had a prominent place. His name has not been associated with any major innovation; partly, one suspects, because he cannot be fitted easily into the conventional categories of antitrust advocate or opponent, his ideas and positions have received relatively little attention. Yet, for a dozen years, from 1921 to 1933, Hoover was a major participant in debates about the role of antitrust law.").

123 **Hart-Scott-Rodino Antitrust Improvements Act of 1976:** In 1976, Congress also voted to repeal the Miller-Tydings Act (1937), which exempted retail price-maintenance agreements from the federal antitrust laws. In essence, the law allowed manufacturers to set the minimum price at which their goods could be sold by retailers. In 1911, the U.S. Supreme Court had declared resale price maintenance per se illegal, but the Miller-Tydings Act basically gave antitrust immunity to retail resale price-maintenance clauses (which eliminate price competition among retailers, meaning consumers pay more). In 2007, a conservative majority of the U.S. Supreme Court overturned the 1911 case (*Dr. Miles v. John D. Park & Sons*). Instead of being per se illegal, resale price-maintenance agreements were subjected to a "rule of reason" analysis. In 2011, Senator Herb Kohl of Wisconsin introduced a bill to reestablish the per se rule against resale price maintenance, the Discount Pricing Consumer Protection Act. That bill—as it made clear—sought "to restore the rule that agreements between manufacturers and retailers, distributors, or wholesalers to set the minimum price below which the manufacturer's product or service cannot be sold violates the Sherman Act." I was an original co-sponsor of that bill. www .congress.gov.

123 **Representative Andrew Volstead of Minnesota:** Andrew Volstead represented Minnesota's Seventh Congressional District (later represented by my friend Collin Peterson, who chaired the House Agriculture Committee) for two full decades, from 1903 to 1923. A Republican lawyer, Volstead is mostly remembered today for the National Prohibition Act of 1919—the legislation, informally known as the Volstead Act, that put into effect the nationwide prohibition on the production, sale, and consumption of intoxicating beverages. That act followed the passage and ratification of the U.S. Constitution's Eighteenth Amendment (later repealed) establishing prohibition of alcoholic beverages in the United States. In an ironic twist of fate, a portrait of a thick-mustached, somewhat glum-looking Andrew Volstead, made entirely of beer

bottle caps, can be seen today at the Freehouse, a popular Minneapolis brew-pub. Volstead, who teamed up with the Anti-Saloon League and others to draft his Prohibition Era legislation, might be turning over in his grave, but the locally made craft beer is excellent. While Prohibition ended in 1933, the less controversial Capper-Volstead Act, exempting agricultural cooperatives from the antitrust laws, still endures to this day.

123 **agricultural cooperatives:** 5A William Meade Fletcher, *Part Two Fletcher Corporation Forms* § 4194, 4th ed. (Jan. 2017 update).

123 **exempt from the antitrust laws:** Ibid.; *In re Mushroom Direct Purchaser Antitrust Litigation,* 655 F.3d 158, 161 (3d Cir. 2011) ("The Capper-Volstead Act of 1922 allows certain agricultural producers to form cooperatives without incurring antitrust liability."); *Gregory v. Fort Bridger Rendezvous Ass'n,* 448 F.3d 1195, 1202 (10th Cir. 2006) ("An agricultural cooperative and its board members constitute a single entity and are thus exempt from antitrust liability when the cooperative is not engaged in one of the excepted activities that removes it from the protections of the Clayton and Capper-Volstead Acts."). It makes good sense that farmers and union members are exempt from the antitrust laws. Indeed, the 1922 Capper-Volstead Act has aptly been described as "the 'Magna Carta' of cooperatives." 1 *Callmann on Unfair Competition, Trademarks, and Monopolies* § 4:5, 4th ed. (Dec. 2016 update by Louis Altman and Malla Pollack). While the Magna Carta (Great Charter) agreed to by King John in 1215 was written in Latin, the Capper-Volstead Act ensured that American farmers would have the economic freedom to associate with one another. As that law reads, "Persons engaged in the production of agricultural products as farmers, planters, ranchmen, dairymen, nut or fruit growers may act together in associations, corporate or otherwise, with or without capital stock, in collectively processing, preparing for market, handling, and marketing in interstate and foreign commerce, such products of persons so engaged." 7 U.S.C.A. § 291.

123 **"labor antitrust exemption":** Comment, "The Antitrust Laws and Labor," 30 *Fordham Law Review* 759 (1962).

123 **established their exemption:** In the late 1890s, farmers and labor unions had tried, but failed, to obtain antitrust exemptions for agricultural cooperatives and unions. The Sherman Act did not address agricultural cooperatives, but such cooperatives, started by farmers in places like Iowa, Minnesota, and North Dakota, continued to be formed and to thrive. "In the early 1900's, when agricultural cooperatives were growing in effectiveness," the U.S. Supreme Court later emphasized of the relevant history, "there was widespread concern because the mere organization of farmers for mutual help was often considered to be a violation of the antitrust laws." *In re Mushroom Direct Purchaser Antitrust Litigation,* 655 F.3d at 165; *Md. & Va. Milk Producers Ass'n v. United States,* 362 U.S. 458, 464–65 (1960); *In re Fresh and Process Potatoes Antitrust Litigation,* 834 F. Supp.2d 1141, 1151 (D. Idaho 2011); *Case-Swayne Co. v. Sunkist Growers Inc.,* 389 U.S. 384, 390–91 (1967). "This concern led to the passage of section 6 of the Clayton Act and eventually the Capper-Volstead Act in 1922." Section 6 of the Clayton Act provided that "nothing contained in the antitrust laws shall be construed to forbid the existence and operation of labor, agricultural, or horticultural organizations, instituted for the purposes

of mutual help, and not having capital stock or conducted for profit," and the Capper-Volstead Act made "associations" of those producing agricultural products exempt from the antitrust laws. In other words, a group of farmers could act together to produce, and then collectively market, their products, all in an effort to improve their economic conditions. *In re Mushroom Direct Purchaser Antitrust Litigation,* 655 F.3d at 165; *Ewald Bros., Inc. v. Mid-America Dairymen, Inc.,* 877 F.2d 1384, 1386 (8th Cir. 1989) ("Section 6 of the Clayton Act, originally enacted in 1914, provides that the antitrust laws shall not be construed 'to forbid the existence and operation of labor, agricultural, or horticultural organizations, instituted for the purposes of mutual help, and not having capital stock or conducted for profit.' The effect of section 6 is that a group of farmers acting together in a single association cannot be restrained 'from lawfully carrying out the legitimate objects' of their association, i.e., the collective marketing of farm products so as to improve economic conditions for individual farmers.") (citations omitted).

123 **against organized labor:** Robert W. Kaps, *Air Transport Labor Relations* (Carbondale: Southern Illinois University Press, 1997), 17–18.

124 **Robinson-Patman Act:** *Arnold Chevrolet LLC v. Tribune Co.,* 418 F. Supp. 2d 172, 184n4 (E.D.N.Y. 2006) ("Price discrimination, charging buyers different prices for the same products, is not a cognizable claim under the Sherman Act, and instead, may be brought under the Robinson-Patman Act."); *Laidlaw Waste Systems, Inc. v. City of Fort Smith, Ark.,* 742 F. Supp. 540, 542 (W.D. Ark. 1990) ("The interstate commerce requirements of the Robinson-Patman Act differ distinctly from those of the Sherman Act. Accordingly, the court will address each of plaintiff's claims separately."). One of the supporters of the Robinson-Patman Act was Charles Hoyt March, a federal trade commissioner from Minnesota. He had managed President Coolidge's Minnesota campaign in 1924 and was appointed to the FTC in 1929. Jill A. Johnson, *Little Minnesota: 100 Towns Around 100* (Cambridge, Minn.: Adventure, 2011). He once characterized his philosophy in this way: "My political creed is death to Fascism. And monopoly is the root of Fascism. I'm going to smash it if I can." *Hearst's International Combined with Cosmopolitan* 104 (1938): 124.

124 **large-chain retailers:** Timothy L. Hall, ed., *U.S. Laws, Acts, and Treaties, 1929–1970* (Pasadena, Calif.: Salem Press, 2003), 2:663.

124 **Sears, Roebuck:** Mark Solheim, "What Sears Meant to Us," Kiplinger, Oct. 31, 2018, kiplinger.com.

124 **grocer A&P:** Marc Levinson, *The Great A&P and the Struggle for Small Business in America* (New York: Hill and Wang, 2011).

124 **these days, think Walmart:** John L. Daly, *Pricing for Profitability: Activity-Based Pricing for Competitive Advantage* (New York: John Wiley & Sons, 2002), 66 ("Today, the companies that are most often litigated under the Robinson-Patman Act are manufacturing companies that are suppliers to 'big box' retailers that give deep discounts to high-volume customers such as Wal-Mart, Kmart, Best Buy, Borders, or Office Max. These suits are often brought by groups of small retailers that lose business when these large retailers open up nearby.").

124 **one federal appellate court:** *Rebel Oil Co. v. Atlantic Richfield Co.,* 51 F.3d 1421, 1446 (9th Cir. 1995).

124 **price discrimination:** Douglas Broder, *U.S. Antitrust Law and Enforcement: A Practice Introduction,* 2nd ed. (Oxford: Oxford University Press, 2012), 7.

124 **one antitrust expert:** Tim Wu, *The Curse of Bigness: Antitrust in the New Gilded Age* (New York: Columbia Global Reports, 2018), 81–82.

124 **The law sought to erect:** Ibid., 128–29.

125 **Celler-Kefauver Act:** Celler-Kefauver Act, P.L. 81-899; Salinger, *Encyclopedia of White-Collar and Corporate Crime,* 1:147.

125 **barred vertical mergers:** Vertical mergers, which give companies control over their supply chains, can result in increased efficiencies and, potentially, reduced prices. Such mergers, however, can be anticompetitive. It all depends on the nature of the particular merger. An example of a vertical merger would be an automobile manufacturer buying a tire company.

125 **practice guide notes:** Peter C. Ward, *Federal Trade Commission: Law, Practice, and Procedure* § 8.04[3] (New York: Law Journal Press, 2005); compare Roger D. Blair and David L. Kaserman, *Law and Economics of Vertical Integration and Control* (New York: Academic Press, 1983), 142 ("Prior to 1950, the government had to deal with vertical integration and vertical mergers under the Sherman Act. From 1914 until 1950, Section 7 of the Clayton Act dealt only with horizontal mergers. In 1950, however, Section 7 was amended to extend its prohibition to vertical and conglomerate mergers as well. The amended Section 7 prohibits a vertical merger whenever its effect may be substantially to lessen competition or tend to create a monopoly. A review of the legislative history of the amendment sheds no light on the standards that the courts were expected to use in evaluating vertical mergers. The statute is similarly unenlightening.").

125 **noteworthy vertical merger:** In 2020, the Trump administration's Department of Justice and Federal Trade Commission released final Vertical Merger Guidelines over the dissent of both Democratic FTC commissioners. "Klobuchar Statement on Final Justice Department, FTC Vertical Merger Guidelines," press release, July 1, 2020, www.klobuchar.senate.gov.

125 **The $7.5 billion deal:** Mark Landler, "Turner to Merge into Time Warner; a $7.5 Billion Deal," *New York Times,* Sept. 23, 1995.

125 **significant concerns:** Federal Trade Commission, "FTC Requires Restructuring of Time Warner/Turner Deal: Settlement Resolves Charges that Deal Would Reduce Cable Industry Competition," press release, Sept. 12, 1996, www.ftc.gov.

126 **a 2016 report:** Federal Communications Commission, Report on Cable Industry Prices, Oct. 12, 2016, transition.fcc.gov.

126 **outpaced inflation:** Nathan McAlone, "Cable TV Price Increases Have Beaten Inflation Every Single Year for 20 Years," *Business Insider,* Oct. 31, 2016, www.businessinsider.com.

126 **Hart-Scott-Rodino Antitrust Improvements Act:** Edwin L. Miller Jr., *Mergers and Acquisitions: A Step-by-Step Legal and Practical Guide* (Hoboken, N.J.: John Wiley & Sons, 2008), 131.

126 **filing is required:** A filing must be made, for example, where one of the parties has annual sales or total assets exceeding approximately $151 million and the other party has sales or assets of more than approximately $15 million, or where the amount of stock of the acquirer is valued at more than approximately $272 million. The HSR's dollar thresholds adjust periodically. On February 15, 2019,

the FTC published a notice to revise the premerger notification thresholds for mergers and acquisitions under the HSR Act. Andrew G. Berg and Stephen M. Pepper, "Revised Jurisdictional Thresholds Under the HSR Act and for the Prohibition of Interlocking Directorates," GreenbergTraurig, Feb. 19, 2019, www.gtlaw.com.

126 **the waiting period:** The review process for mergers and acquisitions, known as M&A in the world of private equity companies, investment bankers, and big law firms, takes time and significant resources. After receiving HSR filings, the FTC and the U.S. Department of Justice must scrutinize the proposed transaction to determine if it would adversely affect U.S. commerce under America's antitrust laws. Parties are allowed to conduct due diligence and make post-merger integration plans, but no steps can be taken to immediately integrate operations for thirty days (fifteen days for all-cash tender offers) while the FTC and DOJ antitrust reviews are conducted. "The waiting period prior to consummation of an acquisition," one practice guide to mergers and acquisitions observes, "is the cornerstone of HSR. . . . While the waiting period preserves the status quo, the agencies, armed with the information obtained from the parties and their own research, can and do challenge proposed mergers. Complex remedial problems of undoing anticompetitive transactions are thereby avoided." Miller, *Mergers and Acquisitions,* 135; see also *Merger Review,* Federal Trade Commission, www.ftc.gov (describing how, under the Hart-Scott-Rodino Act, the FTC and the DOJ do a "preliminary review" of a proposed deal "to determine whether it raises any antitrust concerns that warrant closer examination" and that, "if the initial review has raised competition issues," the parties to the proposed transaction may be asked "to turn over more information" in what is referred to as a "second request"). It is, it turns out, much easier to halt a merger (or to require conditions, such as the divestiture of certain corporate asserts, before one moves forward) than it is to undo one that has already taken place.

126 **"midnight mergers":** Harry Cendrowski et al., *Private Equity: History, Governance, and Operations,* 2nd ed. (New York: John Wiley & Sons, 2012), 237.

127 **Christopher Sagers:** Christopher L. Sagers, *Examples and Explanations for Antitrust* §20.1, 2nd ed. (New York: Wolters Kluwer Law & Business, 2014).

127 **statutory and non-statutory antitrust exemptions:** Michael McCann, ed., *The Oxford Handbook of American Sports Law* (Oxford: Oxford University Press, 2018), 216 ("A foundational principle of federal labor law is that employees may form unions to gain leverage at the bargaining table *by eliminating competition* among themselves. Courts and Congress have struggled with this conflict. For more than twenty years after the passage of the Sherman Act, courts routinely held that unions were illegal restraints of trade in violation of antitrust law. Congress minimized this conflict by creating the 'statutory labor exemption' in the Norris LaGuardia Act (29 U.S.C. § 101 (2006)) and Sections 6 and 20 of the Clayton Act (15 U.S.C. § 12). This exemption protects unilateral union conduct—including strikes and the formation of unions—from antitrust challenge. . . . As the Supreme Court explained in *United States v. Hutcheson,* the statutory labor exemption establishes that 'labor unions are not combinations or conspiracies in restraint of trade, and exempt[s] specific union activities . . . from the operation of the antitrust laws.' . . . The non-statutory labor

exemption recognizes that antitrust law must give way to labor law when necessary to allow the collective bargaining process to work. This implied repeal of antitrust in favor of labor policy reflects a preference for resolving labor disputes through voluntary agreement (and labor policy) rather than through judicial interference (and antitrust law). The Supreme Court first established the nonstatutory labor exemption in *Local Union No. 189, Amalgamated Meat Cutters & Butcher Workmen of North America v. Jewel Tea Co.*").

127 **In fact, antitrust exemptions:** "Exemptions and Immunities," American Bar Association, apps.americanbar.org.

127 **more than twenty statutory exemptions:** Theodore Voorhees Jr., "The Political Hand in American Antitrust—Invisible, Inspirational, or Imaginary?," 79 *Antitrust Law Journal* 557, 558n8 (2014) (citing American Bar Association, Antitrust Law Section, *Federal Statutory Exemptions from Antitrust Law* (Chicago: American Bar Association, 2007), 319 table 1).

127 **McCarran-Ferguson Act:** 15 U.S.C. §§ 1011–15. The McCarran-Ferguson Act, passed after the U.S. Supreme Court held in 1944 that insurance could be regulated by Congress, allows states to regulate insurance. *United States v. South-Eastern Underwriters Ass'n,* 322 U.S. 533 (1944). In late December 2020, Congress passed the Competitive Health Insurance Reform Act to eliminate the antitrust exemption for the insurance industry. John D. Huh, Scott M. Vernick, and Joseph Baker, "Senate Approves Bill Eliminating Antitrust Exemption for Health Insurers," DLA Piper Publications, Dec. 29, 2020, www.dlapiper.com.

127 **insurance industry:** McCarran-Ferguson Act and the Current Crisis in Liability Insurance, House of Representatives, Subcommittee on Monopolies and Commercial Law, Committee on the Judiciary (1986), 438–39 ("In the early 1940s, the anticompetitive activities of the insurance industry caused the U.S. Attorney General to investigate a six-state association of over 200 insurance companies which were jointly setting their rates. After several years in court, the Supreme Court ruled in 1944 in the South-Eastern Underwriters case that the insurance industry was part of 'interstate commerce,' and therefore, was covered by federal antitrust laws. Although this court decision did not abolish the tradition of state regulation of the insurance industry, many people in the industry feared that strong federal regulation would soon follow. Pressure from the insurance industry led to the passage of the McCarran-Ferguson Act by the Congress in 1945."); see also Peter M. Lencsis, *Workers Compensation: A Reference and Guide* (Westport, Conn.: Quorum Books, 1998), 83 (describing the history of the adoption of the McCarran-Ferguson Act, discussing the Supreme Court's 1944 decision in *United States v. South-Eastern Underwriters Association,* and noting that "there have been proposals over the years to repeal or substantially amend the McCarran-Ferguson Act, but it still remains in its original form"). The Competitive Health Insurance Reform Act of 2020, which passed the U.S. Senate by unanimous consent on December 22, 2020, repealed the seventy-five-year-old law that exempted health insurers from the antitrust laws. Matthew McCormick, "Opinion/Letter: Finally, Some Good News for Health Care Consumers," *Portsmouth Herald,* Dec. 29, 2020, www.seacoastonline.com.

127 **Other statutory exemptions:** Local Government Antitrust Act of 1984, 15

U.S.C. §§ 34–36; American Bar Association, Antitrust Law Section, *Federal Statutory Exemptions from Antitrust Law,* 2007), 359–60 (listing various statutory exemptions); "Exemptions and Immunities," American Bar Association, apps.americanbar.org.

127 **uniformly applied across industries:** In *United States v. Socony-Vacuum Oil Co.,* 310 U.S. 150 (1940), the U.S. Supreme Court ruled that "the Sherman Act, so far as price-fixing agreements are concerned, establishes *one uniform rule applicable to all industries alike.*" Ibid., 222 (emphasis added). Well, it seems, not *all* industries, for various kinds of commerce, whether through lobbying or judicial fiat, have gotten exemptions from the antitrust laws.

127 **In that case:** *Federal Baseball Club of Baltimore, Inc. v. National League of Prof'l Baseball Clubs,* 259 U.S. 200 (1922).

127 **More than thirty years later:** *Toolson v. New York Yankees, Inc.,* 346 U.S. 356 (1953).

128 **the Court again reaffirmed:** *Flood v. Kuhn,* 407 U.S. 258 (1972). Compare Leo H. Kahane and Stephen Shmanske, eds., *The Oxford Handbook of Sports Economics* (Oxford: Oxford University Press, 2012), 1:92 ("At the NFL's urging, Congress passed the Sports Broadcasting Act of 1961 (SBA). The SBA allowed the professional sports leagues in football, baseball, basketball, and hockey to pool their TV broadcast rights for sale to a network. By doing so, it removed the threat of antitrust prosecution under §1 of the Sherman Act.").

128 **no blanket antitrust exemption:** *United States v. International Boxing Club of New York,* 348 U.S. 236 (1955); *Radovich v. National Football League,* 352 U.S. 445 (1957); *American Needle, Inc. v. National Football League,* 560 U.S. 183 (2010); see also Scott A. Freedman, "An End Run Around Antitrust Law: The Second Circuit's Blanket Application of the Non-statutory Labor Exemption in *Clarett v. NFL,*" 45 *Santa Clara Law Review* 155, 163 (2004) ("The NFL is a private entity that enjoys a monopoly on professional football in the United States. With the exception of a limited antitrust exemption allowing for the formation of the current league system, the actions of the NFL are otherwise subject to antitrust scrutiny.").

128 **judicial quirk of history:** Stuart Banner, *The Baseball Trust: A History of Baseball's Antitrust Exemption* (Oxford: Oxford University Press, 2013).

128 **the U.S. Supreme Court ruled:** *Radovich v. National Football League,* 352 U.S. 445 (1957).

129 **settled with Radovich:** "60 Heroes: The Father of Sports Labor Action," NFLPA, Aug. 10, 2016, www.nflpa.com.

129 **television broadcast deal:** Steven Malango, "Bench the NFL," *City Journal,* Sept. 28, 2017, www.city-journal.org.

129 **Congress also approved:** R. D. Griffith, *To the NFL: You Sure Started Somethin': A Historical Guide to All 32 NFL Teams and the Cities They've Played In* (Pittsburgh: Dorrance, 2012), 243; "President's Signature Will Assure NFL–AFL Clash," *Naugatuck Daily News,* Oct. 22, 1966, 5; "House Okays Grid Merger," *Nashville Tennessean,* Oct. 21, 1966, 33. NFL commissioner Pete Rozelle appeared before the House antitrust subcommittee chaired by New York congressman Emanuel Cellar prior to Congress authorizing the merger. "Pros May Get Limited Exemption," *Austin American,* Oct. 12, 1966,

26; "Merger Action Hopes Grow Dim," *Miami Herald*, Oct. 14, 1966 (sports section).

129 **were secretly promised:** Dale Van Atta, With Honor: *Melvin Laird in War, Peace, and Politics* (Madison: University of Wisconsin Press, 2008), 72–73 (describing discussions with Senator Russell Long and Representative Hale Boggs); Patrick Gallivan, *Pro Football in the 1960s: The NFL, the AFL and the Sport's Coming of Age* (Jefferson, N.C.: McFarland & Co., 2020), 155 ("Senate Whip Russell Long and House Whip Hale Boggs jointly worked the legislation. Both Long and Boggs hailed from Louisiana and wanted to see professional football move to their state. Once Rozelle promised that New Orleans would get an expansion franchise, the legislation approving the merger moved through Congress. Soon after exemption was approved, the owners granted New Orleans an NFL expansion franchise."); Ben Thomas, "Rozelle Denies Deal to Take in N. Orleans," *Evening Sun*, Oct. 26, 1966, D1 ("Sen. Russell B. Long (D., La.), assistant Senate majority leader, and Representative Hale Boggs (D., La.), assistant House majority leader, were instrumental in gaining passage of legislation to give the National and American leagues immunity from anti-trust laws in their merger. The linking of the two leagues will be completed by 1970."); "Congress Okays Title Game," *Courier-Post*, Oct. 22, 1966, 29, 31 ("One of the 1968 franchises is expected to go to New Orleans. Sen. Russell B. Long, D-La., who helped push the bill through Congress, said the chances were '100 to 1' that New Orleans would be one of the two cities."). Compare "Rozelle Denies Commitment Made to Place NFL Team in New Orleans," *Gazette and Daily*, Oct. 26, 1966, 26.

130 **a non-statutory labor exemption:** Matt Nichol, *Globalization, Sports Law, and Labour Mobility: The Case of Professional Baseball in the United States and Japan* (Cheltenham, U.K.: Edward Elgar, 2019), 113 ("The non-statutory labour exemption is particularly important for professional sport as the exemption applies to restrictive labour practices. The elements of the non-statutory labour exemption expressed in *National Football League v Mackey* [543 F.2d 606 (8th Cir. 1976), *cert. dismissed*, 434 U.S. 801 (1977)] were that the restrictive practice only affect the parties to the collective agreement, relate to a mandatory subject of collective bargaining and be the product of good faith bargaining. . . . The Supreme Court expanded the non-statutory labour exemption to antitrust law in 1996 in *Brown v Pro Football Inc[.]* [116 U.S. 231 (1996)] by applying the exemption to agreements between employees in a multi-employer bargaining unit. It was held that when an impasse occurs during collective bargaining, management has the right to unilaterally impose its last offer to the union without being subject to antitrust law."). Some of the history of the non-statutory exemption that has been held applicable to the National Football League—and that goes back to the 1970s in a series of cases initially heard in the U.S. District Court for the District of Minnesota—is set out in *Brady v. National Football League*, 779 F. Supp.2d 992 (D. Minn. 2011).

130 **judicially created antitrust exemptions:** In addition to the baseball exemption, the courts have created a virtual judicial cornfield maze of antitrust dead ends: the state action doctrine—per a series of U.S. Supreme Court cases beginning with *Parker v. Brown* (1943)—allows state governments and certain private actors to show that state regulatory schemes preclude antitrust liability;

the *Noerr-Pennington* doctrine says there is no antitrust liability for petitioning the government; the filed rate/*Keogh* doctrine prohibits an antitrust action for unreasonable rates if the rates are filed with and approved by a state or federal agency; and finally, the "implied immunities" doctrine shields parties from liability if antitrust enforcement would disrupt or be "repugnant" to a regulatory scheme. The filed rate doctrine originated with a U.S. Supreme Court decision, *Keogh v. Chicago & Northwest Railway Co.*, 260 U.S. 156 (1922).

130 **"Antitrust law is complicated"**: Ben Sheffner, "Collusion Course: Does Today's Hush-Hush Meeting of Newspaper Executives Violate Antitrust Law?," *Slate*, May 28, 2009, slate.com. The current state of antitrust law is complicated, so even basic generalizations are sometimes hard to make. For example, the U.S. Supreme Court has retreated from finding per se antitrust violations to examining conduct under a "rule of reason" test. *Broadcast Music, Inc. v. Columbia Broadcasting System, Inc.*, 441 U.S. 1 (1979) (examining the question of "whether the issuance by ASCAP and BMI to CBS of blanket licenses to copyrighted musical compositions at fees negotiated by them is price fixing per se unlawful under the antitrust laws," and holding that such blanket licenses did not necessarily constitute price-fixing but should be examined under the rule of reason to determine if the practice was unlawful); see also *Antitrust Laws*, Legal Information Institute, https://www.law.cornell.edu/wex/antitrust_laws ("Violations under the Sherman Act take one of two forms—either as a per se violation or as a violation of the rule of reason. A per se violation requires no further inquiry into the practice's actual effect on the market or the intentions of those individuals who engaged in the practice. Some business practices have both pro-competitive effects and anti-competitive effects. For these cases, the court applies a 'totality of the circumstances test' and asks whether the challenged practice promotes or suppresses market competition. Courts often find intent and motive relevant in predicting future consequences during a rule of reason analysis.").

130 **judicial decisions**: For example, in *Copperweld Corp. v. Independence Tube Corp.*, 467 U.S. 752 (1984), the Supreme Court held that a parent company is incapable of conspiring with its own wholly owned subsidiary for purposes of section 1 of the Sherman Act because the companies cannot be considered separate economic entities. The nature of a business relationship or, say, the particular terms of a restraint on trade can thus affect whether an antitrust violation is found, with the courts finding some restraints to be per se unlawful while others are judged by what have come to be called the rule of reason or quick look approaches. Peter C. Ward, *Federal Trade Commission: Law, Practice and Procedure* (New York: Law Journal Press, 2005), § 4.02[1] ("The *per se* rule applies only to a practice that 'facially appears to be one that would always or almost always tend to restrict competition and decrease output.' . . . A more thorough rule of reason analysis is called for if the agreement is one whose competitive effect can be evaluated only by analyzing the facts peculiar to the business, the history of the restraint, and the reasons why it was imposed. In some contexts, the agreement involved may justify a *per se* approach, while in others a rule of reason analysis may be required. An analytical compromise between the two approaches has come to be known as 'quick-look' analysis. That approach is used in situations where 'an observer with even a rudimen-

tary understanding of economics could conclude that the arrangements in question would have an anticompetitive effect on customers and markets.'").

130 **made use of common-law concepts:** Donald Dewey, "The Common-Law Background of Antitrust Policy," 41 *Virginia Law Review* 759 (1955); Frank J. Nawalanic, "Motives of Non-profit Organizations and the Antitrust Laws," 21 *Cleveland State Law Review* 97, 98 (1972); Daniel M. Tracer, "Stare Decisis in Antitrust: Continuity, Economics, and the Common Law Statute," 12 *DePaul Business and Commercial Law Journal* 1, 9, 41–44 (2013); compare Fred S. McChesney and William F. Shughart II, eds., *The Causes and Consequences of Antitrust: The Public-Choice Perspective* (Chicago: University of Chicago Press, 1995), 330 ("the Supreme Court's earliest antitrust decision specifically held that 'the common law cases on restraint of trade would not be precedents in Sherman Act cases'"); *United States v. Trans-Missouri Freight Ass'n,* 166 U.S. 290, 327 (1897) ("It is said that, when terms which are known to the common law are used in a federal statute, those terms are to be given the same meaning that they received at common law, and that, when the language of the title is 'to protect trade and commerce against unlawful restraints and monopolies,' it means those restraints and monopolies which the common law regarded as unlawful, and which were to be prohibited by the federal statute. We are of opinion that the language used in the title refers to and includes, and was intended to include, those restraints and monopolies which are made unlawful in the body of the statute. It is to the statute itself that resort must be had to learn the meaning thereof, though a resort to the title here creates no doubt about the meaning of, and does not alter the plain language contained in, its text."); ibid., 327–28 ("It is now, with much amplification of argument, urged that the statute, in declaring illegal every combination in the form of trust or otherwise, or conspiracy in restraint of trade or commerce, does not mean what the language used therein plainly imports, but that it only means to declare illegal any such contract which is in *unreasonable* restraint of trade, while leaving all others unaffected by the provisions of the Act; that the common law meaning of the term 'contract in restraint of trade' includes only such contracts as are in *unreasonable* restraint of trade; and, when that term is used in the federal statute, it is not intended to include all contracts in restraint of trade, but only those which are in unreasonable restraint thereof. The term is not of such limited signification. Contracts in restraint of trade have been known and spoken of for hundreds of years, both in England and in this country, and the term includes all kinds of those contracts which, in fact, restrain or may restrain trade. Some of such contracts have been held void and unenforceable in the courts by reason of their restraint's being unreasonable, while others have been held valid because they were not of that nature. A contract may be in restraint of trade and still be valid at common law. Although valid, it is nevertheless a contract in restraint of trade, and would be so described either at common law or elsewhere. By the simple use of the term 'contract in restraint of trade,' all contracts of that nature, whether valid or otherwise, would be included, and not alone that kind of contract which was invalid and unenforceable as being in unreasonable restraint of trade. When, therefore, the body of an act pronounces as illegal every contract or combination in restraint of trade or commerce among the several states, etc., the plain and ordinary

meaning of such language is not limited to that kind of contract alone which is in unreasonable restraint of trade, but all contracts are included in such language, and no exception or limitation can be added without placing in the act that which has been omitted by Congress. Proceeding, however, upon the theory that the statute did not mean what its plain language imported, and that it intended in its prohibition to denounce as illegal only those contracts which were in unreasonable restraint of trade, the courts below have made an exhaustive investigation as to the general rules which guide courts in declaring contracts to be void as being in restraint of trade, and therefore against the public policy of the country.").

130 **Senator George Hoar:** Barry E. Hawk, ed., *International Antitrust Law and Policy* (Huntington, N.Y.: Juris, 2004), 22.

131 *Swift & Co. v. United States* **(1905):** *Swift & Co. v. United States,* 196 U.S. 375 (1905).

131 *United States v. American Tobacco Co.:* *United States v. American Tobacco Co.,* 221 U.S. 106 (1911).

131 *United States v. United States Steel Corp.* **(1920):** *United States v. United States Steel Corp.,* 251 U.S. 417, 457 (1920). It was only through relentless union organizing—and the power of collective bargaining—that the behemoth U.S. Steel Corporation was ultimately forced to abandon Andrew Carnegie's stridently anti-union approach. In due time, the twelve-hour workday was jettisoned in favor of the standard eight-hour workday, and the Norris-LaGuardia Act further strengthened the rights of workers. It was the National Labor Relations Act of 1935 that guaranteed collective bargaining rights, allowing workers to more effectively seek better terms of employment and conditions in the workplace. That act created the National Labor Relations Board (NLRB), an independent U.S. government agency headquartered in Washington, D.C. The NLRB enforces U.S. labor laws and polices unfair labor practices. Indeed, it took the formation, in 1942, in Cleveland, of the United Steelworkers—a union previously led by Leo Gerard and now led by Tom Conway—for American steelworkers to achieve some balance in relation to U.S. Steel's enormous corporate and political power.

131 **President Herbert Hoover:** Hawley, "Herbert Hoover and the Sherman Act."

131 **continued to ebb and flow:** Since the days of Teddy Roosevelt's Square Deal and Franklin Delano Roosevelt's New Deal, the debates over antitrust doctrine and policy have played out largely in the academy, in federal agencies, and in the courts, with a bevy of lawyers, economists, and law professors—and a handful of presidential appointees—setting the tone and playing prominent roles in the debate. During FDR's administration, one individual, Thurmond Arnold, played a particularly effective role in rejuvenating antitrust enforcement and taking on monopolists. A native of Laramie, Wyoming, who had practiced law in Chicago and in his hometown, Arnold became a West Virginia law dean before being put in charge of the Justice Department's Antitrust Division. A World War I veteran and a Harvard Law School graduate, Arnold indicted the American Medical Association in 1939 for antitrust violations relating to its anticompetitive actions pertaining to health plans. After a series of appellate battles, the AMA's criminal conviction for violating the antitrust laws was affirmed in 1943. As part of FDR's broader plan to

revitalize the economy, Arnold vigorously prosecuted cartels and monopolies, setting new records for prosecutions and convictions. Spencer Weber Waller, *Thurman Arnold: A Biography* (New York: New York University Press, 2005), 12–13, 18, 20–50; *Managed Care and Antitrust: The PPO Experience* (American Bar Association, Antitrust Law Section, 1990), 4; see also Guy Rolnik, "140 Years of Antitrust: 'Competition' in Democratic and Republican Platforms," *ProMarket,* Oct. 11, 2016, promarket.org ("In March 1938, FDR put [Thurman Arnold] in charge of the Antitrust Division in the Department of Justice, a job he kept until 1943. By 1942, during Arnold's tenure, the Antitrust Division's lawyer headcount grew dramatically: from 15 to 583.").

131 **into stark view:** Broder, *U.S. Antitrust Law and Enforcement,* 8. Even before the end of World War II, Thurmond Arnold understood the importance of antitrust enforcement—both to the health of America's economy and to the American people. In *The Bottlenecks of Business* (1940), Arnold wrote about the critical importance of the antitrust laws and advocated for "the American consumer." Consumers, he explained, depend on private enterprise to give them goods at competitive prices. "Most of the books in the past on the antitrust laws," Arnold stressed, "have been written with the idea that they are designed to eliminate *the evil of bigness.* What ought to be emphasized is not the evils of size but the evils of industries which are not efficient or do not pass efficiency on to consumers." As Arnold wrote after the onset of World War II, "If the antitrust laws are simply an expression of a religion which condemns largeness as economic sin they will be regarded as an anachronism in a machine age. If, however, they are directed at making distribution more efficient, they will begin to make sense, and, incidentally, they will also solve the problem of bigness wherever bigness is blocking the channels of trade." In the very first section of his book, Arnold graphically illustrated the importance of antitrust enforcement to America's middle class, reproducing a chart depicting the distribution of income among American families. The chart, titled "Income Levels in American Life," broke down American families by income, comparing the sliver of those at the very top—the 283,000 families then making more than $10,000 per year and the 800,000 families earning between $5,000 and $10,000 annually (those said to be "not only living luxuriously but piling up fortunes")—with the much larger numbers making up "The Comfortable Middle Class (8,000,000 families)," those "Fighting Poverty (11,000,000 families)," and those "Continually Facing Starvation (8,000,000 families)." Arnold specifically rejected the idea of "a planned economy" and embraced "free exchange in a free market." But he railed against price-fixing and cartels and called for consumer complaints to be addressed by the Justice Department's Antitrust Division for the public's sake. "If that organization is on the job ripples of one antitrust investigation will spread in all directions," Arnold emphasized, alluding to the deterrent effect of antitrust proceedings. Thurman W. Arnold, *The Bottlenecks of Business* (Washington, D.C.: Beard Books, 1940), 1, 3–4, 7–8, 10, 15, 27, 30.

132 *United States v. Columbia Steel Co.* **(1948):** *United States v. Columbia Steel Co.,* 334 U.S. 495, 526 (1948).

132 **In the dissenting opinion:** Ibid., 534–36 (Douglas, J., dissenting).

133 **Chicago school:** Richard A. Posner, "The Chicago School of Antitrust Analy-

sis," 127 *University of Pennsylvania Law Review* 925 (1979). The essential features of the "Chicago school"—per Richard Posner, a longtime professor at the University of Chicago Law School—arose out of the work of Aaron Director in the 1950s. In summarizing the principles and outlook of the Chicago school, Posner wrote that "the focus of the antitrust laws should not be on unilateral action," which he defined as "action that does not involve agreement with a competitor." Ibid., 928n6. The focus of antitrust laws, Posner wrote, "should instead be on: (1) cartels and (2) horizontal mergers large enough either to create monopoly directly, as in the classic trust cases, or to facilitate cartelization by drastically reducing the number of significant sellers in the market." Ibid., 928; see also ibid. ("Since unilateral action, as I have defined the term, had been the cutting edge of antitrust policy for a great many years, to place it beyond the reach of antitrust law, as Director and his followers seemed to want to do, implied a breathtaking contraction in the scope of antitrust policy.").

133 **the University of Chicago:** Academics at the University of Chicago have long been involved in antitrust policy. Nicola Giocoli, *Predatory Pricing in Antitrust Law and Economics: A Historical Perspective* (New York: Routledge, 2014) ("In 1968 a White House Task Force on Antitrust Policy, chaired by Phil Neal, Dean of Chicago Law School, recommended in its final report (the so-called Neal Report) a 'specific legislation dealing with entrenched oligopolies [that] would rectify the most important deficiency in the present antitrust laws.'").

133 **a critique of then-existing law:** "Antitrust 2: The Paradox," NPR, Feb. 20, 2019, www.npr.org.

133 **a series of Supreme Court precedents:** In *Brown Shoe Co. v. United States,* 370 U.S. 294 (1962), the Supreme Court affirmed a district court judgment that a merger would increase concentration in the shoe industry and enjoined the merger. In *United States v. Von's Grocery Co.,* 384 U.S. 270 (1966), the Court held that the merger of two grocers in a market violated section 7 of the Clayton Act. And in *Utah Pie Co. v. Continental Baking Co.* (1967), the Court held that evidence of predatory intent bears on the likelihood of injury to competition.

133 **Richard Posner:** William Domnarski, *Richard Posner* (Oxford: Oxford University Press, 2016), 47, 53, 89. The prolific Posner wrote books such as *Economic Analysis of Law* (1973) and *Antitrust Law: An Economic Perspective* (1976), and in addition to teaching courses on those subjects, he wrote extensively about antitrust issues in academic journals. Richard A. Posner, "A Program for the Antitrust Division, 38 *University of Chicago Law Review* 500 (1971); see also "The Honorable Richard A. Posner Receives Justice Department's 2003 John Sherman Award—Award Presented in Recognition of Judge Posner's Lifetime Contribution to Antitrust Law and Policy," U.S. Department of Justice, press release, Oct. 30, 2003, www.justice.gov (noting that Posner worked as an assistant to FTC commissioner Philip Elman and as an assistant to Solicitor General Thurgood Marshall).

134 **In his treatise:** Kenneth Heyer, "Consumer Welfare and the Legacy of Robert Bork," 57 *Journal of Law and Economics* S19 (2014).

134 **the assessment of scholars:** Robert H. Lande, "A Traditional and Textualist Analysis of the Goals of Antitrust: Efficiency, Preventing Theft from Consumers, and Consumer Choice," 81 *Fordham Law Review* 2349 (2013).

134 **a twisted argument:** Stephen Martin, "Dispersion of Power as an Economic

Goal of Antitrust Policy," in *Power in Economic Thought,* ed. Manuela Mosca (Cham, Switzerland: Palgrave Macmillan, 2018), 269.

135 **ignoring the intent and history:** Robert H. Lande, "Wealth Transfers as the Original and Primary Concern of Antitrust: The Efficiency Interpretation Challenged," in *The Political Economy of the Sherman Act: The First One Hundred Years,* ed. E. Thomas Sullivan (New York: Oxford University Press, 1991), 71–84; John B. Kirkwood and Robert H. Lande, "The Fundamental Goal of Antitrust: Protecting Consumers, Not Increasing Efficiency," 84 *Notre Dame Law Review* 191 (2008); Robert H. Lande, "Proving the Obvious: The Antitrust Laws Were Passed to Protect Consumers (Not Just to Increase Efficiency)," 50 *Hastings Law Journal* 959 (1999).

135 **purported to document it:** Robert H. Bork, "Legislative Intent and the Policy of the Sherman Act," 9 *Journal of Law and Economics* 7 (1966).

135 **two antitrust experts:** Kirkwood and Lande, "Fundamental Goal of Antitrust," 199.

135 **a limited role for judges:** See Robert H. Bork, *The Tempting of America: The Political Seduction of the Law* (New York: Simon & Schuster, 1990), 196–97, 332 (discussing Bork's views on antitrust, with Bork observing, "The Supreme Court now takes the position that consumer welfare is the goal of antitrust and has cited my book *The Antitrust Paradox* in support of that conclusion"); 266n12 ("According to Robert Bork in *The Antitrust Paradox,* courts should almost never credit the possibility that a firm could exclude rivals through predatory pricing or by refusing to deal with suppliers or distributors or otherwise forcing rivals to bear higher distribution costs.").

135 **and Congress:** Bork believed that "Congress as a whole is institutionally incapable of the sustained, rigorous and consistent thought that the fashioning of a rational antitrust policy requires." Richard Lacayo, "The Law According to Bork," *Time,* June 24, 2001, content.time.com.

135 **believing that plaintiffs:** J. Thomas Rosch (commissioner, Federal Trade Commission), "Striking a Balance? Some Reflections on Private Enforcement in Europe and the United States" (International Chamber of Commerce Annual Meeting, New York City, Sept. 24, 2008), 26, www.ftc.gov ("Robert Bork has said treble damages 'attracts bad lawsuits, lawyers interested only in the enormous cash awards, and compels even innocent businesses to settle rather than risk trial with potentially catastrophic damages.'"); Jason Rathod and Sandeep Veheesan, "The Arc and Architecture of Private Enforcement Regimes in the United States and Europe: A View Across the Atlantic," 14 *University of New Hampshire Law Review* 303, 332 (2016) ("In 1976, Robert Bork wrote that '[w]e are sitting in the center of an explosion of federal litigation,' while Francis R. Kirkham, then chair of the Antitrust Law Section of the American Bar Association, 'stridently complained about notice pleading, juries, class actions, abusive discovery, and forced settlement of meritless claims due to the high cost of litigating.' Judge Bork laid blame for the litigation explosion on an imprudent expansion of government.").

135 **should be relaxed:** Jonathan B. Baker, *The Antitrust Paradigm: Restoring a Competitive Economy* (Cambridge, Mass.: Harvard University Press, 2019), 1–2 ("For Bork, the antitrust paradox (his title) was that antitrust enforcement had popular support even though, in his view, antitrust law was a policy at

war with itself (his subtitle). Bork contended that the antitrust law then in force was based on an intellectually incoherent mix of procompetitive and protectionist premises. Its doctrines could not be other than contradictory—sometimes preserving competition and sometimes suppressing it. His prescription was to eliminate the contradictions, and the inefficiencies they created, by relaxing antitrust rules and their enforcement.").

135 **industry concentration:** Industry concentration continues to pose a problem to the health of America's free-enterprise system. Sarah Hubbard, *Monopolies Suck: Seven Ways Big Corporations Rule Your Life* (New York: Simon & Schuster, 2020), 11 ("In spite of our broad antitrust statutes and the antitrust agencies empowered to enforce them, America faces a monopoly crisis. Between 1997 and 2014, corporate concentration increased in 80 percent of industries by an average of 90 percent, according to economists.").

135 **Harvard school:** Donald F. Turner, "The American Antitrust Laws," 18 *Modern Law Review* 244 (1955).

135 **their own influential treatise:** Phillip E. Areeda and Donald F. Turner, *Antitrust Law* (Boston: Little, Brown, 1980).

136 ***Regulation and Its Reform:*** Stephen Breyer, *Regulation and Its Reform* (Cambridge, Mass.: Harvard University Press, 1982), 156–57.

136 **members of the Harvard school:** Barry J. Rodger and Angus MacCulloch, *Competition Law and Policy in the EU and UK,* 5th ed. (London: Routledge, 2015), 19.

136 **competitive market structures:** Brendan J. Sweeney, *The Internationalisation of Competition Rules: The Approach of European States* (London: Routledge, 2010), 164n113.

136 **Professor Herbert Hovenkamp:** Tony Freyer, "Deregulation Theories in a Litigious Society: American Antitrust and Torts," in *Government and Markets: Toward a New Theory of Regulation,* ed. Edward J. Balleisen and David A. Moss (Cambridge, U.K.: Cambridge University Press, 2010), 492.

136 **"Battle for the Soul of Antitrust":** Thomas A. Piraino Jr., "Reconciling the Harvard and Chicago Schools: A New Antitrust Approach for the 21st Century," 82 *Indiana Law Journal* 345 (2007).

136 **William F. Baxter:** Wenonah Hauter, *Frackopoly: The Battle for the Future of Energy and the Environment* (New York: New Press, 2016), 62.

136 **describe Robert Bork:** David G. Savage, "Skeptical of Government Action: Bork Takes Narrow View on Antitrust Legislation," *Los Angeles Times,* Aug. 26, 1987, www.latimes.com.

137 **Bill Baxter's appointment:** Domnarski, *Richard Posner,* 94 ("When Baxter was appointed head of the Antitrust Division, Posner wrote in February 1980 that he was 'delighted—overjoyed, really—to read that you are going to be head of the Antitrust Division. Reagan couldn't have made a better choice.' ").

137 **in an op-ed:** Howard M. Metzenbaum, "Is William Baxter Anti-antitrust?," *New York Times,* Oct. 18, 1981.

137 **number of enforcement actions:** Richard A. Posner, "A Statistical Study of Antitrust Enforcement," 13 *Journal of Law and Economics* 365, 366 (1970).

137 **greater uptick in litigated matters:** Joseph C. Gallo et al., "Department of Justice Antitrust Enforcement, 1955–1997: An Empirical Study," 17 *Review of Industrial Organization* 75, 78–79 (2000).

137 **In the 1980s:** Ibid., 79.

138 **who is put in charge:** William E. Kovacic, "The Modern Evolution of U.S. Competition Policy Enforcement Norms," 71 *Antitrust Law Journal* 378, 396 (2003) ("The president influences the development of agency enforcement norms through the nomination of leadership for the enforcement authorities. New appointees can bring views that catalyze changes in an agency's existing internal enforcement norms. The executive also affects agency enforcement norms by preparing the budget.").

138 **the government's share of civil antitrust cases:** For a source on the relationship between public and private antitrust enforcement, see Working Party No. 3 on Co-operation and Enforcement, "Relationship Between Public and Private Antitrust Enforcement," June 15, 2015, www.justice.gov. Private litigation is the predominant means by which the antitrust laws are enforced. Daniel A. Crane, "Optimizing Private Antitrust Enforcement," 63 *Vanderbilt Law Review* 675 (2010).

138 **over the decades:** From 1949 to 2008, Democratic administrations filed an annual average of 34.8 civil cases, while Republican administrations filed an annual average of 28.6 civil cases. In contrast, Republican administrations during that time frame filed an annual average of 35.9 criminal cases, while Democratic administrations filed an annual average of 28.9 criminal cases. Each presidential administration has varied, with both antitrust suits and criminal prosecutions dropping substantially during the George W. Bush years. While there was an annual average of 27 civil cases and 40.5 criminal cases filed during the Clinton administration (1993–2001), there was only an annual average of 16 civil cases and 19.4 criminal cases during the George W. Bush administration (2001–2009).

138 **MCI, filed a thirty-six-page civil antitrust complaint:** Christopher H. 138, Phyllis W. Bernt, and Martin B. H. Weiss, *Shaping American Telecommunications: A History of Technology, Policy, and Economics* (New York: Routledge, 2014), 147.

138 **brought its own antitrust lawsuit:** James E. Katz, ed., *Mobile Communication: Dimensions of Social Policy* (New Brunswick, N.J.: Transaction, 2011), 52. MCI executives met in the fall of 1973 with the Justice Department's Antitrust Division to persuade that division to file a civil antitrust suit against AT&T to break up the company. Steve Coll, *The Deal of the Century: The Breakup of AT&T* (Open Road Media, 2017), chap. 5 (noting that only the Justice Department "could seek such 'structural' relief in a lawsuit"; "in its own antitrust lawsuit," MCI "was entitled to pursue only monetary damages to compensate for revenues lost because of AT&T's behavior").

139 **Ma Bell:** Robert A. Burgelman, Andrew S. Grove, and Philip E. Meza, *Strategic Dynamics: Concepts and Cases* (Boston: McGraw-Hill, 2006), 472.

139 **its monopoly network:** "In the early 1900s," Steve Coll writes in *The Deal of the Century*, "AT&T had built its basic network monopoly through ruthless business practices that rivaled the tactics of such notorious nineteenth-century monopolists as John D. Rockefeller. When a rival company built a new local telephone exchange, AT&T would refuse to interconnect the exchange with its own network, and it would pressure the upstart company until it sold out to AT&T on favorable terms." Coll, *Deal of the Century*, chap. 5. After President

Woodrow Wilson hammered out a deal in 1919 known as the Kingsbury Commitment with AT&T's then chairman, Theodore Vail, the federal government left AT&T alone for decades. The giant telephone company basically became a regulated monopoly, much akin to a utility. Theodore Vail—the first president of AT&T—subordinated short-term profits and corporate dividends to the principle of "service first," and he was responsible for the motto "One policy, one system, and universal service." Theodore N. Vail, Telecommunications History Group, www.telcomhistory.org. At his death, *The New York Times* wrote glowingly in its obituary, "Mr. Vail was a genius, a great American, and if we venture to call him a Napoleon of communications the description will not be criticized as inappropriate." "Theodore Vail, Whose 'Folly' Is His Monument," *Literary Digest*, May 15, 1920, 76.

139 **computer industry:** AT&T attempted to lift this ban in 1981 but was met with opposition by the Department of Justice and others. "Justice, 11 Others in Opposition: Bell Attempt to Lift Consent Decree to Hit Court," *Computer World,* April 13, 1981. In 1982, as part of what became known as the Modification of Final Judgment, AT&T was allowed to enter the computer market, thus ending the prohibition put in place by the 1956 consent decree. David E. M. Sappington and Dennis L. Weisman, *Designing Incentive Regulation for the Telecommunications Industry* (Cambridge, Mass.: MIT Press, 1996), p. 41 and n46.

139 **James Roosevelt:** *Pipe Line News* 28 (1956): 54.

140 **until that restriction was lifted:** William Lazonick, *Sustainable Prosperity in the New Economy? Business Organization and High-Tech Employment in the United States* (Kalamazoo, Mich.: W. E. Upjohn Institute for Employment Research, 2009), 99 ("The 1982 modification of the 1956 consent decree that underlay the breakup of the Bell System . . . left AT&T free to enter the computer industry. Toward that end, in a 1991 $7.4 billion hostile takeover, AT&T acquired NCR, a company that (as National Cash Register) itself dated back to 1884.").

140 **Judge Harold Greene:** William Yurcik, "Judge Harold H. Greene: A Pivotal Judicial Figure in Telecommunications Policy and His Legacy," ethw.org.

140 **Greene also played a key role in drafting:** Hearing before the Committee on the Judiciary, United States Senate, One Hundred Tenth Congress, First Session, September 5, 2007 (Washington, D.C.: U.S. Government Printing Office, 2009), 65 (noting that "Civil Rights Division lawyers, particularly Harold Greene," drafted "the initial proposal and language" included in the Voting Rights Act of 1965); Norman I. Silber, *With All Deliberate Speed: The Life of Philip Elman* (Ann Arbor: University of Michigan Press, 2004) (noting of Harold Greene, "Born in Germany, Greene escaped from the Nazis and reached the United States in 1943. He then joined U.S. Army Intelligence and went back to fight in Germany. Graduating after the War at the top of his night law school class, he joined the Justice Department and rose to become chief of the Appellate Section of the Civil Rights Division. Greene played a major role in the drafting of the Civil Rights Act of 1964 and the Voting Rights Act of 1965."); Steve Coll, *The Deal of the Century*, chap. 12 (observing of Harold Greene's relationship with Attorney General Robert Kennedy, "Working closely with Kennedy, Greene wrote the Civil Rights Act of 1964

and the Voting Rights Act of 1965, arguably the two most important pieces of legislation passed by Congress in twenty years. When Kennedy made his only appearance before the U.S. Supreme Court to argue a civil rights case, Greene was there with him, helping to put the finishing touches on the argument. As Kennedy himself put it at Greene's Justice department going-away party, 'Harold was the guy who had the answers.' ").

140 **independently owned:** Peter Humphreys and Seamus Simpson, *Globalisation, Convergence, and European Telecommunications Regulation* (Cheltenham, U.K.: Elgar, 2005), 26.

141 **Alexander Graham Bell said:** Steven Shepard, preface to *Telecom Crash Course: Wi-Fi and Wi-MAX Digital Wireless Softswitch CDMA vs. GSM*, 2nd ed. (New York: McGraw-Hill/Osborne, 2005).

141 **Irwin Hirsh:** Philip L. Cantelon, *The History of MCI, 1968–1988: The Early Years* (Dallas: Heritage Press, 1993), 107.

141 **telecommunications law practice:** Amy Klobuchar, *The Senator Next Door: A Memoir from the Heartland* (New York: Henry Holt, 2015), 105.

141 **When Congress passed:** Telecommunications Act of 1996, www.fcc.gov.

142 **one million employees:** Charles Heckscher et al., *Agents of Change: Crossing the Post-Industrial Divide* (Oxford: Oxford University Press, 2003), 13.

142 **the decision to break up AT&T:** OECD, *Supporting Investment in Knowledge Capital, Growth, and Innovation* (Paris: OECD, 2013), 161.

142 **the facts don't lie:** Wu, *Curse of Bigness*, 96–97 (noting of the breakup of AT&T, "Some economists point to lower prices in the wake of the dissolution, but the real impact was different and far more important. It became apparent, in retrospect, just how much innovation the Bell system monopoly had been holding back. For out of the carcass of AT&T emerged entirely new types of industries unimagined or unimaginable during the reign of AT&T.").

142 **As one account notes:** John M. Jordan, *Information, Technology, and Innovation: Resources for Growth in a Connected World* (Hoboken, N.J.: John Wiley & Sons, 2012), 173.

142 **AT&T's forced restructuring:** Steven F. Hayward, *The Age of Reagan: The Conservative Counterrevolution, 1980–1989* (New York: Three Rivers Press, 2009), 216; Barry G. Cole, ed., *After the Breakup: Assessing the New Post-AT&T Divestiture Era* (New York: Columbia University Press, 1991), 6.

143 **Caspar Weinberger:** Cole, *After the Breakup*, 6.

143 **extensive delay:** Leslie A. Pal and R. Kent Weaver, eds., *The Government Taketh Away: The Politics of Pain in the United States and Canada* (Washington, D.C.: Georgetown University Press, 2003), 125 ("Pressured by senior White House personnel and officials from other departments, Baxter agreed to join with AT&T to ask the presiding judge to suspend the court case for approximately one year to see if a legislative solution could be developed.").

143 **In the end:** Cole, *After the Breakup*, 5–6; see also Sappington and Weisman, *Designing Incentive Regulation for the Telecommunications Industry*, 39 ("Commerce Secretary Malcolm Baldrige supported Weinberger's position. President Reagan expressed no clear opinion on the merits of pursuing the case. For political reasons, the administration was reluctant to order Mr. Baxter to drop the case, and he ignored more gentle suggestions to do so.").

143 **recuse himself from the case:** Jim Patterson, "The Sunday Brief: Chronicling AT&T's Divestiture," *RCR Wireless News,* Jan. 2, 2020, www.rcrwireless .com.

143 **put together the deal to break up AT&T:** Barbara Rosewicz, "The Justice Department Under the Direction of Attorney General . . . ," UPI, Jan. 22, 1984, www.upi.com; Caroline E. Mayer, "Government Trying to Settle Antitrust Suit Against AT&T," *Washington Post,* Jan. 1, 1982, www.washingtonpost .com (noting that "the talks were being conducted very privately, involving only a few high-ranking AT&T lawyers and William F. Baxter, the assistant attorney general in charge of the antitrust division, and two of his top aides," and that "Justice Department lawyers who have been trying the case in court and who were involved in previous negotiations during the Carter administration have been left out of the current round of talks").

143 **As one source:** Dick W. Olufs III, *The Making of Telecommunications Policy* (Boulder, Colo.: Lynne Rienner, 1999), 55.

144 **as one Federal Trade Commission representative:** David A. Balto, "Antitrust Enforcement in the Clinton Administration," 9 *Cornell Journal of Law and Public Policy* 61, 62–63 (1999).

144 **"The broad bipartisan consensus":** Marc Allen Eisner, *Antitrust and the Triumph of Economics: Institutions, Expertise, and Policy Change* (Chapel Hill: University of North Carolina Press, 1987).

144 **In what has been called:** Sweeney, *The Internationalisation of Competition Rules,* 90n66.

144 **price-fixing agreements:** Toward the end of the Reagan administration, one federal judge—to the surprise of both the government and the corporate defendant—sentenced the Allegheny Bottling Company to three years' imprisonment (and to pay a $1 million fine) in a price-fixing scheme involving the soft drink industry. Jonathan P. Hicks, "Corporate Prison Term for Allegheny Bottling," *New York Times,* Sept. 1, 1988; see also Sharon Warren Walsh, "Bottling Firm Is Sentenced in Conspiracy," *Washington Post,* Sept. 1, 1988 ("In a corporate sentencing called 'wild' and 'unprecedented' by some legal experts, U.S. District Judge Robert G. Doumar has imposed a prison term and a $1 million fine on the Allegheny Bottling Co. because its previous owners engaged in a price-fixing conspiracy. Doumar ordered a three-year prison term for Allegheny, saying he could send a U.S. marshal to padlock the plant's doors, but then suspended the sentence on the condition that four executives of the Pepsi-Cola bottler perform a total of six years of community service. . . . Even Justice Department attorneys who prosecuted the case seemed nonplused by the sentence. 'Certainly it was not expected,' said David C. Jordan, the government's lead attorney in the case.").

144 **Merger Guidelines:** American Bar Association, Antitrust Law Section, *Mergers and Acquisitions: Understanding the Antitrust Issues,* 3rd ed. (Chicago: ABA, Antitrust Law Section, 2008), 19; Victor J. Tremblay and Carol Horton Tremblay, *The U.S. Brewing Industry: Data and Economic Analysis* (Cambridge, Mass.: MIT Press, 2005), 245.

145 **One antitrust commentator:** Thomas E. Kauper, "The 1982 Horizontal Merger Guidelines: Of Collusion, Efficiency, and Failure," 71 *California Law Review* 497, 498–99 (1983).

145 **another antitrust scholar wrote:** Eisner, *Antitrust and the Triumph of Economics.*

145 **From 1982 to 1987:** Brent W. Huber, "Target Corporations, Hostile Horizontal Takeovers, and Antitrust Injury Under Section 16 of the Clayton Act After *Cargill*," 66 *Indiana Law Journal* 625, 647n141 (1991).

145 **dropped an antitrust case:** Irvin B. Tucker, *Microeconomics for Today,* 7th ed. (Mason, Ohio: South-Western Cengage Learning, 2011), 355.

145 **James Stewart:** James B. Stewart, "Whales and Sharks," *New Yorker,* Feb. 15, 1993, 37–43; "Here's What Apple, Facebook and Other Big Tech Investors Can Learn from IBM's Antitrust Ordeal," Morningstar, July 1, 2019, news.morningstar.com.

146 **the birth of Apple:** James Ciment, ed., *Postwar America: An Encyclopedia of Social, Political, Cultural, and Economic History* (London: Routledge, 2015), 270.

146 **The court case:** Mark V. Siegler, *An Economic History of the United States: Connecting the Present with the Past* (London: Palgrave, 2017), 357.

146 **Microsoft:** Eric G. Flamholtz and Yvonne Randle, *Growing Pains: Building Sustainably Successful Organizations,* 5th ed. (Hoboken, N.J.: Wiley, 2016), 256; see also Andrew I. Gavil and Harry First, *The Microsoft Antitrust Cases: Competition Policy for the Twenty-First Century* (Cambridge, Mass.: MIT Press, 2014), 1 ("Microsoft Corporation's origins are legendary in the world of technology firms. Microsoft was founded in 1975 by Bill Gates and Paul Allen. Its most significant early product breakthrough came in the early 1980s, when it spearheaded the development of the first operating system for the IBM PC: the Microsoft disk operating system (MS-DOS). Late in 1985, building on the success of MS-DOS, Microsoft launched the first version of Windows.").

146 **the modern, personal computing age:** Wu, *Curse of Bigness,* 112.

146 **a history of the FTC's Bureau of Economics:** James Langenfeld and Edwin Galeano, eds., *Healthcare Antitrust, Settlements, and the Federal Trade Commission* (Bingley, U.K.: Emerald, 2018), 28:253.

146 **Caspar Weinberger:** Study on Federal Regulation: Prepared Pursuant to S. Res. 71 to Authorize a Study of the Purpose and Current Effectiveness of Certain Federal Agencies, Committee on Government Operations, United States Senate (Washington, D.C.: U.S. Government Printing Office, 1977), 1:210 ("The Senate confirmed Weinberger on November 19, 1969, but because of previous commitments in California, he did not assume the duties of Chairman until January 13, 1970."); Paul A. Pautler, "A History of the FTC's Bureau of Economics," American Antitrust Institute, AAI Working Paper No. 15–03 (Sept. 8, 2015), 34n144 ("Caspar Weinberger, FTC Chairman, suggested in his 1969 Congressional testimony that the business line data would be useful.").

147 **Its first survey forms:** *1975 Food Price Study,* U.S. Senate, Select Committee on Nutrition and Human Needs (Washington, D.C.: U.S. Government Printing Office, 1975), 180.

147 **FTC's inquiries were criticized:** American Bar Association, Antitrust Law Section, *The FTC as an Antitrust Enforcement Agency: Its Structure, Powers, and Procedures* (1981), 2:102.

147 **Court challenges ensued:** Ibid., 84, 99, 102 (citing *FTC Line of Business Report Litigation,* 595 F.2d 685 (D.C. Cir.), *cert. denied,* 439 U.S. 958 (1978)).

147 **FTC released reports:** Ibid., 9.

147 **one source emphasizes:** Eisner, *Antitrust and the Triumph of Economics* (section on FTC).

147 **line-of-business data collection program:** Oliver Grawe, "Populism, Economists, and the FTC," Antitrust Source, April 2017, n12, www.americanbar.org.

148 **"young liberals did not perceive":** Matt Stoller, "How Democrats Killed Their Populist Soul," *Atlantic,* Oct. 24, 2016, www.theatlantic.com. In 2019, Matt Stoller published an entire book, *Goliath: The 100-Year War Between Monopoly Power and Democracy* (New York: Simon & Schuster, 2019), which builds on his *Atlantic* article and explains how we arrived at the perilous place in which we now find ourselves.

148 **Congress and the president deregulated:** "A History of US Airline Deregulation," Travel Insider, old.thetravelinsider.info; Robert E. Litan, *Trillion Dollar Economists: How Economists and Their Ideas Have Transformed Business* (Hoboken, N.J.: John Wiley & Sons), 185–206 (discussing airline, trucking, and railroad deregulation); Charles W. Calomiris, *U.S. Bank Deregulation in Historical Perspective* (Cambridge, U.K.: Cambridge University Press, 2000), xiv (offering a description of the forces that led to the deregulation of the American banking system in the 1980s).

148 **trickle-down economics:** Joseph E. Stiglitz, *People, Power, and Profits: Progressive Capitalism for an Age of Discontent* (New York: W. W. Norton, 2019), xxv, 38, 82–83.

148 **Senator Howard Metzenbaum:** Eisner, *Antitrust and the Triumph of Economics,* chap. 1.

148 **The Reagan administration's policies:** In his introduction to *How the Chicago School Overshot the Mark,* antitrust expert Robert Pitofsky writes of the shift in approach that occurred in the Reagan era. "Antitrust," Pitofsky explains of its long, storied history in American life, "had been fueled by a general popular mistrust of Big Business and a desire to divide, diffuse, and control economic power for political reasons." "But now a band of economists and economically trained lawyers and academics," Pitofsky observed, pointing to the work of Robert Bork and Richard Posner, "began to challenge that premise." As Pitofsky declared of such economists, lawyers, and academics, "Their approach was to examine business behavior from a purely economic point of view and to exclude from consideration any political or social values—for example, protection of small business for the sake of social values inherent in smallness—and place their faith in an automatic beneficial free market system. Considerations of noneconomic factors—for example, concern that a wave of mergers among television outlets or book publishers—might have adverse effects on opportunities for free speech were dismissed as vague and therefore irrelevant." Robert Pitofsky, ed., *How the Chicago School Overshot the Mark: The Effect of Conservative Economic Analysis on U.S. Antitrust* (Oxford: Oxford University Press, 2008), 4–5.

148 **As one commentator notes:** Broder, *U.S. Antitrust Law and Enforcement,* 9.

149 **first economist:** Fred S. McChesney, "Consumer Protection and James Miller at the Federal Trade Commission," in *The Regulatory Revolution at the FTC: A Thirty-Year Perspective on Competition and Consumer Protec-*

tion, ed. James Campbell Cooper (Oxford: Oxford University Press, 2013), 71, 73.

149 **fewer people were talking about monopolies:** Stacy Mitchell, "The Rise and Fall of the Word 'Monopoly' in American Life," *Atlantic,* June 20, 2017, www .theatlantic.com.

149 **"lawyers and economists":** Harry First and Spencer Weber Waller, "Antitrust's Democracy Deficit," 81 *Fordham Law Review* 2543 (2013) ("Critics of lax antitrust enforcement have long bemoaned the slide of antitrust into political irrelevance. Richard Hofstadter famously sounded the theme nearly fifty years ago. Pointing out that the political impulses animating antitrust in its first half century had faded as the United States became comfortable with big business, he argued that postwar enforcers had transformed antitrust into a technical exercise managed by lawyers and economists: '[O]nce the United States had an antitrust movement without antitrust prosecutions; in our time there have been antitrust prosecutions without an antitrust movement.'"); ibid., 2544 ("The shift that Hofstadter first described has led to an antitrust system captured by laws and economists advancing their own self-referential goals. . . . We characterize the result of this shift toward technocracy as antitrust's democracy deficit.").

149 **the party's platform:** Matt Stoller, "The Return of Monopoly," *New Republic,* July 13, 2017, newrepublic.com; Stoller, "How Democrats Killed Their Populist Soul"; see also Daniel A. Crane, "Technocracy and Antitrust," 86 *Texas Law Review* 1159 (2008) (noting that the Democratic Party's 1988 platform made "only two curt references to antitrust" and that "antitrust dropped out completely of the 1992, 1996, 2000, and 2004 Democratic platforms"); Stoller, *Goliath,* 417 (noting of the Democratic Party's 1992 platform that "for the first time since 1880 there was no mention of antitrust or corporate power" in it).

149 **Democratic Leadership Council:** For a discussion of the history of the Democratic Leadership Council, a nonprofit 501(c)(4) formed in 1985 and disbanded in 2011, see Curtis Atkins, "Forging a New Democratic Party: The Politics of the Third Way from Clinton to Obama" (PhD thesis, York University, 2015), 133–36, yorkspace.library.yorku.ca; see also Samuel L. Popkin, *The Candidate: What It Takes to Win—and Hold—the White House* (Oxford: Oxford University Press, 2012), 184–85 (discussing the Democratic Leadership Council).

149 **"The last significant mention":** Daniel A. Crane, *The Institutional Structure of Antitrust Enforcement* (Oxford: Oxford University Press, 2011), 77.

149 **2016 platform:** Stacy Mitchell, "After Three Decades of Neglect, Antitrust Is Back on the Democratic Platform," Institute for Local Self-Reliance, Aug. 4, 2016, ilsr.org ("For the first time in 28 years, the Democratic Party platform calls for vigorous, stepped-up enforcement of our anti-monopoly laws. 'Large corporations have concentrated their control over markets to a greater degree than Americans have seen in decades,' the platform reads. It defines concentrated corporate power as more than an economic problem, calling it 'corrosive to a healthy democracy,' and declares that Democrats 'will make competition policy and antitrust stronger and more responsive.'").

149 **Anne Bingaman:** Stephen Labaton, "Profile: Anne K. Bingaman; Rousing Antitrust Law from Its 12-Year Nap," *New York Times,* July 25, 1993, www .nytimes.com; Anne K. Bingaman, "Antitrust Enforcement, Some Initial

Thoughts and Actions" (address, U.S. Department of Justice, Aug. 10, 1993), www.justice.gov.

149 **as one source puts it:** Lee B. Burgunder, *Legal Aspects of Managing Technology,* 5th ed. (Mason, Ohio: South-Western Cengage Learning, 2011), 530.

150 **profile of Anne Bingaman:** Labaton, "Profile: Anne K. Bingaman."

150 **more activist approach:** "By the late 1990s," litigator Douglas Broder wrote, "antitrust enforcement had staged a strong comeback, although the amount of antitrust litigation, both government and private, did not approach the level of the late 1970s." Broder, *U.S. Antitrust Law and Enforcement,* 11.

150 **criminal antitrust enforcement:** Anne K. Bingaman (assistant attorney general, Antitrust Division), "The Clinton Administration: Trends in Criminal Antitrust Enforcement," Nov. 30, 1995, www.justice.gov.

150 **"is handling U.S. antitrust cases":** Stephen Labaton, "When It Comes to Antitrust, Washington Is Antibust," *New York Times,* May 5, 2006, www.nytimes .com. Taking note of the news of the day, Labaton wrote, "When the Justice Department cleared Whirlpool's $1.7 billion acquisition of the rival appliance maker Maytag a few weeks ago, the decision demoralized the career ranks of the department's antitrust division, officials there have said." "The Whirlpool deal," Labaton emphasized, "would create an entity with a dominating share of the marketplace, controlling about three-quarters of the American market for some home appliances." "They don't even seem to think that monopolies are bad," Albert Foer, the president of the American Antitrust Institute, complained, further lamenting of the views of Bush administration officials, "Big is efficient and efficient is good. This is a story about how ideology has taken over the law enforcement process."

150 **Other academics:** Eugène Buttigieg, *Competition Law: Safeguarding the Consumer Interest: A Comparative Analysis of US Antitrust Law and EC Competition Law* (Alphen on the Rhine, the Netherlands: Kluwer Law International, 2009), 44n94.

150 **antitrust case against Microsoft Corporation:** William H. Page and John E. Lopatka, *The Microsoft Case: Antitrust, High Technology, and Consumer Welfare* (Chicago: University of Chicago Press, 2007), ix–x; Gavil and First, *The Microsoft Antitrust Cases,* 331–35.

150 **a series of antitrust lawsuits:** James W. Cortada, *IBM: The Rise and Fall and Reinvention of a Global Icon* (Cambridge, Mass.: MIT Press, 2019), 334; William E. Kovacic, "Failed Expectations: The Troubled Past and Uncertain Future of the Sherman Act as a Tool for Deconcentration," 75 *Iowa Law Review* 1105, 1109 (1989); "U.S. vs. I.B.M.," *New York Times,* Feb. 15, 1981.

151 **seven judges:** "Microsoft, Government Agree on Appeal Arguments," CNET, Jan. 11, 2002, www.cnet.com (noting that oral argument before the D.C. Circuit was to be heard by Chief Judge Harry Edwards and by six other appellate judges, Douglas Ginsburg, Raymond Randolph, Judith Rogers, David Sentelle, David Tatel, and Stephen Williams).

151 **a unanimous 2001 per curiam opinion:** *United States v. Microsoft Corp.,* 253 F.3d 34 (D.C. Cir. 2001).

151 **Microsoft Corporation:** Ibid.

151 **until the George W. Bush administration ended the case:** "U.S. v. Microsoft: Timeline," *Wired,* Nov. 4, 2002, www.wired.com. Even before the 2000 presi-

dential election, George W. Bush and his allies had strongly suggested that his administration would side with Microsoft in its antitrust dispute with the government. James V. Grimaldi, "Bush Tries to Clarify Remarks on Microsoft," *Washington Post*, March 3, 2000, E1. Indeed, Microsoft sought to delay the resolution of the antitrust dispute until the 2000 election was decided. Mark Tran, "Microsoft Tries to Delay Breakup Order," June 8, 2000, *Guardian*, www.theguardian.com ("Analysts said Microsoft has decided to fight on despite a series of legal defeats in the hope that George W. Bush will win the presidential election in November. The Republican presidential candidate is considered to be more friendly towards Microsoft than vice-president Al Gore, his Democratic rival.").

152 **videotaped testimony:** Michael B. Becraft, *Bill Gates: A Biography* (Santa Barbara, Calif.: Greenwood, 2014), 87–88; *InfoWorld*, April 10, 2000, 20.

152 **Gates testified:** Victor J. Tremblay and Carol Horton Tremblay, *Industry and Firm Studies,* 4th ed. (Armonk, N.Y.: M. E. Sharpe, 2007), 308.

152 **The deposition:** "The Man Who Ate Microsoft," *Vanity Fair,* March 2000, www.vanityfair.com; James V. Grimaldi, "Microsoft Trial—the Gates Deposition: 684 Pages of Conflict," *Seattle Times,* March 16, 1999, archive.seattletimes.com; see also James F. Haggerty, *In the Court of Public Opinion: Winning Your Case with Public Relations* (Hoboken, N.J.: John Wiley & Sons, 2003), 188 (describing the deposition of Bill Gates in the antitrust case against Microsoft).

152 **a paid legal consultant:** "Robert Bork Issues Lengthy New Attack on Microsoft," www.zdnet.com.

152 **After Bork unexpectedly weighed in:** "Judge Bork: Break Up Microsoft," Reuters, Jan. 15, 1999, www.wired.com.

153 **"My own opinion":** A Reuters story reported of Bork's speech suggesting that Microsoft be broken up into three separate entities, "Asked if the company which got Microsoft chief Bill Gates would have an unfair advantage, Bork first joked that the solution was 'human cloning.'" Bork then offered a more serious answer: "I'd be willing to take the chance that Bill Gates couldn't run the other two companies out of business." Microsoft's spokesman, Mark Murray, countered that Bork was "entitled to his opinion, but it's completely inappropriate for anyone to be talking about potential court actions before Microsoft has even had the chance to present its case."

153 **representing Netscape:** Harry First, "Bork and *Microsoft:* Why Bork Was Right and What We Learn About Judging Exclusionary Behavior," 79 *Antitrust Law Journal* 1017, 1019, 1028–30, 1036–38 (2014) (noting that "Robert Bork nearly killed antitrust," but that Bork came "to support an aggressive monopolization suit against a leading high-technology firm" and wrote in a May 4, 1998, op-ed in *The New York Times* that Microsoft, with a market share "at 90 to 95 percent," "specifically intended to crush competition" through anticompetitive practices and, in particular, "intended to preserve the company's monopoly of personal computer operating systems through practices that exclude or severely hinder rivals but do not benefit consumers"; further noting that when attacked by critics, Bork responded, "I'm no Netscape shill," argued in *National Review* that "the advantages to a structural remedy should not be overlooked by freemarket advocates," and submitted an amicus brief

on behalf of AOL and pro-Netscape industry players after Microsoft appealed Judge Jackson's findings to the D.C. Circuit).

153 **As the legal dispute dragged on:** Ken Auletta, *World War 3.0: Microsoft and Its Enemies* (New York: Random House, 2001) (giving a chronology of relevant events).

153 **the D.C. Circuit:** In a stinging rebuke, the D.C. Circuit also took issue with Judge Jackson's communications with the press about the high-profile case. Judge Jackson had done multiple interviews about the case, and he had given speeches at a college and at an antitrust seminar. In his conversations with reporters, he had discussed numerous aspects of the case, including his personal and strongly held views about Microsoft's conduct and the credibility of the company's witnesses. Citing the Code of Conduct, which prohibits federal judges from commenting publicly on the merits of a pending action, the D.C. Circuit found that Judge Jackson had "breached his ethical duty" in speaking to reporters. Because of his press contacts and his "crude characterizations of Microsoft" and its CEO, the D.C. Circuit Court ruled that "the line has been crossed" and that "the District Judge's interviews with reporters created an appearance that he was not acting impartially."

153 **chose to settle the case:** "The settlement," one commentator, David Singh Grewal, writes in his book, *Network Power,* "demanded very little of a company that had been facing a radical restructuring just two years earlier." As Grewal explains, "Microsoft was not broken up, or obliged to open its code to competitors; it simply had to release some technical data to allow other software companies to write programs for Windows, and it promised to refrain from retaliating against computer manufacturers that use rival products. For Microsoft's rivals, these promises amounted to very little, and several parties continued to press private lawsuits against the corporation." In fact, nine states and the District of Columbia refused to settle on those terms and continued to press separate cases against Microsoft. Microsoft's competitors—AOL Time Warner (which had purchased Netscape), Sun Microsystems, and others— also pressed for, and obtained, sizable monetary settlements. David Singh Grewal, *Network Power: The Social Dynamics of Globalization* (New Haven, Conn.: Yale University Press, 2008), 200.

154 **change of presidents:** Joel Klein, who served in President Bill Clinton's administration as the U.S. assistant attorney general in charge of the Antitrust Division, was eager to litigate the Microsoft case. "Where I think there is a case, I want to litigate," he said. But after the 2000 presidential election, the Justice Department under President George W. Bush's administration decided to settle the case without seeking a breakup of Microsoft. As Tim Wu explains, "It was a sign of things to come, for with that, the campaigns against monopoly and overconcentration were about to enter their deepest freeze since the time of William McKinley." Wu, *Curse of Bigness,* 98, 101.

154 **under the consent decree:** Sharon Pian Chan, "Long Antitrust Saga Ends for Microsoft," *Seattle Times,* May 11, 2011, www.seattletimes.com (noting that the Microsoft consent decree expired on May 12, 2011).

154 **It has been noted:** J. Barkley Rosser, Jr., and Marina V. Rosser, *Comparative Economics in a Transforming World Economy,* 2nd ed. (Cambridge, Mass: The MIT Press, 2004), 31.

154 **"While the Obama administration blocked":** Alan Neuhauser, "On Antitrust, Trump Signals a Return to the Bush Years," *U.S. News & World Report,* Dec. 9, 2016, www.usnews.com.

155 **a deal announced:** Stanley Joseph Konoval, "Amazon, or the Modern Prometheus: How the Kindle Is Firing Up a Reading Revolution, and Why the Status Quo Is Resisting," 33 *Journal of Law and Commerce* 119, 121 (2014) (discussing the deal combining Random House and Penguin).

155 **Obama administration's antitrust enforcement efforts:** William Baer and Philip J. Weiser, "Closing Fireside Chat with the Assistant Attorney General for the U.S. Department of Justice Antitrust Division," 15 *Colorado Technology Law Journal* 13, 21, 25 (2016); Statement on the Departure from the Justice Department of Principal Deputy Associate Attorney General Bill Baer, U.S. Department of Justice, Office of Public Affairs, Jan. 18, 2017, www.justice.gov.

155 **Senator Al Franken:** Tony Romm, "Franken Attacks Comcast Merger," *Politico,* April 11, 2014, www.politico.com.

156 **I co-chaired an antitrust hearing:** www.c-span.org/video/?419533-1/att-time -warner-ceos-testify-merger.

156 **proposed Comcast–Time Warner merger:** Hearing on Examining the Competitive Impact of the AT&T–Time Warner Transaction, Senate Committee on the Judiciary, Subcommittee on Antitrust, Competition Policy, and Consumer Rights, Dec. 7, 2016. At this hearing, I pointed out that whether an acquisition will harm consumers depends on factual investigation and careful analysis, not ideological presumptions. In expressing my concerns at the hearing, I emphasized, "AT&T's acquisition of Time Warner combines one of the world's largest wireless, cable (including satellite TV), and broadband providers with one of the world's largest media and entertainment companies."

156 **later called off:** Jacquie McNish and Laura Stevens, "Canadian Pacific Drops Efforts to Merge with Norfolk Southern," *Wall Street Journal,* April 11, 2016 ("Canadian Pacific Railway Ltd. abandoned its nearly $30 billion pursuit of Norfolk Southern Corp. on Monday after it was unable to overcome a wall of opposition from rival railroads, shippers and U.S. politicians warning the merger would diminish competition.").

156 **by only four Class I railroads:** Scott Mall, "FreightWaves Classics: The ICC and the Railroads," FreightWaves, Nov. 14, 2020, www.freightwaves.com ("What has occurred in the rail industry since the Staggers Act was passed? Consolidation—the number of major railroads dropped from about 40 in 1980 to four in 2013 because of consolidation. At this time, four railroads (BNSF Railway, CSX Transportation, Norfolk Southern Railway and Union Pacific Railroad) control over 90% of the rail traffic in the nation.").

156 **there were many acquisitions:** Through the years, dominant tech companies such as Facebook and Google have acquired numerous companies. Investigation of Competition in Digital Markets: Majority Staff Report and Recommendations, U.S. House of Representatives, Subcommittee on Antitrust, Commercial, and Administrative Law of the Committee on the Judiciary (2020), judiciary.house.gov, 149 ("Since its founding in 2004, Facebook has acquired at least 63 companies. The majority of these acquisitions have involved software firms, such as Instagram, WhatsApp, Face.com, Atlas, LiveWire, and Onavo. Facebook has also acquired several virtual reality and hardware com-

panies, such as Oculus. More recently, the company has acquired several niche social apps, a blockchain platform, Oculus game developers, and a prominent GIF-making and sharing company."); ibid., 174 ("In several markets, Google established its position through acquisition, buying up successful technologies that other businesses had developed. In a span of 20 years, Google purchased well over 260 companies—a figure that likely understates the full breadth of Google's acquisitions, given that many of the firm's purchases have gone unreported.").

157 **in a conversation with the *New York Times* opinion writer and journalist Kara Swisher:** "Was the Obama Administration Too Soft on Big Tech?," *New York Magazine*, May 20, 2020, nymag.com.

157 **September 22, 2015:** Health Insurance Industry Consolidation, www.c-span .org/video/?c4551922/savings&start=622.

158 **Trump administration did that:** Annie Gaus, "Trump Is Taking Antitrust 'Very Seriously'—What Does that Mean for Big Tech?," *Street,* Nov. 6, 2018, www.thestreet.com; Berkeley Lovelace Jr., "Trump Says Administration Is Looking into Antitrust Violations by Amazon, Other Tech Giants," CNBC, Nov. 5, 2018, www.cnbc.com; John D. Harkrider, "Antitrust in the Trump Administration: A Tough Enforcer That Believes in Limited Government," *Antitrust* 32, no. 3 (Summer 2018): 11–15. After the Trump administration's first year of antitrust activity, one legal commentator, John Harkrider, offered this assessment of its early antitrust efforts: "Looking at the first year of activity at the antitrust agencies under the Trump administration, it is hard to come up with support for the narrative that Republican antitrust enforcement is more lax or permissive than it is under Democratic administrations. . . . The Trump administration's antitrust enforcement appears to take a more hands-off approach to regulating business conduct, while still adhering to, and enforcing, evidence-based, economically sound antitrust law."

158 **a whole lot of chaos:** During the Trump administration, the FTC and the Justice Department squabbled, with David Balto—a former staffer at both agencies—calling the "disagreement" between the two bodies "unprecedented" and a "sign of government dysfunction at its worst." In 2019, it was reported that the FTC was handling antitrust complaints about Facebook and Amazon, while the Justice Department was dealing with those about Google and Apple. Emily Birnbaum, "Antitrust Enforcers in Turf War over Big Tech," *Hill,* Sept. 17, 2019, thehill.com. At one hearing, while Senator Josh Hawley, a conservative Republican from Missouri, expressed concern about the "turf wars" between the FTC and the Justice Department, a concern echoed by Senator Mike Lee of Utah, I expressed my own frustration in this way: "I am more concerned that consumers are going to get a big pie in their face if we don't do something about this. . . . The American people increasingly understand that competition is important for their well-being." Marcy Gordon, "Democrats Raise Political Influence Issue in Antitrust Probe," Associated Press, Sept. 17, 2019, www.apnews.com.

158 **Makan Delrahim:** Brent Kendall, "Top Antitrust Copy in Spotlight over Big Tech Inquiry," *Wall Street Journal,* July 7, 2019, www.wsj.com.

158 **major Department of Justice antitrust action:** Complaint, *United States of*

America v. Google LLC, Case 1:20-cv-03010 (filed October 20, 2020 in the U.S. District Court for the District of Columbia).

158 **a lack of joint action:** Leah Nylen, "Turbulence in Texas AG's Office to Delay Google Ad Suit," *Politico*, Oct. 23, 2020, www.politico.com (noting that a "coalition of almost every U.S. state has been probing Google since September 2019" but that "several state attorneys general, including many Democrats, opposed filing a suit so close to the election"). Another antitrust lawsuit was filed against Google in mid-December 2020 by thirty-five states, the District of Columbia, Guam, and Puerto Rico that alleges that Google illegally maintains monopoly power over search engine and advertising markets. Rebecca Klar and Chris Mills Rodrigo, "Google Hit with Another Antitrust Lawsuit by States," *Hill*, Dec. 17, 2020, thehill.com.

158 **the filing of the suit was in my mind a net positive:** Avery Hartmans, "Sen. Amy Klobuchar Calls Google's Defense of Its Search Dominance 'Offensive' and 'Defiant,'" *Business Insider*, Oct. 28, 2020, www.businessinsider.com.

158 **at a Commerce Committee hearing:** "Klobuchar Presses CEOs of Facebook and Google on Need to Combat Misinformation and Promote Industry Competition," press release, October 28, 2020 (containing a transcript of my questioning).

159 **action against Facebook:** Press Release, "FTC Sues Facebook for Illegal Monopolization," Federal Trade Commission, Dec. 9, 2020, www.ftc.gov.

159 **Judge Richard Leon:** Sara Salinas, "AT&T Wins: Judge Clears $85 Billion Bid for Time Warner with No Conditions," CNBC, June 12, 2018, www.cnbc.com.

159 **Justice Department appealed:** Hamza Shaban, "It's Not Looking Great for the Justice Department's Appeal of the AT&T–Time Warner Merger," *Washington Post*, Dec. 6, 2018.

159 **Justice Department argued:** Claire Atkinson, "AT&T and Justice Department Continue Battle over $85.4 Billion Time Warner Acquisition," NBC News, Dec. 6, 2018, www.nbcnews.com.

159 **AT&T, which owns DirecTV:** Wu, *Curse of Bigness*, 115 ("*The AT&T monopoly*, which had been forced to divide itself into 8 pieces, was allowed, over the 2000s, to reconstitute itself in two giant firms: Verizon and AT&T. Later, AT&T bought DirecTV and then TimeWarner to return close to its size in the 1980s.").

159 **the appellate court held:** David McLaughlin, Andrew M. Harris, and Scott Moritz, "AT&T Defeats U.S. Bid to Kill $85 Billion Time Warner Deal," Bloomberg, Feb. 26, 2019, www.bloomberg.com.

159 **refusal to challenge:** John Eggerton, "Klobuchar Slams FCC for T-Mobile-Sprint Merger Approval," *Multichannel News*, Oct. 16, 2019, www.multichannel.com; Matthew Yglesias, "Trump Is Approving an Anti-competitive Merger That Will Cost You Money," *Vox*, July 29, 2019, www.vox.com; John Kwoka Jr., "John Kwoka Unpacks Settlement in the Merger of Sprint and T-Mobile, Demonstrates Why the Remedy Is Ineffective and a Worrisome New Development in Merger Control," American Antitrust Institute, Aug. 21, 2019, www.antitrustinstitute.org.

160 **"Applying traditional metrics":** John M. Connor, "Comment on Cartel

Enforcement in the Trump Administration," Competition Policy International, June 2019, www.competitionpolicyinternational.com.

160 **"staffing in the antitrust division":** Kadhim Shubber, "Staffing at Antitrust Regulator Declines Under Donald Trump," *Financial Times,* Feb. 7, 2019, www.ft.com.

160 **the numbers don't lie:** "The State of Antitrust Enforcement and Competition Policy in the U.S.," American Antitrust Institute, April 14, 2020, 2–3 ("Antitrust enforcement is at a crossroads. The U.S. economy struggles with the cumulative effects of decades of under-enforcement *and* a step-down in current enforcement levels under the Trump administration. Despite its anti-corporate concentration rhetoric on the campaign trail, key metrics of cartel and merger enforcement have declined since the Trump administration took over. And in 2017 and 2018, the DOJ did not open one monopolization investigation, the longest span of inattention to dominant firms in the last 50 years."). The number of civil antitrust suits being brought has declined since the start of the Trump administration. "Civil Antitrust Litigation Continues to Decline," TRAC Reports, trac.syr.edu ("According to the case-by-case court records analyzed by the Transactional Records Access Clearinghouse (TRAC) at Syracuse University, there were just 357 antitrust suits for the first eight months of FY 2019. This is the third year such suits have declined under the Trump administration, down by about a third (32.4%) since FY 2016.").

160 **$164.7 million:** Antitrust Division (ATR), FY 2018 Budget Request at a Glance, www.justice.gov.

160 **fiscal year 2019 budget request:** Antitrust Division (ATR), FY 2019 Budget Request at a Glance, www.justice.gov.

161 **budget allocation:** "Appropriation Figures for the Antitrust Division," U.S. Department of Justice, www.justice.gov (listing appropriation figures for the Antitrust Division).

161 **in February 2020:** Leah Nylen, "DOJ Seeks 71 Percent Bump from Congress for Antitrust," *Politico,* Feb. 10, 2020, www.politico.com.

161 **Congress increased the budget:** Margaret Harding McGill and Ashley Gold, "Spending Bill Boosts Funding for Tech's Antitrust Cops," Axios, Dec. 21, 2020, www.axios.com.

161 **highly improper meddling:** Amy Klobuchar, "Klobuchar to Attorney General on AT&T/Time Warner Merger: 'Political Interference in Antitrust Enforcement Is Unacceptable," press release, July 7, 2017 ("In a letter sent to U.S. Attorney General Jeff Sessions, Klobuchar requested information on contacts between the White House and the Department of Justice regarding the pending merger between AT&T and Time Warner, a parent company of CNN. Klobuchar's effort followed a *New York Times* report that White House advisers have discussed the pending merger as a potential point of leverage against adversary CNN.").

161 **"The evidence continues":** Joe Nocera, "Cohn Didn't Have to Stop the AT&T–Time Warner Merger," Bloomberg, March 4, 2019, www.bloomberg.com.

161 **Eleanor Fox:** Ryan Goodman, "11 Top Antitrust Experts Alarmed by Whistleblower Complaint Against A.G. Barr—and Office of Professional Responsibility's Opinion," Just Security, June 26, 2020, www.justsecurity.org.

162 **hearing in September 2019:** Marcy Gordon, "Democrats Raise Political Influence Issue in Antitrust Probe," Associated Press, Sept. 17, 2019, www.apnews .com; see also "A Cruel Parody of Antitrust Enforcement," *New York Times,* Sept. 6, 2019, www.nytimes.com.

162 **automobile emissions standards:** Kevin Liptak and Gregory Wallace, "Trump Revokes Waiver for California to Set Higher Auto Emissions Standards," CNN, Sept. 18, 2019, www.cnn.com; Diane Bartz, "Top U.S. Antitrust Regulators Admit to Infighting on Big Tech Probe," Reuters, Sept. 17, 2019, www .reuters.com.

163 **a whistleblower:** Ben Remaly, "DOJ Whistleblower Says Agency Misused Investigative Powers," GCR, June 25, 2020, globalcompetitionreview.com.

163 **extremely hostile:** "Jeff Sessions's Endless War on Marijuana," *New York Times,* Jan. 7, 2018; Nina Godlewski, "Attorney General Barr Says He Would Favor Making Marijuana Illegal Across the United States," *Newsweek,* April 10, 2019, www.newsweek.com; see also Igor Derysh, "William Barr Inappropriately Targeted Marijuana Industry with Antitrust Probes: DOJ Whistleblower," *Salon,* June 24, 2020, www.salon.com.

163 **in a public letter:** Delrahim to Jerrold Nadler and Jim Jordan, July 1, 2020, 2, www.politico.com.

163 **he challenged the whistleblower's complaints:** Betsy Woodruff Swan, "Senior DOJ Official Pushes Back Against Former Top Aide's Testimony," *Politico,* July 1, 2020, www.politico.com.

163 **the day after:** Ryan Beene, "DOJ Blasted for Automaker Probe Following Angry Trump Tweets," *Automotive News,* June 24, 2020, www.autonews.com ("The memo opening the automaker investigation was dated Aug. 22, 2019, one day after Trump issued a series of tweets blasting executives for refusing to back the administration's August 2018 plan that called for capping efficiency requirements after 2020 and revoking California's authority to regulate vehicle greenhouse gas emissions to combat climate change.").

164 **an astonishing 29 percent:** Caroline Kelly, "DOJ Whistleblower to Testify That Barr's Personal Anti-marijuana Sentiment Fueled Cannabis Industry Investigations," CNN, June 23, 2020, www.cnn.com.

164 **highly politicized comments:** Hadas Gold, "AT&T Brings Trump Back into Justice Department's Antitrust Case," CNN, Sept. 20, 2018, money.cnn.com; see also Tom Campbell, "Is the Trump Administration Using Antitrust Laws to Go After CNN?," *Press-Enterprise,* Nov. 13, 2017, www.pe.com ("If CNN were divested, it would have neither AT&T nor Time Warner as a wealthy parent. Companies ordered to be divested in antitrust proceedings often go for fire sale prices, and sometimes don't survive under a new and less well resourced parent. . . . In the campaign, candidate Trump publicly announced that he might, as president, direct antitrust scrutiny against those who criticized him. Trump attacked Jeff Bezos, who both owns the *Washington Post* and runs Amazon. After unfavorable coverage from the *Post,* Trump speculated about going after Bezos under the antitrust laws, because of Amazon's 'monopolistic tendencies that have led to the destruction of department stores and the retail industry.'"). At a meeting in January 2017 with then president-elect Trump, the CEOs of Bayer and Monsanto discussed their $66 billion merger, which was at the time under DOJ review. Brandon Moseley, "What

Will Trump Decide About Proposed Super Merger of Bayer and Monsanto?," *Alabama Political Reporter,* Jan. 25, 2018, www.alreporter.com.

164 **reportedly told:** Tom Porter, "Trump Tried to Block the $85 Billion AT&T–Time Warner Merger to Spite CNN, According to a Scathing New Profile of His Cozy Relationship with Fox News," *Business Insider,* March 4, 2019, www.businessinsider.com. *The New Yorker* reported that "in the late summer of 2017, a few months before the Justice Department filed suit" to stop AT&T's acquisition of Time Warner, "Trump ordered Gary Cohn, then the director of the National Economic Council, to pressure the Justice Department to intervene." "The President does not understand the nuances of antitrust law or policy," one former official blandly, if accurately, observed before emphasizing, "But he wanted to bring down the hammer." Jane Mayer, "The Making of the Fox News White House," *New Yorker,* March 11, 2019, www.newyorker.com.

164 **personal dislike:** President Trump, like President Nixon before him, attempted to interfere in an arena that should be driven by antitrust law and sound, objective policy making. Campbell, "Is the Trump Administration Using Antitrust Laws to Go After CNN?"; Ciara Torres-Spelliscy, "The I.T.T. Affair and Why Public Financing Matters for Political Conventions," Brennan Center for Justice, March 19, 2014, www.brennancenter.org (describing how President Nixon directed a deputy attorney general, Richard Kleindienst, to "stay the hell out" of "the I.T.T. thing"—a reference to the International Telephone and Telegraph Corporation, which pledged $400,000 to the Republican National Convention in exchange for a Justice Department antitrust settlement, with ITT also needing Justice Department approval for a merger); E. W. Kenworthy, "The Extraordinary I.T.T. Affair," *New York Times,* Dec. 16, 1973 ("It was April, 1971. Richard G. Kleindienst was Deputy Attorney General. The Government had three antitrust suits going against the International Telephone and Telegraph Corporation. And President Nixon ordered Mr. Kleindienst not to appeal one of the suits to the Supreme Court. . . . [T]op I.T.T. and Administration officials met repeatedly in secret in 1970 and 1971 on the antitrust suits and on a consent agreement; and that, while these negotiations were going on, I.T.T. pledged $400,000 for the 1972 Republican convention then scheduled for San Diego."). Google controls more than 90 percent of internet search traffic globally. Hayley Tsukayama, "Alphabet Shares Soar Despite Hit to Profit from Google's European Union Fine," *Washington Post,* July 23, 2018, www.washingtonpost.com; see also PCMag Staff, "Google Is Still the Search King, but Keep an Eye on Amazon," *PCMag,* June 5, 2018, www.pcmag.com ("Google controls over 90 percent of the search market, with 63 percent coming from its traditional search textbox and 23 percent coming from Google image search, according to VisualCapitalist.com."); Owen Williams, "Google Is Tightening Its Grip on Your Website," Medium, Aug. 20, 2019, onezero.medium.com ("Google is by far the dominant search engine, with 92% market share worldwide and 94.5% on mobile."). The European Union took a more aggressive antitrust stance than U.S. regulators, with European antitrust officials imposing a $5 billion fine on Google for marketing its own apps in an allegedly anticompetitive manner. Jillian D'Onfro, "Google's $5 Billion Fine: What You Need to Know," CNBC, July 18, 2018, www.cnbc.com. In October 2020, the U.S. Department of Justice—along

with eleven state attorneys general—did bring a civil antitrust suit against Google for violating the nation's antitrust laws. "Justice Department Sues Monopolist Google for Violating Antitrust Laws," U.S. Department of Justice, Office of Public Affairs, press release, October 20, 2020, www.justice .gov (noting that the lawsuit sought "to stop Google from unlawfully maintaining monopolies through anticompetitive and exclusionary practices in the search and search advertising markets and to remedy the competitive harms").

164 **the New Jersey Generals:** Paul Reeths, *The United States Football League, 1982–1986* (Jefferson, N.C.: McFarland, 2017), 148–49; Jeff Pearlman, "When Trump Made the U.S.F.L. Great Again," *New York Times,* Oct. 9, 2018, www .nytimes.com.

164 **brought antitrust claims in 1984:** The USFL's thirty-nine-page complaint, filed in 1984, had been signed by two USFL lawyers, one of whom, the later disbarred Roy Cohn, once served as counsel for Senator Joseph McCarthy. Gary Pomerantz and John Kennedy, "USFL Is Awarded $1 in Suit Against NFL," *Washington Post,* July 30, 1986, www.washingtonpost.com. After a 1986 trial in U.S. District Court in New York in which the USFL charged that the NFL had willfully acquired and maintained monopoly power and in which the USFL sought $1.69 billion in damages, the NFL was found to have violated the law. One of the other issues at the trial involved lucrative NFL television contracts with ABC, CBS, and NBC. The jury, however, was not impressed with the USFL's case or with Donald Trump's testimony. Roger D. Blair, *Sports Economics* (Cambridge, U.K.: Cambridge University Press, 2012), 190. With Rozelle denying that he had ever offered Trump an NFL franchise, the jury awarded only nominal damages on the USFL's claims.

164 **just $1 in damages:** Pomerantz and Kennedy, "USFL Is Awarded $1 in Suit Against NFL."

164 **USFL's bankruptcy:** Brendan J. Sweeney, *The Internationalisation of Competition Rules: The Approach of European States* (New York: Routledge, 2010), 90n66.

164 **founded in 1982:** *Football Rising to the Challenge: The Transition from College to Pro,* ed. Geoffrey R. Scott (Sudbury, Mass.: Jones and Bartlett Publishers, 2006), 34n13 (noting that the United States Football League "was formed in 1982 and debuted in 1983"; that in July 1986 "a U.S. district court in New York found in favor of the USFL and awarded the league $1 in damages"; that the USFL "failed prior to the fall season" and "was $160 million in debt at the time"; and that the district court's decision "was affirmed by the Second Circuit Court of Appeals in 1988").

164 **David Dixon:** David Z. Morris, "Donald Trump Fought the NFL Once Before. He Got Crushed," *Fortune,* Sept. 24, 2017, fortune.com.

164 **Trump got involved:** Jacob Pramuk, "How Trump's Time Running a Doomed Football Team Fueled His Political Fight with the NFL," CNBC, Sept. 16, 2018, www.cnbc.com.

164 **high-profile players:** Arash Markazi, "5 Things to Know About Donald Trump's Foray into Doomed USFL," ESPN, July 14, 2015, www.espn.com.

165 **an NFL team:** Through the years, Donald Trump has been involved in multiple attempts to purchase an NFL team. Michael McCann, "Donald Trump

Allegedly Falsified Finance Records in Buffalo Bills Bid. Could President Face Legal Action?," *Sports Illustrated*, March 1, 2019, www.si.com.

165 **unsuccessfully attempted to buy:** John Hartley, "Donald Trump's History of Failed Sports Ventures," *That One Sports Show,* Jan. 16, 2018, thatonesports show.com; see also "Irsay Turns Down $50M Bid for Baltimore Colts," *Hazleton Standard-Speaker,* July 14, 1981, 11 (noting that Robert Irsay, the owner of the Baltimore Colts, rejected a $50 million bid for his NFL team made by "a six-member syndicate headed by New York real estate tycoon Donald Trump"); compare Cameron C. Snyder, "Colts Cut Ben Garry, Will Sign Randy McMillan Today," *The Baltimore Sun,* July 14, 1981, 29 (noting that "Robert Irsay says he has rejected a $50-million offer from a New York real-estate man" and that a news story in *The Evening Sun* from the day before "said the bidder was Donald Trump, who says he talked to Irsay but did not make an offer").

165 **according to one account:** Jeff Pearlman, *Football for a Buck: The Crazy Rise and Crazier Demise of the USFL* (Boston: Houghton Mifflin Harcourt, 2018), 182.

165 **the 1986 antitrust trial:** Reeths, *United States Football League,* 350–66; Pearlman, *Football for a Buck,* 182.

165 **the USFL's lawsuit seeking $1.69 billion:** Pomerantz and Kennedy, "USFL Is Awarded $1 in Suit Against NFL."

165 **Rozelle vehemently denied:** Pearlman, *Football for a Buck,* 304.

165 **one of the NFL's lawyers:** Richard Hoffer, "USFL Awarded Only $3 in Antitrust Decision: Jury Finds NFL Guilty on One of Nine Counts," *Los Angeles Times,* July 30, 1986, www.latimes.com ("Rothman characterized Trump, a wealthy New York builder, as the worst kind of snake who was selling his colleagues down the river so he could affect a merger of a few rich teams.").

166 **Jerry Argovitz:** Sean Gregory, "The NFL Fought Donald Trump's Bullying 30 Years Ago and Won. Should It Do It Again?," *Time,* Sept. 12, 2018, time.com.

166 **One of the jurors:** Hoffer, "USFL Awarded Only $3 in Antitrust Decision."

166 **Another juror:** Jeff Pearlman, "The Day Donald Trump's Narcissism Killed the USFL," *Guardian,* Sept. 11, 2018, www.theguardian.com.

166 **this time as a defendant:** James Rowley, "Trump Agrees to Pay $750,000 Penalty to Settle Antitrust Lawsuit," Associated Press, April 5, 1988, www.apnews .com.

166 **a $750,000 fine:** Patrick A. Gaughan, *Mergers, Acquisitions, and Corporate Restructurings,* 2nd ed. (New York: Wiley, 1999), 94; David Corn, "The Time Donald Trump Was Hit with a $750,000 Fine by the Feds," *Mother Jones,* June 24, 2016, www.motherjones.com; see also Lisa Belkin, "Company News: Donald Trump Gets 9.6% of Bally Corp.," *New York Times,* Nov. 21, 1986, www.nytimes.com; Complaint for Civil Penalties for Violation of Premerger Reporting Requirements for Hart-Scott-Rodino Act, *United States of America v. Donald J. Trump,* Civil Action No. 88–0929, www.justice.gov (dated April 5, 1988, and filed in the U.S. District Court for the District of the District of Columbia).

166 **Makan Delrahim:** Brian Fung, "Trump's Antitrust Chief Questions Whether There's 'Credible Evidence' Big Tech Is Harming Innovation," *Washington Post,* Sept. 28, 2018.

166 **Joe Simons:** Federal Trade Commission, "Joseph Simons Sworn In as Chairman of the FTC," press release, May 1, 2018, www.ftc.gov.

166 **Trump's time in office:** The Trump administration frequently moved in the wrong direction on antitrust issues. In 2018, in one telling news item, the administration's Justice Department announced that it would be reviewing seventy-year-old rules that bar major movie studios from owning movie theaters. Those decades-old rules, the result of consent decrees that followed a 1948 Supreme Court ruling against Paramount Pictures, outlawed "block booking," a practice that required movie theater operators to screen B movies from a movie studio in order to be able to screen the most popular releases. Jeremy Fuster, "Justice Department to Review 70-Year-Old Rules That Barred Major Studios from Owning Theaters," The Wrap, Aug. 2, 2018, www.thewrap .com. The Trump administration's perspective? "The Paramount Decrees," the Trump administration's chief antitrust official announced of the review, "have been on the books with no sunset provisions since 1949. . . . It is high time that these and other legacy judgments are examined to determine whether they still serve to protect competition," he said, referring to nearly thirteen hundred legacy antitrust decisions. Seeing yet another opportunity to expand its reach, Amazon—the mega-company that already has enormous monopoly power— quickly expressed an interest in acquiring Landmark Theatres and getting into the movie theater business, even though Amazon itself already makes and distributes movies. Open Markets Institute, "Why the Paramount Consent Decrees Matter," *Corner,* Aug. 23, 2018, openmarketsinstitute.org; Melissa Locker, "Amazon Is Getting into the Movie Business," *Vanity Fair,* Jan. 19, 2015, www.vanityfair.com ("Amazon announced today that it is planning to produce and acquire original movies for release in theaters and through its Amazon Prime streaming video service."). "A DOJ decision to end the Paramount Decrees," the nonprofit Open Markets Institute has warned, "would allow major studios to buy up theater chains and impose the same anticompetitive practices on filmmakers and consumers barred 70 years ago. More troubling is that this would come at a time of increased concentration in the studio, movie theater, and online distribution markets." "Why the Paramount Consent Decrees Matter" ("Disney's recent purchase of 20th Century Fox means that four corporations now control 75 percent of the movie production business. In theaters, three firms now control 60 percent of the domestic market. Online, two companies dominate the streaming market, where 30 percent of consumers report using Amazon Prime Video and 50 percent report using Netflix as of 2017.")

166 **the appointment of two U.S. Supreme Court justices:** At the time of this writing, the antitrust views of Trump's third conservative Supreme Court appointment, Amy Coney Barrett, are still unknown. I asked her questions about antitrust issues at her hearing, but her prior record and her answers at the hearing give us little sense of where she will land in specific cases. It is highly unlikely, however, that she will decide antitrust cases like Justice Ruth Bader Ginsburg, the legendary justice she replaced. "Senate Confirmation of Justice Amy Coney Barrett Tightens Conservative Grip on Antitrust Law in the Courts," American Antitrust Institute, Oct. 28, 2020, www.antitrustinstitute .org ("Unlike President Trump's previous two nominees to the High Court,

the 48-year-old Barrett appears to have had only a passing acquaintance with antitrust law during her three years on the federal bench and 15 years as a law professor at Notre Dame. . . . Although her record affords little-to-no basis to speculate as to how she might rule in particular cases, Justice Barrett is a self-professed originalist and textualist who was vetted and supported by the Co-Chairman of the Federalist Society. She therefore can be expected to fit a familiar conservative mold, and a 6–3 conservative majority on the Court has important implications for antitrust law.").

166 **extremely conservative views on antitrust:** Rachel Frank, "Judge Gorsuch on Antitrust," *Stanford Law Review Online,* March 2017, www.stanfordlawreview .org; Chris Sagers, "Antitrust, Political Economy, and the Nomination of Brett Kavanaugh," Sept. 6, 2018, available at SSRN: ssrn.com; see also Lydia Wheeler, "Supreme Court Sides with American Express in Antitrust Case," *Hill,* June 25, 2018, thehill.com ("The Supreme Court on Monday sided with American Express, upholding a provision in its contract that prohibits merchants from persuading shoppers to use credit cards with lower swipe fees. In a 5–4 ruling, the court held that the company's anti-steering provisions do not violate federal antitrust laws. . . . Justice Clarence Thomas delivered the majority opinion, which Chief Justice John Roberts and Justices Anthony Kennedy, Samuel Alito and Neil Gorsuch joined.").

167 **At the Senate Judiciary Committee's hearing:** *Confirmation Hearing on the Nomination of Hon. Neil M. Gorsuch to Be an Associate Justice of the Supreme Court of the United States: Hearing Before the Committee on the Judiciary, United States Senate, One Hundred Fifteenth Congress, First Session, March 20, 21, 22, and 23, 2017* (Washington, D.C.: U.S. Government Publishing Office, 2018), 366–68, www.govinfo.gov.

167 **three Court decisions:** *Verizon Communications, Inc. v. Law Offices of Curtis V. Trinko, LLP,* 540 U.S. 398 (2004); *Credit Suisse Securities (USA) LLC v. Billing,* 551 U.S. 264 (2007); *Leegin Creative Leather Products, Inc. v. PSKS, Inc.,* 551 U.S. 877 (2007).

167 *Trinko:* In *Trinko,* the Supreme Court rejected a Sherman Act claim, and Justice Scalia—the majority opinion's author—went out of his way to *extol the virtues* of monopoly power. In his majority opinion in *Trinko,* Justice Scalia wrote, "The mere possession of monopoly power, and the concomitant charging of monopoly prices is not only not unlawful; it is an important element of the free-market system. The opportunity to charge monopoly prices—at least for a short period—is what attracts 'business acumen' in the first place; it induces risk taking that produces innovation and economic growth." *Trinko,* 540 U.S. 398 (2004) (pt. 3 of majority opinion). "To safeguard the incentive to innovate," Scalia continued, "the possession of monopoly power will not be found unlawful unless it is accompanied by an element of anticompetitive *conduct.*" Ibid. (italics in original). Although innovation is very desirable and the promise of the exclusivity of patents—even for a limited period of time— can entice and incentivize entrepreneurs to invent new products, Justice Scalia's majority opinion did not cite any of the academic literature showing that monopolies actually innovate far less than non-monopoly enterprises.

167 *Credit Suisse:* In *Credit Suisse,* the Court held that the creation of the U.S.

Securities and Exchange Commission exempted the securities markets from the antitrust laws.

167 *Leegin:* In *Leegin,* the Supreme Court overruled a long-standing precedent, from 1911, that had established that vertical price restraints were illegal per se. The precedent that the Court overruled in *Leegin* was *Dr. Miles Medical Co. v. John D. Park & Sons Co.,* 220 U.S. 373 (1911).

167 **represented both plaintiffs and defendants:** Lauren Salins, "Supreme Court Nominee Neil Gorsuch Has Significant Antitrust Experience," *Antitrust Alert* (blog), Feb. 24, 2017, www.antitrustalert.com (noting that Gorsuch, as a lawyer, handled "both plaintiff and defense litigation in antitrust matters," and observing that "Gorsuch and his co-counsel helped secure a judgment of $1.05 billion in trebled damages for tobacco company Conwood Co. after a jury found that defendant United States Tobacco Co. engaged in anticompetitive marketing practices").

167 **asked Judge Kavanaugh:** "US: Klobuchar Questions Kavanaugh on Antitrust," Competition Policy International, Sept. 6, 2018, www.competitionpolicyinternational.com.

167 **As I said at the time:** Ibid.

168 *Federal Trade Commission v. Whole Foods Market Inc.: Federal Trade Comm'n v. Whole Foods Market, Inc.,* 533 F.3d 869 (D.C. Cir. 2008).

168 **Whole Foods' $565 million acquisition:** Notably, Whole Foods hired Kellyanne Conway—later Donald Trump's political adviser—as a pollster to design a survey to support the testimony of a former FTC official who testified for Whole Foods. That former official, David Scheffman, argued that Whole Foods and Wild Oats shoppers frequently shopped at other grocery store chains and thus competed for business of customers. The U.S. District Court, however, found Conway's survey methodology and results unreliable. Maxwell Tani, "As an Expert Witness for Whole Foods, Kellyanne Conway Gave Testimony That Was Deemed 'Fundamentally Flawed' and Thrown Out," *Business Insider,* March 14, 2017, www.businessinsider.com.

168 *United States v. Anthem* (2017): *United States v. Anthem,* 855 F.3d 345 (D.C. Cir. 2017).

170 **American Express:** Adam Liptak, "Supreme Court Sides with American Express on Merchant Fees," *New York Times,* June 25, 2018, www.nytimes.com. American Express charges higher fees than Visa and MasterCard, with Stephanie Martz—of the National Retail Federation—calling the ruling "a blow to competition and transparency in the credit card market." "The American Express rules in question," she said, "have amounted to a gag order on retailers' ability to educate their customers on how high swipe fees drive up the price of merchandise."

170 **Justice Breyer:** Jessica Gresko, "Supreme Court Rules for American Express in Credit Card Case," Associated Press, June 25, 2018, www.apnews.com.

170 *Apple Inc. v. Pepper: Apple Inc. v. Pepper,* 139 S. Ct. 1514 (2019). The majority opinion was written by Justice Kavanaugh, with Justices Ginsburg, Breyer, Sotomayor, and Kagan joining it.

170 **direct purchasers:** The absence of an intermediary in the distribution chain between Apple and consumers was found to be dispositive. Although the law-

suit has yet to be resolved, the consumers argued in their case that Apple had monopolized the market for the sale of apps and used its monopoly power to charge consumers higher-than-competitive prices.

170 **at her nomination hearing:** "SCOTUS Nominee Says Antitrust Law Is 'Controlled by Precedent,'" Competition Policy International, Oct. 15, 2020, www .competitionpolicyinternational.com.

171 **new health and economic challenges:** In mid-2020, some members of Congress proposed legislation to ensure medical treatments and any COVID-19 vaccine would be affordable. Representative Jan Schakowsky of Illinois, taking note of the track record of price gouging by pharmaceutical companies, was the sponsor of one of the bills—one that would require "reasonable, affordable pricing" of new drugs to diagnose or treat the virus. As Representative Schakowsky said in June 2020, "Now, during a global health crisis, many pharmaceutical companies will see another opportunity to benefit themselves by 'pandemic profiteering.' That cannot stand." "A public health crisis should not be allowed to be a for-profit bonanza," her colleague Representative Rosa DeLauro of Connecticut concurred. Mitchell Miller, "Federal Legislation Seeks to Prevent 'Pandemic Profiteering,'" WTOP News, June 22, 2020, wtop .com.

171 **increasing consolidation:** In the United States, while some large companies— and many small businesses—are declaring bankruptcy during the COVID-19 pandemic, other large businesses are thriving and have reported increased revenue and earnings. Compare Nicole Lauren and Lincoln Saunders, "Big Name Stores Filing for Bankruptcy amid COVID-19 Pandemic," Wink News, June 4, 2020, www.winknews.com, with Jordan Valinsky, "Business Is Booming for These 14 Companies During the Coronavirus Pandemic," CNN.com, May 7, 2020.

171 **Reuters reported:** "U.S. Senator Klobuchar Blasts Uber, Grubhub Deal Talks," Reuters, May 17, 2020, www.reuters.com. The pandemic has decimated many small businesses, with a significant number of closures of bars, restaurants, arts and entertainment venues, and retail stores. Khalida Sarwari & Eunice Esomonu, "What Does the Second Wave of COVID-19 Mean for Small Businesses?" News@Northeastern, Nov. 12, 2020, https://news.northeastern.edu.

171 **sent a letter:** Lauren Hirsch, "Klobuchar and Democrats Push Antitrust Regulators to Scrutinize Uber's Potential Deal for Grubhub," CNBC, May 20, 2020, www.cnbc.com.

171 **approximately 90 percent of the national market:** Ben Coley, "Grubhub to Merge with Just Eat in $7.3 Billion Deal," *QSR,* June 2020, www.qsrmagazine .com ("Data from analytics firm Edison Trends showed that in April, DoorDash commanded 47 percent of the food delivery market while Grubhub controlled 23 percent and Uber Eats represented 26 percent. Second Measure had DoorDash at 44 percent of sales in April, followed by Grubhub at 23 percent, and Uber Eats at 22 percent. Using either metric, an Uber and Grubhub merger would result in two brands—DoorDash and Uber/Grubhub— commanding roughly 90 percent or more of the market.").

172 **one news report:** Paul Ausick, "No Deal for Grubhub, More Pain for Uber Stock?," 24/7 Wall St., June 16, 2020, 247wallst.com.

172 **I said around that time:** As I said in a statement, "I have repeatedly raised concerns and advocated against a potential merger between Uber and GrubHub.

During this pandemic, when millions are out of work and many small businesses are struggling to stay afloat, our country does not need another merger that could squelch competition." Alex Sherman and Lauren Feiner, "Grubhub Expected to Reach Deal with European Food Delivery Company Just Eat Takeaway Today, Sources Say," CNBC, June 10, 2020, www.cnbc.com.

172 **one headline blared:** "Just Eat Takeaway Acquires Grubhub for $7.3 Billion to Create Largest Food Delivery Firm Outside China," VentureBeat, June 11, 2020, venturebeat.com.

172 **Uber announced its acquisition:** Erin DeJesus, "Uber Acquires Postmates, Merging Two of the Biggest Delivery Companies," Eater, July 6, 2020, www .eater.com.

172 **Facebook was fined:** Harper Neidig, "Critics Slam $5 Billion Facebook Fine as Weak," *Hill,* July 16, 2019, thehill.com; John Eggerton, "Klobuchar: We Will Grill FTC on Facebook Settlement," BroadcastingCable.com, July 15, 2019, www.broadcastingcable.com; "Klobuchar Statement on Reported Federal Trade Commission Settlement with Facebook," press release, July 13, 2019, www.klobuchar.senate.gov.

173 **"Facebook's stock increased":** Jon Swartz, "Facebook Stock Hits Highest Price in Nearly a Year After Reports of $5 Billion FTC Fine," MarketWatch, July 14, 2019, www.marketwatch.com ("Facebook Inc. shares closed at their highest price in nearly a year Friday after reports that the Federal Trade Commission has approved a $5 billion fine, a record amount that would still be less than a quarter of Facebook's annual profit."); Mike Sonnenberg, "Why Facebook Stock Jumped 1.8% on $5 Billion Fine," Market Realist, July 2019, marketrealist.com ("On Friday, Reuters reported that the US Federal Trade Commission (or FTC) approved a $5 billion fine on Facebook (FB) in relation to the Cambridge Analytica scandal that rocked the world last year. Facebook stock jumped on the news."); Carla Herreria Russo, "Critics Say Facebook Penalty Is a Slap on the Wrist as Stock Prices Surge," *HuffPost,* July 12, 2019, www.huffpost.com.

173 **My colleague:** Eric Cortellessa, "To Fix a Broken System, a Jewish Democrat Wants to Bust Corporate Monopolies," *Times of Israel,* June 17, 2019, www .timesofisrael.com.

173 **resources:** Resources for the Justice Department's Antitrust Division are critical. Alex Kantrowitz, " 'It's Ridiculous': Underfunded U.S. Regulators Can't Keep Fighting the Tech Giants Like This," *OneZero,* Sept. 17, 2020, onezero .medium.com (" 'The agencies are severely resource-constrained,' Michael Kades, an ex-FTC trial lawyer who spent 11 years at the agency, told *Big Technology.* The Federal Trade Commission and Department of Justice's antitrust division have a combined annual budget below what Facebook makes in three days. The FTC runs on less than $350 million per year, the DOJ's antitrust division on less than $200 million. Facebook made $18 billion last quarter alone."). However, appropriations for the Antitrust Division were not a priority for the Trump administration except at the very end of the administration. Leah Nylen, "DOJ Seeks 71 Percent Bump from Congress for Antitrust," *Politico,* Feb. 10, 2020, www.politico.com; Leah Nylen, "FTC Suffering a Cash Crunch as It Prepares to Battle Facebook," Politico, Dec. 10, 2020, www. politico.com.

173 **he appointed many judges:** "Confirmed Judges, Confirmed Fears: The Continuing Harm Caused by Confirmed Trump Federal Judges," People for the American Way, April 2019, www.pfaw.org.

6. WE THE PEOPLE

175 **"curse of bigness":** Jeffrey Rosen, "The Curse of Bigness," *Atlantic,* June 3, 2016, www.theatlantic.com; see also Thomas K. McCraw, *Prophets of Regulation: Charles Francis Adams, Louis D. Brandeis, James M. Landis, Alfred E. Kahn* (Cambridge, Mass.: Belknap Press of Harvard University Press, 1984), 82, 108, 136.

175 **"the evils of monopoly":** Tim Wu, *The Curse of Bigness: Antitrust in the New Gilded Age* (New York: Columbia Global Reports, 2018), 36.

176 **corporate consolidation:** What *The Economist,* in May 2016, called "the creep of consolidation across America's corporate landscape" is an incredibly serious issue and one that presents a major problem for American consumers, American workers, and the future health of America's economy. "Concentrated industries, in which the top four firms control between a third and two-thirds of the market," *The Economist* reported, "have seen their share of revenues rise from 24% to 33% between 1997 and 2012." "Daily Chart: Corporate Concentration," *Economist,* May 24, 2016, www.economist.com.

176 **for a very long time:** One 1948 law review article gave these sobering statistics: "In 1929, 130 corporations, each capitalized at more than $100,000,000, controlled nearly 82% of all the assets of the 573 corporations whose stock was traded on the New York Stock Exchange. By 1933, 0.15% of the corporations of the nation owned 53.2% of all corporate assets." "Corporate Consolidation and the Concentration of Economic Power: Proposals for Revitalization of Section 7 of the Clayton Act," 57 *Yale Law Journal* 613, 613n1 (1948).

176 **Open Secrets:** Top Spenders, OpenSecrets.org, Center for Responsive Politics, www.opensecrets.org.

177 **corporations are not people:** The whole notion in the law that "corporations are people" is built on a bit of nineteenth-century chicanery perpetrated by Roscoe Conkling, a Republican U.S. senator from New York and a U.S. Supreme Court justice with close ties to the railroad industry. A lawyer, Conkling represented the Southern Pacific Railroad Company, a powerful corporation owned by American industrialist and tycoon Leland Stanford—the man who, with his wife, founded Stanford University. After making his way to California during the gold rush, Stanford had served as California's governor in the midst of the Civil War, and he later became a U.S. senator from that state from 1885 to 1893. A true robber baron, Stanford also founded the Central Pacific Railroad, the Pacific Mutual Life Insurance Company, and the Pacific Union Express Company, which merged with Wells Fargo and Company, of which Stanford became a director. Adam Winkler, *We the Corporations: How American Businesses Won Their Civil Rights* (New York: Liveright, 2018); Jack Beatty, *Age of Betrayal: The Triumph of Money in America, 1865–1900* (New York: Alfred A. Knopf, 2007); Naomi R. Lamoreaux and William J. Novak,

eds., *Corporations and American Democracy* (Cambridge, Mass.: Harvard University Press, 2017); Adam Winkler, " 'Corporations Are People' Is Built on an Incredible 19th-Century Lie," *Atlantic,* March 5, 2018, www.theatlantic .com; see also David H. Gans and Douglas T. Kendall, "A Capitalist Joker: The Strange Origins, Disturbing Past, and Uncertain Future of Corporate Personhood in American Law," 44 *John Marshall Law Review* 643, 660 (2011) ("Fourteen years after the ratification of the Fourteenth Amendment, Roscoe Conkling—who in 1866 had served as a member of the Joint Committee on Reconstruction that drafted the Fourteenth Amendment—served as counsel to a railroad in a Supreme Court case dealing with the tax on railroads that ultimately led to the *Santa Clara* opinion. . . . In a famous presentation to the Justices high on theatrics, Conkling produced a copy of the Journal of the Joint Committee's deliberations and quoted heavily from the then-unpublished Journal to suggest that the Framers of the Fourteenth Amendment had used the phrase 'person' in the Fourteenth Amendment to protect the rights of corporations. Conkling's argument has been called a 'masterpiece of inference and suggestion.' For example, Conkling created the false impression that corporations were the Framers' concern by observing that '[a]t the time the Fourteenth Amendment was ratified . . . individuals and joint stock companies were appealing for congressional and administrative protection against invidious and discriminating State and local taxes. Conkling forgot to mention to the Justices that the Reconstruction Congress had rejected the companies' pleas.").

In 1881, the Southern Pacific Railroad Corporation—faced with a new state law taxing railroad property—argued that the law constituted unlawful discrimination in violation of the Fourteenth Amendment, which guarantees "equal protection of the laws" and which was designed to protect the rights of persons who had been enslaved. Asserting that the railroad was a "person" entitled to Fourteenth Amendment protection, Conkling—who had served as a U.S. senator from New York from 1867 to 1881, in the House of Representatives before that, and on the Fourteenth Amendment's drafting committee—essentially misled the U.S. Supreme Court by telling its justices that corporations were meant to be covered by the Fourteenth Amendment. In a later case involving Southern Pacific, the Supreme Court declined to decide if corporations were "persons," but one jurist, Stephen Field, had complained of a failure to address that "important constitutional question." Field himself had a major conflict of interest. He had previously advised Leland Stanford's railroad interests, though Field refused to recuse himself from matters involving Southern Pacific and, worse yet, actually shared information with Southern Pacific's lawyers while Southern Pacific's first case—ultimately settled—was still pending.

And Field was not the only person with a serious conflict of interest; Representative John Bingham of Ohio, who spoke about the Fourteenth Amendment's intent, was also a railroad lawyer. Indeed, in the 1880s J. C. Bancroft Davis, a Supreme Court reporter tasked with summarizing Court opinions, wrote up an unofficial headnote that misleadingly summarized a decision—*Santa Clara County v. Southern Pacific Railroad* (1886)—for the proposition that "corporations are persons within the meaning of the Fourteenth Amendment." In fact, the chief justice in that very case had expressly stated the Court did not wish to hear any argument on that specific question. Davis had once been the president of the Newburgh and New York Railway Company, so he was hardly a disinterested lawyer. Later, Justice Field—piggybacking off that inaccurately prepared summary—wrote in *Minneapolis & St. Louis Railway Co. v. Beckwith* (1889) that "corporations are persons within the meaning" of the Fourteenth Amendment, falsely saying that "it was so held in *Santa Clara County v. Southern Pacific Railroad.*" The idea that corporations are "persons" was thus built upon a deception and then enshrined into law in railroad cases by close friends of the powerful railroad industry. See Howard Jay Graham, "The 'Conspiracy Theory' of the Fourteenth Amendment," 47 *Yale Law Journal* 371, 373 (1938); George R. Tyler, *Billionaire Democracy: The Hijacking of the American Political System* (Dallas: BenBella Books, 2018), chap. 3; Zachariah J. DeMeola, "The Corporate Person: How U.S. Courts Transformed a Legal Phantom into a Powerful Citizen" (master's thesis, College of William and Mary, 2015), 57–58, scholarworks.wm.edu ("In Congress' first session after the ratification of the Fourteenth Amendment, John Bingham, who drafted Section One of the Amendment, sponsored a bill to apply the privileges and immunities of the United States to corporations. . . . Accordingly, although the railroads could claim that one of the prominent drafters of the Fourteenth Amendment may have intended for it to cover corporate rights, Congress abjectly and explicitly refused to enact that intention into law."); see also Eugene Francis McCarthy, "Corporate Personhood(s): The Incorporation of Novel Persons in American Law, Society, and Literature, 1870–1914" (PhD diss., University of California, Berkeley, 2016), 8–9, digitalassets.lib.berkeley .edu; *Santa Clara County v. Southern Pacific Railroad,* 118 U.S. 394 (1886); *Minneapolis & St. Louis Railway Co. v. Beckwith,* 129 U.S. 26 (1889).

177   **When America's founders set up our country:** In 1800, there were a total of 335 corporations in the United States, of which only 7 had been organized during colonial times. Eighty-eight percent of those corporations were formed in the last decade of the eighteenth century, and 65 percent of them operated bridges, canals, and turnpikes, with only 1.8 percent of the corporations engaged in manufacturing. Leslie A. White, *Modern Capitalist Culture,* ed. Robert L. Carneiro, Ben Urish, and Burton J. Brown (Walnut Creek, Calif.: Left Coast Press, 2008), 355.

177   **one 2018 news headline:** Marc Sollinger, "From Beer to Airlines, Corporate Consolidation Is All Around Us," *Innovation Hub,* WGBH and PRI, June 1, 2018, blogs.wgbh.org.

177   **plagued the press:** Anthony R. DiMaggio, *Mass Media, Mass Propaganda: Examining American News in the "War on Terror"* (Lanham, Md.: Lexington Books, 2009), 307.

177   **dry cat food market:** Emily Stewart, "America's Monopoly Problem, in One Chart," *Vox,* Nov. 26, 2018, www.vox.com.

177   **during the 2020 presidential campaign:** "US: Klobuchar Says 'We Have a Major Monopoly Problem,'" *Competition Policy International,* March 5, 2019, www.competitionpolicyinternational.com.

178   **a hearing:** Amy Klobuchar, Senate Committee on the Judiciary, Subcom-

mittee on Antitrust, Competition Policy, and Consumer Rights, Hearing on Ensuring Competition Remains on Tap: The AB InBev/SABMiller Merger and the State of Competition in the Beer Industry, Dec. 8, 2015.

178 **"This merger," I said:** Niels Lesniewski, "Proposed Budweiser-Miller-Coors 'Beerhemoth' Draws Senate Scrutiny," *Roll Call,* Oct. 15, 2015, www.rollcall .com.

178 **As of the end of 2018:** Brian Kaufenberg, "Year in Review: Minnesota Beer & Cider in 2018," *Growler,* Dec. 3, 2018, growlermag.com.

179 **co-sponsored the constitutional amendment:** "On Fifth Anniversary of Citizens United Decision, Klobuchar Continues to Push for Campaign Finance Reform," press release, Jan. 21, 2015, www.klobuchar.senate.gov.

179 *Citizens United: Citizens United v. Federal Election Commission,* 558 U.S. 310 (2010).

179 *McCutcheon: McCutcheon v. Federal Election Commission,* 572 U.S. 185 (2014).

179 **Justice John Paul Stevens:** *Citizens United,* 558 U.S. at 466 (Stevens, J., concurring in part and dissenting in part).

179 **From 1895 to 1904:** Wu, *Curse of Bigness,* 24–25.

179 **Since 2000, a leading index:** Ibid., 21.

180 **a complicated field:** Antitrust is an incredibly complex subject, with economists, lawyers, and judges having to concern themselves with economic models, cross elasticity of demand, relevant markets and market power, and antitrust injury. In *Illinois Brick Co. v. Illinois,* 431 U.S. 720 (1977), the State of Illinois and seven hundred local government entities brought an antitrust lawsuit against concrete block manufacturers—companies that sold their products to masonry contractors, which, in turn, dealt with general contractors. In that case, the Supreme Court held that only the person who purchases directly from the defendant has suffered an antitrust injury. In other words, the Supreme Court held that indirect purchasers did not have standing to sue antitrust violators in federal court.

180 **The sheer complexity of antitrust law:** There are multiple legal standards that lawyers and courts regularly use to assess whether an antitrust violation has occurred, but without trust and confidence in the ability of antitrust officials to root out anticompetitive conduct, it is all just a bunch of legal mumbo jumbo. The experts speak of *clustering* (a company's efforts to concentrate its operations in a particular market), *deadweight loss* (a loss in allocative efficiency caused by a price increase above the competitive level, thereby inducing some customers not to purchase the relevant good or service), *predatory pricing* (pricing below cost to exclude competitors and to monopolize a market), and *naked restraints* (agreements having no purpose but to suppress competition and that are per se illegal under section 1 of the Sherman Act). In spite of all the antitrust jargon and terminology, what really matters is preserving competition. In that regard, the American public—and experts, regulators, and the courts—need to do a much better job in tracking and taking on monopolistic behavior.

180 **State of the Union message:** Theodore Roosevelt, State of the Union address, Dec. 3, 1901, www.theodore-roosevelt.com.

181 **to remedy the problem of trusts:** In his State of the Union address, President Roosevelt had this to say:

Artificial bodies, such as corporations and joint stock or other associations, depending upon any statutory law for their existence or privileges, should be subject to proper governmental supervision, and full and accurate information as to their operations should be made public regularly at reasonable intervals. The large corporations, commonly called trusts, though organized in one state, always do business in many states, often doing very little business in the state where they are incorporated. There is utter lack of uniformity in the state laws about them; and as no state has any exclusive interest in or power over their acts, it has in practice proved impossible to get adequate regulation through state action. Therefore, in the interest of the whole people, the nation should, without interfering with the power of the states in the matter itself, also assume power of supervision and regulation over all corporations doing an interstate business. This is especially true where the corporation derives a portion of its wealth from the existence of some monopolistic element or tendency in its business. There would be no hardship in such supervision; banks are subject to it, and in their case it is now accepted as a simple matter of course.

181 **For example, Google:** Will Sommer, "House Judiciary Committee Launches Antitrust Investigation of Tech Giants," *Daily Beast,* June 3, 2019, www.thedailybeast.com.

181 **"google" is a verb:** Virginia Heffernan, "Just Google It: A Short History of a Newfound Verb," *Wired,* Nov. 15, 2017, www.wired.com.

181 **stock price skyrocketing:** Carmen Reinicke, "Amazon Could Jump Nearly 16% This Year as the Coronavirus Pandemic Continues to Boost Demand, According to New Biggest Wall Street Bull," *Business Insider,* July 13, 2020, markets.businessinsider.com; Daniel Sparks, "Amazon Stock at $3,200: Buy, Sell, or Hold?," Nasdaq, October 20, 2020, https://www.nasdaq.com ("Shares of Amazon (NASDAQ: AMZN) have surged this year, reflecting consumers' growing appetite for e-commerce amid the coronavirus pandemic. The stock is up a whopping 75% year to date, crushing the S&P's 6% gain over this same time frame.").

181 **purchased the grocer Whole Foods:** Paul R. La Monica and Chris Isidore, "Amazon Is Buying Whole Foods for $13.7 Billion," CNN Business, June 16, 2017, money.cnn.com.

181 **reshaping the grocery industry:** Ensuring the health and safety of the nation's food supply is critical, but antitrust officials have their own obligation to protect competition and free enterprise. For example, they must ensure the health of the $800 billion grocery industry, which is already a low-margin one. Associated Press, "No Checkout Needed: Amazon Opens Cashier-less Grocery Store," Feb. 26, 2020, https://retail.economictimes.indiatimes.com; Jason Goldberg, "The Race to Reinvent Grocery: How Amazon, Walmart and More Are Trying to Conquer the Space," *Forbes,* March 1, 2020, www.forbes.com; see also William Klepper, *The CEO's Boss: Tough Love in the Boardroom,* 2nd ed. (New York: Columbia University Press, 2019) (noting that the grocery industry is "a high-volume, low-margin business," with profit margins ranging from 1.5 to 3 percent). Even before the coronavirus pandemic, analysts predicted that the U.S. grocery industry margin might shrink, by 2023, by one-third, due in part to Amazon's influence. As Chris Campbell of the Food Institute, examin-

ing industry research, wrote in October 2018, "Food retailers are likely to be pressured by low online penetration and a highly competitive market through 2023, according to research from Morgan Stanley." While online penetration in the grocery industry then stood at 10 percent in South Korea, the massive U.S. grocery market had not yet seen the same level of online shopping penetration. As Campbell noted, "While the U.S. grocery industry generated $840 billion in sales in 2017, growing 4% annually, and is the largest retail category at 18.5% of sales, the grocery category has the lowest online penetration in the U.S., at 3%, compared to more than 10% for total retail sales." Since the onset of the pandemic, though, far more American consumers have shopped online for groceries through Amazon, Instacart, Target, and Walmart. Daniel Keyes, "The Online Grocery Report," *Business Insider*, May 29, 2020, www.businessinsider.com. Indeed, in November 2020, Amazon also announced it was opening an online pharmacy service, causing the stock prices of CVS, Walgreens, and Rite Aid to tumble. Joseph Pisani and Tom Murphy, "Amazon Opens Online Pharmacy, Shaking Up Another Industry," Associated Press, November 17, 2020, https://apnews.com; Matthew Fox, "Pharmacy Stocks Are Getting Amazon'd as the Consumer Giant Pushes into Online Prescription Drugs—and CVS and Walgreens Are Tanking," *Business Insider,* November 17, 2020, https://markets.businessinsider.com.

182 **in June 2019:** "Klobuchar Statement on Lawsuit to Block T-Mobile/Sprint Merger," press release, June 11, 2019, www.klobuchar.senate.gov.

182 **grew to sixteen states:** Corinne Reichert, "Another State Joins the Fight to Block T-Mobile's Sprint Merger," CNET, Sept. 3, 2019, www.cnet.com.

182 **T-Mobile/Sprint merger was approved:** Ibid.; Yuki Noguchi, "T-Mobile and Sprint Merger Finally Wins Justice Department's Blessing," NPR, July 26, 2019, www.npr.org.

182 **state attorneys general still sued:** Merrit Kennedy, "10 State Attorneys General Sue to Block T-Mobile, Sprint Merger," NPR, June 11, 2019, www.npr.org.

183 **completed its acquisition of Sprint:** "Sprint and T-Mobile Merge, Creating New Wireless Giant," News4JAX, April 1, 2020, www.news4jax.com.

183 **a federal court blessed it in February 2020:** Jules Wang, "US District Court Approves Merger Between T-Mobile and Sprint, Denying Claims Brought by States," Android Police, Feb. 11, 2020, www.androidpolice.com.

183 **demise of Lehman Brothers:** Nick K. Lioudis, "The Collapse of Lehman Brothers: A Case Study," *Investopedia,* June 7, 2019, www.investopedia.com.

183 **"I think these companies":** Nilay Patel, "Tech Companies Are 'Too Big, and We've Allowed Them to Exercise Monopoly Power,' Says House Antitrust Chairman David Cicilline," *Verge,* Jan. 23, 2020, www.theverge.com.

183 **monopoly secret:** www.bookingholdings.com (listing ownership of Booking .com, Kayak, Priceline, Agoda, Rentalcars.com, and OpenTable); www .expediagroup.com (listing ownership of various brands); Michael Hiltzik, "Online Travel Agencies, Supermarkets, Laptops: The Hidden Monopolies That May Cost You Money," *Los Angeles Times,* Jan. 28, 2019, www.latimes .com ("As it happens, Expedia, Orbitz, Travelocity, Trivago and Hotels.com all are owned by Expedia Group. The parent company, according to a class action lawsuit filed in San Francisco in 2016, holds a 75% market share among U.S. online travel agencies. It's fair to think of Expedia as a hidden monopoly.

Most customers have no idea that the travel websites they consult are all the same company."); Reid Bramblett, "The New 'Big Three' of Travel Search Engines: Competition Dies," *Frommer's,* www.frommers.com.

184 **Consumers' Checkbook:** John Matarese, "Why Many Travel Sites Now Show the Same Prices," WMAR Baltimore, June 13, 2018, www.wmar2news.com.

184 **called on the U.S. Department of Justice:** "Klobuchar, Lee Call on Department of Justice to Closely Scrutinize Expedia-Orbitz Merger," press release, July 30, 2015; "Senators Ask for Close Scrutiny of Expedia-Orbitz Merger," *Palm Beach Post,* July 30, 2015, www.palmbeachpost.com.

184 **$1.6 billion acquisition:** Ingrid Lunden, "Expedia Buys Orbitz for $1.6B in Cash to Square Up to Priceline," *TechCrunch,* Feb. 12, 2015, techcrunch.com.

184 **weren't the only ones:** Aaron M. Kessler and Julie Weed, "Hotels Fight Back Against Sites Like Expedia and Priceline," *New York Times,* Aug. 31, 2105; Brian Fung, "Group Says Travel Sites Deal Would Hit Consumers," *Boston Globe,* Aug. 7, 2015, www.bostonglobe.com.

184 **Katherine Lugar:** Craig Karmin and Drew FitzGerald, "Hotel Industry Assails Expedia-Orbitz Deal," *Wall Street Journal,* Aug. 6, 2015, www.wsj.com.

184 **approved the merger:** Diane Bartz, "Expedia, Orbitz Win U.S. Approval to Merge," Reuters, Sept. 16, 2015, www.reuters.com.

184 **online travel industry:** The online travel companies have enormous power, as illustrated by the experience of one city in the South—Columbus, Georgia— with a population of approximately 190,000 people. That city refused to play by the rules of the big online travel companies, and it paid the price following its court battle with Expedia—one of dozens of lawsuits filed against online travel companies by cities and counties seeking tax revenue from online hotel bookings. Joseph Henchman, "Taxation of Online Travel Services: Lawsuits Generally Not Succeeding in Effort to Expand Hotel Taxes," Tax Foundation, Special Report, No. 198, May 2012, 1 ("A number of lawsuits have been filed recently by cities and counties claiming that online travel companies (OTCs, such as Expedia, Hotels.com, Orbitz, Priceline, and Travelocity) are in violation of their hotel occupancy tax ordinances. The suits claim that hotel occupancy tax should be paid on the amount of hotel reservation transactions that accrues to the OTC, described variously as a facilitation fee, service fee, commission, markup, or difference between the 'retail' and 'wholesale' rates. Altogether, some 70 lawsuits have been filed in 25 states and the District of Columbia.").

In May 2006, the City of Columbus had sued Expedia in Georgia, alleging that Expedia was selling hotel rooms to the public and had a duty to remit hotel occupancy or excise taxes in accordance with the Columbus Code of Ordinances. Expedia denied that it was required to collect or remit such taxes. The taxes charged to and collected from consumers and remitted *to the hotels* by Expedia for remittance to municipalities were based on the *wholesale* price and not the *actual room rate.* In bringing its lawsuit, Columbus was simply insisting that Expedia pay local taxes on its website-booked rooms just as existing, non-online-booked brick-and-mortar hotels did in the community. Stated differently, Columbus contended that the hotel occupancy taxes had to be collected and remitted to Columbus based on the amount that Expedia disclosed to the consuming public as the charge for each room. In a blatant form of retaliation arising out of that lawsuit, though, all of the room listings for the entire city of Columbus suddenly disappeared from the Expedia travel website (as if Columbus no longer existed and had been wiped off the map). As the American Hotel & Lodging Association put it, "Subsequent to the Columbus, Georgia decision, Expedia, Orbitz, Travelocity, hotels.com, (and possibly others) delisted hotels in Columbus." "Hotel Online: News for the Hospitality Executive," American Hotel & Lodging Association, www.hotel -online.com. Thus, potential consumers got the message that there were no hotels to find in Columbus because the city simply had the audacity to charge the online sites the exact same tax rate as existing local hotels for non-online customers. Order and Decree on Permanent Injunction, Order of Sept. 22, 2008, Docket/Court: SU-06-CV-1794-7, Georgia Superior Court, ¶ 55, riles52 .blogspot.com.

Outraged by the delisting of Columbus, Georgia, from the OTC's websites, I led an effort in the U.S. Senate to call out Expedia and other online travel sites on their conduct. I got many U.S. senators, including Mark Warner (D-Va.) and Lindsey Graham (R-S.C.), to come out and take on this issue with me. As a result, the online travel companies were unsuccessful in attaching an amendment to a major bill that would have allowed the travel websites to permanently pay lower taxes all over the country with no consequences. That they could even *try* to do what they did was because they controlled the modern-day distribution system on the internet's online travel marketplace. Most lawsuits by cities and counties against the online travel companies have been unsuccessful to date. Henchman, "Taxation of Online Travel Services," 3 ("To date, judges have shown skepticism of the cities' claims, with OTCs prevailing in 18 of the 25 states where lawsuits have been filed; cases in five states remain pending while the governments have prevailed, at least initially, in three states plus the District of Columbia. Many cities have backed off pursuing litigation as it became clear that easy revenue would not be forthcoming, contrary to proponents' claims."); Peter J. Reilly, "Online Travel Companies Win Another Round in Fight over Occupancy Taxes," *Forbes,* Dec. 13, 2016, www.forbes .com ("In the seemingly endless dispute between municipalities and online travel companies, the online travel companies have scored another win. This time it was in the Supreme Court of California. . . . The Tax Foundation toted up the score on these cases in a paper by Joseph Henchman early this year noting that over the past decade state and local governments in 34 states, the District of Colombia [*sic*] and Puerto Rico have filed law suits against the likes of Expedia, Hotels.com, Priceline and Travelocity. Overall the online companies have been winning prevailing [*sic*] in 39 cases in 23 states while losing in ten cases in six states and the District of Columbia."); *City of San Antonio v. Hotels .com,* 876 F.3d 717, 724 (5th Cir. 2017) ("the hotel occupancy tax applies only to 'the discounted [room]' rate paid by the OTC to the hotel"). But the online travel companies sought to ensure, through federal legislation and by exerting their political clout, that they would be exempt from suits and would not have to pay the same taxes as hotel rooms booked through non-online means. Jeri Clausing, "Lobby Effort Divides Hotels and OTAs on Who Pays Room Tax," *Travel Weekly,* Feb. 8, 2010, www.travelweekly.com; AH&LA's 2011 Annual Report, 7 ("Draft legislation created by the online travel companies (OTCs), the Internet Travel Tax Fairness Act (ITTFA), was successfully blocked, and a massive consumer campaign designed to confuse the public was thwarted. . . . If passed, the legislation would have legalized a tax loophole that would allow OTCs to remit occupancy tax based on the wholesale rate."). In a world in which corporate lobbyists for industries sometimes outnumber elected officials, they were almost successful. But for a concerted organizing effort to take them on, there was a real possibility that Expedia and other online travel companies might have forever etched their anticonsumer, pro-OTC wish list into federal law.

184 **one 2019 news story:** Steven Yoder, "Rx for Merger Madness," *Comstock's Magazine,* Sept. 5, 2019, www.comstocksmag.com.

185 **Leemore Dafny:** Roy Smythe, "Fighting Bad Guys with Health System Consolidation," *Forbes,* Aug. 25, 2015, www.forbes.com.

185 **American Medical Association:** American Medical Association, "10 States with the Least Competitive Health Insurance Markets," Sept. 17, 2019, www.ama-assn.org.

185 **CVS's $69 billion acquisition of Aetna:** Joe Cooper, "CVS Completes Historic $69B Aetna Acquisition," *Hartford Business,* Nov. 28, 2018, www.hartfordbusiness.com.

185 **Cigna's $67 billion acquisition of Express Scripts:** Joe Cooper, "Cigna Closes $67B Express Scripts Purchase," *Hartford Business,* Dec. 20, 2018, www.hartfordbusiness.com.

185 **Senator Chuck Grassley:** Joe Cooper, "Top U.S. Senator Asks for Insurance Merger Reviews," *Hartford Business,* Aug. 16, 2018, www.hartfordbusiness.com.

185 **Before Walgreens acquired:** Associated Press, "Walgreens Starts Fiscal 2019 with Boost from Rite Aid Stores," *Chicago Tribune,* Dec. 20, 2018, www.chicagotribune.com.

185 **raised similar concerns:** Sruthi Ramakrishnan and Diane Bartz, "A Top Antitrust Lawmaker Said Walgreens' Plan to Buy Rite Aid 'Raises Serious Issues,'" Reuters, Oct. 28, 2015, www.klobuchar.senate.gov. "I have fought tirelessly to promote competition in the health sector," I said in 2015 after the proposed merger was first announced, "and I believe the proposed merger of two of the three largest drug store chains in the country raises serious issues."

186 **easily digestible video:** Robert Reich, *The Monopolization of America* (Inequality Media, 2018), www.youtube.com.

186 **"When Oakley would not accept":** Patrick A. Gaughan, *Maximizing Corporate Value Through Mergers and Acquisitions: A Strategic Growth Guide* (New York: John Wiley & Sons, 2013).

187 **Peter Parker:** Christopher Robichaud, "With Great Power Comes Great Responsibility: On the Moral Duties of the Super-Powerful and Super-Heroic," in *Superheroes and Philosophy: Truth, Justice, and the Socratic Way,* ed. Tom Morris and Matt Morris (Chicago: Open Court, 2005), chap. 14.

187 **"The U.S. has the highest level":** Joseph E. Stiglitz, "A Rigged Economy," *Scientific American,* Nov. 2018, 57–61.

187 **Economic Policy Institute:** Estelle Sommeiller and Mark Price, "The New Gilded Age: Income Inequality in the U.S. by State, Metropolitan Area, and County," Economic Policy Institute, July 19, 2018, www.epi.org.

187 **Executive Paywatch database:** AFL-CIO, "CEO Pay Soars to 361 Times That of the Average Worker," press release, May 22, 2018, aflcio.org.

188 **For farmers in rural America:** "Real Net Farm Income Trends and Outlook," Farmers National Company, April 29, 2019, www.farmersnational.com.

188 **poverty rate for kids:** "Growing Up Rural in America," Save the Children, U.S. Complement to the End of Childhood Report 2018, 6, www.savethechildren .org ("Many Americans think child poverty is just an urban issue. But in 2016, 23.5 percent of children in rural areas were impoverished as compared to 18.8 percent in urban areas. On the county level, between 2012 and 2016, 41 counties in the United States had child poverty rates of 50 percent or higher, 93 percent of which (38 out of 41) were rural."); see also Andrew Schaefer, Marybeth J. Mattingly, and Kenneth M. Johnson, "Child Poverty Higher and More Persistent in Rural America," Carsey Research (Winter 2016), University of New Hampshire, Carsey School of Public Policy, scholars.unh.edu. In 2019, there were 10.46 million children in the U.S. living in poverty, meaning that 14.4 percent of the country's children were living below the official poverty threshold. Melissa S. Kearney, "We Could Abolish Child Poverty in the U.S. with Social Security Benefits for Poor Kids," Brookings, October 21, 2020, www.brookings.edu.

188 **Poverty is clustered:** *Rural Poverty & Well-Being,* U.S. Department of Agriculture, Economic Research Service, www.ers.usda.gov; Tanvi Misra, "From Gentrification to Decline: How Neighborhoods Really Change," CityLab, April 10, 2019, www.citylab.com.

188 **In a 2017 article:** Brian S. Feldman, "The Decline of Black Business," *Washington Monthly,* May 3, 2017, openmarketsinstitute.org.

188 **Black-owned businesses:** Tanasia Kenney, "Number of Black-Owned Businesses Grow, but Still Lags Behind Growth of Other Groups," *Atlanta Black Star,* Sept. 5, 2016, atlantablackstar.com.

189 **"The number of active":** Francine Knowles, "With Limited Access to Resources, Black-Owned Businesses Hit Especially Hard by Pandemic," *Chicago Tribune,* July 14, 2020, www.chicagotribune.com.

189 **Tulsa Race Riot of 1921:** Tim Madigan, *The Burning: Massacre, Destruction, and the Tulsa Race Riot of 1921* (New York: Macmillan, 2013) (author's note); see also Scott Ellsworth, *Death in a Promised Land: The Tulsa Race Riot of 1921* (Baton Rouge: Louisiana State University Press, 1982); Hannibal B. Johnson, *Black Wall Street: From Riot to Renaissance in Tulsa's Historic Greenwood District* (Fort Worth, Tex.: Eakin Press, 2007).

190 **civil rights movement:** Louis A. Ferleger and Matthew Lavallee, "How Small Black Businesses Supported the Civil Rights Movement" (working paper 67, Dec. 2017), www.ineteconomics.org; see also Candacy Taylor, *Overground Railroad: The Green Book and the Roots of Black Travel in America* (New York: Abrams Books, 2020) ("Since black Montgomery residents weren't taking the bus downtown during the bus boycott, they did all their shopping in their own neighborhoods, supporting local, black-owned businesses. And because they weren't spending their money on bus fare, even more money was being funneled back into the black community. Supporting black-owned businesses was critical to the success and the health of black neighborhoods, not only in Montgomery but throughout the country as well. Black entrepreneurs rarely

had access to capital, so it was hard enough to start a business, let alone maintain one, so they relied on a steady stream of black patrons.").

190 **social and economic justice:** Alfred Dennis Mathewson, "Race in the Ordinary Course: Utilizing the Racial Background in Antitrust and Corporate Law Courses," 23 *Journal of Civil Rights and Economic Development* 667, 695 (2008) ("Civil rights groups can also use the antitrust laws."); Bettye Collier-Thomas and V. P. Franklin, *My Soul Is a Witness: A Chronology of the Civil Rights Era, 1954–1965* (New York: Henry Holt, 2015) (noting how, in 1961, "members of the Chicago Federation of Labor declared that the group would not contribute support to or cooperate with any agency whose funds were allocated to any hospital or institution that practiced discrimination or segregation" after "ten black doctors filed an antitrust suit charging that fifty-six hospitals had carried out a boycott against black physicians since 1938").

190 **inequalities of wealth:** Robert M. Sapolsky, "The Health-Wealth Gap," *Scientific American,* Nov. 2018, 63 ("Economic disparity has only gotten worse during the past several decades, particularly in the U.S. In 1976 the richest 1 percent of U.S. citizens owned 9 percent of the country's wealth; today they own nearly 24 percent.").

190 **"10|20|30 formula":** Congressman James E. Clyburn, "10|20|30 Formula to Fight Persistent Poverty," clyburn.house.gov. "For far too long," Majority Whip James Clyburn of South Carolina observes, "persistent poverty communities have suffered from neglect and indifference, leading to a lack of access to quality schools, affordable quality health care, and adequate job opportunities." Union of Black Episcopalians, "Clyburn and Booker Introduce Sweeping Anti-poverty Bill," April 9, 2019, www.ube.org. Sadly, with declining social mobility and a widening income gap, the chances of escaping poverty and achieving the American Dream are too often just a dream for many Americans. Intergenerational upward mobility, a recent study showed, is the exception rather than the rule, though 70 percent of Americans still believe that the American Dream is attainable. Patricia Cohen, "Southerners, Facing Big Odds, Believe in a Path Out of Poverty," *New York Times,* July 4, 2019; Mairead McArdle, "Poll: 38 Percent of Democrats Say American Dream Is Unattainable for Them," *National Review,* July 18, 2019, www.nationalreview .com. To make the American Dream a reality, we must fight poverty and give people the educational and job opportunities that they deserve. Among other things, we need to bridge the urban-rural divide by making sure everyone has access to high-speed internet and broadband.

190 **comprehensive broadband infrastructure legislation:** "Klobuchar, Clyburn Introduce Comprehensive Broadband Infrastructure Legislation to Expand Access to Affordable High-Speed Internet," news release, July 1, 2020, www .klobuchar.senate.gov.

190 **excesses of the 2017 Trump tax bill:** Cody Nelson, "Klobuchar Takes Aim at Tax Bill, Trump Ahead of His Minnesota Visit," MPR News, April 14, 2019, www.mprnews.org.

191 **community college degrees:** Sara Boboltz, "Amy Klobuchar Outlines Support for Free 2-Year Community College," *HuffPost,* March 30, 2019, huffpost .com; see also Derek Silva, "Who Benefited Most from the Tax Cuts and Jobs Act?," Policygenius, March 17, 2020, www.policygenius.com ("The Tax Cuts

and Jobs Act of 2017 (TCJA), passed by President Trump and congressional Republicans, was the biggest reform of the U.S. tax code since 1986. The TCJA lowered income tax rates, especially for higher-income Americans, and it lowered the corporate tax rate from 35% to 21%.").

191 *universal* **health care:** Andrew Kugle, "Klobuchar in Response to Judge Striking Down Obamacare: 'We Need Universal Health Care,'" *Washington Free Beacon,* Dec. 16, 2018, freebeacon.com.

191 **need to invest:** Amy Klobuchar's Response to the Action for Opportunity Survey, actionforopportunity.org.

191 **minimum wage:** Abigail Abrams, "Here's What All the 2020 Candidates Have Said and Done About Equal Pay," *Time,* April 2, 2019, time.com. Some states and municipalities have already taken steps to raise the minimum wage, but the federal minimum wage—now $7.25 an hour—has not been raised since 2009. "Minimum Wage Tracker," Economic Policy Institute, July 12, 2019, www.epi.org; David Cooper, "Congress Has Never Let the Federal Minimum Wage Erode for This Long," Economic Policy Institute, June 17, 2019, www.epi .org.

191 **Paycheck Fairness Act:** The Paycheck Fairness Act seeks to end gender-based wage discrimination. It passed the U.S. House of Representatives in March 2019. Ella Nilsen, "The House Just Passed a Bill to Close the Gender Pay Gap," *Vox,* March 27, 2019, www.vox.com.

191 **gender and racial pay disparities:** Today, women make far less than men for the same work, though estimates vary. Anna North, "You've Heard That Women Make 80 Cents to Men's Dollar. It's Much Worse Than That," *Vox,* April 2, 2019, www.vox.com; Nikki Graf, Anna Brown, and Eileen Patten, "The Narrowing, but Persistent, Gender Gap in Pay," Pew Research Center, March 22, 2019, www.pewresearch.org ("The gender gap in pay has narrowed since 1980, but it has remained relatively stable over the past 15 years or so. In 2018, women earned 85% of what men earned.").

191 **even the playing field:** We must change our tax laws to make them more equitable. For example, we must change the way the capital gains tax works; we must start taxing the income on trust funds set up by billionaires and millionaires for their kids to help finance long-term care for our seniors and a cure for Alzheimer's; and we must put in place the "Buffett Rule," named for the legendary Omaha investor Warren Buffett. The Buffett Rule, which Warren Buffett himself supports, recognizes the galling unfairness of a billionaire investor (him) paying a lower tax rate than his secretary. As President Obama once put it, "Middle-class families shouldn't pay higher taxes than millionaires and billionaires. That's pretty straightforward. It's hard to argue against that." We, as a country, must reward hard work, and the tax system needs to treat working people much more fairly. Teachers or nurses shouldn't have to work two jobs just to get by, and those who work forty hours a week (1) should be able to live on the income they make from that work and (2) shouldn't be paying a higher percentage of their income in taxes than passive investors. "Are Millionaires Taxed Less Than Secretaries?," Associated Press, Sept. 20, 2011, www.cnbc.com.

191 **credit card debt:** Credit card debt is on the rise, and 55 percent of Americans don't regularly pay their credit card balances in full, with the average indi-

vidual credit card debt standing at $5,331 in 2019. Brian O'Connell, "What's the Average U.S. Credit Card Debt by Income and Age in 2019?," *Street,* Feb. 16, 2019, www.thestreet.com; see also Alina Comoreanu, "Credit Card Debt Study," WalletHub, Sept. 9, 2020, wallethub.com ("Americans began 2020 owing more than $1 trillion in credit card debt after a $76.7 billion net increase during 2019."). In addition to credit card debt held by Americans, there are forty-five million people in the U.S. who collectively owe $1.5 trillion in student debt. Margaret Talbot, "The Faces of Americans Living in Debt," *New Yorker,* Nov. 5, 2020, www.newyorker.com.

191 **some Americans need to work two—or even three or more—jobs:** Jessica Hall, "For Many Mainers, Working Multiple Jobs Isn't Unusual," *Portland Press Herald,* Sept. 2, 2012, www.centralmaine.com; Aparna Mathur, "Are Most People Actually Working Two or Three Jobs? Not Really," *Forbes,* Aug. 4, 2019, www.aei.org.

191 **"side hustles":** In May 2019, the Census Bureau published survey data compiled in 2013 which showed that 8.3 percent of respondents held multiple jobs, with 6.9 percent of those individuals holding three or more jobs. Emily Cole, "Work Week Doesn't End at 40 Hours or One Job for Some Workers," *Jefferson City (Mo.) News Tribune,* Aug. 18, 2019, www.newstribune.com.

192 **Union workers earn, on average:** Susan Dynarski, "Fresh Proof That Strong Unions Help Reduce Income Inequality," *New York Times,* July 6, 2018, www .nytimes.com (citing Henry S. Farber et al., "Unions and Inequality over the Twentieth Century: New Evidence from Survey Data" (working paper 620, Princeton University, Industrial Relations Section, May 2018), dataspace .princeton.edu. The Bureau of Labor Statistics reported in January 2018 that the union membership rate was 10.7 percent of wage and salaried workers in 2017 and that "nonunion workers had median weekly earnings that were 80 percent of earnings for workers who were union members ($829 versus $1,041)." Bureau of Labor Statistics, U.S. Department of Labor, USDL-18-0080, press release, Jan. 19, 2018, www.bls.gov. Not only do union members earn higher wages, but they are more likely to have employer-provided pensions and health insurance and safer, more flexible working conditions. AFL-CIO, "What Unions Do," aflcio.org.

192 **"right-to-work" laws:** Cedric de Leon, *The Origins of Right to Work: Antilabor Democracy in Nineteenth-Century Chicago* (Ithaca, N.Y.: Cornell University Press, 2015), ix–x, 1–2. One of the earliest supporters of these right-to-work laws was Vance Muse, an anti-Semitic lobbyist from Texas who openly supported Jim Crow laws and "white supremacy." He also opposed woman's suffrage, sought repeal of the eight-hour workday, and lobbied throughout the South on behalf of corporate interests. Michael Pierce, "Vance Muse and the Racist Origins of Right-to-Work," American Constitution Society, Feb. 22, 2018, www.acslaw.org.

193 **new rules of the road:** "Senator Klobuchar's Plan for the Future of Work and a Changing Economy," Medium, Dec. 5, 2019, medium.com. Senator Warner frequently talks about the need to protect gig economy workers. Ruth Reader, "Senator Mark Warner Has a New Plan to Protect Gig Economy Workers," *Fast Company,* Feb. 26, 2019, www.fastcompany.com.

193 **some of the most productive:** Melanie Dimmitt, "15 of the World's Most

Productive Countries," Collective Hub, Feb. 13, 2018, collectivehub.com; see also William M. Rodgers III and Amanda Novello, "Making the Economic Case for a $15 Minimum Wage," Century Foundation, Jan. 28, 2019, tcf.org ("The productivity of American workers has roughly doubled since 1968 (the peak of the minimum wage in inflation-adjusted dollars), but workers making the minimum wage today make 25 percent less than they did in 1968, once adjusted to today's dollars.").

193 **"From 1973 to 2017":** "The Productivity-Pay Gap," Economic Policy Institute, updated Aug. 2018, www.epi.org.

193 **increases in the minimum wage:** Rodgers and Novello, "Making the Economic Case for a $15 Minimum Wage" ("The most recent piece of federal minimum wage legislation, the Fair Minimum Wage Act, was passed in 2007, which raised the rate to $7.25 by 2009.").

194 **Jason Furman:** Jason Furman, Professor of the Practice of Economic Policy, www.hks.harvard.edu.

194 **"Today's labor markets increasingly":** Marina N. Bolotnikova, "The New Monopoly," *Harvard Magazine,* March–April 2019, harvardmagazine.com.

195 **"Nurses filed class-action lawsuits":** Steven Greenhouse, "Suit Claims Hospitals Fixed Nurses' Pay," *New York Times,* June 21, 2006, www.nytimes.com.

195 **to settle similar claims:** Diana J. Mason et al., eds., *Policy and Politics in Nursing and Health Care,* 7th ed. (St. Louis: Elsevier, 2016), 452.

195 **exchanged the relevant information:** Kenneth M. York, *Applied Human Resource Management: Strategic Issues and Experiential Exercises* (Thousand Oaks, Calif.: SAGE, 2010), 227.

195 **In 2010, tech companies:** Dan Levine, "Apple, Google Agree to Settle Lawsuit Alleging Hiring Conspiracy," Reuters, April 24, 2014, www.reuters.com.

195 **Steve Jobs:** Jeremy Quittner, "How Steve Jobs Undercut Silicon Valley's Greatest Asset: Engineers," *Inc.,* April 22, 2014, www.inc.com.

195 **class-action litigation:** Brian Fung, "64,000 Software Engineers Have Settled with Tech Companies over Wage Collusion," *Washington Post,* April 24, 2014, www.washingtonpost.com.

195 **Intuit, Lucasfilm, and Pixar settled:** Dana Shilling, *Lawyer's Desk Book,* 2017 ed. (New York: Wolters Kluwer, 2017), § 8.01 (noting that a $324.5 million settlement "was negotiated by Google, Apple, Adobe, and Intel with 64,000 tech workers," but that "the settlement was rejected by Judge Lucy H. Koh of the Central District of California, who found that the settlement was inadequate" because the conspiracy evidence "was strong, and plaintiffs did not receive enough," with a larger settlement—$415 million—reached that was approved by the district court in September 2015); Courtney Jorstad, "Apple, Google Anti-Poaching Antitrust Class Action Settlement," Top Class Actions, August 12, 2015, https://topclassactions.com ("A $415 million antitrust class action settlement was reached with tech workers and Apple, Google, and other tech companies to resolve allegations that the tech companies had a secret agreement not to recruit software engineers from each other's companies, keeping salaries artificially low. If you worked for Adobe, Apple, Google, Intel, Intuit, Lucasfilm or Pixar, you may qualify for benefits from this class action settlement.").

196　**"deep fakes":** Stephanie Ruhle, "'Deep Fakes' Are a Major Threat to 2020 Campaigns," MSNBC, June 5, 2019, www.msnbc.com.

196　**a crudely edited video:** "Trump Retweets Doctored Video of Pelosi to Portray Her as Having 'Lost It,'" Reuters, May 24, 2019, www.reuters.com.

197　**when a profit motive is involved:** Stephen Battaglio, "How Will Cable News Thrive without Donald Trump in the White House?," *Los Angeles Times*, Nov. 23, 2020, www.latimes.com (noting that "Trump has fueled a five-year run of record ratings and profit for Fox News"). Roger Ailes turned Fox News into an arm of the Republican Party, promoting that political party's daily talking points and then candidate Donald Trump, even though he had shamelessly embraced "birtherism," the baseless conspiracy theory that Barack Obama was not born in the United States. The close relationship between Fox News and Trump continued even after his Electoral College victory in 2016. "The White House and Fox," Jane Mayer, writing for *The New Yorker,* observed in March 2019, "interact so seamlessly that it can be hard to determine, during a particular news cycle, which one is following the other's lead. All day long, Trump retweets claims made on the network; his press secretary, Sarah Sanders, has largely stopped holding press conferences, but she has made some thirty appearances on such shows as 'Fox & Friends' and 'Hannity.'" David Brock, Ari Rabin-Havt, and Media Matters for America, *The Fox Effect: How Roger Ailes Turned a Network into a Propaganda Machine* (New York: Anchor Books, 2012); Jane Mayer, "The Making of the Fox News White House," *New Yorker,* March 11, 2019.

197　**If barriers to media consolidation are eroded:** In 2017, for example, the Federal Communications Commission endeavored to make it easier for the same individual to own a newspaper and a broadcast station in the same market. In November of that year, the Republican-led FCC—on a 3–2 party line vote—eliminated the decades-old ban on cross-ownership of a newspaper and TV station in a major market. "The vote," *The New York Times* reported at the time, "was the latest action in a deregulatory blitz at the agency cheered on by media, broadband and cable corporations, but opposed by many Democrats and consumer advocates, who say Americans will be hurt from greater consolidation in those industries." A federal appeals court, however, struck down that effort, saying the FCC "did not adequately consider the effect its sweeping rule changes will have on ownership of broadcast media by women and racial minorities." "U.S. Court Deals Setback to FCC Push to Revamp Media Ownership Rules," Reuters, Sept. 23, 2019, www.reuters.com. The Trump administration's FCC chairman, Ajit Pai, said he intended to eliminate the current media ownership rules. "We're getting to a point where if they weaken it even further in small markets you could have one media voice across the board," warned Gigi Sohn, an adviser to former FCC chairman Tom Wheeler, of any further loosening of the media ownership rules. Ironically, while Donald Trump repeatedly railed against "fake news," he was the one who constantly spread lies, conspiracies, and false information online. Cecilia Kang, "F.C.C. Opens Door to More Consolidation in TV Business," *New York Times,* Nov. 16, 2017, www.nytimes.com; Michael Balderston, "Oral Arguments for Media Ownership Case Set for June," *TVTechnology,* May 21, 2019, www.tvtechnology.com; John Eggerton, "FCC's Pai Plugs Broadcast Rule

Forbearance Authority," *Multichannel News,* May 15, 2019, www.multichannel
.com.

197 **repeal of federal net neutrality rules:** Cecilia Kang, "F.C.C. Repeals Net
Neutrality Rules," *New York Times,* Dec. 14, 2017.

197 **allows big companies:** Tony Romm, "The Trump Administration Just Voted
to Repeal the U.S. Government's Net Neutrality Rules," *Vox,* Dec. 14, 2017,
www.vox.com.

197 **James Madison warned:** Madison to W. T. Barry, Aug. 4, 1822, in *The Founders' Constitution,* ed. Philip B. Kurland and Ralph Lerner, press-pubs.uchicago
.edu.

197 **"will harm consumers":** "Klobuchar Statement on Net Neutrality Vote," press
release, Dec. 14, 2017, www.klobuchar.senate.gov.

197 **John Oliver:** Gregory Wallace, "That Was No Cyberattack on the FCC,
Inspector General Says—Just John Oliver Fans," CNN, Aug. 9, 2018, www
.cnn.com.

198 **protecting consumer choice:** Thomas J. Horton and Robert H. Lande,
"Should the Internet Exempt the Media Sector from the Antitrust Laws?,"
65 *Florida Law Review* 1521, 1525–26 (2013) ("The impact of a merger should
be separately analyzed for its likely impact on investigative journalism, local
coverage, etc. The evidence demonstrates that the quality and variety of several
specific media functions, such as investigative reporting and local reporting,
are often much better in the 'old' media that they should be considered distinct markets for antitrust purposes.").

198 **Tip O'Neill:** Tip O'Neill, *All Politics Is Local: And Other Rules of the Game*
(Avon, Mass.: Bob Adams, 1994).

198 **a review of its media ownership rules:** David McCabe, "FCC Starts Second
Round of Media Consolidation Wars," *Axios,* Dec. 18, 2018, www.axios.com;
see also "FCC Broadcast Ownership Rules," Federal Communications Commission, www.fcc.gov; see also David Shepardson, "U.S. Supreme Court Will
Consider FCC Effort to Loosen Media Ownership Rules," Reuters, Oct. 3,
2020, www.reuters.com; Cynthia Littleton, "Supreme Court to Tackle Media
Ownership Case," Variety, Oct. 2, 2020, variety.com.

198 **Right now:** "FCC Broadcast Ownership Rules," Federal Communications
Commission, www.fcc.gov (describing the FCC's limits on the number of
broadcast stations—radio and TV—that an entity can own).

199 **wrote an article:** John Light, "How Media Consolidation Threatens Democracy: 857 Channels (and Nothing On)," Moyers Spotlight, May 12, 2017, bill-
moyers.com.

199 *Associated Press v. United States* **(1945):** *Associated Press v. United States,* 326
U.S. 1 (1945).

199 **Writing for the Court:** Ibid., 20.

200 **Two political scientists:** Kevin L. Dooley and Joseph N. Patten, *Why Politics
Matters: An Introduction to Political Science* (Boston: Wadsworth, 2013), 247.

200 **owned 90 percent of American media:** "Media Consolidation: The Illusion of
Choice," Visually, visual.ly.

200 **just six media giants:** In 2009, Comcast and GE formed a joint venture—
51 percent owned by Comcast, 49 percent owned by GE—that consists of
NBCUniversal and Comcast's cable networks and regional sports networks.

"Comcast and GE to Create Leading Entertainment Company," Dec. 3, 2009, corporate.comcast.com.

200 **A new study:** Edmund L. Andrews, "Media Consolidation Means Less Local News, More Right Wing Slant," Insights by Stanford Business, July 30, 2019, www.gsb.stanford.edu.

200 **Sinclair Broadcast Group:** "About," Sinclair Broadcast Group, sbgi.net.

201 **62 percent of Americans:** Will Oremus, "How Many People Really Get Their News from Facebook?," *Slate,* Dec. 20, 2016, slate.com.

201 **social media sites:** Emily Dreyfuss, "Who Gets Their News from Which Social Media Sites?," *Wired,* Sept. 13, 2018, www.wired.com.

201 **online platforms:** While newspaper subscriptions have fallen substantially, website audience traffic has increased. "Newspapers Fact Sheet," Pew Research Center, June 13, 2018, www.journalism.org.

201 **monthly active users:** Jan Pokrop, "Instagram Statistics That Matter for Marketers in 2019," NapoleonCat, Sept. 12, 2019, napoleoncat.com.

201 **U.S. digital ad market:** John Koetsier, "Digital Duopoly Declining? Facebook's, Google's Share of Digital Ad Dollars Dropping," *Forbes,* March 19, 2018, www.forbes.com; "Google's US Ad Revenues to Drop for the First Time," Insider Intelligence, June 22, 2020, www.emarketer.com; see also Megan Graham, "Facebook, Google and Pinterest Are 'Top Picks' to Lead 20% Growth in Online Advertising in 2021, Morgan Stanley Analysts Say," CNBC, Nov. 12, 2020, www.cnbc.com ("Third-quarter earnings by tech giants like Facebook, Google, Snap, Twitter, Pinterest and Amazon showed that digital ad revenue came roaring back in recent months, and suggested some of the digital ad trends tied to the explosion of e-commerce could be here to stay."); Nina Goetzen, "Google and Facebook's Share of the UK Digital Ad Market Will Drop to 65.9% This Year," *Business Insider,* July 27, 2020, www.businessinsider.com ("Google and Facebook made up 67.8% of the UK digital ad market last year, which we expect will drop slightly to 65.9% this year.").

201 **nearly $14.1 billion:** Ginny Marvin, "Amazon's Booming Ad Business Grew by 40% in 2019," Marketing Land, Feb. 3, 2020, marketingland.com.

201 **analysts projecting growth:** "Report: Amazon Gains Significant Ground in Digital Ad Market as COVID-19 Drags Google," *Fast Company,* June 22, 2020, www.fastcompany.com; Robert Williams, "Amazon Ad Revenue Jumps 51% to $5.4B as Marketers Eye Online Shoppers," Marketing Dive, Oct. 30, 2020, www.marketingdive.com.

201 **comes to digital distraction:** Maggie Jackson, *Distracted: Reclaiming Our Focus in a World of Lost Attention* (New York: Prometheus Books, 2018).

201 **distracted driving:** Mohamed Ibrahim, "Hands-Free Bill to Go into Effect as Distracted Driving Citations Rise," *Minnesota Daily,* July 9, 2019, www.mndaily.com.

201 **took 2,841 lives:** "Distracted Driving," National Highway Traffic Safety Administration, www.nhtsa.gov.

202 **smartphone addictions:** Nathan Toups, "I Quit My iPhone Habit Using WebMD's Advice for Dealing with Drug Addiction," Quartz, May 2, 2018, qz.com.

202 **60 percent of U.S. college students:** "Cell Phone Addiction," PsychGuides.com, www.psychguides.com.

202 **A poll conducted by NBC News:** Leo Sun, "Analysis: Are Social Media Users Abandoning Facebook and Instagram?," *USA Today,* Sept. 12, 2019, www .usatoday.com.

202 **the massive shift:** In the 1920s, there were more than 2,000 daily newspapers. That number, however, has fallen substantially in the last hundred years, and the decline in daily papers has been accelerating even more rapidly in the internet and cable news network era. In a recent four-year period, the number of dailies fell from 1,425 in 2012 to 1,286 in 2016. Mergers have also led to greater consolidation of the TV and radio industries, with one nonprofit, Free Press, pointing out the genuine threat this poses to keeping a diversity of voices in the marketplace. According to Free Press's deputy director and senior counsel, Jessica González, "It's become painfully evident that media consolidation leaves us with far less of the local news and information communities need to stay informed. Despite the growth in digital-media options, free over-the-air broadcasting remains a critical news source for people of color and low-income communities." Richard Benedetto, "Demise of Print Newspapers May Have Far-Reaching Consequences for Communities and the Nation," *Hill,* Aug. 18, 2018, thehill.com; Bob Batchelor, *American Pop: Pop Culture Decade by Decade* (Westport, Conn.: Greenwood Press, 2009), 1:273; Kathleen Drowne and Patrick Huber, *The 1920s: American Popular Culture Through History* (Westport, Conn.: Greenwood Press, 2004), 189; "In Lawsuit, Free Press Condemns the FCC for an Appalling Lack of Diversity in Radio and TV Ownership," press release, Dec. 21, 2018, www.freepress.net.

202 **"old" media to the "new" media:** Traditional news outlets—newspapers, magazines, and major television news networks—have a long track record, but they've had to rapidly adapt to the digital age, with its 24/7 news cycle and its online advertising and paid subscription-revenue models. Companies that don't adapt risk going bankrupt (some already have), and all too often that has meant implementing cost-cutting measures such as laying off journalists—a profession that, as I know from my dad's career, is so critical to safeguarding America's democracy. Anyone can get online these days to express themselves, but media companies have huge megaphones, and what they produce gets distributed and amplified in ways that a small-town newspaper or local radio station could only dream of. In addition, off-the-cuff Twitter messages or hastily written blog or Facebook posts are just not the same as superior, award-winning journalism, fueled by intensive investigative reporting. Consolidation of newspapers and media companies, which often produces smaller newsroom staffs and reduces new content, thus poses a real and substantial threat to the public's ability to express themselves freely and to get the facts they need to shape and monitor the activities of federal, state, and local governments. At a panel at the Newseum in Washington, D.C., titled "Media Ownership and the Public Interest," Bernie Lunzer—the Newspaper Guild's president—specifically warned of the dangers of media conglomerates in 2013. "It's a good time to be a corrupt congressman," Lunzer observed of the sparser news-gathering environment that is producing shallower political news coverage. It is only when the media— the Fourth Estate—is vigilant that abuses of power and the misuse of public funds get exposed. "Media Consolidation Endangers Democracy, Unions

and Others Say," Workday Minnesota, Jan. 27, 2013, www.workdayminnesota
.org.

202 **newspaper advertising revenue:** Michael Barthel, "Despite Subscription
Surges for Largest U.S. Newspapers, Circulation and Revenue Fall for Industry Overall," Pew Research Center, June 1, 2017, www.pewresearch.org;
"Newspapers Fact Sheet," Pew Research Center, July 9, 2019, www.journalism
.org.

202 **total U.S. newspaper circulation:** "Newspapers Fact Sheet," Pew Research
Center, June 13, 2018, www.journalism.org.

202 **two largest newspaper groups:** David Folkenflik, "Gannett Plans to Merge
with New Media Investment Group," NPR, Aug. 5, 2019, www.npr.org.

202 **a deal completed in November 2019:** "New Media and Gannett Complete
Merger, Creating Leading U.S. Print and Digital News Organization," Business Wire, Nov. 19, 2019, www.businesswire.com.

202 The *Pottstown Mercury:* Jack Shafer, "This Is How a Newspaper Dies," *Politico,* May 13, 2018, www.politico.com.

202 *St. Paul Pioneer Press:* William Bornhoft, "Hedge Fund Gets Rich by Gut-
ting Pioneer Press: Report," Patch, May 4, 2018, patch.com.

202 *The Denver Post:* Shafer, "This Is How a Newspaper Dies"; see also Denver
Newspaper Guild, "Where Have All These Denver Post Journalists Gone?,"
March 26, 2018, denvernewspaperguild.org.

202 **an ad taken out:** Jon Levine, "Denver Post Staff Makes Desperate Plea amid
Layoffs: The Paper 'Must Be Saved,'" The Wrap, April 6, 2018, www.thewrap
.com ("The Denver Post issued what could only be described as a cry for help
on Friday, publishing an editorial pleading with its hedge fund owners to support the iconic city paper. The piece also informed readers of impending layoffs."); see also Laurel Wamsley, "'Denver Post' Calls Out Its 'Vulture' Hedge
Fund Owners in Searing Editorial," NPR, April 9, 2018, www.npr.org.

203 **Pew Research Center:** Elisa Shearer, "Social Media Outpaces Print Newspapers in the U.S. as a News Source," Pew Research Center, Dec. 10, 2018, www
.pewresearch.org.

203 **stories floating around internet sites:** Katy Steinmetz, "How Your Brain
Tricks You into Believing Fake News," *Time,* Aug. 9, 2018, time.com. In 2016,
Russian efforts to manipulate the presidential election through disinforma-
tion and fake social media accounts are clear. Scott Shane and Sheera Frenkel,
"Russian 2016 Influence Operation Targeted African-Americans on Social
Media," *New York Times,* Dec. 17, 2018 ("The Russian influence campaign
in 2016 was run by a St. Petersburg company called the Internet Research
Agency, owned by a businessman, Yevgeny V. Prigozhin, who is a close ally
of President Vladimir V. Putin of Russia. Mr. Prigozhin and a dozen of the
company's employees were indicted last February as part of the investigation
of Russian interference by Robert S. Mueller III, the special counsel.").

204 **media outlets have consolidated:** One example of what even more media consolidation and a further lack of competition could portend was the recent
attempt by Sinclair Broadcast Group to acquire Tribune Media, which would
have meant that those combined media giants would own enough stations to
reach nearly three-quarters of all U.S. households. Fortunately, the Federal
Communications Commission—asserting that the merger would not be in the

public interest—stepped in to stop it. Makena Kelly, "FCC Claims Sinclair-Tribune Media Merger Would Not Be 'in the Public Interest,'" *Verge*, July 19, 2018, theverge.com. After the FCC chairman, Ajit Pai, said he had "serious concerns" about the proposed $3.9 billion acquisition, successful efforts were made to block it. John D. McKinnon, Joe Flint, and Keach Hagey, "FCC Chairman Has 'Serious Concerns' with Sinclair-Tribune Deal," *Wall Street Journal*, July 16, 2018, www.wsj.com. The proposed merger was ultimately abandoned, although an FCC administrative law judge, Jane Hinckley Halprin, concluded that "extremely serious charges" regarding misrepresentations might warrant a further investigation. Harper Neidig, "FCC Warns of Future Probe into Sinclair Allegations," *Hill*, March 5, 2019, thehill.com; Ari Meltzer, "An Early Look at the FCC's New Administrative Law Judge," Wiley on Media, July 8, 2019, www.wileyonmedia.com. One of the "side transactions" that had been floated to bring the proposed merger in line with media ownership restrictions, *The Hill* reported, was a potential sale of WGN-TV "to a man named Steven Fader for a price that was considered well below market value and with terms that would effectively allow Sinclair to remain in control of the station." Neidig, "FCC Warns of Future Probe into Sinclair Allegations." WGN-TV, based in Chicago, was to be sold to Fader, the CEO of a Towson, Maryland–based auto dealership group in which David Smith—the executive chairman of Sinclair Broadcast Group—held a controlling interest. "Sinclair's executive chairman," *The Hill* emphasized, "owned a stake in Fader's Maryland car dealership, the FCC alleged." Robert Channick, "Sinclair Deal to Sell WGN to Chairman's Business Partner Gives Broadcaster Control," *Chicago Tribune*, March 1, 2018, www.chicagotribune.com. In the end, amid the swirl of controversy, this consolidation scheme went nowhere. But why did they even try? The answer? Because given the current state of the law and the lax enforcement we've seen, why not?

204 **fewer investigative reports:** One 2013 study found that the vast majority of award-winning journalism (for example, producing a Pulitzer Prize) is still being done by traditional media sources. Horton and Lande, "Should the Internet Exempt the Media Sector from the Antitrust Laws?," 1553.

204 **one op-ed:** "Give Newspapers the Tools to Fight Facebook and Google (Editorial)," Syracuse.com, Nov. 13, 2018, www.syracuse.com.

204 **Michael Copps:** "GateHouse-Gannett Merger Further Consolidates News Industry, Undermines Democracy," Common Cause, Aug. 5, 2019, www.commoncause.org.

205 **more than 70 percent:** Ron Clapp, "Trends of the Month: Ad Challenges, Sports and Mobile Video," WARC, Sept. 11, 2020, www.warc.com; "Google, Facebook, and Amazon: From Duopoly to Triopoly of Advertising," *Forbes*, Sept. 4, 2019, www.forbes.com; Anders Hjorth, "The Triopoly of Digital Advertising Exposed to the Great Disturbance in the Data (Q3 Retrospective)," Innovell, Nov. 3, 2020, www.innovell.com; "Safe Harbor Bill Needed to Promote Local Journalism," *Bowling Green Daily News*, Dec. 24, 2019, www.tribunecourier.com.

205 **attracted a lot of support:** The Journalism Competition and Preservation Act, cicilline.house.gov (noting, for example, the following endorsement of the bill by Andrew Johnson, the president of the National Newspaper Association:

"Facebook and Google love us for our local content. But they are not contributing to the cost of gathering our intensely local and interesting news, and publishers do not receive any compensation when our material travels out over these mega-giant networks. This bill would give newspapers the ability to work as an industry for fairness in the digital environment. We hope Congress will move quickly to pass the legislation.").

205 **the health of the journalism industry:** In 2020, I also joined Senators Brian Schatz and Michael Bennet in introducing the Future of Local News Commission Act. That legislation would create a commission to study the state of local journalism and offer recommendations to Congress on the actions it can take to support local news organizations. "As Local News Organizations Across the Country Struggle to Stay in Business, Klobuchar, Schatz, Bennet Introduce New Legislation to Bolster Local Journalism," press release, Sept. 29, 2020, www.klobuchar.senate.gov.

206 **protect our democracy:** It's an issue that's dominated the news in recent years, especially with the release of Special Counsel Robert Mueller's report, his public congressional testimony, and President Trump's admission while in office that he'd accept dirt on a political opponent from a foreign power. Lucien Bruggeman, " 'I Think I'd Take It': In Exclusive Interview, Trump Says He Would Listen if Foreigners Offered Dirt on Opponents," ABC News, June 13, 2019, abcnews.go.com. It is crystal clear (and long has been) that Russia—a country controlled by Vladimir Putin—invaded the 2016 U.S. presidential election in a blatant effort to influence the electoral outcome to help Donald Trump. That invasion didn't involve the use of tanks or missiles, but it was an attack—a massive cyberattack, one involving all fifty states—nonetheless. Karoun Demirjian and Colby Itkowitz, "Russians Likely Targeted Election Systems in All 50 States, Senate Intelligence Report Says," *Philadelphia Inquirer,* July 26, 2019, www.inquirer.com. To add insult to injury, after the 2020 presidential election Donald Trump fired via Tweet Christopher Krebs, the director of the U.S. government's Cybersecurity and Infrastructure Security Agency, for debunking Trump's false and baseless claims about election fraud. Kevin Collier, Katy Tur, Julia Ainsley, and Ken Dilanian, "Trump Fires Head of Election Cybersecurity Who Debunked Conspiracy Theories," NBC News, Nov. 17, 2020, www.nbcnews.com.

206 **foreign interference:** To make sure that what happened in 2016 never happens again, Congress must pass my bipartisan legislation—the Secure Elections Act—so that federal officials and secretaries of state around the country have the cybersecurity resources they need and so every American state has backup paper ballots and proper auditing of election results. If an election system is hacked, it is absolutely critical that states—and the American people—have a physical record of how individual voters cast their ballots. We must also know who is actually paying for all those social media ads that have come to so dominate political campaigns, something that another one of my bipartisan bills—the Honest Ads Act—would do. The Honest Ads Act would impose disclosure requirements for all political ads that appear on social media sites. We need to be honest about the fact that social media platforms are not just public arenas to share information, they are run by profit-making media companies that should be governed by the same rules as print, radio, and TV.

206 **$1.4 billion was spent:** Dow Jones, "Facebook Ends Commissions for Political Ad Sales," May 23, 2019, eresearch.fidelity.com.

206 **Russian rubles:** David S. Cloud, "Lawmakers Slam Social Media Giants for Failing to Block Russian Ads and Posts During 2016 Campaign," *Los Angeles Times,* Nov. 1, 2017, www.latimes.com.

206 **good work of people like Chris Krebs:** Alana Wise, "Trump Fires Election Security Director Who Corrected Voter Fraud Disinformation," NPR, Nov. 17, 2020, www.npr.org.

207 **$8.5 billion:** Steve Passwaiter, "Political Ad Spending This Year Reached a Whopping $8.5 Billion," *AdAge,* Nov. 23, 2020, adage.com. See also Alexandra Bruell, "Political Ad Spending Will Approach $10 Billion in 2020, New Forecast Predicts," *Wall Street Journal,* June 4, 2019, www.wsj.com. In 2018, $8.7 billion was spent in congressional midterm elections, far more than in 2016, when $6.3 billion was spent. A large percentage of political advertising dollars are spent online. A report from September 2018 noted that since 2014 there has been a staggering 2,539 percent growth in digital advertising. While digital ads accounted for less than 1 percent of spending for political ads in 2014, that number was projected—at one point—to be more than 20 percent of overall political advertising for 2018. Kaitlin Washburn, "Digital Ad Use Continues to Skyrocket with Little Oversight," Open Secrets, Sept. 26, 2018, www.opensecrets.org. Approximately $1.8 billion was spent on digital advertising alone in 2018, and the total cost of the 2020 election, according to the Center for Responsive Politics, was an unprecedented $14 billion. Hamsini Sridharan and Margaret Sessa-Hawkins, "Federal Action and Inaction on Digital Deception," MapLight, May 30, 2019, maplight.org; "2020 Election to Cost $14 Billion, Blowing Away Spennding Records," OpenSecrets.org, October 28, 2020, www.opensecrets.org.

207 **At a 2020 post-election hearing:** "Klobuchar Questions CEO of Facebook about Competition, Antitrust Investigation, and Political Advertising," press release, Nov. 17, 2020, klobuchar.senate.gov.

207 **highly paid lobbyists:** Former Members, Open Secrets, Center for Responsive Politics, www.opensecrets.org.

207 **Some politicians:** There are, sadly, numerous examples. David Madland, *Hollowed Out: Why the Economy Doesn't Work Without a Strong Middle Class* (Oakland: University of California Press, 2015), 106 ("in 2009 a Louisiana congressman was convicted of corruption after FBI agents found $90,000 of cash stashed in a freezer that they traced back to a briefcase the Congressman received"); Julian E. Zelizer, "Without Restraint: Scandal and Politics in America," in *The Columbia History of Post–World War II America,* ed. Mark C. Carnes (New York: Columbia University Press, 2007), 240 ("In 1980, the FBI rented a house in Washington, D.C., where FBI officers disguised themselves as Arab employees of a Middle Eastern oil sheik. Six congressmen were convicted of accepting bribes in the so-called Abscam affair.").

207 **effective campaign ad:** Dennis J. McGrath and Dane Smith, *Professor Wellstone Goes to Washington: The Inside Story of a Grassroots U.S. Senate Campaign* (Minneapolis: University of Minnesota Press, 1995), 219.

208 **"Politics," Paul said:** Bill Lofy, *Paul Wellstone: The Life of a Passionate Progressive* (Ann Arbor: University of Michigan Press, 2005), 157.

208 "The moral test of government": Suzy Platt, ed., *Respectfully Quoted: A Dictionary of Quotations* (New York: Barnes & Noble Books, 1993), ix.

208 *Citizens United:* In the *Citizens United* case, the Supreme Court held, in a case involving a conservative group's release of a ninety-minute, highly partisan film about U.S. senator and then-presidential candidate Hillary Clinton shortly before the 2008 Democratic primaries, that corporations have an unrestricted constitutional right to finance campaign speech. *Citizens United,* which declared unconstitutional a key provision of the Bipartisan Campaign Reform Act of 2002 co-sponsored by John McCain and Russ Feingold, encourages special interests with substantial resources to engage in political action in their self-interest rather than promoting the common good or the public interest. John Paul Stevens, *Six Amendments: How and Why We Should Change the Constitution* (New York: Little, Brown, 2014), chap. 3.

208 **we need to make sure:** Bridget Bowman, "Amy Klobuchar Launches 2020 Presidential Campaign," *Roll Call,* Feb. 10, 2019, www.rollcall.com.

208 **fight back against gerrymandering:** Erick Trickey, "Where Did the Term 'Gerrymander' Come From?," *Smithsonian Magazine,* July 20, 2017, www .smithsonianmag.com (discussing Governor Elbridge Gerry, who signed the bill that created a bizarrely shaped Massachusetts district, and observing of the origins of the word "gerrymander," "The word 'gerrymander' was coined at a Boston dinner party hosted by a prominent Federalist in March 1812, according to an 1892 article by historian John Ward Dean. As talk turned to the hated redistricting bill, illustrator Elkanah Tisdale drew a picture map of the district as if it were a monster, with claws and a snake-like head on its long neck. It looked like a salamander, another dinner guest noted. No, a 'Gerrymander,' offered poet Richard Alsop, who often collaborated with Tisdale.").

208 **the bill I introduced with Senator Ron Wyden:** "Senators Klobuchar and Wyden Introduce 'Natural Disaster and Emergency Ballot Act,'" National Low Income Housing Coalition, May 4, 2020, nlihc.org.

210 **trying to pick their voters:** Max Labaton, "Politicians Choosing Their Voters," *Chronicle,* Feb. 7, 2018, www.dukechronicle.com.

210 **Donald Trump's false claims of systemic voter fraud:** Jeremy Roebuck, "'Not how the Constitution works': Federal Judge Tosses Trump Suit Seeking to Disrupt Pa. Election Results," *Philadelphia Inquirer,* Nov. 21, 2020, www .inquirer.com.

210 **hired an operative:** Michael Wines, "Deceased G.O.P. Strategist's Hard Drives Reveal New Details on the Census Citizenship Question," *New York Times,* May 30, 2019, www.nytimes.com.

210 **only after that operative died:** Paul Waldman, "How a Dead Man's Hard Drives Are Exposing the GOP Attack on Democracy," *Washington Post,* June 7, 2019, www.washingtonpost.com.

211 **rise in insurance costs:** Gretchen Frazee, "How Climate Change Is Changing Your Insurance," *PBS NewsHour,* Nov. 27, 2018, www.pbs.org ("Home insurance rates already increased more than 50 percent from 2005 to 2015, the year with the latest available date. The National Association of Insurance Commissioners attributes the increase to natural disasters, inflation, rising real estate values and construction costs."); Lena Borrelli, "How Climate Change Has Impacted Home Insurance Rates," Reviews.com, Oct. 2, 2020, www.reviews

.com (noting the effect of climate change and global warming on insurance rates).

211 **as the Ojibwe people say:** Thomas Peacock and Marlene Wisuri, *Ojibwe Waasa Inaabidaa: We Look in All Directions* (Afton, Minn.: Afton Historical Society Press, 2008), 62.

212 **made calls to stop it:** Tim Starks, "What's Next for Postponed Secure Elections Act," *Politico,* Aug. 23, 2018, www.politico.com; Marianne Levine and Tim Starks, "Election Security Push Stumbles amid White House Resistance," *Politico,* May 1, 2019, www.politico.com.

212 **For the People Act:** H.R. 1—For the People Act of 2019, www.congress.gov; see also Melissa Harris-Perry, "To Honor Representative John Lewis' Legacy, Restore the Voting Rights Act," *Harper's Bazaar,* July 20, 2020, https://www .harpersbazaar.com ("Four years after Representative Lewis commemorated the 50th anniversary of his own bloody sacrifice in Selma, Alabama, he presided over the House of Representatives as it passed *HR1: For the People Act of 2019.* The bill restores key protections of the Voting Rights Act, which was gutted six years earlier by the Supreme Court's 5–4 decision in *Shelby County v. Holder* (2013).").

212 **two-thirds of Americans:** "Growing Partisan Divide over Fairness of the Nation's Tax System," Pew Research Center, April 4, 2019, www.people-press .org ("Currently, 63% of Americans say the 'economic system unfairly favors powerful interests,' while just 34% say it is 'generally fair to most Americans.'").

213 **As Brandeis put it:** Erica Schoenberger, *Nature, Choice, and Social Power* (London: Routledge, 2015), 195.

213 **annual visits:** Maya Rao, "High Profile, and Seeking Third Term: A Look Inside Amy Klobuchar's Quest for Senate," *Minneapolis Star Tribune,* Oct. 16, 2018.

213 **nearly won in 2016:** Associated Press, "Trump Campaign Eyes Chances to Vie for States Lost in 2016," MPR News, April 13, 2019, www.mprnews.org (noting that Donald Trump lost Minnesota to Hillary Clinton by fewer than forty-five thousand votes in 2016).

213 **who cast their votes:** Tom Nehil and Greta Kaul, "Where Trump Did Better Than Mitt Romney in Minnesota, and Where He Did Worse," *MinnPost,* Nov. 11, 2016, www.minnpost.com.

213 **the greatest number of citizens casting their ballots in our nation's history:** Celine Castronuovo, "Biden-Harris Ticket the First in US History to Surpass 80 Million Votes," *Hill,* Nov. 24, 2020, thehill.com.

213 **As I said when I announced my own campaign for president:** Amy Klobuchar, "Announcement of Candidacy for President of the United States—Boom Island Park, Minneapolis, Minnesota, February 10, 2019," in Amy Klobuchar, *The Senator Next Door: A Memoir from the Heartland,* new ed. (Minneapolis: University of Minnesota Press, 2019), xxi.

214 **more concentrated markets:** "Klobuchar Presses Heads of DOJ Antitrust Division and FTC on Critical Issues of Competition in the U.S. Economy," news release, Sept. 17, 2019, www.klobuchar.senate.gov.

7. MODERN-DAY ANTITRUST CHALLENGES

215 **strict enforcement:** Arnold A. Offner, *Hubert Humphrey: The Conscience of the Country* (New Haven, Conn.: Yale University Press, 2018), chap. 5; see also Jeff Greenfield, "What Makes Hubert Not Run?" *New York Times,* April 4, 1976, www.nytimes.com.

215 **In 1952, on the Senate floor:** Benjamin R. Barber, *A Place for Us: How to Make Society Civil and Democracy Strong* (New York: Hill and Wang, 1998), 153n8. In 1945, Humphrey's own father, after reading in the newspaper that his son, then the mayor of Minneapolis, had dined with a group of bankers, telephoned to warn the youthful Hubert not to get too cozy with bankers. Telling him to be wary of their wealth and flattery, he reminded Hubert of how the banks had foreclosed on so many farmers during the Great Depression. Carl Solberg, *Hubert Humphrey: A Biography* (St. Paul: Minnesota Historical Society Press, 2003), 469.

215 **throughout our history:** To fight the monopolies, American lawmakers created the Interstate Commerce Commission in 1887 to regulate railroads, then passed the Sherman Act in 1890 to curb monopolies and trusts. Over the ensuing decades, they passed other laws to close loopholes and to fight consolidated power.

215 **in recent decades:** For example, in the transportation area, a series of mergers in the airline and rail industries—including a large number of airline mergers approved during the Reagan administration after the Airline Deregulation Act (1978) was signed into law by President Carter—led to heavily consolidated industries. "Railroad Mergers & Takeovers," Trains 21, trains21.org (listing railroad mergers and takeovers after World War II and through 2013); Philip H. Burch, *Reagan, Bush, and Right-Wing Politics: Elites, Think Tanks, Power, and Policy* (Greenwich, Conn.: Jai Press, 1997), 163 (noting that "in just a brief two-year period, the Reagan administration sanctioned 26 airline mergers"); see also Ted Reed and Dan Reed, *American Airlines, US Airways, and the Creation of the World's Largest Airline* (Jefferson, N.C.: McFarland, 2014), 3, 165 (discussing a meeting at a restaurant in St. Paul in 1985 that led to the merger of Republic Airlines and Northwest Airlines, as well as telling the story of how three airlines—American, America West, and US Airways—combined in 2013 to form the world's largest airline). The U.S. Department of Transportation has granted antitrust immunity for international airline alliances. Diana L. Moss, "Revisiting Antitrust Immunity for International Airline Alliances," Competition Policy International, Feb. 28, 2019, www .competitionpolicyinternational.com.

   The airline, trucking, and rail industries were all deregulated by President Carter in the late 1970s and in 1980 before he left office, with Carter—in his 1976 campaign—having pledged to restructure those industries to eliminate antiquated regulations. W. Carl Biven, *Jimmy Carter's Economy: Policy in an Age of Limits* (Chapel Hill: University of North Carolina Press, 2002); Mark H. Rose, Bruce E. Seely, and Paul F. Barrett, *The Best Transportation System in the World: Railroads, Trucks, Airlines, and American Public Policy in the Twentieth Century* (Philadelphia: University of Pennsylvania Press, 2006), 166, 185–86, 194, 200, 208, 218, 220, 222. Airline deregulation changed the market landscape for travelers, but it was the lax antitrust enforcement that followed that led to greater corporate consolidation as major airlines merged and created their hub-and-spoke systems. Paul Stephen Dempsey and Andrew R. Goetz, *Airline Deregulation and Laissez-Faire Mythology* (Westport, Conn.: Quorum Books, 1992), 228; "U.S. Airline Mergers and Acquisitions," Airlines for America, www.airlines.org (containing an "unofficial compilation of completed (not merely proposed) mergers and acquisitions since the inception of the U.S. airline industry").

215 **have languished:** In 1978, President Carter, trying to eliminate obsolete regulations and to fight inflation, signed the Airline Deregulation Act, although he could not have anticipated the lax antitrust enforcement that followed in the Reagan administration. B. E. Hawk, "Airline Deregulation After Ten Years: The Need for Vigorous Antitrust Enforcement and Intergovernmental Agreements," 34 *Antitrust Bulletin* 267 (1989). The Airline Deregulation Act abolished the Civil Aeronautics Board—a body that had, since 1938, tried to ensure regional parity in the cost of airline service. In 1980, both the rail and the trucking industries were deregulated, too, changing the regulatory structure that had existed since the Interstate Commerce Act (1887). Motor Carrier Act of 1980, Pub. L. No. 96-296, 94 Stat. 793; Staggers Rail Act of 1980, Pub. L. 96-448. But as in the airline industry, the lack of rigorous antitrust enforcement in the years to come meant that many mergers went forward without appropriate scrutiny. "As a result," antitrust historian Phillip Longman observes, "midwestern grain farmers, Texas and Gulf Coast petrochemical producers, New England paper mills, mines, and the country's steel, automobile, and other heavy-industry manufacturers, all now typically find their economic competitiveness in the hands of a single carrier that faces no local competition and no regulatory restraints on what it charges its captive shippers."

It was not deregulation, however, that ultimately led to highly concentrated markets. Instead, the powerful tool of antitrust enforcement, previously used in the 1960s and 1970s to balance the American economy and to check monopoly power, became far less potent in the 1980s as it fell out of favor, antitrust enforcers lost interest, and the tool was placed in the hands of those who did not value it and, in many instances, chose not to use it. Sigrid Stroux, *US and EC Oligopoly Control* (The Hague, the Netherlands: Kluwer Law International, 2004), 69 (noting that in 1969 a staff memo to the Federal Trade Commission urged that an antitrust investigation be launched into the ready-to-eat breakfast cereal industry, and that a formal complaint, filed in 1972, charged that Kellogg, General Mills, General Foods, and Quaker Oats, which collectively controlled 91 percent of the ready-to-eat cereal market, had "shared monopoly power" over the cereal market); W. Kip Viscusi, Joseph E. Harrington, Jr., and John M. Vernon, *Economics of Regulation and Antitrust*, 4th ed. (Cambridge, Mass.: The MIT Press, 2005), 304 ("The 'shared monopoly' theory presented by the FTC against Kellogg, General Mills, and General Foods was a novel approach to a highly concentrated oligopoly. The three firms had collectively 81 percent of the ready-to-eat cereals market, with Kellogg, the largest of the three, holding 45 percent. The FTC charged that the companies had engaged 'in certain interdependent acts and practices in order to achieve a highly concentrated, noncompetitive market structure and shared monopoly power.'"); Merrill Brown, "FTC Staff Says Cereal Monopoly Cost $1.2 Billion," *Washington Post*, Oct. 1, 1980, www.washingtonpost.com (noting that the FTC charged that, between 1958 and 1972, the nation's consumers paid more than $1.2 billion in higher grocery store prices because of a monopoly among the nation's major producers of ready-to-eat cereals and that there was a "tacit conspiracy" involving the sharing of current advertising data and limitations on the use of discounts to grocery wholesalers and retailers, but that Quaker Oats Co. had been dismissed from the case in 1978); Michael Decourcy Hinds, "U.S. Drops 10-Year Antitrust Suit Against 3 Largest Cereal Makers," *New York Times*, Jan. 16, 1982, www.nytimes.com (noting that the Federal Trade Commission, on a 3–1 vote, "decided today to dismiss the 10-year-old antitrust case against the nation's three biggest breakfast cereal makers, Kellog, General Mills and General Foods," thus accepting the recommendation of an FTC administrative law judge that the agency's staff had failed to prove the original charges); Merrill Brown, "Cereal Maker Antitrust Case Is Dismissed," *Washington Post*, Jan. 16, 1982, www.washingtonpost.com (noting the FTC's dismissal of the case against the cereal makers and observing that the case "had become a cause celebre in Congress, where industry fears that the break-up of the leading manufacturers might cost Michigan and other grain areas jobs found a ready audience"); "Antitrust Division and President Reagan: Changes in Enforcement Policies, Activities," GAO Report (Chicago: Commerce Clearing House, 1990), 31 ("After a period of growth throughout the 1970s, the Antitrust Division experienced a decade of significant reductions in its funding and staff levels. The Reagan administration shifted Justice resources toward other priorities and away from antitrust. Consequently, between fiscal years 1980 and 1989, the Division's appropriations fell by nearly 30 percent in constant dollars. . . . Antitrust enforcement was a relatively low priority for the Reagan administration."); Tony A. Freyer, *Antitrust and Global Capitalism, 1930–2004* (Cambridge, U.K.: Cambridge University Press, 2006), 139 ("Reagan's reliance on Chicago economic efficiency theories dominated the deregulation movement during the 1980s. Under Reagan, antitrust cases against mergers declined to the lowest point in eight decades. William Baxter, the Assistant Attorney General in charge of the Antitrust Division, did break up AT&T on the ground that it was a monopoly, but the Reagan administration's approach to market concentration allowed most mergers.").

The lack of rigorous antitrust enforcement has led to higher levels of concentration in various industries, regional disparities in economic power, and exacerbated disparities between the haves and the have-nots. The failure of Congress to eliminate unnecessary antitrust exemptions—for example, to pass one of my bills, the Railroad Antitrust Enforcement Act—has also been a big part of the problem. My bill seeks to eliminate the antitrust exemption for railroads and to address "captive shipping," whereby many agricultural producers and businesses in rural communities have access to only one rail company to ship their commodities or goods to market. "Klobuchar, Vitter Introduce Legislation to Address Captive Shipping and Promote Fairness and Competition in the Railroad Industry," news release, March 21, 2013, www.klobuchar .senate.gov. "Beginning in the late 1970s," Phillip Longman writes in a recent article, Americans "struggled with how to keep railroads from engaging in price discrimination against specific areas or otherwise favoring one town or region over another." Phillip Longman, "Why the Economic Fates of America's Cities Diverged," *Atlantic,* Nov. 28, 2015, www.theatlantic.com.

Now, not only is our country still struggling with how to make the railroad industry competitive, but we are also living in a world in which our communications, our interactions, and much of our commerce are conducted through a few online companies. These days, goods still make their way to market by rail, but the rapid growth in technology and internet sales has created a whole new set of antitrust issues and concerns—issues and concerns that have yet to be addressed, in great part, because those that benefit immensely from the status quo have no reason whatsoever to see change. The American economy, of course, does not stand still and never has throughout the country's history. Driven by capitalism, it is constantly in motion, with companies, for example, using drones in agriculture and obtaining FAA approval for their use for package deliveries. In 2019, as part of a pilot project, Walgreens began making drone deliveries of a hundred of its products in Christiansburg, Virginia, through Wing, a drone company owned by Google's parent company. "With this pilot," Vish Sankaran, the chief innovation officer at Walgreens, observed, "Walgreens will be in a unique position to capitalize on the convenience of drone delivery if and when it should expand, with approximately 78 percent of the U.S. population living within five miles of a Walgreens store." Amanda Shiffler, "10 Companies Using Drones to Disrupt the Agriculture Industry," *Disruptor Daily,* Dec. 20, 2017, www.disruptordaily.com; Bill Chappell, "FAA Certifies Google's Wing Drone Delivery Company to Operate as an Airline," NPR, April 23, 2019, www.npr.org; Eric Adams, "Drone Delivery Services Are Actually, Finally Almost Here," *Wired,* April 27, 2019, www.wired; Catherine Thorbecke, "Small Virginia Town to Be the Site of Drone Delivery Program for Walgreens," ABC News, Sept. 23, 2019, abcnews.go.com.

215 **antitrust enforcement reached its apex:** Phillip Longman points out that in 1966 the U.S. Supreme Court blocked the merger of two supermarket chains that, had the merger gone forward, would have controlled just 7.5 percent of the Los Angeles market—a paltry market share compared with what we now see permitted by antitrust regulators. "Today, by contrast," Longman explains in his 2015 article, "there are nearly 40 metro areas in the U.S. where Walmart controls half or more of all grocery sales." Longman, "Why the Economic Fates of America's Cities Diverged."

215 **in the 1970s:** In the 1970s, the Justice Department's Antitrust Division was pursuing major monopolization cases against IBM and AT&T. Liliane Kerjan, "Antitrust Laws: The IBM and AT&T Cases," 35 *Revue Française d'Études Américaines* 95, 98 (1988) (noting that that antitrust case against IBM was filed on January 17, 1969, but "went to trial six years later and then the battle for liability lasted for another six years" and that "AT&T's reactions to new comers in the telecommunications market . . . prompted the government in late 1974 to file a complaint under Section 2 of the Sherman Act, charging that AT&T and two of its subsidiaries Western Electric and Bell Laboratories had conspired to monopolize interstate communications services and equipment and had engaged in various restraints of trade"). In addition, in the 1970s, the Federal Trade Commission was still pursuing a massive case against the

nation's three biggest cereal makers, a case that lasted roughly ten years and that was not dropped until 1982. Michael Decourcy Hinds, "U.S. Drops 10-Year Antitrust Suit Against 3 Largest Cereal Makers," *New York Times,* Jan. 16, 1982, www.nytimes.com ("The Federal Trade Commission, in a 3-to-1 vote, decided today to dismiss the 10-year-old-antitrust case against the nation's biggest three breakfast cereal makers, Kellogg, General Mills and General Foods. The commission thus accepted the recommendation of an F.T.C. administrative law judge that the agency's staff had failed to prove the original charges. These had accused the three companies, whose products are consumed by tens of millions of Americans every day, of having operated a 'shared monopoly' that limited competition among themselves and prevented new competition from entering the market."). After the FTC dropped the antitrust case against the cereal makers, the price of "cereal breakfast foods"—as the director of the Bureau of Economics, who was involved in the case as a witness, later pointed out—"rose from approximately 47.5 percent between 1972 and 1977—i.e., while the case was actively pending—to an average of 61.7 percent over the ten years 1982 through 1991—among the five highest such margins evident among 459 four-digit manufacturing industries." The consequences? As that economist, Frederic M. Scherer, argues: "One finds that the additional prices paid by retailers for breakfast cereals amounted to approximately $10 billion. Assuming not implausibly that cereal producers no longer found it prudent to restrain their prices and margins once the antitrust threat had ended, this was a high cost indeed for American consumers." F. M. Scherer, "The F.T.C., Oligopoly, and Shared Monopoly," Faculty Research Working Paper Series, RWP13-031 (Sept. 2013), Harvard Kennedy School, John F. Kennedy School of Government, 2–3, 19.

215 **in the 1980s:** Alison Jones, Brenda Sufrin, and Niamh Dunne, *Jones and Sufrin's EU Competition Law: Text, Cases, and Materials,* 7th ed. (Oxford: Oxford University Press, 2019), 36–37 ("During the 1970s Chicago School thinking became increasingly influential and its ascendancy from the 1980s Reagan administration onwards led to a fundamental change of direction in the application and enforcement of antitrust law. This change saw the Supreme Court describe the antitrust rules as 'a consumer welfare prescription' and deliver a number of landmark Chicago-inspired judgments which often cite Bork directly. These, for example, overruled the per se rule against non-price intrabrand restraints in vertical restraints, the per se rule against maximum resale price maintenance (RPM), and the per se rule against fixed and minimum RPM. The Court also adopted a standard for proving predatory pricing which makes it extremely difficult for plaintiffs to win and it is inimical to claims of refusal to supply.").

216 **"We haven't changed our business":** Michael B. Becraft, *Bill Gates: A Biography* (Santa Barbara, Calif.: Greenwood, 2014), 76; Luca Rubini, ed., *Microsoft on Trial: Legal and Economic Analysis of a Transatlantic Antitrust Case* (Cheltenham, U.K.: Edward Elgar, 2010), 217; Chris Taylor, "Gates: What, Me Worry?," *Time,* Nov. 11, 1998, content.time.com.

216 **stand-alone section 2 cases:** The depicted data—as scholar Fiona Scott Morton puts it—"understates the division's enforcement against exclusionary conduct, or actions in the marketplace that deny a competitor access to either

suppliers or customers. Conduct that violates Section 2 of the Sherman Antitrust Act may also violate Section 1, which bars agreements in restraint of trade." For example, she emphasizes, "exclusive contracts signed by a monopolist and another party that harm competition could be illegal under both sections" and that "if Section 1 is the dominant theory, the division only reports it as a Section 1 case." Fiona Scott Morton, "Modern U.S. Antitrust Theory and Evidence amid Rising Concerns of Market Power and Its Effects," Washington Center for Equitable Growth, May 29, 2019, equitablegrowth.org. Other charts show Americans are more likely to work for large employers than in the past. "Why Americans Are More Likely to Work for a Large Employer, in 20 Charts," *Wall Street Journal,* April 6, 2017, www.wsj.com.

217 **Wealth Inequality:** William A. Galston and Clara Hendrickson, "A Policy at Peace with Itself: Antitrust Remedies for Our Concentrated, Uncompetitive Economy," Brookings, Jan. 5, 2018, www.brookings.edu ("Declining competition has also resulted in rising income inequality. Consolidation in the health-care industry, for instance, has meant that for some patients, the cost of routine health services have increased by as much as several hundred percent. Facing few competitors, today's cable providers have raised the price of subscriptions. Concentration in the airline industry has led to fare surges for some routes."); Jordan Brennan, *A Shrinking Universe: How Concentrated Corporate Power Is Shaping Income Inequality in Canada,* Canadian Centre for Policy Alternatives, 2012, bnarchives.yorku.ca (finding a relationship between corporate concentration and rising income inequality).

217 **Stagnant Wages:** Marshall Steinbaum, Eric Harris Bernstein, and John Sturm, *Powerless: How Lax Antitrust and Concentrated Market Power Rig the Economy Against American Workers, Consumers, and Communities,* Roosevelt Institute, Feb. 2018, 2, rooseveltinstitute.org ("Because fewer firms mean less competition between firms for employees, workers have less power to bargain for fair wages and less economic mobility to find better jobs. In fact, the labor share of income has decreased most in consolidated industries, and firm consolidation is a major factor contributing to the suppression of workers' wages.").

217 **Higher Prices for Consumers:** Ibid., 3 ("Firms in consolidated industries tend to lower production and raise prices, reducing the demand for labor. In 2009, pharmaceutical giant Pfizer acquired Wyeth and announced it would cut 20,000 jobs worldwide. After combining in 2015, Kraft-Heinz announced plans to cut 5 percent of its workforce.").

217 **Racial Disparities:** Stacy Mitchell and Susan R. Holmberg, "Fighting Monopoly Power—America's Monopoly Problem: Why It Matters and What We Can Do About It," Institute for Local Self-Reliance, July 2020, ilsr.org ("Monopoly works hand-in-hand with systemic racism to impose barriers on communities of color while extracting wealth from them. The consolidation of banking has deprived Black and Latinx business owners of capital, while levying higher interest rates on those who do receive credit. Consolidation in the grocery industry—and its byproduct, the proliferation of dollar store chains—means poor communities of color especially have limited access to fresh, healthy food. The grip of incumbent telecom monopolies is driving a digital divide that leaves many Black and Latinx households without fast, affordable Internet.").

218 **more than $6.5 trillion:** Wolf Richter, "'Wild Ride to Nowhere': APPL, MSFT, AMZN, GOOG, FB Soar to New High. Rest of Stock Market Is a Dud, Has Been for Years," News Break, July 11, 2020, www.newsbreak.com.

218 **the stock market:** The American economy is, increasingly, in the hands of the very powerful. Seventy percent of the stock market is now controlled by institutional investors (for example, banks, hedge funds) that are frequently the largest shareholders in companies that compete against one another. David Peartree, "The Stock Market Isn't What It Used to Be," Worth Considering, Oct. 19, 2017, www.worthconsidering.com ("The individual investor who directly owns stock no longer dominates the stock market. Institutional investors do. In 1950, over 90 percent of the stock market was owned directly by individual investors. Today, that number is believed to be less than 30 percent."); see also ibid. ("The shift in stock ownership and management has contributed to a third significant change, a shift in trading patterns. Decades ago, individual investors were responsible for most of the trades placed. In recent years, however, about 90 percent of stock trades are made by institutional investors."); Maureen Burton and Bruce Brown, *The Financial System and the Economy: Principles of Money and Banking*, 5th ed. (London: Routledge, 2009), 323 ("Large institutional investors such as pension funds, insurance companies, and mutual funds have come to dominate the market. The institutional investors tend to trade large blocks of stocks (more than 10,000 shares of a given stock or trades with a market value higher than $200,000). Institutional investors, who owned only 7.2 percent of all equities in 1950, now own over 60 percent of the market valuation of all stock."); Ben W. Heineman Jr. and Stephen Davis, "Are Institutional Investors Part of the Problem or Part of the Solution? Key Descriptive and Prescriptive Questions About Shareholders' Role in U.S. Public Equity Markets," Yale School of Management, Millstein Center for Corporate Governance and Performance, Oct. 2011, 1, web.law .columbia.edu ("institutional investors own more than seventy percent of the largest 1,000 companies in the United States"); Luca Enriques and Alessandro Romano, "Institutional Investor Voting Behavior: A Network Theory Perspective," 2019 *University of Illinois Law Review* 223, 225 ("Pension funds, whether state-sponsored or privately sponsored, mutual funds, banks' trust departments, hedge funds, and insurance companies are today the predominant holders of shares in U.S. (and non-U.S.) listed companies."). Cross-ownership, coupled with the growing consolidation of industry players, is creating novel legal issues and, frankly, the conditions for a perfect storm that threatens American capitalism—the economic system that, in prior decades, produced America's vast middle class and that is, frankly, still the envy of the world. When companies that should be competing fiercely against one another are owned by the exact same small group of institutional investors and big money firms, bad things—including collusion and price-fixing cartels—are bound to happen.

218 **too few, to date, even acknowledge exists:** The first step to addressing a problem, I would suggest, is something I learned from my dad's many years in Alcoholics Anonymous, that is, *admitting* that a problem actually exists, which it clearly does. The statistics for new start-ups are all over the map, though there is a consensus that it's become harder to successfully start a business

in the United States. The U.S. Census Bureau and economists at the Federal Reserve, the University of Maryland, and the University of Notre Dame have recently teamed up, leading to the release of a new measure—Business Formation Statistics—that uses modeling and data on applications from firms to the IRS for an employer identification number (EIN). EIN applications provide forward-looking information on business formation activities, though not all EIN applications result in new businesses that actually get off the ground and hire people. Ron S. Jarmin, "Evolving Measurement for an Evolving Economy: Thoughts on 21st Century US Economic Statistics," 33 *Journal of Economic Perspectives* 165, 171 (2019); Center for Economic Studies and Research Data Centers Research Report: 2018—Research and Methodology Directorate, June 2019, 1; U.S. Census Bureau, "Census Bureau Debuts New Data Product: Business Formation Statistics," news release, July 17, 2019, www.census .gov. Prior to the pandemic, the data showed that the number of national and state business applications, seasonally adjusted, rose over time—from around fewer than 650,000 applications per quarter in 2005 to more than 850,000 applications per quarter in 2018. Business Formation Statistics, Historic Time Series, 2004—present, www.census.gov. But even though pre-pandemic applications were up and Americans' entrepreneurial spirit is alive and kicking, with TV shows like *Shark Tank* inspiring start-ups and entrepreneurship, the newly formed companies are creating jobs at a slower pace than they have in the past. According to a 2017 report of the nonprofit Kauffman Foundation, start-up activity climbed above 2008 levels, reflecting progress since the Great Recession. The number of employer businesses, however, reportedly remained "roughly 20 percent below pre-recession levels and down from the previous three decades." "Despite the rebound in recent years, high-growth firms create fewer jobs than they did in the past," notes Arnobio Morelix, a researcher who authored the report. "The overarching story is the decline in dynamism," Morelix observes. Leigh Buchanan, "Small-Business Growth Is Improving. Just Don't Expect It to Be What It Once Was," *Inc.*, Oct. 25, 2017, www.inc .com.

219 **John Oliver:** Melissa Locker, "John Oliver Breaks Down Corporate Consolidation on *Last Week Tonight*," *Time*, Sept. 25, 2017, time.com.

219 **control 82 percent of the coffin industry:** Fiona Zublin, "Why the Coffin Industry Is Dying for Disruption," OZY, June 26, 2019, www.ozy.com; Michael Waters, "Can the American Casket Monopoly Be Disrupted," Hustle, Dec. 20, 2019, thehustle.co.

219 **the number of new businesses:** Heather Long, "Where Are All the Startups? U.S. Entrepreneurship Near 40-Year Low," CNN, Sept. 8, 2016, money.cnn .com.

219 **start-up activity:** To kick-start more jobs and economic growth in light of the start-up slump, I have paired up with Senator Tim Scott—a Republican from South Carolina—to create the first bipartisan entrepreneurship caucus to explore why the rate of new business creation fell below historic levels. Leigh Buchanan, "The Senate Just Made a Bold Move to Jump-Start the Creation of New Businesses," *Inc.*, March 7, 2019, www.inc.com. The new caucus will bring together political leaders from both parties—and across committees and issue areas—to figure out what can be done to spur more innovation, drive

economic growth, and move America's economy forward, as well as jump-start new businesses, including in communities of color and by women entrepreneurs. "This is big news," John Dearie, the president and founder of the nonpartisan Center for American Entrepreneurship, said after we announced the formation of the caucus, adding that it would provide a "coherent framework for caucus members to learn about a subject like entrepreneurship and lead, hopefully, to greater understanding, consensus, and legislative momentum." "Small businesses and entrepreneurship are the backbone of the American economy," Senator Scott pointed out, talking about America's more than thirty million small businesses.

219 **a recent report:** "2016 Was Best Year for Business Formation Since the Recession, but Hold the Fireworks," Economic Innovation Group, Jan. 10, 2019, eig .org.

219 **venture capital:** The Center for American Entrepreneurship and the National Center for Women & Information Technology have documented that the U.S. venture capital industry—as well as the high-tech start-ups funded by it—has a long-entrenched gender gap. "In 2017," those organizations observed in February 2019, just "16 percent of the nearly $83 billion invested in U.S. venture-backed startups went to companies with at least one female founder, and just 2.5 percent went to startups with all-female founders." "CAE Releases New Report: 'The Ascent of Women-Founded Venture-Backed Startups in the United States,'" press release, Feb. 19, 2019, www.startupsusa.org. The statistics, in fact, show both gender and racial disparities when it comes to venture capital funding. As the *MIT Technology Review* pointed out in mid-July 2020, "Most of the people who allot venture cash are white men, and they mostly fund startups led by white men. Fully 65% of venture capital firms have no female partners, and 81% have no Black investors. Only 2% of the cash distributed by venture firms in 2017–18 went to women-led startups, and over the period from 2013 to 2017, only 1% of venture money went to Black entrepreneurs." Wade Roush, who's been following technology start-ups for twenty years, summarized it this way: "The statistics show that only a tiny fraction of the startups backed by venture capital are led by women or people of color." Wade Roush, "Podcast: Lassoing the Venture Capital Cowboys," *MIT Technology Review,* July 15, 2020, www.technologyreview.com.

220 **Bloomberg News:** Davide Scigliuzzo et al., "Covid-19 Is Bankrupting American Companies at a Relentless Pace," Bloomberg, July 9, 2020, www .bloomberg.com.

220 **In mid-July 2019 testimony:** Tim Wu, "Where New Industries Get Their Start: Rebooting the Startup Economy," Testimony Before the Committee on the Judiciary, Subcommittee on Antitrust, Commercial, and Administrative Law, U.S. House of Representatives, July 16, 2019, docs.house.gov.

221 **led to more new start-ups:** "Startups Are Finding the Sweet Spot in a Downturn," Knowledge@Wharton, Wharton School of the University of Pennsylvania, Nov. 3, 2020, https://knowledge.wharton.upenn.edu/article/mollick -pandemic-startups/ (podcast).

221 **getting bigger:** Dorothy Neufeld, "Visualizing the Size of Amazon, the World's Most Valuable Retailer," Visual Capitalist, July 2, 2020, www.visualcapitalist .com (chart depicting "10 Largest Public U.S. Retailers 2010 vs 2020").

221 **one analyst:** Rich Duprey, "Analyst Predicts Amazon Will Hit $2 Trillion Valuation," Motley Fool, July 31, 2020, www.fool.com; see also Taylor Soper, "Amazon Earnings Preview: Analysts Expect Another Big Quarter for Retail and Cloud Giant," GeekWire, Oct. 29, 2020, www.geekwire.com ("The company's stock is up 90% since March, trading at around $3,187 on Thursday. Its market capitalization has risen to $1.6 trillion, right alongside Microsoft. They trail Apple ($2 trillion) for the title of most valuable publicly-traded U.S. company.").

221 **Apple and Microsoft:** Nicolas Vega, "A Day After Congressional Grilling, Big Tech Stocks Add $250 Billion," *New York Post,* July 31, 2020, nypost.com.

221 **to more than $2 trillion:** Amrith Ramkumar, "Apple Surges to $2 Trillion Market Value," *Wall Street Journal,* Aug. 19, 2020, www.wsj.com.

221 **a *Wall Street Journal* article:** Theo Francis and Ryan Knutson, "Wave of Megadeals Tests Antitrust Limits in U.S.," *Wall Street Journal,* Oct. 18, 2015, www.wsj.com.

222 **David Leonhardt reported:** Steve Dubb, "Nonprofit Study Charts Rising US Corporate Concentration," *Nonprofit Quarterly,* Nov. 27, 2018, nonprofitquarterly.org.

222 **three largest pharmacy chains:** Charley Grant, "A Prescription for Pain at the American Drugstore," *Wall Street Journal,* July 19, 2019, www.wsj.com.

223 **"Residents may need to travel":** Lisa Esposito, "Rural Pharmacies Are Closing: Where Does That Leave Patients?," *U.S. News & World Report,* Oct. 17, 2018, health.usnews.com.

223 **Amazon launched its own online pharmacy:** Aislinn Antrim, "Amazon Launches Amazon Pharmacy, Prescription Delivery Service," *Pharmacy Times,* Nov. 17, 2020, www.pharmacytimes.com.

223 **"If your local small town pharmacy":** "Rep. Forbes: Putting an End to Gaming the System," *Des Moines Register,* Jan. 25, 2020, www.desmoinesregister.com.

223 **a University of Illinois study:** Maia Anderson, "Pharmacy Closures 'Disproportionately' Affect Independent Pharmacies, Low-Income Neighborhoods, Study Finds," *Becker's Hospital Review,* Oct. 21, 2019, www.beckershospitalreview.com.

224 **consumer products:** The prices for other common products have been manipulated by monopoly power. One example? Canned tuna. In September 2019, StarKist—the market leader for packaged tuna—was ordered to pay a $100 million fine for its part in a conspiracy to inflate prices. As *The Wall Street Journal* summarized the court filings and the federal judge's order that the company pay that penalty, "StarKist worked with rivals Bumble Bee Foods LLC and Chicken of the Sea for almost a two-year period that ended in December 2013 to fix prices for canned tuna." While Chicken of the Sea managed to avoid criminal charges by exposing the conspiracy, Bumble Bee pleaded guilty for its role in the price-fixing conspiracy and got fined $25 million. "Millions of American households and businesses," *The Wall Street Journal* observed, had purchased canned-tuna products at inflated prices. Micah Maidenberg, "StarKist Hit with $100 Million Fine in Tuna Price-Fixing Case," *Wall Street Journal,* Sept. 11, 2019, www.wsj.com. Christopher Lischewski—Bumble Bee's former CEO—was later sentenced to forty months in prison and fined

$100,000 for his role in the price-fixing conspiracy after a jury, following a four-week trial in late 2019, convicted him. Dave Sebastian, "Former Bumble Bee CEO Sentenced for Role in Tuna Price-Fixing Scheme," *Wall Street Journal,* June 17, 2020, www.wsj.com. In mid-2020, Washington State's attorney general, Bob Ferguson, sued StarKist and a former canned-tuna industry CEO for price-fixing that he asserts bilked consumers of millions of dollars. The price-fixing scheme, he continued, cost Washington State residents alone at least $6 million by artificially inflating the cost of canned tuna. The lawsuit alleges that Lischewski, at a 1999 industry conference, expressed alarm that the companies in the industry were losing $200 million annually in an "unwinnable" war and that the price-fixing agreement—one that included telephone calls, emails about collusive prices, and assurances not to compete—was in place by 2004. Geoff Baker, "Washington State Lawsuit Alleges Price-Fixing by StarKist and Rival Tuna Conglomerates," *Seattle Times,* June 2, 2020, www.seattletimes.com ("In the early stages of the conspiracy, the lawsuit states, the companies agreed to follow any competitor's price increase with one of their own. Later, they each downsized their cans from six ounces to five without reducing prices—then later colluded in increasing prices on those smaller containers."). In its report on the lawsuit, *The Seattle Times* observed that Attorney General Ferguson "is saying 'Sorry Charlie' to StarKist tuna and the former CEO of competitor Bumble Bee." See also "Who Knew There Was So Much Drama in the Canned Tuna Industry?," *Market Crumbs,* Dec. 5, 2019, www.marketcrumbs.com ("In August 2015, a class-action lawsuit filed in a federal court alleged that the three major U.S. tuna producers—StarKist, Bumble Bee Foods and Tri-Union Seafoods—colluded to inflate prices for years. . . . At the time of the lawsuit, the three companies controlled 73% of the $1.7 billion U.S. canned tuna market. Tri-Union and Bumble Bee had been in discussions to merge when the lawsuit was filed, which would've created a duopoly. The merger was abandoned less than four months after the lawsuit was filed, with the United States Department of Justice's Antitrust Division saying 'Consumers are better off without this deal.' "). The global market for canned tuna stood at $7.74 billion in 2019, and it is expected to reach more than $9 billion by 2027. "Canned Tuna Market Size to Reach USD 9.22 Billion by 2027," Fortune Business Insights, July 6, 2020, www.globenewswire.com. In calling for a prison term for Lischewski, prosecutors stated, "When defendant decided to engage in this crime, he already was a wealthy man and CEO of a major company. . . . And he led a multi-year conspiracy to raise the price of canned tuna—all to satisfy his own greed." Cliff White, "Chris Lischewski Hopes to Avoid Prison, While Prosecutors Push for 10-Year Sentence," SeafoodSource, May 15, 2020, www.seafoodsource.com.

224 **multinational accounting firms:** Karthik Ramanna, *Political Standards: Corporate Interest, Ideology, and Leadership in the Shaping of Accounting Rules for the Market Economy* (Chicago: University of Chicago Press, 2015), 70.

224 **the Final Four:** James Brock, *The Structure of American Industry,* 12th ed. (Long Grove, Ill.: Waveland Press, 2009), 333.

224 **the Big Five:** Jane Friedman, *The Business of Being a Writer* (Chicago: University of Chicago Press, 2018), 44–45. The consolidation of publishing companies began in the 1980s and 1990s, with the Big Five imprints accounting for

approximately 75 percent of the shelf space in bookstores. As Jane Friedman explains in her book, "Larger publishers have bought smaller ones, and multi-media companies have bought the big publishers. Eventually, the Big Five are expected to become the Big Four, or perhaps even the Big Three." In November 2020, a bidding war broke out between Rupert Murdoch's News Corp and German media group Bertelsmann to buy Simon & Schuster. As the *Financial Times* reported: "ViacomCBS is expecting final bids for its Simon & Schuster publishing arm this week, according to people familiar with the process, with a floor for offers set at $1.7bn, significantly in excess of initial estimates. Interest from trade bidders including News Corp, the owner of HarperCollins, and Bertelsmann's Penguin Random House, the world's biggest publisher, appears to have priced out potential financial buyers and private equity, according to the people." Alex Barker, Leila Abboud, James Fontanella-Khan, and Anna Nicolaou, "News Corp to Join Battle for Simon & Schuster," *Financial Times*, Nov. 17, 2020, www.ft.com.

224 **controlled by a German media company:** "Bertelsmann to Take Full Control of Penguin Random House," Associated Press, Dec. 18, 2019, apnews.com.

224 **One recent megamerger:** Kate Holton, "Random House and Penguin Merge to Take on Amazon, Apple," Reuters, Oct. 29, 2012, www.reuters.com.

224 **agreed to combine:** Authors and agents naturally expressed concern that further industry consolidation would drive down author advances and agent commissions. But the deal, estimated to be worth $3 billion and reportedly driven by the threat posed by Amazon, which had amassed a 90 percent market share of e-book sales, went forward anyway. The deal itself was announced after the U.S. government had sued Apple and five publishers—Hachette Book Group, HarperCollins, Holtzbrinck (d/b/a Macmillan), Penguin Group (USA), and Simon & Schuster—for allegedly conspiring, in violation of the Sherman Act and state laws, to raise and fix e-book prices. All of the publishers ultimately settled those antitrust claims with federal and state authorities out of court, leaving only Apple in the crosshairs when the case went to trial in a federal district court in June 2013.

It was, there is little doubt, Amazon's power, massive size, and e-book industry dominance that led to joint venture discussions between Penguin and Random House in the first place. As one October 2012 headline announcing the joint venture read, "Battling Amazon: Pearson and Bertelsmann to Form Global Consumer Publishing Giant, Penguin Random House, to Build 'New Digital Publishing Models.'" "In their joint announcement," the news story reported, "there is no mention of Amazon but the ecommerce giant is the elephant in the room—having disrupted traditional bookselling models, driving down the price of books by selling physical books online and championing the sale of digital books via its Kindle readers. Amazon is also treading directly on publishers' toes by taking on a publishing role itself." Natasha Lomas, "Battling Amazon: Pearson and Bertelsmann to Form Global Consumer Publishing Giant, Penguin Random House, to Build 'New Digital Publishing Models,'" *TechCrunch,* Oct. 29, 2012, techcrunch.com.

224 **in a joint venture:** The deal gave Bertelsmann, a giant German media company, a 53 percent share of the new venture, while Britain's Pearson received a 47 percent stake. In the lead-up to the deal, traditional publishers were being

hit particularly hard because many consumers were swapping bookshops and printed books for the convenience of e-books and digital downloads. At the time of the combination, Pearson's chief executive, Marjorie Scardino, said it would allow Penguin and Random House "to share a large part of their costs, to invest more for their author and reader constituencies and to be more adventurous in trying new models." Thomas Rabe, Bertelsmann's chief executive, said the deal would allow the combined businesses "to publish even more effectively across traditional and emerging formats and distribution channels." Monira Matin, "Penguin and Random House to Merge and Compete Against Amazon and Apple," *ITProPortal,* Oct. 29, 2012, www.itproportal.com. Bertelsmann later bought out all of Pearson's interest in Penguin Random House. Katherine Cowdrey, "Bertelsmann Formally Completes Full Acquisition of Penguin Random House," *The Bookseller,* April 2, 2020, www.thebookseller .com.

224 **an antitrust dispute:** Matthew Lasar, "Apple, Publishers Conspired Against $9.99 Amazon E-books: Lawsuit," *Wired,* Aug. 10, 2011, www.wired.com; "Apple Colluded on E-book Prices, Judge Finds," Reuters, July 10, 2013, www .reuters.com.

224 **a protracted court battle:** In 2010, *The New York Times* called the e-book industry fight "a formidable high-tech face-off: Amazon.com versus Apple for the hearts and minds of book publishers, authors and readers." Brad Stone and Motoko Rich, "Apple Courts Publishers, While Kindle Adds Apps," *New York Times,* Jan. 20, 2010, www.nytimes.com. In the dispute, Amazon had complained to the FTC that the book publishing companies had signed agreements with Apple simultaneously. Cynthia E. Clark, Kabrina K. Chang, and Sean P. Melvin, *Business and Society: Ethical, Legal, and Digital Environments* (Thousand Oaks, Calif.: SAGE, 2020), 116. On July 10, 2013, Judge Denise Cote described how the price for e-books rose significantly in the United States in April 2010, leading to the antitrust lawsuit by the U.S. government, as well as thirty-three states and U.S. territories, against Apple and the five book publishers originally named in the lawsuit. Following a bench trial in which the government called twelve fact witnesses and two expert economists, Judge Denise Cote, of the U.S. District Court for the Southern District of New York, issued her lengthy written opinion. In that opinion, she concluded that "Apple conspired to raise the retail price of e-books" and that "without Apple's orchestration of this conspiracy, it would not have succeeded as it did in the Spring of 2010." *United States v. Apple Inc.,* 952 F. Supp. 2d 638 (S.D.N.Y. 2013); Chris Sagers, *United States v. Apple: Competition in America* (Cambridge, Mass.: Harvard University Press, 2019), 2.

Before Apple met with book publishers, Judge Cote found, it knew that the then "Big Six" publishers wanted to raise e-book prices above the $9.99 prevailing price charged by Amazon for many e-book versions of *New York Times* best sellers and other newly released hardcover books. "Apple," Judge Cote determined, "also knew that Publisher Defendants were already acting collectively to place pressure on Amazon to abandon its pricing strategy." After the publishers conveyed to Apple their disdain for Amazon's $9.99 pricing regime, Apple—planning to launch its iBookstore when Steve Jobs announced the original iPad on January 27, 2010—had assured the publishers that it would work with them to raise e-book prices, suggesting prices such as $12.99 and $14.99. As Judge Cote summarized her findings, "Taking advantage of the Publisher Defendants' fear of and frustration over Amazon's pricing, as well as the tight window of opportunity created by the impending launch of the iPad on January 27 (the 'Launch'), Apple garnered the signatures it needed to introduce the iBookstore at the Launch. It provided the Publisher Defendants with the vision, the format, the timetable, and the coordination that they needed to raise e-book prices. Apple decided to offer the Publisher Defendants the opportunity to move from a wholesale model—where a publisher receives its designated wholesale price for each e-book and the retailer sets the retail price—to an agency model, where a publisher sets the retail price and the retailer sells the e-book as its agent." Virtually overnight," Judge Cote concluded, "Apple got an attractive, additional feature for its iPad and a guaranteed new revenue stream, and the Publisher Defendants removed Amazon's ability to price their e-books at $9.99." See also Alan Hess, *The New iPad Fully Loaded* (Indianapolis, Ind.: John Wiley & Sons, 2012), 3 ("The original iPad was announced by Steve Jobs on January 27, 2010, and shipped on April 3, 2010—the longest 66 days ever. It changed personal computing forever.").

On appeal, the U.S. Court of Appeals for the Second Circuit, by a 2–1 vote, affirmed Judge Cote's ruling. "We conclude," the Second Circuit ruled, "that the district court's decision that Apple orchestrated a horizontal conspiracy among the Publisher Defendants to raise ebook prices is amply supported and well-reasoned, and that the agreement unreasonably restrained trade in violation of § 1 of the Sherman Act." *United States v. Apple Inc.,* 791 F.3d 290 (2d Cir. 2015). The Second Circuit's opinion, which led to Apple paying out $450 million in 2016 because of the U.S. Supreme Court's discretionary decision to decline to hear Apple's appeal, describes the novel context of the antitrust case against Apple. "Apple to Pay $450m Settlement over US Ebook Price Fixing," Reuters, March 7, 2016, www.theguardian.com. "Since the invention of the printing press," the majority opinion began, "the distribution of books has involved a fundamentally consistent process: compose a manuscript, print and bind it into physical volumes, and then ship and sell the volumes to the public." "In late 2007," however, the Second Circuit observed, Amazon.com "introduced the Kindle, a portable device that carries digital copies of books, known as 'ebooks.'" "This innovation," the court stressed, taking note of Amazon's $9.99 pricing, "had the potential to change the centuries-old process for producing books by eliminating the need to print, bind, ship, and store them. . . . Publishing companies, which have traditionally stood at the center of the multi-billion dollar book-producing industry, saw Amazon's ebooks, and particularly its $9.99 pricing, as a threat to their way of doing business."

224 **the Society of Children's Book Writers and Illustrators:** Lee Wind, "Will the 'Big Five' Become the 'Big Four'?", SCBWI: The Blog (the official blog of the Society of Children's Book Writers and Illustrators), Nov. 19, 2020, scb .blogspot.com.

224 **it was announced in late November 2020:** Bhuma Shrivastava and Natalia Drozdiak, "Bertelsmann to Buy Simon & Schuster for $2.18 Billion," Bloomberg, Nov. 25, 2020, www.bloomberg.com. Thomas Rabe, Bertelsmann's chairman and chief executive, downplayed any antitrust concerns relating to

the acquisition of Simon & Schuster, citing "the strength of Amazon" and figures from the American Association of Publishers showing that the two companies' combined revenue would amount to less than 20 percent of the market. Ibid.; Alex Barker and Erika Solomon, "Bertelsmann Joins Race to Acquire Simon & Schuster," *Financial Times,* Sept. 1, 2020, www.ft.com. Compare Jill Goldsmith, "Simon & Schuster Bids Due by Thanksgiving; News Corp., Bertelsmann, Vivendi Contenders for ViacomCBS Publisher," Deadline, Nov. 17, 2020, deadline.com ("The question of antitrust could come up. . . . The sector has been squeezed by competition, especially by Amazon, and seen major consolidation in recent years.").

225 **against other big companies:** By July 2018, on the fifth anniversary of the merger, Penguin Random House did $3.4 billion in sales, had 275 imprints, and was selling 700 million books a year. Although it now has to compete against Amazon, another mega-company, Penguin Random House is currently larger than its four largest rivals put together. Alex Shephard, "Penguin Random House Is Building the Perfect Publishing House," *New Republic,* Sept. 12, 2018, newrepublic.com. "The point of a Penguin Random House is to create scale," *The New Republic* reported in September 2018, noting the competition from Amazon and quoting Penguin Random House's spokesperson Claire von Schilling. "We are able to leverage scale in direct marketing to consumers and in our supply chain to support our retailers and to get our books into the hands of readers quickly," she wrote in an email. "We have the largest book sales force in the world, with unparalleled reach into every different kind of bookseller globally," she said.

225 **Amazon.com:** In some cases, Amazon has led, in the short term, to lower prices. Martin Moore and Damian Tambini, eds., *Digital Dominance: The Power of Google, Amazon, Facebook, and Apple* (Oxford: Oxford University Press, 2018), 39. However, the dominance of Amazon, when combined with the failure to update our country's antitrust laws, has created a grave risk to marketplace competitors who are, very frequently, now heavily reliant on that company—in some cases, for their very survival. Jason Del Rey, "Amazon Was Already Powerful. The Coronavirus Pandemic Cleared the Way to Dominance," Recode, April 10, 2020, www.vox.com; "Survey: Independent Businesses See Major Threats in Amazon, Corporate Concentration," Institute for Local Self-Reliance, Aug. 6, 2010, https://ilsr.org.

225 **local bookstores:** Virginia Wardell, "Penn Book Center to Close in May, Another Store Beaten Out by Amazon," The Triangle, April 19, 2019, www.thetriangle.org; J. Oliver Conroy, "Why Are New York's Bookstores Disappearing?," *Guardian,* March 4, 2019, www.theguardian.com; Alexandra Alter and Tiffany Hsu, "Barnes & Noble Is Sold to Hedge Fund After a Tumultuous Year," *New York Times,* June 7, 2019, www.nytimes.com; Erica Pandey, "How Barnes & Noble, the Last Big Bookstore, Fell to Amazon," *Axios,* Oct. 7, 2018, www.axios.com. See also Bryce Covert, "How Bookstores Are Weathering the Pandemic," Vox, Oct. 25, 2020, www.vox.com (noting that "according to the American Booksellers Association (ABA), 35 member bookstores have closed during the pandemic, with roughly one store closing each week").

225 **"the most dominant force":** Rachelle Hampton, "Amazon Is Putting Book

Deliveries into the Slow Lane Thanks to the Coronavirus," *Slate,* March 17, 2020, slate.com.

225 **bad news for most authors:** Adam Rowe, "Why Authors Are Earning Less Even as Book Sales Rise," Forbes.com, Aug. 11, 2018, www.forbes.com.

226 **Back in 2015:** David Streitfeld, "Accusing Amazon of Antitrust Violations, Authors and Booksellers Demand Inquiry," *New York Times,* July 13, 2015, www.nytimes.com.

226 **Amazon's dominance:** A new market entrant can disrupt an entire market and take on big players, but when the new entrant is, itself, a massive corporation, the result can be that individual creators or consumers get hurt. At one point, during the bitter fight over whether book publishers could control the pricing of e-books, Amazon removed preorder buttons from book titles published by Hachette, a subsidiary of the French company Lagardère Publishing, and refused to restock Hachette titles. Nick Statt and Donna Tam, "Amazon and Hachette Settle Bitter E-book Dispute," CNET, Nov. 13, 2014, www.cnet .com. While Amazon wanted to offer most e-books at the same price, Hachette sought to control the price of their own e-books. Hachette is the publisher of popular authors such as James Patterson, though all Hachette authors—and all American consumers—were affected by the battle of the titans. The companies settled their dispute in 2014, but as one account notes, during the dispute Amazon came under scrutiny "for its aggressive tactics," which included "delaying delivery and deleting the pre-order facility for Hachette titles." Kelvin Smith and Melanie Ramdarshan Bold, *The Publishing Business: A Guide to Starting Out and Getting On,* 2nd ed. (London: Bloomsbury, 2018).

In March 2019, Amazon—citing antitrust concerns—announced that it would no longer dictate how sellers price their products. Ahiza Garcia, "Amazon Will No Longer Dictate How Sellers Price Their Products," CNN Business, March 11, 2019. Plainly, Amazon's dominance in the book industry has put tremendous pressure on authors and traditional publishers. Authors can distribute their own books through Amazon, the top retailer of books, but they don't have a lot of leverage to negotiate the best terms. "It's estimated," Friedman writes, "that across all formats—print, e-book, and audio—more than 60 percent of book sales in the United States are now made through Amazon." "Looking solely at e-books," she points out, picking out one major category, "Amazon is believed to account for 70 to 80 percent of all US book sales." One watchdog group found in 2017 that as much as 80 percent of dollars spent on e-books likely goes to Amazon, leaving less money for the writers who create the content. "As publishers feel increased pressure to meet the bottom line, authors' advances are often the one negotiable line item in the budget," Mary Rasenberger, the executive director of the Authors Guild, has said, identifying industry consolidation as a major reason why authors now make less money. Since Amazon released its Kindle product in November 2007, Amazon has fought a series of battles with traditional book publishers and authors, and there is a lot of money at stake. David Guion, "How Amazon Has Disrupted the Book Industry," *Reading, Writing, Research* (blog), Jan. 31, 2018, www.allpurposeguru.com.

In a more recent incident, after Amazon mailed out copies of the novelist Margaret Atwood's highly anticipated (but embargoed) sequel to *The Hand-*

maid's Tale a week ahead of its planned release date, Amazon apologized, but independent booksellers went ballistic. "Amazon's latest actions only further underscore how important it is that the appropriate federal agencies thoroughly investigate Amazon's destructive business practices," the American Booksellers Association declared. Keith J. Kelly, "Booksellers Blast Amazon's Apology for Early Release of 'The Handmaid's Tale' Sequel," *New York Post,* Sept. 5, 2019, nypost.com.

226 **a twenty-two-page letter:** David Grogan, "ABA Provides DOJ Antitrust Division with Information Ahead of Its Big Tech Review," American Booksellers Association, Aug. 28, 2019, www.bookweb.org.

226 **with one analyst:** Matthew Fox, " 'COVID-19 Has Been Like Injecting Amazon with a Growth Hormone': Here's What 4 Analysts Had to Say About Amazon's Earnings Report as $4,000 Price Targets Start to Roll In," *Business Insider,* July 31, 2020, markets.businessinsider.com.

226 **Amazon has opened:** Nat Levy, "Amazon Continues Physical Retail Expansion with Plans for New Bookstore in Nashville and 4-Star Store in Boston," *GeekWire,* Aug. 15, 2019, www.geekwire.com.

226 **2018 holiday shopping season:** Dan Alaimo, "80% of Online Shoppers Will Use Amazon This Holiday Season," *Retail Dive,* Oct. 15, 2018, www.retaildive.com.

226 **Amazon sells books and electronics:** "How Many Products Does Amazon Sell?—April 2019," ScrapeHero, www.scrapehero.com.

226 **PillPack:** Charley Grant, "A Prescription for Pain at the American Drugstore," *Wall Street Journal,* July 19, 2019, www.wsj.com. After acquiring PillPack, Amazon launched Amazon Pharmacy approximately two years later. Jonathan Shieber and Ingrid Lunden, "Amazon Launches Amazon Pharmacy, a Delivery Service for Prescription Medications," TechCrunch, Nov. 17, 2020, techcrunch.com.

226 **recently published statistics:** Jeff Desjardins, "The Impressive Stats Behind Amazon's Dominance of the Cloud," Visual Capitalist, July 8, 2019, www.visualcapitalist.com.

227 **in a market:** Capitalism is driven by market-based transactions. While corporate deals are, long have been, and no doubt forever will be a common feature of America's capitalist system, the sheer size of many modern-day mergers and acquisitions has created massive, now dominant companies. Those huge companies dwarf small businesses and thus can easily—because of their immense power—squash or stifle competition or make things miserable for their competitors. One common strategy they employ is simply buying up their competition. When competitors are gobbled up, competition simply vanishes altogether. Writing in November 2018, three equity investment analysts emphasized that 2018 was "on track to be an unprecedented fourth consecutive year with more than $2 trillion in proposed M&A transactions. There have been more than two dozen deals valued at more than $10 billion each year, most notably megadeals between Disney and 21st Century Fox, CVS and Aetna, and AT&T and Time Warner." Brad Freer, Martin Jacobs, and Shailesh Jaity, "The Global Consolidation Wave in 5 Charts," Capital Ideas, Nov. 21, 2018, www.thecapitalideas.com.

227 **cable industry:** Nathan McAlone, "Cable TV Price Increases Have Beaten

Inflation Every Single Year for 20 Years," *Business Insider,* Oct. 31, 2016, www
.businessinsider.com (noting that for U.S. cable TV, "price increases have outpaced inflation for every single one of the past 20 years," with cable TV's
increases "more than double that of inflation"; whereas in 1995, cable cost
$22.35 per month, in 2015 it had gone up to $69.03); see also Tali Arbel, "TV
Rate Hikes: Why Cable Bills Are Rising Again and What Can You Do," *USA
Today,* Jan. 8, 2018, www.usatoday.com ("Over the past decade, prices for TV
service have risen almost twice as fast as inflation, according to an analysis of
government data.").

227 **The FTC challenged:** Michael B. Bernstein, Justin P. Hedge, and Franc-
esca M. Pisano, "FTC's Success in Staples/Office Depot Showcases Trends
in Agency Merger Enforcement Strategy," Arnold & Porter Advisory, June 8,
2016, www.arnoldporter.com.

227 **in May 2016:** Less than three years later, in March 2019, Office Depot
announced that it was teaming up with China-based Alibaba, with its global
network of 150,000 suppliers, to help the Boca Raton office supply company
compete more effectively against Amazon. Marcia Heroux Pounds, "Office
Depot Teams Up with Global Supply Network Alibaba," *South Florida Sun
Sentinel,* March 4, 2019, www.sun-sentinel.com.

227 **in the tech area:** Omri Wallach, "How Big Tech Makes Their Billions," Visual
Capitalist, July 6, 2020, www.visualcapitalist.com.

227 **global online search market:** Sissi Cao, "Google CEO Sundar Pichai Struggles
to Defend Monopoly in Big Tech Hearing," *Observer,* July 7, 2020, observer
.com.

228 **"While the vast majority of dairies":** Adam Belz, "Milking Cows on an Industrial Scale Arrives in Western Minnesota, and Some Farmers Shudder," *Minneapolis Star Tribune,* Aug. 11, 2018, www.startribune.com. In agriculture, the
shift from smaller to much larger operations is clear, with many dairy farmers
and corn and soybean growers struggling to make ends meet. As the *Star Tribune's* reporter Adam Belz notes in his story about America's dairy industry
and those who cultivate the land, "In 2001, dairy farms with fewer than 500
cattle produced two-thirds of the nation's milk. By 2009, their share fell to 40
percent." "For 30 years," Belz adds, "farms in the Upper Midwest have gotten
bigger and farmers who used to work a couple hundred acres now work a couple thousand." Other experts, including ones in my own state, have made dire
predictions for what lies ahead given the trend line. Marin Bozic, a University
of Minnesota economist, recently predicted that 80 percent of Minnesota's
surviving dairies may be "last generation" farms. That is a sobering assessment,
especially for someone like me who believes strongly that kids who grow up in
rural America should be able to stay in rural America. Although Bozic emphasized that the recent farm bills aim to provide a safety net for dairy farmers, he
said that despite his sympathy for "the little guy," more consolidation is on the
horizon, raising grave concerns about whether the children of family farmers
will be able to continue to farm—and to live on—the homesteaded land they
and their ancestors grew up on.

228 **Heartland Forum:** "Presidential Candidates to Discuss Farm Issues: Heartland Forum Set for March 30 at Buena Vista University in Storm Lake," press
release, March 18, 2019, iowafarmersunion.org.

229 **runaway executive compensation:** Collin Eaton, "CEO Pay Towers over Median Salary of Workers," *Houston Chronicle,* May 17, 2018, www.houston chronicle.com.

229 **income and wealth inequality:** Shana Lynch, "Stanford Profs: U.S. Income Inequality Is Only Getting Worse. Now What?," *Fast Company,* July 30, 2019, www.fastcompany.com; Juliana Menasce Horowitz, Ruth Igielnik, and Rakesh Kochhar, "Trends in Income and Wealth Inequality," Pew Research Center, Jan. 9, 2020, www.pewsocialtrends.org.

229 *Wall Street Journal* **analysis:** Erik Sherman, "CEOs Get Big Pay Raises for Being in the Right Place at the Right Time," *Forbes,* March 25, 2019, www .forbes.com.

229 **report of the Economic Policy Institute:** Elise Gould, *State of Working America Wages 2018: Wage Inequality Marches On—and Is Even Threatening Data Reliability,* Economic Policy Institute, Feb. 20, 2019, 9, www.epi.org.

229 **another report:** Lawrence Mishel and Julia Wolf, "CEO Compensation Has Grown 940% Since 1978," Economic Policy Institute, Aug. 14, 2019, www.epi .org.

229 **to decrease such inequality:** Back in 1774, even before the Revolutionary War (1775–1783) broke out, the Continental Congress—as a whole—quoted a then-famous Italian thinker, Cesare Beccaria, about inequality, the abuse of power that can occur in a society, and how the law can fight those ills. As the Continental Congress wrote, " 'In every human society,' says the celebrated Marquis Beccaria, 'there is an effort, continually tending to confer on one part the height of power and happiness, and to reduce the other to the extreme of weakness and misery. The intent of good laws is to oppose this effort, and to diffuse their influence universally and equally.' " *Journals of the Continental Congress, 1774–1789* (Washington, D.C.: Government Printing Office, 1904), 1:106; John D. Bessler, *The Baron and the Marquis: Liberty, Tyranny, and the Enlightenment Maxim That Can Remake American Criminal Justice* (Durham, N.C.: Carolina Academic Press, 2019), xl–xli.

229 **if the antitrust laws are vigorously enforced:** When antitrust enforcement is neglected, there are extremely adverse societal consequences, including for American consumers, workers, and low-income communities. According to a recent study of the Roosevelt Institute, "The results of the 40-year experiment in the Chicago School antitrust have spelled disaster for the American work-force, middle class, and economy overall. While corporate profits have risen, wages and investment have stagnated." In its 2018 report, *Powerless: How Lax Antitrust and Concentrated Market Power Rig the Economy Against American Workers, Consumers, and Communities,* the authors of the Roosevelt Institute study emphasize, "A 40-year assault on antitrust and competition policy—the laws and regulations meant to guard against the concentration of power in private hands—has helped tip the economy in favor of powerful corporations under the false pretense that the unencumbered ambitions of private business will align with the public good." Noting that most Americans believe the economy is "rigged" in favor of corporations, the Roosevelt Institute report offers this fitting commentary: "Healthy markets depend on rules to create an equitable balance of market power between workers, consumers, and businesses. And when those rules skew the balance of power, markets favor the

most powerful to the detriment of others." Steinbaum, Bernstein, and Sturm, *Powerless;* see also Nathan Wilmers, "Wage Stagnation and Buyer Power: How Buyer-Supplier Relations Affect U.S. Workers' Wages, 1978 to 2014," *American Sociological Review* 83, no. 2 (2018), journals.sagepub.com ("During the 1970s, U.S. workers' wages ended three decades of steady increase and have since stagnated. In the same period, market restructuring, lax antitrust enforcement, and supply chain innovation left many supplier companies dependent on sales to large corporate buyers.").

229 **wealth and income inequality:** Joshua Gans et al., *Inequality and Market Concentration, When Shareholding Is More Skewed Than Consumption,* IZA Institute of Labor Economics, IZA DP No. 12034, Dec. 2018, 8, ftp.iza.org ("The lowest-income fifth of families had 1.1 percent of corporate equity in 1989, and 2.0 in 2016 (over the same timespan, the second-bottom quintile share went from 3.5 percent to 1.6 percent, so the total share of corporate equity of the bottom 40 percent fell). By contrast, the highest-income quintile had 77 percent of corporate equity in 1989, and 89 percent of corporate equity in 2016."); see also ibid., 11 (noting that "monopoly power effectively acts to transfer resources from low-income families to high-income families").

229 **"Antitrust is an important policy tool":** Diana L. Moss, "Antitrust and Inequality: What Antitrust Can and Should Do to Protect Workers," American Antitrust Institute, April 25, 2017, www.antitrustinstitute.org.

230 **racial disparities:** Steinbaum, Bernstein, and Sturm, *Powerless* ("Companies with market power charge consumers of color more for products. Exploiting the structural absence of market access, some companies engage in price discrimination—charging different prices to different customers—in communities of color. Mortgage companies and car insurance providers have been discovered charging consumers of color more, and there is some evidence that major retailers and travel sites offer different prices based on digital activity—opening the door to discrimination based on technological characteristics tied to race.").

230 **racial profiling:** Melissa Repko, "As Black Buying Power Grows, Racial Profiling by Retailers Remains Persistent Problem," CNBC, July 5, 2020, www.cnbc .com; Alison Marie Behnke, *Racial Profiling: Everyday Inequality* (Minneapolis: Twenty-First Century Books, 2017) (noting that "individual acts of profiling can be traced" to businesses and observing that "while racial profiling is closely tied to law enforcement, any institution or individual can engage in profiling"); see also "How Some Algorithm Lending Programs Discriminate Against Minorities," NPR, Nov. 24, 2018, www.npr.org.

230 **discriminatory hiring and promotion practices:** Walter Haessel and John Palmer, "Market Power and Employment Discrimination," 13 *Journal of Human Resources* 545 (1978) (noting that the results of a study "generally confirm that firms in more highly concentrated industries discriminate more"); see also Tejvan Pettinger, "The Economics of Discrimination," Economics, March 23, 2017, www.economicshelp.org ("If firms have monopoly/monopsony power, discrimination enables firms to cut costs and receive more profits (at the expense of workers).").

230 **redlining:** Martin A. French and Simone A. Browne, "Profiles and Profiling Technology: Stereotypes, Surveillance, and Governmentality," in *Criminaliza-*

tion, Representation, Regulation: Thinking Differently About Crime, ed. Deborah Brock, Amanda Glasbeek, and Carmela Murdocca (Toronto: University of Toronto Press, 2014), 272 (noting that *"redlining* is a practice that saw a denial of services by lending institutions, insurance companies, and other financial services," with that form of discrimination particularly affecting "Black individuals in the United States beginning in the 1930s. It initially involved drawing red lines on maps that delineated areas where the privileged would be served and the disadvantaged would be underserved"); see also "Beyond Redlining: Black Lives Matter and Community Development," American Bar Association, June 17, 2020, www.americanbar.org ("Racial discrimination in mortgage lending in the 1930s shaped the demographic and wealth patterns of American communities today, a new study shows, with 3 out of 4 neighborhoods 'redlined' on government maps 80 years ago continuing to struggling economically.").

230   **a report of the Open Markets Institute:** "Income Inequality & Monopoly," Open Markets Institute, www.openmarketsinstitute.org. The report also states,

> One of the easiest ways to see monopoly's effect on America's unequal, concentrated economy is to look at the history of retail business in America in the 20th century. Beginning with state and local laws in the 1920s and continuing with federal legislation passed in the 1930s, Americans crafted an anti-chain store policy that ensured independent business owners would control retail trade.
>
> Sam Walton was a beneficiary of that system. In 1950, he bought one of the three variety stores in Bentonville, Arkansas and opened Walton's 5&10 on the downtown square of the small, rural town. That Bentonville supported three such stores, and other small, independent businesses, was not unusual for small towns in the United States during that time. Walton, like so many thousands of other Americans, then was able to carve out this own slice of the American Dream when he opened his own businesses.
>
> But, radical changes in antimonopoly law and policy in the late 1970s and early 1980s eliminated almost all the traditional constraints on chain stores. In the years since, a few corporations—led by Walmart—steadily took over the American retail market. Today, Walmart controls 72 percent of all warehouse clubs and super centers in the US, and in nearly 40 metro areas, the firm claims at least 50 percent of all grocery spending.
>
> Walmart today runs 5,229 stores across the United States, the equivalent of many tens of thousands of 1950s-era stores. In short, Walmart captures wealth that was once distributed among many tens of thousands of families, taking it out of areas that once benefitted from small business economies that fueled civic engagement and gave back to local communities.

230   **"In concrete terms, monopoly pricing":** Lina Khan and Sandeep Vaheesan, "Market Power and Inequality: The Antitrust Counterrevolution and Its Discontents," 11 *Harvard Law and Policy Review* 235, 236 (2017).

230   **"the potential for unfair":** Andrew Smith, "Using Artificial Intelligence and Algorithms," Federal Trade Commission, April 8, 2020, www.ftc.gov.

231   **Chicago-area hospitals:** "Javits to Address National Conference on Hospital-

ization," *Alabama Tribune*, Feb. 16, 1962, 8 ("A group of Chicago physicians has filed suit against 56 Chicago hospitals and five hospital organizations alleging violation of the Sherman antitrust act in the exclusion of Negro physicians from the local hospital staffs."); see also Bob Queen, "Negroes on Hospital Staffs," *Pittsburgh Courier*, March 18, 1961, 11 ("Nearly 100 Philadelphia medical doctors, assembled in the offices of a leading law firm here, heard Chicago radiologist, Dr. Robert Morris, relate the details of a law suit filed against the Windy City's 56 hospitals and medical services that utilize the Sherman Anti-Trust Law as a unique vehicle in fighting for the acceptance of Negro medics on all hospital staffs.").

231 **Brian Feldman:** Brian S. Feldman, "The Decline of Black Business," *Washington Monthly*, March/April/May 2017, washingtonmonthly.com.

231 **"Reginald Johnson":** "Advocates Use of Anti-trust Act on Housing Bias," *Alabama Tribune*, May 22, 1964, 3 (noting that in an address to the Conference on Discrimination convened by the College of Law and the School of Social Work of Washington University in St. Louis, Missouri, Reginald Johnson of the National Urban League advocated the use of the Sherman Antitrust Act "to break up housing segregation in the nation's cities"); "Trust Act's Use Urged to Halt Bias in Housing," *St. Louis Post-Dispatch*, May 8, 1964, 8 (observing of Reginald Johnson's addresss attended by about 150 people representing housing, welfare, and social agencies, "The use of the Sherman Anti-trust Act to break up housing segregation in the nation's cities was advocated here today by the administrative director of the National Urban League.").

231 **"While there were 70,000":** Louis A. Ferleger and Matthew Lavallee, "Lending a Hand: How Small Black Businesses Supported the Civil Rights Movement" (working paper 67, Dec. 2017); see also Lerone Bennett Jr., "Money, Merchants, Markets: The Quest for Economic Security," *Ebony*, Feb. 1974, 66, 77 (noting that "according to the first comprehensive survey of the black business field (*Minority-owned Businesses: 1969*) there were 163,000 black owned businesses in 1969" in comparison to "the 70,000 black-owned businesses reported in 1930").

231 **"the Civil Rights Movement":** The relationship between the civil rights movement and antitrust is complicated. Black-owned businesses were critical to the success of the civil rights movement. At the same time, local white-owned businesses were the staunchest defenders of Jim Crow laws. By contrast, the large national chains like Woolworth's were far more susceptible to public and social pressure because they had to worry about adverse publicity—and their corporate images—in the North. It was the ability of civil rights' workers to end segregation at Woolworth's that marked the end of Jim Crow in restaurants. Jonathan Scott Holloway, *Jim Crow Wisdom: Memory and Identity in Black America Since 1940* (Chapel Hill: University of North Carolina Press, 2013), 188 ("The lunch counter sit-ins that began at Woolworth's on February 1, 1960, are generally understood as the seedbed for change, as they sparked a nationwide wave of similar protests against racism and segregation that ultimately led to the formation of the Student Nonviolent Coordinating Committee, one of the most influential national protest organizations for most of the decade."; "The Woolworth's in Greensboro . . . was part of one of the largest convenience store chains in the country. As such, the company had much

greater flexibility in how it wanted to respond and recognize its own role in the civil rights struggle. Clarence Lee 'Curly' Harris, the local Woolworth's manager, acknowledged from the very beginning that the company's decision to integrate its lunch counter was as much a nod to a basic sense of decency as it was a recognition of the financial bottom line. The store needed the money and could no longer afford the negative publicity."). Similarly, in the 1920s and 1930s, Sears, Roebuck—what might be thought of as the Amazon of its day— was a lifeline to minorities in the South. White merchants were notorious for not dealing fairly with their Black customers. But Sears, which relied on sales from mailed catalogs, did not know the skin color of its customers when they placed their orders. Although Sears still followed Jim Crow laws in its Atlanta department store until the middle of the twentieth century, the Sears catalog allowed Black shoppers to avoid dealing with local merchants who discriminated against them. Antonia Noori Farzan, "How Sears Mail-Order Catalogs Undermined Jim Crow Racism," *Chicago Tribune,* Oct. 16, 2018, www .chicagotribune.com (noting that "Julius Rosenwald, who had become a part owner of the company after Alvah Roebuck sold his share of the business in 1895, became a well-known philanthropist to the black community," donating $4.3 million—"the equivalent of more than $75 million today"—to open nearly five thousand schools in the rural South that were called Rosenwald schools).

231 **Proper enforcement of the nation's:** The "antitrust" terminology may be a vestige from another era, one that long predates America's civil rights movement and Dr. Martin Luther King Jr.'s "I Have a Dream" speech. However, only vigorous antitrust enforcement can guarantee robust, diverse competition, thriving markets, and cutting-edge innovation, thus allowing everyone—of whatever background or race—to have a fair shot at the American Dream. The antitrust laws set the rules of the road for competition, much the way stop signs, yield signs, and traffic lights direct drivers on how to behave on the roads. But the laws are only meaningful if they are enforced by federal and state authorities and put to good use. Without antitrust enforcement, you get anticompetitive conduct. "Put simply," University of Michigan law professor Daniel Crane observes, "antitrust is the body of rules about how individuals and companies . . . are allowed to compete in order to make money."

232 **an honest opportunity to compete:** When antitrust enforcement is not prioritized, Americans end up paying higher prices for necessities and other goods and services, whether it's everyday consumer products, pharmaceuticals, or health care. That's why it's so critically important that the FTC and the Justice Department's Antitrust Division pay attention to the concerns of lawmakers and their constituents when it comes to doing their antitrust reviews. An example that has major implications for the health of Americans and their ability to afford their medications? In September 2019, I led a letter to Joseph Simons, the chair of the FTC, that began, "In light of ongoing consolidation in the pharmaceutical sector, we write to urge the Federal Trade Commission (FTC) to closely scrutinize pharmaceutical mergers that raise competition issues, including AbbVie Inc.'s (AbbVie) $63 billion bid for Allergan plc (Allergan) and Bristol-Myers Squibb Company's (Bristol-Myers) proposed $74 billion acquisition of Celgene Corporation (Celgene)." Eight other U.S. senators

joined me in asking the FTC to carefully examine the implications of those proposed mergers.

232 **President Theodore Roosevelt:** *Addresses and Presidential Messages of Theodore Roosevelt, 1902–1904* (New York: C. P. Putnam's Sons, 1904), 15.

232 **Justice Thurgood Marshall:** Justice Marshall wrote more than one antitrust opinion. See *Fisher v. City of Berkeley,* 475 U.S. 260, 270 (1986) ("Because, under settled principles of antitrust law, the rent controls established by Berkeley's Ordinance lack the element of concerted action needed before they can be characterized as a *per se* violation of § 1 of the Sherman Act, we cannot say that the Ordinance is facially inconsistent with the federal antitrust laws."); see also Rudolph J. R. Peritz, *Competition Policy in America, 1888–1992: History, Rhetoric, Law* (Oxford: Oxford University Press, 1996), 356 ("In Fisher v. City of Berkeley, 475 U.S. 260 (1986), the Court made it clear that the preemption doctrine applied as well to municipalities. The Court determined, even before reaching the 'state action' question, that the Sherman Act had not preempted the city's rent control ordinance. Justice Marshall determined that since the ordinance 'on its face' did not conflict 'irreconcilably' with the Act, the antitrust laws simply did not apply and thus, the Supremacy Clause was not offended."). In *Hawaii v. Standard Oil Co. of California,* 405 U.S. 251 (1972), Justice Marshall also emphasized the importance of this area of law: "Every violation of the antitrust laws is a blow to the free enterprise system envisaged by Congress. This system depends on strong competition for its health and vigor, and strong competition depends, in turn, on compliance with antitrust legislation."

232 **"Antitrust laws in general":** *United States v. Topco Assocs., Inc.,* 405 U.S. 596, 610 (1972).

233 **their analysis of sixty-five pharma mergers:** Justus Haucap and Joel Stiebale, "Research: Innovation Suffers When Drug Companies Merge," *Harvard Business Review,* Aug. 3, 2016, hbr.org.

233 **the cable industry:** The first two sentences of a 2019 column in the *Los Angeles Times*—about AT&T raising the price for its DirecTV Now online streaming service by $10 per month—pretty much says it all about the broken promises of big companies who say mergers will help, not harm, consumers. "From the day in 2016 when AT&T announced its $85.4 billion merger with Time Warner, through three years of antitrust wrangling over the deal," that column began, "the big telecommunications company promised that it would mean lower prices and more choices for consumers. Now AT&T has a message for everyone who believed the pitch: Suckers!" Michael Hiltzik's column went on to point out how the price increases mock the representations AT&T made about the consequences of its merger, with Hiltzik noting that AT&T's new packages no longer carry cable channels owned by AT&T competitors such as A+E Networks and Discovery but that they all include HBO, now owned by AT&T. Michael Hiltzik, "AT&T Raises DirecTV Now Prices, Making Chumps of Those Who Backed Time Warner Merger," *Los Angeles Times,* March 18, 2019, www.latimes.com.

233 **while that decree was in effect:** Meredith Rose, Policy Counsel, Public Knowledge, Roundtable on Antitrust Consent Decrees, Written Statement of Public Knowledge, www.justice.gov.

233 **conditions expired:** Sarah Barry James, "Fresh Concerns Rise as Comcast-NBC Merger Conditions Sunset," S&P Global Market Intelligence, Aug. 31, 2018, www.spglobal.com.

233 **American Cable Association:** "Cable Group Urges Antitrust Probe of Comcast and Trump Tweets Support," Reuters, Nov. 12, 2018, www.reuters.com; see also David McLaughlin, "Comcast Gets Notice That NBC Antitrust Scrutiny Will Persist," Bloomberg, Aug. 28, 2018, www.bloomberg.com ("The department's antitrust division wrote a letter to Comcast this month warning that it would continue to monitor developments in how the company handles TV programming and distribution. It also asked for notice by Wednesday of any changes that the cable giant plans to make when the decree runs out on Sept. 1, according to the Aug. 14 letter, which was obtained by Bloomberg News.").

234 **depends on antitrust enforcement:** In the American economy, mergers and acquisitions occur with some frequency. They can create economic efficiencies, and they are a regular and healthy part of American capitalism. *Anticompetitive* mergers and acquisitions, however, can do great harm to America's economy and to its market participants, the farmers, workers, and consumers operating within it. "The time has come to reinvigorate antitrust enforcement," William Galston writes in *The Wall Street Journal.* An International Monetary Fund study, in fact, specifically found that, initially, higher markups are associated with increasing investments in both physical plants and research and development. But innovation then lags—and is stifled and withers—as markups and market concentration rise. "At higher levels of markups, or at higher levels of market concentration," the IMF study's authors concluded, "the marginal relation between innovation and markups becomes negative." In other words, as a company's market power and profit margins become too high, the company's incentive to invest in R&D and innovation decreases. "Rising market concentration," Galston emphasizes, "means more for profit and less for labor. This helps explain why wages have increased so slowly since the Great Recession even as the stock market has soared." Galston's warning: "If we have reasons to care about workers' ability to share in the growth of their firms—and we do—we have little choice but to rein in market concentration when it upsets the balance that makes the American dream possible." William A. Galston, "The Perils of Corporate Concentration," *Wall Street Journal,* June 19, 2018.

234 **to protect competition:** Charles A. James, "Reconciling Divergent Enforcement Policies: Where Do We Go from Here?," in *International Antitrust Law & Policy: Annual Proceedings of the Fordham Corporate Law Institute,* ed. Barry E. Hawk (Huntington, N.Y.: Juris, 2002), 15 ("Perhaps the single most quoted aphorism in U.S. antitrust jurisprudence is that the antitrust laws 'protect competition not competitors,'" quoting *Brown Shoe Co. v. United States,* 370 U.S. 294, 320, 344 (1962)).

234 **As antitrust expert Tim Wu points out:** Tim Wu, *The Curse of Bigness: Antitrust in the New Gilded Age* (New York: Columbia Global Reports, 2018), 132.

234 **breakup of AT&T:** Andrew Beattie, "AT&T's Successful Spinoffs: The Breakup of Ma Bell," *Investopedia,* Oct. 31, 2019, www.investopedia.com.

235 **Staffing levels:** Premerger filings have increased by more than 50 percent since

2010 alone. That statistic, as one FTC commissioner, Rebecca Kelly Slaughter, points out, does not even reflect "the many additional mergers we investigate that fall beneath the Hart-Scott-Rodino Act's reporting threshold." As Slaughter describes the existing resource problem, "Over the past several years, merger filings have increased and the cost to investigate and challenge anticompetitive mergers has skyrocketed. Yet, our funding levels have largely remained flat—which in reality is not flat but declining, because each year . . . the cost of compensation and benefits for the same number of employees rises, so 'flat' funding provides for fewer staff." Remarks of Commissioner Rebecca Kelly Slaughter, "Merger Retrospective Lessons from Mr. Rogers," Hearings on Competition and Consumer Protection in the 21st Century: Merger Retrospectives, April 12, 2019, 4, www.ftc.gov.

235 **Facebook's acquisition of Instagram and WhatsApp:** I asked Facebook CEO Mark Zuckerberg about Facebook's acquisition of both Instragram and WhatsApp at a recent Senate Judiciary Committee hearing. "Klobuchar Questions CEO of Facebook about Competition, Antitrust Investigation, and Political Advertising," press release, Nov. 17, 2020. Emails between Zuckerberg and Facebook's chief financial officer, David Ebersman, revealed that Zuckerberg viewed nascent businesses such as Instragram as a competitive threat and potentially "very disruptive to us." Casey Newton and Nilay Patel, "'Instagram Can Hurt Us': Mark Zuckerberg Emails Outline Plan to Neutralize Competitors," Verge, July 29, 2020, www.theverge.com.

236 **heavily dependent on filing fees:** "Appropriation Figures for the Antitrust Division Fiscal Years 1903–2019," U.S. Department of Justice, www.justice .gov.

236 **changes to premerger filing notification:** "Major Changes to Hart-Scott-Rodino Premerger Notification Requirements to Take Effect February 1, 2001," Federal Trade Commission, www.ftc.gov.

236 **split equally:** Federal Trade Commission, Fiscal Year 2020 Congressional Budget Justification (submitted March 11, 2019), 5, www.ftc.gov.

236 **filing fees:** *Merger Notification Filing Fees: A Report of the International Competition Network* (April 2005), 13, www.internationalcompetitionnetwork.org ("In the United States, filing fee revenue is deposited into a Treasury Department account and allocated equally to the FTC and the Antitrust Division of the Department of Justice ('Antitrust Division') to offset their total appropriations. Filing fees cover a portion of the agencies' total appropriations.").

236 **At the end of 1980:** *Federal Antitrust Enforcement and Its Impact on Small Business: Hearing Before the Committee on Small Business, United States Senate, Ninety-Eighth Congress, Second Session, on Federal Antitrust Enforcement and Its Impact on Small Business, February 7, 1984* (Washington, D.C.: U.S. GPO, 1984), 167.

236 **At the end of fiscal year 2017:** Directorate for Financial and Enterprise Affairs, Competition Committee, Organisation for Economic Co-operation and Development, DAF/COMP/AR(2018)18 (June 13, 2018), 6.

236 **Bureau of Competition:** Compare *The Federal Trade Commission Since 1970,* in *Oversight of Federal Trade Commission Law Enforcement: Fiscal Years 1982 and 1983: Hearing Before a Subcommittee of the Committee on Government Operations, House of Representatives, Ninety-Eighth Congress, First Session, November*

9, 1983 (Washington, D.C.: U.S. GPO, 1984), 359 ("The number of full-time employees in the Bureau of Competition went from 326 when I arrived to 284, a diminution of 12.9 percent."), with "Inside the Bureau of Competition," Federal Trade Commission, June 2018 ("D. Bruce Hoffman, Director, manages the Bureau's almost 300 employees.").

236 **number of employees at the FTC has fallen off:** "FTC Appropriation and Full-Time Equivalent (FTE) History," Federal Trade Commission, www.ftc.gov; Robert H. Lande, "Beyond Chicago: Will Activist Antitrust Arise Again?," 39 *Antitrust Bulletin* 1, 17 (1994). "Before the 1980s," Professor Robert Lande writes, "antitrust was generally thought to serve a variety of social, political and moral objectives." "Part of the Chicago school revolution," he explains, putting in context the decline in U.S. government resources dedicated to antitrust enforcement, "was to replace this belief structure with the narrow view that efficiency is the only original and legitimate concern of antitrust." Ibid., 5. Although federal antitrust enforcement dropped off in the 1980s, the states reemerged as important antitrust enforcers. As Lande explains, "During the 1930s, 1940s and 1950s no state appears to have filed a merger case. Two were filed during the 1960s and another two during the 1970s. During the 1980s the states collectively or individually filed twenty-nine merger cases and another sixteen amicus briefs or interventions. During 1988 . . . the states collectively filed more merger cases than the U.S. Department of Justice's Antitrust Division."

237 **the FTC's full-time staff:** "FTC Appropriation and Full-Time Equivalent (FTE) History," Federal Trade Commission, Financial Management Office, www.ftc.gov.

237 **in its fiscal year 2021 budget:** Letter of FTC Chairman Joseph J. Simons to Rep. Mike Quigley and Sen. John Kennedy, Feb. 10, 2020, www.ftc.gov.

237 **a sobering report:** Michael Kades, "The State of U.S. Federal Antitrust Enforcement," Washington Center for Equitable Growth, Sept. 2019, 2, equitablegrowth.org. A few of the statistics from the report? The sixteen criminal cases filed in 2018 were the fewest filed since 1990; that the number of merger filings increased nearly 80 percent from 2010 to 2018 but the number of enforcement actions has been constant, hovering at around 40 actions per year; that, on average, the two federal antitrust enforcement agencies brought 10.9 non-merger cases a year between 1999 and 2008 but only 7.5 cases a year before 2009 and 2018; that "in real terms (after accounting for inflation), appropriations are 18 percent lower in 2018 than in 2010"; and that "the two federal antitrust enforcement agencies had slightly fewer resources in 2018 ($471 million) as they did nearly 20 years earlier, in 2001 ($491 million)."

237 **American economy has expanded:** Kimberly Amadeo, "US GDP by Year Compared to Recessions and Events: The Strange Ups and Downs of the U.S. Economy Since 1929," The Balance, Jan. 20, 2019 (listing growth rates by year), www.thebalance.com; compare Harriet Torry, "U.S. Economy Shrank in 2020 Despite Fourth-Quarter Growth," *Wall Street Journal,* Jan. 28, 2021.

237 **adds to the work:** Antitrust Division Workload Statistics (FY 2008–2017), www.justice.gov.

237 **in the second quarter of 2020:** Carmen Reinicke, "US GDP Plunged by a Record 33% Annual Rate in the 2nd Quarter as Coronavirus Lockdowns

Raged," *Business Insider,* July 30, 2020, www.businessinsider.com. The Bureau of Economic Analysis later said that real GDP in the second quarter of 2020 decreased by 31.4 percent, with real GDP growth estimated to have bounced back—to have increased at an annual rate of 33.1 percent—in the third quarter of 2020. "Gross Domestic Product, Third Quarter 2020 (Advance Estimate)," Bureau of Economic Analysis, press release, Oct. 29, 2020, www.bea .gov.

237 **much more to do:** The country's economic data reveals just how overdue we are for meaningful antitrust reform. America's economy—in terms of gross domestic product (GDP), the total value of everything produced in the country—increased considerably between 2012 and 2018, and although the COVID-19 pandemic has suppressed economic activity, once effective vaccines for the coronavirus are widely administered, economic conditions will improve substantially. Kimberly Amadeo, "Gross Domestic Product and How It Affects You," The Balance, March 28, 2019, www.thebalance.com. In 2018, nominal U.S. GDP—a raw measurement that includes price increases—was $20.494 trillion. Kimberly Amadeo, "Nominal GDP, How to Calculate It, When to Use It," The Balance, April 3, 2019, www.thebalance.com. Real GDP, which removes the effects of inflation, is lower, but that figure also provides a snapshot of economic activity. The U.S. Bureau of Economic Analysis, by way of background, calculates real GDP by using a price deflator, using 2012 as a base year. In 2012, the country's GDP was $16 trillion. For 2018, by contrast, the real U.S. GDP was $18.566 trillion. Either way it is measured, America's GDP growth rate exceeded 15 percent from 2012 to 2018, meaning significantly more economic activity for antitrust authorities to monitor. Amadeo, "US GDP by Year Compared to Recessions and Events."

238 **merging or contemplating mergers:** Micki Wagner, "How the Pandemic Has Affected Mergers and Acquisitions," *Worth,* June 30, 2020, www.worth.com; see also Mark Herndon and John Bender, "What M&A Looks Like During the Pandemic," *Harvard Business Review,* June 10, 2020, hbr.org ("companies such as Google Cloud, Nestle SA, BlackRock, the British clothing company Boohoo, and others have all publicly stated that they are open to acquisitions despite the uncertainty created by coronavirus").

238 **lack of sufficient resources:** Hart-Scott-Rodino Annual Report, Fiscal Year 2017 (Fortieth Annual Report), Federal Trade Commission and Department of Justice, www.ftc.gov ("In fiscal year 2017, 2,052 transactions were reported under the HSR Act, representing about a 12.0 percent increase from the 1,832 transactions reported in fiscal year 2016. . . . Over the past five years, the number of HSR reportable transactions has increased significantly—in FY2013, 1,326 HSR transactions were reported and in FY2017, 2,052 HSR transactions were reported, an increase of over 50%. This is in the face of flat, or effectively decreasing, budgets and restrictions on hiring.").

238 **"a $10 trillion wave":** "The Problem with Profits," *Economist,* May 26, 2016, www.economist.com.

238 **Between 2015 and 2018:** Robert H. Lande and Sandeep Vaheesan, "Preventing the Curse of Bigness Through Conglomerate Merger Legislation," 52 *Arizona State Law Journal* 75 (2020).

239 **"The making of monopoly":** Barry C. Lynn, *Cornered: The New Monopoly*

Capitalism and the Economics of Destruction (Hoboken, N.J.: John Wiley & Sons, 2010), 17.

239 **cartels:** A recent empirical study—one conducted by economist John Connor and University of Baltimore law professor Robert Lande—found that cartels are not being punished severely enough to deter monopolistic behavior. The authors note that cartels "overcharge consumers many billions of dollars every year." Yet, they point out, "the combined level of U.S. cartel sanctions has been only 9% to 21% as large as it should be to protect potential victims of cartelization optimally." John M. Connor and Robert H. Lande, "Cartels as Rational Business Strategy: Crime Pays," 34 *Cardozo Law Review* 427, 441, 478 (2012). In their study, Connor and Lande found that "the best evidence is that, historically, cartels in the United States have faced only a 20% to 24% chance of being discovered and convicted," and that many of the corporate executives who are caught and convicted for their unlawful participation end up working in the same industry—or even for the same offending company—after serving their prison sentences. As Connor and Lande write, "We were able to determine the present whereabouts of 35 (34%) out of 103 managers known to have received a prison sentence in cartel cases between 1995 and 2010. Of those 35, 9 (26%) are currently employed by the company for which they worked during the cartel, and another 9 (26%) seem to be working at a different company within the same industry." In a more recent analysis, Connor found that cartel enforcement in the Trump administration "is very weak compared to all recent presidents, except for President George H. W. Bush. . . . Indeed, the Obama record is *eleven times* higher on an annual basis than the first two years of the Trump administration." Those who engage in monopolistic behavior should be barred from rejoining the industries they manipulated, not financially rewarded for their misdeeds. John M. Connor, "Comment on Cartel Enforcement in the Trump Administration," *Antitrust Chronicle* (June 2019): 29, 33.

239 **must be held accountable:** Douglas H. Ginsburg et al., "DOJ Has the Power to Crush Price-Fixers," *USA Today,* May 25, 2015, www.usatoday.com. Monetary fines can be imposed by antitrust enforcers. In 2015, the Obama Justice Department's Antitrust Division obtained a record $3.6 billion in criminal fines. However, much anticompetitive conduct still goes unchecked or is not deterred, or punished, enough. Those engaged in price-fixing, bid rigging, and monopolistic customer allocation are plainly damaging the American economy, and such anticompetitive behavior must be stopped. As I put it at a March 9, 2006, Senate Judiciary Committee subcommittee hearing called "Oversight of the Enforcement of the Antitrust Laws," "Make no mistake about it; although their weapon may be a handshake, a wink, or a nod, those who fix prices are stealing just as surely as the burglar who picks the lock on your front door."

239 **increasingly hostile to antitrust claims:** Thomas A. Lambert, "The Roberts Court and the Limits of Antitrust," in *Business and the Roberts Court,* ed. Jonathan H. Adler (Oxford: Oxford University Press, 2016), chap. 6. As the federal judiciary has raised the bar for antitrust plaintiffs, companies have become more willing than ever before to engage in anticompetitive conduct or undertake riskier mergers, which taxes the government's already slim antitrust resources even further.

239 **Adam Feldman:** Adam Feldman, "Empirical SCOTUS: The Big Business Court," *SCOTUSblog,* Aug. 8, 2018, www.scotusblog.com; see also Andrew Hamm, "Announcing Partnership with Adam Feldman of Empirical SCOTUS," *SCOTUSblog,* March 21, 2018, www.scotusblog.com.

239 **golden age of antitrust enforcement:** If the period from 1945 to 1976—the period that begins with Judge Learned Hand's decision in the *ALCOA* case— is rightfully seen as the golden age of antitrust enforcement, the year 1977 witnessed the beginning of a rightward shift on the U.S. Supreme Court. In the latter year, the U.S. Supreme Court narrowly interpreted the notion of "antitrust injury" in *Illinois Brick Co. v. Illinois,* 431 U.S. 720 (1977). Likewise, in *Continental Television v. GTE Sylvania,* 433 U.S. 36 (1977), the Supreme Court overturned an earlier antitrust case. In *Continental Television,* GTE Sylvania— a television manufacturer—attempted to curtail the number of competing retailers selling its products by limiting the number of franchisees. When the plaintiff, Continental Television, was denied a franchise, it sued, alleging a Sherman Act violation. Although the Supreme Court, in a prior case, had held such restrictions to be per se unlawful, the Court overruled that precedent and held that "per se rules of illegality are appropriate only when they relate to conduct that is manifestly anticompetitive." The *Continental Television* case, which jettisoned a ten-year-old precedent, *United States v. Arnold, Schwinn & Co.,* 388 U.S. 365 (1967), in favor of a "rule of reason" approach, is now seen as part of the ascendency of the Chicago school of antitrust.

240 **Senator Sheldon Whitehouse:** Sheldon Whitehouse, "There's a 'Crisis of Credibility' at the U.S. Supreme Court," *National Law Journal,* Feb. 15, 2019.

240 **At the Kavanaugh hearing:** "Whitehouse Reveals Kavanaugh's Pro-corporate, Right-Wing Record in SCOTUS Hearing Opener," press release, Sept. 4, 2018, www.whitehouse.senate.gov.

240 **"voted to advance far-right":** Statement of U.S. Senator Sheldon Whitehouse, "Nomination of Brett Kavanaugh to the Supreme Court," Oct. 6, 2018, www .whitehouse.senate.gov.

240 **The Trump administration:** Carrie Johnson and Renee Klahr, "Trump Is Reshaping the Judiciary," NPR, Nov. 15, 2018, www.npr.org.

240 **Judge Merrick Garland:** After Justice Antonin Scalia's death in 2016, the Republican-controlled Senate simply refused to take any action on Judge Garland's nomination.

240 **reversing himself on no-election-year appointments:** "For McConnell, Ginsburg's Death Prompts Stark Turnabout from 2016 Stance," *New York Times,* Sept. 18, 2020 www.nytimes.com.

240 **one of the fastest Supreme Court confirmations in recent history:** Claudia Grisales, "Senate to Vote on Amy Coney Barrett's Confirmation for Supreme Court," NPR, Oct. 26, 2020, www.npr.org.

240 **further to the right on business issues:** See discussion of my questioning of U.S. Supreme Court nominees in chapter 5.

240 **Affordable Care Act:** "Supreme Court Upholds Health Care Law, 5–4, in Victory for President Obama," *New York Times,* June 29, 2012, www.nytimes .com.

240 **DREAMers:** Nina Totenberg, "Supreme Court Rules for DREAMers, Against Trump," NPR, June 18, 2020, www.npr.org.

240 **LGBTQ community:** Nina Totenberg, "Supreme Court Delivers Major Victory to LGBTQ Employees," NPR, June 15, 2020, www.npr.org.

240 **minority voting rights:** For example, *Shelby County v. Holder*, 570 U.S. 529 (2013) (invalidating a key provision of the Voting Rights Act); see also Joan Biskupic, "How the Supreme Court Is Changing the Rules on Voting," CNN, June 26, 2018, www.cnn.com.

240 **union rights:** Scott Horsley and Nina Totenberg, "Supreme Court Deals Blow to Government Unions," NPR, June 27, 2018, www.npr.org ("In a blow to organized labor, the U.S. Supreme Court ruled Wednesday that government workers who choose not to join a union cannot be charged for the cost of collective bargaining.").

240 **Lilly Ledbetter:** David L. Hudson Jr., *The Handy Presidents Answer Book,* 2nd ed. (Detroit: Visible Ink, 2012), 458 ("The first bill that Obama signed into law was the Lily [*sic*] Ledbetter Fair Pay Act, which extends the time period an individual has to file a suit under the Equal Pay Act. Congress had passed the law in response to the U.S. Supreme Court's decision in *Ledbetter v. Goodyear Tire & Rubber Co.* (2007), when the Court ruled that Lily [*sic*] Ledbetter did not file her Equal Pay Act lawsuit in time. The Court had reasoned that the limitations period began when the pay agreement was made, not at each new paycheck."). Justice Ruth Bader Ginsburg—as she did in so many cases—played a key role in fighting the gender discrimination at issue. Teri Kwal Gamble and Michael W. Gamble, *The Gender Communication Connection*, 2nd ed. (Armonk, N.Y.: M.E. Sharpe, 2014), 254 ("Ginsburg was also a force for equality in Congress's passage of the Lilly Ledbetter law. Shortly before her retirement from Goodyear Tire & Rubber Company in 1998, Ledbetter became aware that she was making less money than men in the same position. Ledbetter sued Goodyear and was awarded $3.8 million by a jury. The case went to the Supreme Court, which in a 5–4 vote threw it out—citing that claims for pay discrimination had to be brought within 180 days of the violation. Ledbetter's case was filed much later. Ginsburg dissented, urging Congress to undo the Court's work.").

240 **In one of those 5–4 decisions:** *Epic Systems Corp. v. Lewis,* 138 S. Ct. 1612 (2018).

241 **Obama's election to the presidency:** During the Obama administration, the FTC won a few Supreme Court victories, but they are still few and far between. See *Federal Trade Commission v. Phoebe Putney Health System, Inc.,* 568 U.S. 216 (2013); *North Carolina State Board of Dental Examiners v. Federal Trade Commission,* 135 S. Ct. 1101 (2015); *Federal Trade Commission v. Actavis, Inc.,* 133 S. Ct. 2223 (2013); see also *Financial Services and General Government Appropriations for 2015: Hearings Before a Subcommittee of the Committee on Appropriations, House of Representatives, One Hundred Thirteenth Congress, Second Session* (Washington, D.C.: U.S. Government Printing Office, 2014), 433 ("In June 2013, the FTC won a significant victory in the Supreme Court. In *FTC v. Actavis,* the Court held that pay-for-delay agreements are subject to antitrust scrutiny, thus reversing a lower court dismissal of the case.").

241 **"It has been more than fifteen years":** Thomas A. Lambert, "The Roberts Court and the Limits of Antitrust," in *Business and the Roberts Court*, ed. Jonathan H. Adler (Oxford: Oxford University Press, 2016), 164–65.

242 **make it harder:** The U.S. Supreme Court has also made significant legal rulings against unions. For example, in 2018, the Court—in a 5–4 decision that
overturned a forty-year-old precedent—held that it was unconstitutional
for public employee unions to require the payment of collective bargaining
fees from those employees who choose not to join the union. The ruling was
described by *The Washington Post* as "a major blow for the U.S. labor movement." Robert Barnes and Ann E. Marimow, "Supreme Court Rules Against
Public Unions Collecting Fees from Nonmembers," *Washington Post,* June 27,
2018, www.washingtonpost.com.

242 **the Court—contorting the law:** *Bell Atlantic Corp. v. Twombly,* 550 U.S. 544
(2007).

242 **forcing antitrust plaintiffs to plead more:** The *Twombly* case, in which the
Supreme Court jettisoned a decades-old precedent, shows the lengths to which
the Court is willing to go to deep-six antitrust lawsuits against large companies. In that case, the plaintiffs—subscribers to local telephone services—
filed a class-action lawsuit against major American telephone companies, Bell
Atlantic Corporation, BellSouth Corporation, Qwest Communications International Inc., SBC Communications Inc., and Verizon Communications Inc.
The complaint alleged that those companies had violated the Sherman Act
through efforts to inhibit the growth of local phone companies and to eliminate competition among themselves in their respective territories. Among the
allegations in the plaintiffs' complaint: the Consumer Federation of America's
conclusion that "the major telephone companies have not sought to provide
local telephone service outside of their home territories" and that the failure
of those companies "to compete with one another would be anomalous in
the absence of an agreement . . . not to compete with one another in view of
the fact that in significant respects, the territories that they service are non-
contiguous."

The allegations in the plaintiffs' complaint in *Twombly,* brought by consumers who purchased local telephone and high-speed internet services,
strongly suggested that anticompetitive, monopolistic behavior was afoot.
For example, the complaint referenced a statement made in October 2002 by
Richard Notebaert, Ameritech's former chief executive officer who was then
serving as the CEO of Qwest, one of the lawsuit's defendants. Notebaert was
quoted in a *Chicago Tribune* article as saying it would be wrong to compete
in the SBC Communications–Ameritech territory, adding, "It might be a
good way to turn a quick dollar but that doesn't make it right." In November 2002, after Notebaert's remarks, the Illinois Coalition for Competitive
Telecom specifically called them "evidence of potential collusion among
regional Bell phone companies to not compete against one another and kill off
potential competitors in local phone service." Consolidated Amended Class
Action Complaint, *Twombly v. Bell Atlantic Corp.,* No. 02 Civ. 10220 (GEL),
April 11, 2003, ¶¶ 40, 42, 44. Indeed, in the wake of Notebaert's comments,
members of Congress called for a full-blown antitrust investigation. As the
plaintiffs pleaded in the complaint, "On December 18, 2002, United States
Representatives John Conyers, Jr. of Michigan and Zoe Lofgren of California
sent a letter to United States Attorney General John Ashcroft requesting that
the U.S. Department of Justice, Antitrust Division investigate whether the

RBOCs [Regional Bell Operating Companies] are violating the antitrust laws by carving up their market territories and deliberately refraining from competing with one another. . . . Representatives Conyers and Lofgren questioned the extent to which the RBOCs' 'very apparent noncompetition policy in each others' markets is coordinated.' " Ibid., ¶ 45.

The civil litigation process is designed to sort out good, meritorious claims from bad or frivolous ones. Under ordinary circumstances, the major telephone companies—as a matter of routine procedure—would have had to at least serve an answer to the plaintiffs' complaint and then engage in a judicially managed discovery process in which documents and information would be produced and exchanged to see if the plaintiffs' case should go to trial or be dismissed. Under the pleading standard articulated by the U.S. Supreme Court way back in *Conley v. Gibson,* 355 U.S. 41, 45–46 (1957), a litigant's complaint could not be dismissed for a failure to state a claim unless "it appears beyond doubt that the plaintiff can prove *no set of facts* in support of his claim which would entitle him to relief." But in *Twombly,* a majority of the Supreme Court justices rejected the *Conley* standard, holding that, instead, the plaintiffs' complaint had to contain "enough factual matter . . . to suggest that an agreement was made" in order to state an antitrust claim.

In summarily dismissing the class-action lawsuit in *Twombly,* the Supreme Court emphasized that "antitrust discovery can be expensive" and that "allegations of parallel conduct" by major telephone companies were insufficient to withstand a motion to dismiss. While the Court acknowledged that in the plaintiffs' complaint "a few stray statements speak directly of agreement," it provided no support for why antitrust discovery is more expensive than it would be in any complex, commercial dispute. The Court also dismissively described "the nub of the complaint" as simply alleging non-actionable "parallel behavior" by the telephone companies. Certainly, companies would incur some attorneys' fees and expenses in answering a complaint and providing information and documents in the discovery process to antitrust plaintiffs. But American consumers, it must be remembered, are greatly harmed when anticompetitive behavior occurs, with the Court tossing out the antitrust lawsuit before even the most basic information was obtained and failing to consider the potential for plaintiffs to recover large sums of money to rectify harmful conduct. One recent study found that in sixty private antitrust enforcement actions, the plaintiffs recovered $33.8 to $35.8 billion (or more that $500 million per case), making litigation discovery costs look like chump change in comparison to the benefits of letting antitrust lawsuits proceed. Joshua P. Davis and Robert H. Lande, "Defying Conventional Wisdom: The Case for Private Antitrust Enforcement," 48 *Georgia Law Review* 1, 16–17 (2013).

242 **Supreme Court reversed the class-action:** *Comcast Corp. v. Behrend,* 569 U.S. 27 (2013).

242 **the majority opinion in *Twombly*:** The *Twombly* ruling, in fact, is a far cry from what the U.S. Supreme Court said in a much earlier antitrust case, *Poller v. Columbia Broadcasting System Inc.,* 368 U.S. 464 (1962). In *Poller,* the Supreme Court wrote that "summary procedures should be used sparingly in complex antitrust litigation where motive and intent play leading roles, the proof is largely in the hands of the alleged conspirators, and hostile witnesses thicken

the plot." As the Court added in *Poller,* "It is only when the witnesses are present and subject to cross-examination that their credibility and the weight to be given their testimony can be appraised." Even before *Twombly,* the Supreme Court had undermined what it once said in *Poller* about the ability of antitrust plaintiffs to successfully bring cases. Douglas Broder, *U.S. Antitrust Law and Enforcement: A Practice Introduction,* 2nd ed. (Oxford: Oxford University Press, 2012), 212 ("In *Matsushita Electric Industrial Co. v. Zenith Radio Corp.,* and a series of subsequent cases, the Supreme Court made it clear that the standard for obtaining summary judgment is no different in antitrust cases than in any other."); American Bar Association, Antitrust Law Section, *Nonprice Predation Under Section 2 of the Sherman Act* (American Bar Association, 1991), 60 ("The Supreme Court addressed summary judgment standards in the context of a predation claim in *Matsushita Electric Industrial Co. v. Zenith Radio Corp.,* one of the Court's trilogy of summary judgment cases in the 1986 term. Matsushita involved a Section 1 claim by two American television manufacturers against twenty-four Japanese television manufacturers. The plaintiffs alleged a wide-ranging conspiracy to exclude foreign competition from the Japanese market and to reap monopoly profits therein, and to drive plaintiffs out of business in the United States market by predatory pricing. The district court entered summary judgment for defendants. The Third Circuit reversed, finding that plaintiffs' evidence of conspiracy (including plaintiffs' expert testimony) had been erroneously excluded and, when considered, created a genuine issue of fact for trial. The Supreme Court reversed in a 5–4 decision, reflecting sharp divisions on the proper standard for summary judgment. Citing the works of economically conservative commentators, the Court in dictum concluded that predatory pricing schemes are economically implausible, particularly when numerous conspirators are involved."); see also *Ashcroft v. Iqbal,* 556 U.S. 662 (2009) (noting that the ruling in *Twombly* "expounded the pleading standard for 'all civil actions,' and it applies to antitrust and discrimination suits alike") (citations omitted).

243 **very troubling:** Notably, a spirited dissent in *Twombly,* written by Justice John Paul Stevens, made this telling observation about the antitrust laws: "This is a case in which there is no dispute about the substantive law. If the defendants acted independently, their conduct was perfectly lawful. If, however, that conduct is the product of a horizontal agreement among potential competitors, it was unlawful. Plaintiffs have alleged such an agreement and, because the complaint was dismissed in advance of an answer, the allegation has not even been denied." "Respondents' amended complaint," Stevens added, "describes a variety of circumstantial evidence and . . . allege[s] that petitioners entered into an agreement that has long been recognized as a classic *per se* violation of the Sherman Act." Finding that the antitrust plaintiffs should have been entitled to at least some sort of response (and to at least some discovery, however limited in scope), Justice Stevens wrote, "The Court and petitioners' legal team are no doubt correct that the parallel conduct alleged is consistent with the absence of any contract, combination, or conspiracy. But that conduct is also entirely consistent with the *presence* of the illegal agreement alleged in the complaint."

243 *Verizon Communications Inc. v. Law Offices of Curtis V. Trinko, LLP* (2004),

Leegin Creative Leather Products, Inc. v. PSKS, Inc. (2007), **and** *Ohio v. American Express Co.: Verizon Communications Inc. v. Law Offices of Curtis V. Trinko, LLP,* 540 U.S. 398 (2004); *Leegin Creative Leather Products, Inc. v. PSKS, Inc.,* 551 U.S. 877 (2007); *Ohio v. American Express Co.,* 138 S. Ct. 2274 (2018).

243 **the *American Express* decision:** The Supreme Court's decision in the *American Express* case, which upheld that anti-steering provision prohibiting merchants from suggesting the use of competing credit cards with lower fees, has been heavily criticized. "Steering," antitrust scholar Herbert Hovenkamp has explained in his critique of the decision, "is fundamental to competition of any kind, including competition among platforms." "It offers market participants an incentive to seek out lower cost alternatives," he notes, teasing out the adverse implications of the Court's decision for consumers using ride-hailing services such as Uber and Lyft, web browsers, and computer search engines. "Competition among platforms," he stresses, pointing out that other jurisdictions around the world have acted against anti-steering policies and high interchange fees, "can help ensure competitive prices and high-quality service, but an antisteering rule, such as Amex's, eliminates a consumer's incentive to use the least costly alternative." Herbert J. Hovenkamp, "Platforms and the Rule of Reason: The *American Express* Case," 2019 *Columbia Business Law Review* 35, 44–45, 77, 91 ("On a typical transaction, the Amex merchant acceptance fee may be fifty percent greater than the fee charged by competing cards. Suppose that on a particular purchase Amex's merchant fee was $30, but $20 for Visa. This $10 difference creates bargaining room—a 'surplus,' in Coasean terms—for the merchant and the cardholder to strike a mutually beneficial deal. Suppose that the merchant offers the customer a $6 discount for using a Visa card instead, which would make the customer $6 better off for that particular transaction and the merchant $4 better off. The customer would agree if the value it placed on Amex's perks was less than the $6 price discount. The antisteering provision prevents this transaction from occurring, however. As a result, the customer stays with the Amex card and experiences a $6 loss. The merchant loses $4 as well."); see also Michael Katz and Jonathan Sallet, "Multisided Platforms and Antitrust Enforcement," 127 *Yale Law Journal* 2142 (2018) (containing the views of an economist and a lawyer involved in the U.S. government's antitrust case against American Express).

244 **played a detrimental role:** "Sabre, Farelogix Deal Called Off but U.S. Defeat Still Stands," Bloomberg Law, May 1, 2020, news.bloomberglaw.com.

244 **the deal was ultimately called off:** Mitra Sorrells, "Sabre and Farelogix $360M Merger Deal Cancelled," *PhocusWire,* May 1, 2020, www.phocuswire.com.

244 **is still out there:** At the request of the U.S. Department of Justice, the U.S. Court of Appeals for the Third Circuit vacated the district court's decision in July 2020 "because Sabre Corporation mooted the parties' dispute by terminating its acquisition of Farelogix, Inc." *United States v. Sabre Corp.,* No. 20-1767 (3d Cir. July 20, 2020), www.wlf.org. In its order, however, the Third Circuit emphasized, "We . . . express no opinion on the merits of the parties' dispute before the District Court. . . . As such, this Order should not be construed as detracting from the persuasive force of the District Court's decision, should courts and litigants find its reasoning persuasive."

244 **One illustrative example:** Darren Bush, "The Death of the Tunney Act at the Hands of an Activist D.C. Circuit," 63 *Antitrust Bulletin* 113 (2018).

244 **the Antitrust Procedures and Penalties Act:** Antitrust Procedures and Penalties Act, Pub. L. 93-528, 88 Stat. 1708 (Dec. 21, 1974) (codified at 15 U.S.C. § 16).

244 **John Tunney:** Claude R. Marx and Kirk Victor, "Former Senator John Tunney, Who Pushed for Antitrust Reform, Dies," *FTC Watch,* Jan. 19, 2018, www .mlexwatch.com; Miles Parks, "Former U.S. Sen. John Tunney, Inspiration for Redford's 'The Candidate,' Dies at 83," NPR, Jan. 13, 2018, www.npr.org.

244 **Tunney's 1970 Senate race:** "Tunney-Murphy Coast Race Is Close," *New York Times,* Sept. 18, 1970, www.nytimes.com.

244 **one involving an acquisition:** In 1971, Nixon had directed that Deputy Attorney General Richard Kleindienst settle a Clayton Act lawsuit filed two years earlier against ITT. But during Kleindienst's subsequent confirmation hearings to become attorney general, the journalist Brit Hume—as one book puts it—"broke a news story that linked the settlement of the suit to a $400,000 contribution to help finance the 1972 Republican National Convention." Kleindienst later pleaded guilty to a misdemeanor for not telling the Senate panel that Nixon had directed him to settle the case. Anthony Ripley, "Kleindienst Admits Misdemeanor Guilt over Testimony in Senate on I.T.T. Case," *New York Times,* May 17, 1974, www.nytimes.com.

244 **"sweetheart" antitrust deals:** Gary L. Reback, *Free the Market! Why Only Government Can Keep the Marketplace Competitive* (New York: Portfolio, 2009), chap. 15.

244 **the modest legislative proposal:** The Tunney Act is a law that covers only a narrow set of circumstances. For example, the Department of Justice can circumvent the Tunney Act process by using what is known as a fix-it-first remedy, whereby the parties come and propose a deal, without filing it. If the Justice Department spots something problematic about the deal from an antitrust perspective, a problematic asset can be divested before the acquisition actually occurs. If the Justice Department never challenges the deal, there is no consent decree and thus no judicial review. Section of Antitrust Law, *The Merger Review Process: A Step-by-Step Guide to Federal Merger Review,* ed. Ilene K. Gotts, 2nd ed. (Chicago: American Bar Association, 2001), 300 ("At the Antitrust Division, the parties at any point in the process may fix-it-first without a consent order. This is true even after the Antitrust Division has announced that it will challenge the transaction in the form initially proposed. In fact, the Antitrust Division favors fix-it-first as a solution for competitive concerns, since any divestiture occurs before consummation of the transaction, eliminating any diminution of competition during the period before the assets are sold, as well as the need for a consent order and Tunney Act proceedings.").

244 **"a Watergate-era statute":** Andrew I. Gavil and Harry First, *The Microsoft Antitrust Cases: Competition Policy for the Twenty-First Century* (Cambridge, Mass.: MIT Press, 2014), 331.

244 **undermined the law's purpose:** It did so by asserting judicial review presented separation of powers issues. Prior to the Tunney Act, it was difficult for nonparties to Justice Department consent decrees to express their disapproval

of their terms. In a prior case, *Sam Fox Publishing Co. v. United States,* 366 U.S. 683 (1961), the U.S. Supreme Court found that courts should defer to the DOJ as regards the imposition of consent decrees. The Tunney Act, however, abrogated that Supreme Court ruling, with Senator Tunney—in the lead-up to that law's passage—observing that the district court had an "independent duty" (not just a "ministerial" role) to determine if a consent decree was in the public interest. In spite of the Tunney Act, and a 2004 amendment to that law designed to strengthen it, the D.C. Circuit ignored the law's plain language and the law's legislative history in finding that courts should play a very minimal role in reviewing Justice Department–negotiated consent decrees. Antitrust Criminal Penalty Enhancement and Reform Act of 2004; see also Darren Bush, "The Death of the Tunney Act at the Hands of an Activist D.C. Circuit," 63 *Antitrust Bulletin* 113, 122 (2018); 150 Cong. Rec. S. 3610 (April 2, 2004) ("The amendments to the Tunney Act found in our bill will restore the original intent of the Tunney Act, and make clear that courts should carefully review antitrust consent decrees to ensure that they are in the public interest. It will accomplish this by, No. 1, a clear statement of congressional findings and purposes expressly overruling the improper judicial standard of recent D.C. Circuit decisions; No. 2, by requiring, rather than permitting, judicial review of a list of enumerated factors to determine whether a consent decree is in the public interest; and No. 3, by enhancing the list of factors which the court now must review."). In a 2014 interview, Tunney himself had expressed his own disappointment. "I am deeply offended," he said of how courts had ignored the intent of the law that bears his name. "The purpose of the act was to have judicial review to make sure that the public interest is being protected." In that interview, Tunney had added, "I was always a keen advocate for effective implementation of the antitrust laws and am just horrified that these days it seems that big is better and let's not in any way try and stop the concentration of capital and monetary interests in the corporate sector." In *The Candidate,* Robert Redford's character—after a long, very arduous campaign that ultimately ends in a stunning victory—earnestly asks his adviser, "What do we do now?" Eileen Button, *The Waiting Place: Learning to Appreciate Life's Little Delays* (Nashville: Thomas Nelson, 2011), 225. In real life, though, Senator Tunney knew what to do—certainly, what he thought needed to be done to help take on monopoly power. Sadly, the courts frustrated the purpose of the law he ushered through Congress, essentially by ignoring it.

245   **thwarted by the D.C. Circuit:** Darren Bush—of the University of Houston Law Center—describes how that court "chose to ignore legislative intent and cast judicial review of consent decrees back to the days when rubber-stamping was prevalent" and reopened "the potential for political abuse in the settlement of antitrust cases by closed-door negotiation and settlement of significant cases—one of the very abuses Congress sought to end with the passage of the Tunney Act." After John Tunney's death in 2018, Seth Bloom—the former longtime general counsel to the U.S. Senate's Antitrust Subcommittee—made this comment about the law that bears Tunney's name: "It is sad—the Tunney Act has fallen short. It was a very good idea but because of the application of it by the courts, Senator Tunney's vision has not been realized." Bush, "Death of the Tunney Act at the Hands of an Activist D.C. Circuit," 119–20.

245 **conservative U.S. Supreme Court:** In fact, the addition of three new conservative justices—Neil Gorsuch, Brett Kavanaugh, and Amy Coney Barrett—will not do much of anything at all to change the Supreme Court's disposition and character.

245 **"Evidence of conspiracy":** Christopher L. Sagers, *Antitrust: Examples and Explanations,* 2nd ed. (New York: Wolters Kluwer, 2014), § 12.1, 162.

246 **"unreasonable" restraints of trade:** Charlotte Slaiman, "Decoding Antitrust Law: A Primer for Advocates," Public Knowledge, 7, www.publicknowledge.org.

246 **the U.S. Supreme Court has made clear:** Ibid., 9.

246 **it must currently be shown:** Ibid., 11–12.

246 **have long existed:** Oliver E. Williamson, "The Merger Guidelines of the U.S. Department of Justice—in Perspective," www.justice.gov (noting that Donald Turner "was the first Ph.D. economist to head the Antitrust Division"; that after getting his law degree at Yale and clerking for the U.S. Supreme Court, Turner joined the Harvard Law School faculty in 1954 and specialized in antitrust; and that "the first Department of Justice Merger guidelines were issued on Turner's last day (May 30, 1968) as Assistant Attorney General" and were "more stringent than . . . the later 1982 Guidelines," with "the 1968 Guidelines adopt[ing] market share limits that could be inferred from recent merger decisions by the courts").

246 **Stephen Weissman:** Stephen Weissman, "Pardon the Interruption: Competition and Disruptive Business Models" (remarks at the 32nd Annual Antitrust & Consumer Protection Seminar, Washington State Bar Association, Nov. 4, 2015), 3, 11, www.ftc.gov.

247 **"Merger analysis is almost always":** Herbert J. Hovenkamp and Carl Shapiro, "Horizontal Mergers, Market Structure, and Burdens of Proof," 127 *Yale Law Journal* 1996, 2024 (2018).

247 **To make it easier to challenge mergers:** In the world of antitrust, legal standards and presumptions carry a lot of weight, and shifting the way the law looks at harmful conduct will help. That is exactly what my bill—the Anticompetitive Exclusionary Conduct Prevention Act—seeks to do. S. 3426: Anticompetitive Exclusionary Conduct Prevention Act of 2020 (introduced March 10, 2020), www.congress.gov. For example, under that legislation, exclusionary conduct shall be *presumed* to present "an appreciable risk of harming competition" if the exclusionary conduct is undertaken in a relevant market by a person or group with a market share above a certain level or if the individual or group "has significant market power in the relevant market." While that presumption can be rebutted if the defendant can show distinct pro-competitive benefits that eliminate the risk of harming competition, putting in place a presumption of harm will serve to deter anticompetitive exclusionary conduct. Going forward, Congress, the courts, and federal agencies must all reevaluate the standards and procedures by which anticompetitive exclusionary conduct—as well as mergers and acquisitions—is evaluated. To help, my Anticompetition Exclusionary Conduct Prevention Act, which I'll discuss more in the next chapter, would abrogate the *Trinko* decision. *Trinko* strongly suggests that a refusal to deal can be illegal only if the monopolist and the competitor had a prior course of dealing or the monopolist refuses to deal

with competitors but does deal with noncompetitors. If *Trinko* had been the law in the 1980s, the Antitrust Division's case against AT&T would have been far more difficult to prove. The heart of the Justice Department's concern was that AT&T would not connect MCI's long-distance service to AT&T's local monopolies. There was no prior relationship between MCI and AT&T, meaning it would have been difficult to argue that AT&T was treating MCI differently than noncompetitors because AT&T—the monopolist—interconnected very few companies. Notably, the *Trinko* decision has also made it very hard for antitrust to address what has been termed the "REMS" issue. Under the Food and Drug Administration Amendments Act of 2007, the Food and Drug Administration may require the use of risk evaluation and mitigation strategies (REMS) in addition to professional labeling to ensure that a drug's benefits outweigh its risks. In the pharmaceutical industry, brands regularly defend their refusal to sell product to generics based on *Trinko*. As one source summarizes the situation, "The Federal Trade Commission and the generic drug industry have raised concerns that branded drug companies are using these REMS to delay or prevent generic entry. They assert that branded firms are using REMS-mandated distribution restrictions to inappropriately limit access to product samples generic drug developers need for bioequivalence testing, a predicate for FDA approval of generic drugs." Darren S. Tucker, Gregory F. Wells, and Margaret E. Sheer, "REMS: The Next Pharmaceutical Enforcement Priority?," *Antitrust* 28, no. 2 (Spring 2014), www.morganlewis .com. I have led a bipartisan charge to solve the REMS problem with the CREATES Act. "Klobuchar, Grassley Introduce New Bipartisan Legislation to Crack Down on Pharmaceutical Pay-for-Delay Deals," press release, Dec. 19, 2018, www.klobuchar.senate.gov.

247 **"is clearly intended to strengthen":** Hovenkamp and Shapiro, "Horizontal Mergers, Market Structure, and Burdens of Proof," 2021.

247 **reject the *Illinois Brick* doctrine:** American Bar Association, Antitrust Law Section, *Antitrust Federalism: The Role of State Law* (Chicago: American Bar Association, 1988), 25.

247 **Antitrust Modernization Commission report:** The bipartisan Antitrust Modernization Commission, created by Congress in 2002 but later disbanded, recommended the statutory repeal of the *Illinois Brick* ruling. Paul Stancil, "Atomism and the Private Merger Challenge," 78 *Temple Law Review* 949, 993 (2006); Barak D. Richman and Christopher R. Murray, "Rebuilding *Illinois Brick:* A Functionalist Approach to the Indirect Purchaser Rule," 81 *Southern California Law Review* 69, 71 (2007).

247 **Andrew Finch:** Kathy L. Osborn and Justin R. Olson, "Bringing Back Indirect Purchasers—DOJ Considers Seeking Reversal of *Illinois Brick*," Faegre Drinker, Jan. 31, 2018, www.faegredrinker.com.

248 **went in the opposite direction:** American Antitrust Institute, "The State of Antitrust Enforcement and Competition Policy in the U.S.," April 14, 2020, www.antitrustinstitute.org ("Our analysis of agency advocacy reveals that the Trump DOJ has framed a new policy of intervening in private antitrust cases through the unprecedented use of amicus briefs and statements of interest. Several examples stand out. One was an uninvited appearance in the Ninth Circuit with an amicus brief in *Stromberg v. Qualcomm*. The Antitrust Divi-

sion reversed, without explanation, a decadees-old policy position that the federal *Illinois Brick* indirect purchaser rule does not irreconcilably conflict with
state Illinois-Brick repealer rules that allow indirect purchaser suits under state
antitrust law.").

248 **must be done in the right way:** Randy M. Stutz, "Cracking *Pepper:* An Analy-
sis of the Supreme Court's Latest Pronouncement on the Indirect Purchaser
Rule," American Antitrust Institute, May 2019, www.antitrustinstitute.org
("During the Supreme Court briefing in *Pepper,* thirty states and the District
of Columbia submitted an amicus brief urging the Court to overrule *Illinois
Brick.* The DOJ had also highlighted criticism of the current regime under
Illinois Brick and *California v. Arc America* (which sanctioned state *Illinois
Brick* 'repealer' laws) and questioned whether the rationale underlying *Illinois
Brick* had withstood the test of time. The AAI brief argues that the issue is
appropriately left to Congress. If undertaken without due care, reform to the
existing regime threatens to undermine the deterrent value of antitrust treble
damages class actions.").

248 **"Predatory pricing":** Jeffrey F. Beatty and Susan S. Samuelson, *Business Law
and the Legal Environment,* 4th ed. (Mason, Ohio: Thomson West, 2007), 941.

248 **the Supreme Court held in 1993:** *Brooke Group Ltd. v. Brown & Williamson
Tobacco Corp.,* 509 U.S. 209 (1993).

248 **"Today, succeeding on a predatory pricing claim":** Lina M. Khan, "Amazon—
an Infrastructure Service and Its Challenge to Current Antitrust Law," in *Digital Dominance: The Power of Google, Amazon, Facebook, and Apple,* ed. Martin
Moore and Damian Tambini (Oxford: Oxford University Press, 2018), 103.

248 *Philadelphia National Bank: United States v. Philadelphia National Bank,* 374
U.S. 321 (1963).

249 **"Since the Supreme Court's landmark":** Hovenkamp and Shapiro, "Horizontal Mergers, Market Structure, and Burdens of Proof," 1996.

249 **as Hovenkamp and Shapiro note:** Ibid., 2022–23.

249 **"Although critics argued":** Constance E. Bagley, *Managers and the Legal Environment: Strategies for Business,* 9th ed. (Boston: Cengage, 2019), 508.

250 *Philadelphia National Bank* **standard:** In *Philadelphia National Bank,* Justice Potter Stewart noted, the Court had highlighted the relevance of industry concentration to antitrust law in these words: "The intense congressional
concern with the trend toward concentration warrants dispensing, in certain
cases, with elaborate proof of market structure, market behavior, or probable
anticompetitive effects. Specifically, we think that a merger which produces a
firm controlling an undue percentage share of the relevant market, and results
in a significant increase in the concentration of firms in that market, is so
inherently likely to lessen competition substantially that it must be enjoined
in the absence of evidence clearly showing that the merger is not likely to have
such anticompetitive effects."

250 **undermined and eroded:** Richard S. Markovits, *Economics and the Interpretation and Application of U.S. and E.U. Antitrust Law: Basic Concepts and
Economics-Based Legal Analyses of Oligopolistic and Predatory Conduct* (Heidel-
berg: Springer, 2014), 1:246.

250 *United States v. General Dynamics Corp.: United States v. General Dynamics
Corp.,* 415 U.S. 586 (1974). In an opinion written by Justice Potter Stewart,

the Supreme Court in *General Dynamics* emphasized that "in prior decisions involving horizontal mergers between competitors, the Court has found *prima facie* violations of § 7 of the Clayton Act from aggregate statistics of the sort relied on by the United States in this case."

250 **focus on market concentration:** Jay Greenfield and Mark S. Olinsky, eds., *The Use of Economists in Antitrust Litigation* (American Bar Association, Antitrust Law Section, 1984), 11.

250 **increased the market share of the two biggest firms:** Richard A. Posner, *Antitrust Law,* 2nd ed. (Chicago: University of Chicago Press, 2001), 129.

250 **heavily criticized:** Chris Sagers, "Ohio v. American Express: Clarence Thomas Sets Sail on a Sea of Doubt, and, Mirabile Dictu, It's Still a Bad Idea," ProMarket, June 27, 2018, promarket.org ("Justice Clarence Thomas does not write any antitrust opinions. When he does they tend to be kind of doozies, and not in a good way. The last big one that comes to mind was a 2006 decision called *Texaco, Inc. v. Dagher,* which strongly implied that a gasoline marketing joint venture was a 'single entity' not even subject to Sherman Act § 1. That was so even though it was mainly just a price-fixing agreement covering a quarter of its market, between two firms that otherwise remained quite separate, and though the record showed that it caused price increases with no offsetting benefit. . . . And then there was *United States v. Baker Hughes,* a merger opinion by then Judge Thomas for the DC Circuit. It approved a merger on breathtaking concentration numbers, largely on the mere conjectural possibility of entry, because he thought it 'onerous' were defendants required actually to prove likely entry.").

250 **the shift in approach:** The loosening of the *Philadelphia National Bank* standard, as evidenced by the Supreme Court's *General Dynamics* decision, gave license to lower courts to follow suit and to let other mergers and acquisitions go forward. For instance, in *United States v. Baker Hughes Inc.,* 908 F.2d 981 (D.C. Cir. 1990), the U.S. Court of Appeals for the District of Columbia—in an opinion authored by the future U.S. Supreme Court justice Clarence Thomas—held that "evidence of market concentration simply provides a convenient starting point for a broader inquiry into future competitiveness," with the importance of the *Philadelphia National Bank* standard cut back sharply by such cases. In the *Baker Hughes* case, a Finnish corporation, through its subsidiary Tamrock AG, sought to acquire Eimco Secoma, S.A., a French subsidiary of the Texas-based Baker Hughes Inc. In December 1989, the U.S. government sought to block the transaction, charging that it would substantially lessen competition in the U.S. market for hard-rock hydraulic underground drilling rigs (HHUDRs). The federal government obtained a temporary restraining order to stop the transaction, but the district court—after a bench trial—later rejected the government's request for a permanent injunction. The D.C. Circuit later affirmed the trial court's rejection of the government's antitrust claims, citing the Supreme Court's decision in *General Dynamics* and ruling that "high concentration has long been the norm in this market." The acquisition thus went forward, even though the two firms, when combined, had a 76 percent share in the HHUDRs market. The result: yet another industry was allowed to become highly consolidated.

The *Baker Hughes* case illustrates the shift in approach to antitrust cases that we have seen in the federal courts. In that Clayton Act case, the government had asserted that the merger would hurt competition, but the government's argument had been turned aside. Citing the *Philadelphia National Bank* case, the opinion of then judge Clarence Thomas began by emphasizing that "the basic outline of a section 7 horizontal acquisition case is familiar." As Thomas's opinion then stressed, "By showing that a transaction will lead to undue concentration in the market for a particular product in a particular geographic area, the government establishes a presumption that the transaction will substantially lessen competition. The burden of producing evidence to rebut this presumption then shifts to the defendant. If the defendant successfully rebuts the presumption, the burden of producing additional evidence of anticompetitive effect shifts to the government, and merges with the ultimate burden of persuasion, which remains with the government at all times."

Although the merger at issue in *Baker Hughes* plainly increased market concentration for the rigs in question, the D.C. Circuit affirmed the district court's finding that the relevant market share was "volatile and shifting" and "easily skewed." Robert S. Schlossberg, ed., *Mergers and Acquisitions: Understanding the Antitrust Issues,* 2nd ed. (Chicago: ABA Book Publishing, 2004), 146. The *Philadelphia National Bank* case found that a high market concentration creates what has been called "a nearly-conclusive presumption of harm from a merger." Markovits, *Economics and the Interpretation and Application of U.S. and E.U. Antitrust Law,* 1:246. But the D.C. Circuit's *Baker Hughes* decision found that "concentration simply provides a convenient starting point" for a "totality-of-the-circumstances approach." "In the wake of *General Dynamics,*" the D.C. Circuit ruled, "the Supreme Court and lower courts have found section 7 defendants to have successfully rebutted the government's prima facie case by presenting evidence on a variety of factors other than ease of entry." See also Hovenkamp and Shapiro, "Horizontal Mergers, Market Structure, and Burdens of Proof," 2010–11 ("The *Baker Hughes* opinion also produced a startling conclusion about the burden-shifting framework— namely, that '[i]mposing a heavy burden of production' on defendants' rebuttal to structural evidence would be 'anomalous where, as here, it is easy to establish a prima facie case.' The court appeared to be saying that where high market shares make the government's prima facie structural case strong, and thus easy to make, some sense of justice requires that the defendant's case be correspondingly easy to make as well. This makes little sense to us. When the plaintiff's case is stronger, the defendant's case is accordingly weaker and will naturally be harder to prove.").

250 **issued at the end of June 2020:** U.S. Department of Justice, Office of Public Affairs, "Department of Justice and Federal Trade Commission Issue New Vertical Merger Guidelines," press release, June 30, 2020, www.justice.gov.

250 **draft Vertical Merger Guidelines:** Federal Trade Commission, "FTC and DOJ Announce Draft Vertical Merger Guidelines," press release, Jan. 10, 2020, www.ftc.gov.

250 **Rebecca Kelly Slaughter:** In re FTC-DOJ Vertical Merger Guidelines, Commission File No. P810034 (June 30, 2020), Dissenting Statement of Commissioner Rebecca Kelly Slaughter, U.S. Federal Trade Commission, www.ftc .gov.

250 **Rohit Chopra:** Regarding the Publication of Vertical Merger Guidelines—Commission File No. P810034 (June 30, 2020), Dissenting Statement of Commissioner Rohit Chopra, U.S. Federal Trade Commission, www.ftc.gov.

251 **As I noted in early July 2020:** "Klobuchar Statement on Final Justice Department, FTC Vertical Merger Guidelines," press release, July 1, 2020, www.klobuchar.senate.gov (noting that "I called on the agencies to incorporate improvements from prior public comments into revised draft guidelines and to seek further comments, but the agencies finalized their guidelines without additional input.").

252 **anticompetitive "tying" arrangements:** Greenfield and Olinsky, *Use of Economists in Antitrust Litigation,* 19 ("A tying arrangement, or tie-in, exists where a seller offers to sell a (tying) product, but only on the condition that the buyer purchase a second (tied) product, or at least refrain from purchasing that product from any other supplier.").

253 **As *The New York Times* recently reported:** Ben Lovejoy, "AAPL Has Doubled Its Value in 21 Weeks in 'Unprecedented' Tech Giant Rise," 9to5Mac, Aug. 19, 2020, 9to5mac.com.

253 **higher prices for consumers:** Michael Bluhm, "The Pandemic Is Setting Off a Wave of Mergers. And That's a Problem," Open Markets, June 30, 2020, www.openmarketsinstitute.org ("Industry concentration costs each American family roughly $5,000 per year in higher prices for goods and services, calculated author Thomas Philippon, in his 2019 book *The Great Reversal: How America Gave Up on Free Markets.*").

253 **in a monopsony:** Julie Young, "Monopsony," *Investopedia* (updated Feb. 3, 2020), www.investopedia.com.

253 **in a Medium blog:** Thales Teixeira, "Big Tech's Power Is in Monopsony," Medium.com, Jan. 10, 2020, medium.com.

254 **"help clarify and emphasize":** Hovenkamp and Shapiro, "Horizontal Mergers, Market Structure, and Burdens of Proof," 2022.

254 **study of monopsony power:** "Labor Market Monopsony: Trends, Consequences, and Policy Responses," Council of Economic Advisers Issue Brief (Oct. 2016), obamawhitehouse.archives.gov.

254 **with much of the interest focused on:** In early 2017, when Lina Khan, then a Yale law student, published her nearly hundred-page law review note, titled "Amazon's Antitrust Paradox," it went viral—at least in the tight-knit antitrust community. Lina M. Khan, "Amazon's Antitrust Paradox," 126 *Yale Law Journal* 710 (2017). Khan pointed out that in addition to being a retailer and book publisher, Amazon is now a delivery and logistics network, a marketing platform, a credit lender, an auction house, a fashion designer, a hardware manufacturer, a payment service, and a host of cloud server space. "Although Amazon has clocked staggering growth," she explained, "it generates meager profits, choosing to price below-cost and expand widely instead." For years, Amazon reported losses, even as its revenues grew exponentially. "Through this strategy," Khan observed, "the company has positioned itself at the center of e-commerce and now serves as essential infrastructure for a host of other businesses that depend upon it." As she concluded of Amazon, "Elements of the firm's structure and conduct pose anticompetitive concerns—yet it has escaped antitrust scrutiny." Although the tech industry is finally

coming under intense scrutiny in Washington, D.C., the prevailing antitrust framework of the U.S. courts, pegged to short-term price effects, Khan has explained, "is unequipped to capture the architecture of market power in the modern economy."

Amazon's tactics—forgoing short-term profits while establishing its market dominance, including by pricing products below cost—raise a whole series of new questions for antitrust professionals to consider. "Amazon," David Streitfeld reported in *The New York Times* in 2018 in the aftermath of the publication of Khan's law review note, "dominates online commerce, employs more than half a million people and powers much of the internet itself through its cloud computing division. . . . If competitors tremble at Amazon's ambitions, consumers are mostly delighted by its speedy delivery and low prices. . . . Few of Amazon's customers, it is safe to say, spend much time thinking they need to be protected from it." David Streitfeld, "Amazon's Antitrust Antagonist Has a Breakthrough Idea," *New York Times*, Sept. 7, 2018, www.nytimes.com. The article in the *Times* specifically highlighted Khan's work, noting that her paper had gotten 146,255 hits—making it "a runaway best-seller" that had "rocked the antitrust establishment." After members of Congress—forced to confront how laws need to be updated—questioned social media executives, Streitfeld pointed out that "not since the Department of Justice took on Microsoft in the mid-1990s has Big Tech been scrutinized like this."

254 **testified via video before a House committee:** Alina Selyukh, "4 Big Tech CEOs Testified Before House Panel's Anti-trust Hearing," NPR, July 30, 2020, www.npr.org.

254 **before Senate committees:** Irina Ivanova, " 'Who the Hell Elected You?' Big Tech Defends Itself against Charges of Political Bias," CBS News, Oct. 29, 2020, www.cbsnews.com; Lauren Feiner, "Mark Zuckerberg and Jack Dorsey Testify before the Senate Tuesday—Here's What They'll Say," CNBC, Nov. 17, 2020, www.cnbc.com.

254 **the CEOs were grilled:** Matt Rosoff, "Congress Grills Tech CEOs amid Backdrop of Coronavirus and Economic Struggles," CNBC, July 29, 2020, www.cnbc.com.

254 **App Store:** Increased antitrust scrutiny recently prompted Apple to reduce its App Store commissions for smaller businesses. Sarah Perez, "Apple Dropping App Store Fees to 15% of Users with under $1 Million in Revenues," TechCrunch, Nov. 18, 2020, techcrunch.com ("Amid increased regulatory scrutiny over how it runs its App Store, Apple today announced it will reduce the App Store commissions for smaller businesses. Under the new guidelines of the 'App Store Small Business Program,' as it's called, developers earning up to $1 million per year will only have to pay a 15% commission on in-app purchases, rather than the standard 30% commission.").

254 **section 230 of the Communications Decency Act:** Lauren Feiner, "Both Trump and Biden Have Criticized Big Tech's Favorite Law—Here's What Section 230 Says and Why They Want to Change It," CNBC, May 28, 2020, www.cnbc.com.

254 **I later asked Zuckerberg:** "Klobuchar Questions CEO of Facebook about Competition, Antitrust Investigation, and Political Advertising."

254 **At a similar U.S. Senate Commerce Committee hearing:** "Klobuchar Presses

CEOs of Facebook and Google on Need to Combat Misinformation and Promote Industry Competition."

255 **as I noted:** Steven Overly, "Klobuchar: Republicans Are 'Politicizing' Tech while Legislation Stalls," *Politico*, Oct. 28, 2020, www.politico.com; "Tech CEOs Senate Testimony Transcript October 28," Rev, Oct. 28, 2020, www.rev .com.

255 **dozens of questions:** Ben Popken, "From Snacks to Snafus, 10 Highlights from Wednesday's Tech Hearing," NBC News, July 29, 2020, www.nbcnews .com.

255 **"have monopoly power":** "Big Tech Testifies: Bezos Promises Action if Investigation Reveals Misuse of Seller Data, Zuckerberg Defends Instagram Acquisition," CNBC, July 30, 2020, www.cnbc.com.

255 **In the Senate hearings:** "Klobuchar Questions CEO of Facebook about Competition, Antitrust Investigation, and Political Advertising."

255 **most of the questioning focused on section 230 issues:** Abram Brown, "5 Big Takeaways from Dorsey and Zuckerberg's Contentious Trip to the Senate," *Forbes*, Oct. 28, 2020, www.forbes.com.

255 **after Twitter launched Vine:** Adi Robertson, "Mark Zuckerberg Personally Approved Cutting Off Vine's Friend-Finding Feature," Verge, Dec. 5, 2018, www.theverge.com.

255 **Cicilline concluded:** Adi Robertson, "Everything You Need to Know from the Tech Antitrust Hearing," *Verge*, July 29, 2020, www.theverge.com.

255 **a portion of news coverage:** Popken, "From Snacks to Snafus, 10 Highlights from Wednesday's Tech Hearing."

256 **449-page report:** Adi Robertson and Russell Brandom, "Congress Releases Blockbuster Tech Antitrust Report," *Verge*, Oct. 6, 2020, www.theverge.com; Investigation of Competition in Digital Markets: Majority Staff Report and Recommendations, U.S. House of Representatives, Subcommittee on Antitrust, Commercial, and Administrative Law of the Committee on the Judiciary (2020), judiciary.house.gov.

256 **much-talked-about law review article:** Khan, "Amazon's Antitrust Paradox," 716, 722–23, 729–30.

257 **revolutionized order fulfillment:** Kiri Master, "Amazon Revolutionized Order Fulfillment, but This Company Is Creating Prime-Like Shipping for All," *Forbes,* June 21, 2018, www.forbes.com.

257 **once a company has cornered a market:** In today's business environment, individual companies or just a handful of companies already control large segments of particular markets. Google—a very successful enterprise—reportedly controls about 90 percent of the search engine market. Daisuke Wakabayashi, "Google Prepares to Brief Congress on Its Role in Election amid Investigation into Russian Interference," *New York Times,* Oct. 1, 2017, www.nytimes.com ("Google's search engine, with about a 90 percent market share, is an inescapable part of the internet, so it was no surprise that congressional investigators turned toward the company. Google is the only company that sells more digital advertising than Facebook, and its YouTube service is the go-to place for videos on the internet."). Likewise, Amazon—another mega-company that has its tentacles into just about everything these days, from apparel to toys to electronics—has tremendous power. "Amazon doesn't just dominate the

online market; it controls access to it," Stacy Mitchell, the co-director of the Institute for Local Self-Reliance, has pointed out. Samuel R. Miller, "Is Amazon Violating the Antitrust Laws?," *Verdict: Legal Analysis and Commentary from Justia,* July 25, 2019, verdict.justia.com. Indeed, Amazon recently purchased a brick-and-mortar grocer, Whole Foods, and started a pharmacy service, raising important new questions about Amazon's marketplace ambitions and growing corporate power. Richard Kestenbaum, "Amazon and Whole Foods After a Year: Supermarkets Will See Massive Changes," *Forbes,* Dec. 16, 2018, www.forbes.com; Nicolas Vega, "Amazon Pharmacy Announcement Sends Stocks of Drugstore Chains Tumbling," New York Post, Nov. 17, 2020, https://nypost.com. Not only are Amazon Echoes now sold at Whole Foods, but Amazon Prime members get special benefits for shopping in Whole Foods stores. The launching of Amazon Pharmacy and Amazon's plans to rapidly expand the number of Whole Foods locations, coupled with its ongoing efforts to get grocery buyers to shop online, have already changed the market landscape for the pharmacy and grocery industries. "Amazon Shakes Up Health Care," *Wall Street Journal,* Nov. 18, 2020, www.wsj.com; Zee Krstic, "Insiders Say Amazon Could Soon Turn Sears Stores into Whole Foods Locations," *Cooking Light,* Jan. 11, 2019, www.cookinglight.com.

258 **predatory pricing tactics:** Although the U.S. Supreme Court has asserted that "predatory pricing schemes are rarely tried and even more rarely successful," empirical research shows that simply is not true. Predatory pricing can be—and in fact long has been—used by dominant companies to squash or reduce competition. Predatory pricing involves a relatively simple two-step process: first, a company prices its goods or services below cost to drive competitors out of the market by forcing them to sell at a loss; and second, the company—during the recoupment stage—then charges a monopoly price to recoup the losses it incurred in establishing its market dominance. Christopher R. Leslie, "Predatory Pricing and Recoupment," 113 *Columbia Law Review* 1695 (2013). If the company, through monopoly pricing, is able to make more money during the recoupment phase than it was forced to expend in the initial predation phase, the company—unless deterred by the antitrust laws—will have employed what one scholar calls "an attractive anticompetitive strategy." Sandeep Vaheesan, "Reconsidering *Brooke Group:* Predatory Pricing in Light of the Empirical Learning," 12 *Berkeley Business Law Journal* 81, 82 (2015). Predatory pricing violates the antitrust laws, but the current difficulty in bringing such claims (especially in an era of "dynamic pricing" that technology and algorithms so easily facilitate) is inhibiting our ability to protect the free-enterprise system. A ProPublica investigation of 250 products frequently purchased through Amazon found that Amazon's algorithm prioritizes its own products. "Roughly 75% of the time," *Investor's Business Daily* reported in 2018 of the results of that study, "Amazon prioritized these products as 'suggested purchases'—even when there were substantially cheaper offers available." Richard Berman, "Consumers Beware: Amazon Monopoly Will Price Gouge," *Investor's Business Daily,* Jan. 25, 2018, www.investors.com.

258 **A less publicized issue:** See C. Scott Hemphill and Marcel Kahan, "The Strategies of Anticompetitive Common Ownership," 129 *Yale Law Journal* 1392, 1395 (2020) ("The Department of Justice has acknowledged concerns about

the anticompetitive effects of common ownership and investigated common ownership of competing airlines. In 2018, the Federal Trade Commission took these concerns a step further, conducting an all-day hearing on the subject.").

258 **common shareholders:** Einer Elhauge, "How Horizontal Shareholding Harms Our Economy—and Why Antitrust Law Can Fix It," Dec. 4, 2018, 4, 7–8, 13, 18–19, 31, 60, 65, 78, 104. Available at SSRN: ssrn.com.

258 **a November 2020 news report:** Julie Segal, "There's an Oligopoly in Asset Management. This Researcher Says It Should Be Broken Up," Institutional Investor, Nov. 24, 2020, www.institutionalinvestor.com.

259 **"share of corporate ownership":** John C. Bogle, "Bogle Sounds a Warning on Index Funds," *Wall Street Journal,* Nov. 29, 2018, www.wsj.com; Erin Arvedlund, "John Bogle Pens WSJ Op-Ed Warning Index Funds Becoming Too Big," *Philadelphia Inquirer,* Nov. 29, 2018, www.inquirer.com.

259 **Jenny Luna reports:** Jenny Luna, "The Biggest Antitrust Story You've Never Heard," Stanford Business, Aug. 6, 2018, www.gsb.stanford.edu.

259 **Luna traces the rise:** Luna points out that since 1970 "the share of the American stock market owned by large investment firms has grown from 7% to 70%." A lot of individual investors still like picking their own stocks, but these days huge institutional investors—Fidelity and Vanguard, for example—own the vast majority of shares. "At the end of the day, what we really need is a policy," one expert, Fiona Scott Morton, asserts, adding, "We need to understand exactly where the harm comes from and build a policy for mutual funds that protects consumers from the lack of competition."

260 **Elhauge explains:** Einer Elhauge, "The Causal Mechanisms of Horizontal Shareholding" (August 2, 2019), 3, corpgov.law.harvard.edu.

261 **U.S. seed market:** Mohammad Torshizi and Jennifer Clapp, "Price Effects of Common Ownership in the Seed Sector," posted March 14, 2019, papers.ssrn .com.

261 **"market concentration":** The primary tool for assessing market concentration since 1982 is the obscure Herfindahl-Hirschman Index, which—as Professor Daniel Crane observes—measures market concentration "by summing the square of the market share of each participant in the relevant market." Daniel A. Crane, *Antitrust* (Frederick, Md.: Wolters Kluwer, 2014), 192.

261 **airline industry:** Martin C. Schmalz, "Common-Ownership Concentration and Corporate Conduct," *Annual Review of Financial Economics* 10 (Nov. 2018): 413. At one time, Berkshire Hathaway was the largest shareholder in United Airlines and Delta Air Lines. "Lunch with Warren Buffett—How High Was This Year's Bid?," CGTN Live, June 3, 2018, news.cgtn.com. Berkshire Hathaway was also the second-largest shareholder in American Airlines and Southwest Airlines. Dan Burrows, "10 Stocks Warren Buffett Is Buying (and 6 He's Selling)," Kiplinger, Nov. 15, 2018, www.kiplinger.com. After the onset of the COVID-19 pandemic, Berkshire Hathaway sold its positions in the Big Four U.S. carriers: American Airlines, Delta Air Lines, Southwest Airlines, and United Airlines. Victor Ferreira, "Investors Sour on Airline Sector as Warren Buffett Exits Top U.S. Carriers," *Financial Post,* May 5, 2020, https:// financialpost.com.

261 **economic consequences:** The economist Paul Krugman has offered an explanation for the lag in corporate investment: "The most significant answer, I'd

suggest, is the growing importance of monopoly rents: profits that don't represent returns on investment but instead reflect the value of market dominance." Robin Harding, "Corporate Investment: A Mysterious Divergence," *Financial Times,* July 24, 2013, ft.com. There is, in fact, one little-discussed reason why for so long the wages of American workers have remained stagnant; it has a lot to do with the concentration of corporate power through consolidation and with the huge disparity of bargaining power that now exists between large corporations and individual workers, especially those who do not belong to a union. Jordan Weissmann, "Why Is It So Hard for Americans to Get a Decent Raise?," *Slate,* Jan. 16, 2018, slate.com ("Since 1979, inflation-adjusted hourly pay is up just 3.41 percent for the middle 20 percent of Americans while labor's overall share of national income has declined sharply since the early 2000s. There are lots of possible explanations for why this is, from long-term factors like the rise of automation and decline of organized labor, to short-term ones, such as the lingering weakness in the job market left over from the great recession. But a recent study by a group of labor economists introduces an interesting theory into the mix: Workers' pay may be lagging because the U.S. is suffering from a shortage of employers. . . . [I]t's clear that American industry has consolidated enormously over the decades. Years of mergers and the rise of exceedingly profitable superstars like Google and Facebook have concentrated economic power in fewer corporate boardrooms, and research suggests that America's transformation into a life-size Monopoly board may be cutting into labor's share of the economy.").

262 **anticompetitive impact of horizontal shareholding:** George S. Dallas, "Common Ownership: Do Institutional Investors Really Promote Anti-competitive Behavior?," Harvard Law School Forum on Corporate Governance, Dec. 2, 2018, corpgov.law.harvard.edu (noting that the International Corporate Governance Network "believes that this challenge to common ownership is ill-founded, and lacking in both an understanding of institutional investment practice and clear evidence. . . . [W]e believe that any blunt legislative initiatives to quell the perceived problem of common ownership would be retrograde, reducing the rights of investors and resulting in unintended consequences anathema to good corporate governance and good stewardship.").

262 **New empirical studies:** "A growing body of empirical literature," the experts Fiona Scott Morton and Herbert Hovenkamp write in *The Yale Law Journal* of horizontal shareholding, "concludes that under these conditions, market output is lower and prices are higher than they would otherwise be." As they explain the problem, "Due to the twin trends of increases in the mutual fund industry and the rise of concentration in the U.S. economy, the impact of lessening competition due to common ownership by mutual funds has a potentially adverse effect on consumer welfare." Fiona Scott Morton and Herbert Hovenkamp, "Horizontal Shareholding and Antitrust Policy," 127 *Yale Law Journal* 2026, 2027 (2018).

262 **non-compete agreements:** Scott Morton, "Modern U.S. Antitrust Theory and Evidence amid Rising Concerns of Market Power and Its Effects" ("Further evidence of monopsony power in labor markets come from the use of non-compete clauses in employment contracts, which have become pervasive in low-skilled jobs.").

262 **cover 30 million:** "Workers & Monopoly," Open Markets Institute, openmarketsinstitute.org.

262 **One study published in 2018:** Alan B. Krueger and Orley Ashenfelter, "Theory and Evidence on Employer Collusion in the Franchise Sector" (NBER working paper 24831, July 2018), www.nber.org.

263 **almost always dictated exclusively by the employer:** Evan Starr, J. J. Prescott, and Norman Bishara, "Noncompetes in the U.S. Labor Force" (University of Michigan Law and Economics research paper 18-013), available at SSRN: ssrn.com; see also Evan Starr, "Are Noncompetes Holding Down Wages?" (delivered at "Unrigging the Labor Market: Convening to Restore Competitive Labor Markets," June 13, 2018, Harvard Law School), lwp.law.harvard.edu; Michael Lipsitz and Evan Starr, "Low-Wage Workers and the Enforceability of Non-compete Agreements," April 20, 2020, available at SSRN: ssrn.com (finding that Oregon's ban on non-compete agreements (NCAs) for hourly paid workers increased hourly wages by 2–3 percent on average, and—according to the paper's abstract—that "the effect on employees actually bound by NCAs may be as great as 14–21%, though the true effect is likely lower due to labor market spillovers onto those not bound by NCAs").

263 **Jimmy John's:** Sarah Whitten, "Jimmy John's Drops Noncompete Clauses Following Settlement," CNBC, June 22, 2016, www.cnbc.com.

263 **Forced arbitration clauses:** Brianna Holt, "Why Forced Arbitration Policies Are a Huge Red Flag for Women at Work," *Quartz,* Sept. 19, 2019, qz.com.

264 **the Economic Policy Institute study:** Alexander J. S. Colvin, "The Growing Use of Mandatory Arbitration," Economic Policy Institute, April 6, 2018, www.epi.org.

264 **pay-for-delay:** In *FTC v. Actavis, Inc.,* 133 S. Ct. 2223 (2013), one of the litigated cases, the Federal Trade Commission sought to establish that pay-for-delay agreements are presumptively illegal. In that case, Solvay Pharmaceuticals had obtained a patent for a brand-name FDA-approved drug, but two other companies, Actavis and Paddock, had filed applications for generic drugs modeled after the brand-name drug. The FDA ultimately approved Actavis's generic product, but instead of bringing its product to market, Actavis entered into what is known as a "reverse payment" settlement agreement with Solvay, whereby Actavis agreed not to bring its generic product to market for a number of years and to instead promote Solvay's brand-name drug in exchange for millions of dollars. Paddock also entered into a similar reverse-payment agreement. Those agreements prompted the FTC to file suit, alleging that by refraining from engaging in competition (and instead agreeing to share in Solvay's monopoly profits), companies such as Actavis and Paddock were violating the law.

The Supreme Court in *FTC v. Actavis* held that reverse-payment settlements "can sometimes violate the antitrust laws," though it declined to find that they are "presumptively unlawful" as the FTC had urged. That was a missed opportunity to stop pay-for-delay, but it is now crystal clear that Congress must act to end the abuse of patent rights and the use of pay-for-delay agreements. Pay-for-delay agreements have real and undeniable consequences for consumers, especially when so many Americans are struggling to afford their prescriptions. "Apparently," a majority of the justices ruled in *FTC v.*

Actavis, "most if not all reverse payment settlement agreements arise in the context of pharmaceutical drug regulations, and specifically in the context of suits brought under statutory provisions allowing a generic drug manufacturer (seeking speedy marketing approval) to challenge the validity of a patent owned by an already-approved brand-name drug owner." Despite the by now well-known adverse price effects for consumers, the Supreme Court did not hold that all such settlements are illegal. Instead, it held that each such agreement must be evaluated by a "rule of reason" analysis, thus necessitating that Congress pass legislation to end pay-for-delay. While not outlawing the practice outright, the Court did freely admit in its ruling in the case that consumers would be hurt. As the Court emphasized, "Settlement on the terms said by the FTC to be at issue here—payment in return for staying out of the market—simply keeps prices at patentee-set levels, potentially producing the full patent-related $500 million monopoly return while dividing that return between the challenged patentee and the patent challenger. The patentee and the challenger gain; the consumer loses."

For many goods or services, the prices in America should be lower than in other countries because the market is larger. But in general, American prices are not lower than in countries with smaller markets. The high cost of prescription drugs in the United States is but one example. Yoni Blumberg, "Here's Why Many Prescription Drugs in the US Cost So Much—and It's Not Innovation or Improvement," CNBC.com, Jan. 14, 2019, www.cnbc.com ("Americans spend about $1,200 on prescription drugs a year, according to the latest figures from the Organization for Economic Cooperation and Development. That's more than people pay in any other developed country in the world."). Per se violations (for example, horizontal agreements to fix prices, bid rigging among competitors) of the antitrust laws are those violations determined to be so inherently anticompetitive that there is no need for a plaintiff to demonstrate the conduct's negative competitive effects in the relevant product and geographic markets. The more commonly employed rule of reason test, on the other hand, analyzes the definition of such markets, the market power of economic players in them, and the existence of anticompetitive effects, with lawyers and economists distinguishing between those effects harmful to consumers and any restraints stimulating competition that may benefit them. In contrast, the quick look test—an abbreviated version of the rule of reason analysis—allows courts to adjudicate antitrust claims without conducting such a rigorous analysis of the marketplace and a particular restraint's anticompetitive effects. The rule of reason, the U.S. Supreme Court has held, can sometimes be applied in "the twinkling of an eye," see *National Collegiate Athletic Association v. Board of Regents,* 486 U.S. 85, 109n39 (1984), with the Supreme Court emphasizing that a quick-look rule-of-reason analysis is appropriate when "an observer with even a rudimentary understanding of economics could conclude that the arrangements in question would have an anticompetitive effect on customers and markets." *California Dental Ass'n v. FTC,* 526 U.S. 756, 770 (1999). Most antitrust claims are subjected to the rule of reason test, with courts analyzing such things as the history, effects, and intent and purpose of the restraint in question, any offered justification for it, the defendant's market position, and any barriers to entry in the market. The overriding goal: deciding if the restraint on trade is *unreasonable* in nature.

264 **$3.5 billion a year:** "California Tackles Big Pharma's Anticompetitive 'Pay for Delay' Practices that Slow Down Lower-Cost Generic Drug Development," *National Law Review,* Oct. 17, 2019, www.natlawreview.com; *Pay for Delay,* Federal Trade Commission, www.ftc.gov.

264 **As one source notes:** Michael L. Fialkoff, "Pay-for-Delay Settlements in the Wake of *Actavis,*" 20 *Michigan Telecommunications and Technology Law Review* 523, 525 (2014).

265 **prescription drug costs increased by $63 billion:** Michael Kades, "Competitive Edge: Underestimating the Cost of Underenforcing U.S. Antitrust Laws," Washington Center for Equitable Growth, Dec. 13, 2019, equitablegrowth.org.

265 **For years:** David S. Savage, "High Court Rules 'Pay-for-Delay' Drug Deals Can Face Antitrust Suits," *Los Angeles Times,* June 18, 2013, www.latimes.com (taking note of the bill Senator Grassley and I introduced to crack down on anticompetitive pay-for-delay deals).

265 **$613 million over ten years:** Congressional Budget Office Cost Estimate, April 26, 2019, www.cbo.gov; see also "Policy Proposal: Banning or Limiting Reverse Payment Agreements," Pew Charitable Trusts, June 2017, www.pewtrusts.org ("The Congressional Budget Office has estimated that the Preserve Access to Affordable Generics Act would reduce federal spending by $2.4 billion over 10 years.").

265 **benefits the pharmaceutical industry:** The glaring examples of runaway greed in the pharmaceutical industry are almost too numerous to mention. Amy Klobuchar, "Klobuchar Calls for FTC Investigation of Mylan Pharmaceuticals for Possible Antitrust Violations in Light of Dramatic Price Increase of EpiPen Packs," press release, Aug. 22, 2016 ("Time and again, we see reports of a pharmaceutical company buying a prescription drug product and then raising the price dramatically. For example, Turing Pharmaceuticals, after purchasing the infectious disease drug Daraprim, increased its price from $13.50 to $750 a pill. Similarly, after acquiring two heart drugs, Nitropress and Isuprel, Valeant Pharmaceuticals immediately increased their prices by 525 and 212 percent, respectively. In letters to the CEOs of Eli Lilly, Sanofi, and Novo Nordisk, Klobuchar called for action to help people with diabetes afford insulin and asked for an explanation of the extreme price increases."). In 2014, Americans spent more than $297 billion on prescription drugs—a 12.2 percent increase from 2013 and the largest increase since 2012. Yet the prices of prescription drugs just keep going up, putting health care and drug treatments out of reach for many Americans. A recent study found that one out of four Americans whose prescription drug costs went up say they were unable to pay their medical bills. One out of five Americans, unable to afford medicines, actually skipped doses of their medications. An Associated Press investigation published in September 2018 found that pharmaceutical prices—despite President Donald Trump's campaign promise to reduce costs—continue to increase. "Minnesota Lawmakers Discuss Reining in Soaring Insulin Costs," *U.S. News & World Report,* Dec. 12, 2018, www.usnews.com. Over the first seven months of 2018, the Associated Press found, there were ninety-six price hikes for every price cut. The stories of all the people and all the families who

have been so tragically affected by the unaffordability of prescription drugs give urgency to this fight.

265 **hurting consumers:** Federal Trade Commission, "Pay-for-Delay: How Drug Company Pay-Offs Cost Consumers Billions," Jan. 2010, www.ftc.gov.

265 **abused their patent rights:** Robin Feldman and Evan Frondorf, *Drug Wars: How Big Pharma Raises Prices and Keeps Generics Off the Market* (New York: Cambridge University Press, 2017), 8–9.

265 **bill I introduced:** Mike Lee, "Opening Statement on the CREATES Act," June 21, 2016, www.lee.senate.gov.

266 **almost $4 billion in savings:** "Klobuchar, Grassley Legislation to Crack Down on Anticompetitive Pay-for-Delay Deals Gains Support in Senate," press release, Jan. 29, 2019, www.klobuchar.senate.gov.

266 **incorporated into another law:** H.R. 965: CREATES Act of 2019, www .govtrack.us.

266 **the outsized influence of money:** Money (a whole lot of which is undisclosed dark money, as documented in Jane Mayer's eye-opening book *Dark Money*) has literally flooded our political system and American elections. Jane Mayer, *Dark Money: The Hidden History of the Billionaires Behind the Rise of the Radical Right* (New York: Doubleday, 2016). All of that cash, some of which has come from foreign sources, presents nothing less than a clear and present danger to America's democracy. Alex Finley, "How Russian Money and Influence Slipped Through Cracks in the US Legal System," *Vox,* Oct. 25, 2018, www.vox .com.

266 **Dark money groups:** Robert Maguire, "$1.4 Billion and Counting in Spending by Super PACs, Dark Money Groups," OpenSecrets.org, Center for Responsive Politics, Nov. 9, 2016, www.opensecrets.org.

266 **$150 million:** Simone Pathé, "Liberal 'Dark Money' Groups Spent More in 2018 Than Conservative Groups," *Roll Call,* Jan. 23, 2019, www.rollcall.com.

266 **"$100 Million May Just Be the Tip of an Iceberg":** Ciara Torre-Spelliscy, "$100 Million May Just Be the Tip of an Iceberg," Brennan Center for Justice, Nov. 20, 2020, www.brennancenter.org.

266 **OpenSecrets research:** Anna Massoglia, "'Dark Money' Groups Find New Ways to Hide Donors in 2020 Election," OpenSecrets—Center for Responsive Politics, Oct. 30, 2020, www.opensecrets.org.

266 **"Americans who are running":** Jonathan Berr, "Election 2016's Price Tag: $6.8 Billion," CBS News, Nov. 8, 2016, www.cbsnews.com.

266 **super PACs:** 2016 Presidential Race, OpenSecrets.org, Center for Responsive Politics, www.opensecrets.org.

266 **$14 billion:** "So How Many Billions of Dollars Did the 2020 Election Cost?," Now This, Nov. 19, 2020, www.nowthisnews.com.

266 **amount of money spent on lobbyists:** Fredreka Schouten, "Washington Lobbying Business Surges to Eight-Year High," CNN, Jan. 26, 2019, www.cnn .com.

267 **lobbying activity in Washington, D.C.:** The health-care industry regularly employs multiple lobbyists for every member of Congress. Earl H. Fry, *Revitalizing Governance, Restoring Prosperity, and Restructuring Foreign Affairs: The Pathway to Renaissance America* (Lanham, Md.: Lexington Books, 2014), 34. OpenSecrets listed 1,451 pharmaceutical/health industry lobbyists in 2018—or

roughly 2.7 lobbyists for every member of Congress. "The 1,451 pharma/health products lobbyists," PolitiFact observed in 2019, "outnumbered lobbyists in all 89 other categories, according to an analysis by Daniel Auble, a senior researcher at OpenSecrets." Julie Appleby, "Klobuchar Says There Are Enough Drug Lobbyists in D.C. to Double-Team Lawmakers," PolitiFact, July 26, 2019, www.politifact.com. The numbers change constantly, but the pattern is the same year to year. Whenever the snapshot is taken, it shows a disturbing portrait of influence peddling gone amok. Alex J. Rouhandeh, "Big Pharma's Game of Control," *American Prospect*, Sept. 11, 2020, prospect.org ("In 2019 alone, the pharmaceutical/health products lobby spent $295 million, nearly double the next-highest spender, electronics manufacturing and equipment. For each member of Congress, there are 2.7 pharmaceutical/health products lobbyists.").

267 **U.S. Chamber of Commerce:** Alyssa Katz, *The Influence Machine: The U.S. Chamber of Commerce and the Corporate Capture of American Life* (New York: Spiegel & Grau, 2015), xii–xiii (noting that the U.S. Chamber of Commerce, through contributions from member corporations, "has in recent years invested more than a billion dollars in lobbying and campaign spending").

268 **nonprofit, public option:** Julie Rovner, "Obama Renews Call for a 'Public Option' in Federal Health Law," NPR, July 11, 2016, www.npr.org.

268 **the public option was dropped:** Wendell Potter, *Deadly Spin: An Insurance Company Insider Speaks Out on How Corporate PR Is Killing Health Care and Deceiving Americans* (New York: Bloomsbury Press, 2010), 193–95, 205–6 (discussing the debate in Congress over the public option); see also *Guide to U.S. Health and Health Care Policy,* ed. Thomas R. Oliver (Thousand Oaks, Calif.: CQ Press, 2014), 387. *Politico* estimated that in the fight over health care, including in the debate over Obamacare and the possibility of creating a public option, health-care players spent an estimated $1 million a day on Washington, D.C., lobbyists. All of that money and lobbying affected the law that was passed, illustrating the enormous power that corporations—including Big Pharma—wield in American life.

268 **a public option:** Like me, Joe Biden has long supported the creation of a public option. Selena Simmons-Duffin, "What Biden's Election Means for U.S. Health Care and Public Health," NPR, Nov. 9, 2020, www.npr.org.

268 **Tim Wu writes:** Wu, *Curse of Bigness,* 116.

268 **EpiPens:** Our daughter, Abigail, has a severe nut allergy and carries an EpiPen everywhere she goes. A few years ago, the price of EpiPens suddenly spiked, making them unaffordable for many Americans. It was an outrageous situation. According to an August 2016 *Washington Post* article about Mylan, the drug company that makes EpiPens and that has had more than $1 billion in annual sales, "A two-pack of the injectors, which release epinephrine to stop an allergic reaction, has risen from less than $100 in 2007 to $608 today. . . . Having a virtual monopoly has facilitated the rapid price hike." Carolyn Y. Johnson and Catherine Ho, "How Mylan, the Maker of EpiPen, Became a Virtual Monopoly," *Washington Post,* Aug. 25, 2016, www.washingtonpost.com.

Mylan had run into antitrust issues in the past, once settling a case brought by the Federal Trade Commission for $100 million. Federal Trade Commission, "FTC Reaches Record Financial Settlement to Settle Charges of

Price-Fixing in Generic Drug Market," press release, Nov. 29, 2000, www.ftc
.gov ("The Federal Trade Commission today approved a $100 million settle-
ment with Mylan Laboratories, Inc., the largest monetary settlement in Commission history. If the settlement is approved by the federal district court,
Mylan will pay the money into a fund for distribution to injured consumers
and state agencies. The settlement would resolve the Commission's charges
that four companies, including Mylan, conspired to deny Mylan's competitors ingredients necessary to manufacture two widely-prescribed anti-anxiety
drugs, lorazepam and clorazepate. The companies also agreed to the entry of
an injunction barring similar unlawful conduct in the future."). A class action
lawsuit involving the EpiPen price hike is currently pending.

268　**insulin:** The price of insulin has essentially tripled in the past decade, with
three companies—Eli Lilly, Novo Nordisk, and Sanofi, which sell 95 percent
of the world's insulin—raising their prices without any evidence of increased
production costs. Ken Alltucker, "Struggling to Stay Alive: Rising Insulin
Prices Cause Diabetics to Go to Extremes," *USA Today*, March 21, 2019, www
.usatoday.com; Linda Stein, "House Committee Discusses Rising Costs of Prescription Drugs," *Main Line Times*, Sept. 13, 2019, www.mainlinemedianews
.com. The price of one vial of Eli Lilly's Humalog, for example, jumped from
$35 in 2001 to $234 in 2015, while Novo Nordisk's NovoLog surged from $289
in 2013 to $540 in 2019. As a recent story in *USA Today* reports of insulin, the
drug originally discovered in 1921 by Canadian scientists and sold to the University of Toronto for three Canadian dollars, "The price of modern versions
of a drug that more than 7 million Americans need to live nearly tripled from
2002 to 2013, according to one study. Type 1 diabetics paid an average of $5,705
for insulin in 2016—nearly double what they paid in 2012, according to the
Health Care Cost Institute." Sadly, the goal of those pioneering, twentieth-
century scientists—to make insulin, the life-saving drug, available and affordable to all—has been thwarted by Big Pharma in the twenty-first century.
　　One Republican state legislator in my home state touted the availability
of insulin vials at Walmart that cost approximately $25 and that can be pur-
chased over the counter. But that type of insulin, which became widely available in the early 1980s, is not the same as newer, now much more expensive
analog insulin products that emerged in the mid-1990s. As Matt Petersen, a
vice president at the American Diabetes Association, told the Minneapolis
Star Tribune in 2019, "The analog insulin kicks in faster than the traditional
version and is more predictable, helping people avoid potentially dangerous
peaks that lead to low blood sugar." As the newspaper story reported, "The
older, cheaper version requires diabetics to be regimented about when they eat
and can increase the likelihood that they have to wake up in the night with
low blood sugar, doctors said. For people who are used to the analog versions,
switching to the cheaper option requires careful assistance from a health care
provider." Jessie Van Berkel, "Minnesota GOP Legislator Touts $25 Insulin at
Walmart; Diabetics Say It Has Drawbacks," *Minneapolis Star Tribune*, Sept.
24, 2019, m.startribune.com.

268　**Humira:** Lisa L. Gill, "The Shocking Rise of Prescription Drug Prices," *Consumer Reports*, Nov. 26, 2019, www.consumerreports.org (noting a 78 percent
price spike in Humira); see also Thomas Sullivan, "Humira and Lyrica Top

List of Drugs with Steep Price Hikes," *Policy and Medicine,* Dec. 8, 2019, www
.policymed.com ("The Institute for Clinical and Economic Review ('ICER')
recently released a revised study entitled Unsupported Price Increase Report,
which evaluates price hikes for drugs. The study found that AbbVie's Humira
and Pfizer's Lyrica, which showed the steepest price increases, topped a list of
7 drugs that accounted for a combined $4.8 billion increase in US spending in
2017 and 2018.").

268 **are galling:** Klobuchar, "Klobuchar Calls for FTC Investigation of Mylan
Pharmaceuticals for Possible Antitrust Violations in Light of Dramatic Price
Increase of EpiPen Packs" (seeking Federal Trade Commission investigation
of Mylan Pharmaceuticals for possible antitrust violations in light of dramatic
price increase of EpiPen packs, noting some reports of consumers paying $600
or more for the life-saving drug); Amy Klobuchar, "Klobuchar Presses Three
Pharmaceutical Companies for Action on High Insulin Prices; Urges Vigilance Against Anticompetitive Conduct," press release, July 3, 2017 ("According to recent reports, the price of insulin has more than tripled in the last
decades—likely due in part to limited competition. In the United States, three
companies have raised the list prices of insulin in near lock step, without providing evidence of increased production costs.").

268 **Alec:** Bram Sable-Smith, "Insulin's High Cost Leads to Lethal Rationing,"
NPR, Sept. 1, 2018, www.npr.org. "My son died because he could not afford
his insulin," Nicole Smith-Holt recently told CBS News. Megan Trimble,
"Minnesota Woman Says Son Died Because He Couldn't Afford Insulin,"
U.S. News & World Report, Jan. 4, 2019, www.usnews.com. And Alec's story is
not unlike that of Meaghan Carter, who died alone in her suburban apartment
in Dayton, Ohio, in 2018. Alltucker, "Struggling to Stay Alive." Another type
1 diabetic, Carter—an uninsured forty-seven-year-old nurse—died on Christmas after she tried to ration her insulin while she was between jobs. "There
was no insulin at all in the refrigerator," her sister-in-law, Mindi Patterson,
reported after Carter died, adding, "She had gauze, bandages and all her nursing supplies. She had plenty to take care of others but not enough to take care
of herself." As insulin prices have risen, people with diabetes have been forced
to choose between paying for their medications and paying for other necessities, like groceries, rent, and utilities. William T. Cefalu et al., "Insulin Access
and Affordability Working Group: Conclusions and Recommendations," *Diabetes Care* 41, no. 6 (June 2018): 1299–311, care.diabetesjournals.org.

269 **Nicole was my guest:** Associated Press, "Minnesotans Make Statements with
State of the Union Guests," *Pioneer Press,* Feb. 5, 2019, www.twincities.com.

269 **State of the Union address:** "Klobuchar to Be Joined at State of the Union
Address by Nicole Smith-Holt to Highlight Need to Bring Down Prescription
Drug Costs," press release, Feb. 1, 2019, www.klobuchar.senate.gov.

269 **broke his promises:** Ronnie Shows, "Trump Hasn't Kept His Promises to
Reduce Drug Prices," RealClearPolitics, Feb. 14, 2019, www.realclearpolitics
.com.

269 **American media:** "Media Consolidation: The Illusion of Choice," Visually,
visual.ly.

269 **media companies that do exist:** Take Comcast. Comcast Corporation, headquartered in Pennsylvania, also owns all of the common equity interests in

NBCUniversal Media, LLC, a Delaware entity. As a global media and technology company, Comcast operates its cable business under the Xfinity brand to residential and business customers, selling video, high-speed internet, voice, and other services. But that is not all. It also owns Universal Pictures, which acquires, produces, markets, and distributes films; theme parks, consisting primarily of its Universal theme parks in Hollywood, California, Orlando, Florida, and Osaka, Japan; major broadcast networks, NBC and Telemundo, that provide news, sports, and other entertainment content; and Sky, one of Europe's top entertainment companies, which operates the Sky News and Sky Sports networks and provides video, high-speed internet, and voice and wireless phone services. Comcast 2018 Annual Report on Form 10-K, www.sec.gov.

Or consider Viacom. Another multinational media conglomerate, Viacom owns movie studios, including Paramount Pictures Corporation, founded in 1914 and purchased by Viacom in 1994; popular television channels, including Nickelodeon, MTV, Comedy Central, and BET Network, which runs the Black Entertainment Television (BET) channel; music labels, Nick Records and Comedy Central Records; Nick, a radio network; various websites; and Nickelodeon Universe, its own theme park located in the Mall of America in Minnesota. Although Viacom, as originally constituted, included CBS, the two companies split in 2005. But in August 2019, it was announced that CBS and Viacom—both controlled by the Redstone family—would be getting back together, with the merged entity to be called ViacomCBS Inc. "Your Complete Guide to Everything Owned by Viacom," Nasdaq.com, July 10, 2017, www.nasdaq.com. As reported in *USA Today,* the combined company would have annual revenue of $28 billion—a truly staggering number. Kelly Tyko, "CBS and Viacom Are Reuniting with New Deal and Set to Become ViacomCBS Inc. by End of Year," *USA Today,* Aug. 13, 2019, www.usatoday .com. To facilitate the merger, Viacom and CBS announced in mid-2019 that they had set up an integration management office. Georg Szalai, "Viacom, CBS Set Up Integration Management Office," *Hollywood Reporter,* Sept. 3, 2019, www.hollywoodreporter.com.

269 **lead to censorship:** Marissa Moss, "One More Scoop of Vanilla: A New Proposal Looks to Loosen Radio Ownership Rules," NPR, June 7, 2019, www.npr .org; Edmund Sanders, "Senators Scold Radio Chain for Tuning Out Dixie Chicks," *Los Angeles Times,* July 9, 2003, www.latimes.com.

270 **some Clear Channel stations:** Michael Fitzgerald, "Dixie Chicks Axed by Clear Channel," *Jacksonville Business Journal,* March 17, 2003, www.bizjournals .com.

270 **iHeartMedia:** iHeartMedia, "Clear Channel Becomes iHeartMedia," press release, Sept. 16, 2014, www.iheartmedia.com; Josh Mandell, "Radio Broadcaster iHeartMedia Files for IPO," *Forbes,* April 3, 2019, www.forbes.com.

270 **Nasdaq listing:** Marsha Silva, "iHeartMedia Withdraws Its Estimated $1.5 Billion Public Offering," *Digital Music News,* June 29, 2019, www.digitalmusic news.com.

270 **then-named Dixie Chicks:** Gary Younge, "Anti-Bush Remark Hits Band CD Sales," *Guardian,* March 20, 2003, www.theguardian.com; Anastasia Tsioulcas, "Dixie Chicks Change Band Name to the Chicks," NPR, June 25, 2020, www.npr.org.

270 **"This is an aspect":** "Radio Under Fire: Chicks Ban Comes Back to Haunt Chain," *Billboard*, July 19, 2003, 62.

270 **co-chair of the Canada–United States Inter-Parliamentary Group:** "Klobuchar Welcomes Canadian Prime Minister Justin Trudeau to the United States," press release, March 10, 2016, www.klobuchar.senate.gov; Kelly Dittmar, Kira Sanbonmatsu, and Susan J. Carroll, *A Seat at the Table: Congresswomen's Perspectives on Why Their Presence Matters* (Oxford: Oxford University Press, 2018), chap. 2 ("Early in her Senate career, Democratic Majority Leader Harry Reid appointed Klobuchar to co-chair the Canada–United States Interparliamentary Group, and in this capacity she is 'always pushing things with Canada and our relationship.'").

271 **one of America's largest trading partners:** Wayne C. Thompson, *Canada, 2018–2019*, 34th ed. (Lanham, Md.: Rowman & Littlefield, 2018), 179; Dan Kopf, "Mexico Is Finally the US's Number-One Trading Partner," *Quartz*, Aug. 8, 2019, qz.com.

271 **Reuters reported:** Greg Roumeliotis and Pamela Barbaglia, "Global Mergers and Acquisitions Reach Record High in First Quarter," Reuters, March 30, 2018, www.reuters.com.

271 **Qualcomm:** Notably, in 2019, the FTC and the Justice Department's Antitrust Division publicly diverged on the handling of an issue pertaining to Qualcomm. "On May 2," one story reported, "the Antitrust Division of the U.S. Department of Justice (DOJ) took the unusual step of submitting a Statement of Interest in the Federal Trade Commission's (FTC's) case against Qualcomm to take a position contrary to the FTC." This divergence of views also showed the continual chaos within the Trump administration. Timothy Syrett, "The FTC's Qualcomm Case Reveals Concerning Divide with DOG on Patent Hold-Up," IP Watchdog, June 28, 2019, www.ipwatchdog.com.

271 **the proposed deal called off:** Daniel Shane and Sherisse Pham, "Why the US Killed Broadcom's Giant Bid for Qualcomm," CNN Business, March 13, 2018, money.cnn.com.

272 **criminal charges:** Julie Gordon and Steve Stecklow, "U.S. Accused Huawei CFO of Iran Sanctions Cover-up; Hearing Adjourned," Reuters, Dec. 7, 2018, www.reuters.com; David E. Sanger, Katie Benner, and Matthew Goldstein, "Huawei and Top Executive Face Criminal Charges in the U.S.," *New York Times*, Jan. 28, 2019, www.nytimes.com; "Chinese Telecommunications Conglomerate Huawei and Huawei CFO Wanzhou Meng Charged with Financial Fraud," U.S. Department of Justice, press release, Jan. 28, 2019, www.justice .gov (noting the unsealing of a 13-count indictment).

272 **"Effective enforcement of U.S. antitrust laws":** International Program, U.S. Department of Justice, www.justice.gov.

272 **Office of International Affairs:** Randolph Tritell and Elizabeth Kraus, "The Federal Trade Commission's International Antitrust Program," Feb. 2018, www.ftc.gov.

272 **Europe's antitrust regulators:** Kelvin Chan and Raf Casert, "Europe Fines Google $1.7 Billion in Antitrust Case," Associated Press, March 20, 2019, www .apnews.com.

272 **online advertising business:** There are two major forms of online advertising: display advertising and search advertising. J. Howard Beales III, "Pub-

lic Goods, Private Information: Providing an Interesting Internet," *Antitrust Chronicle* 1, no. 2 (Spring 2019): 14, 16, www.competitionpolicyinternational .com. Whereas the former involves display, digital video, and banner ads, the latter involves ad purchases based on keywords that consumers enter into a search engine, with sales revenue generated on a cost-per-click basis. In 2018, Google had a whopping 78 percent market share of the $44.2 billion search-ad market. Suzanne Vranica, "Amazon Puts a Dent in Google's Ad Dominance," MarketWatch, April 4, 2019, www.marketwatch.com.

272 **under investigation:** Sean Keane, "Google Job Search Service Draws Antitrust Complaint," CNET, Aug. 13, 2019, www.cnet.com.

272 **antitrust investigations:** Elizabeth Schulze, "If You Want to Know What a US Tech Crackdown May Look Like, Check Out What Europe Did," CNBC, June 7, 2019, www.cnbc.com.

272 **the sixty-four-page antitrust lawsuit:** The complaint against Google was filed on October 20, 2020.

273 **"The underlying aim":** Shunsuke Tabeta, "China's Decade-Old Antitrust Law Still Vexes Foreign Companies," *Nikkei Asian Review,* Aug. 2, 2018, asia.nikkei .com.

273 **China has an antimonopoly law:** "Competition Policy and Enforcement in China," US–China Business Council, Sept. 2014, www.uschina.org (describing China's antimonopoly law, the relevant Chinese agencies, and concerns about unequal treatment between domestic and foreign companies, with many U.S. companies expressing concerns about competition law, due process, and transparency—in China). In December 2020, China's State Administration of Market Regulation opened an antitrust investigation of Alibaba, that country's biggest tech company. Ryan McMorrow and Tom Mitchell, "Beijing Launches Antitrust Investigation into Alibaba," *Financial Times,* Dec. 24, 2020, www.ft.com.

274 **the word "antitrust":** No hyphenation is used these days, though "anti-trust" was once a common usage.

275 **"a horrible word":** Daniel A. Crane, *Antitrust* (Frederick, Md.: Wolters Kluwer Law & Business, 2014), 3.

275 **Antitrust Law Section:** Robert Connolly, "A Plug for the Section of Antitrust Law of the American Bar Association," *CartelCapers* (blog), Aug. 14, 2018, cartelcapers.com.

275 **two American presidents:** While Bill Clinton taught an antitrust course before becoming president, William Howard Taft became a professor at Yale Law School after his presidency and spent a considerable amount of his time there thinking about antitrust policy. Theodore P. Kovaleff, "Grading the Clinton Antitrust Policy as Enforced by the Antitrust Division of the Department of Justice," *Antitrust Bulletin* 53, no. 4 (Winter 2008): 1027 ("Having taught a course in trade regulation at the School of Law at the University of Arkansas in Fayetteville, William Jefferson Clinton was the only elected President with a firm grounding in antitrust."); Michael A. Carrier, "The Rule of Reason in the Post-*Actavis* World," 2018 *Columbia Business Law Review* 25, 26n1 ("Taft . . . contributed to antitrust law in his capacity as U.S. President, 'launching twice as many antitrust prosecutions as had his progressive predecessor' and, in his 1911 State of the Union address, defending Supreme Court decisions that had

adopted a Rule-of-Reason analysis. He further contributed to antitrust law as a scholar at Yale Law School, where he authored *The Anti-trust Act and the Supreme Court,* which, again, defended the Supreme Court's antitrust jurisprudence."). Notably, one of Bill Clinton's mentors, former Arkansas U.S. senator J. William Fulbright, had himself worked in the Justice Department's Antitrust Division. "Former Sen. Fulbright Dies," UPI Archives, Feb. 9, 1995, www.upi.com.

276 **special assistant:** Martha Minow, "Essays in Honor of Justice Stephen G. Breyer," 128 *Harvard Law Review* 416 (2014); see also Charles J. Russo, ed., *Encyclopedia of Education Law* (Thousand Oaks, Calif.: SAGE, 2008), 114 (noting that after finishing his clerkship with Supreme Court justice Arthur Goldberg, "Breyer served as a special assistant to the assistant attorney general in the antitrust division of the Justice Department").

276 **drew laughter:** Crane, intro. to *Antitrust* ("Laughter filled the courtroom. Staying awake during antitrust! Funny stuff indeed.").

276 **pop culture:** For a comprehensive list of antitrust references in pop culture, see "Antitrust in Pop Culture: A Guide for Antitrust Gurus," Institute for Consumer Antitrust Studies, jobs.luc.edu (compiled by Sarah Riddell, William Schubert, and Spencer Weber Waller).

276 **an NPR podcast:** Julia Simon, Kenny Malone, and Jacob Goldstein, "Antitrust in America," *Planet Money,* NPR, Feb. 23, 2019, www.npr.org (discussing NPR's three-part *Planet Money* podcast, with episode 1 titled "Standard Oil," episode 2 "The Paradox," and episode 3 "Big Tech").

276 **John Grisham novel:** John Grisham's novel *The Summons* (2002) features a law professor teaching a spring semester antitrust class with fourteen students in it. In the novel, Grisham notes of the professor that in that semester "he was supposed to be writing a book, another drab, tedious volume on monopolies that would be read by no one but would add handsomely to his pedigree." John Grisham, *The Summons* (New York: Delta Trade Paperbacks, 2010), 3, 119–20. The treatise was to be an "eight-hundred-page brick on monopolies" that "he'd promised to deliver by either this Christmas or the one after." Ibid., 14. Another of Grisham's novels, *The Street Lawyer* (1998), also features a lawyer who specializes in antitrust law. John Grisham, *The Street Lawyer* (New York: Delta, 2005), 7, 46, 118, 121, 176.

276 *Fair Fight in the Marketplace: Fair Fight in the Marketplace,* which focused on the history of the nation's antitrust laws and their use over time, is narrated by Mara Liasson. See vimeo.com.

276 *Louis Brandeis: The People's Attorney:* Another documentary, *Long Distance Warrior* (2011), is about Bill McGowan, the former CEO of MCI who took on AT&T in a historic antitrust case. Caroline Van Hasselt, *High Wire Act: Ted Rogers and the Empire That Debt Built* (Somerset: Wiley, 2010) (noting that "MCI, which originally stood for Microwave Communications Inc.," spent years taking on AT&T "to become America's first alternative long-distance telephone carrier," and offering this description of some of the history: "In 1974, when MCI unveiled Execunet, which used private lines and customer-owned switches to offer long-distance service to business customers, AT&T tried to crush the fledgling service by tripling the access fees it charged MCI to let customers connect to Execunet. MCI sued, accusing the world's largest corporation of violating antitrust laws. Led by its maverick leader, Bill McGowan,

who hated AT&T, MCI hired a battalion of lawyers and relocated the company to Washington DC. The cigar-chomping McGowan, a voracious reader who despised bureaucracy, once told his employees that they wouldn't succeed in the long-distance business until they succeeded in the litigation business. MCI won its case, and the U.S. Supreme Court refused to hear AT&T's appeal in 1978. MCI was awarded US$600 million in damages, which under U.S. law was trebled to a stunning US$1.8 billion, the largest monetary award in U.S. history. The case paved the way for the U.S. Department of Justice's antitrust case to break up the Bell System.").

276 *A View to a Kill:* Tony Nourmand, *James Bond Movie Posters: The Official 007 Collection* (San Francisco: Chronicle Books, 2004), 150; Nader Elhefnawy, *The Many Lives and Deaths of James Bond,* 2nd ed. (CreateSpace, 2015), 78–79.

276 **David E. Kelley:** Alessandra Stanley, "Television Review: Same Old Law Firm, New Snake," *New York Times,* Sept. 27, 2003, www.nytimes.com.

277 *Billions:* Damian Lewis, www.damian-lewis.com.

277 **in the music industry:** Michael Busler, "Antitrust Issues Continue to Rage in America's Music Industry," *Communities Digital News,* March 31, 2019, www.commdiginews.com. The auction house industry also became the subject of an antitrust scandal. *The Art of the Steal: Inside the Sotheby's-Christie's Auction House Scandal* (New York: G. P. Putnam's Sons, 2004), a book by Christopher Mason, bills itself in this way: "*The Art of the Steal* tells the story of several larger-than-life figures—the billionaire tycoon Alfred Taubman; the most powerful woman in the art world, Dede Brooks; and the wily British executive Christopher Davidge—who conspired to cheat their clients out of millions of dollars. It offers an unprecedented look inside this secretive, glamorous, gold-plated industry, describing just how Sotheby's and Christie's grew from clubby, aristocratic businesses into slick international corporations. And it shows how the groundwork for the most recent illegal activities was laid decades before the perpetrators were caught by federal prosecutors." The antitrust dispute involving price-fixing charges against the auction houses Sotheby's and Christie's, however, involved lots of tedious, attorney-driven court filings, including motions to certify a class action, to appoint class counsel, and to approve the settlement under Rule 23(e) of the Federal Rules of Civil Procedure. In ruling on motions to approve a $512 million settlement of the matter, the U.S. district judge Lewis A. Kaplan wrote a lengthy memorandum opinion that contained ninety-four footnotes. Opinion, In re Auction Houses Antitrust Litigation (S.D.N.Y. Feb. 22, 2001), casetext.com.

277 **a lengthy judicial opinion:** *Polygram Holding, Inc. v. Federal Trade Commission,* 416 F.3d 29 (D.C. Cir. 2005). That opinion focused on section 5 of the FTC Act, an assortment of prior precedents, a "rebuttal presumption of illegality," and the "substantial evidence" standard of review.

278 **once prompted Pearl Jam:** Eric Boehlert, "Pearl Jam: Taking On Ticketmaster," *Rolling Stone,* Dec. 28, 1995, www.rollingstone.com (noting that "the saga dates back to early '94," when Pearl Jam, "committed to paring hidden costs passed on to concert fans and emboldened by their newfound status as America's best-selling rock act," laid down guidelines for their upcoming concert tour (that is, "$1.80 service fees clearly spelled out on $18 tickets"), but Ticketmaster "was used to charging concertgoers a service fee that was two or three

times that amount with fees on top-dollar tickets reaching as high as $18"; after Pearl Jam abandoned their tour plans, they filed an antitrust suit against Ticketmaster, with Pearl Jam claiming Ticketmaster had abused its market dominance).

278 **smaller venues:** To alleviate financial woes of venues such as First Avenue, where Prince got his start in Minneapolis, Republican senator John Cornyn and I introduced the Save Our Stages Act. "Klobuchar, Cornyn Introduce Relief Bill for Independent Live Music Venues During Pandemic," news release, July 22, 2020, www.klobuchar.senate.gov. That bill became law in 2020.

278 **"furiously for days":** Bert Foer, Essay, "As U.S. Attorney General Gonzales Confidentially Reports, There Is Nothing Funny About Antitrust," American Antitrust Institute, April 1, 2006, www.antitrustinstitute.org.

278 **"AT&T is reportedly interested":** These days, of course, we should be more concerned about companies like AT&T reassembling the kind of monopoly power that the old AT&T once possessed. AT&T's recent merger with Time Warner—an $85 billion deal—has made a big company even bigger, even as the company has taken on substantial debt to finance its acquisition of entities like DirecTV and Time Warner. Robert Teitelman, "Here's Why the Government Lost the AT&T Antitrust Case," *Barron's,* Feb. 28, 2019, www.barrons .com; Mitchell Schnurman, "What's Ailing AT&T's Stock? One Year After Time Warner, Investors Worry About Debt, Disney, and Netflix," *Dallas News,* June 14, 2019, www.dallasnews.com.

278 **Twitter posts:** See Twitter posts of Carolyn Lander, Terri Mascherin, Janelle Filson Wrigley; Alex Harman and Josh Srago.

278 **students using antitrust law:** April Rockstead Barker, "Antitrust Case Targets Taverns for Cutting Drink Specials," *Wisconsin Law Journal,* Sept. 15, 2004, wislawjournal.com; Leigh Mills, "Bars Blame UW Professor for Lawsuit; Professor Says He's Not at Fault," WMTV, www.nbc15.com; *Eichenseer v. Madison-Dane County Tavern League Inc.,* 748 N.W.2d 154 (Wis. 2008).

278 **The law-student-led lawsuit:** Ann Althouse, "Do You Crack Jokes About Antitrust Law?,' *Althouse* (blog), April 8, 2004, althouse.blogspot.com.

8. THE PATH FORWARD

281 **higher costs for consumers:** Joseph E. Stiglitz, "A Rigged Economy," *Scientific American,* Nov. 2018.

281 **Two-thirds of U.S. industries:** Jacob Greenspon, "How Big a Problem Is It That a Few Shareholders Own Stock in So Many Competing Companies?," *Harvard Business Review,* Feb. 19, 2019, hbr.org; see also ibid. ("A different form of monopoly has largely escaped the limelight. An emerging body of research alleges that trusts have returned in a more insidious form as 'horizontal shareholdings': investors that own significant shares in several competing firms. For example, there is substantial common ownership among U.S. airlines. Between 2013 and 2015, the seven shareholders who controlled 60% of United Airlines also controlled 28% of Delta, 27% of JetBlue, and 23% of Southwest. Together these airlines have over half of domestic market share.").

282 **overturn *Citizens United:*** In its 5–4 decision in *Citizens United v. Federal*

Election Commission, 558 U.S. 310 (2010), the Supreme Court held that the free speech clause of the First Amendment prohibits the government from restricting independent expenditures in political campaigns. I have long argued that the U.S. Supreme Court should overturn its disastrous decision in *Citizens United,* which held that the Constitution prohibits the government from restricting independent expenditures in political campaigns. After seeing the distorting and corrupting influence of money on our politics, I believe that now more than ever. Because I see no evidence that the Supreme Court plans to reverse that decision, we should pass a constitutional amendment to make that happen, as I've advocated for years. It's hard to pass a constitutional amendment, but it's absolutely necessary to do just that for the health of our democracy.

282 **For the People Act:** "On Senate Floor, Klobuchar Calls on Republican Colleagues to Bring For the People Act to the Senate Floor," press release, March 10, 2020 ("Today, U.S. Senator Amy Klobuchar (D-MN), Ranking Member of the Senate Rules Committee with jurisdiction over federal elections, spoke on the floor of the Senate and called on her Republican colleagues to bring H.R. 1, the *For the People Act* to the Senate Floor for a vote. Today marks one year since the House of Representatives passed H.R. 1, the *For the People Act,* to restore ethics and transparency to government, which includes over a dozen Klobuchar provisions, including the *Honest Ads Act* and the *Election Security Act.*").

282 **Accessible Voting Act:** Special Committee on Aging, "Casey, Klobuchar Introduce Bill to Remove Barriers to Voting for Seniors and People with Disabilities," press release, Jan. 16, 2020, www.aging.senate.gov ("Today, U.S. Senators Bob Casey (D-PA), Ranking Member of the U.S. Senate Special Committee on Aging and Amy Klobuchar (D-MN), Ranking Member of the U.S. Senate Committee on Rules and Administration, introduced the Accessible Voting Act, which would support state and local efforts to improve voter accessibility and remove barriers to voting. In the 2016 general election, 16 million votes, representing 11.5 percent of the total votes, were cast by people with disabilities. However, a GAO study found that only 17 percent of the polling places it examined during the 2016 election were fully accessible.").

282 **antitrust enforcement:** For an in-depth primer on antitrust law, see E. Thomas Sullivan et al., *Antitrust Law, Policy, and Procedure: Cases, Materials, Problems,* 8th ed. (Durham, N.C.: Carolina Academic Press, 2019).

283 **"good trouble":** Representative John Lewis regularly told activists to get into "good trouble, necessary trouble" to help "save our democracy." Emily Birnbaum, "John Lewis Urges Young Activists to Get into 'Good Trouble' to Save Democracy," *Hill,* June 5, 2018, thehill.com.

283 **cable TV:** Associated Press, "Cable TV Prices Keep Going Up as More People Cut the Cord," *New York Post,* Jan. 5, 2018, nypost.com; Daniel Frankel, "Pay TV Bills Up 74% Since 2000, Are a Leading Cause of Cord Cutting, Kagan Says," FierceVideo, April 25, 2018, www.fiercevideo.com; see also Todd Shields, David McLaughlin, and Scott Moritz, "DirecTV to Hike Prices After Owner AT&T Promised Cheaper Bills," Bloomberg, March 14, 2019, www .bloomberg.com ("AT&T Inc. is hiking prices on its pay TV services for the second time since January, even after telling a judge during the U.S. antitrust trial last year that prices would go down if it was allowed to buy Time Warner Inc."). No one likes the cable companies' power to charge exorbitant prices,

and the battle over cable TV pricing has gone on for years. Until 1984, cable TV prices were regulated (just like other utilities such as electricity, water, gas, and local phone service). But in 1984, Congress prohibited municipalities from regulating cable prices. Paul Krugman, Robin Wells, and Martha L. Olney, *Essentials of Economics* (New York: Worth, 2007), 290. That law caused cable TV prices to rise sharply, leading to a backlash and the passage of a new law. In 1992, Congress once again gave local governments the authority to set limits on pricing. Along with protracted battles over cable TV bills, the issue of innovation in the provision of services has been at the forefront. For years, the cable companies had no incentive to update their cable boxes, while they had plenty of incentive—that is, profit maximization—to increase rental fees. Suddenly with Apple TV, Roku, Hulu, and Netflix, competition set in and innovation finally came to cable in terms of how you select the things you want to view, and the options you have to choose from in the marketplace. "For some of us," Apple's Peter Stern said during a press conference, "the big bundle is more than we need, so we designed a new TV experience where you can pay for only the channels you want all in one app." Cable prices remain far too high, however, and a lot of that has to do with lax antitrust enforcement and the power of certain companies. Todd Haselton, "Apple Unveils Streaming TV Services," CNBC, March 25, 2019, www.cnbc.com.

283 **beer:** The price of a six-pack of beer has gone from $1.57 in 1953 to $9.03 in 2018, though the price depends somewhat on the type of beer. Talia Lakritz, "What a 6-Pack of Beer Cost the Year You Were Born," *Insider,* April 7, 2019, www.insider.com; see also Victor J. Tremblay and Carol Horton Tremblay, *The U.S. Brewing Industry: Data and Economic Analysis* (Cambridge, Mass.: The MIT Press, 2005), 167 (listing the price differential between premium and popular-priced beer for a six-pack of 12-ounce cans from 1953 to 2001). The price of beer in the United States was thus 475.62% higher in 2018 than it was in 1953. Compare Samuel Stebbins, "The Price of Beer the Year You Were Born," 24/7 Wall St., April 5, 2019, 247wallst.com ("Throughout the 1950s and 1960s, the average price of a six-pack of beer was less than $2.00. While this may sound like a bargain, adjusting for inflation shows that beer actually costs less now than it did in the mid-20th century."). One study of the merger of Miller and Coors breweries—a merger approved by the U.S. Department of Justice in 2008—found that the average price of MillerCoors beer increased in the short run and that rivals in the market also increased their prices in response to the increased market concentration. Orley C. Ashenfelter, Daniel Hosken, and Matthew C. Weinberg, "Efficiencies Brewed: Pricing and Consolidation in the U.S. Beer Industry" (working paper 19353, National Bureau of Economic Research, Aug. 2013), www.nber.org. That's a double whammy for consumers. That 2013 National Bureau of Economic Research study of the combined joint venture of the industry's second- and third-largest firms reached this conclusion: "We estimate that, all else equal, the average market experienced a price increase of just under two percent because of the merger." Although the study's authors found that "despite the price increases associated with the merger, on net it had little effect on pricing because of efficiencies resulting from the combined Miller/Coors," they also noted that "the price decreases associated with the reductions in shipping distance

occurred more slowly than the price increases associated with the increases in concentration."

A subsequent follow-up study of the price effects of the MillerCoors joint venture, one published in 2017, documented "abrupt increases in retail beer prices just after the consummation of the MillerCoors joint venture, both for MillerCoors and its major competitor, Anheuser-Busch." Nathan H. Miller and Matthew C. Weinberg, "Understanding the Price Effects of the Miller-Coors Joint Venture," Feb. 24, 2017, www.nathanhmiller.org. The craft brewing industry has injected much-needed competition into the market, with craft beer sales now amounting to $114 billion—or 24 percent—of the U.S. beer market. And this nascent industry, which is growing rapidly, must be allowed to grow unimpeded by unfair competition from the industry's biggest players. As of 2018, there were 7,346 small, independent microbreweries, brewpubs, and breweries, up from 6,490 at the end of 2017. Mike Snider, "Craft Beer Sales Continue Growth, Now Amount to 24% of Total $114-Billion U.S. Beer Market," *USA Today,* April 2, 2019, www.usatoday.com. But a lot of people still don't realize that when they walk through the aisles of a liquor store, a lot of the major beer brands are owned by just a handful of big companies. After the merger of Anheuser-Busch InBev and SABMiller, the combined enterprise controlled more than two thousand beer brands, including such recognizable ones as Beck's, Bass, Budweiser, Corona, Labatt, Michelob, and Stella Artois. Tim Wu, *The Curse of Bigness: Antitrust in the New Gilded Age* (New York: Columbia Global Reports, 2018), 117. Making sure small craft brewers can easily distribute their products is key to making sure true competition exists.

283 **health care:** Emily Gee and Ethan Gurwitz, "Provider Consolidation Drives Up Health Care Costs," Center for American Progress, Dec. 5, 2018, www .americanprogress.org ("Prices for medical care have generally risen faster than overall inflation, even for common procedures such as appendectomies and knee replacements. Any serious effort to bend the cost curve must address the prices Americans currently pay for health care, including the price markups that result from insufficient competition in U.S. health care markets. Put simply, less competition leads to higher prices for care.").

283 **start doing something about it:** Hearings are one way to inform the public, but we need much more than that; we need more vigorous antitrust enforcement, too. Opening Statement of Sen. Amy Klobuchar, Senate Committee on the Judiciary, Subcommittee on Antitrust, Competition Policy, and Consumer Rights, Hearing on Ensuring Competition Remains on Tap: The AB InBev/SABMiller Merger and the State of Competition in the Beer Industry, Dec. 8, 2015 ("Over the last decade, Anheuser-Busch, Miller, and Coors all have been involved in major acquisitions. Today, Anheuser-Busch InBev (ABI, owners of what was Anheuser-Busch) and SABMiller account for 70 percent of the beer sales in the United States."). According to ten-year workload statistics published by the Antitrust Division of the Department of Justice, the number of investigations is down—from seventy-four section 1 and 2 Sherman Act investigations in 2009 to forty-four in 2018, and from sixty-eight section 7 Clayton Act investigations in 2009 to sixty-five in 2018. "Antitrust Division Workload Statistics FY 2009–2018," U.S. Department of Justice, www.justice .gov.

284 **anticompetitive and exclusionary conduct:** For example, there is behavior that creates unjustified barriers to entry or that improperly raises the costs of rivals to compete in a market; price-fixing or bid-rigging agreements; pricing below cost, otherwise known as "predatory pricing"; market divisions, whereby companies collude and divide up territories and agree to stay out of each other's respective territories; behavior that leads to output reductions (think OPEC), thus driving up prices; and tying or bundling of products or services together without a complementarity need.

284 **Anticompetitive Exclusionary Conduct Prevention Act:** Anticompetitive Exclusionary Conduct Prevention Act of 2020, www.klobuchar.senate.gov; "Senator Klobuchar Introduces Sweeping Bill to Promote Competition and Improve Antitrust Enforcement," press release, Feb. 4, 2021, www.klobuchar .senate.gov.

284 **"The proposed legislation":** Michael Kades, "Hearing with Tech CEOs Sets Stage for New Legislation to Tackle Anticompetitive Conduct by Dominant Firms in the U.S. Economy," Washington Center for Equitable Growth, Aug. 10, 2020, equitablegrowth.org. Prior to joining the Washington Center for Equitable Growth, Kades—a graduate of the University of Wisconsin Law School—worked for me as my antitrust counsel and spent twenty years investigating and litigating antitrust cases as an attorney at the Federal Trade Commission, where he worked directly with former FTC chair Jon Leibowitz. Michael Kades, equitablegrowth.org/people/michael-kades/.

285 **formed the Antitrust Caucus:** Tess Townsend, "Keith Ellison and the New 'Antitrust Caucus' Want to Know Exactly How Bad Mergers Have Been for the American Public," *New York*, Dec. 4, 2017, nymag.com.

286 **a number of antitrust hearings:** "Lee, Klobuchar Hold Antitrust Subcommittee Hearing on CREATES Act, Bipartisan Legislation to Address Rising Prescription Drug Prices," press release, June 21, 2016, votesmart.org; Elise Reuter, "Sprint/T-Mobile Merger Now Faces Legislative Hearing," *Kansas City Business Journal*, May 24, 2018, www.bizjournals.com.

287 **since 1903:** U.S. Department of Justice Antitrust Division, www.revolvy.com; *Oversight and Authorization Hearings into the Policies and Enforcement Record of the Antitrust Division (DOJ): Hearings Before the Subcommittee on Monopolies and Commercial Law of the Committee on the Judiciary, House of Representatives, One Hundredth Congress, First and Second Sessions, February 26 and March 4, 1987; February 24, 25, and March 3, 1988* (Washington, D.C.: U.S. Government Printing Office, 1989), 4:587. The FTC and the Department of Justice's Antitrust Division (first referenced in a 1919 DOJ annual report) only came into being after the passage in 1914 of the Clayton Act (Pub. L. No. 63–212, 38 Stat. 730) and the FTC Act (Pub. L. No. 63–203, 38 Stat. 717), but enforcement efforts ramped up over the decades that followed, though the commitment to these efforts varied by administration. The number of attorneys and staff dedicated to antitrust enforcement at the DOJ's Antitrust Division and at the FTC has grown substantially since 1903, albeit with a noticeable decline in staffing levels in recent times. Meanwhile, the size and complexity of the mergers and acquisitions those agencies are tasked with reviewing have gotten exponentially larger. In truth, modern antitrust enforcement efforts just haven't kept pace with the acceleration of corporate consolidation and

multibillion-dollar megadeals. See Kadhim Shubber, "Staffing at Antitrust Regulator Declines Under Donald Trump," *Financial Times,* Feb. 7, 2019, www.ft.com; see also *Annual Report on Competition Policy Developments in the United States (1st October 1996–30 September 1997)* (DIANE, 1998), 8 ("At the end of FY97, the [Antitrust] Division had 804 employees: 345 attorneys, 49 economists, 186 paralegals and 224 support staff. . . . At the end of FY97, the FTC's Bureau of Competition had 224 employees: 141 attorneys, 44 other professionals and 33 clerical staff. The FTC also employs about 40 economists who participate in its antitrust enforcement activities.").

287 **full-time equivalents:** "FTC Appropriation and Full-Time Equivalent (FTE) History," Federal Trade Commission, www.ftc.gov.

287 **congressional appropriations to the Antitrust Division:** "Appropriation Figures for the Antitrust Division, Fiscal Years 1903–2021," U.S. Department of Justice (updated Feb. 2020), www.justice.gov.

287 **a "daunting" workload:** In his testimony on March 9, 2016, Baer referenced the Antitrust Division's "daunting" workload while highlighting some of the division's successes in spite of that crushing workload. For example, he spoke of the division's legal challenge to Electrolux's acquisition of General Electric's appliance business, a merger that—as he put it—"would have left millions of Americans vulnerable to price increases for ranges, cooktops, and wall ovens, products that represent large purchases for many households." That proposed merger, he noted, was abandoned after four weeks of trial, "thereby preserving the head-to-head competition that leads to lower prices, better services, and greater innovation for consumers." Baer also noted that the division's challenge to a "merger-to-monopoly between the nation's two largest cinema advertising networks (which provide preshow advertisements services to movie theaters)." It was the kind of "anticompetitive transaction," he said, "that never should have made it out of the boardroom." Statement of Bill Baer, Assistant Attorney General, Antitrust Division, Before the Subcommittee on Antitrust, Competition Policy, and Consumer Rights, Committee on the Judiciary, U.S. Senate, Hearing on Oversight of the Enforcement of the Antitrust Laws, presented on March 9, 2016, www.justice.gov.

287 **we need to be bold:** A major part of beefing up antitrust enforcement—and amending our country's laws to help do that more effectively—is simply about having the will to do it. But the other part of the equation is less obvious: having the grit and the resources—as well as the legal tools—to do it right. The neglect of our country's antimonopoly and antitrust tradition, which dates back to America's founding, is a huge mistake. Instead of being *proactive,* as antitrust regulators were in prior decades and as they should be today, the Justice Department's Antitrust Division and the Federal Trade Commission have all too often been largely *reactive* and not getting the job done. The lack of resources being devoted to keeping America's free-enterprise system strong and healthy is incredibly shortsighted because a free-enterprise system will endure only if there is robust competition. Recently, antitrust investigations were opened to examine the activities of Big Tech (and that is a good thing), but we need more than investigations and inquires. Makena Kelly, "Justice Department Announces Broad Antitrust Review of Big Tech," *Verge,* July 23, 2019, www.theverge.com. Investigations form the prelude to antitrust enforce-

ment actions, and if violations are found, investigations are utterly meaningless without proper enforcement. The Justice Department's commencement of an antitrust lawsuit against Google in October 2020 and the FTC's December 2020 lawsuit against Facebook are a start, but it should be seen as just that—a start. Brian Fung, "The US Government Sues Google for Alleged Anticompetitive Abuses in Search," CNN, Oct. 21, 2020, www.cnn.com.

289　**since 2001:** "Premerger Notification; Reporting and Waiting Period Requirements," Federal Trade Commission, 16 CFR Parts 801, 802, and 803, Federal Register, vol. 66, no. 22, p. 8680 (Feb. 1, 2001) (noting the implementation of a "tiered fee structure" in which a fee of $45,000 would be paid for proposed transactions less than $100 million, $125,000 for transactions between $100 and $500 million, and $280,000 for transactions involving $500 million or more).

289　**urgently addressed:** Back when the premerger filing requirement was set up in 1976 with the Hart-Scott-Rodino Antitrust Improvements Act, no one anticipated today's complex megamergers—mergers that can mean large sums of money for those involved in them. These days, the parties' advisers and lawyers routinely receive hundreds of thousands of dollars—into the millions—for completing a deal and getting it approved. James B. Stewart, "$11 Million a Year for a Law Partner? Bidding War Grows at Top-Tier Firms," *New York Times,* April 26, 2018, www.nytimes.com (noting that a law partner "will earn $10 million in 2018 to lead Paul Weiss's global mergers and acquisitions practice, according to people familiar with the arrangement"); "M&A Advisor Fees for Selling a Business," Strategic Exits, May 1, 2016, www.exits.com (noting of "M&A Advisor Success Fees," "For transactions over $100 million, success fees had been in the 2% to 4% range. This means that a firm executing a $100 million exit will typically receive a success fee in the $2 to 4 million range."). Bottom line: there are a lot of powerful interests who have an awful lot at stake in preserving the system we have now.

289　**criminal antitrust fines:** "Doing Hard Time: The Antitrust Division Sets Records in Number of Individuals Sentenced and in Number of Criminal Trials," U.S. Department of Justice, Division Update Spring 2018, www.justice .gov ("From 2012 through 2015, the [Antitrust] Division assessed fines over $1 billion each year, with a high of $3.6 billion in 2015.").

290　**the acquiring party:** Filing Fee Information, Premerger Notification Program, Federal Trade Commission, April 3, 2019, www.ftc.gov.

290　**Merger Enforcement Improvement Act:** Merger Enforcement Improvement Act, S. 1811, 115th Cong. (introduced Sept. 14, 2017), www.congress.gov; "Klobuchar, Senators Introduce Legislation to Modernize Antitrust Enforcement," press release, Sept. 14, 2017, www.klobuchar.senate.gov.

291　**the FTC:** The FTC's mission statement: "Protecting consumers and competition by preventing anticompetitive, deceptive, and unfair business practices through law enforcement, advocacy, and education without unduly burdening legitimate business activity." About the FTC, Federal Trade Commission, www.ftc.gov.

291　**multibillion-dollar megamergers:** Amy Klobuchar, "Klobuchar, Merkley, Senators Urge DOJ Antitrust Division to Conduct Thorough and Impartial Analysis of Bayer AG Acquisition of Monsanto Company," press release, July 21, 2017 ("U.S. Senators Amy Klobuchar (D-MN) and Jeff Merkley (D-OR) today led 17 senators in urging the U.S. Department of Justice Antitrust Division to conduct a thorough and impartial analysis of Bayer AG's proposed $66 billion acquisition of Monsanto Company.").

291 **capitalist system:** Capitalism, by its very nature, involves the formation of corporations and the issuance and sale of stocks. Companies own assets and the owners of those companies—often very ambitious entrepreneurs—naturally seek to grow those companies. But the American people are right to ask why certain companies have been allowed to get so big and what should be done about it.

291 **bill would authorize:** There are a lot of people who have long seen the need to beef up antitrust enforcement budgets, so I'm hardly alone in asking for this step. Because antitrust enforcement is now so inadequately funded, it's not surprising that the bill I'm sponsoring drew the immediate support of important pro-competition consumer groups and their leaders. For example, George Slover, senior policy counsel at Consumers Union, said this about the legislation: "This bill makes several constructive improvements to keep merger law strong and up to date. The proposal to collect concrete information on the actual results of divestitures and other conditions merging companies agree to will help make enforcement more accountable to the public for preventing the harms to competition and consumer choice that mergers can leave in their wake." Diana Moss, the president of the pro-consumer, pro-competition American Antitrust Institute, another important watchdog group, had this to say about our bill: "We are greatly encouraged to see lawmakers recognize key issues in merger enforcement that have emerged over the last several years. The elements of the proposed bill go to resources, process, and substance—all of which will support more vigorous enforcement."

291 **appropriations for the FTC:** FTC Appropriation and Full-Time Equivalent (FTE) History, Federal Trade Commission, www.ftc.gov.

291 **Senator Grassley:** "Klobuchar, Grassley Introduce Legislation to Ensure Antitrust Authorities Have the Resources They Need to Protect Consumers," press release, June 20, 2019, www.grassley.senate.gov.

293 **runaway corporate consolidation:** One of the policy choices made since the early 1980s is not to vigorously enforce the antitrust laws in the way they once were from the 1940s through the late 1970s—what has been characterized as the "golden era of antitrust." Maurice E. Stucke and Ariel Ezrachi, "The Rise, Fall, and Rebirth of the U.S. Antitrust Movement," *Harvard Business Review,* Dec. 15, 2017, hbr.org. Not only have lawmakers and antitrust officials not paid sufficient attention to the effect of corporate consolidation on American paychecks and the costs of goods and services for working families, but the sheer number of mergers and acquisitions approved by the Justice Department's Antitrust Division and the Federal Trade Commission has allowed the level of corporate consolidation to reach new heights, and that has only continued in recent years. From 2008 to 2017, American firms transacted more than $10 trillion in mergers and acquisitions. Matt Stoller, "With Amazon on the Rise and a Business Tycoon in the White House, Can a New Generation of Democrats Return the Party to Its Trust-Busting Roots?," Open Markets Institute, July 13, 2017, openmarketsinstitute.org.

293 **In September 2017, I introduced:** Consolidation Prevention and Competi-

tion Promotion Act of 2017, 115th Congress (introduced Sept. 14, 2017), www
.congress.gov; Amy Klobuchar, "In Effort to Lower Costs for Consumers,
Help Even Playing Field for Business, and Encourage Innovation—Klobuchar,
Senators Introduce Legislation to Promote Competition," press release, Sept.
14, 2017.

293 **shift the burden of proof:** The bill would shift the burden of proof to merging
parties when a proposed merger (1) substantially increases concentration, (2)
involves more than $5 billion, or (3) involves a party worth $100 billion or more
acquiring assets of $50 million or more.

293 **which party has the burden of proof:** This issue has gotten some attention in
the scholarly literature. See Andrew I. Gavil, "Burden of Proof in U.S. Antitrust Law," in *Issues in Competition Law and Policy* (Chicago: ABA Antitrust
Law Section, 2008), vol. 1.

293 **The bill requires:** Jim Spencer, "Deals by UnitedHealth, Other Health Giants
Draw Antitrust Scrutiny in D.C.," *Minneapolis Star Tribune,* June 22, 2019,
www.startribune.com.

293 **prove it won't reduce competition:** Ilene Knable Gotts, "Back to the Future:
Should the 'Consumer Welfare' Standard Be Replaced in U.S. M&A Antitrust Enforcement," *Antitrust Report,* 1, 25, www.law.berkeley.edu (noting that
the Consolidation Prevention and Competition Promotion Act would "shift
the burden of proof from the agencies to the transaction parties, making the
merger presumptively unlawful unless the parties establish by a preponderance
of the evidence that the merger will not have an anticompetitive result").

294 **congressional testimony:** Submission of Bill Baer, Visiting Fellow, Governance Studies, Brookings Institution, Before the U.S. House Committee on
the Judiciary, Subcommittee on Antitrust, Commercial, and Administrative
Law, May 19, 2020, 3–4. In addition to addressing how courts have interpreted
section 7 of the Clayton Act, Baer's testimony made a similar point about section 2 of the Sherman Act. As Baer testified, "The same bias against the risk
of over-enforcement has resulted in court hostility to monopolization challenges under Section 2 of the Sherman Act." He noted that a joint response to
the House subcommittee by "twelve experienced antitrust scholars and former
public servants" emphasized that the antitrust laws, *as interpreted and enforced
today,* are inadequate to confront and deter growing market power in the U.S.
economy. Ibid., 4 (citing Jonathan B. Baker et al., Joint Response to the House
Judiciary Committee on the State of Antitrust Law and Implications for Protecting Competition in Digital Markets, 116th Cong. (2020)).

294 **my proposed legislation:** Senators Kirsten Gillibrand of New York, Ed Markey
of Massachusetts, and Richard Blumenthal of Connecticut are co-sponsors of
the bill.

294 **lower the applicable standard:** Gotts, "Back to the Future," 1, 25 (noting
that the Consolidation Prevention and Competition Promotion Act would
"change the substantive injunctive standard from the current requirement that
has been in effect for over a century, whereby the agencies must prove that
merger would substantially lessen competition or tend to create a monopoly
to a lesser standard such that a transaction is 'materially likely' to cause more
than *de minimis* harm to competition," and that "under the revised standard, a
transaction would be illegal if it would lead to a significant increase in market

concentration *unless* the transaction parties establish by a preponderance of the evidence that the effect of the acquisition will not tend to materially lessen competition or create a monopoly or a monopsony").

295 **vertical mergers:** *United States v. AT&T,* involving the merger of AT&T and Time Warner, is one example. "D.C. Circuit Holds That DOJ Failed to Prove AT&T/Time Warner Merger Is Anticompetitive," Shearman & Sterling, March 12, 2019, www.lit-antitrust.shearman.com.

295 *Federal Trade Commission v. Steris Corp.: Federal Trade Commission v. Steris Corp.,* 133 F. Supp.3d 962 (N.D. Ohio 2015); "FTC Dismisses Complaint Against Steris and Synergy," press release, Oct. 30, 2015, www.ftc.gov.

296 **monopoly power:** These days, companies such as Amazon can exert enormous monopoly power, including on the merchants that rely on Amazon's online platform to bring their goods to market. As one 2019 news report notes, "Amazon has evolved from partner to competitor" for sellers who use Amazon's site to sell their products. Although that news report observes that merchants who sell their goods on Amazon.com make up 58 percent of all sales on the site, it also contains this tidbit that reveals just how much merchants are getting squeezed: "Amazon captures 50 cents of every dollar spent online in the U.S. EBay Inc., its closest competitor, gets just six cents." In recounting the story of merchants' trying to bring their goods to the online market, the news report concluded, "Amazon takes a bigger bite of each sale. Its share has almost tripled to more than 40 percent in the past few years, merchants say, mostly due to the new cost of advertising." "If you're going to have a marketplace," Jason Boyce, a seller of sporting goods, complained of the rising cost of using Amazon's platform and how Amazon is now selling competing or knockoff products, "you shouldn't be able to piggyback off the hard work and labor of your sellers to beat them. . . . Amazon is constantly throwing curve balls at you." While Amazon has run television ads touting how many small- and medium-sized businesses use its services, it is the sheer power of Amazon that everyone must be concerned about. The fact that so many small- and medium-sized businesses use Amazon's services certainly does not mean that Amazon's business model should escape antitrust scrutiny. "Amazon Merchants Feel Market-Clout Pain Bezos Disputes," *NewsMax Finance,* April 17, 2019, www.newsmax.com.

296 *Brooke Group: Brooke Group Ltd. v. Brown & Williamson Tobacco Corp.,* 509 U.S. 209 (1993).

296 **recouping its losses:** American Bar Association, Antitrust Law Section, *Model Jury Instructions in Civil Antitrust Cases* (Chicago: ABA Publishing, 2005), C-48 (discussing the holding of the U.S. Supreme Court in *Brooke Group*).

297 **empirical research:** Sandeep Vaheesan, "Reconsidering *Brooke Group:* Predatory Pricing in Light of the Empirical Learning," 12 *Berkeley Business Law Journal* 81 (2015); see also Richard O. Zerbe Jr. and Donald S. Cooper, "An Empirical and Theoretical Comparison of Alternative Predation Rules," 61 *Texas Law Review* 655 (1982).

298 **antitrust cases:** For a link to the Department of Justice's antitrust case filings, see www.justice.gov. My Anticompetitive Exclusionary Conduct Prevention Act sets out a general test for exclusionary conduct that is presumptively harmful to competition and requires a preponderance of the evidence to overcome

the presumption. In terms of the standard of proof, Congress—if it chose—could set an even stricter standard of proof, one of "clear and convincing evidence," to rebut a presumption of anticompetitive conduct.

298 **can be so subjective:** See Harry First and Spencer Weber Waller, "Antitrust's Democracy Deficit," 81 *Fordham Law Review* 2543, 2547 (2013) ("The Sherman, Clayton, and Federal Trade Commission Acts are broadly worded, with Congress intentionally leaving it to the courts to fill in the exact meaning of phrases like 'restraint of trade,' 'monopolization,' 'substantially lessen competition,' and 'unfair methods of competition,' none of which was statutorily defined.").

298 ***Philadelphia National Bank:*** *United States v. Philadelphia National Bank,* 374 U.S. 321 (1963).

298 **in its incipiency:** Peter Carstensen and Robert H. Lande, "The Merger Incipiency Doctrine and the Importance of 'Redundant' Competitors," 2018 *Wisconsin Law Review* 783 (2018).

299 **create a presumption:** This presumption could be overcome by a showing of a "preponderance of the evidence" or, if Congress chose to make it even tougher to counteract, by the heightened "clear and convincing evidence" standard.

299 **Richard Posner:** J. Robert Robertson, "Editor's Note, *Philadelphia National Bank* at 50," 80 *Antitrust Law Journal* 189, 197, 200 (2015); "*Philadelphia National Bank* at 50: An Interview with Judge Richard Posner," 80 *Antitrust Law Journal* 205, 206, 216 (2015) (Judge Posner notes that "Justice Brennan assigned the writing of the *Philadelphia Bank* opinion to me."). Of course, the government would still be required to establish the relevant market. In antitrust law, how the relevant market is defined is obviously of great importance. Indeed, merger analysis begins with defining the relevant product market. *FTC v. Swedish Match,* 131 F. Supp.2d 151, 156 (D.D.C. 2000) (citing *Brown Shoe Co. v. United States,* 370 U.S. 294, 324 (1962)). As has been emphasized: "Defining the relevant market is critical in an antitrust case because the legality of the proposed merger in question almost always depends upon the market power of the parties involved." Ibid. (quoting *FTC v. Cardinal Health, Inc.,* 12 F. Supp.2d 34, 45 (D.D.C. 1998)).

300 **recently pondered aloud:** Sandeep Vaheesan, "American Prosperity Depends on Stopping Mega-mergers," *Financial Times,* April 25, 2019, ftalphaville.ft.com.

300 **Jonathan Baker writes:** Jonathan B. Baker, *The Antitrust Paradigm: Restoring a Competitive Economy* (Cambridge, Mass.: Harvard University Press, 2019), 1–2.

300 **the former chief economist:** Baker served as the chief economist at the FCC from 2009 to 2011. He also served as the director of the Bureau of Economics at the Federal Trade Commission from 1995 to 1998. Jonathan B. Baker, www.wcl.american.edu.

300 **an expansion of U.S. competition policy:** Many challenges have been identified, including the lack of adequate antitrust enforcement resources. Alison Jones and William E. Kovacic, "Antitrust's Implementation Blind Side: Challenges to Major Expansion of U.S. Competition Policy," 65 *Antitrust Bulletin* 227, 248 (2020).

301 **"consumer welfare" misnomer:** The Trump administration promoted the "con-

sumer welfare standard." "CPI Talks . . . with Makan Delrahim," *Antitrust Chronicle,* Sept. 2019, www.justice.gov.

301 **section 7 of the Clayton Act:** 15 U.S.C. § 18.

301 **Borkian manner:** In his article "The 'Borking' of America," Jordan Haedtler explains that "Robert Bork set in motion pro-monopoly policies that have ravaged the middle class, particularly in small-town and rural America." While Bork is most remembered today for having his nomination to the U.S. Supreme Court rejected by the Senate, Bork's perverse definition of "consumer welfare"—as Haedtler notes—led to a dramatic decline in antitrust enforcement and thus caused serious and lasting damage. "The victims of the 'Bork antitrust era,'" Haedtler observes, have been small businesses and consumers, with mergers producing higher—not lower—consumer prices. As Haedtler wrote before the COVID-19 pandemic of some of the adverse effects, "Black-owned businesses have been crushed by growing concentration, the Big Four airlines use their market power to gouge consumers with fees, and major mergers have led to deep regional inequality, spurred by the closure of hospitals, retail stores, rural airports and more." Jordan Haedtler, "The 'Borking' of America," *Washington Monthly,* Feb. 6, 2018, washingtonmonthly.com.

301 **"tying" by dominant firms:** In *Northern Pacific Railway Co. v. United States,* 356 U.S. 1, 5–6 (1958), the Supreme Court defined a "tying arrangement" as "an agreement by a party to sell one product, but only on the condition that the buyer also purchases a different (or tied) product, or at least agrees that he will not purchase that product from any other supplier."

302 *Jefferson Parish: Jefferson Parish Hospital District No. 2 v. Hyde,* 466 U.S. 2 (1984).

302 **That standard is complicated:** For a tie to violate the per se standard, the following elements must be met: (1) there must be two products and/or services, not just one; (2) both relevant product and geographic markets must be defined; (3) market power or "dominance" in at least one market is required, with a 30 percent market share plus market imperfections found not to be enough in the *Jefferson Parish* case to constitute market power or dominance; (4) there must be a tie that forces customers to purchase something they otherwise might not want to purchase; and (5) the tie is not explained by efficiencies.

302 **the presumption of anticompetitive conduct:** In my bill, the presumption could be rebutted if the defendant establishes, by a preponderance of the evidence, that "(A) distinct procompetitive benefits of the exclusionary conduct in the relevant market eliminate the risk of harming competition presented by the exclusionary conduct"; "(B) one or more persons, not including any person participating in or facilitating the exclusionary conduct, have entered or expanded their presence in the market with the effect of eliminating the risk of harming competition posed by the exclusionary conduct"; or "(C) the exclusionary conduct does not present an appreciable risk of harming competition." Obviously, if Congress chose to be stricter, it should require the presumption to be rebutted by clear and convincing evidence.

302 **a market investigations law:** "Market Investigations," Thomson Reuters, Practical Law, uk.practicallaw.thomsonreuters.com ("The Enterprise Act 2002 replaced the complex and scale monopoly provisions of the Fair Trading Act 1973 with new powers in relation to 'market investigations.' This allows the

UK competition authorities (currently the Competition and Markets Authority (CMA)) to investigate and take action where any feature or features of a market have an adverse effect on competition."); see also Jonathan Reuvid, ed., *Investors' Guide to the United Kingdom 2015/16* (London: Legend Press, 2015) ("Generally speaking, these market investigations focus on industry practices rather than the actions of specific firms."); "The UK's New Market Studies and Market Investigations Regime," Insights, Jones Day, April 2014, www .jonesday.com ("Market studies and market investigations enable the competition authorities to examine any market in the UK, assess whether there are obstacles to competition functioning well in those markets, and propose actions (often wide-ranging, including business divestments) to address any such obstacles. Under the current regime, the Office of Fair Trading ('OFT') (and sectoral regulators, such as Ofgem) carries out market studies and can refer markets to the Competition Commission ('CC') for a market investigation. During market investigations, which are more detailed examinations into particular markets, the CC must decide whether there is an adverse effect on competition in the markets in question and, if so, what remedial action is appropriate.").

302 **As Tim Wu explains:** Wu, *Curse of Bigness,* 134.

303 **As Wu suggests:** Ibid., 132–33.

304 **Consolidation Prevention and Competition Promotion Act:** Consolidation Prevention and Competition Promotion Act of 2017, 115th Congress (introduced Sept. 14, 2017), www.congress.gov; Klobuchar, "In Effort to Lower Costs for Consumers, Help Even Playing Field for Business, and Encourage Innovation."

305 **As one economist:** William A. McEachern, *Microeconomics: A Contemporary Introduction,* 8th ed. (Mason, Ohio: Cengage Learning, 2009), 238.

305 **Monopolization Deterrence Act of 2019:** Shiva Stella, "Public Knowledge Applauds Sen. Klobuchar for Bill Enhancing FTC, DOJ Antitrust Fines," Public Knowledge, press release, Aug. 2, 2019, www.publicknowledge.org; Amy Klobuchar, "Klobuchar Introduces Legislation to Crack Down on Monopolies That Violate Antitrust Law," press release, Aug. 2, 2019, www .klobuchar.senate.gov.

306 **Public Knowledge:** About Us, Public Knowledge, www.publicknowledge.org; see also Klobuchar, "Klobuchar Introduces Legislation to Crack Down on Monopolies That Violate Antitrust Law."

306 **their 2012 article:** John M. Connor and Robert H. Lande, "Cartels as Rational Business Strategy: Crime Pays," 34 *Cardozo Law Review* 428 (2012). Connor and Lande have suggested that cartel sanctions be increased fivefold to counter the problem of price-gouging cartels. The total expected costs of cartel activity (for example, in civil or criminal penalties) are, they point out, significantly less than the sum of expected gains to cartels and individual decision makers involved in such unlawful activity. The chance of hidden cartels being detected is estimated to be only 10 percent to 30 percent, while the financial rewards to cartel participants are extremely high and very lucrative for those who get away with practices such as bid rigging and other monopolistic, cartel-driven price gouging. Douglas H. Ginsburg and Joshua D. Wright, "Antitrust Sanctions," 6 *Competition Policy International* 3 (2010). Cartel overcharges cost

American consumers billions of dollars each year. Consequently, increasing fines and the amounts demanded in antitrust settlements is the right thing to do from both an economic and a moral perspective. Upping criminal sanctions and penalties for cartel participants would also help to deter cartels from operating and being formed in the first place. A "slap on the wrist" is not the kind of rigorous antitrust enforcement we need in this day and age of monopoly power run amok, and would-be cartel participants need to be better deterred.

307 **cartel activity:** Connor and Lande, "Cartels as Rational Business Strategy."

307 **That formula:** See ibid., 435–47.

307 **average cartel overcharge:** Ibid., 455–57.

307 **have recommended:** See Douglas H. Ginsburg et al., "DOJ Has the Power to Crush Price Fixers: Column," *USA Today Weekend,* May 29–31, 2015, 11A, www.usatoday.com.

307 **No new legislation is needed:** Ibid.

308 **Just as the SEC:** Alan R. Palmiter, *Securities Regulation: Examples and Explanations,* 7th ed. (New York: Wolters Kluwer, 2017), §§ 12.2.1–12.2.2.

308 **OPEC:** Alfred A. Marcus, *Controversial Issues in Energy Policy* (Newbury Park, Calif.: SAGE, 1992), 63–66.

308 **bipartisan legislation:** "Klobuchar, Grassley Introduce Bipartisan Bill to Fight Price Fixing by the Organization of the Petroleum Exporting Countries (OPEC)," press release, July 16, 2018, www.klobuchar.senate.gov.

309 *Illinois Brick* **decision:** *Illinois Brick Co. v. Illinois,* 431 U.S. 720 (1977).

309 **it has been shown:** John M. Connor and Robert H. Lande, "Not Treble Damages: Cartel Recoveries Are Mostly Less Than Single Damages," 100 *Iowa Law Review* 1997 (2015).

309 **allow indirect purchasers:** Robert H. Lande, "New Options for State Indirect Purchaser Legislation: Protecting the Real Victims of Antitrust Violations," 61 *Alabama Law Review* 447 (2010).

309 **needs to be done very carefully:** Randy M. Stutz, "Cracking *Pepper:* An Analysis of the Supreme Court's Latest Pronouncement on the Indirect Purchaser Rule," American Antitrust Institute, May 2019, www.antitrustinstitute .org (noting that "the opinion [in *Apple Inc. v. Pepper*] leaves intact, for now, both the *Illinois Brick* rule barring indirect purchaser suits and the *Hanover Shoe* ruling barring defendants from asserting a 'pass-on' defense" and observing, "AAI [American Antitrust Institute] is concerned that overturning *Illinois Brick* likely means overturning *Hanover Shoe* (often described as *Illinois Brick*'s 'corollary') as well, notwithstanding that the States did not propose to do so. Allowing a pass-on defense would burden direct-purchaser class actions with complex new class certification issues under Rule 23, involving predominance of common issues (including the ability to prove impact (or injury) on a class-wide basis), ascertainability, and damages calculation. These matters currently tend not to arise under the indirect purchaser rule, but if *Illinois Brick* and *Hanover Shoe* were overturned, they would present challenges to effective private antitrust enforcement.").

309 **indirect purchaser legislation:** Lande, "New Options for State Indirect Purchaser Legislation," 448 ("Many states enacted laws, called *Illinois Brick* Repealers ('IBRs'), to give indirect purchasers the right to sue when firms vio-

late analogous state antitrust laws. The majority of states now have some form of IBR.").

309 **A model statute:** Ibid., 447–48 ("In *Illinois Brick v. Illinois Co.,* the Supreme Court held that, under federal antitrust law, only direct purchasers have standing to sue antitrust violators for damages. Since most products travel through one or more intermediaries before reaching consumers, this decision left most true victims of illegal cartels and other antitrust violations without a remedy to compensate them.").

309 **prejudgment interest:** The empirical significance of the absence of prejudgment interest in antitrust cases is explored in Robert H. Lande, "Are Antitrust 'Treble' Damages Really Single Damages?," 54 *Ohio State Law Journal* 115, 130–36 (1993). A provision of federal law, 15 U.S.C. § 15, titled "Amount of Recovery; Prejudgment Interest," currently reads as follows: "The court *may* award under this section, pursuant to a motion by such person promptly made, simple interest on actual damages for the period beginning on the date of service of such person's pleading setting forth a claim under the antitrust laws and ending on the date of judgment, or for any shorter period therein, if the court finds that the award of such interest for such period is just in the circumstances." 15 U.S.C. § 15 (italics added). But that statutory provision goes on to state, "In determining whether an award of interest under this section for any period is just in the circumstances, the court shall consider only—(1) whether such person or the opposing party, or either party's representative, made motions or asserted claims or defenses so lacking in merit as to show that such party or representative acted intentionally for delay, or otherwise acted in bad faith; (2) whether, in the course of the action involved, such person or the opposing party, or either party's representative, violated any applicable rule, statute, or court order providing for sanctions for dilatory behavior or otherwise providing for expeditious proceedings; and (3) whether such person or the opposing party, or either party's representative, engaged in conduct primarily for the purpose of delaying the litigation or increasing the cost thereof."

310 **hardly ever end up paying prejudgment interest:** Robert H. Lande, "Five Myths About Antitrust Damages," 40 *University of San Francisco Law Review* 651, 652 (2006); Connor and Lande, "Not Treble Damages," 2004 and n26 (noting just one instance, a case from New Jersey in 2014, in which a plaintiff was awarded prejudgment interest in an antitrust case).

310 **mandating prejudgment interest:** *Handbook of Research in Trans-Atlantic Antitrust,* ed. Philip Marsden (Cheltenham, U.K.: Edward Elgar, 2006), 534 ("Allowing prejudgment interest . . . would likely enhance the potential for settlement of private actions.").

311 **bounty system:** See William E. Kovacic, "Private Participation in the Enforcement of Public Competition Laws," in *Current Competition Law,* ed. Mads Andenas, Michael Hutchings, and Philip Marsden (London: British Institute of International and Comparative Law, 2004), 2:167, 173–75.

311 **based on a true story:** "The Serious Story Behind 'The Informant,'" NPR, Sept. 20, 2009, www.npr.org.

311 **price-fixing scheme:** For a narrative of the price-fixing scheme and a chronology of major events, see James B. Lieber, *Rats in the Grain: The Dirty Tricks*

and Trials of Archer Daniels Midland (New York: Four Walls Eight Windows, 2002).

311 **Mark Whitacre:** "Price-Fixing Whistleblower and FBI Informant to Deliver Shoemaker Lecture," *Penn State News,* Oct. 15, 2014, news.psu.edu.

311 **exposed serious wrongs:** Avinash K. Dixit and Barry J. Nalebuff, *The Art of Strategy: A Game Theorist's Guide to Success in Business and Life* (New York: W. W. Norton, 2008), 92.

311 **the motto:** Kurt Eichenwald, *The Informant: A True Story* (New York: Broadway Books, 2000).

311 **a $100 million fine:** Sharon Walsh, "ADM to Pay $100 Million to Settle Price-Fixing Case," *Washington Post,* Oct. 15, 1996, www.washingtonpost.com.

311 **the right to sue:** 15 U.S.C. § 15 ("Any person who shall be injured in his business or property by reason of anything forbidden in the antitrust laws may sue therefor in any district court of the United States in the district in which the defendant resides or is found or has an agent, without respect to the amount in controversy, and shall recover threefold the damages by him sustained, and the cost of suit, including a reasonable attorney's fee.").

311 **treble damages:** Roger D. Blair and D. Daniel Sokol, eds., *The Oxford Handbook of International Antitrust Economics* (Oxford: Oxford University Press, 2015), vol. 1, § 11.2.1.2 ("Under Section 4 of the Clayton Act, persons injured by antitrust violations can sue for treble damages.").

312 *qui tam:* Under the English common law, a writ of *qui tam* allowed a private individual who assisted a prosecution to receive part of the penalty imposed. The writ is an abbreviation of the Latin *qui tam pro domino rege quam pro se ipso in hac parte sequitur*—that is, "[he] who sues in this matter for the king as well as for himself."

312 **Criminal Antitrust Anti-retaliation Act:** Criminal Antitrust Anti-retaliation Act of 2019, www.congress.gov; "Senate Unanimously Passes Grassley-Leahy Criminal Antitrust Anti-retaliation Act," press release, Oct. 18, 2019, www.grassley.senate.gov; Bernard Archbold and Mark Krotoski, "US Senate Passes Criminal Antitrust Anti-retaliation Act," Morgan Lewis, Oct. 22, 2019, www.jdsupra.com; "Grassley Marks Policy Oversight Accomplishments in 2020," U.S. Senator Chuck Grassley, www.grassley.senate.gov.

312 **at a recent hearing:** Robert Connolly, "Some Antitrust Whistleblower News," *CartelCapers* (blog), Sept. 25, 2019, cartelcapers.com.

313 **a 2020 editorial:** John W. Mayo and Mark Whitener, "Five Myths About Antitrust Law," *Washington Post,* March 20, 2020, www.washingtonpost.com.

313 **power to hold hearings:** Hearings on Competition and Consumer Protection in the 21st Century, Federal Trade Commission, www.ftc.gov (noting the FTC held "a series of public hearings during the fall 2018–spring 2019 examining whether broad-based changes in the economy, evolving business practices, new technologies, or international developments might require adjustments to competition and consumer protection law, enforcement priorities, and policy").

314 **private antitrust enforcement:** Reed Albergotti and Jay Greene, "When Regulators Fail to Rein in Big Tech, Some Turn to Antitrust Litigation," *Washington Post,* Aug. 21, 2020, www.washingtonpost.com.

314 **the rule of reason doctrine:** Barak Orbach and D. Daniel Sokol, "Symposium: 100 Years of *Standard Oil* Antitrust Energy," 85 *Southern California Law*

Review 429, 435 (2012) ("In *Standard Oil,* Chief Justice White declared that courts should use the rule of reason to construe the Sherman Act: The 'standard of reason which has been applied at the common law' should guide interpretation of the phrase 'restraint of trade' in Section 1 of the Sherman Act."); Robert W. Kolb, ed., *The SAGE Encyclopedia of Business Ethics and Society,* 2nd ed. (Thousand Oaks, Calif.: SAGE, 2018), 142 (noting that the Sherman Act was interpreted to prohibit only unreasonable restraints against trade, though certain practices were held to be per se violations). Of course, the whole point of the nation's antitrust laws, no matter what the applicable standard, is to protect competition. Representative Dick Morgan of Oklahoma once emphasized, for example, that "the thing we wish to maintain, and retain and sustain, is competition. We want to destroy monopoly and restore and maintain competition." 51 Cong. Rec. 9265 (1914); Wu, *Curse of Bigness,* 136–37. In *Chicago Board of Trade v. United States* (1918), Justice Louis Brandeis—writing for the U.S. Supreme Court—himself emphasized of restraints against trade: "The true test of legality is whether the restraint imposed is such as merely regulates and perhaps thereby promotes competition or whether it is such as may suppress or even destroy competition." *Chicago Board of Trade v. United States,* 246 U.S. 231, 238 (1918).

314 **outdated and discredited economic theories:** Submission of Jonathan B. Baker, Joseph Farrell, Andrew I. Gavil, Martin S. Gaynor, Michael Kades, Michael L. Katz, Gene Kimmelman, A. Douglas Melamed, Nancy L. Rose, Steven C. Salop, Fiona M. Scott Morton, and Carl Shapiro, "Joint Response to the House Judiciary Committee on the State of Antitrust Law and Implications for Protecting Competition in Digital Markets" April 30, 2020, 4–5 (describing how the courts have handled antitrust cases and noting that many antitrust precedents "rely on unsound economic theories or unsupported empirical claims about the competitive effects of certain practices"); Fiona Scott Morton, "Modern U.S. Antitrust Theory and Evidence amid Rising Concerns of Market Power and Its Effects," Washington Center for Equitable Growth, May 29, 2019, equitablegrowth.org ("The bulk of the research featured in our interactive database on these key topics in competition enforcement in the United States finds evidence of significant problems of underenforcement of antitrust law. The research that addresses economic theory qualifies or rejects assumptions long made by U.S. courts that have limited the scope of antitrust law. And the empirical work finds evidence of the exercise of undue market power in many dimensions, among them price, quality, innovation, and marketplace exclusion. Overall, the picture is one of a divergence between judicial opinions on the one hand, and the rigorous use of modern economics to advance consumer welfare on the other.").

314 **private litigants:** Although the U.S. Department of Justice and the Federal Trade Commission are the primary federal enforcers of the nation's antitrust laws, states, companies, and individuals who are harmed by anticompetitive activities can sue too. To incentivize private litigants to take very complicated and often very expensive antitrust cases to court, victorious plaintiffs can receive treble (that is, three times the actual) damages. Most legal cases settle out of court and never actually get to a jury. Although the law allows for the recovery of treble damages for plaintiffs who prevail in court, one 2015

study found that only fourteen of seventy-one cases were settled for amounts that exceeded single damages. In fact, the median average settlement was just 37 percent of single damages. Connor and Lande, "Not Treble Damages." Private antitrust lawsuits make up the lion's share of antitrust actions filed in the federal courts today. Paul E. Godek, "Does the Tail Wag the Dog? Sixty Years of Government and Private Antitrust in the Federal Courts," *Antitrust Source,* Dec. 2009, www.americanbar.org. Private antitrust settlements grew to $5 billion in 2018, with plaintiffs recovering an estimated $19 billion in federal court settlements since 2013. Victoria Graham, "Private Antitrust Settlements Total Grew to $5 Billion in 2018," Bloomberg Law, May 14, 2019, news.bloomberglaw.com; see also "Antitrust Experts Assess New Data on Private U.S. Antitrust Enforcement, Highlight Trends in Compensating Victims and Deterring Illegal Conduct," American Antitrust Institute, Sept. 21, 2020, www.antitrustinstitute.org (observing that private antitrust enforcement "continues to be effective" and citing a report finding that in antitrust class actions in federal court from 2009 to 2019, cases settled during that time frame "recovered more than $24 billion on behalf of victims of antitrust violations"). But the number of private antitrust cases filed in federal courts has declined in recent years, in part because of existing judicial skepticism of antitrust claims. "The explanation for the decline," University of Michigan law professor Daniel Crane observed in February 2019, "can be largely found in a number of currents of judicial hostility to private antitrust enforcement." As Crane explained, "The creation of the antitrust injury requirement, tightening of standing requirements, and Chicago School era contraction of liability norms in such areas as vertical restraints and exclusionary conduct created a less hospitable environment for new federal claims." Daniel A. Crane, "Private Enforcement of U.S. Antitrust Law—a Comment on the U.S. Courts Data," *Antitrust Chronicle,* Feb. 2019, 3, www.competitionpolicyinternational.com.

315 **House tech investigation and report:** Investigation of Competition in Digital Markets: Majority Staff Report and Recommendations, U.S. House of Representatives, Subcommittee on Antitrust, Commercial, and Administrative Law of the Committee on the Judiciary (2020), judiciary.house.gov, 6, 12–13.

316 **"serial innovation killers":** John Eggerton, "Big Tech: Senate Drills Down on Potential Serial (Innovation) Killers," *Multichannel News,* Sept. 24, 2019, www .multichannel.com.

316 **Diana Moss:** "Competition in Digital Technology Markets: Examining Acquisitions of Nascent or Potential Competitors by Digital Platforms," Testimony of Dr. Diana Moss, President, American Antitrust Institute, Before the U.S. Senate, Committee on the Judiciary, Subcommittee on Antitrust, Competition, and Consumer Rights, Sept. 24, 2019, www.judiciary.senate.gov.

317 **In order to acquire ITA Software:** Final Judgment, *United States of America v. Google Inc.,* Case: 1:11-cv-00688 (RLW), Oct. 5, 2011, 1 (reciting that the United States "filed its Complaint on April 8, 2011" and that the United States, Google, and ITA Software "have consented to entry of this Final Judgment" requiring Google and ITA Software "to undertake certain actions and refrain from certain conduct for the purpose of remedying the loss of competition").

317 **a series of acquisitions:** Nicolás Rivero, "The Acquisitions That Made Google

a Search Monopoly," Quartz, Oct. 20, 2020, qz.com (taking note of Google's "2005 takeover of Android" for $50 million, its 2007 purchase of ad vendor DoubleClick for $3.1 billion as well as "a slew of rival ad vendors, including AdMob, Invite Media, Admeld, Applied Semantics, and Sprinks," Google's $700 million purchase of ITA Software, and Google's $1.1 billion purchase of Waze in 2013).

317 **In Europe, Amazon:** Mary Hanbury, "The EU Just Launched a Big Antitrust Probe into Amazon, and It Could Lead to a Fine of Up to $23 Billion," *Business Insider,* July 17, 2019, www.businessinsider.com; Laurence Norman, "Qualcomm Hit by Second Antitrust Fine in Europe," *Wall Street Journal,* July 18, 2019, www.wsj.com.

317 **as much as $28 billion:** Duncan Oleinic, "Amazon.com, Inc. (NASDAQ: AMZN) Expects to Pay $28 Billion for Violating Bloc's Rules: EU Will File a Complaint Soon," *Wall Street PR,* June 15, 2020, www.wallstreetpr.com; see also Kelvin Chan, "EU Files Antitrust Charges against Amazon over Use of Data," Associated Press, Nov. 10, 2020, apnews.com ("Amazon faces a possible fine of up to 10% of its annual worldwide revenue. That could amount to as much as $28 billion, based on its 2019 earnings. The Seattle-based company rejected the accusations.").

317 **new laws and tactics:** Adam Satariano, " 'This Is a New Phase': Europe Shifts Tactics to Limit Tech's Power," *New York Times,* July 30, 2020, www.nytimes .com (noting that "European Union leaders are pursuing a new law to make it illegal for Amazon and Apple to give their own products preferential treatment over those of rivals that are sold on their online stores").

317 **a May 2019 op-ed:** Chris Hughes, "It's Time to Break Up Facebook," *New York Times,* May 9, 2019, www.nytimes.com.

318 **Mark Zuckerberg has made clear:** Jason Del Rey and Shirin Ghaffary, "Leaked: Mark Zuckerberg Threatens 'Major Lawsuit' if President Warren Tries to Break Up Facebook," *Vox,* Oct. 1, 2019, www.vox.com.

318 **which calls for:** In his op-ed, Hughes calls upon the U.S. government to take two actions: first, "break up Facebook's monopoly," and second, "regulate the company to make it more accountable to the American people." In particular, Hughes has called upon the FTC and the Justice Department to "enforce antitrust laws by undoing the Instagram and WhatsApp acquisitions and banning future acquisitions for several years. . . . There is precedent for correcting bad decisions—as recently as 2009, Whole Foods settled antitrust complaints by selling off the Wild Oats brand and stores that it had bought a few years earlier." See also Sheppard Mullin, "The Food Fight Is Over: Whole Foods and FTC Settle Dispute Over Merger of Organic Markets," SheppardMullin (blog post, April 13, 2009) (noting that under a consent order, Whole Foods agreed to sell 32 Wild Oats stores and related assets to one or more FTC-approved buyers and to divest the intellectual property of Wild Oats).

318 **regulation of Facebook:** "Just breaking up Facebook is not enough," Hughes observes, writing in his op-ed, "We need a new agency, empowered by Congress to regulate tech companies. Its first mandate should be to protect privacy." The law, of course, requires due process before a divesture occurs, and even Hughes acknowledges that there would need to be a legal process to break up Facebook or federal legislation to create a new agency. The benefits of

an aggressive legal proceeding, Hughes asserts, could be considerable, regardless of the outcome of the judicial process. A Justice Department suit against Facebook, even if unsuccessful, Hughes emphasizes, "would persuade other behemoths like Google and Amazon to think twice about stifling competition in their own sectors, out of fear that they could be next. . . . If we do not take action," Hughes warns, "Facebook's monopoly will become even more entrenched." Taking specific note of the calls for "more oversight" by me and others on Capitol Hill, Hughes ended his op-ed on a more hopeful note about what is possible: "An era of accountability for Facebook and other monopolies may be beginning. Collective anger is growing, and a new cohort of leaders has begun to emerge."

318 **breaking it up:** "How would a breakup work?" Hughes asks. His answer: "Facebook would have a period to spin off the Instagram and WhatsApp businesses, and the three would become distinct companies, most likely publicly traded." He adds, speaking of his friend Mark Zuckerberg, "Facebook shareholders would initially hold stock in the new companies, although Mark and other executives would probably be required to divest their management shares." Hughes argues that banning Facebook from engaging in short-term acquisitions "would ensure that competitors, and the investors who take a bet on them, would have a space to flourish." Putting a pause on new acquisitions would, certainly, give its competitors and new market entrants some breathing space. "Digital advertisers," he adds, analogizing to the benefits produced by AT&T's breakup, "would suddenly have multiple companies vying for their dollars." In other words, what is being sought by Hughes is the modern-day equivalent of the 1980s breakup of AT&T and the Bell System.

318 **calling for change:** Ben Brody, "Biden's Antitrust Police Would Crack Down on Mergers, Ally Says," Bloomberg, Aug. 27, 2020, www.bloomberg.com; see also Diane Bartz, "House Democrats Discuss Tougher Antitrust Law, Some Republicans Agree," Reuters, Oct. 1, 2020, www.reuters.com ("The U.S. House of Representatives Judiciary Committee's antitrust panel discussed ways to tighten antitrust laws on Thursday, with two Republicans on the Democrat-dominated panel indicating potential support for some changes.").

318 **marketplace consequences:** As Hughes writes, "Because Facebook so dominates social networking, it faces no market-based accountability. This means that every time Facebook messes up, we repeat an exhausting pattern: first outrage, then disappointment and, finally, resignation." I myself have been incredibly frustrated and disappointed with Facebook and the way it has handled its business. "The F.T.C.'s biggest mistake was to allow Facebook to acquire Instagram and WhatsApp," Hughes wrote in his op-ed of the lax antitrust enforcement that allowed Facebook to grow so big, noting that Facebook has "acquired its way to dominance" and "used its monopoly position to shut out competing companies."

318 **Facebook acquired:** B. Rajesh Kumar, *Wealth Creation in the World's Largest Mergers and Acquisitions: Integrated Case Studies* (Cham, Switzerland: Springer, 2019), 327; Baker, *Antitrust Paradigm*.

319 **Tim Wu writes:** Wu, *Curse of Bigness*, 123.

319 **Google Maps:** Greg Bensinger, "Google Redraws the Borders on Maps Depending on Who's Looking," *Washington Post*, Feb. 14, 2020, www

.washingtonpost.com ("With some 80 percent market share in mobile maps and over a billion users, Google Maps has an outsize impact on people's perception of the world—from driving directions to restaurant reviews to naming attractions to adjudicating historical border wars.").

319 **a hearing entitled:** "Sen. Lee Announces Antitrust Subcommittee Hearing on Online Advertising Market," press release, July 27, 2020, www.lee.senate.gov.

320 **the investigation of the House of Representatives:** Investigation of Competition in Digital Markets: Majority Staff Report and Recommendations, U.S. House of Representatives, Subcommittee on Antitrust, Commercial, and Administrative Law of the Committee on the Judiciary (2020), judiciary.house .gov, 15–16.

320 **Amazon itself is a seller:** Amazon, for example, now sells close to half of all physical books and 90 percent of e-books in the United States, and books and the sale of other products are just the beginning of Amazon's quest for even greater market power. Julia Gray, "America Is Reading More in Quarantine, but Indie Booksellers Are Missing Out," Thinknum, May 15, 2020, media .thinknum.com ("According to BookStat, the online retailer accounts for over 90 percent of ebooks and audiobooks, and around 42 to 45 percent of print sales.").

320 **a study published in 2018:** Robin Feldman, "May Your Drug Price Be Evergreen," *Journal of Law and the Biosciences,* Dec. 7, 2018, academic.oup.com.

321 **"Daraprim":** In 2015, I specifically called on the FTC to investigate pharmaceutical companies for antitrust violations after the price of the life-saving drug Daraprim increased by more than 4,000 percent. See "Klobuchar Statement on Federal Trade Commission, NY Attorney General Complaint Against Vyera Pharmaceuticals, Martin Shkreli, and Others for Anticompetitive Scheme to Protect Massive Daraprim Price Increase," press release, Jan. 28, 2020, www.klobuchar.senate.gov.

321 **a bill to lift the ban:** "Klobuchar Introduces Legislation to Unleash the Bargaining Power of Seniors for a Better Deal on Prescription Drug Costs," press release, Aug. 1, 2017, www.klobuchar.senate.gov.

321 **forty-three million seniors:** "Medicare Must Be Allowed to Negotiate Drug Prices," National Committee to Preserve Social Security and Medicare, June 12, 2019, www.ncpssm.org.

321 **spent $116 million:** Wu, *Curse of Bigness,* 56–57.

322 **my Medicare negotiation bill:** "Klobuchar Leads 34 Senators in Introducing Legislation to Unleash the Bargaining Power of Seniors for a Better Deal on Prescription Drug Costs," press release, Jan. 9, 2019 ("U.S. Senator Amy Klobuchar (D-MN) reintroduced legislation today to unleash the bargaining power of seniors for a better deal on prescription drug costs. The Empowering Medicare Seniors to Negotiate Drug Prices Acts would allow for Medicare to negotiate the best possible price of prescription drugs to cut costs for nearly 43 million seniors enrolled in Medicare Part D.").

322 **my plan for 100 things a president can do:** Amy Klobuchar, "Senator Amy Klobuchar Releases Plan of More Than 100 Actions for Her First 100 Days as President," Medium, June 18, 2019, medium.com.

322 **(CREATES) Act:** The Senate Judiciary Committee's Subcommittee on Antitrust, Competition Policy, and Consumer Rights held a hearing on the CRE-

ATES Act in June 2016. This is important legislation that will help American families. As I said at that hearing in pushing for the legislation's adoption, "When families get sick, their focus should be on getting well, not on affording their prescriptions." Generic alternatives are critical to controlling prescription drug prices, I pointed out. Hearing on the CREATES Act: Ending Regulatory Abuse, Protecting Consumers, and Ensuring Drug Price Competition, Senate Committee on the Judiciary, Subcommittee on Antitrust, Competition Policy, and Consumer Rights, June 21, 2016.

322 **Preserve Access to Affordable Generics and Biosimilars Act:** Preserve Access to Affordable Generics and Biosimilars Act, www.congress.gov; Steve Brachmann, "Congress Adds TERM Act and No Combination Drug Patents Act to List of Drug Patent Bills Being Considered," IP Watchdog, June 20, 2019, www.ipwatchdog.com. An earlier version of this bill, the Preserve Access to Affordable Generics Act, was introduced in 2015 and co-sponsored by Republican senator Chuck Grassley of Iowa. Preserve Access to Affordable Generics Act, www.congress.gov.

323 **safe importation of drugs:** Matt Taibbi, "Republicans and Democrats Continue to Block Drug Reimportation—After Publicly Endorsing It," *Rolling Stone,* June 2, 2017, www.rollingstone.com ("Back in January, Sens. Bernie Sanders and Amy Klobuchar introduced an amendment to a budget resolution that would have paved the way for drug importation. Twelve Republicans, including John McCain, Rand Paul and Lisa Murkowski, voted for it. But the measure died when thirteen Democrats voted no.").

323 **one headline:** Glenn Howatt, "Insulin Outlaws: High Cost of Medication Drives Minnesotans Across the Border to Canada," *Minneapolis Star Tribune,* May 12, 2019, www.startribune.com.

323 **between $3 and $7 a vial:** Pete Kotz, "The Assault: How Big Pharma and Insurers Are Leaving Minnesotans Sick, Hospitalized, Even Dead," *City Pages,* July 24–30, 2019, 6, 8.

324 **first Merger Guidelines:** 1968 Merger Guidelines, www.justice.gov.

324 **revised multiple times:** Eleanor M. Fox, "The New Merger Guidelines—a Blueprint for Microeconomic Analysis," 27 *Antitrust Bulletin* 519 (1982); § 4.3.6 ("In 1968, the Justice Department issued its first set of merger guidelines. The guidelines were meant to help reduce the uncertainty regarding the legality or illegality of a particular merger. Especially with regard to horizontal mergers, the 1968 guidelines tended to be quite strict."); see also ibid., n20 ("Since 1968 the Department of Justice has established merger guidelines suggesting which mergers the Department is likely to challenge. The guidelines were amended in 1982, 1984, 1992, 1997, and 2010. The changes resulted in fewer mergers that would be challenged.").

325 **just accepted the representations:** Ibid., n19 ("Public policy toward horizontal mergers was lax until 1950, then strict for 25 years until the mid-1970s. Since then, the modern trend in the lower courts is to recognize cost-saving efficiencies as a defense in horizontal mergers."); Herbert J. Hovenkamp, "Appraising Merger Efficiencies," 24 *George Mason Law Review* 703, 704 (2017) ("attitudes toward mergers are heavily driven by assumptions about efficiency gains"); compare ibid., 705 ("In highly competitive, undifferentiated markets anticompetitive price increases (or quality reductions) are unlikely to be a motivating

factor for a merger. The post-merger firm still lacks significant market power, and the market is no more conducive to collusion than it had been prior to the merger. In that case efficiency gains must be the rationale for the merger. But as markets become more concentrated or differentiated, anticompetitive consequences become more plausible. More concentrated markets encourage collusion or other forms of coordinated interaction, particularly when there are only three, four, or a few more firms in the post-merger market. In markets that are differentiated by product or geography, mergers between relatively 'proximate' firms in product or geographical space can facilitate unilateral price increases.").

325 **first being issued in 1984:** 1984 Merger Guidelines, www.justice.gov.

325 **Rohit Chopra:** Dissenting Statement of Commissioner Rohit Chopra Regarding the Publication of Vertical Merger Guidelines, Commission File No. P810034 (June 30, 2020), www.ftc.gov.

325 **Rebecca Kelly Slaughter:** Dissenting Statement of Commissioner Rebecca Kelly Slaughter, *In Re FTC-DOJ Vertical Merger Guidelines,* Matter No. P810034 (June 30, 2020), www.ftc.gov.

325 **opposed vertical mergers:** "Klobuchar Statement on AT&T–Time Warner Merger Ruling," press release, June 12, 2018, www.klobuchar.senate.gov.

325 **Diana Moss:** "Competition in Digital Technology Markets."

326 **agency transparency:** At all times, there must be far more transparency by antitrust enforcers about what is being done to probe the activities of the tech companies. Public relations efforts aimed at mollifying the American people are not enough; the public expects—and deserves—up-to-date information and concrete actions taken to protect their interests. That's why I've been so critical of companies like Facebook and its policies, and why I've led efforts to request details about the FTC's actions in regard to Amazon and Facebook and the Justice Department's actions in regard to Apple and Google. Jon Swartz, "Facebook and Trump Are Amy Klobuchar's Dual Targets in Presidential Bid," *Barron's,* Feb. 11, 2019, www.barrons.com; see also Emily Birnbaum, "Bipartisan Senators Ask FTC to Disclose Whether It Is Investigating Google," *Hill,* April 8, 2019, thehill.com. "Over the years," I wrote in a June 2019 letter to the FTC and the Justice Department on which I was joined by a number of my Senate colleagues, "We have heard numerous complaints about potential anti-competitive conduct by large technology firms, and we have held hearings that have explored these issues. . . . But given the silence of the FTC and the Justice Department, the truth is that we still do not know if these investigations have actually been initiated and neither do the American people." Donna Goodison, "FTC, DOJ Queried on Potential Antitrust Probes of Amazon, Other Tech Giants," *CRN,* June 24, 2019, www.crn.com. Our letter—signed by me and Senators Patrick Leahy, Richard Blumenthal, Cory Booker, Tammy Baldwin, Ed Markey, and Tina Smith—sought "basic disclosures" about any ongoing probes. "The significant public interest in and allegations surrounding the business conduct of big tech and the leaks concerning the clearance process relating to potential investigations of Amazon, Apple, Facebook and Google have made these matters highly unusual," we wrote. Given how much the actions of Big Tech affect our lives, the American people deserve to know what their government is doing on their behalf. In a

world in which information moves at lightning speed, the public is entitled to receive information about what federal and state antitrust officials are doing to combat monopoly power and corporate consolidation.

327 **cross-ownership of competing companies:** For example, the largest shareholders of Apple and Microsoft are BlackRock and Vanguard. The same patterns also show up in pharmacies, soft drink companies, and banks. It is easy to see how cross-ownership could incentivize anticompetitive conduct and thus hurt consumers.

327 **Einer Elhauge:** Einer R. Elhauge, "How Horizontal Shareholding Harms Our Economy—and Why Antitrust Law Can Fix It," *Harvard Business Law Review* 10, no. 2 (2020), www.hblr.org. Available at SSRN: ssrn.com.

328 **Modified Herfindahl-Hirschman Index:** C. Scott Hemphill and Marcel Kahan, "The Strategies of Anticompetitive Common Ownership," 129 *Yale Law Journal* 1392, 1404 (2020) ("As the name suggests MHHI is a modification of the Herfindahl-Hirschman Index (HHI), a commonly used measure of market concentration. In any market, the HHI is the sum of the squared market shares of each competitor. In a monopoly market, where one firm has a 100% share, the HHI is 100^2, or 10,000. In a duopoly . . . equally sharing the market, the HHI is $50^2 + 50^2$, or 5,000. In a market with a very large number of small competitors, the HHI approximates zero. MHHI adjusts the HHI to account for ownership overlap among competing firms. In the absence of any ownership overlap, the HHI is equal to the MHHI. But if competitors have common owners, the MHHI exceeds the HHI."); see also Thom Lambert, "Lowering the Barriers to Entry to the Common Ownership Debate: A (Relatively) Non-technical Explanation of MHHI Delta," Truth on the Market, Aug. 16, 2018, truthonthemarket.com; Michael Sykuta, "What to Make of MHHI? A Policy Problem," Truth on the Market, Aug. 27, 2018, truthonthemarket.com.

329 **a major problem:** To Elhauge, the problem is clear. "New empirical studies," he has written, responding proactively to critics of his work, "confirm my prediction that horizontal shareholding can help explain the rapid increases over recent decades both in the gap between corporate profits and investment and in economic inequality. This new literature shows that we had a sharp rise in horizontal shareholding from 1999 to 2014, with the probability of two competing firms in the S&P 1500 having a large horizontal shareholder increasing from 16% to 90% over that period." Explaining that the sharp rise in horizontal shareholding coincided with a large divergence between corporate profits and investment, he also observes that the sharp rise "coincides with the period during which we have had the highest growth in corporate profits and greatest decline in labor's share of national income since World War II." A new cross-industry empirical study, he points out, "found that the gap between corporate investment and profitability is mainly driven by the level of horizontal shareholder ownership in concentrated markets."

329 **European antitrust officials:** Hemphill and Kahan, "Strategies of Anticompetitive Common Ownership," 1395–96 ("In Europe, antitrust enforcers have taken a more aggressive approach: in addition to announcing a potentially wide-ranging inquiry into the effects of common ownership, the European Commission actually relied on theory and evidence about the anticom-

petitive effects of common ownership in a 2017 decision analyzing a major merger.").

329 **potential solutions:** Elhauge, "How Horizontal Shareholding Harms Our Economy" ("I provide new legal theories for tackling the problem of horizontal shareholding. I show that when horizontal shareholding has anticompetitive effects, it is illegal not only under Clayton Act §7, but also under Sherman Act §1. In fact, the historic trusts that were the core target of antitrust law were horizontal shareholders.").

329 **index funds:** Most individual investors have neither the time nor the resources to build their own portfolios. Over the long term, it is also unlikely that the average small investor will be able to outperform an index fund. Not only do index funds perform better, but they charge much lower fees. We should be able to have the benefits of index and mutual funds while eliminating the potential harm caused by horizontal shareholding.

330 **the anticompetitive power of institutional investors:** Eric A. Posner, Fiona M. Scott Morton, and E. Glen Weyl, "A Proposal to Limit the Anti-competitive Power of Institutional Investors," Competition Policy International, Nov. 22, 2016, www.competitionpolicyinternational.com.

330 **common stock ownership:** Einer Elhauge, "Horizontal Shareholding," 100 *Harvard Law Review* 1267 (2016).

331 **FTC revises annually:** See Clayton Act., sec. 8 (1990), 15 U.S.C. § 19. The law contains a number of exceptions. Section 8(a)(5) requires the Federal Trade Commission to revise these thresholds annually, based on changes in the gross national product. The thresholds as of January 29, 2018, were $34,395,000 for section 8(a)(1), and $3,439,500 for section 8(a)(2)(A).

331 **"it may be tempting to follow":** Hemphill and Kahan, "Strategies of Anti-competitive Common Ownership," 1447–48.

331 **the ill effects of conglomerate mergers:** Robert H. Lande and Sandeep Vaheesan, "Preventing the Curse of Bigness Through Conglomerate Merger Legislation," 52 *Arizona State Law Journal* 75 (2020) (discussing a proposal to block conglomerate mergers between firms with assets exceeding $10 billion, noting that "reasonable approaches to the conglomerate merger problem could be stricter or looser," and noting that studies show that firm size is correlated to political activity and thus political influence). This is something an Iowa politician, Representative Neal Smith, and members of his congressional committee considered decades ago. Smith, the chairman of the Committee on Small Business in the U.S. House of Representative, transmitted to the then House Speaker, Tip O'Neill, a report titled *Conglomerate Mergers—Their Effects on Small Business and Local Communities.* That report shows that the problems we face today are actually just newer versions of the same old problem: the power of BIG. The product of a series of hearings and the work of the Subcommittee on Antitrust and Restraint of Trade Activities Affecting Small Business, the 1980 report began by noting that another Iowan, Representative Berkley Bedell, the chair of the subcommittee, had opened the seven-day hearing by stating, "In the 1960's and 1970's we saw a remarkable increase in the concentration of ownership of America's business assets. Progressively largely portions of the American economy have come under the control of fewer and fewer people." The third chapter of the report contained the following statement

from Sanford Litvack, the Justice Department's assistant attorney general for antitrust: "Those concerned about the recent wave of conglomerate mergers, the Antitrust Division among them, have noted that conglomerate mergers may contribute to needless concentration of economic and political power in the hands of a relatively small number of major corporations, removing independent voices from the business community." *Conglomerate Mergers—Their Effects on Small Business and Local Communities,* Report of the Committee on Small Business, House of Representatives, 96th Cong., 2d Sess., House Document No. 96-343 (Washington, D.C.: U.S. Government Printing Office, 1980), iii–iv, 1, 18.

331 **From 2015 to 2019 alone:** Lande and Vaheesan, "Preventing the Curse of Bigness Through Conglomerate Merger Legislation," 91, 118–27 (containing appendix and supporting data compiled by Nicholas Jordan, a recent graduate of the University of Baltimore School of Law).

332 **only three of the seventy-eight:** Robert H. Lande to Chairman Cicilline and Ranking Member Sensenbrenner, Subcommittee on Antitrust, Commercial, and Administrative Law, Committee on the Judiciary, U.S. House of Representatives, 3, papers.ssrn.com.

332 **some scholars:** Lande and Vaheesan, "Preventing the Curse of Bigness Through Conglomerate Merger Legislation."

332 **"Bigness" alone:** Don Alan Evans, *The Legal Environment of International Business: A Guide to United States Firms* (Jefferson, N.C.: McFarland, 1990), 186 ("Bigness alone is not an antitrust violation, nor is possession of great power in the market. What the would-be monopolist does with its power is the determining factor.").

332 **automobile manufacturers:** Elizabeth Blessing, "Big Three Automakers," Investopedia, Oct. 9, 2020, www.investopedia.com (noting the "Big Three" automakers in the United States are General Motors Company, Ford Motor Company, and Fiat Chrysler Automobiles).

332 **As one source:** Janice E. Rubin, "General Overview of United States Antitrust Law," in *Antitrust Policy Issues,* ed. Patrick Moriati (New York: Nova Science, 2006), 44.

332 **A "no-fault approach":** Bernice Rothman Hasin, *Consumers, Commissions, and Congress: Law, Theory, and the Federal Trade Commission, 1968–1985* (New Brunswick, N.J.: Transaction Books, 1987), 158 ("The no-fault approach, argued first in 1969 by Donald F. Turner in the *Harvard Law Review,* assumes that monopoly power itself is objectionable, suggesting that some questionable behavior rather than economic efficiency is fundamental to it, and determining that its social, political, and economic effect on the nation can only be detrimental. Just before his death in 1976, Democratic Senator Philip A. Hart of Michigan had introduced a no-fault bill but it went nowhere at all. Later, staff members of Metzenbaum's Senate Judiciary Subcommittee on Antitrust, Monopoly and Business Rights did some work on no-fault. They hoped to continue with it in 1981 but were not especially optimistic about its prospects.").

332 **another article:** Harry First, "Woodstock Antitrust," *Antitrust Chronicle,* April 17, 2018, 3, papers.ssrn.com (discussing the history of no-fault (or no-conduct) monopolization proposals).

333 **stopped in the mid-1980s:** William E. Kovacic, *The Federal Trade Commission at 100: Into Our 2nd Century: The Continuing Pursuit of Better Practices,* Federal Trade Commission, Jan. 2009, 53n185.

333 **antitrust scrutiny:** In his book, *The Myth of Capitalism* (2018), Jonathan Tepper wrote in blunt terms about America's economic system and the problems we face: "Capitalism has been the greatest system in history to lift people out of poverty and create wealth, but the 'capitalism' we see today in the United States is a far cry from competitive markets. What we have today is a grotesque, deformed version of capitalism." Pointing to the relative lack of competition in the airline industry, especially at regional hubs, where specific airlines tend to dominate those markets, he emphasized that "capitalism without competition is not capitalism." "Many states," Tepper added, ticking off a number of industries (for example, beef, corn seeds, banking, high-speed internet access) where true competition is wanting, "have health insurance markets where the top two insurers have an 80–90% market share." Jonathan Tepper, *The Myth of Capitalism: Monopolies and the Death of Competition* (Hoboken, N.J.: John Wiley & Sons, 2018).

333 **One model in the U.K.:** Sandra Marco Colino, *Competition Law of the EU and UK,* 8th ed. (Oxford: Oxford University Press, 2019), 406–12; Bruce Kilpatrick, Pierre Kobel, and Pranvera Këllezi, eds., *Compatibility of Transactional Resolutions of Antitrust Proceedings with Due Process and Fundamental Rights and Online Exhaustion of IP Rights* (Switzerland: Springer, 2016), 421.

333 **International Antitrust Enforcement Act of 1994:** U.S. Department of Justice, "Attorney General Reno Unveils New Proposal to Strengthen International Antitrust Efforts," press release, June 13, 1994, www.justice.gov.

333 **signed into law:** Nina Hachigian, "Essential Mutual Assistance in International Antitrust Enforcement," 29 *International Lawyer* 117, 119 (1995) ("A new U.S. law, the International Antitrust Enforcement Act of 1994, represents an important first step in the direction of better cooperation. The Act allows the Antitrust Division to enter into international cooperation agreements with its sister agencies.").

334 **establishing the ICN:** Andrew T. Guzman, ed., *Cooperation, Comity, and Competition Policy* (Oxford: Oxford University Press, 2011), 231.

334 **According to the ICN:** About, International Competition Network, www.int ernationalcompetitionnetwork; see also Oliver Budzinski, "The Economics of International Competition Policy: New Challenges in the Light of Digitization?" (Ilmenau Economics Discussion Papers 135, Jan. 2020), 1 ("The International Competition Network (ICN) celebrates its 20th birthday in 2020. It governs global competition by providing a cooperative forum for (mostly national) competition authorities from all around the world. In the absence of binding global competition rules and antitrust laws, it attempts to coordinate national and supranational competition policies by providing best practice recommendations and exercising peer pressure on deviating regimes.").

334 **ICN publishes papers:** *2020 Annual ICN Work Product,* International Competition Network, June 28, 2020, www.internationalcompetitionnetwork.org.

334 **already have in place:** U.S. Department of Justice and Federal Trade Commission, Antitrust Guidelines for International Enforcement and Cooperation, Jan. 13, 2017, www.justice.gov.

335 **dumping of subsidized steel:** "Klobuchar Statement on Administration Action Against Foreign Steel Dumping," press release, April 12, 2017, www .klobuchar.senate.gov.

335 **Tim Wu writes:** Wu, *Curse of Bigness*, 108.

336 **America Invents Act:** Amy Klobuchar, "America Invents Act Will Promote Innovation, Modernize Patent System," Vote Smart, press release, March 8, 2011, votesmart.org; "Klobuchar: America Invents Act Will Help Minnesota Businesses Compete in Global Economy," press release, June 20, 2012, www .klobuchar.senate.gov.

336 **(PATENT) Act:** "Klobuchar Cosponsors Bipartisan Bill to End Patent Abuses That Cost U.S. Economy Billions of Dollars Every Year," press release, April 29, 2015, www.klobuchar.senate.gov.

337 **U.S. Constitution:** U.S. Constitution, art. 1, sec. 8.

337 **Thomas Jefferson's view:** Jefferson to Isaac McPherson, Aug. 13, 1813, in *The Founders' Constitution,* ed. Philip B. Kurland and Ralph Lerner, press-pubs .uchicago.edu.

338 **reasonable restrictions on the use:** Tal Axelrod, "Warren, Klobuchar Call on FTC to Curtail Use of Non-compete Clauses," *Hill,* March 20, 2019, thehill .com.

338 **restricting their use:** The Open Markets Institute is doing a lot of work on the issue of non-compete agreements and recently published a white paper on this subject.

338 **"Every contract by which anyone":** California Business and Professions Code § 16600.

339 **I joined a letter:** Blumenthal et al. to Joseph Simons, March 20, 2019, www .blumenthal.senate.gov.

340 **Restoring Justice for Workers Act:** "Murray, Nadler, Scott Introduce Bill to End Forced Arbitration in the Workplace, to Allow Workers to Band Together to Enforce Their Legal Rights," press release, May 15, 2019, judiciary.house .gov.

340 ***Epic Systems Corp. v. Lewis:*** *Epic Systems Corp. v. Lewis,* 138 S. Ct. 1612 (2018).

340 **Al Franken:** Al Franken and Mignon Clyburn, "How Your Internet Provider Restricts Your Rights," *Time,* Oct. 23, 2016, time.com.

340 **his own legislation:** Arbitration Fairness Act, www.workplacefairness.org.

340 **stand up for workers and unions:** "Senator Klobuchar on Standing Up for Our Workers and Unions," Medium, Sept. 29, 2019, medium.com.

341 **coming to America for centuries:** Roger Daniels, *Coming to America: A History of Immigration and Ethnicity in American Life,* 2nd ed. (New York: Perennial, 2002).

341 **DREAMers:** Nancy Pelosi and Charles E. Schumer, "DREAMers Are as American as Apple Pie," CNN, Sept. 29, 2017, www.cnn.com.

341 **a 5–4 ruling:** Marcia Coyle, "Chief Justice Roberts Leads Ruling Against Trump's Effort to End DACA," *National Law Journal,* June 18, 2020, www .law.com.

341 **Chief Justice John Roberts:** *Department of Homeland Security v. Regents of the University of California,* 140 S. Ct. 1891 (2020).

341 **AFL-CIO and its president:** Immigration, AFL-CIO, aflcio.org ("Enacting meaningful immigration reform is critical to our long-term efforts to lift labor

standards and empower workers, and the labor movement will continue to stand in solidarity with all working people.").

341 **it was estimated:** "A Guide to S. 744: Understanding the 2013 Senate Immigration Bill," American Immigration Council, July 10, 2013, www .americanimmigrationcouncil.org.

341 **Center for American Entrepreneurship:** "Immigrant Founders of the 2017 Fortune 500," Center for American Entrepreneurship, startupsusa.org; see also Cassie Werber, "New Research Finds That US Immigrant Entrepreneurs Score Higher on Innovation," *Quartz,* Feb. 21, 2019, qz.com ("A 2018 report by Mary Meeker, a prominent analyst of the internet, found that over half of America's most highly-valued tech companies were founded by first or second generation immigrants.").

342 **undocumented DREAMers:** Patrick McGee, "Apple CEO Puts Employees at Centre of 'Dreamer' Appeal," *Financial Times,* Oct. 2, 2019, www.ft.com.

342 **More than 30 percent:** Michael Greshko, "Who Are the Nobel Prize Winners? We've Crunched the Numbers," *National Geographic,* Oct. 3, 2018, www .nationalgeographic.com.

342 **Bruce Stillman:** Bruce Stillman, "Why Has America Been Such a Magnet for Immigrant Scientists?," *Scientific American,* Oct. 3, 2018, blogs .scientificamerican.com.

342 **U.S. Census Bureau estimates:** U.S. Census Bureau, "Annual Business Survey Release Provides Data on Minority- and Women-Owned Businesses," press release, May 19, 2020, www.census.gov.

342 **employer firms:** An *employer firm* is a firm or company with employees on payroll at one or more establishments or locations. "Philadelphia's Small and Midsize Business Landscape," Pew Charitable Trusts, Aug. 26, 2020, www .pewtrusts.org. By contrast, a *nonemployer firm* is defined as one that has no paid employees, has annual business receipts of $1,000 or more, and is subject to federal income taxes. Annual Report of the Office of Economic Research FY 2018, U.S. Small Business Administration, Office of Advocacy, 17, cdn .advocacy.sba.gov.

342 **one 2015 report:** Michael S. Barr, "Minority and Women Entrepreneurs: Building Capital, Networks, and Skills," Hamilton Project, Brookings, March 2015.

342 **"Small businesses":** U.S. Small Business Administration, "Small Businesses Generate 44 Percent of U.S. Economic Activity," press release, Jan. 30, 2019, advocacy.sba.gov.

343 **December 2018 report:** Kathryn Kobe and Richard Schwinn, *Small Business GDP, 1998–2014,* U.S. Small Business Administration, Office of Advocacy, Dec. 2018, cdn.advocacy.sba.gov.

343 **30.2 million small businesses:** "2018 Small Business Profile," U.S. Small Business Administration, Office of Advocacy, www.sba.gov.

343 **in their incipiency:** Marcus Glader, *Innovation Markets and Competition Analysis: EU Competition Law and US Antitrust Law* (Cheltenham, U.K.: Edward Elgar, 2006), 59 ("Formally, US antitrust policy has never been confined to merely assessing the instantaneous effects of a transaction or current markets. In *FTC v. Proctor & Gamble Co.,* the Supreme Court held that the standard of Section 7 of the Clayton Act—testing whether a merger might substantially

lessen competition—requires 'a prediction of the merger's impact on competition, present and future.'") (citing *Federal Trade Commission v. Proctor & Gamble Co.,* 386 U.S. 586 [1967]); ibid., 59–60n2 ("The Supreme Court furthermore stated: 'Section 7 of the Clayton Act was intended to arrest the anticompetitive effects of market power in their incipiency. The core question was whether a merger may substantially lessen competition, and necessarily requires a prediction of the merger's impact on competition, present and future. . . . The section can deal only with probabilities, not with certainties. . . . And there is certainly no requirement that the anticompetitive power manifest itself in anticompetitive action before 7 can be called into play. If the enforcement of [section] 7 turned on the existence of actual anticompetitive practices, the congressional policy of thwarting such practices in their incipiency would be frustrated.'") (quoting *Proctor & Gamble Co.,* 386 U.S. at 477); see also ABA, Antitrust Law Section, *Private Litigation Under Section 7 of the Clayton Act: Law and Policy* (American Bar Association, 1989), 93 ("Congress did not enact Section 7 [of the Clayton Act] in 1914, or amend it in 1950 and 1980, merely to duplicate the Sherman Act. Section 7 was intended to halt the accumulation of market power gained by merger *before* it reached Sherman Act levels, even where the anticompetitive effects associated with the acquisition 'may not be so far reaching as to amount to a violation of the Sherman Act.'"); ABA, Antitrust Law Section, *Antitrust Law Developments,* 5th ed. (Chicago: American Bar Association, 2002), 2:1658 ("The Celler-Kefauver amendments retained and strengthened the 'incipiency' standard by extending the coverage of the law to acquisitions of assets.").

344 **Enhancing Entrepreneurship for the 21st Century Act:** "Klobuchar, Scott Introduce Legislation to Enhance Entrepreneurship for the 21st Century," press release, Sept. 24, 2019, www.klobuchar.senate.gov.

344 **In announcing support:** "Scott, Klobuchar Introduce Legislation to Enhance Entrepreneurship for the 21st Century," press release, Sept. 24, 2019, www .scott.senate.gov.

344 **a 2015 Brookings report:** Barr, "Minority and Women Entrepreneurs," 6.

345 **Zebrafish Facility:** "Laboratories—Zebrafish Facility: Stephen C. Ekker," Mayo Clinic, www.mayo.edu ("The zebrafish facility supports the thesis projects of undergraduates, grad students and post docs in user laboratories. In addition, the zebrafish is a fantastic model for outreach and K–12 science education. The zebrafish facility has already helped sponsor a visit to a local Rochester grade school as a part of a health science outreach effort."); Caitlin Doran, "Mayo InSciEd Out Program Teaches Students How to Test the Effects of Vaping on Zebrafish," Center for Leading Innovation and Collaboration, Jan. 16, 2020, clic-ctsa.org.

345 **Harvey Mackay:** Harvey B. Mackay, *Swim with the Sharks Without Being Eaten Alive: Outsell, Outmanage, Outmotivate, and Outnegotiate Your Competition* (New York: Harper Business, 2005).

346 **a sweeping bill:** "Klobuchar, Senate Democrats Unveil Strong Online Privacy Rights," press release, Nov. 26, 2019, www.klobuchar.senate.gov ("Today, U.S. Senator Amy Klobuchar (D-MN) joined Commerce, Science, and Transportation Committee Ranking Member Maria Cantwell (D-WA) and fellow senior members Senators Brian Schatz (D-HI) and Ed Markey (D-MA) in

unveiling comprehensive federal online privacy legislation to establish privacy rights, outlaw harmful and deceptive practices, and improve data security safeguards for the record number of American consumers who now shop or conduct business online.").

346 **Mark Zuckerberg:** Maya Rao, "Minnesota Sen. Amy Klobuchar Queries Facebook's Mark Zuckerberg on Privacy," *Minneapolis Star Tribune,* April 10, 2018, m.startribune.com.

347 **consumer data breaches:** Kenneth Kiesnoski, "5 of the Biggest Data Breaches Ever," CNBC, July 30, 2019, www.cnbc.com; Prachi Bhardwaj, "A Capital One Breach Has Affected over 100 Million People—Here's How to Tell if You Were Hit and What to Do," *Money,* July 30, 2019, finance.yahoo.com.

347 **protect our democracy:** The Russian government's interference in American elections is appalling, and it was certainly no "hoax" as President Trump, when he was in office, liked to portray it. The Russian government actively invaded our democracy, and American tech companies must be vigilant and do a better job of making sure we don't have foreign interference in our elections.

347 **One possibility I've floated:** Sami Sparber, "At SXSW, Sen. Amy Klobuchar Pitches New Tax for Big Tech Profits on Consumer Data," *Houston Chronicle,* March 9, 2019, www.chron.com; Adi Robertson, "Amy Klobuchar Suggests Taxing Companies Making Money off User Data," *Verge,* March 9, 2019, www.theverge.com.

348 **higher prices:** In a 2018 op-ed in *The Wall Street Journal,* aptly titled "The Perils of Corporate Concentration," William Galston cited an International Monetary Fund paper finding that "between 1980 and 2016, markups by U.S. companies have increased by an average of 42%." That's a big, eye-popping number, and one that should get everyone's attention. Higher prices in the marketplace mean that Americans have less money in their pockets to spend or save, with many Americans finding it increasingly hard to buy what they need, let alone to save for their retirement years or send their kids to college. "Although markups have risen in all major industry sectors," Galston writes, summarizing the paper's disturbing findings, "some have experienced increases far above the average, led by 419% for biotechnology." "Since the mid-1990s," Galston adds, "the standard measure of concentration used in antitrust analysis, the Herfindahl-Hirschman Index, has risen by 50%." William A. Galston, "The Perils of Corporate Concentration," *Wall Street Journal,* June 19, 2018, www.wsj.com.

348 **stagnant or lower wages:** The Economic Policy Institute found that since 1979 wages for the 90 percent of Americans on the lower end of the income scale have declined by 10 percent, resulting in a loss of $10,800 in total wages per household. Galen Hendricks, Daniella Zessoules, and Michael Madowitz, "The State of the U.S. Labor Market: Pre-March 2019 Jobs Release," Center for American Progress, April 4, 2019, www.americanprogress.org. Some places and some people—particularly those individuals already at the higher end of the income scale—have done better than others. Rebecca Koenig, "Where Is the Wage Growth?," *U.S. News & World Report,* Feb. 12, 2019, money.usnews .com ("Over the past four decades, workers at the top of the pay scale have seen the largest percent increase in real wages (pay adjusted for inflation), while those in the bottom fifth have actually seen their real wages decline in value.").

Wage growth at the 10th percentile in states with at least one minimum-wage increase from 2013 to 2018 was nearly 50 percent faster than in states without minimum-wage increases in that time period. Elise Gould, "Wage Growth for Low-Wage Workers Has Been Strongest in States with Minimum Wage Increases," Economic Policy Institute, March 5, 2019, www.epi.org. But many hourly wage workers, including in manufacturing, have struggled mightily. In an August 2018 analysis titled "For Most U.S. Workers, Real Wages Have Barely Budged in Decades," Drew DeSilver of the Pew Research Center observed that "today's real average wage (that is, the wage after accounting for inflation) has about the same purchasing power it did 40 years ago. And what wage gains there have been have mostly flowed to the highest-paid tier of workers. . . . After adjusting for inflation, . . . today's average hourly wage has just about the same purchasing power it did in 1978, following a long slide in the 1980s and early 1990s and bumpy, inconsistent growth since then." Drew DeSilver, "For Most U.S. Workers, Real Wages Have Barely Budged in Decades," Pew Research Center, Aug. 7, 2018, www.pewresearch.org.

348 **Robert Reich video:** Robert Reich, *The Monopolization of America* (Inequality Media, 2018), www.youtube.com.

348 **American Antitrust Institute:** American Antitrust Institute, www.antitrust institute.org; see also Wu, *Curse of Bigness*, 108 ("A new group, the American Antitrust Institute, was founded in 1998 by Albert Foer to create an institutional counterweight to antitrust erosion.").

348 **Open Markets Institute:** The Open Markets Institute bills itself as "a team of journalists, researchers, lawyers, and advocates working together to expose and reverse the stranglehold that corporate monopolies have on our country." About Us, Open Markets Institute, openmarketsinstitute.org.

349 **Washington Center for Equitable Growth:** equitablegrowth.org.

349 **American Economic Liberties Project:** www.economicliberties.us.

349 **Roosevelt Institute:** rooseveltinstitute.org.

349 **Antitrust Law Section:** Antitrust Law Section, American Bar Association, www.americanbar.org.

349 *Antitrust* **magazine:** www.americanbar.org.

349 **21.7 million comments:** Lee Rainie, "Our Response to Concerns Raised About Our Analysis of the FCC's Net Neutrality Public Comments," Pew Research Center, Nov. 30, 2017, www.pewresearch.org; see also "Public Comments to the Federal Communications Commission About Net Neutrality Contain Many Inaccuracies and Duplicates," Pew Research Center, Nov. 29, 2017, www.pewresearch.org ("From April 27 to Aug. 30, 2017, the FCC allowed members of the public to formally submit comments on the subject. In total, 21.7 million comments were submitted electronically and posted online for review. This figure dwarfs the number received during the initial comment period when the FCC last accepted comments on this topic in 2012, as well as the nearly four million total submissions received during the entirety of the comment process that year.").

349 **the FCC's server crashed:** Jeff John Roberts, "John Oliver Gets Fired Up over Net Neutrality—and FCC's Site Goes Down," *Fortune*, May 8, 2017, fortune .com.

349 **high-speed broadband:** For example, Stacy Mitchell, "6 Ways to Rein in

Today's Toxic Monopolies," *Nation,* Feb. 16, 2018, www.thenation.com ("Cities are also sidestepping monopolies by creating their own public options. Half of US households have, at most, only one provider to choose from for high-speed Internet access. While the federal government has been content to let these monopolies maintain their chokehold, many municipalities have not been. Dozens have built their own publicly owned high-speed fiber networks.").

350 **millions of dollars in damages:** ABA, Antitrust Law Section, *Telecom Antitrust Handbook* (Chicago: Antitrust Law Section, ABA, 2005), 287 ("MCI claimed that AT&T had engaged in anticompetitive actions in violation of Sections 1 and 2 of the Sherman Act, including predatory pricing, denial of interconnections, negotiation in bad faith, and unlawful tying arrangements. After trial, the jury found in favor of MCI on ten claims, and awarded damages of $600 million, which was then trebled to a judgment of $1.8 billion, exclusive of costs and attorneys fees. On appeal, the Seventh Circuit affirmed portions of the liability finding, reversed other portions, and remanded to the district court for a separate trial on damages. The case then settled."); Jeffrey E. Cohen, *The Politics of Telecommunications Regulation: The States and the Divestiture of AT&T* (London: Routledge, 2015), 68 (noting that in 1980 MCI, in *MCI v. AT&T,* "won a stunning victory and an antitrust award of $1.8 billion" and further observing, "Jolted by the magnitude of the defeat, AT&T appealed the case and won . . . a new jury trial, which began in 1985. This time the award was reduced to $37.8 million (trebled to $113.3 million).").

CONCLUSION

351 **Adam Smith:** "Adam Smith on the Crisis of Capitalism," Machinery of Politics, Jan. 4, 2012, machineryofpolitics.wordpress.com.

351 **dumped all that tea:** Matt Stoller, "The Boston Tea Party Was a Protest Against Monopoly," *Big,* July 1, 2019, mattstoller.substack.com. Of the history of the tea trade and what preceded the American Revolution, Stoller writes:

> In the 1770s, the tea trade was a highly regulated global business. The East India Company, founded in 1600, brought tea to London from China, but it wasn't allowed to sell direct. It had to auction its tea to middlemen in London, who would then sell it in the colonies. As a result, there was a thriving colonial business of tea merchants, including many key political leaders in port cities across America—men such as John Hancock, who would later become leaders in the revolution. These merchants sold East India tea, but they also sold rival tea, sometimes smuggled.
>
> The East India Company was a stagnant and corrupt monopoly. Insiders manipulated the company's stock, and officers used their position in the company to retire with massive wealth, with nouveau riche named "Nabobs" buying seats in Parliament. The company was so systemically important to British finance that falls in its stock caused banking crises. It was a Too Big to Fail corporation. By 1772, it was borrowing from the Bank of England to stay afloat. . . .
>
> Restructuring the tea trade threatened to overturn the power structure of the colonies. The Tea Act was a miscalculation, an attempt to use low

prices to impose a new governing regime. After some attempts to negotiate, the British government simply imposed the laws on the colonies, thus proving valid the fears colonists had about political oppression. The colonists eventually engaged in an act of political desperation, which was throwing the company's tea in the ocean to destroy it, with the British Navy in the harbor.

Why didn't warships act? In 1773, colonists were fully British and thought of themselves as such. Their opposition to the East India Company was rooted in their belief that the behavior of the corporation violated their rights as Englishmen. The protest was at first an internecine struggle—an act of civil disobedience—about what it meant to be British. And firing on one's own people is a tougher bar to meet for a military than opposing a rival faction in a revolution. The stubbornness of British leaders in protecting their corrupt monopoly ended up radicalizing colonists, but when they threw that tea in the harbor, they had not yet been radicalized to independence.

351 **John Sherman:** *Bills and Debates in Congress Relating to Trusts: Fiftieth Congress to Fifty-Seventh Congress, First Session, Inclusive* (Washington, D.C.: Government Printing Office, 1903), 95 (reprinting speech of John Sherman in the Senate on March 21, 1890).

351 **first federal antitrust law:** Martin J. Sklar, *The Corporate Reconstruction of American Capitalism, 1890–1916: The Market, the Law, and Politics* (Cambridge, U.K.: Cambridge University Press, 1988), 107 ("The Sherman Act was considered by its principal authors and floor managers in the United States Senate—Republican senators John Sherman of Ohio, George F. Hoar of Massachusetts, and George F. Edmunds of Vermont—as a federal enactment of the common law with respect to restraints of trade and monopoly."); compare Roger K. Newman, ed., *The Yale Biographical Dictionary of American Law* (New Haven, Conn.: Yale University Press, 2009), 495 (noting that John Sherman's "biggest contributions to federal policy" included the Sherman Antitrust Act (1890), "the first attempt to control the power of large-scale enterprise," but that while Sherman "initially contemplated a system of fines as well as forfeiture of corporate charters for firms that engaged in monopolistic practices," subsequent amendments "removed corporate forfeiture as a possible penalty and articulated more clearly what was to be covered—namely, contracts, combinations, and conspiracies in restraint of trade and monopolistic practices'; also observing that "the final statute resembled Sherman's initial proposal only vaguely" and that Massachusetts senator George Hoar "was at least as responsible as Sherman was for the final text"); *The Trust Problem: Replies of 16,000 Representative Americans to a Questionnaire Sent Out by Department on Regulation of Industrial Corporations of the National Civic Federation* (New York: M. B. Brown, 1912), 507 ("The Sherman Act, so-called because the original measure was introduced by Senator John Sherman, of Ohio, was really the work of Senator Hoar, of Massachusetts, and of Senator Edmunds of Vermont, who co-operated in preparing the Senate Judiciary Committee substitute for the Sherman bill. This substitute was finally passed without any change by both houses of Congress, and approved by President Harrison, July 2, 1890."). George F. Edmunds, the Vermont senator, later gave his own recitation of the

Sherman Act's complex legislative history. George F. Edmunds, "The Interstate Trust and Commerce Act of 1890," *North American Review* (Dec. 1911), 194:801–17.

352 **vertically integrated enterprises:** Karin Shedd, "Why the $49 Billion Merger of Eyewear Giants Luxottica and Essilor Worries Some Antitrust Experts," CNBC, May 18, 2019, www.cnbc.com (noting that Luxottica's "vertically integrated strategy helped it pull in $10 billion in sales in 2018 and control 40% and 76% of the U.S. glasses and sunglasses market, respectively"; "this strategy has also raised eyebrows among antitrust experts, who worry the company has too much power over the industry").

352 **Amazon to Google:** "Amazon, Apple, Google: Are They the New Conglomerates?," *Content in Context* (blog), May 13, 2014, contentincontext.me.

352 **trust certificates:** Robert Sobel, *The Entrepreneurs: Explorations Within the American Business Tradition* (Washington, D.C.: Beard Books, 2000), 142.

352 **America's "rigged" economy:** Robert B. Reich, *The System: Who Rigged It, How We Fix It* (New York: Alfred A. Knopf, 2020).

352 **leaves so many families and working people behind:** Tens of millions of Americans are uninsured or underinsured, have no retirement savings other than Social Security benefits, struggle to pay their medical expenses, or cannot afford a $400 emergency medical expense. Peter Baker, Michael Tackett, and Linda Qiu, "Trump Wants to Neutralize Democrats on Health Care. Republicans Say Let It Go," *New York Times,* June 16, 2019; Susan Jones, "Klobuchar and Coons Propose Subsidies for People 'Who Need Help in Their Everyday Lives,'" CNS News, April 29, 2019, www.cnsnews.com; Sheila Rustgi et al., "Losing Ground: How the Loss of Adequate Health Insurance Is Burdening Working Families—Findings from the Commonwealth Fund Biennial Health Insurance Surveys, 2001–2007," Commonwealth Fund, Aug. 1, 2008, www.commonwealthfund.org; Anna Bahney, "40% of Americans Can't Cover a $400 Emergency Expense," *Business Insider,* May 22, 2018, money.cnn.com. In fact, the inability to pay medical bills is the leading cause of U.S. bankruptcies. Hillary Hoffower, "Staggering Medical Bills Are the Biggest Driver of Personal Bankruptcies in the U.S.," *Business Insider,* June 24, 2019, www .businessinsider.com ("In fact, 66.5% of all bankruptcies are related to medical issues, either because of expensive medical bills or time away from work, reported Lorie Konish for CNBC, citing a study by the American Journal of Public Health.").

352 **who suffer the most:** In 2015, the median household income—per U.S. census data—was $56,516, with women earning far less than their male counterparts for doing the same or similar work. According to the Institute for Women's Policy Research, women earn, on average, 20 percent less than men for work in the same jobs. When compared with a Fortune 500 company CEO's average salary, the average take-home pay of an American worker, whether male or female, is not even close—not even in the same league or ballpark. According to the AFL-CIO's new Executive Paywatch database, a CEO of an S&P 500 Index company hauled in, on average, $13.94 million in 2017—an average that was *361 times* the compensation of the average American worker. "When adjusted for inflation," the AFL-CIO notes of production and nonsupervisory workers, "the average wage has remained stagnant for more than 50 years."

Emmie Martin, "Here's How Much Money American Women Earn at Every Age," CNBC, Sept. 12, 2017, www.cnbc.com.

352 **New business formation has been declining:** Maurice E. Stucke and Ariel Ezrachi, "The Rise, Fall, and Rebirth of the U.S. Antitrust Movement," *Harvard Business Review,* Dec. 15, 2017, hbr.org ("'In 1982, young firms [those five years old or younger] accounted for about half of all firms, and one-fifth of total employment,' observed Jason Furman, Chairman of the Council of Economic Advisers. But by 2013, these figures fell 'to about one-third of firms and one-tenth of total employment.' Competition is decreasing in many significant markets, as they become concentrated. Greater profits are falling in the hands of fewer firms.").

352 **address income inequality:** The 2017 tax bill that rewrote the nation's tax laws exemplifies how greed and corporate power have co-opted America's political system—all the while only further exacerbating economic inequality. "The rich will not be gaining at all with this plan," President Trump promised in September 2017. "Our framework," he said the following month, "ensures that the benefits of tax reform go to the middle class, not to the highest earners." But in December 2018, after the tax bill had become law, an analysis by Bloomberg rated both of those claims as false. While taxes declined for the lowest income quintile group by a measly 0.4 percent, the top income quintile reaped a 2.9 percent change in after-tax income. In addition, the top tax rate fell from 39.6 percent to 37 percent, while the corporate tax rate got slashed from 35 percent to 21 percent, a huge benefit for corporations and their shareholders. Indeed, while the reduced tax rates for individuals were set to expire in 2026, meaning tax *hikes* for almost 70 percent of middle-class families in 2027, the tax cuts for corporations were made permanent in the law. "The alternative-minimum tax, or AMT, dreaded by affluent Americans," the Bloomberg article further emphasized, "lost much of its bite in the legislation." Under prior law, the estate tax—paid by the estates of only two out of a thousand deceased taxpayers—applied only to estates larger than $5.49 million. But under the new tax law, the amount of money exempt from the estate tax doubled to $11.18 million. "The rich," the Bloomberg reporters pointed out in their analysis, "are already using the new limits to create dynasty trusts for generations of their descendants." Like the Trump administration's failure to adequately fund antitrust enforcement, Donald Trump's tax policies and budget priorities utterly failed to tackle the problem of income inequality. Ben Steverman, Dave Merrill, and Jeremy C. F. Lin, "A Year After the Middle Class Tax Cut, the Rich Are Winning," Bloomberg, Dec. 18, 2018, www.bloomberg .com.

353 **Bill Gates:** Clare Duffy, "Big Tech Must Be Regulated Now, Bill Gates Says," CNN, June 24, 2019, www.cnn.com.

353 **that works for everyone:** Already, many have called for a new way of thinking, what some have termed "a progressive, anti-monopoly, New Brandeis School." Jake Walter-Warner and Jonathan H. Hatch, "A Brief Overview of the 'New Brandeis' School of Antitrust Law," *Antitrust Update* (blog), Patterson Belknap, Nov. 8, 2018, www.pbwt.com (noting that "the 'New Brandeis' or 'Neo-Brandeis' movement" is "concerned with the downsides of business and economic concentration"); Jake Walter-Warner and William F. Cava-

naugh Jr., "The New Brandeis School Manifesto," *Antitrust Update* (blog), Patterson Belknap, Feb. 5, 2020, www.pbwt.com ("The 'New Brandeisians' challenge the Chicago School 'consumer welfare' standard that has dominated policymaking for decades. They assert that the authors of the statutes that form the backbone of American antitrust law were primarily focused on the manifold danger of concentrated market power beyond simply the economic effects on the ultimate consumer."); Lina Khan, "The New Brandeis Movement: America's Antimonopoly Debate," 9 *Journal of European Competition Law and Practice* 131, 131–32 (2018) (sketching out some of the core tenets of the New Brandeis school and noting that the New Brandeis school was "largely driven by the work of a small group of scholars, journalists, lawyers, and organisers" who "sounded the first alarms about the extreme and growing concentration in most sectors of the American economy" and "signals a break with the Chicago School, whose ideas set antitrust on a radically new course starting in the 1970s and 1980s and continue to underpin competition policy in the USA today").

Louis Brandeis—the American attorney and jurist—became known as "the People's Lawyer" for his antimonopoly and social justice advocacy and for fighting for people's rights in the courts. Diana Klebanow and Franklin L. Jonas, *People's Lawyers: Crusaders for Justice in American History* (Armonk, N.Y.: M. E. Sharpe, 2003), 66; Clyde Spillenger, "Elusive Advocate: Reconsidering Brandeis as People's Lawyer," in *Lawyers' Ethics and the Pursuit of Social Justice: A Critical Reader,* ed. Susan D. Carle (New York: New York University Press, 2005), 72–73. "Shall the industrial policy of America be that of competition or that of monopoly?" Brandeis once queried, asking a very important question. Tim Wu, *The Curse of Bigness: Antitrust in the New Gilded Age* (New York: Columbia Global Reports, 2018), 17. As Maurice Stucke and Ariel Ezrachi explain of the new scholarship and the general public's reawakening to antimonopoly and Brandeisian impulses, "An emerging group of young scholars are inquiring whether we truly benefitted from competition with little antitrust enforcement. The mounting evidence suggests no. New business formation has steadily declined as a share of the economy since the late 1970s." Stucke and Ezrachi, "Rise, Fall, and Rebirth of the U.S. Antitrust Movement." Regardless of the specific label or terminology that is employed, both sides of the political aisle are, at long last, starting to see the errors of the past, whether brought on by apathy or an intentional, misguided desire to allow big companies to get away with whatever they wanted to get away with. As Stucke and Ezrachi emphasize, "Liberals and conservatives are increasingly warning that consumers are not benefitting from the meager competition in many markets. Their concern is that the current state of competition law (and crony capitalism) benefits the select few at the expense of nearly everyone else."

353   **rural Georgia:** Modern-day corporate consolidation has hit rural communities hard, with bankruptcies on the rise. Diana Moss, "Consolidation and Concentration in Agricultural Biotechnology: Next Generation Competition Issues," Competition Policy International, Jan. 9, 2020, www .competitionpolicyinternational.com ("The most recent wave of consolidation in agricultural biotechnology has sharply reduced the number of rivals from the 'Big 6' to the 'Big 3.' "). The average income of all farm households in

2016 was $117,918 compared with the $83,143 average income of all U.S. households. The median income of farm households was $76,250 compared with the $59,039 median income of all U.S. households. A great deal of the income for farm households is actually *nonfarm* income, however, with farmers often working jobs off the farm in order to make ends meet. See U.S. Department of Agriculture, "Farm Household Income and Characteristics," www.ers.usda .gov (containing spreadsheet for "Mean and Median Farm Operator Household Income and Ratio of Farm Household to U.S. Household Income, 1960–2017"). Scott VanderWal, the president of the South Dakota Farm Bureau, explained the economic strain on farmers: "There's a lot of stress situations where bankers are really concerned about people that aren't very well capitalized anymore, whether it's young farmers and ranchers who haven't had a chance to build up that capital yet. Or if it's people that have been in the business for a long time and they're just losing their equity." Farm income is down while farm debt is up. "What's in the 2018 Farm Bill? The Good, the Bad, and the Offal . . . ," Farm Aid, Dec. 20, 2018, www.farmaid.org ("Since 2013, America's farmers and ranchers have weathered a 50% drop in net farm income. The 1-800-FARM-AID hotline has had its busiest year yet, with more farmers calling us stressed, desperate and with a shrinking number of viable options for keeping their farms running."); "Farm Bureau: Lenders Say Farmers Dependent on Off-Farm Income," *Fence Post,* Feb. 20, 2019, www .thefencepost.com ("Farm debt is at a record level of $410 billion. . . . The debt to asset ratio is not as high as it was during the farm crisis of the 1980s, . . . but it is at 13.5 percent and has been rising for the last six years."). And the suicide rate among American farmers is more than double that of veterans. Debbie Weingarten, "Why Are America's Farmers Killing Themselves?," *Guardian,* Dec. 11, 2018, www.theguardian.com. Low prices for beef, corn, grain, milk, and soybeans are an economic reality, too, one exacerbated by the Trump administration's retaliatory tariffs. Adam Belz, "Farm Bankruptcies Are on the Rise, and Bankers Worry That Far More Are on the Way," *Minneapolis Star Tribune,* Nov. 26, 2018, www.startribune.com. A recent report of the Federal Reserve Bank of Minneapolis found that from 2017 to 2018, chapter 12 bankruptcy filings in Minnesota, North Dakota, Montana, South Dakota, and Wisconsin were up, more than double the level from 2013 to 2014. Sammi Bjelland, "Farmers Facing Tough Times," Keloland Media Group, Dec. 20, 2018.

353 **judges who get it:** We need more judges who will forthrightly acknowledge what the U.S. Supreme Court itself said about the purpose of the nation's antitrust laws back in 1958. In *Northern Pacific Railway Co. v. United States,* 356 U.S. 1, 4 (1958), the Court declared in no uncertain terms, "The Sherman Act was designed to be a comprehensive charter of economic liberty aimed at preserving free and unfettered competition as the rule of trade. It rests on the premise that the unrestrained interaction of competitive forces will yield the best allocation of our economic resources, the lowest prices, the highest quality, and the greatest material progress, while at the same time providing an environment conductive to the preservation of our democratic political and social institutions." In short, economic opportunity and greater material progress for Americans were expressly linked to enforcing the country's antitrust

laws—a key to protecting the integrity of our economy and our representative democracy, which is governed by "We the People."

354 **Thurman Arnold:** Spencer Weber Waller, *Thurman Arnold: A Biography* (New York: New York University Press, 2005); Donald R. Stabile and Andrew F. Kozak, *Markets, Planning, and the Moral Economy: Business Cycles in the Progressive Era and New Deal* (Cheltenham, U.K.: Edward Elgar, 2012), 210. In 1937, Thurman Arnold wrote a book, *The Folklore of Capitalism,* that brought him considerable attention. Thurman W. Arnold, *The Folklore of Capitalism* (New Haven, Conn.: Yale University Press, 1937).

354 **President Franklin D. Roosevelt's administration:** On January 11, 1944, President Franklin Delano Roosevelt spoke of every American being entitled to various economic rights. One of the rights on the list: "The right of every businessman, large and small, to trade in an atmosphere of freedom from unfair competition and domination by monopolies at home or abroad." Cass R. Sunstein, *The Second Bill of Rights: FDR's Unfinished Revolution and Why We Need It More Than Ever* (New York: Basic Books, 2004), pp. 13, 187.

354 **like other antitrust officials:** Lee Loevinger—a graduate of the University of Minnesota Law School and the son of one of the founders of Minnesota's Democratic-Farmer-Labor Party who became President John F. Kennedy's antitrust chief—was another leader of the Justice Department's Antitrust Division who truly believed, with a passion, in the mission of that division. Joseph M. Siracusa, *Encyclopedia of the Kennedys: The People and Events That Shaped America* (Santa Barbara, Calif.: ABC-CLIO, 2012), 1:479; James R. Williamson, *Federal Antitrust Policy During the Kennedy-Johnson Years* (Westport, Conn.: Greenwood Press, 1995), 57. Loevinger, who himself had worked for Arnold before being tapped by JFK to head up the division, once testified before Congress, "The problems with which the antitrust laws are concerned—the problems of distribution of power within society—are second only to the questions of survival in the face of threats of nuclear weapons." Wu, *Curse of Bigness,* 78. "I believe in antitrust almost as a secular religion," Loevinger famously told Attorney General Robert Kennedy. Loevinger said antitrust violators were guilty of "economic racketeering." Williamson, *Federal Antitrust Policy During the Kennedy-Johnson Years,* 57.

354 **During his tenure:** Wu, *Curse of Bigness,* 79.

354 **"size in itself":** Xu Yi-chong, *Sinews of Power: The Politics of the State Grid Corporation of China* (Oxford: Oxford University Press, 2017), 181.

354 **"Arnold is credited":** John R. Vile, *Great American Lawyers: An Encyclopedia* (Santa Barbara, Calif.: ABC-CLIO, 2001), 1:16–17.

354 **"curse of bigness":** Thomas K. McCraw, *Prophets of Regulation: Charles Francis Adams, Louis D. Brandeis, James M. Landis, Alfred E. Kahn* (Cambridge, Mass.: Belknap Press of Harvard University Press, 1984), 108.

355 **"If we are unwilling":** Senator Hubert H. Humphrey, address, University of Wisconsin-Milwaukee, March 31, 1960, 12, www2.mnhs.org.

Index

Page numbers in *italics* refer to illustrations.

Nebraska, 70
NeoProfen, 4–9, 361–62n, 364n
Nestlé, 177
Netscape Communications
    Corporation, 150, *151*, 152, 153,
    429–30n
Network Power (Singh), 430n
Neuhauser, Alan, 154
"New Colossus, The" (Lazarus), 382n
New England Journal of Medicine, 185
New Freedom, 115
New Gilded Age, 239–40
New Jersey, and Standard Oil, 100,
    397n
New Jersey Generals, 164
New Media Investment Group, 202
New Orleans Saints, 129–30
New Republic, 482n
news
    newspapers, 198, 199, 201–4, 206,
        269, 282, 458n, 460n, 461n, 464n
    on social media, 201, 203
    see also journalism; media
News Corp, 200, 269, 479n, 482n
Newspaper Guild, 461n
New York American, *43*
New York and Long Branch
    Railroad, 81
New York City
    Tammany Hall in, 28, 32, 43, 375n
    Uber Eats and Grubhub in, 171
New Yorker, 145, *225*, *235*, *241*, *277*, 436n,
    458n
New York State Agricultural
    Association, 90
New York Stock Exchange, 68
New York Times, 12, 31, 35, 36, 83, 137,
    150, 157, 195, 222, *222*, 253, 317,
    377n, 422n, 428n, 429n, 434n,
    458n, 480n, 511n
New-York Tribune, *108*
NFL (National Football League), 128–
    30, 164–65, 412n, 413n, 437n, 438n
Niagara Movement, 113–14, *114*
Nineteenth Amendment, 114
Nitropress, 518n
Nixon, Richard, 137, 164, 244, 436n,
    503n
Nobel Prize winners, 342

Nocera, Joe, 161
Noerr-Pennington doctrine, 163
non-compete agreements (NCAs), 195,
    262–63, *263*, *337*, 338–40, 515n,
    516n
No Oil Producing and Exporting
    Cartels (NOPEC) Act, 308–9
Norfolk Southern Railway, 156, 431n
Norris-LaGuardia Act, 123, 393n, 410n,
    416n
North, Lord, 21, 23
North Carolina, 19
North Dakota, 70
Northern Pacific Railway, *41*, 93, 565n
Northern Securities Company, 30, *41*,
    93–98, *95*, *96*, *97*, 100, 109, 396n
Northrup Grumman, 176
Northwest Airlines, 468n
Northwestern Bell, 141
Norton, Mary Beth, 22
Notebaert, Richard, 499n
Novo Nordisk, 518n, 521n
nurses, 195
NYNEX, 144

Oakland Tribune, *101*
Obama, Barack, 5, 154–57, 194, 213,
    240, 241, 254, 266, 268, 271,
    289–90, 335, 344, 455n, 496n, 498n
    birtherism conspiracy about, 458n
Obamacare (Affordable Care Act), 157,
    240, 267–68, 520n
Oculus, 432n
Office Depot, 227, 485n
Ohio, and Standard Oil, 100–102, 397n
Ohio v. American Express Co., 243–45,
    502n
oil industry, 28, 40, *101*, 150, 211, 269,
    354
    No Oil Producing and Exporting
        Cartels (NOPEC) Act and, 308–9
    OPEC and, 308, 532n
    Standard Oil, *see* Standard Oil
Ojibwe people, 211, 467n
oligopoly, 136
Oliver, John, 197, 219, 349
Oliver Iron Mining Company, 54
Olson, James, 87
O'Neill, Tip, 198

Illustration Credits

All other images are in the public domain or courtesy of the author.